MODERN ARMENIAN DRAMA

Scene from G. Sundukian's *Pepo*. Diocese of the Armenian Church of America Players (1975). Director, N. Parlakian; (left) as Pepo, G. Achian and as Giko, S. Kilerciyan.

MODERN ARMENIAN DRAMA

AN ANTHOLOGY

EDITED BY

NISHAN PARLAKIAN

S. PETER COWE

COLUMBIA UNIVERSITY PRESS

NEW YORK

THIS PUBLICATION WAS MADE POSSIBLE BY A
GENEROUS GRANT FROM THE DOLORES ZOHRAB
LIEBMANN FUND.

COLUMBIA UNIVERSITY PRESS WISHES TO EXPRESS ITS
APPRECIATION FOR ASSISTANCE GIVEN BY THE PUSHKIN
FUND TOWARD THE COST OF PUBLISHING THIS BOOK.

Columbia University Press
Publishers Since 1893
New York Chichester, West Sussex
Copyright © 2001 Columbia University Press

Library of Congress Cataloging-in-Publication Data

Modern Armenian drama : an anthology / edited by
Nishan Parlakian and S. Peter Cowe.
   p. cm.
  Includes bibliographical references.
  ISBN 0–231–11630–6 (cloth)
    1. Armenian drama—19th century—Translations into
English.   2. Armenian drama—20th century—
Translations into English.   I. Parlakian, Nishan, 1925–
II. Cowe, S. Peter.

PK8831.E5 M6 2000
891'.992508—dc21

                               00–043162

Designed by Chang Jae Lee
c 10 9 8 7 6 5 4 3 2

CONTENTS

PREFACE

By Armenian drama this anthology understands that body of plays originally composed in the Armenian language, and hence it excludes works in other languages written by playwrights of Armenian descent. The selections for this volume were arrived at in consultation with theater critics Professors Levon Hakhverdyan and Henrik Hovhannisyan of the Institute of Fine Arts in Erevan and in light of the judgment of its editors, who had experienced the dramas by reading, viewing, or staging them in both Armenia and the United States. The two interlocking principles that have guided the present choices are, first, the establishment of modern professional theater companies in the 1860s and the continuing popularity of plays within that repertory up to the present. The seven plays published in this collection span the years 1871 to 1992. The first four emanate from the rapid development of the pre-Soviet Armenian stage, and the next two represent the early and later phases of the Soviet period. The final item exemplifies the current era of transition to democracy and a market economy being charted by the post-Soviet Armenian republic. All but one of these pieces was written expressly for theatrical performance. Though Baronian's *Medzabadiw muratsganner* [Honorable beggars] appeared in novel form, the portions in dialogue outweighed the narrative frame, so that soon after its author's death the work was readily adapted for the stage, where it has enjoyed widespread success ever since.

The translation process, of necessity, involves a creative tension between the idiom of the original and target languages. The plays comprising this anthology present a particular challenge in that they span a wide diversity of linguistic levels. The register of Demirchyan's farcical *Nazar the Brave*, for example, is obviously slangy and colloquial, whereas that of *Ancient Gods* is elevated for the most part. In others, such as *For the Sake of Honor*, all the characters possess their own idiolect, depending on their personality traits. Often the unity of the spirit and the letter innate in the original cannot be re-created in the transfer, and hence the translator must devise some compromise to cope with this disjunction. In the present collection every attempt has been made to remain as faithful as possible to the thought of the original, and so we have often been constrained to recast its form. On occasion, when the sociopolitical and cultural gap between a play's Armenian ambience and that of projected English readers demanded it, the editors had recourse to adaptation of the original scripts. Humor being one of the great human imponderables, not all jokes in Armenian are funny in English. Roman transliterations of Armenian terms follow a modified version of the system employed by the *Journal of the Society for Armenian Studies* obviating the use of diacritics, as laid out in the equivalency table at the end of the volume.

One of the goals behind the present endeavor has been to make available for performance in English representative plays of the Armenian repertoire that should appeal to theatrical groups of all levels. Consequently the editors considered it appropriate to insert supplemental stage directions in square brackets in an effort to facilitate readers' visualization and for assistance in stage production.

It is our pleasant obligation to acknowledge the kind permission of the playwrights Perch Zeytuntsyan and Anahit Aghasaryan for their works to be translated and the valuable comments of Professor Kevork Bardjakian of the University of Michigan, Ann Arbor, at the project's initial stage. Aris G. Sevag and Aram Arkun of the Zohrab Information Center, New York, provided bibliographical assistance, and Dr. Nona Manoukian shared her linguistic expertise in certain nuances of translation. Our thanks go as well to the faculty of St. Nersess Armenian Theological Seminary, New Rochelle, for their hospitality and the use of their computer resources. John Taveras, computer expert at John Jay College of the City University of New York, also offered important advice. Archbishop Torkom Manoogian, formerly primate of the Eastern Diocese of the Armenian Church of America and currently Patriarch of Jerusalem, is to be credited for having created an interest in staging Armenian drama in the 1970s and 1980s, which has borne fruit in this volume. The editors express their appreciation for a grant from the Dolores Zohrab Liebmann Fund, represented by co-trustee Suren D. Fesjian, to facilitate publication and for the interest of Ms. Jennifer Crewe of Columbia University Press. Lastly, the editors would like to express their thanks for the patience and generosity of time lent to this effort by Anahit Tutunjian and Florence Parlakian.

INTRODUCTION

Armenian literature arguably has one of the longest and most varied dramatic traditions of Eurasia, though it has not been continuous. By its nature, drama, in contrast to poetry, is an urban art dependent on the institution of a theater and associated groups of actors, as well as the existence of a sizable and relatively sophisticated audience. For Armenian theater, these conditions were met by the cities of Constantinople, capital of the Ottoman Empire, and Tiflis, administrative center of the Russian viceroyalty of Transcaucasia. By the second half of the nineteenth century both possessed large Armenian communities with a burgeoning middle class, developed educational system, and significant socioeconomic and cultural contacts with Western Europe.

Similar conditions prevailed in Armenia during the Roman period, which witnessed a significant degree of urban construction. Some of these cities were equipped with theaters, for example, Artashat, capital of King Artashes I (188–c.160 B.C.), and Tigranocerta, capital of Tigran the Great (95–56/5 B.C.). The historian Dio Cassius records a memorable performance of Euripides' *Bacchae* in 53 B.C., in which the skull employed at Agave's dramatic entrance with her son's head was that of the Roman general Crassus. The production was overseen by King Artawazd II (55–34 B.C.), who also composed tragedies in Greek, which were valued by the writer Plutarch (A.D. 50–125) but have not survived.[1]

Although from that time until the second half of the seventeenth century no dramatic text exists, spectacle and theatrical performance of various kinds maintained their appeal. Despite the conversion of the Armenian court to Christianity in the early fourth century A.D. and the increasing importance of the new religion as a significant element in Armenian identity, the recitation of legends of ancient deities and heroes, orally transmitted by the bard (*gusan*) to instrumental accompaniment and improvised gesture, continued well into the medieval period over the opposition of the church. Court performances of mime and dance paralleled the dramatic elaboration of ecclesiastical ritual, for example, in the Palm Sunday *Dṛnbatsek* [The opening of the doors] and the Washing of the Feet on Maundy Thursday.[2] In the early modern period, Armenians were also involved in shadow theater (*karagöz*) and various types of farce, such as *orta oyunu* (central staging), about which more will be said later.[3]

Jesuit school drama exercised a marked influence on Eastern and Western European theater. Under its impact, the school became the first institution to nurture a new movement in Armenian dramaturgy. Its first fruit was a neoclassical tragicomedy of 1668 at the Papal Academy in Lvov on the role of the Roman martyr St. Hripsime in the Christianization of Armenia. The work is emblematic of Counter-Reformation proselytism among Armenian merchant communities in different parts of the Middle East and sought to advance the union of the Armenians of Poland with Rome. During the next century and a half this tradition became firmly rooted in Armenian culture through the efforts of the Armenian Catholic Mkhitarist Brotherhood of San Lazzaro, Venice.

This religious community played a major role in the development of Armenian publishing through the support of merchant munificence, issuing a series of grammars, dictionaries, and translations, as well as inaugurating the literary movement of Armenian classicism and producing the first modern critical history of the Armenian people. These Mkhitarist dramas were in-house productions at Mardi Gras and other holidays. Mainly drawn from biblical and ecclesiastical themes and composed in classical Armenian, the tragedies also treat episodes of secular history, for example, *The Perfidious Death of King Khosrov*. Plays of Metastasio, Alfieri, and Corneille were also performed in translation. The comedies, in contrast, were lively farces mostly written in the Armenian vernacular of Constantinople, involving

---

1. For a somewhat dated overview of preclassical Armenian theatrical activities, see V. Arvanian and L. G. Murad, *Two Thousand Years of the Armenian Theater* (New York: The Armenian National Council of America, 1954).

2. See H. H. Hovhannisyan, *Tatrone mijnadaryan Hayastanum* [The theater in medieval Armenia] (Erevan: Armenian Academy of Sciences, 1978).

3. See L. S. Myrsiades, *The Karagiozis Heroic Performance in Greek Shadow Theater* (Hanover, N.H.: University Press of New England, 1988), pp. 3, 7–8.

stock characters drawn from the motley Ottoman capital (Jew, Greek, Albanian, etc.), supplemented by works of Goldoni and Molière.[4]

In 1808 Mkhitarist school drama was brought to Constantinople and in 1820 to the Crimea, where in the 1860s the former Mkhitarist, Khoren Kalfayian, wrote the tragedy *Arshak II* and the rollicking farce *Alafranka* critiquing Armenian xenophilia. The Armenians of Tiflis, capital of Georgia, passed from Iranian to Russian rule in 1801, to be followed, in 1828, by those in the Khanate of Erevan. This period witnessed a significant expansion of Armenian educational establishments in what was now called Transcaucasia, the most important of which was the Nersisian school, whose first director was the Moscow-trained cleric Harutiwn Alamdarian (1795–1834). He introduced drama in a more Romantic vein, which influenced the sentimental work *Theodora or Filial Love* (1841) by his pupil Khachatur Abovian, more famous for his novelistic treatment of the Armenian struggle for liberation from Iran in *Wounds of Armenia* (1858).

The second social institution to promote Armenian drama was the voluntary association. Founded in a number of cities during the nineteenth century with the aim of fostering educational and cultural projects, these organizations performed plays such as Mkrtich Martirosian's comedy *Physiognomist of Duplicity* written in Calcutta in 1821 and works of Romantic nationalism written by the Mkhitarist-educated playwrights of Constantinople Mkrtich Beshigtashlian and Tovmas Terzian in the 1860s. Soon after the entry of the Khanate of Erevan into the Russian Empire, an Armenian amateur group there also premiered Griboedov's hugely successful comedy *The Woes of Wit* in 1827.[5]

The first step toward creating a professional theater in Tiflis was made by the dramatist Galust Shermazanian, who, in 1836, turned the first floor of his house into a hall where he staged plays satirizing social ills such as bribery, clerical backwardness, and tsarist bureaucracy. This more realist, secular approach is also manifest in the first works of serious Armenian drama criticism by Sargis Tigranian in the introduction to a translation of Racine's *Athalie* (1834) and in the writings of the social revolutionary Mikayel Nalbandian in the 1850s. During that decade students at Moscow University such as Nikoghayos Pughinian and Mikayel Ter-Grigorian began to write and produce vaudevilles in the Armenian dialect of Tiflis, making fun of the manners of the city's Armenian mercantile class, transferring these to the Caucasus upon graduation. Out of this matrix emerged the first East Armenian theater company in 1863, which staged in the same year *Sneezing at Night Is Good Luck*, the first work of Gabriel Sundukian. Though his predecessors' works have

---

4. See L. Zekiyan, *Hay tadroni sgzpnakaylere* [The initial steps of the Armenian theater] (Venice: St. Lazar's Press, 1975).

5. See V. A. Parsamyan, *Griboyedove ew hay-rusakan haraberutyunnere* [Griboedov and Armeno-Russian relations] (Erevan: Armenian Academy of Sciences, 1947).

passed into oblivion, Sundukian's oeuvre is continually reprised on the Armenian stage.

GABRIEL SUNDUKIAN

The incorporation of Transcaucasia into the Russian Empire introduced a more developed money economy into the region, which gradually transformed many of its social mores. Over his dramatic career spanning half a century, Sundukian was to explore realistically the effects of incipient capitalism and modernism on urban life in the tradition of Gogol and Ostrovsky, as the novelist Perch Proshian had done more romantically for the countryside. One of the best illustrations of his approach is provided by *Pepo* (1871), which has established itself as probably the most popular work in the whole Armenian dramatic repertoire.[6] Composed under the inspiration of Molière's *Le Mariage forcé*, the play highlights changes in business practice through the clash of the chief characters created for Chmshkian and Amerikian, two of the most talented Armenian actors of the day. This contrast in values is immediately evident from the details of dress and the décor of their respective houses, Pepo the fisherman, Sundukian's only lower class hero, appearing in traditional Caucasian garb, while the moneylender Arutin Zimzimov follows European fashion in his dress and domestic furnishings.

The more widespread utility of the usurer's services is indicated by Pepo 's father depositing a large sum with Zimzimov to secure his daughter Kekel's dowry, one of the largest expenses the family would have to incur. The promissory note had been entrusted to Giko, the play's chief comic character, who indulges in long-winded stories interrupted by stuttering and snuff taking and peppered with proverbs and apothegms.

When the note is temporarily lost, Zimzimov exploits this technicality to deny any record of the debt, even forswearing himself before Pepo, who holds the traditional view that a man's word is his honor, and chides him with the question: "Don't you have a record in the ledger of your heart?" When Pepo remonstrates, the other has him removed from the premises and charged with trespassing and aggravated assault. However, in a powerful reversal triggered by the note's miraculous reappearance, Pepo idealistically ignores the pleas of his friend (and foil) Kakuli, a typical carefree representative of the Tiflis bazaar, to accept the usurer's bribe, preferring instead to bring his adversary to trial and expose him, as he tells his mother, Shushan, in the following speech:

---

6. Some notion of its charisma and magnetism can be measured from entries of its performances recorded in a commemorative log of the Erevan State Theater. See *The Sundukian Theater, 1922–1972* (Erevan: Hayastan, 1972).

Shall I give it [the promissory note] to him [Zimzimov] so he can make a
fool and liar out of me in public? Shall I sell my soul for fear of prison?
No Mama! This note is a sword handed to me by God and with it I shall
lop off his head . . . People have to know that the man they bow to, hon-
or and respect, and magnify and exalt to high heaven is really someone for
whom there is nothing sacred in the world!

Pepo's conduct provokes Zimzimov 's comment: "The distinction between great
and small has gone now . . . A beggar without a bean to his name has the nerve to
bawl me out!"

The fisherman's resolute defiance echoes the liberalism of the era of Alexan-
der II's reforms, which led to the abolition of serfdom in the Tiflis province in 1864
and the integration of local courts into the imperial system in 1866. Other social
changes of the time are also significant for the background of the play, such as the
unprecedented mass protest of the Tiflis merchants and artisans against, and successful revocation of, an unpopular new tax in 1865. The growing impact of capitalism manifest in *Pepo* also emerges in *Ruined Family*. There the merchant Par-
sigh Leprunts sets about destroying his rival's business by making an immediate
court-ordered call on a huge debt that he was honor-bound by word and hand-
shake to delay for a month, with devastating effect on the other's family.

By the end of the nineteenth century, money had also loosened rigid class distinctions that had previously been determined by land tenure and breeding, fuel-
ing a new movement for upward mobility. Thus in *Ruined Family* Salome, wife of
merchant Osep Gulabints, over her husband's objections, desires to marry her
daughter Nato to the civil servant Aleksandr Marmarov. Similarly Pepo promises a
large dowry to raise his sister to the middle class by marriage to a merchant, despite
Kakuli's insistence that he is wading out of his depth.

Many of Sundukian's other dramas treat other aspects of the mating game.
Thus *Khatabala*, for example, highlights the lack of contact intending couples had
before their wedding. Margrit is an "old maid" daughter unable to attract a suitor
because she is unappealing, if not ugly. Georg Masisiants, a suitor who has been
love-smitten by a distant window view of the beautiful Natalia, is lured into the
household by Garasim Yakulich Zambakhov, who deliberately misconstrues the
situation and plans to offer his ugly daughter to the young man. But at the climax
when finally introduced to Margrit, the young man is horrified by her appearance.
As a result, a pleasant, humorous drama suddenly takes on near tragic proportions
in an excruciating reversal.

These various social changes also impacted the structure of the Caucasian
family. The old aunt Khakho, in *Ruined Family*, waxes lyrical on the living conditions of former days when several brothers would live under the parental roof, contrasting it with the current weakening of such ties. Similarly, in *Pepo*, we are struck
by the cohesion and solidarity of the main character's extended family against the

marriage of convenience contracted by Epemia and Zimzimov. The wife has all the characteristics of a gold digger, enticing money and favors from a sugar daddy. The husband so craves to relive his youth with his young bride that his embarrassingly elderly billing, cooing, and kissing is a delight to behold. Their scenes together afford the dramatist the opportunity to reveal something of the human frailty of the usurer, who otherwise might appear a veritable monster.

Sundukian's plays also contribute to the contemporary debate on the status of women and their eligibility for higher education, employment, and increasing social emancipation. Epemia has such control over her husband as to alienate him from his daughter, and Salome, in Ruined Family, flouts her husband's wishes in arranging Nato's dowry, while in Spouses (1888) Margarit actually has the self-confidence to leave her husband. Nonetheless, many of Sundukian's female characters, particularly those of the lower class, are presented in more passive roles. Hence Kekel succumbs to a deep melancholia when her suitor rejects her after kissing her in public, while her mother, Shushan, is beside herself with grief and constantly appeals to divine intervention to impact her condition indirectly.

Dramatically Sundukian's works tend to follow the traditional mold. In particular, he deftly uses the device of soliloquy in plays like Pepo as a means of conveying to the audience the innermost thoughts of the principal characters in speeches of great power and memorable effect. Similarly he underlines the significance of certain episodes by halting the action through the convention of tableaux adopted from melodrama. As noted by Arnot, the Ibsenesque quality of Sundukian's Ruined Family is striking.[7] Dealing as they do with middle-class morality, a number of Sundukian's works are somewhat reminiscent in structure and theme of several of Ibsen's realistic social plays (1879–1890), but the tone in the Armenian works is often lighter—a bittersweet mixture—not at all in the style of the stolid Norwegian playwright.

HAGOP BARONIAN

In contrast to the German and Russian influences that predominated in Transcaucasia, the cultures of Italy, and more particularly France, had far more of an impact on the Armenian and Turkish intelligentsia of Constantinople. Touring Italian operatic groups performed there periodically from the eighteenth century on, and French plays were staged under the later Tanzimat period in which the Ottoman Empire became more amenable to European influence. Thus Hagop Baronian's early adaptation of Goldoni's A Servant of Two Masters (1865) reflected the artistic

7. R. Arnot, "Special Introduction," Armenian Literature, rev. ed. (New York: Colonial Press, 1901), p. vii.

predilections of the time. The dramatists Beshigtashlian and Terzian, encountered above, were also active during the same decade in making works from those cultures available to Armenian audiences. Indeed, the repertoire of both early Armenian drama companies, the Arevelean Tadron [Eastern Theater] and Gedikpasha Theater, relied so heavily on translated material that they provoked the censure of critics like the short story writer and legal expert Krikor Zohrab.[8] In contrast to the penchant for Romantic tragedies manifested by the Armenian poets of Mkhitarist training, Baronian's natural genius lay in comedy. There, as his output clearly indicates, his greatest inspiration was Molière.[9]

At the same time, some of Baronian's works bear a certain similarity to the indigenous theatrical tradition of *orta oyunu*, or central staging, mentioned above. Like the Italian commedia dell'arte on which Goldoni drew inspiration, the form consisted of typical scenes involving a lively range of stock characters.[10] It is likely that Baronian would have witnessed such performances either outdoors or in some of the large coffeehouses. Moreover, the repartee between its chief characters, the clever conjuror Peshikiar and the trader, comic, artisan, servant Kavaklu, seems reminiscent of features in the satirist's novel *Honorable Beggars*, although the work's main literary models are Molière's *Les Fâcheux* and *Monsieur de Pourceaugnac*. However, its opening scene exploits the same topos as Kavaklu's narrative in *The Sorcery* of begging for alms from travelers disembarking from small steamers at the pier.[11]

From the time he wrote *Honorable Beggars* Baronian was precluded from producing plays to be staged because of a general ban on Armenian theater imposed by the reactionary sultan Abdülhamid II. Nevertheless, a number of his works were later adapted for the theater and have been continually reprised in the homeland and in different parts of the Armenian Diaspora.

Like Sundukian, Baronian explores the changes occurring in urban Armenian society of the later nineteenth century. Some of his satirical writings focus on the central Armenian political figures and issues of the day, such as the power struggle between the *amira* establishment of bankers and influential civil servants, on the one hand, and the guilds and European-educated intellectuals. The latter's success led to the promulgation of the Armenian National Constitution in 1860 that assured much greater lay participation in the deliberative process regarding the af-

---

8. For further details, see T. S. Halman, *Modern Turkish Drama* (Minneapolis: Bibliotheca Islamica, 1976), pp. 30–36, and the literature cited there.

9. For further details, see K. B. Bardakjian, "Baronian's Debt to Molière," *Journal of the Society for Armenian Studies* 1 (1984): 139–62; and E. Alexanian, "19th Century Armenian Realism and Its International Relations," *The Review of National Literatures* (Armenia) 13 (1984): 50–51.

10. N. N. Martinovich, *The Turkish Theatre* (Boston: Benjamin Blom, 1968), p. 14.

11. Ibid., p. 49

fairs of the Armenian *millet* in the Ottoman Empire.[12] However, two of his works, *Eastern Dentist* (1869) and *Brother Balthazar* (1886–87), are satires on adultery, focusing on the contemporary clash between traditional sexual mores and the introduction of more liberal European attitudes. The first depicts a philandering dentist who rendezvous at the homes of women "patients." His suspicious wife chases after him through his shenanigans on a given day, including a hot session at a costume party, before resolving their marital problem.

The second relates to the infidelity of a wife who is bored by her rather boorish, older merchant husband and has assignations with a sophisticated, savvy family friend ironically named Kibar (lit., upright, honest). The piece also satirizes the venal, perfunctory hearings by members of the Armenian judicial council of Balthazar's suit to divorce his wife. In conclusion, it highlights the contrast between the older position of a wife's fidelity to her husband regardless of his treatment of her and a woman's right to greater freedom of action in her love life, as asserted in Srpuhi Diwsap's controversial novel *Mayda* (1884).

Tame from a sexual point of view, *Honorable Beggars* deals with every other vice and folly known to man, especially the cardinal sins of vanity and greed. The play opens as the rich provincial land owner, Apisoghom Agha, arrives at Constantinople from Trebizond, hoping, at age forty, to find a decent girl to marry in the capital. Baronian directs satire not only at the city slickers he encounters there but also at the agha himself for his philistinism in neglecting Armenian culture, unless his name is prominently displayed on any publication. He creates laughter by the use of the age-old comedic techniques of derision, incongruity, and automatism.[13] In other words, the agha is ridiculed as a country bumpkin, shown to be out of his element by his supposed betters, and turned into an automaton with machinelike responses, lacking the ability to communicate intelligently.

The method of each beggar — editor, poet, writer, priest, doctor, matchmaker, barber, or photographer — is to shower the agha with flattery. For example, in trying to get Apisoghom to subscribe to his newspaper, an editor pretends to know his entire family history. Lying through his teeth, he starts a syllogism. Major premise:

---

12. The term *millet* relates to confessional communities within the Ottoman Empire outside the Islamic majority. The Armenian *millet* was constituted by communicant members of the Armenian Apostolic Church under the jurisdiction of the Armenian patriarch of Constantinople, who as ethnarch represented his community at the Sublime Porte. As a result of the constitution a greater measure of lay participation was introduced into the *millet*'s deliberative process. During the second half of the nineteenth century the community's profile gradually changed from one determined by religion to one increasingly influenced by nationalism. For further details, see M. Ashjian, *Armenian Church Patristic and Other Essays* (New York: The Armenian Prelacy, 1994), pp. 227–51.

13. See T. Hatlen, *Orientation to the Theater*, 5th ed. (Englewood Cliffs, N.J.: Prentice Hall, 1992), pp. 125–38.

Your father was a subscriber (unlikely in view of Trebizond's distance from the capital). Minor premise: He was a very good person. Conclusion: The agha will also be a good person, if he subscribes. But the agha is being deliberately dense so the editor tries flattery.

EDITOR: You can speak Turkish I believe?

AGHA: No.

EDITOR: French?

AGHA: No.

EDITOR: German?

AGHA: No.

The robotlike repartee is pure Molièrian automatism.

Eventually he is outraged by having to treat several sycophants who join his restaurant table. Cheated by everyone under the sun, and all but pulled apart physically by a clergyman and a matchmaker with eligible women to offer him as a wife, Apisoghom Agha decides to leave. Even then, his landlord, who has harassed him with the latest gossip from the Armenian National Assembly, demands a huge loan. When his wife ups the request by a hefty sum, the agha finally packs and heads for the steamboat back to Trebizond. With Apisoghom's departure, the dog-eat-dog world is brought into temporary quiescence and, one hopes, a time to reflect on human shortcomings. Baronian has performed the work of the satirist in seeking to cleanse society of its foibles and follies with a word rapier of the sharpest quality.

ALEKSANDR SHIRVANZADE

In the last quarter of the nineteenth century Transcaucasia underwent rapid change. We have observed the impact of incipient capitalism on Tiflis in Sundukian's plays. However, Baku became the hub of the region's industrial development from the 1870s with the opening of the oilfields to long-term leases. This paved the way for large-scale mechanized production, which sets the scene for Shirvanzade's masterpiece *For the Sake of Honor*. Foreign investment was involved from early on, attracting the interest of the Nobel brothers of Sweden and the Rothchilds of Paris. With the expansion in the job market, rail and steamship links were forged to ease worker transportation. Baku became a city of contrasts ranging from the poverty and inadequate conditions of the slums to the flamboyance and vulgar ostentation of the nouveaux riches. By the 1890s trade unions were formed to curb the owners' exploitation, and in 1903 a strike was organized that concluded in December 1904 with the first labor agreement in the Russian Empire.

In that very month Shirvanzade's play opened in Baku. Its enthusiastic reception there led to a successful run in Tiflis in 1905. That same year its script was published in the newspaper *Lumay*, as well as in book form. Its 1908 staging in Constantinople was viewed with approbation by the critic Krikor Zohrab, who later commented that "the structure of the play is superb in its simplicity and reminds one of the construction of northern literature."[14] By 1911 it had enjoyed three hundred performances, a record unprecedented in Armenian theater history.

Zohrab's allusion presumably relates to Ibsen, many of whose plays were translated into Armenian and performed in the 1890s, for example, *Ghosts* in 1891 and *A Doll's House* the following year. And indeed Shirvanzade adopts an Ibsenesque psychological approach in his plays, realistically presenting his characters' positive and negative traits and adopting an ironic stance toward the convention in melodrama of identifying with the hero and vilifying the villain. The plot construction of *For the Sake of Honor* also owes something to the dramaturgy of the Scribean "well-made play," whose impact on Ibsen is well established, to generate suspense through carefully placed foreshadowing, discoveries, turning-point crises, and ironic climaxes.

The dramatist's increasing involvement in social and political causes manifests itself in his commitment to the improvement of women's rights, already featured in the play *Princess* (1891). This was followed by *Evgine* (1901), *Did She Have the Right?* (1902), and *Armenuhi* (1909). The second of these seems particularly dependent on Ibsen's *Doll's House*. Like the latter, it suffered critics' affront over a mother who abandons her children to escape a husband who has made her life unbearable. Shirvanzade directs an ironical apologia at his conservative detractors: "You would instruct Shirvanzade to have his heroine motivate her leaving by saying something patriotic such as 'Goodbye, my children, I'm going off to fight the Turks and preserve Armenia.'" He ends by observing that a true understanding of the situation will only result from future enlightenment.[15] *For the Sake of Honor* also promotes women's greater independence of thought and action in society in the characterization of Margarit.

That play sketches three generations of a dysfunctional family of provincial origins that had become caught up in the "get rich quick" atmosphere of the time. Intermittently we hear of one of the grandfathers who, as a village priest, embodies the traditional values of Transcaucasian agrarian life. In his novel *Namus* of 1885 Shirvanzade had treated the fiercely held code of sexual propriety maintained in that milieu. In a more cosmopolitan context, however, the concept of honor is capable of multiple constructions. In the present work the family represents society

———

14. A. B. Kaghtzrouni, ed., *Alexandre Shirvanzade* (New York: Armenian National Council of America, 1959), p. 18. For some negative criticism the play generated, see H. S. Tamrazyan, *Shirvanzade* (Erevan: Haypethrat, 1961), pp. 449–50.

15. *Shirvanzade: amboghjakan erker* [Shirvanzade: Collected works] (Erevan: Haypethrat, 1950), vol. 6, pp. 232–33.

"writ small," each of its members interpreting the term *honor* with significant nuance.

The patriarch of the current generation is Andreas Elizbarian. Something of a family man from his origins, he misses the affection of his children, who seem to him cold, calculating, and highly individualistic. A self-made pragmatist, he has not been above lying and cheating when this served his purpose. Now, though, he enjoys esteem as a philanthropist and pillar of society, an honor he safeguards by burning documents incriminating him of defrauding the family of his deceased business partner Otarian.

The other two figures of that generation, Andreas's wife, Eranuhi, and her brother, Saghatel, act as foils for each other. Eranuhi's sense of honor owes much to her formation in a priestly household. She opposes the moral relativism around her but maintains a subordinate silence. Her brother, in contrast, is a self-centered, small-minded, unscrupulous rogue. Totally devoid of any finer feelings, he steals from his brother-in-law, for whom he works as a clerk, and appears ready to countenance any action to increase his hoard, assisting Andreas in destroying the documents in order to blackmail him.

The siblings of the younger generation are also presented as foils. Of these, the elder son Bagrat is a chip off the old block. Building on his father's achievements, he nurses ambitious plans to expand the family business into a much larger complex. Consonant with this, he observes a greater distinction between manager and workmen, and holds the latter (even his uncle) to a much stricter code of accountability. In keeping with the times, he praises engineers over the old professional elite of lawyers and doctors, and supports science against religion, about which he favors skepticism. Fearing his credit would be damaged by scandal, he urges his sister, Margarit, to destroy the documents in the family's interest.

Bagrat's younger brother, Suren, has a more delicate, artistic disposition and affects the lifestyle of an upper-class beau. Despising the business of making money, he prefers to squander it on love affairs with opera stars and by gambling. According to this code, one must honor one's debts, and so he borrows large sums from his uncle in anticipation of his inheritance.

Although Rozalia, like Suren, has a penchant for extravagance, whereas the latter splurges on others, his sister is a materialist. Playing the socialite, she loves being driven in a carriage but, typical of her nouveau riche status, overly insists on distinctions between herself and the servants. Rozalia's sense of honor seems based on family expectations. As she says to Margarit, "I'm my father's daughter. I have to love and protect him-if you wish-even if he's a thief."

Margarit takes after her mother in the significance she accords to ethics. However, where Eranuhi derives her values from religion, her daughter, as Saghatel remarks, "talks like a philosopher," a propensity nurtured by her more extensive education and voracious reading. Her role in the play is that of a bourgeois Armenian Antigone, pitting principle against authority in confronting Andreas: "Father . . .

I'd die for your honor. But what about mine? Must I defile it for your riches? Spare me this shame. That's your duty as my father. Give me my honor. Without it I cannot live."

Having little experience of the world, she is prepared to sacrifice her life to maintain her sense of integrity, which she perceives as compromised by her father's destruction of the papers she had faithfully promised to guard. It is the mood of what Hegel calls "abstract right" that drives those who suffer its loss to seek satisfaction in the subjective depths of conscience. A shot heard offstage alerts us to the suicide. The melodramatic effect tempts modern audiences to smile. But, as in Ibsen's *Hedda Gabler*, the temptation is quickly dispelled in the genuinely tragic denouement.

LEWON SHANT

Shant's early plays (*The I Man*, 1901; *For the Sake of Others*, 1903; *On the Road*, 1904) coincide chronologically with those of Shirvanzade and maintain the same approach of treating contemporary problems in a realistic mode, despite differences in political philosophy. The former adhered to the more nationalist Armenian Revolutionary Federation founded in Tiflis in 1890, whereas the latter belonged to the social democratic Hnchakian Revolutionary Party organized in Geneva in 1887. His seven-year study of philosophy and psychology in Germany left its imprint in those works on his handling of the exercise of the will. However, his next play, *Ancient Gods*, written after a four-year hiatus, while exploring similar questions, did so within a radically different mise-en-scène and from an entirely new dramatic perspective. The work was totally epoch making. When staged in 1913, it took the Armenian literary and theatrical world by storm. Controversial in its subject matter, no less than its arresting sensual appeal, it became a runaway smash hit and a best-seller overnight, the debate it engendered spilling into Armenian newspaper columns for several years.

As a potent force in Europe and the Middle East during the nineteenth century, nationalism played a major role in Armenian culture. At its core lay a new definition of Armenian identity, explained no longer in terms of affiliation to a religious community but by ties to a common homeland, shared history, and collective symbols. Interest in folklore and ethnography led to a more serious preoccupation with Armenian mythology, both in the pre-Christian Armenian legends recorded by the historian Movses Khorenatsi and the living oral epic of Sasun. In the first two decades of the twentieth century this lore inspired a coterie of writers in avant-garde journals to renew Armenian literature by appealing to the powerful pristine symbols of the pagan era. One of the first of these, *Anahit* [goddess of nature], was begun in Constantinople by Arshag Chobanian in 1898 and continued in Paris. Another, *Mehean* [temple of Mithra], was founded by a group of writers, including the poet and novelist Gosdan Zarian, the novelist and critic Hagop Oshagan, and the poet Taniel Varuzhan (1884–1915), whose seminal collection *Hetanos erger* [Pagan songs] appeared in 1913.

It is against this background that Shant, seeking a broader canvas for his dramatic creation, began to mine the deep veins of Armenian myth. In *Ancient Gods*, an elemental dichotomy subsists between the ascetic, world-denying life of the monks on their island desert and the celebration of strength and beauty in the pagan temple scene, in which the young monk is moved to join. That scene, which culminates in the awesome epiphany of the deities Vahagn and Astghik, is one of impressive visual pomp and splendor, suggestive of the cinematographic treatment of a Cecil B. De Mille film epic. Its extravagant spectacle is characteristic of the playwright's heightened use of music, song, and dance in the play, as well as greater sophistication and elaboration in stage sets and lighting, commensurate with the richness of his theme. The overall effect is reminiscent of Wagner's concept of the *Gesammtkunstwerk*, uniting all the arts in the service of drama.

As in the rest of his mature dramas, Shant based the plot of *Ancient Gods* on an episode of the Armenian past, in this case, the founding of a monastery on the island (now a peninsula) in Lake Sevan in A.D. 874. According to historical accounts, the project was undertaken by the future catholicos,[16] Mashtots, and commissioned by Princess Mariam Bagratuni, wife of the local prince Vasak Siwni. This setting was particularly appropriate since, by report, Mashtots had had a liaison with a high-born lady before becoming a monk. In the play the motif is developed to powerful effect in the father superior's encounters with Princess Mary, creating dramatic tension by the juxtaposition of opposites: male and female, clerical and lay, sacred and profane, this-worldly and other-worldly.

In most sexually overlaid dialogue, the princess seeks to rekindle the flame of passion between them. Confessing she is largely a stranger to her two offspring, she confronts the abbot with the fact that the monastic church they have been laboring over is actually their "child," dedicated not to Mary, Mother of God, but to herself, Princess Mary. The revelation devastates the cleric, who determines forthwith that their common edifice must be destroyed, as an abomination to his faith.

This interchange is paralleled by another between the young monk and the prince's daughter, Seda, who are united by a storm on the lake, from which the monk rescues the girl. Afterward, he is obsessed by fantasies of her, which disturb his devotions. The broad outline of this incident echoes that of Krikor Zohrab's short story *Potorige* [The storm] of 1889 in which a young man becomes withdrawn and delusional after sharing physical intimacy with a beautiful widow while on a boat in a storm at sea. Moreover, Shant had already constructed a similar scenario

---

16. The term *catholicos* designates the highest office in the Armenian ecclesiastical hierarchy.

in his novella *Dartse* [The turning point] of 1897, in which a monk embraces a young woman in order to assist her across a brook. Their physical contact arouses new emotions in him, which affirm his manhood and ultimately cause him to abandon his life of celibate austerity.

When the young monk divulges his innermost thoughts, the blind monk, a Teiresias figure, informs him that these elemental stirrings within himself are demonic apparitions, against which he must contend in spiritual warfare. However, in the midst of the long monastic office in church, the young man drifts into a reverie, his imagination spiriting him off to participate in pagan rites and renounce the ascetic struggle for the instant gratification of the senses. In another quasi-dream sequence he sees a hermit, whose only sense of value comes from a pit he has been digging. In keeping with the biblical book of Ecclesiastes, the latter avers that "all is vanity." However, in a crucial transformation of the scene, the hermit disappears, the pit is filled up, and the monk's beloved Seda appears on top of it, only to vanish again. Finally, she appears mermaid-like and beckons him to unite with her once more in the sea. In the end, the other monks scramble to retrieve his body from the waves to give him burial at the threshold of the church, one already acknowledged as the dwelling of the ancient gods, not that of the new faith.

Shant is the first Armenian dramatist to employ such expressionistic techniques. In this play he puts them to effective use in objectifying the residual worldliness in the mind of the father superior and the blind monk in the person of the man in white. They are even more evident in the onstage representation of the workings of the young monk's unconscious in his fantasies of Seda, the natural elements of the winds and the waves, and the hermit.

These parts of the play contrast significantly with the linear realism of the main plot. In the latter, the abbot decides that the church must be demolished, as we have noted, and informs the brotherhood of his decision. The majority oppose him, citing its external beauty and traditional form, their lack of ability in construction, the offense that such a move would cause to their patrons, and the possible repercussion of having their food rations suspended. Hence the father superior leaves on his own to embark on a continuous process of building and destroying on a higher plane, stating: "This shrine shall have my reason as foundation, my will for columns, my faith its dome!"

This section of the drama is reminiscent of the conclusion of Ibsen's romantic tragedy *Brand* of 1866, in which the main character abandons the church he is having built in the town, regarding it as corrupt, and leads the townspeople up the mountain to worship in the natural Ice Church. However, half way up, the exhausted community are easily won over by the mayor and his collaborator, the bishop, to return to their homes, after falsely promising them a redistribution of wealth on their return. The Armenian dramatist's keen interest in Ibsen's work is evident from his translation of the latter's *Enemy of the People* (1882). Although more prevalent in later plays such as *The Master Builder* (1892) and *When We Dead*

Awaken (1899), already in *Brand* Ibsen utilized elements of symbolism to convey his dramatic message.

In *Ancient Gods* Shant follows Ibsen in his depiction of what might be called the Apollonian and Dionysian principles of Nietzsche's *Birth of Tragedy* in contrasting the father superior's more cerebral path with the young monk's sensuous journey, which had provoked the former's retort: "Through you speaks primitive mankind." The young monk's susceptibility to fantasy, full of nostalgia for a previous world beyond the strictures of the critical mind, parallels the mood of other symbolist playwrights of the time, such as Hauptmann or Maeterlinck. Indeed, the love scenes in the latter's *Pelléas and Mélisande* of 1893 bear comparison with the passionate exchanges between Seda and the young monk in the present play.

The decade and a half separating *Ancient Gods* from *Nazar the Brave* (1923), the next work in the anthology, witnessed unprecedented turmoil internationally, which was to engulf the Armenian communities of both the Ottoman and Russian empires. In the course of World War I and its aftermath, the first genocide of the twentieth century was perpetrated against the Armenian population of the Ottoman capital and the eastern provinces, causing widespread death and destruction. Large numbers were deported from their traditional homeland into exile in Syria, thus precipitating the creation of the current worldwide Armenian Diaspora. The immediate impact of this catastrophe is reflected in the dramatic works of Suren Bartewian (1876–1921), such as *The Eternal Flame*.[17]

Meanwhile, the collapse of Romanov rule in Russia offered Armenians in Transcaucasia the opportunity to declare independence. However, squeezed between the advancing Kemalist Turkish forces in the west and the Red Army from the north, the government of the Armenian Revolutionary Federation capitulated to the latter in December 1920. Heralded by poets of the revolution like Eghishe Charents (1897–1937) and Shushanik Kurghinyan (1876–1927), the first years of socialist rule inaugurated a period of intellectual ferment resulting in the foundation of the Institute of Science and Art, and of artistic experimentation, which led to the establishment of the State Dramatic Theater in 1922, a music conservatory in the following year, and a film studio in 1925. The atmosphere in the Armenian capital

---

17. More recently, dramatic reflections of the Genocide include Perch Zeytuntsyan's *Mets Lrutyune* [The great silence] (1984), depicting the life of the poet Taniel Varuzhan, and *Otki, Datarann e galis* [All rise, the court is in session] (1988), dealing with the trial of Soghomon Tehlirian. The latter was produced under the impact of glasnost, which permitted greater freedom of speech on nationalist issues. Moreover, the past decade has seen the proliferation of four treatments, in English, of different facets of the subject in America: (1) *Grandma, Pray for Me*, by Nishan Parlakian (1990); (2) *Beast on the Moon*, by Richard Kalinoski (1995); (3) *Mirrors*, by Herand Markarian (1996); and *Nine Armenians*, by Leslie Ayvazian (1998).

is vividly captured in Zabel Esayian's travelogue *Prometheus Liberated* of 1926. By the following year, however, the situation started to change as deviation and dissension from the ascendant Stalinist position began to be purged from the party and positions of authority in public life.

DERENIK DEMIRCHYAN

One of the first Armenian dramas of the Soviet period treats the common folkloric motif of the rise of a total nonentity to kingly power. Armenian tradition had embodied the theme in the story of the ne'er-do-well peasant Nazar. One day he strikes dead several flies in an incident reminiscent of the delightful tale of "Seven in One Blow." In an English version of the latter, a tailor swatted dead one fly and the number was overblown to seven. In the Armenian tale Nazar is too lazy to count the number killed, and so he rounds out the figure to a thousand.[18] This folk tale received its first literary adaptation at the hands of the poet Avetik Isahakyan under the title *Agha Nazar* in 1911. A year later another important poet of the time, Hovhannes Tumanian, produced a second version, also close to the folk idiom. Demirchyan's play *Kaj Nazar* [Nazar the brave] of 1923 represents a more independent handling of the material. First appearing in the literary magazine *Nork*, it was subsequently published several times in Armenian and Russian, as well as in Turkish and Georgian. Its immense popularity secured its transformation into other artistic media, first as an opera by Hamo Stepanyan and then in 1940 as a film.

Although the main character seems doomed to failure, thanks to a fortuitous series of events he realizes the fantasies of the man in the street, living in palatial luxury like the tyrant of Plato's *Republic*. What is laughable is that his glorious achievements are always dependent on inadvertent actions, which at first seem to be ridiculous and potentially harmful. When Nazar retreats, this is viewed as a subterfuge to cut off the enemy at the flank. Carrying his banner into Zorbastan, he escapes a tiger, which strays into his ranks, by climbing a tree. Accidentally falling onto the beast's back, he seems to be fearlessly riding the animal. In the Land of the Giants he must fight to displace the king. This time his willful horse foils his escape plan by charging into the fray. Nazar grabs a tree limb to stop his forward movement, but, the limb being dead, it snaps off. His enemies think he has uprooted a tree in the fierceness of his attack, and the king abdicates in his favor.

In keeping with the earlier legend, Demirchyan's Nazar is thus a potent embodiment of the workings of fate and fortune, having had "greatness thrust upon"

---

18. The Armenian rhyme between the hero's name, Nazar, and the number one thousand (*hazar*) is aptly exploited in the jingle the hero creates to celebrate his feat: "I'm Nazar the Brave, I'll have you know. I slay a thousand with a single blow."

him quite literally by Lady Luck. So uncanny is Nazar's winning streak that he ends up believing implicitly in his unassailability. Reassuring his wife Ustian, who had earlier driven Nazar out of the house but has now rejoined him after hearing of his precipitate prosperity, he promises her, "We'll live a comfortable and secure life."

The human face of his unprecedented advancement lies in the effective use of publicity, or, in current parlance, "spin." The credibility of the written account on Nazar's banner of his slaying a thousand creates an aura about Nazar, predisposing people to show him deference as an intrepid warrior. Others then jump on the bandwagon of Nazar's increasing fame, fabricating memories of common exploits to ingratiate themselves.

In the Tumanian account, it is Nazar who goes to the village priest as the only literate person around, and the latter humors him by emblazoning his watchword on a piece of cloth, merely as a joke. However, Demirchyan expands the episode into a somewhat anticlerical satire. The idea of publicizing Nazar's achievements arises from a wacky, decrepit subdeacon, who mutters incoherently about their forming part of a larger picture of eschatological speculation, vouchsafed to him in dreams and visions. Then, in token of divine protection, he gives the peasant a few specks of earth in a charm and sends the coward off, saying, "Go vanquish your enemies."

Tumanian's Nazar is merely pitiful and timid and reigns as a *bon viveur*. Demirchyan's character, however, is more complex, acquiring the attributes of guile, opportunistic aggression, and flamboyance. In the course of acts 4 and 5, he becomes corrupted by the adulation of the courtiers and the absolute power he wields, and he begins issuing preposterous commands: that "the sun rise in the east and set in the west," that "people are to be born and die." In his overweening ambition, he aspires to "liberate the entire world from unworthy kings." He has learned that "people are so stupid that they will put up with anything." Exploiting this, he has himself proclaimed a saint, sharply increases taxation, and insists on putting civilian recruits in the front line of battle. People fight and die for him. If they win, he gets the credit. If they lose, "I am not to blame, what do I care?" he cynically remarks.

Man's gullibility and its power to facilitate tyranny are thus central to the play's theme. As Hakhverdyan contends, the work is on a par with Bertolt Brecht's caricature of Hitler's rise to power in *The Career of Arturo Ui.*[19] Nothing in English compares to it except, perhaps, Henry Fielding's *Tragedy of Tragedies, or the Life and Death of Tom Thumb the Great* (1730), which was inspired by the digit-sized hero of folklore. Just as that play contains political overtones, so in *Nazar the Brave* we

---

19. See L. Hakhverdyan, "Armenian Classical Drama and Its International Context," *Review of National Literatures* (Armenia) 13 (1984): 193.

note allusions to the troops' refusal to fight for Nazar latterly and the people's fomenting revolt. His luck finally runs out, however, when he tries to send Ustian away in order to ennoble himself by consorting with queens of the blood royal.

Ustian, that last vestige of his real-life self, is provoked to expose him as the poseur and fraud he really is, by venting her ire at him as she had done in act 1. His imploding fall is as mercurial as his rise. Immediately the courtiers begin plundering the palace fixtures, dismantling Nazar's glory before his very eyes, while the common people laugh and scorn him for his being pusilanimously hen-pecked. The motif of an authority figure facing the consequences of his actions adumbrates the main focus of Demirchyan's play *Phosphoric Ray* of 1932.

Ustian had always mistrusted her husband's intrinsic belief in their luck. Considering that their rags-to-riches story had a dreamlike quality, she braced herself for fortune's fickle turn. Now that the bubble is burst, she joins in the scrimmage to salvage some valuables to take back with her. As is often the case in folk tales, the moral is underscored at the end, in this case by the house manager's epilogue. Characterizing the play as a "bad dream," he denies that this is the effect of luck but rather the result of people allowing themselves "to be hoodwinked by scarecrows," inspiring Muradyan to argue that the work unequivocally sounds the alarm against despotism.[20] However, he concludes the comedy on a lighter note, by a theatrical analogy. Just as he plunges the stage in darkness to indicate that the performance is over, so he expresses his hope for the future by affirming that the real-life "dream" is also over: "There's no more king, no Nazar now."

In transposing the material from narrative to dramatic voice, Demirchyan renders the characters virtually Hirschfeldian caricatures set into motion. He had to write a hyperbolic travesty of reality, an outsized burlesque, a circus with a linear plot not dissimilar to the comedies of Aristophanes. The play's grotesque and phantasmagorical aspects are reminiscent of Gogol's *Revizor* [The inspector general] of 1836. The latter's plot is similar in poking fun at the provincial townspeople for feting a member of the lower classes as a visiting official. Small wonder, then, that the master farceur Danny Kaye played the protagonist in a film version of Gogol's work a few decades ago. Indeed, Kaye would have made a great Nazar!

PERCH ZEYTUNTSYAN

The 1920s marked a significant cultural transition for the Armenian Republic. Traditional classics, European and Armenian, shared the stage of the Erevan State Theater with newer works like Demirchyan's *Kaj Nazar* and Shant's *Ancient Gods*,

---

20. H. Muradyan, *Derenik Demirchyan: Kyankn u gortse* [Derenik Demirchyan: Life and work] (Erevan: Armenian SSR Academy of Sciences, 1961), p. 300.

despite the latter author's political views, which subsequently kept his oeuvre off the repertoire until the final years of the Soviet Union.[21] At the same time, other writers like the poet Eghishe Charents experimented with novel theatrical forms, improvising large-scale spectacles with mass nonprofessional participation on the theory that the new society demanded a radically new kind of art.

With the growth of Stalinism, the role of ideology, centrally formulated and implemented by the increasingly encompassing organs of the Communist Party, began to obtrude more palpably on the republic's cultural milieu. Strict censorship imposed limits on artistic freedom, harnessing it to the tenets of socialist realism. This tended toward the publication of rather two-dimensional works, unmasking the bourgeois enemy within Soviet society or extolling the virtues of exemplary citizens in the factory or collective farm, while overlooking societal faults and inspiring confidence in the future. Similarly, during World War II, the arts were pressed into service in support of the defense of the homeland against Nazi aggression (e.g., Aramashot Babayan's play *Our Struggle Is Just* in 1941). In the aftermath they also had their role to play in the cold war.

Significant change did not occur until the thaw under Krushchev and its aftermath, when a new generation of writers and artists like the poet Paruyr Sevak and the film director Frunze Dovlatyan were allowed to explore topics previously taboo, such as nationalism and the significance of the individual. Examples of this greater latitude on stage include Aleksandr Araksmanyan's *Sixty Years and One Hour* (1965), treating Stalinist purges in Siberia, and Zhora Harutyunyan's *Your Last Haven*, on two brothers who emigrate to Armenia from the Diaspora after the war, one of whom resettles in the United States because of the degree of corruption he finds in his homeland. Social criticism was also more incisive, as in Zhirayr Ananyan's farce *My House Is Not Your House*, which pokes fun at the rigors of Soviet bureaucracy in allocating city apartments.

Perch Zeytuntsyan is a younger contemporary of these playwrights, who began his literary career in the 1960s. His drama *Unfinished Monologue* (1981) provides a panorama of three generations of Soviet society from its pioneers to their offspring, who led its postwar industrial expansion, and their children, who are now growing up under its moral decline in Brezhnev's era of stagnation (1964–82). The work thus anticipates Gorbachev's belated appeal for perestroika, or reconstruction, in its critique of the widening gulf between sociopolitical rhetoric and actual practice.

It focuses on a traditional Armenian household where grandfather, father, and son live under one roof. Arsen Avetyan, now a pensioner, has a large circle of friends on whose behalf he continually appeals to his son, Rafayel, to circumvent

---

21. In contrast, the play was recently revived in Erevan during an International Day of Theater before an audience including President Robert Kocharian. See the report in *Marmara* (Istanbul), April 1, 1999.

bureaucratic red tape.[22] Rafayel, in turn, grew up under wartime deprivations to become the director of a construction works, a responsible position, in which he is constantly called on to make decisions. Consequently he yearns for the reassurance of a bygone era of greater idealism and sharply defined moral judgment on "how to live, how to tell good from evil, white from black. After all, there are so many shades in between." Obsessively he asks his father to retell the story of the trial of a coworker for stealing four biscuits from a Russian supply train in the 1920s. He is also anxious about his son, Vigen, who is on the threshold of adulthood, making the transition from school to university. His son is street-smart on the importance of cronyism and a "sweetener" to facilitate acceptance into higher education. Like a dutiful father, Rafayel has made the necessary arrangements, yet his conscience is not at peace. He apologizes for his action, when on the phone about it in the presence of colleagues, and insists on going through the motions of congratulating Vigen on attaining his goal by his own efforts.

Hard work and dedication are the essence of Rafayel's life, as he says about himself in his final monologue: "He came into the world as a laborer and that's how he lived and died." So devoted is he to what he perceives to be his public duty that he has totally neglected his individual needs and those of his family. Striving to do what he feels is right has led him to take a stand against the ministry's rigid command structure over a rail link to service an industrial complex. Perceiving the inadequacy of the partial four-kilometer track, which has been approved, he sets about the necessary wheeling and dealing and finessing of the accounts to extend it to thirteen kilometers so that it connects the plant directly with its workforce in the neighboring villages.

Although even his superior, Markosyan, acknowledges that right may be on Rafayel's side, the latter has exposed himself to censure by disobeying orders and abusing his office. Laboring under this tension, Rafayel disintegrates physically and emotionally: First he suffers a heart attack, and then, when it appears that proceedings will be brought against him, he tries to commit suicide. Frail and vulnerable in his stream of consciousness confession, which he tapes for his family, he is perhaps honest with himself for the first time since the age of ten, when he forced himself to wear the mask of a strong man at the expense of his real nature. Admitting his mistakes in allowing himself to "float with the current," he sees himself and the surrounding society careening out of control without a sense of common purpose. In keeping with this, the pace of the play in performance is absolutely frenetic. In productions by the Sundukian Theater, use of the revolving stage had the effect of melding scenes together into a single forward thrust.

---

22. The main character's name sheds light on his role. His second name is based on an Armenian root signifying good news, while his first name is that of an angel ("God has healed") familiar from the apocryphal book of Tobit on.

Although a conservative at heart, striving for the selfless pursuit of justice, he has also compromised his principles, as when he bought someone else's winning ticket to surprise his wife with winning a Zhiguli make of car in the lottery. At the same time, while insisting she give up her career and stay at home to assuage his male jealousy, he is prepared to indulge in assignations with married women, ostensibly to solicit their intercession with their husbands to further his projects at work.

In indicting himself with failure, Rafayel questions the health of the culture in which he lives. Straining to bring together rhetoric and practice has ripped him apart, fragmented his identity, and brought him to the verge of self-negation. In the brief final scenes, however, the dramatist pulls us back from the edge. The impending disaster has not yet arrived, and in the interim there is time to commend the heroism of Rafayel's moral struggle and searing self-scrutiny, leaving us to ponder its broader implications.

ANAHIT AGHASARYAN

One of the most significant, if unintended, results of Gorbachev's policy of glasnost was to provide an outlet for pent-up nationalist tensions, which hastened the downfall of the Soviet edifice. Armenia was one of the first republics to take advantage of the new freedom of speech. From the autumn of 1987 on, meetings, often numbering in the thousands, would be convened at Opera Square (now renamed Liberty Square) to protest ecological issues, as well as the situation of the ethnic Armenian majority in the region of Nagorno Karabagh located in Azerbaijan. This proved a training ground for the new cadre of the first post-Soviet government. The Republic of Armenia declared independence on September 23, 1991, and proceeded to set in place the apparatus of a democratic society, holding parliamentary and presidential elections in the same year and drafting a constitution.

A vital element in the construction of civil society is the tolerance of political satire, the genre to which the last play in the collection, Anahit Aghasaryan's *Madmen of the World, Unite!* (1992), belongs.[23] Focusing on the novel electioneering process, her work captures excellently the instability of the transition charted above, highlighting its potential either as a vehicle for real change or simply as political business as usual but under new management. She pointedly contrasts the

---

23. Though present in Armenia under the Soviet period in periodicals like *Vosni*, the satirical genre has burgeoned since independence, resulting in such popular rambunctious farces as Mikayel Poghosyan's *Khatabalada*, a lightly veiled parody on the Faust legend applied to the career of the poet/politician Vano Siradeghyan, who has been indicted on charges of corruption in office.

narrow interests of the political parties jockeying for position with the demands of the wider electorate for a more responsive administration, a radically democratic style of government truly representative of the people. Tracing the movement from a grass-roots to a national level, the playwright envisions its global implications, as the center of attention moves from Erevan's Liberty Square to New York's Statue of Liberty. Its charter of human rights becomes a new ideology replacing the discredited Soviet shibboleths. In keeping with this, the play's title is a spoof on the socialist watchword "Workers of the World, Unite!"[24] Consequently, though the scene is set in a manifestly Armenian environment, the fundamental issues it raises are of universal concern.

The representatives of the two sides, the officials of the five parties contesting the election, on the one hand, and a former suicidal maniac named Mher, who has committed himself to a psychiatric facility, on the other, have more in common than first meets the eye: Both are professional con artists. As an actor, Mher is a master of disguise, while his counterparts display the prevarication of career politicians. Although they are drawn as two-dimensional caricatures, Mher's character undergoes significant growth as he becomes more politicized.[25] The uncertainty of whether he will allow himself to be corrupted in the process is the main engine of suspense until the last scene.

The portrayal of Mrs. Amatuni's misandric barbs and use of feminine wiles to seduce her opponent pokes fun at platforms like that of the actual Armenian feminist party Shamiram. Meanwhile, Hasratyan, a socialist leader, comes across as a party hack with a shady past, who tries to divert voters' attention by appealing to serious-sounding imponderables like *Realpolitik* and the *Zeitgeist*. Shamamyan, a member of the sitting government, is ruthless in silencing the opposition with his sinister hit squad. Brtujyan, in contrast, represents the Armenian Revolutionary Federation, the party that governed Armenia during the first republic (1918–20), now reestablishing its base in Armenia. Not to be outdone in stealth by his colleagues, the Communist Party representative disguises himself as a statue prepared to adorn Mher's grave. The image of the gravestone implies the death of the party and its message, belonging, as Mher states, in Erevan's Historical Museum, where the statue of Lenin, which used to dominate the eponymous central square, now rests.

---

24. The idea had already been applied by the political satirist Aramayis Sahakyan in an article entitled "Armenians of the World, Unite!" (1989). See his *Khorhrdavor khorhrdaran* [Mysterious parliament] (Erevan: Parberakan, 1992), pp. 11–16.

25. Their names already reveal a great deal about their characters. Shamamyan derives from the root of muskmelon and suggests the incumbent politician's rotundity from overindulgence in the high life. The significance of Hasratyan is yearning and desire, suggesting his driving ambition for office. The root underlying Brtujyan signifies bluster and bombast, a stereotype of political rhetoric.

The final figure of significance is Aramyan, who, despite his amiable appearance as the unwilling stooge compelled to perform dirty work, ultimately emerges as the consummate Machiavellian *macher*, a political parasite ready to lend his services to the highest bidder. His connivance with Davtyan to procure a similar victim willing to immolate himself at Mher's inauguration powerfully encapsulates the eternal struggle between means and ends in the political process.

Aramyan's counterpart among Mher's ranks of seeming misfits at the psychiatric facility is the professor. In combining astronomy with religious speculation, he resembles the "mad scientist" of science fiction, expatiating on the metaphysical dimension of the evil at work in political machinations. So firmly does he espouse his principles that compromise is impossible, and hence, perceiving himself betrayed, he commits suicide rather than sully his integrity. Although the professor does not live to see the arresting play-within-a-play opening of act 3 in Betelgeyze, it certainly manifests his utopian ideals of purity and harmony unattainable in the real world of politics.

Mher, in contrast, develops into more of a political animal. Dazzled at first by the unheard of sum offered for his services to the opposition parties, he seizes the initiative on realizing his marketability and determines to undermine the system from within by mounting his own campaign for the presidency. The symbolist scene of the operation to remove his heart potently suggests the impact of the political process, which might leave Mher "heart-less," callous, and uncaring. However, like the invincible cock of the folktale, remarkably he survives, invigorated to advance his crusade for justice.

His comeback is a kind of resurrection from which he emerges as a savior figure somewhat larger than life, in keeping with the professor's apocalyptic speculation. His second name Astuatsatryan already indicates that he is the bearer of divine favor. Moreover, a previous scene prepares us for his role by alluding to his namesake, Little Mher, of Armenian legend, who, after being enclosed in Raven's Rock near Lake Van, will reappear at the end of time when evil has been dispelled from the world.[26] By triumphing over venality and narrow party politics, Mher ends up vindicating his championship of the professor's principles, highlighting the "prophetic" sociopolitical role of the artist and intellectual, so important a theme in modern Armenian literature.

In overall technique the play invites comparison with the American drama *One Flew over the Cuckoo's Nest* in stage and film versions. In it the world of the insane has a logic that operates as well in its own context as does the ostensible clear logic of an alleged sensible world. Aghasaryan develops the theme of the theatri-

---

26. It is significant that Shant employs the parallel Armenian legend of Artavazd and Zabel Esayian, as has been stated, the related Greek legend of Prometheus regarding the downfall of the Russian Empire and the new era of constructing socialism in the 1920s.

cality of life, especially the political process, along with the interplay between illusion and reality. In doing so, she has not only exploited various absurdist techniques to good effect but has liberally drawn on the works of Shakespeare, which, in the translation by Mahseyan, have exercised an enormous influence on Armenian culture.[27] She liberally employs *King Lear* to assist in her project of subverting the polar opposition between madness and sanity, monarch and fool, in addition to Leoncavallo's opera *I Pagliacci*. Similarly *Hamlet* serves as a model for avenging corruption in high places by a hero with theatrical affinities. All in all, while making a serious comment on the absurdities of democratic governance, Aghasaryan provides an exciting, provocative theatrical extravaganza.

It is impossible for an anthology of this kind to convey a fully comprehensive impression of the vast range and diversity of plays composed in Armenian within the century and a half surveyed in this volume. Nevertheless, the seven examples selected here include some of the best known and best loved works from that repertoire, all of which have been tried and tested on stage. Hence they may provide a reliable insight into the characteristic themes of the Armenian tradition, its historical evolution, and its particular contribution to Western drama.

Sharing in the many upheavals and dislocations of Armenian history during the modern age, the theater continues to play an important cultural role both in the communities of the Diaspora and in the homeland. Surviving the transition from state funding in the Soviet period to increased private sector sponsorship, theatrical companies in the capital and provincial cities of the republic are restructuring for the future, and a new generation of dramatists is entering the field, vying with more established names to propel Armenian drama into the new millennium.

---

27. See N. Parlakian, "Shakespeare and the Armenian Theater," *Council on National Literatures Quarterly World Report* 5, no. 4 (1982): 3-12.

MODERN ARMENIAN DRAMA

GABRIEL SUNDUKIAN

Gabriel Sundukian was born in Tiflis, the administrative center of Russian Transcaucasia, on June 29,
1825. His father, Mkrtum, was a merchant who had
settled there as a convenient hub on a trade axis between the North Caucasus and Iran. He had also
traveled to different parts of Europe. Mrktum died
when Gabriel was six, leaving him and his two siblings, Mikayel and Hripsime. Gabriel received his
early training from his mother, before attending the
private school of Hakob Shahan Jrpetian, later first
incumbent of the professorship in the Armenian
language at the Ecole Pratique des Langues Orien-
tales Vivantes in Paris. During the five-year course
of study Sundukian learned classical and modern
Armenian, as well as French and Italian from Jrpetian's French wife. Subsequently he attended the
Arzanov brothers' school for the gentry for two years,
where he developed greater skills in Russian to facilitate entry to the Russian gymnasium in 1840. On
completion of the six-year curriculum there, Sundukian was selected as one of six youths sent to attend the University of St. Petersburg to train as official translators for the Transcaucasian viceroyalty.

During his course of study at the imperial capital (1846–50) Sundukian majored in Arabic, Turkish, and Persian and submitted a dissertation on the
principles of versification in the latter language.
While there, he came under the influence of Russian literary experts like Nikitenko and read widely
in the works of Shakespeare, Schiller, and Hugo.

His interest in drama was whetted by attending performances of works such as Gogol's *Inspector General* and Griboedov's *Woes of Wit*, as well as French plays at the Michael Theater.

Back in Tiflis he entered the civil service, as artists often did to earn a living (e.g., Rimsky Korsakov). Additionally, he volunteered as a teacher of geometry at the Nersisian School, established by Nerses Ashtaraketsi, activist bishop of the Armenian community of Tiflis in 1824. Two years later he was relieved of his position along with M. F. Akhundov, founder of modern Azerbaijani drama, and was sent on an assignment to the North Caucasian port of Derbent as an engineering and architectural inspector. In part as a result of the intercession of the Georgian aristocratic poet Grigol Orbeliani, Sundukian was reposted to Tiflis in September 1858 and given a position in the development of rail communications in the region. He remained in the civil service till 1907.

The year 1863 proved extremely significant for Sundukian in several ways. First, it marked his marriage to Sopia Mirimanian, with whom he had five children. In the same year, a regular Armenian theater company opened in Tiflis through the efforts of a group that had been involved a few years earlier in student theatricals in Moscow. That year also saw the staging of Sundukian's first work for the stage, *Gisheruan sabre kher e* [Sneezing at night's good luck], inspired by the zany vaudeville *Dalal Ghalo* by Nikoghayos Pughinian, one of the theatrical enthusiasts. There is a hint in this light farce of a theme to be developed in the dramatist's later major plays, those on the subject of marriage and social mobility. The local paper *Meghu Hayastani* [Bee of Armenia] critiqued the play, highlighting, among other things, weakness in characterization, which gave him reason to pause for three years before writing again for the stage.

The rest of his production in the sixties continues the trend of light, humorous representations of the life and manners of the Armenian community of Tiflis. *Khatabala* [Quandary] (1866) focuses on the issue of dowry, the role of the matchmaker, and the lack of any real courtship between the bride and groom. *Oskan Petrovich en kinkume* [Oskan Petrovich in the afterlife] of the same year is another farce. *Ev ayln kam nor Diogenese* [Et cetera or the new Diogenes] (1869) also treats the topic of marriage but from the intended groom's point of view. He and his father differ as to who should be his bride, the former seeking to elope with his lower-class fiancée while the latter insists he marry the daughter of the wealthy Briliantov.

With *Pepo* (1871) a new phase begins in which the dramatist starts to handle the same overall themes of bourgeois domestic drama with more maturity, probing more deeply into the underlying social trends that gave rise to the problems and the inequalities facing his main characters. A more serious discussion of the impact of incipient capitalism followed in *Kanduats ochakhe* [Ruined family] (1873). Consonant with this, a more critical rewrite of *Khatabala* was staged in 1879.

His next three plays, *Amusinner* [Spouses] (1893), *Baghnesi bokhcha* [Bath bag] (1907), and *Ser ew azatutiwn* [Love and liberty] (1910) continued the theme of matrimony inaugurated by *Sneezing at Night's Good Luck*. Of these, two should be of considerable interest to the modern reader. In the first of the three, which is Sundukian's only play written in the new standard East Armenian rather than the local dialect of Tiflis, the heroine actually leaves her philandering husband, who ultimately divorces her. Preceding by some eight years Shirvanzade's play on the same theme *Did She Have the Right?* it enunciates the idea that mutual love is the most important quality in a marriage. It also advances the cause of women's rights by commenting on the inequality of local law, which favors the husband in divorce cases.[1]

Bath Bag is a more bitter satire of the impact of capitalism in Transcaucasia and its negative influence on personal relationships. It seeks to explore the circumstances that might draw together figures like the moneylender Zimzimov and his beautiful young, status-conscious wife, Epemia, from his play *Pepo*, concluding that poor men look for rich wives, whereas rich men want beautiful wives.

Not only was Sundukian devoted to the Armenian theater, but he was also quite closely associated with the Georgian stage. Moreover, he would often direct Georgian troupes of actors in Tiflis and the second city of Kutaisi for productions of his works in Georgian translation, in which his critique of contemporary social mores was equally appreciated.

Sundukian's plays were performed in the Tiflis State Theater until it burned down in 1874. Subsequently productions were staged in various clubs and educational institutions, as well as in parks during the summer. In a letter to an intimate friend, he writes, "My plays have been presented and published many, many times, but I have never received a kopeck in profit from them." A man of great compassion, by all reports he gave much of his income to charity and helped the needy families of actors. Many of his satiric articles appeared in daily and weekly publications under the name *Hammal*, a pseudonym meaning street porter. Popular with his fans, very often he received ovations after performances of his plays and was carried home on the shoulders of adulatory members of the audience.

Sundukian's intrinsic interest in dramatic writing was such that in his last years he became involved in reinterpreting some of his works for the new medium of film. Though he did not live to see his plays in cinematographic adaptation, in due course some of them did find their way onto the screen. Of these, his masterpiece, *Pepo*, had the honor of being selected as the first Armenian talkie in 1935 under the doyen of early Armenian directors, Hamo Beknazaryan.

---

1. The inequality of women's rights in divorce law figured in a speech to the Ottoman parliament by the Armenian jurist and short story writer Krikor Zohrab in 1911, which marked a significant *volte face* from his earlier reactionary stance. See Rita Vorperian, "A Feminist Reading of Krikor Zohrab," Ph.D. thesis, University of California, Los Angeles, 1999.

Gabriel Sundukian died on March 29, 1911, at the age of eighty-five, retaining his mental acuity to the last. Only a few days before his death he was correcting printer's proofs of his ironically written comedy, *Ktak* [Testament], which appeared the following year.

E.D.M.

PEPO

(PEPO, 1871)

Translated by Ervant D. Megerditchian

CAST OF CHARACTERS

ARUTIN ZIMZIMOV: A rich merchant, sixty years old, medium height, stocky build, ruddy complexion, round face, heavy eyebrows, and trimmed mustache. His short gray hair is dyed jet black. He wears a European costume, white shirt, colored collar, vest and trousers, black coat, derby hat, watch and chain, and carries his pocketbook inside his vest pocket. He sports a colored silk handkerchief and worry beads. His speech and motions are slow, and he appears to be an honest man.

EPEMIA: ARUTIN's second wife, thirty years old, a handsome woman with auburn hair. She wears a beautiful European-style sky-blue dress, Georgian hat—a flat cap from which a white veil, attached with a silver pin, hangs to her waist. She is adorned with a gold watch and chain, many rings with precious stones on her fingers, and a red band round her neck. Her speech and motions are quick and full of life. She walks smartly and quickly.

PEPO: A fisherman, thirty-five years old, tall, strong, muscular, broad shoulders, regular features, short black hair growing low over his forehead, thin eyebrows and mustache. He has two suits of clothes. One for everyday use, like that of a Georgian workman, is dark and plain with wide trousers, tucked in woolen leggings, and a narrow silver girdle. He wears a reddish brown Caracal hat (with bent top), made of the fur of the Asian lynx, and carries a red cotton handkerchief. The other, his best suit, is in the same style, made from more expensive material. His walk is firm, his voice sweet but forceful, and his speech and personality very pleasant. Most often he wears a hat.

SHUSHAN: PEPO's widowed mother, fifty years old, medium height. She wears a Georgian ladies costume, black mantilla on the back of her head, a plain black dress, cut high in front, and a simple black shawl. When outdoors she wears a sable wrap.

KEKEL: PEPO's sister, eighteen years old, medium height, long black hair, fresh attractive features, a sweet voice and modest demeanor. She wears a handkerchief and veil on her head.

GIKO: PEPO's relative, sixty-five years old, medium height, slightly bent, has gray hair and a mustache, and is close shaven. He wears a Georgian costume, white shirt with black edges,wide blue trousers, plain woolen belt, black shoes, and Caracal hat dyed black with its top bent back. He always carries a cane, a snuffbox, and a large blue handkerchief. His walk, speech, and all his motions are very slow. He stutters profusely throughout.

KAKULI: PEPO's friend, twenty-five years old, a bit shorter than PEPO with a ruddy face and handsome features, dark hair combed over his forehead, thin eyebrows and mustache, and sparse short beard. He wears showy clothes like a carefree Caucasian redneck young blood, a large Caracal hat dyed Baku-style blue, and a loose-fitting red silk shirt,wide blue (or black) trousers, tucked-in woolen leggings, and a broad silver girdle embroidered with gold thread. His handkerchief is as beautiful as it is large. His voice is gruff and speech coarse. Very often he keeps his hat on.

GIGOLI: ARUTIN's store salesman, twenty-five years old. He wears a white Georgian costume buttoned in front, a narrow silver girdle, and a skullcap that is often in his hand.

SAMSON: ARUTIN's butler, eighteen, with long black hair combed in the latest style. He wears a Parisian shirt open in front, a white bandoleer slung across the shoulders with five silver cartridges on each side, close-fitting trousers, a silver girdle with dagger and small box on the side, black shoes in the latest mode and nicely polished. He is always hatless.

TWO OTHER SERVANTS: Employed in ARUTIN's house, hatless, wearing white gloves and dress suits.

The action of the play takes place in Tiflis, Russian Transcaucasia, 1870

Act 1: PEPO's house, at noon.
Act 2: ARUTIN's house at 1:45 P.M.
Act 3: PEPO's house, the next morning.

ACT 1

The scene is set in a multipurpose room in an old-fashioned house. Poorly furnished, it contains a china closet with shelves, one window, and three doors-right, left, and back center. At left, there is an immovable high takht,[2] *covered with a rug and cushions. At corner right is a kitchen table with a colored table cloth and a clothes-line hanging above it. On the china closet shelves are old-fashioned copper, wood, and clay pots, and various shaped wineglasses. A few chairs complete the room's furnishings.*

Scene 1

SHUSHAN (*seated on the sofa, knitting stockings*): Didn't you hear me?

KEKEL (KEKEL, *seated on the chair near the table busy sewing, takes another thread from her scrap bag.*): Just let me finish this first, Mama.

SHUSHAN: Leave it, rest a while; finish it later.

KEKEL: I can't, Mother. The customer will be here soon.

SHUSHAN: Devil take him! It'd be okay if only he were a more generous man!

KEKEL: That's the way it is, Mama. If I don't have things ready before he comes, he won't pay in full. You know he's a man without a conscience.

SHUSHAN: You're going to go blind. You didn't sleep a wink last night, and then you started work before dawn.

KEKEL: What can we do, Mama? It's not easy for poor people like us to make a living.

SHUSHAN: That's enough, Kekel! Damn our luck! We'll get by somehow.

KEKEL: Right this minute, Mama. As God's my witness, there's only a little more.

SHUSHAN: I couldn't sleep, thinking about you and your brother. You with your problems and your brother with his worries. (*Pause, then to herself*) I wonder why he's so late? I hope nothing's happened to him.

KEKEL (*anxious to placate her*): You mean he's never been out all night before, Mama?

SHUSHAN: He usually comes home by early morning. But it's almost noon now, and there's no sign of him.

KEKEL: Maybe he's busy in the market.

SHUSHAN (*sighing*): God willing, you're right, my child! My heart's uneasy. Who

---

2. A Middle Eastern form of rectangular couch/table suitable for lying on, dining, or performing various household tasks. Traditionally set in a hole dug in the ground, in which a fire may be kindled, family members would slide their legs under it for warmth during cold weather.

knows? Maybe the river rose and swept him away. Maybe he jumped in to save someone and drowned.

KEKEL: Now Mama, why are you talking like this?

SHUSHAN: If anything happens to him, we're lost.

KEKEL: In God's name, Mama dear, stop worrying. He's not a child. All your talk's only upsetting me.

SHUSHAN: What kind of a life is this? (*She looks up.*) Oh, Arutin! May Almighty God be your judge.

(*Footsteps are heard offstage.*)

KEKEL: I think he's here, Mother!

SHUSHAN (*listening*): Is that really him? (*Shaking her head*) No!

KEKEL (*also listening*): Oh, it's only Giko!

Scene 2

The Same, GIKO

GIKO (*He enters by center door, wearing a hat and with cane in hand, stuttering.*): G-good m-morning to y-you!

SHUSHAN (*sadly*): Good morning, Giko! Come in!

KEKEL (*She stands and nods to* GIKO. *To herself*): I dropped a dish towel this morning. I knew someone was going to come. (*She sits and resumes her work.*)

GIKO (*sitting on a chair close to* SHUSHAN): How are y-you? A-Are things g-good?

SHUSHAN: Thank God, we're still alive!

GIKO: Thank G-God! Where's Pepo? Isn't he home y-yet?

SHUSHAN: No! Any news?

GIKO: Y-yes! I have.

SHUSHAN: I knew it. May I go blind! What news have you brought?

GIKO (*soberly*): What news?

SHUSHAN: Yes!

GIKO: It isn't such good news, Sh-Shushan!

SHUSHAN (*more frightened*): What is it? Has he drowned?

(KEKEL *drops her sewing and stares at them, more frightened.*)

GIKO (*calmly*): Who's drowned? What are you talking about?

SHUSHAN: He hasn't drowned then?

GIKO (*crossing himself*): For the love of God, I don't know what you're talking about.

SHUSHAN: Last night, around midnight, he took his net and went to the river, and he hasn't returned since.

GIKO: G-God bless your soul! You frightened me for a minute! He's not afraid of drowning. A river wilder than our own Kura couldn't drown him.

SHUSHAN: Then what news were you talking about?

GIKO: What n-news?

SHUSHAN: Out with it, for the love of God!

GIKO: W-wait a minute! Have a little p-pa-tience! The Lord have mercy on your mother's soul. God has written a lot of things on people's brows, sometimes h-happiness, sometimes s-sadness. (*He takes his snuffbox from his vest pocket.*)

KEKEL (*to herself*): Whatever he says is always disturbing.

SHUSHAN: Sadness! That's what God gives us, morning, noon, and night.

GIKO: What can you do, Sh-Shushan? Our fate's in God's hands. Both s-sadness (*yawning*) and h-happiness. (*Yawning again, he inhales some snuff.*) Hum, hoh. A man's affairs go as G-God wishes.

SHUSHAN: So be it! What can we do?

GIKO: That's so, Sh-Shushan. This morning I heard some bad news. I was uneasy so I went to see your future son-in-law and talked to him face to face. (*To* KEKEL) He asked about you and sends his compliments, Kekel!

(KEKEL *bows her head slightly to* GIKO, *dries her tears and continues sewing.*)

He said he misses you a lot. (*He inhales more snuff and splutters.*)

(KEKEL *wipes her eyes again.*)

SHUSHAN: You've worn us out waiting for you to get to the point. In Heaven's name! Tell us what you've got to say and be done with it!

GIKO: Okay, okay, Shushan! (*Inhaling snuff*) Heavenly, believe me! Hum! When God created men, He gave them patience, too. (*Wiping his nose with a handkerchief*).

SHUSHAN: Oh, you and your sayings!

GIKO (*inhaling snuff again*): Hmm. I was going to say that . . . (*building into a sneeze*) that . . . (*He sneezes.*) Achew! (*About to sneeze again*) A-a-a (*He sneezes.*) Achew. Oh, ho, ho, ho, ho, some snuff this. You s-see, I sneezed twice. That's a sign of good luck.

SHUSHAN: Bless you!

GIKO: Long life . . . (*About to sneeze*) . . . to, to, to, y-your family. (*He sneezes.*) Achew!

SHUSHAN (*aside*): Oh, damn you and your gibberish.

GIKO: That one was for good luck and a half more (*About to sneeze*) and this, this,

this. (*He sneezes again.*) That's double luck. At this rate, there'll be no end to my good luck.

SHUSHAN: What are you blabbering about? Luck has nothing to do with sneezing.

GIKO: Luck's in the hands of God, Sh-Shushan. (*He puts snuffbox in his pocket.*) It's real nippy, this cursed stuff. Still it's a thousand to one I'll sneeze with the first pinch. I don't think they gave me the usual snuff. Everybody's in a racket nowadays, Sh-Shushan! (*He again takes the snuffbox out of his pocket and opens it.*) I'm afraid it's been cut with something. (*Examining the snuff*) But I can't see anything wrong with it. Shushan, your eyesight's better. (*He shows the box to* SHUSHAN.)

SHUSHAN (*to herself*): Damn your eyes.

KEKEL (*to herself*): I can't stand it anymore.

GIKO: Take a look, for the love of God!

SHUSHAN (*to herself*): This is just too much! (*She takes the box and examines it.*) It looks all right to me. But, for the love of God, give us the news you have. You're killing us with your stalling. (*She puts the box on the couch.*)

GIKO: Why are you in such a hurry? Let's wait till Pepo gets back so we'll all hear what I have to say. (*Continuing to wipe his nose.*)

KEKEL (*to herself*): I see, now. He wants to join us for dinner! (*To* SHUSHAN) He thinks we've plenty to eat, so he's come to scrounge.

SHUSHAN (*to herself*): Aih! (*To* KEKEL) Watch your mouth or you'll break out in spots. (*To* GIKO) Out with it. Give us your news.

GIKO: I will, Shushan. (*In a low voice*) Send your daughter out for a minute.

SHUSHAN (*softly*): She's busy with her work and won't hear. Tell me quietly.

GIKO: It'd be bad if she overheard, Shushan! You don't know what Khikar (*putting his index finger on his forehead*) says about such things.[3]

SHUSHAN: Khikar? Who's this old fool Khikar? How did he get mixed up in all this?

(GIKO *bursts out laughing and then begins to cough.*)

SHUSHAN(*to herself*): May you roast in hellfire if you don't tell us.

GIKO (*continuing to cough*): Khikar . . . (*He coughs.*) . . . was a philosopher. (*He coughs.*)

PEPO (*singing the first verse of a song off stage*):

> Wine is from Damascus grapes,
> Come share with me its rich, full blend.

KEKEL (*running to the door, full of joy*): It's Pepo! Pepo's here!

———

3. Khikar (Akhikar) was a legendary sage to monarchs in the ancient Near East.

Scene 3

The same and PEPO

PEPO (*He enters by the center door, with his hat on, in his working clothes, sleeves turned up above the elbows, carrying a net on his shoulder and a red handkerchief full of live fish hanging from his belt in front. He continues singing the song.*):

> Wine is from Damascus grapes,
> Come share with me its rich, full blend.
> Brandy is from Persian grapes.
> Raise your glass and drink, my friend.

KEKEL: Heaven help us, Pepo! We've been worried sick wondering where you were.

SHUSHAN: What's the matter with you? You go off and then disappear.

PEPO (*happy*): Ha! If I didn't go off and disappear, we'd need manna from heaven to eat. Ooh, Giko! You've come at the right time. I'm going to treat you to some trout. But if you drop any of your snuff on them, you won't even get a whiff. (*He draws out a big fish from his handkerchief.*) You see! (*Patting* GIKO'S *cheeks with its tail*) Oh boy! Look at that, will you!

GIKO: Hey! What do you think you're doing?

(KEKEL *laughs.*)

SHUSHAN (*laughing*): Take it easy! This is no time for practical jokes! He was about to say something!

PEPO (*retying the handkerchief and laughing*): About to say something? I'd say he was talking like hailstones, showering word after word. (*He grabs hold of* GIKO'S *left hip and shakes it vigorously.*) How are you, Giko? How are you?

GIKO: My, oh my! You've got a hand of iron.

PEPO (*laughing*): Did you think something had happened to me? I'm not decrepit like you. (*Giving handkerchief of fish to* KEKEL) Now! Take those and put them in water. And make a good fire. (*In a low voice*) We've enough wood, haven't we?

KEKEL (*happy, softly*): We've enough for two more meals. (*She takes the fish.*) Shall I fillet them?

PEPO: No! No! No! Kakuli asked us to wait for him. He loves to fillet fish. (*Taking the fish that was in* KEKEL'S *hand*) Look at this frisky one, will you? He must have been hiding at the bottom. Take them away. I'd give my life for those beauties. If the fish weren't free, who'd give them to us? (*Tapping his vest pock-*

et and in low voice to KEKEL) Don't worry, Kekel. You see, I've money, too. I sold ten rubles worth in the market.

KEKEL: That's why you were so late.

PEPO: Yes! I'd like to go fishing tonight, too. You see, God's been good to me lately.

KEKEL: Oh, Pepo! You work too hard and long for us. (*She goes out the door to the left, taking with her the sewing bag and handkerchief of fish.*)

Scene 4

The same without KEKEL

PEPO: What else can I do? Giko! Tell me! What's best, money or health?

GIKO: It's better to have both if God grants it.

PEPO: You've lived all these years, and still you don't know that God doesn't dole out money. If God gives a man health, the money follows. (*Opening the net*) Did I get this with money? (*He slaps his chest.*) Let this heart tick on. (*He bends, examines the net, and laughs.*) What a net this is! I've cast it so many times, but it's still in good condition. The best spot for fishing on the Kura is Peter Morev's place. When I throw my net, zoom, zoom, the frisky fish leap into it. If people had any sense, they'd do nothing but fish. Casting your net into the water and drawing it out makes your heart pound with excitement. Life and death pulses before you. And at night, you converse with the stars, as the moon hovers over your head like a fluttering moth. And when you're done and come home, you feel so good as you lay out your wet net. (*He throws his net over* GIKO's *head, as he speaks.*) Giko, what a wonderful fish you make! All we need is a big pot to cook you in. (*He laughs.*)

SHUSHAN (*laughing*): What the devil's gotten into you, Pepo?

GIKO (*throwing off the net*): You frightened me, my boy! What sort of joke is this?

PEPO (*folding the net*): We have to have some fun sometimes.

GIKO: You seem so excited today.

PEPO (*spreading the net on the line*): What am I supposed to be? Half-baked stew like you, inhaling snuff all the time and chomping my words like a camel chewing Turkish delight? (*He laughs.*)

GIKO (*sighing*): Ooh, Pepan, my dear boy.

SHUSHAN: No more jokes. I told you before . . . listen! My heart's racing! (*To* PEPO) He's heard some bad news about your brother-in-law to be, I'm sure.

PEPO (*wary*): Bad news? What is it?

GIKO: Sit down, Pepo! Bless you!

PEPO: I'm okay as I am. Go on, tell us.

GIKO: No! It'd be much better if you sat.

PEPO (*irritated*): Oh, merciful God! (*He takes a chair and sits.*) All right. I'm sitting.

GIKO: Wait a minute! We can't work things out if you're going to get irritated. We've got to think and plan ahead. (*Looking for his snuffbox*) What happened to my snuffbox? It was right here.

PEPO (*finding the box and handing it to* GIKO): Here! Take it. I know you can't say a word without taking a pinch.

GIKO (*taking some snuff*): You see, Nephew! This morning I smelled a rat. (*Inhaling snuff, to* SHUSHAN) Hmm! Word is, they've found another girl for your son-in-law to-be!

SHUSHAN: Damn our luck!

(*Alarmed,* PEPO *emits a prolonged cry.*)

GIKO: Yes! And the new fiancée is a very good girl, they say, and her dowry is much more than you promised for Kekel. (*He inhales snuff again.*) Hmm.

PEPO (*angrily*): Heavens! Will you stop taking snuff? (*Snatching the snuffbox, he spills some into* GIKO's *palm and pushes it up his nose.*) Here, take your fill!

GIKO: Oh, oh! My snuff! What a crazy creature you are! (*He puts the snuff back into the box.*)

PEPO: On my soul, Giko, you won't get out of here alive if you don't tell us everything right now!

GIKO: Just give me a chance.

SHUSHAN (*to* PEPO): Heavens! You're confusing him.

PEPO: Come on! Hurry up!

GIKO: Yes! I was going to say that . . . What was it I was going to say? I've forgotten!

PEPO (*to himself in a low voice*): Oh, what pain and grief you are.

GIKO (*continuing*): Yes! I heard that news this morning!

PEPO: Damn it! What kind of a man are you? You already said that. Then what?

GIKO: Oh yes! Then, I went to confront your brother-in-law to be, but he wasn't at home. Then I went to his store. What do you suppose I saw? That hustler, Mrs. Natale—you know, the matchmaker—whispering to him. Seeing that, I bit my little finger. (*He puts his little finger in his mouth.*) I thought it looked serious, so I waited awhile, and as soon as that devil left, I approached him and grilled him in detail.

PEPO (*impatiently*): And what did he say?

GIKO: Just a minute! I'm telling it in order, don't you see?

PEPO (*raising his fist*): Giko! Watch it! As God's my witness, you're going to get it!

GIKO (*drawing himself back*): Stop mixing me up!

SHUSHAN (*impatiently rubbing her knee during this conversation*): What's gotten into you, Pepo?

GIKO: First, he pretended not to hear, then he broke down and confirmed what I'd heard earlier. I can say by all that's holy, I almost swallowed my tongue.

SHUSHAN: May the earth open up and swallow him!

PEPO (*angrily*): Are you going out of your mind or playing games?

GIKO: Upon my soul it's true!

PEPO: So what did he say then?

GIKO: He said, "I like Kekel very much, but since things haven't come to a head, what can I do?"

SHUSHAN (*striking her knees with both hands and referring to the fiancé*): Just listen to that cad!

PEPO (*angrily*): What does he mean, "things haven't come to a head?"

GIKO: Just that. He said, "Why don't you give me the dowry you promised?" (*Sighing*) Oh, God!

PEPO: Who said we won't give what we promised? Do you mean to tell me he doesn't know why we haven't paid him yet?

GIKO: "How long do I have to wait?" he asked.

SHUSHAN: Is he waiting? Who's telling him to wait? Why didn't he ask for his money? Let him ask. When we get it, it's his! (*To herself, looking up*) May God be your judge, Arutin!

GIKO: What he says is that he wants a girl, not a headache. (*He shakes his head.*)

PEPO: We discussed all this a hundred times. Where to go from here?

GIKO: That's just it, Pepo! He says, "The matter could drag on for a year, and I can't wait any longer. I want to get married, right away. (*He cries.*) I've sinned, Oh, Lord! It's all my fault!

SHUSHAN: In a word, Giko, he's jilting Kekel.

PEPO: So that's it?

GIKO: If we don't come across with the money, the deal's off.

PEPO: Just like that?

GIKO: Right!

PEPO (*He jumps up angrily from his chair, leans forward, strikes his fist to his palm, and speaks out to the brother-in-law to be.*): You'll get what's coming to you. (*He goes to* GIKO *with open arms.*) What did you say to him after that, Giko?

GIKO (*Drawing back, he stands up.*): Tell me what I was supposed to say.

PEPO (*moving toward him*): Couldn't you get across to him that we're honest?

GIKO (*pulling back*): Ah! Of course I did!

PEPO (*moving forward again*): Then?

GIKO (*eyes averted*): Then? He just repeated himself.

PEPO (*pressing forward*): And you went along with that?

GIKO (*turning away*): Ah!

PEPO (*nearing him*): Why didn't you use your head?

GIKO (*He gradually reaches stage right but finds no way out*): Ah! May your father rest in peace! How could I top what he said?

PEPO: So you didn't say a damn thing?

SHUSHAN: Pepo! Control yourself! That's no way to talk.

GIKO: Oh Pepo, I told him what I've already said. I said, "Wait until Arutin pays up, then you can get married." "Or," I said, "Get married now and then get the money from Arutin yourself."

PEPO: And then?

GIKO: Then he gave me an ultimatum and said, "I've no head for headaches. If you can bring me the money today, I'll marry her tonight. I'm a man of my word."

PEPO: Oh, Giko! As if that's something to boast about. Saying, "I'm a sensible man, I've read the wise man Khikar's writings from beginning to end." Is that all you could do?

GIKO: But (*He coughs.*) What have I done wrong? (*Intensely coughing*)

PEPO: With friends like you, who needs enemies?

SHUSHAN: Pepo! What's gotten into you?

PEPO (*leaving* GIKO): Nothing! I've got to see the man and get the story straight.

SHUSHAN (*She stands.*): Wait here for me, Pepo! Let me go and see that bitch Natale first. (*She puts on her cloak and goes out in hurry.*) Giko! Come with me for the love of God and help me out of this corner. (*She exits by the center door.*)

GIKO (*severe choking cough, to himself*): Working with you's a real headache. (*He follows* SHUSHAN.)

PEPO (*as* GIKO *leaves*): And we took you for a man.

Scene 5

PEPO *alone, after a brief silence*

So you want another girl! Over my dead body! (*Silence again, then to himself*) No Pepo! You're a decent guy. You like things straight and businesslike. Your brother-in-law isn't in the wrong! You made him a promise. You have to keep to it. That's all! You must give him the shirt off your back if you have to, even if it kills you, but you have to come through. But how am I going to produce that damn money? Who'll lend me such a large sum? (*Looking at the walls*) Who'd give me anything for what's in here? If I mortgage the house and try to sell our furniture and clothing, what would I get for them? Not even half what they're worth. This is it—the end! This is what you wanted, Arutin. You've tormented me long enough, and now I've come to this. That's it! I'll be disgraced in people's eyes. How am I going to face my friends after this? What'll they think of me? (*He throws his hat on the floor.*) I spit on your honor!

Scene 6

PEPO *and* KEKEL

KEKEL (*entering door left, confused*): What's up, Pepo?

PEPO: Nothing! (*Lifting his hat and shaking it clean*) Nothing! What did you think could be up?

KEKEL: Why are you trying to conceal things from me? (*Crying*) I heard. I know all about it, Pepo!

PEPO (*putting his hat on*): What did you hear, Kekel?

KEKEL (*in anguish, drying her tears with a handkerchief*): I heard, Pepo dear. I heard Mama and Giko talking as they left the house just now. He's jilting me.

PEPO: Have patience, Kekel! Have patience! God is merciful.

KEKEL: If He's merciful, why's He been so hard-hearted to me. We were engaged and congratulated by everybody. That man kissed me in public, and now he discards me. Did God create me to be a useless rag thrown in a corner? Am I dust under everyone's feet? Where's my honor? (*She cries and dries her tears.*)

PEPO: Kekel, there's no need to cry.

KEKEL (*continuing to cry*): I'd rather be dead and buried. How am I going to face my girlfriends after this? They'll all gossip about me. They'll ridicule me and laugh at me. (*Sobbing, she dries her tears.*)

PEPO (*embracing her*): Kekel! Oh, my dear!

KEKEL: Tie a stone around Kekel's neck, Pepo, and throw her into the Kura. How can I go on living after this?

PEPO: Cheer up, Kekel dear! All this is only a question of money. We'll find it, no matter what. If Arutin doesn't give us what he owes, I'm going to sell everything. I'll beg and borrow, but I won't desert you.

KEKEL: No! No! Pepo! I heard that the money is due today, and who would lend it to us so quickly? And besides, you've already pawned yourself to the hilt. If it weren't for money, I wouldn't be in this disgrace. (*She cries.*)

KAKULI (*behind the stage*): Pepo!

KEKEL: I'm better off dead! (*Drying her tears, she runs out of door left.*)

PEPO (*slapping hands on knees*): Your Pepo's luck has run out, Kekel! (*He sits on couch bemoaning his fate*)

Scene 7

PEPO *and* KAKULI

KAKULI (*Hat on, he enters from center door, holding a handkerchief full of provisions in one hand and carrying a half-gallon wine bottle in the other.*): I've got some wine here, a wine to turn your head! Believe me, that took some doing!

PEPO (*crestfallen*): Just in time for a party.

KAKULI: What's up?

PEPO: Nothing!

KAKULI: You think I can't tell? I'd know you even if you turned on a spit.

PEPO: We'll talk about it later, okay?

KAKULI: Hey! Have you been going out with those louts again? Steer clear of them, if you know what's good for you.

PEPO: They don't let me alone.

KAKULI: Let's drown your worries in a glass. I used to worry all the time. But now (*tapping the half-gallon bottle*), say no more. I've found a way to deal with them. When I see a drinking horn, that's it. (*He drinks long and deep, directly from the wine bottle and starts to sing.*)

> My dearest, don't cry I pray.
> Give only a day to sorrow.
> For whoever locks a door today,

PEPO (*shaking his head and in a low voice reciting the last line of poem*):

> Shall open it tomorrow.

KAKULI (*He continues singing and finishes.*): Shall open it tomorrow. Don't cry! Now! (*Raising the half-gallon to* PEPO) Drink! It'll cut your miseries like a sword.

PEPO: Eh!

KAKULI: You're full of headache and pain. Hmm! I see you're in a damn rut. You've got some damn big problems plaguing you today. How big are they? (*He puts the laden handkerchief and half-gallon on the table and raises his hands to his head to indicate horns.*) My God, look here! Let's play leapfrog.

PEPO: I've no time for jokes, Kakuli. Leave me alone for the love of God. They've got us by the throat. (*He stands up.*)

KAKULI: What's the trouble?

PEPO: Nothing could be worse. He's breaking off with my sister.

KAKULI: Your brother-in-law to be?

PEPO: Who else?

KAKULI: No kidding?

PEPO: As God is my witness!

KAKULI: That son of a bitch. (*To* PEPO) Let's go and give him a good beating, Pepo! I'll give him such a shot he'll spin like a top. You see! I kept telling you, Pepo. You'd no business getting mixed up with a merchant.

PEPO: It's all over, Kakuli! What's the use of rehashing it? The point now is if we don't give him what we promised immediately, he's going to announce his engagement to another girl tonight.

KAKULI: Wrap it up then. (*He unbuckles his silver girdle.*) If you're short, throw this in. It'll net a hundred rubles. (*He holds up the girdle with his left hand.*) Otherwise, Pepo (*displaying his right fist*), I have this! That's all I have to offer.

PEPO: Those amount to nothing, Kakuli. You know very well we've promised a thousand rubles, and that cursed Arutin keeps putting me off.

KAKULI: I'm giving it to you straight. We'll never get a cent out of that guy, till we beat his belly like a drum.

PEPO: Oh, Kakuli! You settle everything with your fists.

KAKULI: If he really owes you, why wouldn't he shell out? (*He puts on his girdle again.*)

PEPO: What do you mean "if he really owes" me?" Am I a liar? It's just that I can't find the damned *iou*.

KAKULI: What *iou*? That's news to me!

PEPO: You mean I didn't tell you?

KAKULI: No!

PEPO: Yes! We had a note from Arutin, and now it's lost.

KAKULI: No, Pepo. The only thing I knew was that the vulture owed your father money. But this is the first I've heard of a note. How did it get lost?

PEPO: God only knows. It's a long story.

KAKULI: Try me!

PEPO: What's the use?

KAKULI: Please.

PEPO: Here's how the story goes. My father had some money and invested it with him at a good rate of interest. My father kept the promissory note so close to his chest that, while he was alive, I'd say I'd seen that damn note maybe twenty times. About a week before his death, the poor man had the note in his hand. After his death, we opened the strongbox, but no hide nor hair of the note.

KAKULI: Why, Pepo! Could it be that Arutin stole the note.

PEPO: Don't be stupid. How could he have gotten into our strongbox?

KAKULI: Who stole it then, Pepo?

PEPO: If I knew who, there wouldn't be a problem.

KAKULI: Maybe your father "took" it with him.

PEPO: We thought so, too. While dressing him for the wake, unbeknownst to us, the note could have been in his clothing.

KAKULI: Oh Pepo! Wait till you see what's going to happen to Arutin in the next life. Four pairs of devils will put the note in front of him. I'd go to hell myself to see that show. (*They laugh.*) Pepo, never mind the joke! Search the house again. It may turn up.

PEPO: What are you talking about? We already turned everything in the house upside down.

KAKULI: Does that "buffalo head" even know that the note is lost?

PEPO: He must know. That's why he's not paying.

KAKULI: Doesn't he know he owes you that money?

PEPO: Of course, he knows!

KAKULI: Then he should cough up.

PEPO: Take the cotton out of your ears and get it straight, will you! The man said, "I can't remember anything." And on top of that, he said, "My books don't show a record of such a note. Bring me the note, and I'll give you the money."

KAKULI: Upon my soul, Pepo, as sure as I'm standing here, I'll have it out with him in the morning. There's no other way. Leave it to me. When he comes back from his gardens and orchards in Ortajala[4] with his hands behind his back like this (*He puts his hands behind his back and walks a few steps like* ARUTIN.), I'll beat him so hard, he'll holler louder than the guy selling ice in the street.

PEPO: You're lucky, Kakuli. You've no sister to marry off.

KAKULI: That's no problem. I wouldn't have run after a merchant like you did. I'd have given her to a friend, even a happy-go-lucky fellow like me. God created us like birds, who work and eat a day at a time. Why think about tomorrow or the next world?

PEPO: All right! All right! Don't strain yourself. That's enough. Go clean the fish. Then we'll sit back and have a few drinks. Afterward we'll see what God gives us.

KAKULI: Right! That's my specialty! But where's the table? I want to lay out the food first. (*He takes hold of the handkerchief of food.*)

PEPO: Just a minute! (*He pushes sofa cushions to one side, takes an old-fashioned blue table cloth, wooden spoons, and a few plates from the china closet.*) Here! Bring it here! (*He spreads the tablecloth on the* takht *and puts the food on it.*)

KAKULI (*Kneeling on the floor, he pushes his hat back on his head with his arm, opens the bundle, takes out some dried fish, green vegetables, flat bread, and cheese preserved in sheepskin and puts everything on the table.*): Look at this variety of food! Here's some flat bread and fish for you. (*He folds the empty handkerchief.*)

PEPO (*inspecting the cheese*): Looks great!

KAKULI: How about these greens? (*He takes a green leaf and shakes it.*) Look at this! It's like velvet!

PEPO (*subdued*): You're a good man, Kakuli! Let me get some glasses.

KAKULI (*jumping up*): Ha! That'd be a damn shame. Whoever heard of anyone drinking wine like this from glasses. Think of your soul. (*He fixes his hat on his head and gets the half-gallon bottle.*) Why don't you bring those glazed clay mugs, so while we drink we can see our saintly reflections in them? (*He puts the half-gallon on the table.*)

PEPO: I know what you want. (*He goes to the china closet and brings two mugs, a few wine glasses and a silver-trimmed wooden pitcher.*) Here's a mug for you. Take this one, too, if you want. (*He arranges them on the tablecloth.*)

KAKULI (*lifting the wooden pitcher*): I'd die for you, Pepo, my friend! What a sport you are! You've got style! That's all there is to it. (*Raising it to his lips as if to*

---

4. Ortajala was a quarter of gardens and vineyards in eastern Tiflis.

drink, to the pitcher) Oh my nightingale, your gurgling song is like a serenade to me. (*Kissing the pitcher*) Lay your problems on me, Pepo.

PEPO: Would that I had none, and we'd both have it made.

KAKULI (*indicating the pitcher*): If a man adopted a child like this, it would raise his spirits out of the doldrums. (*He puts the pitcher on the table.*)

PEPO: Fine! Get going and prepare the fish! I'll take care of these.

KAKULI: I'll cook you a fish that'll get you into the spirit.(GIKO, *hat on, cane in hand, and* SHUSHAN, *with sable wrap, enter by the center door.*)

Scene 8

The same, with GIKO *and* SHUSHAN

KAKULI: Hello, Mama! (PEPO *looks at* SHUSHAN *with anticipation.*)

SHUSHAN (*to* KAKULI): Bless you, my son!

KAKULI: Hi, Giko. (*Coming forward, winking and whispering to* PEPO) Is this the best guest you could find?

PEPO: Hold on! (*To* SHUSHAN) What news?

(KAKULI *goes behind* GIKO, *imitating him inhaling snuff.*)

SHUSHAN: What would you expect? May the ground open up and swallow me! If we can't produce the money by tonight, Pepo, it's all over. (*To herself*) Oh Arutin! May you get what's coming to you. (*She takes off her sable wrap.*) There's no hope he'll cough up today, and who else would trust us? I arrived in time to catch that bitch Natale. She was bringing the last offer from the girl's father to our cad of a son-in-law. Devil take him!

PEPO: Mama! What do you want from the guy? Are we going to give him what we promised or not? He's decent enough. Why should he take the fall? If we take him for a ride, nothing's sacred anymore. How many times did I tell you, Mama? Wait till we get the money before announcing the engagement? But there was no way I could persuade you! You said, "No problem, Arutin's not going anywhere, he wouldn't take advantage of us." Now, Mama, I'd like to see you try to get him to fork over the money.

GIKO (*With a long sigh, he takes a seat near the table.*): Oh, for that note, how did it get lost? (*He slaps his knees.*)

PEPO: Enough, Giko! If you don't stop, there's no telling what I'll do to you this minute. If you hadn't poked your nose into this business, we wouldn't be in disgrace now. To hell with money and the wretch who dreamed it up.

GIKO: Oh Pepo, my boy! You don't know how my heart races. What can I do? What can I say? Why don't you finish me off, so I can be free.

PEPO: Don't give me that stuff, Giko. You see I've got problems galore heaped on

my head! And you pile more sorrow and anguish on me? Think about that before you go shooting off your mouth.

GIKO (*sighing deeply*): Oh dear, oh dear! (*He dries his eyes with his hands.*)

KAKULI: Hold it, Pepo. Wasn't there a witness to the debt?

PEPO: Are you some sort of wise guy? If that'd been the case, we wouldn't be in this
mess now.

GIKO: What the devil am I if not a witness? But what's the use?

KAKULI: How come?

PEPO (*to* KAKULI): Let me set you straight. The scoundrel says a witness's testimony
doesn't count.

KAKULI (*to himself, shaking his head*): Bullshit. In that case I'll have to shake him
up a bit.

SHUSHAN: That blackguard gave us short shrift the day we went to claim the
money.

PEPO: He said, "I can't remember. My books don't show a record. If I gave you a
promissory note, bring it in and take your money."

SHUSHAN: He's pretending it never happened? A rich man like him shouldn't be so
small! What's a thousand rubles to a well-heeled big shot like him? If he wanted to, he could make us a present of it and never miss it.

PEPO: You're right. He's insulting us right to our face.

SHUSHAN: Let's see if that's the lay of the land. (*In a tearful voice*) I'll go to him; I'll
kneel before him; I'll burst out crying and pray for the longevity of his family.
I'll take an oath that if we later present the note, he can have his way with us.
I'll even sign a release before ten witnesses. He has to die some day. How can
he ignore his soul?

PEPO: Wait, wait, Mama! I'll go! I'll be back shortly. Till then, rest easy.

SHUSHAN: Have something to eat first.

PEPO: No! I couldn't swallow a spoonful till I see him. Where are my good clothes?

SHUSHAN: I put them in the chest yesterday.

KAKULI: Shall I come, too, Pepo?

PEPO: No! You've got your hands full. I'll be back soon. (*He exits by door right.*)

KAKULI: You know best. (*Striking his chest*) Oh, Arutin! I'll be damned if I don't
beat you to a pulp! You'll see. (*He exits by center door.*)

Scene 9

SHUSHAN, GIKO

GIKO (*sitting close to the table, inhaling snuff*): Hasten your judgment, Oh Lord!

SHUSHAN (*sitting on* takht, *drawling*): Oh God, You send some people carts full of
wood to burn, while we haven't a straw to start a fire.

GIKO: Yes, yes, Shushan.

SHUSHAN: Blessed be the Lord's dominion. He gives wealth to those unable to enjoy it and denies us our daily bread. Glory be to Him! His will be done. Perhaps that was written on our forehead.

GIKO (*approaching the table*): And yet God is merciful, Shushan! (*Taking a piece of dried bread, he shakes his head.*) There's this. We're not starving. (*He puts the bread back.*)

SHUSHAN (*to herself*): Damn your nonsense! (*To* GIKO) How is God merciful to us when we've been carried away by this flood? If that godless charlatan invents new lies again today and refuses to pay his debt, God only knows what will happen to us. My poor girl's wasting away day by day. How can she keep body and soul together? (*She cries.*) My poor Kekel, the sunshine of your life has left you. Instead of a wedding gown, they'll carry you off in a funeral shroud. (*She cries again.*)

GIKO (*Sobbing, he exits by he door left, drying his eyes.*): Oh, my God!

(PEPO *enters door right, wearing his hat, best suit and girdle, coat half-buttoned, and belt in his hand.*)

Scene 10

SHUSHAN, PEPO

SHUSHAN: Have something to eat before you go.

PEPO: I don't deserve bread. (*He puts on his belt.*) Bread is meant for the likes of Arutin. If I were to eat bread, then what would he eat? Are we equals that we should eat the same food? (*Bitter laugh*)

SHUSHAN: It's a black cloud has darkened my day! (*Drying her tears, she exits by door left.*)

Scene 11

PEPO *alone*

PEPO (*buttoning his coat*): On with it, Pepo! Lick the ground and kiss peoples' boots. Grovel in the dirt before them. Let them walk all over you. Who are you? What are you? Call yourself a man? You're just a doormat. You're not human. You're made for human consumption. You're tormented night and day. Stay up till dawn, struggle with the wind and rain, freeze in the winter cold and burn in the summer sun. Go earn your bread and support your mother and sister. What sort of life is this? It's a dog's life. You're just like a dog ferreting around for food. Where's the human dignity in that, Pepo? (*Pause*) To be a man, you've got to rob people. Got to cheat the poor and murder suckers like me. Make them shed tears of blood for the 25,000 they owe you and make money out of their tears and use the money to build lavish houses and live in them like a lord with horses and carriages and twenty-five servants like me in attendance. Then I'd say you were a man, Pepo, and anything that a man could want or took your fancy, you could come up with. Everybody would bow to you, respect and honor you, and cut each other's throat so your honor would rest on them. (*He exits center door.*)

Curtain

ACT 2

A parlor in ARUTIN*'s house, elegantly furnished. Doors right, left, and center, with magnificent portieres. The center door opens onto a reception hall, whose window looks onto the garden. The floor is covered with rugs and from the ceiling hangs a chandelier with unlighted candles. A takht to the right. On the left, a large mirror and sofa. A table with a very expensive cover and unlighted lamp near the mirror. Chairs, sofas, little tables, vases, candelabra with candles, statuettes; date, citron, and other plants; flowers, pictures and albums suitably placed. A piano to the right of center door with round stool in front. At left, a fireplace; above that, a high-grade clock, the hands indicating 1.45 P.M. At opening, the stage is unoccupied.*

Scene 1

GIGOLI, *then* SAMSON

GIGOLI (*He enters by center door accompanied by grocery boy who is carrying a large basket filled with provisions, such as bottles of champagne, sardines, Swiss cheese, canned caviar, cucumbers, boxes of red and white cherries, and pastry.*): All right! Let me have it! (*He removes his cap and takes a basket from the boy, who exits. He brings it in, puts it down, and drops into the chair near center door, puffing with exhaustion.*) Oh! (*He wipes perspiration from his forehead with his cap, and calls in a low voice.*) Samson! (SAMSON *enters from the same door, his coat unbuttoned, wiping champagne glasses with a long white towel.*) Now, Samson my boy, go tell Madam I'm back.
SAMSON: Oh, you're here. Madam was furious. Why are you so late?
GIGOLI: Why? She ordered the impossible. I looked high and low but couldn't find it.

SAMSON: You don't say.

GIGOLI: Every storekeeper I asked laughed at me. "Whoever heard of strawberries as big as walnuts?"

SAMSON: There must be, if she ordered them. (*Inspecting the contents of the basket*) Did you get everything else?

GIGOLI: Everything. But I couldn't find those damned strawberries. One store promised to get them by tomorrow.

SAMSON: That's too damn late. The party's tonight, not tomorrow!

GIGOLI: What'll I do then, Samson? Can't they have a party without strawberries? Look at those cherries. Each one's as big as a buffalo's eye.

SAMSON: If you ask me, Gigoli, they'd have enough to stuff themselves with, but I know the Master's wife well. I'm sure you'll have to come up with strawberries no matter what. Go to foreign embassies and ask at the German orchard in Calonia.

GIGOLI: What are you talking about? I'm just about out of my mind. Let her know I'm back.

(SAMSON *goes toward left door.*)

(GIGOLI *sits.*) I'm dead to the world. (*Looking toward left door, he suddenly jumps up.*)

Scene 2

The same and EPEMIA

EPEMIA (*She enters from the left door, stylishly dressed, wearing magnificent jewels.*): Oh my! This is impossible. How can you be so late? The guests will be here shortly. There's so much to arrange.

GIGOLI: I've worn out my soles, Madam. My legs are buckling.

EPEMIA: Walk till you drop. Am I supposed to do the errands? Now! Take everything out, and let me see what you've bought. (*She sits.*)

GIGOLI (*Putting the basket in front of* EPEMIA, *he drops to his knees and shows her, one by one, the contents of the basket.*): See, Madam! I couldn't get this champagne for less than four rubles. I bought three bottles, but if there's one bottle left over, they'll take it back. I really had to haggle. This is that red liqueur from the Frenchman. The damn Frenchy charged four fifty for it. These are sardines, first class. An even half dozen, as you ordered. They'll keep for a long time. These are smoked fish from the Don. This large tin has fresh caviar. The small size from last time wasn't very good. They're very fresh, just unpacked.

He swore they were the best. This is imported cheese, the color of genuine amber. Look at these German cherries. They come in two colors and weigh three pounds altogether. (*Taking a few cherries from the box*) I'll cut off my arm if anybody can find any better than these. This is a cucumber. Look, will you Madam! Here's a sweet pastry *extraordinaire*. And the baker will send round the rolls as soon as they're out of the oven.

EPEMIA (*jumping up from chair*): What do you mean "*extraordinaire*"? Let me see! Where did you buy it?

GIGOLI (*Taking out the pastry, he stands up suddenly*): Main Street, Madam!

EPEMIA (*pinching his cheek*): That wasn't very smart, Gigoli! Didn't I tell you to buy all the pastries from the Frenchman?

GIGOLI: Really, Madam, it's all one. Why should we pay half a ruble more for each pound? See, how good it looks!

EPEMIA (*examining the pastry*): Who are you trying to kid? One bite of the Frenchman's creations is better than all this. Why are you so obstinate? Take it back! Return it this minute and get back the money! Do as I say and don't second-guess me. (*Thinking*) What else did I order? I can't remember.

GIGOLI (*stammering*): Straw-b-b-er-ries.

EPEMIA: Oh, yes! Where are they?

GIGOLI: I couldn't find any, Madam!

EPEMIA (*puffing out her cheeks in anger*): Damn it!

GIGOLI: What could I do if there were none to be had?

EPEMIA (*angry*): Are you insane? Last night I had strawberries at the Dardumanian's. What will my guests think? They'll make fun of me. If they had theirs, why can't I have mine? Impossible! Hire a horse and carriage. Go from garden to garden. I don't care where you have to go, as long as you find some. Otherwise, I'll skin you alive! Why are you hanging around? Didn't you hear me? Look lively.

GIGOLI: I'm going, I'm going, Madam! (*He puts the pastry in the basket and starts off.*)

EPEMIA: Don't you have a brain in your head? Take all the pastry back with you.

GIGOLI (*taking the pastry*): I'll take them, all, Madam! (*Muttering to himself*) I don't know whether I'm coming or going. (*He exits quickly by center door.*)

Scene 3

EPEMIA *and* SAMSON

SAMSON: You've got him all confused, Madam!

EPEMIA (*frowning*): Who are you to open your big mouth? Take these away. Put them where they belong and do your best not to embarrass me this evening, Samson! Or else, say your prayers!

SAMSON: Everything'll be fine, Madam!

EPEMIA: Listen carefully to my instructions. All food and drink must be exquisitely prepared. Every course must be served on time. In a word, don't make the slightest mistake.

SAMSON: Everything'll be fine, Madam!

EPEMIA: I want you to dress to the hilt, so everybody will admire you. Wear a silk blouse—that white Russian suit with the cuffs turned in. And wear your silver girdle.

SAMSON (*interrupting*): Shall I wear the dagger, too, Madam?

EPEMIA: Of course! Did you suppose I gave it to you to keep in your chest? Wear your dagger so . . . (*Moving her left hand to her right shoulder, to her chest, and then to her left side*) In a word, dress neatly and make a good appearance, so everybody'll say you're smart-looking and serve in a gentleman's house.

SAMSON: Was there ever a day I didn't look great?

EPEMIA: Do you want a crack in the head? Do you call how you look, great? You run around like a scarecrow. How many times have I told you not to come in my presence like this? What will people think when they see you? Button your shirt. A servant has to look the part. Be smart. Servants of other masters know how to comport themselves. Why don't you? Your Master's just as rich as theirs.

SAMSON: You see I was doing something else . . .

EPEMIA: Don't drivel on, just listen! In a word, enter and exit with elegance and always be immaculately clean and tidy. (*Aside, softly*) So they'll burst with envy when they see you. (*To* SAMSON) Don't leave your post and circle the table like a moth around a light. If you see anything awry, correct it immediately. I also want you to bring in the plates and put them in front of me first.

SAMSON: What will the guests say, Madam?

EPEMIA: Again? Who knows the in-style, you or me? Let them see and learn a thing or two. (*Thinking*) What else was I going to say? (*Remembering*) Ah, yes! (*Taking a few steps toward the provisions*) Take those and put them where they belong, and see you don't forget what I said! (*Threatening him with an index finger, she departs quickly by door left.*)

Scene 4

SAMSON *alone*

SAMSON: Quite a woman, my Master's wife! I'm all stressed out. (*Imitating her*) "Button up! Wear it this way! Walk this way!" I don't know what she wants of me. Phew! What a damned headache she is. (*Referring to her*) What business is it of yours? I know my job. I've worked for many a wife of many a master and followed their orders. But this one's the limit. No one asks who she really is. Whose daughter is she? Word is, she didn't have a shirt on her back in her father's home, and now she's puffed up with airs and graces. (*Striking fist to palm*)

Scene 5

SAMSON *and* ARUTIN

ARUTIN (*entering by center door, hat on*): What's going on? What's all the noise about?

SAMSON: Nothing, Master!

ARUTIN: What do you mean "nothing"? I heard the ruckus with my own ears! Who was in here?

SAMSON: Only your wife, sir.

ARUTIN: My wife? What was she saying?

SAMSON: You see, sir! Gigoli brought these in just now . . . things she sent him for. She told me to put them away.

ARUTIN: Go on then. What other tasks are you about? What's in the basket?

SAMSON: Drinks, fruit, hors d'oeuvres, and—

ARUTIN (*inspecting the basket*): Oh ho! You'd think we were honoring the royal family. All right! Take them away! (SAMSON *is about to take the basket.*) Ah, yes! How many places are you setting?

SAMSON: Your wife ordered twenty-four plates.

ARUTIN: She didn't send you to my daughter, did she?

SAMSON: No, sir!

ARUTIN: Then add two more places and go to my daughter and son-in-law this minute and ask them to honor us with their presence. And tell them if they don't come, I'll be extremely disappointed. Now go! Get on with it, and don't dilly-dally!

SAMSON (*taking the basket*): Right away, sir! (*He exits door right, bent over from the weight of the basket.*)

Scene 6

ARUTIN *alone*

ARUTIN (*taking hat off and placing it on the table*): Whoever heard of eating dinner at three? Whatever! (*He arranges himself, looking in the mirror.*) I'm in pretty good shape still. Nothing to find fault with. I'm erect, tall, and as firm as ebony. My cheeks are red as roses. The hair on my head is jet black. So I dye it, so what. Who can tell? (*He sits on the* takht.) There's nothing in the world like a young wife to keep her husband young! A man's happiness and the age he feels depend on his wife. My first wife—God have mercy on her soul— came from a noble family, but she had no taste! I looked like nothing, then. Now, I look like a man. Now, I have everything a gentleman could wish for. Many handsome young fellows are jealous of me because I have a young wife. Of course, the drawback is she makes me spend so much on her . . . Me, who'd give my very soul for a nickel. (*Feeling the sleeves of his shirt*) My, it's as white as snow. The young studs are no competition. (*Puffing out his chest*) Glory to You, O God! Glory to You. (*As* EPEMIA *enters*) This, too, seems to be Your will . . . to Pepel and defy the evil eye.

Scene 7

ARUTIN *and* EPEMIA

EPEMIA (*entering from left*): Are you laying down the law again?
ARUTIN: What do you mean?
EPEMIA: As if you didn't know. Would you have me faint from public disgrace?
ARUTIN: I don't understand.
EPEMIA (*continuing*): You're going to make a laughing stock out of me.
ARUTIN: How so?
EPEMIA (*crying crocodile tears*): You vowed to love me. And now this? (*Wiping her tears*)
ARUTIN (*speaking in a sweet voice*): Tell me, what troubles you. I'm not the devil, you know!
EPEMIA: What more can I say? I say a thing once, not a thousand times.
ARUTIN: God have mercy!
EPEMIA: Was that a nice thing to do? Inviting your daughter and her husband to dinner?
ARUTIN: Give me a break, Pepel dear! You can't separate the nose from the face.
EPEMIA: That's not my fault!
ARUTIN: Then why are you so opposed to them?
EPEMIA: Opposed? Your daughter insulted me to my face in every way you can imagine. She snubs her nose at me, she mocks me, and then you say that I op-pose her. She gives ten answers to one of my questions. I don't know how many false accusations she's made against me. She wants to grind me into the ground. And you say that I oppose her. She even says my dad lost his senses.
ARUTIN: Is that so?

EPEMIA (*continuing*): She makes believe I've bewitched you to deprive you of your wits and that I can toss you around like a strand of wool and that I'm trying to boss you about. And still you say that I oppose her! How do you think I can look her in the face after all these insults? How can a decent person tolerate all this?

ARUTIN: Surely isn't it you who should have patience, dear? Since you married me, you're considered a parent to her and her husband.

EPEMIA: Who? Me their parent? I'm not their parent. I'm their enemy. I'm like a wolf, a dog, a cat to them. (*Crying*) It was a black day when I entered this house. What's the use of having this magnificence, this honor, these clothes, these diamonds? Better to be thirsty and dying for bread in my father's house than come see this day. (*She falls on the sofa and cries.*)

ARUTIN: All right, Pepel dear! (*Tearfully*) Don't break my heart. I know what kind of fruit they are, too. I just thought we ought not to give people a chance to bad-mouth us.

EPEMIA: I don't care what people say. If you listened to all the gossip, you know where you'd be, don't you? You know what people are saying about you? You're a crook. You've cheated the poor! Are we to believe all this? (*She stands up.*)

ARUTIN: They're false accusations. . . .

EPEMIA (*continuing*): That you're an old man.

ARUTIN (*angry and coughing*): Stop.

EPEMIA (*continuing*): That you dye your hair.

ARUTIN (*coughing again*): Enough.

EPEMIA (*continuing*): That you're trying to make a fool of me! Who believes them? Let people talk all they want.

ARUTIN (*choked by a cough*): People are crazy, Pepel dear! You know very well how young I am. Is there a young man more able than me?

EPEMIA: Now, how would I go about convincing anyone?

ARUTIN: Tell those damn fools that a game, mature man makes a better husband than an uncouth youngster. (*Touching his hair, he approaches* EPEMIA) Now, is this dyed?

EPEMIA (*touching* ARUTIN'*s head and laughing*): Your enemies say a great many things, Artushka dear! (*Kissing* ARUTIN'*s head*) Oh my, my! It smells like violets!

ARUTIN (*embracing her*): Oh, you silky fox! One of your kisses is worth a kingdom. (*Stroking her arms*) I'm crazy about you, Pepel dear, and I'll do anything you say.

EPEMIA: Then we're not going to invite them, are we?

ARUTIN: Who?

EPEMIA: Your daughter and son-in-law.

ARUTIN: That again?

EPEMIA (*crying false tears*): I'm sorry I ever got involved with this family.

ARUTIN (*sweetly*): Okay. Have your own way.

EPEMIA (*embracing him*): Oh, my darling! My pheasant, my gazelle, my black crow . . .

ARUTIN: Crow! That's a nice thing to say!

EPEMIA (*laughing*): Oops, forgive me. I was going to say my dove.

ARUTIN (*laughing*): Oh yes! Dove is good!

EPEMIA (*embracing him*): Of course, you're a dove! What else could you be?

ARUTIN: I have a dove's face, too. (*Embracing her*) Pepel dear! You're a dove, too. You're a rose and a violet, too.

EPEMIA: I'm a rose, you're a nightingale, Artushka dear.

ARUTIN: Quite beautiful! You're a rose, and I'm a nightingale. It's very becoming. (*Patting* EPEMIA's *cheeks, while reciting*)

> Rosebud,
> Don't leave me.
> I'm your slave.

EPEMIA (*Singing, flattering* ARUTIN):

> Jet black eyes in your head,
> Beauty spot on your face,
> I'm yearning to see you.

ARUTIN: Sing the words so they enter my soul.

EPEMIA: This is not the time. I've got so much on my mind.

ARUTIN: Please! Pepel dearest!

EPEMIA: If you won't take no for an answer . . . (*She sings to* ARUTIN *with flattering attention.*)

> Rosebud
> Don't leave me.
> I'm your slave.
> Jet black eyes in your head,
> Beauty spot on your face,
> I'm yearning to see you.

ARUTIN: Oh, I'd die for you, Pepel dear! (*He takes* EPEMIA *in his arms and kisses her.*) Your beauty could turn the whole world upside down.

EPEMIA: That reminds me of something I was going to tell you, Artushka dear! (*Putting her hands on* ARUTIN's *shoulders*) Our mirrors are old-fashioned. I saw a pair of mirrors costing only five hundred rubles.

(*Turning aside*, ARUTIN *screws up his face*.)

I was going to put a deposit on them, but I thought I'd ask you first.

ARUTIN (*touching* EPEMIA's *cheeks*): What a wag you are!

EPEMIA: What would I do without you, Artushka dear?

ARUTIN (*thinking, then in a loud voice*): Five hundred rubles!

EPEMIA: Did the house repairs cost any less?

ARUTIN: Couldn't we do with something less expensive?

EPEMIA: I can't take this anymore. What we have are cheaper. That's why they have to go. I'm ashamed to look at myself in them.

ARUTIN: Give me a chance to breathe! You've turned everything in this house topsy-turvy. "The mirrors are a disgrace. The furniture has to go! The silk draperies are hung wrong! Change your hat. Wear a suit instead of a morning coat."

EPEMIA (*embracing him*): If you love me, Artushka dear!

ARUTIN: If? Who else would I love? (*Silence for a moment*) Pepel dear, do you really love me?

EPEMIA: Who else have I in the world? You're my soul, my body, my breath, my life.

ARUTIN: Could there be someone else you fancy?

EPEMIA: Now, Artushka dear, that would be a sin! What are you saying? A woman with a husband like you . . . How could anyone else catch her eye?

ARUTIN: All right! Send for the mirrors, then! (*Kissing* EPEMIA) I love you too much.

EPEMIA (*embracing him*): Who'd say you're a money grubber now? (*Fixing* ARUTIN's *necktie and collar*)

ARUTIN: You sure throw money around, but you're awfully stylish. No one has a red band like you, Pepel dear.

EPEMIA (*continuing*): Just a moment, dear! (*After fixing* ARUTIN's *shirt and tie, she stands back a little to see how they look.*) Now, who's more elegantly turned out than you?

Scene 8

Same and GIGOLI

GIGOLI (*He enters by the center door, cap under his arm, a small basket of strawberries in one hand covered with leaves, and pastry in the other hand.*): You see, Madam, I found them, but the strawberries are not quite the size of walnuts. The storekeeper said, "Kill me, if you can find any bigger."

EPEMIA (*pinching the strawberries*): You see, these are the ones I was talking about.

GIGOLI (*happy*): I should have asked that rascal of a peddler where he got his strawberries. It took me the whole morning to find them.

EPEMIA (*irritated*): Oh, GIGOLI, your lack of manners disgusts me! Now, when did you ever see me buy anything from a peddler that that should have crossed your mind. Couldn't you go to the garden and find the strawberries yourself?

GIGOLI (*embarrassed*): Madam!

ARUTIN (*to* EPEMIA): Don't fret, Pepel dear. God have mercy on your father's soul. In any event, they're obviously from the garden! (*To* GIGOLI) Peddlers don't make them.

EPEMIA: But their dirty hands get all over them. (*Disgustedly*) If the guests weren't arriving so soon, I'd throw them all out the window. (*To* GIGOLI) What else have you there?

GIGOLI: This is the pastry. I took the other back.

EPEMIA: Yes! (*Looking over the pastry and calling*) Samson! Samson!

ARUTIN (*inspecting strawberries in* GIGOLI's *hand*): They're really fresh, Pepel dear! You'd think they'd never been pawed over. (*He puts one in his mouth and chews.*) They are good. My father Kirakos couldn't live without his strawberries either.

GIGOLI: Have you anything more for me to do, Madam?

(SAMSON *enters right with his coat unbuttoned as usual.*)

Scene 9

The same and SAMSON

EPEMIA (*to* GIGOLI): Of course I have! Wait here. (*To* SAMSON) Take these strawberries to the cold cellar. Place the pastry nicely on plates.

(SAMSON *takes the cake.*)

Again your coat's unbuttoned in my presence? This is your last warning. If I ever see you in that state again, you're fired on the spot.

GIGOLI (*under his breath*): Wow! She's a firebrand!

SAMSON: I was busy, Madam!

EPEMIA (*angrily*): He dares answer me back. (*To* ARUTIN) You see! Aren't you going to do anything about it?

(GIGOLI *shakes the collar of his coat.*)

ARUTIN (*threatening* SAMSON): Watch your step. Go about your business! What are you standing around for?

(SAMSON, *shaking his head, exits door right, carrying strawberries and pastry.*)

(*to* EPEMIA *in a low voice*): You can see the boy has a lot to do. He's covered with perspiration. Why give him such a hard time?

EPEMIA (*continuing*): What do you mean? He's spoiled silly. Today he came in with his coat open. Tomorrow he'll come in without a vest. He has a lot of nerve. There are ladies who fraternize with the help, but you know very well, I'm not one of them. A servant should know his place.

ARUTIN: All right! All right! Excuse him this once. I'll give him a talking to. (*To himself*) I'm a lucky man to have such a soul mate. (*Fingering worry beads with hands behind his back, he takes a few steps and begins singing softly.*)

> Jet black eyes in your head.
> Beauty spot on your face.
> I'm yearning to see you.

(*He exits door left.*)

Scene 10

EPEMIA *and* GIGOLI

EPEMIA: GIGOLI, in heaven's name, can't you make that spoiled brat understand that he should be more formal?

GIGOLI: Yes, Madam! (*He bows his head.*) Are there any further orders, Madam?

EPEMIA: Yes, Gigoli. Go immediately to Taghltiants. I saw a pair of mirrors. They're asking five hundred rubles for the pair. Go and buy them this minute. I don't care if you have to hire four porters. I want them in place here before the guests arrive.

GIGOLI: This minute, Madam. Right away. But has the Master given the okay?

EPEMIA (*angrily*): Now you? I'm the Master! I give the orders around here.

(*Offstage noises*)

GIGOLI: Right away, Madam!

SAMSON (*offstage near center door*): Wait here. Let me announce you.

Scene 11

The same and PEPO

PEPO (*offstage*): No, wait for me! I'm going right in, or else! (PEPO *enters at center door, clad in his best suit, with his hat on; whistles in surprise at the opulent scene and bows to* EPEMIA.)

EPEMIA: What's your business here? Who are you?

PEPO: I'm here as a guest.

EPEMIA: You are our guest?

PEPO: Yes!

EPEMIA (*stamping her foot*): Help! Oh, help! Someone, help me. (*She runs out the door left.*)

Scene 12

PEPO *and* GIGOLI

PEPO (*advancing into the room, to himself*): Whoever eats your bread would throw up.

GIGOLI: What do you want, fellah? What's your business here?

PEPO: I must have some business to walk all this way.

GIGOLI: May we ask what it is?

PEPO: What good would it do you? Tell Arutin I'm here.

GIGOLI: So, who are you?

PEPO: Me? (*He sits on the couch.*) It's me!

GIGOLI: Some people!

Scene 13

Same and ARUTIN

ARUTIN (*running in from door left*): What's this? What's going on here? (*He sees* PEPO *and stops.*)

PEPO (*He stands, takes off his hat, and bows.*): I trust business is well, Mr. Arutin!

ARUTIN (*to* GIGOLI, *in a low voice*): Go see to your tasks.

GIGOLI (*to himself*): Oh, yeah! The mirrors! (*He exits door center.*)

Scene 14

PEPO, ARUTIN

ARUTIN: Now what's your business here, friend?

PEPO: Be seated, please. (*He takes a chair and sits down.*)

ARUTIN (*on the sofa, to himself*): Look at that! He's playing the host in my own house. (*To* PEPO) Now I wonder what brings you here at this hour?

PEPO: You're a fat cat caring about one of the hungry. Might as well slit my throat, Mr. Arutin. If you're not going to give me what you owe me right now, do me the favor of finishing me off.

ARUTIN: I always pay my debts. What's that to you? I welsh on anyone? Why would I welsh? Didn't you say something about a promissory note some time ago? Have you found it? Have you brought it with you?

PEPO (*to himself, patting his breast, he sighs, then aloud*): There's no note, and you know it. You must have a record in your books.

ARUTIN: I've checked my ledgers many times. Before God, I can tell you there's no such record.

PEPO: Where do we go from here?

ARUTIN: You go your way, I go mine. (*He takes amber worry beads from his pocket and fingers them.*)

PEPO: What's that supposed to mean? In your heart you believe you don't owe me money?

ARUTIN: Friend, I owe you nothing. You have no note. I have no record in my books, so how could I owe you money?

PEPO: Don't you have a record in the ledger of your heart?

ARUTIN: The ledger of my heart?

PEPO: Your conscience, does it speak to you? Come clean, Arutin, you owe me money.

ARUTIN: If I knew that, I'd pay you right now and stop all this cross-examination.

PEPO: How come Giko says you owe me money? Everybody knows how pious and honest he is.

ARUTIN: Well! The parable says, "The fox showed his tail as witness."

PEPO: Mr. Arutin, there's a God in heaven who can read your heart and mine. Don't cheat God.

ARUTIN: Are you accusing me of lying, friend? Anyone listening to you might think you spoke the truth.

PEPO: You know very well I'm speaking the truth. Think of your children. Pity us! The money's not for me.

ARUTIN (*interrupting him*): Oh Lord, enough of this.

PEPO (*continuing*): Now hold on! Hear me out. That money is earmarked for my sister's dowry. If we don't hand it over to her fiancé, he'll jilt her and marry someone else tonight. Consider God's awful judgment. You'll be cross-examined as I will. What will your answer be?

ARUTIN (*He whistles in surprise and starts to reflect.*): By God's awful judgment, I cannot recall that debt.

PEPO: I'm telling you the truth. Don't you believe me?

ARUTIN: Impossible, Pepo! If every Tom, Dick, and Harry came in and said I owe them money, ten million rubles—if I had them—wouldn't last me one day. No, friend, that's not how our accounting systems work.

PEPO (*He stands up and puts his hat on.*): So you're not going to pay up?

ARUTIN: Of course not! But you said your sister's getting married. Fine. I'll be glad to help out. (*He takes his wallet from his inside vest pocket.*) Here you are. (*He hands bills to* PEPO.)

PEPO (*taking off his hat and bowing*): May you and your family enjoy a long life. (*He takes the money.*)

ARUTIN: That's twenty-five rubles. Pick up another twenty-five at my office. I'm going to send word right now. Off you go, friend, and enjoy it.

PEPO (*confused, looking at the money*): Twenty-five and twenty-five makes fifty. (*Silent, he puts on his hat.*): What about the rest? You know the dowry's a thousand rubles.

ARUTIN: I don't care. You made a foolish mistake in promising so much. Whose money were you figuring on giving her? Cut your coat according to your cloth. If a family like yours promises a thousand rubles, what should others do? My, my! The world is topsy-turvy, brother, and there's no rule left us to measure values.

PEPO: You know your affairs, I know mine. We promised our own money. What business is it of yours?

ARUTIN: If you promised your own, give your own. What do you expect from me?

PEPO: Pay me the money, so I can pass it on. Don't you realize what you're giving me now is an insult?

ARUTIN: Try being compassionate to these people! (*To* PEPO, *loudly*) Try to understand once and for all. I don't owe you any money! And the alms I gave you are for my soul.

PEPO: Alms! Do you think me a pauper come to beg. I'm here to demand what's mine. I'm not asking for charity.

ARUTIN: Give the money back if you don't want it! I can use it. This is what they mean when they say the proud poor. (*To* PEPO, *directly*) Come on! Let's have it! What are you gaping at?

PEPO: Then you're not going to hand over the whole sum?

ARUTIN: Are you insane? What's the story? What do you want from me? You can't choke me and have me cough it up.

PEPO (*advancing*): Swear you don't owe me anything. Go ahead.

ARUTIN: I swear by my faith, my God, by heaven, by my loved ones, I don't owe you anything.

PEPO (*awestruck at the sacrilege*): May God in heaven bring calamity on your head. (*He throws the money in* ARUTIN's *face.*) Here, take it! Stick it in your eye! You may want to buy something for your wife.

ARUTIN (*jumping up from the chair, crying out*): Help! Help! Police! He's killing me! Flaying me! Help!

(EPEMIA *rushes in from door left,* SAMSON *from door right, wearing his best suit as* EPEMIA *had directed him. Two other servants enter by center door in formal attire, including white gloves.*)

(*Tableau*)

Scene 15

The same and EPEMIA, *Two Other Servants*

PEPO (*pointing to Servants with his left hand*): This is the kind of man you are? (*Long silence*) May you drown in your riches!

ARUTIN (*confused, to the Servants*): Don't just stand there. Do something. Don't you see he wants to kill me?

(SAMSON *and the Servants approach* PEPO.)

PEPO (*pushing Servants back*): Back off! (*To* ARUTIN) These walls of gold, you've built . . . were paid for by robbing thousands like myself. You've mixed our blood with the stone and quick-lime. You blew dust in people's eyes to hide your theft, and now you sit back and enjoy life.

EPEMIA: Throw him out!

ARUTIN (*to* PEPO): Get out, I say. (*To the Servants*) Throw him out. Are you deaf?

(*The Servants attack* PEPO.)

PEPO: Out! (*Pushing back the Servants*) Back off!

(*The Servants retreat a bit and stand near center door.*)

PEPO (*to* ARUTIN): You denied me my money and now you're throwing me out as well. (*Silence*) I'm going! I've no recourse. Might's on your side. You're the boss here. But I want you to know, Mr. Arutin, you won't get away with this.

There's a God above, so you'll pay through the nose for your injustice. (*Pushing the Servants aside*) Get out of my way. (*He exits by center door.*)

ARUTIN (*to the Servants*): Follow him. He may steal something.

(*The Servants run after* PEPO.)

Scene 16

ARUTIN, EPEMIA

ARUTIN: I've never seen a brazen scoundrel like him! (*He stoops down and picks up the bills.*)

EPEMIA: Is that man sane? You don't know how frightened we were.

ARUTIN (*putting the money inside his breast pocket, ironically*): Try to be compassionate to such people, if you can.

EPEMIA: What's the trouble? You're not telling me what's going on.

ARUTIN: I don't know what the devil is the matter with him. "I've a sister to be married," he said. What's that to me?

EPEMIA: What does he mean by saying you're denying him money?

ARUTIN: Now, I'm surprised at you, Epemia! Me denying somebody his money? Especially a man like that! Don't you know me yet?

EPEMIA: The money you just put in your pocket, was it his?

ARUTIN: God rest his father's soul, in that case everything I own would be his. He came in and said, "I'm a poor man. I've no dowry for my sister. You know what it is to have loved ones. Help me out." And I, like a fool, gave him money. (*Fretting*) Instead of thanking me for it, he took the money and threw it in my face, saying, "It's too little!"

EPEMIA (*aghast*): The very idea! Could it really be so, Arutin dear?

ARUTIN: So I'm lying?

EPEMIA (*cunningly*): You exposed your kindness, so he took advantage. If he should know how every Sunday, returning from church, you place money in the hands of a hundred poor people (*imitating the action*) and say, "Take this, take this!" Now, are you going to take this insult lying down?

ARUTIN: What can I do?

EPEMIA: He threw mud in your face.

ARUTIN: But what can I do?

EPEMIA: Impossible! All those insults! Are you going to swallow such a disgrace? What will people say?

ARUTIN: How will people know? Let him rave! He's a poor man.

EPEMIA: What do you mean, "How will people know?" He shouted at you, in front of the servants. (*Exaggerating* PEPO's *words*) He said, "You robbed the whole world. You've ruined twenty-five thousand poor families. You won't get away with what you did." You can't stomach that. Do you suppose the servants will keep household secrets? Don't you know that by this time tomorrow the whole city will hear of it? A respectable man like you shouldn't have to endure the insults of a bum like him, in your house no less. He said, "You're denying me my money!" If the gossip about you is already damning, it's going to be deadly after this. (*She looks toward center door.*)

Scene 17

The same, GIGOLI, SAMSON

GIGOLI (*cap in hand, hastily enters by center door*): I bought the mirrors, Madam!
EPEMIA (*instantly happy*): The mirrors? (*She rushes in the direction of the mirrors and calls to* ARUTIN *rapturously.*) Come here a minute, Artushka. See how beautiful the mirrors are! How exquisitely antique. (*Calling*) Samson! Samson! (*She departs hurriedly by the center door.*)

(SAMSON *enters door right with* GIGOLI, *and both follow* EPEMIA *from the room.*)

Scene 18

ARUTIN *alone*

ARUTIN (*after a long silence*): Really this was some game that lout played at my expense. The distinction between great and small has gone now . . . A beggar without a bean to his name has the nerve to bawl me out! (*Pacing*) Insult me! (*Adjusting his tie in the mirror*) The world is falling apart. (*He moves away from the mirror.*) "You owe me money," he says. He's insane. What debt? Who said I owe him anything? Who knows I owe him? If I owed him, how come I haven't paid him till now? If I pay him now, what will I say to the others? What harm have they done to deserve this? (*He sits down.*) Forget it! I don't owe anything! He accuses me falsely! If I owe him, where's his promissory note? Where is it? Who has it? What note? It's disappeared! It doesn't exist! That low-life fishmonger will shoot his mouth off to everyone. "He owes me and won't pay up." (*He jumps up from the chair.*) No, no! Epemia's right! It's me that should be hollering. I should be shouting from the rooftops to shake up the world to the fact that a man of prominence like me has been dishonored, having false accusations heaped on me. Just wait, you lout! Then I'll fix you! (*He exits door left.*)

Curtain

ACT 3

Scene 1

The same room as act 1. Fishing net spread on a line. Morning.

KEKEL (*on the* takht, *alone, sewing. She takes a piece of cloth from a sewing bag that is lying beside her, continues sewing and begins singing.*):

> Sweetheart, you hate me.
> You hate me, you insult me.
> You've pierced my heart.
> You've made me all bloody.

(*Drying her tears*)

> When you see me, give a greeting,
> Speak your mind in a letter.

(*In a weepy voice*)

> You didn't flay me with a sword,
> You sacrificed me without a sword.

(*She drops her sewing and begins to cry.*) Oh, dear God! I'm human, too. Why did you create me? What am I in the world, a useless burden on the face of the earth? I wish I were buried under the sod. Take my breath, dear Lord. You know it'd be easier for me to die than live. (*Pause*) Let me sink into the water. Or suspend myself from a rope. Pierce my heart with a knife. And yet to take one's life is a sin. (*She cries*) Lord, strike me with a lightning bolt or rip the earth apart and pull me under.

Scene 2

KEKEL *and* SHUSHAN

SHUSHAN (*enters door left*): Crying again, Kekel?

KEKEL (*drying her eyes*): What else is left, Mama? I've no other way to ease my heart! (*She throws her sewing on the* takht.)

SHUSHAN: You've cried your eyes dry, Kekel!

KEKEL: I feel as though there was a stone pressing on my chest. Tears ease the pain. Otherwise, my sorrows would choke me.

SHUSHAN: May your ne'er-do-well come to judgment and bitter grief. Is he worth all this suffering?

KEKEL: I'm an outcast in the world without dignity. How can I face my girlfriends anymore?

SHUSHAN (*seated on the chair near* KEKEL): Don't worry, Kekel dear. God is merciful. He may send you a better man.

KEKEL: Would that I had sewn his eyes when he began to flirt. Do men have a conscience or soul? He took my kiss and gave it to another. (*Striking her head*) How can I look to heaven now?

SHUSHAN: If you take this so badly, how am I to cope? (*Crying*) Don't I deserve some pity? How else would I get through those dark and dreary days? There are many more in our situation and worse. Begging for bread from door to door, if one in one thousand gets it, they're lucky. Thank God for providing our daily bread. Perhaps this fate was written on our brow. Thanks for the life the Lord gives us. Let's be content with what we have in case worse is to follow. God grant Pepo long life and health to sustain us with a modicum of bread.

KEKEL: I pray to die.

SHUSHAN (*approaching and embracing* KEKEL): Don't say that, Kekel. (*She sits beside* KEKEL.) It's a sin before God, my dear!

KEKEL (*in* SHUSHAN's *arms*): Mama, dear Mama! (*She weeps.*)

(*Tableau*)

Scene 3

Same and GIKO

GIKO (*entering by center door with hat on, cane in hand, and stuttering as usual*): Don't you have anything else to do but cry, my dears?

SHUSHAN (*She stands, leaving* KEKEL's *side.*): What else can we do? Why don't you clap out a rhythm and we'll dance.

KEKEL (*taking her sewing*): It's too much. (*Wiping her eyes, she hastily exits door right, leaving sewing bag partly open on the couch.*)

Scene 4

SHUSHAN, GIKO

GIKO: Enough, enough. May God have mercy on your father. People should have a little patience. You're forever crying. Why not enjoy life occasionally? You can't go on like this.

SHUSHAN (*sits on couch*): What can we do? God keep my worst enemy from suffering this way.

GIKO: You don't know the ways of the Lord, Shushan! God created the world in His own way. Life's sometimes sweetly bitter and sometimes bitterly sweet. (*Pulling up the chair close to the* takht, *he takes snuff and sneezes, then puts two index fingers together.*) Yes, just like this! See! As you can't separate a brother and sister, it's the same joy and grief.

SHUSHAN (*to herself*): I've heard that song before!

GIKO: God's handled everything well. He tells a man, "Here's a portion of happiness—enjoy it." And then to the merriment He sometimes adds a touch of sorrow. So we don't forget Him. We thank the Lord!

SHUSHAN: This is no time for a sermon.

GIKO: Wait a minute, Shushan! You haven't caught the drift of my story. I'm burning like a man in Hell, but I'm also curious whether God's hand is behind it. Kill me, if you like, or thank God that Giko is still alive and able to talk.

SHUSHAN: Enough of your nonsense, Giko. I've worries enough.

GIKO: That's what I'm saying, Shushan! See what joy can come out of grief.

(SHUSHAN *looks surprised.*)

Why are you so surprised? Just wait till you've heard the rest. (*From his pocket he takes a blue envelope, covered with red wax and postal cancellations and raises it with his right hand.*) Look at this, Shushan!

SHUSHAN: What is it?

GIKO: This is it, Shushan!

SHUSHAN: I don't know what it is! What are you blathering about?

GIKO: You'll know soon enough! When God apportioned patience he gave the last part to women. Now, muster your God-given patience attentively, so I don't get tongue-tied.

SHUSHAN (*to herself*): Thank goodness there's only one like him.

GIKO (*continuing*): You remember, Shushan, your late husband?

(SHUSHAN *emits a high-pitched guttural sigh.*)

> (GIKO *takes handkerchief from his pocket and wipes his eyes. He speaks with teary voice*) May God have mercy and illumine his soul. He was a respected man; he was a good man.

(SHUSHAN *sighs.*)

Eh, Shushan! It's a hard life.

SHUSHAN: Get on with it!

GIKO: Okay. (*Pause*) A few days before his death—you know that I was always right beside his bed—he ordered me to lock the door. Then there were only the two of us. (*He dries his eyes.*)

SHUSHAN (*sadly*): I recall!

GIKO: Hold on. (*Covering his mouth with his hand*) He took the cabinet keys out of his pocket and asked me for his small black chest. So I gave it to him. He opened it, took out this paper, gave it to me and ordered me to keep it and not to tell you, or Pepo, until the right time. "My son, Pepo," he said, "is young and inexperienced, and may blow it all, and my wife Shushan is a woman, she may let it fall to Pepo's children," he said. "Until then don't tell a soul you have it."(*He takes an old, white, folded paper from the envelope and points to it; then, in a tearful voice*) "This is Kekel's dowry," he said.

SHUSHAN (*jumping up*): What kind of a document is that?

GIKO: Document? It's Arutin's promissory note!

SHUSHAN (*rushing to him*): What are you saying, Giko? (*She snatches the paper from GIKO's hand.*) The shock will kill me! (*She unfolds the paper and recognizes ARUTIN's note.*)This is it! Help! I'm going to faint! (*She drops in her chair. SHUSHAN and GIKO look at each other in wonder. Long pause*) I've had it. You cruel man! Where have you been keeping it all this time? You've killed my dear child Kekel, already. And now?

GIKO: It isn't my fault, Shushan! God knows I'm innocent.

SHUSHAN (*hurriedly*): May God be your judge. (*Sarcastically*) Is this your idea of the proper time to produce the note?

GIKO: Just give me a moment more!

SHUSHAN (*cutting him off*): Oh, you and your deaf ear. May you get an earful of God's wrath! Was that right, what you did?

GIKO: But, Shushan—

SHUSHAN (*again interrupting GIKO, until he stands*): Let's hear it! (*To herself*) Damn you! (*To GIKO*) Oh, you fool.

(GIKO *whistles.*)

But why did you keep it all this time? Why? What account can you give to the Lord?

GIKO: Listen a minute. I'll tell you.

SHUSHAN: Tell me quickly!

GIKO: Eee! Shushan!

SHUSHAN: Say it!

GIKO: Ooh! Eee!

SHUSHAN: Say what you're going to say!

GIKO: Well-

SHUSHAN: Your usual nonsense, that's all.

GIKO: You're not letting me get the words out of my mouth!

SHUSHAN: You'll get what's coming to you!

GIKO (*He stands up and fixes his hat, ironically*): I don't know a thing. (*Going*) You're the typical impatient woman.

SHUSHAN (*loudly*): Wait a minute! Hold on! (*She calls him.*) Giko!

GIKO (*turning back*): Bless you. Have a little patience, I say. Do you think I'm glad things turned out this way? Man proposes; God disposes. (*Sitting, he inhales snuff, and sneezes.*)

SHUSHAN (*to herself*): I'll give you snuff.

GIKO (*wiping his nose*): You don't know what a merry chase I got drawn into.

SHUSHAN: Give it to me straight. No sidetracking. Now, now! For goodness sake, don't slant things this way and that way. (*She drops the note on the* takht.)

GIKO: Just a minute! It's almost over. When your late husband gave me that note, I pleaded with him not to put a heavy burden like that on my shoulders. "I can't take it," I said, but to no avail. " Giko," he said (*tearfully*), "You're a decent man. I've no one else to turn to." Now, Shushan! Tell me, what could I do? So I took the note, and three or four days later he passed away! (*Drying his eyes*) God rest his soul. Maybe he'll intercede for his Kekel.

(*Drying her tears,* SHUSHAN *sighs deeply.*)

We all die sometime. Eh, what was I saying again?

SHUSHAN: He gave you the note.

GIKO: Oh, yes! He gave it to me. I took it, brought it home and kept it. When you lock something in the strongbox, how can you get a good night's sleep? I held onto it. I also had a few old inscribed seals from King Irakli's time.[5] You know

5. The reference is to Erekle II (1720–1798) of Kartli (East Georgia), whose capital was Tiflis. He bequeathed his realm to Russia on his death.

all I have is a hovel, but still I collected them. I'd safeguarded those seals and writings very securely, I thought. Once in a while, I'd get a kick out of taking them out and having someone read the inscriptions to me. I don't think you've seen them, Shushan. First God's name was written on top, then Christ's, and then came the Holy Spirit! Then the four evangelists and many of the saints in order. Lots of blessings and things like that! They all disappeared. How times have changed.

SHUSHAN: Giko! You're way off the mark.

GIKO: On the contrary, I'm right on it. I told you I kept the promissory note with my seals, wrapped them up, and then put them in a corner of my trunk. The keys were in my pocket at all times. I didn't let a month go by without opening and checking the packet. Nothing's harder than guarding valuables. I prayed that God would see to Kekel's good fortune, and he heard me. (*Pause*) One day I opened my trunk and found the packet gone! I searched high and low but found nothing. By the way, I forgot to tell you, I have a few very old coins as well. Very, very old coins! They had also disappeared. The rest of the things in the trunk were safe and just as I'd left them. Now, Sister, listen. If a thief broke in, why didn't he steal my ready cash instead of old, rusty coins? I had more than fifty rubles in the trunk. Tsar Nicholas's issue, mind you. Now, if the devil got in my trunk, I'd like to know how he got in and out without leaving a trace. The trunk was locked, keys in my pocket. I couldn't figure it out. You can imagine how I felt, Shushan! God knows, one day I have to give up the ghost. Yes. I went to the fortune-teller and [following the usual ritual] shook the seven grains of barley to discover what happened to the package. I even consulted the ephemerdist's predictions. And pray? I was on my knees in church for hours. I lost my appetite, my sleep, and became a shadow of my former self. And the more I saw you, the more I heard your sobbing and laments, the more my heart was consumed by raging fire. (*He dries his tears.*)

SHUSHAN: My goodness! We questioned you many times. Why didn't you break your silence? We knew that my late husband, God rest his soul, told you about his will. Why didn't you say a word about it?

GIKO: Shushan, I tried to tell you many times, but I was always afraid to talk about it. What could I do if I became tongue-tied? Not long ago, I was almost going to tell you the whole story. Really it was on the tip of my tongue, but it seemed like a bad time. Pepo was very angry, and I didn't dare open my mouth. I was nervous, not for myself, Shushan, but for you, as God knows. I didn't want an argument to break out that might lead to dire consequences. (*Greatly affected*) Again I swallowed my heart's sorrow fearfully, like a bitter pill. (*Again he dries his tears.*)

(SHUSHAN *shows impatience.*)

Let me tell you, Shushan, that I didn't bear my responsibility lightly. I prayed to God not to let me die until I discharged my duty. I don't want to boast, Shushan! The Lord knows that. I pawned my clothes for you, and I would have gotten the cash in a day or two. But that would have been too late. Perhaps that was how it was meant to be. Glory be to you O Lord God almighty!

SHUSHAN: How did you find the note eventually?

GIKO: How did I find it? I didn't find it, Shushan! It found me! Yes! Now I'll tell you how.

SHUSHAN (*to herself*): He's wiped me out!

GIKO (*continuing*): That, that tricky nephew of mine—

SHUSHAN: You mean the one in Russia?

GIKO: Yes, the one that puts on airs. While he was over here between college semesters, a day before he left, he asked me several times if I would give him those seals. "Give them to me," he said, "they could be useful for my studies because they're old." To tell you the truth, Shushan, I turned him down, so he wouldn't break them or throw them away. Why would anyone need old stuff in a modern course of study? And so he left without them, so I thought. Just before he set off—

SHUSHAN: He's been gone for about three months, hasn't he?

GIKO: Yes, about that! But before going, he reached into my pocket while I was snoozing—Lord knows what I was dreaming of—took my keys, opened the trunk as though he owned it, and swiped the packet and the old coins. Locking the trunk again, he replaced the keys in my pocket and sneaked off. Now, if you want to call me a jerk, I'd like to know what a savvy man would do that Giko couldn't. Come on, Shushan, always hear a guy first, then start throwing out the blame. If you call me a jerk, what would you call the genuine article?

SHUSHAN: Then what happened?

GIKO: Then? The note arrived in today's mail along with a comical letter, belittling and mocking me, mind you, "I've sent your seals to France," he wrote, and if you want, they'll send you a medal for your old coins. The note I return as a favor to you." His letter's there if you want to see it. (*He stands slowly and goes to* SHUSHAN.)

SHUSHAN (*in an outburst*): The devil take your nephew!

GIKO (*presenting his nephew's letter to* SHUSHAN): Take a look, if you don't believe me. I had a great deal of trouble getting the parcel from the post office. I'm dead tired from all that running around.

SHUSHAN: Keep it. I believe you.

GIKO: Now, Shushan, am I to blame for what's happened?

SHUSHAN: My Kekel is at death's door. It doesn't matter to me whether you're to blame or not.

GIKO: Don't worry, Shushan! God is merciful!

SHUSHAN: He's taken the light of my eye, and you say God is merciful.

GIKO: Don't say that, Shushan! Nobody knows the workings of God.

SHUSHAN: To Him all glory! It's all in His hands.

GIKO (*sitting*): A good man wouldn't have jilted her over money. (*He puts the envelope in his pocket.*)

SHUSHAN: That's true. But why beat a dead horse? We've been shamed. We've lost face. We're the butt of jokes all over town. Who'd want to marry my Kekel after this? My poor girl! (*She cries.*) Your candle flickers in the wind!

GIKO: That's enough, Shushan!

SHUSHAN (*crying*): Kekel, dear Kekel!

(GIKO *dries his eyes, lamenting*)

Scene 5

The same, KAKULI

KAKULI (*entering by center door*): I've been looking for you for hours, and I find you jawing!

GIKO: What's new?

KAKULI (*shoving* GIKO *by the hip*): Get up, quick! Come with me!

SHUSHAN: What's happened?

KAKULI: The Lord himself only knows what's going to happen!

SHUSHAN: (*frightened*): What's up?

KAKULI: They took Pepo away this morning.

SHUSHAN: Where did they take him? What are you talking about?

KAKULI: That fiend filed a formal complaint against Pepo.

SHUSHAN: Who? What complaint?

KAKULI: Who do you suppose? That devil, Arutin! The man who owes you money. (*He pounds on his chest and grinds his teeth*) If I ever get the chance—

SHUSHAN: God strike me blind! What are they going to do with Pepo?

KAKULI: I don't know, Mama! It would be a miracle if he doesn't do time. (*To* GIKO) Come on, let's get going, Giko! I was looking for you all day. If we don't get there soon, we'll be too late.

SHUSHAN: He owes us money, and he's filed a complaint against us? Oh, Arutin! May the Lord punish you! (*To* GIKO) Get up, Giko! Do you hear me? (*She takes the note and gives it to* GIKO.) Take it! Take this note with you and shame him.

(GIKO *takes the note and puts it in his pocket.*)

KAKULI: What note?

SHUSHAN: That black-hearted devil's note.

KAKULI (*happy*): Is that right? You found it? (*Jumping with joy*) God bless your soul. How did it come to light?

SHUSHAN(*pointing to* GIKO): He'll tell you on the way.

KAKULI: Giko found it?

SHUSHAN: Yes!

KAKULI (*embracing* GIKO): Good for you, old buddy. You're a sport, a champion. You'll have a place in my heart forever. You'll be like a father to me.

GIKO: My boy! May you live to be my age!

KAKULI (*hurriedly, in a low voice*): Thank you, Giko! (*Raising his voice*) Long life Giko! (*Tapping his chest with his fist*) Arutin! Let's see how you weasel out of this one! (*Taking* GIKO's *arm*) Let's go, Giko.

SHUSHAN: Heaven preserve us!

KAKULI: Don't worry, Mama dear. God is merciful.

SHUSHAN: Hurry up before anything happens to my Pepo!

KAKULI (*pulling* GIKO): Are your shoes nailed down or something?

GIKO (*standing*): Let's go! (*He starts to inhale snuff.*) Let's see what excuse he comes up with.

KAKULI (*snatching the snuffbox from him*): Come on! You can take all the snuff you want on the way. (*Grabbing* GIKO's *arm and leading him away in a hurry*)

(GIKO *walks around, wailing.*)

(KAKULI *puts his arm around* GIKO.) Good old pal, you'll never hear a cruel word from me again.

(*They exit door center.*)

Scene 6

SHUSHAN, *then* KEKEL

SHUSHAN (*standing alone*): What is it you want of us, Oh Lord! What have I done wrong? First you darkened my day by taking my husband, then you wrecked my child's future. I hope there won't be many black days to come. Have pity on us, Oh Lord! I don't ask for fame and fortune. Don't make our lives harder than they are. But preserve my Pepo and give him his freedom. (*Putting on her cape, she calls* KEKEL.) Kekel, dear.

(KEKEL *enters by door right, sad, her sewing in her hand.*)

Come here, Kekel! Come in and lock the doors. I'm going out to kiss the cross in the chapel up the street. I'll be right back, dear!

KEKEL: Right away, Mama!

(SHUSHAN *exits quickly by door left.*)

Scene 7

KEKEL *alone*

KEKEL: Poor Mama! (*Going to the* takht) How the Lord and the Cross have abandoned her. (*She takes up her sewing bag.*) A trial and tribulation—that's what's written on our brow. (*With sewing bag in her hand, she exits door left.*)

Scene 8

PEPO *alone*

PEPO(*entering by center door, hat on and in his best clothes*): What a world. (*He takes his hat off, wipes sweat from his forehead with his index finger, then puts his hat on again.*) A man's innocent through and through and he comes in the wrong. Then punish him and set the culprit free. So go to prison, Pepo. And ponder the ways of the world. You pursue justice and see the whole city's filled with wolves, not men. Who asked you where it gets you? You see, the city's become a den of wolves. Who asked you to go around in a sheep's costume? Whom did you shout at? Why did you shoot your mouth off at him? What cards are you holding? Do you have money in your pocket or brains in your head, or can you write? What have you got going for you, pal? All you can do is bleat like a lamb, you chump, and end up on the butcher block. Lay down quietly, Pepo, let them slit your throat. There'll be ten knives instead of one. (*He sits on a chair at the table, covering his face with his hands.*)

Scene 9

PEPO, KEKEL

KEKEL (*entering door left*): Oh, you're back, Pepo?

PEPO: I'm here, but I'm going off for a while. Good-bye!

KEKEL: Where are you going?

PEPO (*ironically, a smile on his face*): A nice warm place.

KEKEL: What does that mean?

PEPO (*standing*): I'm off to prison Kekel!

KEKEL (*frightened*): What for?

PEPO (*He puts the chair back where it belongs.*): Just for the hell of it.

KEKEL: Pepo dear, what are you talking about?

PEPO: I'm not kidding around, Kekel. Don't worry. You'll get by somehow. Where's Mama? Isn't she home?

KEKEL : She'll be back any minute. She's gone to kiss the cross at the church near-by.

PEPO: Poor Mama!

KEKEL: Seriously, Pepo. Why are you going to prison?

PEPO: Oh, nothing really! (*With a bitter smile*) "You've been wearing out your hips, throwing that net of yours," they said. "Go and have a rest. For throwing your net so often," they said. "Your hips are tired," they said. "You can go to prison and rest them," they said.

KEKEL: Pepo, don't break my heart. I've had as much as I can take.

PEPO: Feelings have nothing to do with it. I have to go to prison. That's all there is to it.

KEKEL: What's your crime?

PEPO (*bitterly*): Robbery.

KEKEL: Robbery? Pepo, tell me what it's all about. My heart's in my mouth.

PEPO: Yes! So is mine. But no one cares about our heartache.

KEKEL (*wiping her tears, crying*): Oh Pepo, dear, your words have cut me to the quick.

PEPO: You know who's responsible.

KEKEL: Who then?

PEPO: Who? Mr. Arutin, of course! (*Laughing bitterly*)

KEKEL: Why?

PEPO: God only knows what runs through his head. "He dishonored me in my house," he said. "I gave him a gift and he threw it in my face," he said. Don't think it's a small thing to trifle with a powerful man's honor. A poor man like me daring to slap a pillar of society in the face is no laughing matter. (*Laughing bitterly, arms outstretched*) Oh God!

KEKEL (*embracing* PEPO): It's all because of me, Pepo dear. I wish I'd never been born so that you wouldn't have had such an unlucky sister. What did you want from me? Who told you to insult that rich man? Why did you add to your troubles? What are you going to do now? What's going to become of Mama? When she hears, she'll have a stroke. (*She cries.*)

PEPO: Mama has come through many hardships. She'll get through this one, too.

KEKEL (*tearfully*): I'd be better off dead.

PEPO: That's enough, Kekel! For the love of God! Crying doesn't help. (*Shouting to Heaven*) Oh Lord, is this Your justice? Arutin did the stealing. Arutin did the injury. Arutin denied his crimes. And we've borne the brunt of the penalty. He's chortling while we tear out our hair. He's making merry while we shed bitter tears. (*He exits right.*)

KEKEL: Pepo, Pepo! (*She follows* PEPO *out.*)

Scene 10

GIKO, ARUTIN, *both wearing hats*

(GIKO *enters by center door, followed by* ARUTIN)

GIKO: You'll see, I haven't lied to you.

ARUTIN (*following* GIKO): Okay.

GIKO (*coming forward*): Wait a minute! Please have a seat, until Pepo comes!

ARUTIN: It's all one, Giko. Just let me see it. What kind of paper is it?

GIKO: Now I'm going to show you, Mr. Arutin. (*Putting his hand in his pocket, he takes out the snuffbox.*) No, no! This is not it. (*He inhales snuff.*) Hmm, now! (*He puts the snuffbox in his pocket and takes out the note.*) Keep your distance, Mr. Arutin.

(ARUTIN *steps back toward the couch.*)

ARUTIN: Are you afraid I'll snatch it from you? My gracious, we're not in a dog-eat-dog world yet!

GIKO: No! No! Mr. Arutin, you wouldn't do that. I don't think you're that sort of man. This paper's a bit of bad luck. That's why I don't want your hand to be infected by it. (*Opening the note*) Now, have a look. Is this it?

ARUTIN (*bending his head toward the note*): Let me see! Let me see!

GIKO (*pointing with his finger*): iou, signed Arutin Zimzimovich.

(*Surprise tableau*)

ARUTIN (*confused and stuttering*): That! That! (*Reaching out*) Is that my handwriting?

GIKO (*bringing the note close to* ARUTIN): It isn't mine.

ARUTIN (*recognizing the note, to himself*): This is punishment from heaven. (*Raising his hand, to* GIKO) Let me have a good look at that paper, will you?

GIKO (*pulling away the note*): Wait a minute, Sir! Do you remember I told you a dozen times, "I'm a witness to the debt"? You thought I was lying, didn't you? It wasn't my fault if you didn't believe me. (*Crying out*) Thanks for Your justice, Oh Lord!

ARUTIN (*looking for a chance to snatch the note*): Let me have a good look.

GIKO (*putting the note in his pocket*): Now, Mr. Arutin, bless your father's soul, take your hands away. I told you this paper is a bit of bad luck, didn't I? Pepo will be here soon. Kakuli will bring him along any minute. You wait here. I'm going to bring word to Shushan (*While leaving he looks behind, suspicious of* ARUTIN, *and exits door left.*)

Scene 11

ARUTIN *alone*

ARUTIN (*dumbstruck, reviving*): I've never played such a game in my life. I've had many a close shave but never anything like this. Where the devil did that damn note come from? How the devil did that damn lout come to life? I must be dreaming. No! I'm not. If this is a dream (*looking around*), what am I doing here? This is Pepo's house, and I (*feeling himself*), Arutin Zimzimov, am here? No! This is punishment direct from heaven. Impossible! I've swallowed many a medicine in life, but this time I seem to have swallowed the bottle. It's curtains. What will people say when they hear about it? Who'll trust me anymore? I was blinded by greed. I didn't distinguish between black and white. It was just a few days ago I said to Pepo before witnesses, "I don't owe you a thing." Now, Arutin, shame on you! How did you get into this mess? (*Long pause*) There's no other way. I have to get my hands on that note, whatever it costs, right here and now. Even if I have to pay double the amount plus interest. Even twenty or thirty percent. Even if I have to pay two rubles for one. I'll pay my debt even if it kills me. (*He falls into chair at right.*)

Scene 12

ARUTIN, PEPO

PEPO (*He enters door right, in his old clothes and hat on as in first act. He is surprised at seeing* ARUTIN.): What are you doing here?

ARUTIN (*He takes his hat off and puts it on the table.*): Are you surprised?

PEPO: Why shouldn't I be? Don't you think it strange you're here? Tell me what wind blew you in? Did a good angel move you to compassion, or did a demon goad you to hound me further.

ARUTIN: Pepo, I'm a guest. I'm sure you know how to treat a guest?

PEPO: You, my guest? Better start saying your prayers. You're my worst enemy.

ARUTIN: Please, have a seat.

PEPO: I'm fine standing. Tell me what you've come for. If it's fish you want, you've come to the wrong place. (*He smiles, bitterly and ironically, to himself.*) It's against city ordinances.

ARUTIN: Come on, Pepo, let's patch things up.

PEPO (*mocking him*): Mr. Arutin, did anyone put you up to this?

ARUTIN: What difference does it make? I'm asking you to make up.

PEPO: There must be something in it for you. You're such a big shot and me a pipsqueak. (*Ironically*) Are you afraid of doing time instead of me? Are your hands shaking because the boys are going to rough you up?

ARUTIN: Listen, I came here to do you a favor.

PEPO (*ironically*): You've done me enough favors already. You owed me money but denied it. I came to your house to plead, and you threw me out. And to top it all off, you're sending me to prison. What other favors have you in store for me, Mr. Arutin? Are you here to mock me? That's enough, Sir! Get out of here, and thank God that you're under my roof. Otherwise, you wouldn't make it home alive. Don't you remember how you kicked me out on the street? Did that become a gentleman like you? Now, I beg you, please don't trouble yourself further. They're coming any minute now to take me away. I've only time to say good-bye to my mother and sister.

ARUTIN: A word from me, and you're off the hook.

(PEPO *looks at him, surprised.*)

KAKULI (*offstage*): Is he here yet?

Scene 13

The same, GIKO, KAKULI

GIKO (*at center door, to* KAKULI): I've lost them! They've disappeared! Nobody's home.

KAKULI (*entering, to* GIKO): Ha, Pepo's here!

ARUTIN (*seeing* KAKULI, *to himself*): Is that hooligan here, too?

GIKO (*entering*): Why Pepo, how did you get here? I didn't see you come in. (*To* ARUTIN) Now, Mr. Arutin, I'll let you have it if (*pointing to* PEPO) Pepo says it's okay.

PEPO: What's this all about?

KAKULI: Don't ask me! You were talking to Mr. Arutin yourself. Didn't he tell you?

PEPO: What he said didn't make sense! (*Ironically*) He's come to make up with me.

KAKULI (*mocking*): Huh! (*humorously, to* ARUTIN) We're most beholden to you, Mr. Arutin.

ARUTIN (*to himself and confused*): The nerve of this lowlife . . .

KAKULI (*to* PEPO): I thought you said Mr. Arutin was not an honest man.

ARUTIN (*to himself*): Oh, you buffoon!

PEPO (*smiling ironically*): How do I know? His conscience finally kicked in.

(GIKO *shakes his head.*)

KAKULI (*to* PEPO): How is he going to patch things up? Is he giving you at least half? (*Approaching* ARUTIN) I pity the life of anyone who calls you a man. (*Raising up his first*) Take off your coat and prepare to die.

PEPO: Kakuli! Control yourself!

GIKO (*to* PEPO): Watch he doesn't skin him alive.

KAKULI (*grabbing* ARUTIN'*s collar and necktie with his left hand*): You bastard! (*He hits him with his right hand.*) Now go and make all the complaints you want. You son of a bitch.

ARUTIN: Are you out of your mind?

PEPO (*separating them*): Not so fast, Kakuli! Easy does it.

ARUTIN (*straightening up and fixing his collar and tie*): And to think I came here to do you a favor.

KAKULI: A favor! (*To* PEPO) What a joker. (*Laughing*) He's always plotting to save his own skin. (*To* ARUTIN) You think I don't know what you're up to. (*Looking at* ARUTIN *he shakes his head, and then turns to* PEPO) Oh sure! You'd like to do us a favor now, now that the note's been found.

PEPO: What note?

KAKULI: You mean you don't know? (*Ironically*) Yes, this fine gentleman's note has been found. (*Going to* GIKO) Come, bring it here! (*To* PEPO) When Giko told him, he went as pale as a ghost. I thought, for a minute, I wanted to bash his brains out, but I guessed you'd want to know the good news first. (*To* GIKO) Come Giko, dear. Hurry up!

GIKO (*taking the note from his pocket*): Wait, wait a minute. I'm going to give it to the rightful owner. (*He offers the note to* PEPO.)

KAKULI (*He snatches the note out of* GIKO'*s hand and gives it to* PEPO.): What do you think of that, old buddy?

(PEPO *examines the note, increasingly puzzled.*)

(*Tableau*)

PEPO: Is this a dream?

KAKULI: A dream and a half . . .

GIKO: Really it's a dream, Pepo. Don't you—

ARUTIN (*to himself*): I've never been so disgraced.

KAKULI (*pointing at* GIKO): Don't get him going, Pepo. The tale about the note is as long as the story about the seven camels.

PEPO:How did it surface?

GIKO (*He sits on the couch and gets ready to relate the story.*): Okay, Pepan. This is how it began.

KAKULI (*covering* GIKO's *mouth with his hands*): Shush! Be quiet, Giko. (*To* PEPO) We'll tell you later how it happened. Look at this villain.

(ARUTIN *is extremely nervous.*)

PEPO (*He looks at* ARUTIN *and then the note. Suddenly turning, he takes off his hat, looks up to heaven, and cries out.*): Thank you, Oh Lord! Again Your judgment prevails over all others. (*Putting his hat on, he turns to* GIKO.) In my heart I always knew—

GIKO: God knows, Pepo, it's not my fault.

(KAKULI *covers* GIKO's *mouth with his hands again and exhorts him to be silent.*)

PEPO: You're my guardian angel, Giko, at this moment. (*In silence, he looks at* ARUTIN *for a long time.*)

GIKO (*in a low voice*): May your guardian angel be with you, my son. (*A long silence*)

PEPO (*He crosses to* ARUTIN *slowly and shows him the note.*): Is this your note or not, Mr. Arutin? (*He takes a long hard look into* ARUTIN's *face, then shakes his head.*) Now I understand why you've come. (*Ironically*) You did me proud. You said you owed me nothing. You swore by your faith, by your children. Do you swear like that every day? Or is that how you deceive people? Did oaths like that get you your millions? May your oaths come back to haunt you. May they tear your body to bits so your soul can see the light of heaven. (*Coming close to him*) Aren't you ashamed? Conscience is an empty word to you. (*Showing him the note again*) What's this? (*Continuing*) What have you to say for yourself? Didn't you sign this with your gnarled hands? But that should pose you no problem. Lies are second nature to you. May the earth swallow you up, you and your fancy clothes.

(ARUTIN *is utterly devastated.*)

KAKULI (*He takes his hat off and exclaims.*): Yes Sir, no Sir, three bags full, Sir, Agha

Arutin. (*Putting his hat on, and in a menacing tone*) I swear I'd hate to be in your shoes.

GIKO (*standing*): I wonder what's happened to Shushan? (*He exits left, shaking his head*)

Scene 14

The same without GIKO

ARUTIN (*reviving, to* PEPO): What's all this spouting off? If I could have remembered, I'd have paid you.

KAKULI (*raising his fists*): Hmm! (*He claps hands, then hooks his thumbs into his girdle.*)

PEPO (*to* ARUTIN): You mean your memory failed you? You poor thing. How do you manage to get by then? Who do you think you're kidding? This morning you told the judge you'd never owed anyone anything and that I'd accused you falsely. It was only recently that you signed this note, and yet you couldn't remember. And you want us to make up now. You tormented us all this time. You put your head in the noose. And now overnight you've become an angel. You're frightened. You're ashamed the whole world will hear of your double-dealing. You're scared stiff you're going to fall apart before the judge. But you lose nothing by reconciling with naïve people like us. It doesn't matter so long as it doesn't go public and people don't get to hear. (*Raising his voice*) Get out of my house!

(KAKULI *takes a threatening position, shakes his head, and beats his chest with his hands.*)

ARUTIN: Have you had your say? Did you unburden your heart? Now let me have my say. Here's my bottom line. Take the money and give me my note, and I'll quash your prison sentence.

PEPO: I'm going to prison. I don't need your favors. (*Showing the note*) I can draw cash on this note at anytime without you.

ARUTIN: Don't be rash, Pepan! (*Putting his hand in his inside vest pocket*) Here! Take this money. It's yours. Take it I'm telling you. (PEPO *shakes his head.*) Take it and an additional sum for your troubles. Come on! How much more? Fifty? Sixty?

PEPO (*After looking at* ARUTIN *disdainfully, he turns to* KAKULI.): Are you following all this, Kakuli? Did you hear what he said? An hour ago he wasn't going to pay the principal, and now he's adding interest. That's the way it is with loan sharks! They're all alike. If they can get away with it, they'll refuse to pay. If there's any danger of being exposed, this is what they do to save face.

KAKULI (*to* PEPO, *softly*): Take the money and screw him. (*Making a fist*) I know how to get even with him.

PEPO (*to* ARUTIN): I'm not taking your handout, Mr. Arutin. Shove it. Keep your eye on it. I'll take your eye and your very head in the very place you lied about me a couple of hours ago. Then the public will see what kind of a con man you are. That's why it won't really be like prison though I'm holed up in a cell.

KAKULI (*to* PEPO): You've taken leave of your senses!

ARUTIN: Take the money and a hundred more.

KAKULI (*approaching* ARUTIN): Give it here. I'll broker the deal.

PEPO (*pushing* KAKULI *back*): This is not your business!

KAKULI (*drawing back*) Don't be a damn fool!

Scene 15

The same, SHUSHAN, GIKO

SHUSHAN (*A sable wrap over her shoulders, she stands on the threshold of the center door, to* GIKO *who is following her.*): God strike me blind! Is that true, Giko? (*Coming in, she takes off the sable wrap.*) Where is he? Is this our tormentor? (*She throws her wrap on the chair, nearby.*)

(GIKO *stands near the* takht.)

PEPO: Yes, Mama! This is the man who wants to make us rich.

SHUSHAN (*to* ARUTIN, *speaking hurriedly*): May the ground open and pull you in! What do you want from us? You denied us our money, you cut my daughter's throat, and now you're putting my Pepo in prison. Do you have some grudge against us, that you want to destroy us completely?

ARUTIN (*to himself*): Instead of water, the gargoyle spews out hailstones.

SHUSHAN (*continuing*): May your name be blotted out! May your house fall and collapse, and the fire you ignited in us burn through your shameless wife's heart.

KAKULI (*to himself, softly*): Amen!

PEPO: Mama!

(KEKEL *enters by door right and stands in the corner near the net, crying silently.*)

Scene 16

The same, KEKEL

ARUTIN (*to* SHUSHAN): Pull yourself together, Mama. You don't know what you're talking about.

SHUSHAN (*to* GIKO): Where is it? Throw it in his face! Where's that confounded note? (*To* ARUTIN) You still say you don't owe us anything?

ARUTIN: Yes, I owe you the money! I owe you and I'm willing to pay. What more do you want?

SHUSHAN: Then why are you sending him to prison?

ARUTIN: I won't let him go to prison. I'll pay my debt and more. What can I do if Pepo doesn't want to make peace?

(SHUSHAN *looks around in surprise.*)

PEPO (*to* ARUTIN): Right now, shall we make peace? (*Approaching* KEKEL) But what have you got to say to *her*? (*Holding* KEKEL's *right arm and advancing with her*) How will you come to terms with *her*? You've buried her alive. You've made an old woman of her. You've messed up her life. How would you go about reconciling with her? How are you going to pay her for what she's lost? With all your riches you can't heal the wound you made in her heart. Go! There can never be a reconciliation. Go, while you still have breath in your body. So long as you live, remember her tears so as not to harm others as you did her.

KEKEL (*trying to free her arm*): Let go my arm, Pepo dear!

(PEPO *lets her arm go.*)

Throw his note in his face. Give it to him!

GIKO (*to* PEPO): Better reconcile.

KAKULI (*to* SHUSHAN): Mama, tell him to patch it up. You can see Mr. Arutin is willing to pay more.

SHUSHAN: Let him keep the extra. And keep his hands off my Pepo.

KEKEL: Make up, Pepo.

ARUTIN: Don't be stubborn, Pepan. Make peace with me.

PEPO: Okay, let's be reconciled. But we'll do it in the place where you lied about me a couple of hours ago. I'll present this note before all to prove that I'm not the one who lied. Come on! Why don't you? Even if I have to take a cut in the principal.

SHUSHAN (*to* ARUTIN): Go! Go and see your name blackened as you blackened ours.

PEPO: Come on, then.

ARUTIN: Why should I have to go through the wringer, when you're now in the clear?

PEPO: You fraud! You scam artist!

(KAKULI *growls under his breath as he bares his chest.*)

(*There's a knock at the center door.*)

KAKULI (*He goes to the door, opens it halfway, and speaks to someone.*): Yes! He's here! (*He rushes back to* PEPO.) Are you crazy? Reconcile! The police sergeant's at the door.

PEPO, SHUSHAN, KEKEL (*together*): Sergeant?

GIKO: Sergeant!

(*Tableau*)

ARUTIN: Give me my note, Pepan, or they'll take you to prison.

PEPO: I'm going to do my time in prison. I'm not going to die there. I know I'll be coming home soon. It's a short sentence. You conned thousands like me with your schemes. And you cut many a throat. I wouldn't be Pepo if I didn't seek vengeance on you for them all. I'll blacken your reputation all over. Good-bye, Mama. Don't cry, Kekel. God is merciful. This is the fate written on the brow of the oppressed.

(KAKULI *slowly goes to the net and stands there in a menacing attitude.*)

ARUTIN (*devastated, to himself*): What shall I do now?

KEKEL (*embracing* PEPO): Don't go, Pepo dear, don't go!

SHUSHAN (*to* PEPO): What are you doing, Pepo? Give him that infernal note.

PEPO: Shall I give it to him so he can make a fool and a liar out of me in public? Is that the right thing to do? Shall I sell my soul for fear of prison? No, Mama, this note is a sword handed me by God, and with it I shall lop off his head. How many hearts like yours has he left to burn? How many (*pointing to* KEKEL) like her? How many like me tear their hair in desperation? Shouldn't somebody come forward and tell the world what he's done? People have to know that the man they bow to, honor, and respect, who they magnify and ex-alt to high heaven, is really someone for whom there is nothing sacred in this world. Now, you can cry all you want. The Lord has created the tears of the poor to wash clean the wrongdoings of the rich.

(*Again a knock at the center door*)

Good-bye! (*He exits by center door.*)

Scene 17

The same without PEPO

SHUSHAN (*crying after* PEPO): Pepo! Pepo!
KEKEL (*at same time*): Pepo, dear brother! Pepo! (*Throwing herself on the* takht, *with her face in the pillow, she remains motionless, sobbing loudly to the end.*)
ARUTIN (*standing near the table, beating his head with both hands, then to himself*): What a load of trouble has fallen on my head.
SHUSHAN (*stretching to full height, to* ARUTIN): May the Heavenly King pass judgment on you. (*She runs out after* PEPO.)

Scene 18

The same without SHUSHAN

GIKO (*to* ARUTIN): May your father rest in peace. Are you satisfied that you got what you wanted? (*Speaking to* KEKEL) Don't cry, Kekel dear, don't cry. God is merciful. (*He stands quietly beside* KEKEL.)
KAKULI (*approaching* ARUTIN *with his left hand akimbo, leaving his right hand free*): Now, Mr. Arutin, It's you and me!

(*Tableau*)

Slow curtain

HAGOP BARONIAN

Hagop Baronian died in 1891, in abject poverty, having laughed himself into financial failure, even while he gained immortality as a writer. He had been eminently successful in making life miserable for many prominent figures of his time with satire aimed at deflating incompetent leaders and mockery of immoderate societal mores.

Born in 1843 into a poor family of Edirne (Adrianople), Baronian received primary and secondary training in Armenian schools. Thereafter he attended the local Greek school for a year, after which he was compelled to abandon formal education in order to find a job. He started work in a chemist's shop and then turned to bookkeeping. Moving to Constantinople in 1864, he worked in a telegraph office and then as a clerk at the Armenian Patriarchate. He also taught for a short time at the Armenian school in Üsküdar, where he mentored the Romantic poet and dramatist Bedros Turian (1851–1872).

A voracious reader, he taught himself several European languages, especially French and Italian, whose literary and theatrical influence at Constantinople was greatest at that time.

In the Ottoman capital he gained experience as a writer by contributing to various periodicals. This served as a training ground for his later major satiric works, in which his ability to capture on paper the humor or absurdity of people and situations in a few lively strokes of the pen raised his work above the ephemera of his own time to continue to amuse new

readers. Soon he learned that satirists may be revered by the masses but unfortunately receive no patronage from the rich they mock. Marrying in 1879, he was
obliged to fall back on the publicly inoffensive nonliterary occupation of bookkeeping repeatedly in subsequent years to earn an adequate living for his large family.

The periodicals he edited proved short-lived. The *Pogh arawodean* [Morning
bugle] was discontinued for financial reasons after the twenty-eighth issue. Within
a seven-year period, *Eprad* [Euphrates], *Meghu* [Bee], and *Tadron* [Theater] were
suppressed by the Ottoman censor's office, *Khigar* after four years, and *Dzidzagh*
[Mirth] within a few months.

Baronian's parting shot at various pernicious elements in society after a hectic
see-saw career in publishing expressed the bitterness of two decades of frustration
and financial loss:

> Farewell injustice, farewell slanderers
> Farewell corrupt officials and
> Farewell nonpaying subscribers.

The "farewell" to "slanderers" doubtless was addressed to the very people who, having suffered his ridicule, had applied to the censors as their only means of silencing
him.

It was Baronian's purpose to expose and ridicule the incompetence of lay and
church leaders, the indolence of monks in the monasteries, the inadequacy of the
Armenian Patriarchate of Constantinople, the futility of deliberation at the National Assembly mandated by the Armenian constitution of 1863, the parsimony of
men of wealth, the adherence to questionable social customs, which destroy family relations, and, last but not least, the improvidence of the sultan's government
and his corrupt, incompetent officials.

He denounced rich merchants bent only on profit making but sympathized
with small merchants, "who broil in their own fat," making a meager living. He
sided with underpaid instructors "invited to teach a week or two and expelled for
not kowtowing to a member of the school committee."

Baronian's deep interest in the theater manifested itself at a young age. The
first Armenian professional company had been founded at Constantinople in 1861,
and this significant event introduced the young writer to the possibility of an acting
career. The previous decade had seen the wide popularity of farces and comedies
by Goldoni and Molière, both of whose plot lines aroused Baronian to creative
adaptation. He produced his first play, a brief farce, *Erku derov dzaray me* [A servant with two masters] in 1865, in close imitation of the Goldoni original. This was
followed four years later by his first comedy *Adamnapoyzh arevelean* [Oriental den-
tist], which treats arranged marriage and marital fidelity in a typically light vein.
He developed his realistic presentation of Armenian society in his later works,
which were serialized in newspapers before appearing in book form. Baronian be-

gan *Shoghokorte* [The flatterer] in 1872 but left it incomplete. Appearing in 1880–81, his broad satire *Medzabadiw muratsganner* [Honorable beggars] highlighted the gaucherie and naïveté of the provincial landed gentry as well as the readiness to exploit these qualities by various artistic, professional, religious, and artisan opportunists. Finally, his *Baghdasar aghpar* [Brother balthazar] takes up the theme of divorce, in which the main character seeks to escape his wife, Anoysh, whom he suspects of adultery, but is forced to accept the status quo when the maid presents convincing, though fabricated, charges that the master has been making advances toward her.

Baronian was also a penetrating theater critic, demanding a high standard from playwrights and performers alike. He particularly disapproved of the Romantic excesses of historical tragedies such as Tovmas Terzian's *Santukhd*, portraying the martyrdom of an early Armenian saint, on grounds of subject matter and treatment. Commenting on the religious apparatus of many of these works, he once stated:

> Every theater-going Armenian knows that an angel and a spirit seem invariably a part of Armenian dramas. Last night I dreamed that God needed an angel in order to take someone's life. There are no available angels, the Archangel informed him, they are all at Armenian plays.

Baronian's satirical collections include a rogue's gallery of prominent Armenian personalities under the overall title *Azkayin chocher* [Bigwigs of the nation]. The thirty-two individual portraits published in the 1870s include a broad spectrum of political, religious, and cultural figures from both the Ottoman and Russian empires, highlighting their inconsistencies and eccentricities with good-natured humor. In the next decade the author began to focus more on social issues. His *Hoshosi tseradedr* [Notes on this and that] in 1880 expressed skepticism at Ottoman reform in the aftermath of the Treaty of Berlin and inveighed against the vanity of the Patriarch of Constantinople as head of the Armenian *millet*, censorship of the press, and price inflation in general but especially that regarding medical costs. That same year he began another collection, *Bdoyd me Bolsoy tagherun mech* [A stroll through the quarters of Constantinople], consisting of thirty-four sections. Forming a more coherent whole, it provides a humorous evocation of the sights and sounds of the different parts of town from the gambling and deception of the upper-class center of Pera ("the Paris of Constantinople") to the drunken carousing associated with the poor fishing neighborhood of Samatia.

Similar to *Honorable Beggars* in tone and character is a series of vignettes published in 1886–87 under the general title *Kaghakavarutean vnasnere* [The perils of politeness]. The work introduces us to a range of variations on a central theme, illustrating the lengths to which some people will go to satisfy their own selfish ends, riding roughshod over others' sense of courtesy and goodwill.

When Sultan Abdülhamid II's suspicions of popular sedition denied the press freedom to criticize specific individuals and institutions, Baronian sought to subvert the ban by couching his censure in allegorical form. He continued to discuss national and international politics, disguising the central players under the ciphers of animals such as the frog, fox, monkey, and ant familiar from Armenian folklore and parable. Unlike most Armenians of his time, who trusted the European powers to redress their grievances against the Sublime Porte, he insisted that they acted solely out of self-interest. He was also outspoken in denouncing the harshness and incompetence of Ottoman officials. When a number of Armenian women in Smyrna were unlawfully evicted from their homes by soldiers led by Ahmed Pasha, Baronian wrote:

> Bravo, princely Ahmed Pasha! Your bravery has impressed the entire world, for it surely requires courage to attack and subdue women. Rest assured that whenever war is declared against women, you will be chosen as the supreme commander of the army. The people are especially grateful to you for your ability to overcome a few women without asking for reinforcements from Constantinople.

After the suppression of *Khigar*, Baronian was again compelled to work as a bookkeeper. However, the long years of worry and deprivation, and the threat of creditors, had taken their toll. He died of tuberculosis in the Surp Prgich Armenian Hospital of Constantinople. But although Hagop Baronian was silenced at last, the echo of his laughter will be heard as long as people read or see his works.

Bedros Norehad

HONORABLE BEGGARS

(MEDZABADIW MURATSGANNER, 1880)

Translated by Jack Antreassian

CAST OF CHARACTERS

APISOGHOM AGHA
LANDLADY
MANUG AGHA
PRIEST
MATCHMAKER
THE BEGGARS:
    EDITOR
    PRIEST
    POET
    PHOTOGRAPHER
    DOCTOR
    TEACHER
    WRITER
    LAWYER
    ACTOR
    PRINTER
    BARBER
    CLERGYMAN
MINOR CHARACTERS:
    FIVE PORTERS
    AGHAWNI
    WAITER
    THREE GUESTS AT RESTAURANT
    PHOTOGRAPHER'S SECRETARY

[In order to highlight the stage directions essential for an understanding of the play, extended authorial narrative intrusions in the original have been isolated and framed between curly brackets. — Eds.]

ACT 1

A man is standing on the dock at Galata, having just gotten off the steamer from Trebizond. It is 1870 something. {The author can't recall the exact year, or the day for that matter, thinking that it might be September 31, until he remembers that September has only thirty days. He does remember that} the man is stout and of medium height, and bundled in a long, heavy overcoat. {The author prides himself on the simple beginning of his tale, and on how resolutely he has resisted the temptation to make it more sensational by opening, for example, with a gale roaring in the harbor, or with a huge crowd surging excitedly toward the square in Galata, or with the police apprehending a beautiful young girl, and attaching such other dramatic details with which writers like to enliven their stories. He may have said all these things, but he does not because on that day there is no wind, no crowd, no rain, and no girl in the hands of the police. Such truthfulness should excite the complete confidence of the reader, and dispel any doubts he may have.} This traveler, APISOGHOM AGHA, is endowed with a pair of large black eyes, a pair of thick long black eyebrows, a pair of large ears, {and a pair of noses . . . no, no, only one nose of course, though it could serve for a pair, so confusing is its size and the varied directions it seems to take}. He has the kind of look in his eyes that would prompt any enterprising director to jump at the chance of casting him in one of his plays, any time the role of an idiot becomes available. As soon as his trunks and bedding, wrapped securely in burlap, are safely on the dock, he pulls out his purse, pays the boatman, and shouts for a porter. Five of them leap to his side {and, according to the established custom of the capital, there is no doubt that if he had called for five porters, twenty-five would have sprung up before him.}

Scene 1

The dock at Galata. PORTERS 1, 2, 3, 4, 5, and APISOGHOM AGHA.

PORTER 1 (*placing a foot on one of the trunks*): Where are you going, Agha?
APISOGHOM AGHA: Number Two, Flower Street, in Pera.
PORTER 1: Good. I know the place. Flower Street in Pera. It's a fine neighborhood.(*He picks up the trunk and starts walking off.*)
PORTER 2: I know where it is, too. (*He grabs another trunk and goes down the street after him.*)

PORTER 3: I go to Flower Street every day. (*He sweeps up the man's bedding and runs off before the last word is out of his mouth. All this happens so quickly that the traveler, now thoroughly confused, does not know which* PORTER *to keep track of, and so loses track of all three.*)

APISOGHOM AGHA (*screaming, stamping his feet*): This is disgraceful. Where did they take my trunks and bedding? What right did they have to interfere in my affairs? It's positively shameless, picking up whatever they see and walking off with it.

PORTERS 4 and 5: We're familiar with Flower Street, too, Agha, give us something to take.

APISOGHOM AGHA: The devil take your Flower Street, and you along with it.

(*The two* PORTERS *laugh as they leave. As* APISOGHOM AGHA *gets ready to go after his trunks, the* EDITOR *of a local Armenian newspaper, a tall dark man with small eyes and a forced smile, approaches him, extending his hand in greeting.*)

EDITOR: Are you Apisoghom Agha? When did you arrive? On which steamer did you travel? How are you? How is your brother? How are local Armenian affairs in Trebizond? How much does bread cost there now? Has it rained recently in your city? Ah, my dear Apisoghom Agha . . .

APISOGHOM AGHA: I am Apisoghom Agha, I've just landed, I came on a Turkish steamer, I'm very well, my brother is well, too, Armenian affairs are fine in Trebizond, the price of bread is one piaster, we have had no rain recently.

EDITOR: I'm so sorry for not having been at the steamer to welcome you. Please forgive me. They wrote from Trebizond that you'd definitely be here sometime this week, but—

APISOGHOM AGHA: Such things don't matter to me.

EDITOR: Our capital city should consider itself fortunate to have such an honorable figure, such a gracious young man, such vigorous intelligence—

APISOGHOM AGHA: My trunks—

EDITOR: Such a kind heart, proud spirit—

APISOGHOM AGHA: The por—

EDITOR: Such a patriotic individual—

APISOGHOM AGHA: . . . ters—

EDITOR: Patriotic, knowledgeable, educated—

APISOGHOM AGHA: . . . took my trunks—

EDITOR: . . . civilized—

APISOGHOM AGHA: . . . and went off—

EDITOR: . . . noble, modest, and handsome man in its midst.

APISOGHOM AGHA: There's nothing like that in my trunks. (*He walks about in search of the* PORTERS.)

EDITOR: You don't know me, but I'm well acquainted with your family. Your blessed father was a subscriber of my newspaper. He was a very good man. He helped the needy. He found suitable husbands for unfortunate girls. He had sympathy for everybody who approached him. Men like him should live a long time. But what can one do? Death is pitiless, and always takes the good ones and leaves the bad ones here to work their evil on our people. But let us talk about other things. Were you comfortable on the steamer?

APISOGHOM AGHA: Very comfortable. I ate, drank and slept royally. (*He tries to move off rapidly.*)

EDITOR: If you'd been inconvenienced in any way, I'd have written about it in tomorrow's paper, and made the company aware of its offense. (*He runs to keep pace with* APISOGHOM AGHA.)

APISOGHOM AGHA: Thank you.

EDITOR: May I ask you, please, how old you are?

APISOGHOM AGHA: Forty.

EDITOR: You are a merchant, I believe.

APISOGHOM AGHA: Yes. If you intend to issue an identity card for me, there's no need. I already have one.

EDITOR: No, no, it's not that at all. In my paper tomorrow I'm going to publish news of the noted merchant, the eminent Apisoghom Agha who's arrived in the capital from Trebizond, and whose linguistic and mercantile accomplishments are well known to all our people. You speak Turkish, I believe?

APISOGHOM AGHA: No.

EDITOR: French?

APISOGHOM AGHA: No.

EDITOR: English?

APISOGHOM AGHA: No.

EDITOR: German?

APISOGHOM AGHA: No.

EDITOR: No matter. I'll refer to you as a linguist and praise you for all your outstanding achievements.

APISOGHOM AGHA (*starting to slow down*): Do you print the names of all visitors to Constantinople?

EDITOR: Almost all of them, if they're eminent figures like you.

APISOGHOM AGHA: How about those who leave the capital?

EDITOR: We write about most of them, too, if they're important national figures.

APISOGHOM AGHA: Very well then, print my name. I'm considered important, too. Back home, I'm the owner of fields, vineyards, cows, and oxen. Print that, too.

EDITOR: Don't worry. We'll print it all as a debt of conscience and justice.

APISOGHOM AGHA: I have two or three servants. Can you put that in your paper some place?

EDITOR: Why not?

APISOGHOM AGHA: I've a gold watch and chain, too, but I didn't wear them because I was afraid they'd be stolen on the steamer. Would you want to mention that? (*He is now almost oblivious of his vanished belongings.*)

EDITOR: There's no need to say anything like that.

APISOGHOM AGHA: Very well, but put the other things in so everybody will know about me.

EDITOR: That's just what I've in mind.

APISOGHOM AGHA: In large letters . . .

EDITOR: Rest assured, in the largest letters we have . . .

APISOGHOM AGHA: You only write about the wealthy people who come and go from the capital, isn't that so?

EDITOR: Of course.

APISOGHOM AGHA: If you write about the poor ones, too, I don't want my name—

EDITOR: By no means. We don't pay any attention to them at all, not even if they were to donate a thousand pounds for the construction of a school.

APISOGHOM AGHA: You mean, then, that you wait here every afternoon to see what rich people arrive and depart, and then print their names in your paper? There's no question, then, that I'll read my name in your paper tomorrow?

EDITOR: No question whatever. Give me your address so I can have a copy sent to you by post.

APISOGHOM AGHA: Number Two, Flower Street, in Pera.

(*The* EDITOR *takes a paper from his pocket and adds* APISOGHOM AGHA's *name to his subscription list, nodding as he does so.*)

APISOGHOM AGHA: You'll send me a copy first thing in the morning.

EDITOR: Toward evening. Our paper is printed in the afternoon.

APISOGHOM AGHA: How happy I'd be if you could print tomorrow's paper in the morning. But no matter. I'll wait . . . as long as my name appears in large letters.

EDITOR: Don't worry about that at all. I'll send the paper tomorrow night with an acknowledgment.

APISOGHOM AGHA: With an acknowledgment? I thought you said that it would come by post. Who is this "acknowledgment"? Does he know my address?

EDITOR: The acknowledgment is merely a piece of paper on which it is written that I received from the honorable Apisoghom Agha one and a half pounds for a year's subscription. It will entitle you to receive our newspaper for a year.

APISOGHOM AGHA: You're going to write about me for a whole year?

EDITOR: No, but you'll be a subscriber for a year by paying me one and a half pounds.

APISOGHOM AGHA: One and a half pounds . . . that's a lot of money . . . won't three-quarters of a pound be enough?

EDITOR: EDITORs don't bargain over subscription rates.

APISOGHOM AGHA: Oh, all right, send the paper with that acknowledgment you're talking about. I'll arrange something.

EDITOR: I hope you don't think that I came to see you just to get a subscription. It's not the case at all. That would be demeaning. My visit was nothing more than a gesture of friendship.

APISOGHOM AGHA: That's obvious.

EDITOR: Don't ever let it enter your mind that this man came to see you for the purpose of snatching a pound and a half from your purse.

APISOGHOM AGHA: I won't.

EDITOR: Because there are some greedy editors who descend on visitors to the capital and rob them by making them subscribers. I can't bring myself to do such things. It's against my nature. I want to be able to live as an honorable man.

APISOGHOM AGHA: I understand . . . you want to live as an honorable man . . .

EDITOR: I beg of you not to mention this meeting to anyone else. There are wretched, unprincipled people who'll distort things deliberately in order to attack my person.

APISOGHOM AGHA: I see . . . they'll attack your person . . . .

EDITOR: Let me ask you, can I be reproached for anything I've done? I came to welcome you and promised to publish your name in my paper. And as a concerned and interested Armenian, you wished to subscribe. I beg of you, tell me, did I squeeze your throat to force you to subscribe?

APISOGHOM AGHA: No, no.

EDITOR: Did I point a gun at you?

APISOGHOM AGHA: Never.

EDITOR: Did I wave a knife in your face?

APISOGHOM AGHA: No, but do others get subscribers by pointing guns or waving knives?

EDITOR: That's not what I mean. What I mean is that you subscribed freely and willingly.

APISOGHOM AGHA: Yes.

EDITOR: And I behaved quite properly.

APISOGHOM AGHA: Without any doubt.

EDITOR: I didn't behave like those miserable editors who, as soon as they learn a stranger's in town, rush to his house to get a subscription.

APISOGHOM AGHA: Those creatures have no right to attack you . . . don't worry about my telling—

EDITOR: I'm grateful to you. Good day, Apisoghom Agha. Come visit our office one day. We can have some coffee together.

APISOGHOM AGHA: I will. Don't forget to write about me in tomorrow's paper.(*The* EDITOR *exits.* APISOGHOM AGHA *muses aloud as he continues on his way, his mind a jumble of thoughts.*) I didn't think I was as important a man as this editor seems to feel. But of course he must know better how big a man I must be, since he's an editor and well educated. Everybody who reads about me in the paper tomorrow will get all excited and will want to see me. I have to wear my Sunday suit, and my gold watch and chain. I should have brought my servants with me. But how was I to know? Everyone will find out tomorrow that an important man has come to Constantinople, noble, educated, a linguist. And the women will say to their husbands, "Let's arrange a match with our daughter." And the husbands will answer, "Will Apisoghom Agha accept her? He'll want a girl from a rich family." The answer will upset the women, husbands and wives will start quarreling, and they'll have a big fight, but why should I care? My name in the paper will serve at least one good purpose; it'll help me settle the matter of finding a rich girl right away. That's all I came to Constantinople for anyway . . . marriage. (*While* APISOGHOM AGHA *talks and wanders aimlessly, beguiled by his musings, one of the* PORTERS *carrying his belongings and apparently lost, bumps into him.*)

PORTER: Look out there.

APISOGHOM AGHA: What the devil? Oh, it's you. Where did you take my belongings?

PORTER (*as he continues walking*): You should be careful about what you're doing.

APISOGHOM AGHA: I could have used that advice before . . . come back . . . my trunks . . . (*He gets up and runs after* PORTER.)

{*The* PORTERS, *of course, had never seen nor even heard of Flower Street but, following the example of certain people who make a great pretense of knowing what they do not know and who are quite numerous in our community, had ventured to assure* APISOGHOM AGHA *that they did indeed know where Flower Street was located. The audacity of the* PORTERS *is not as reprehensible as the boldness of those men who, having studied cooking, deem themselves qualified as critics; having done a bit of surveying, pose as astronomers; having tended two geese and four cows, involve themselves in educational issues; having had one child, hold forth on the first ever born on earth; of all those, in short, who speak endlessly on subjects altogether foreign to them. Yes, their temerity is far more offensive since criticism, astronomy, education are surely more complex than the identification of Flower Street, which one can determine simply by asking someone. And the* PORTERS, *asking directions of everyone they come upon, do indeed find Flower Street without much difficulty; whereas there are lecturers we all have listened to who, even after speaking for seven or eight hours, are incapable of finding the street they are looking for and keep wan-*

dering aimlessly in shady lanes and blind alleys, dragging their innocent audiences with them.}

Scene 2

At the entrance to Number Two, Flower Street. PORTERS 1, 2, 3, *and* LANDLADY

(*When the* PORTERS *knock, the door is opened by the* LANDLADY, *on whose dark, long face time has drawn as many lines, in its compassionate effort to improve it, as the editor of Masis slashes through a short paragraph, be it someone's obituary or another's wedding announcement. The* PORTERS *drop their bundles inside the door and start wiping their perspiration.*)

LANDLADY: These must belong to Apisoghom Agha.

PORTER 1 (*continuing to wipe his face and head with a black handkerchief*): He didn't give us his name.

LANDLADY: What kind of man was he?

PORTER 2: He was wearing a large overcoat.

PORTER 3: Black.

LANDLADY: Black?

PORTER 3: Yes, black but nice . . . anyone hugged and cuddled like that wouldn't be cold in winter.

LANDLADY: What kind of talk is that? What do you mean "hugged and cuddled?" I'm not the kind of woman you can talk to in that manner, do you understand?

PORTER 1 (*spreading his handkerchief on chair to dry*): I didn't say anything wrong. What's the harm in saying "hugged"?

LANDLADY: What can be worse than that?

PORTER 1: Why should we bother our heads with such fine points?

LANDLADY: I'll see that you bother. You don't know who you're dealing with.

PORTER 1: But what harm can come from "hugging"?

LANDLADY: I have a husband. Why should I be hugging someone else?

PORTER 1: A husband is one thing; this is something else. Let's say that you went out some night in winter. You can't hug your husband in the street. But this you can take on your back.

LANDLADY: Apisoghom Agha?

PORTER 1: The overcoat, Madam, the overcoat. How would it be possible to put Apisoghom Agha on your back?

LANDLADY: You've been talking about an overcoat all this time?

PORTER 2: Of course, what did you think?

LANDLADY: I thought you were talking about hugging Apisoghom Agha.

PORTER 1: God have mercy, dear God, have mercy. (*He pulls handkerchief off the chair.*)

LANDLADY (*Calmed by the explanations, she reasserts her position of authority.*): Take these trunks and bedding upstairs.

(*The* PORTERS *pick up their burdens, but are stopped before they reach the first step of the staircase.*)

LANDLADY (*shouting*): Have you come from the hills?

PORTER 2: No, from Grand Avenue.

LANDLADY: I know you came from Grand Avenue. How can you go up in those canal boats you're wearing? Look what you did to my floors! I broke my back cleaning them just today.

PORTER 3: What can we do? We have no other boots.

LANDLADY: Why are you standing there staring at me? Take them off, take them off!

PORTER 1: Don't shout, Madam, don't shout. We'll take them off. (*They take off their boots, which turn out to be cleaner than their feet.*)

LANDLADY (*screaming*): You're going to go up with those feet?

PORTER 1: We have to, we haven't got any others. {*Plaintively, as though ashamed that poverty had prevented them from having more than two feet, and as though the rich could have four, five, even six of them.*}

LANDLADY: Come down. I don't want you to go upstairs. Put the bags down. I'll take them up myself.

PORTER 2: Fine with us.

LANDLADY (*muttering to herself while she rubs the first step with a wet cloth*): Ah, curse that husband of mine. He doesn't go to work, just sits in the coffee house all day arguing about Armenian politics. And I have to rent out rooms to strangers and get into predicaments like this.

PORTER 2: Madam, should we wait?

LANDLADY (*still muttering*): If he had any sense at all, I could be living the life of a queen. I have no children, no other worries. But all he thinks about is electing this representative or defeating the other. God knows where all those representatives come from who are the cause of all our misery. But what's it to you? Let them do what they want. Have all the problems of our country been left in your hands?

PORTER 1: Madam, pay us and we'll be off. We don't want to hang around for nothing.

LANDLADY: Come back tomorrow.

(*The* PORTERS, *accustomed to hearing the word "tomorrow" every day, trail out of the house.*)

Scene 3

In the front room. The LANDLADY, MANUG AGHA, *then* AGHAWNI

LANDLADY (*continuing to grumble*): He's always after his politics, and it doesn't even enter his mind that we might need bread to eat, or butter, or rice; that we need wood or coal for the fire to cook. He doesn't bother about such things. He leaves in the morning, before the light of the sun gets through our window, and comes back after dark. Our guest has arrived and will be here within the hour. He'll be hungry, of course. I'll have to serve him something, and there's nothing in the house. If only he would bring some meat and fish with him when he comes home at night, we might have some food in the house. But no, we have nothing but politics in this house, politics every night . . .

(*She is still muttering to herself when a man, about seventy years old, who has opened the door with a key, enters and greets her with a smile. It is her husband,* MANUG AGHA. *His forehead is wrinkled and protruding, and his face gives the impression that someone is strangling him.* MANUG AGHA *barely crosses the threshold before his wife confronts him.*)

Where have you been all this time, for God's sake?

MANUG AGHA: Don't even ask, Woman. We finally finished work at our council today. The election will be this Sunday, and I must say that all the candidates are fine upright men. Toros Agha offered me a few drinks and was after me to support his candidates. But I voted for my own people, since they entertain me with raki every night, and are good and honorable men, and don't steal from the treasury like others I can name, and the school—

LANDLADY: This is no time for that kind of talk. Hurry down to the butcher for some meat.

MANUG AGHA: Toros Agha got very angry and won't play cards with me anymore. Well, he doesn't have to.

LANDLADY: Don't you hear what I'm saying? Hurry!

MANUG AGHA: Then I'll just play checkers with Deacon Mardiros after this.

LANDLADY: We can talk about that later, Manug Agha. Go get some meat from the butcher.

MANUG AGHA: What about the trouble the Deacon had? His wife came within a hair's breadth of dying last night.

LANDLADY: What happened?

MANUG AGHA: She gave birth to a baby boy, but she had all sorts of problems. There were four midwives and sixteen doctors, and all of them together were barely able to save the child.

LANDLADY: Poor woman.

MANUG AGHA: Go visit her tomorrow.

LANDLADY: I will. Now you go and take care of the meat.

MANUG AGHA: Must we have that meat tonight?

LANDLADY: Of course. Apisoghom Agha's trunks and bedding have already arrived, and he himself should be here any minute.

MANUG AGHA: Are you telling me the truth, Woman?

LANDLADY: Why should I lie?

MANUG AGHA: All right, then. I'll go and get us a good cut of meat.

(MANUG AGHA *has barely taken a few steps out of the house when his wife shouts after him.*)

LANDLADY: Manug Agha, Manug Agha.

(MANUG AGHA *reenters.*)

What are we going to cook the meat with?

MANUG AGHA: You can cook it with potatoes or beans.

LANDLADY: No, no. That's not what I'm talking about. We've no coal. Get some coal, too.

MANUG AGHA: All right. (*He turns to go out again.*)

LANDLADY: Manug Agha, Manug Agha.

(*He comes back in again.*)

We can't do with meat alone. Buy a little rice, too, for pilaf.

MANUG AGHA: That's a good idea, Woman. I'll get some rice, too. (*This time* MANUG AGHA *runs out of the house. He is about to move offstage when he hears his wife shouting after him with all her might.*)

LANDLADY: Manug Agha, Manug Agha.

MANUG AGHA: (*returning, his impatience showing in his face and voice*): What is it now?

LANDLADY: For the love of God, why do you rush out like a steam engine? My throat is sore from shouting. We have no onions or salt, and you ought to buy some oil for the lamps. We can't leave the poor man in the dark.

MANUG AGHA: All right, all right. But tell me everything we need all at once, and I'll get them. You've called me back a hundred times.

LANDLADY: We need a water bottle, too . . . And I have nothing to wrap around my head, no shoes to wear. How can I greet Apisoghom Agha in this condition?

MANUG AGHA: Let's get the food now; we'll worry about your clothes tomorrow.

(*He slams the door behind him when he leaves.*)

LANDLADY: Manug Agha, Manug Agha.

MANUG AGHA (*muttering, moving toward stage left*): Scream as much as you want. I'm not coming back another time. (*As he is about to move offstage, he hears a woman's voice calling after him. He pauses.*) If you've nothing better to do, go on screaming after me all you want. (*He keeps muttering as he turns to move offstage. The calling continues. Deacon Mardiros's ten-year-old daughter, AGHAWNI, enters stage right.*)

AGHAWNI: Manug Agha, Manug Agha. (MANUG AGHA *continues on to stage left.* AGHAWNI *nears him and, out of breath, manages to shout his name one last time.*) Manug Agha. (*Still no response. In one last burst, she rushes offstage left after him, pulling him back onstage by his jacket.*)

MANUG AGHA (*without turning*): Let me alone, Woman.

AGHAWNI: I've something to tell you.

MANUG AGHA: I've no time to listen. I can't even remember what you told me before, and now you've still more to tell me.

AGHAWNI: I just wanted to ask you where the midwife lives.

MANUG AGHA (*Realizing it is not his wife following him, he turns.*): Aghawni, was it you running after me?

AGHAWNI (*gasping*): Yes, it was.

MANUG AGHA: How's your mother?

(AGHAWNI *is still out of breath.*)

Why don't you say something? How's your mother? Is anything wrong?

(AGHAWNI *can only gasp.*)

I'm going to burst with curiosity. Say something. Is this any time to heave like that? Tell me how your mother is.

AGHAWNI (*still gasping*): Mother is well, but the baby won't take her milk. The midwife—

MANUG AGHA: Very well, my child, I understand. You go home now. I'll get the midwife to come over.

(AGHAWNI *exits stage right and* MANUG AGHA *stage left, looking for the midwife's house. On practically every street he stops to chat with friends, informing them about the baby born to Deacon Mardiros's wife, discussing the elections, or relating the news of* APISOGHOM AGHA*'s arrival. {It has been a long established tradition for many living in eastern Anatolia to go to France or Germany for an education, and to Constantinople for a wife. And we already know that* APISOGHOM AGHA *has come to Constantinople for no other purpose but that. After his collision with the* PORTER,

APISOGHOM AGHA *inquires of passersby for directions to Flower Street, since this is the first time he has come to Constantinople, and a friend in Trebizond recommended that house as a comfortable place to eat and sleep. The friend wrote to* MANUG AGHA *accordingly, a week in advance. Following such instructions as he is given,* APISOGHOM AGHA *enters one street and emerges from another, walks up a dead-end street, curses, and turns back, all the time suspecting that the* PORTERS *have run off with his belongings, though he had been assured of their honesty by many people. After tramping through the streets of Pera for about an hour,* APISOGHOM AGHA *finally succeeds in finding Flower Street, which should not be confused with the street of the same name that was reduced to ashes in the Pera fire of 1870 something. This street was named Flower because flowers could always be seen in the windows of the houses there.}* APISOGHOM AGHA *approaches* MANUG AGHA's *wife, who is not known to him and who is waiting out front for her husband's return.*)

Scene 4

MANUG AGHA's *house on Flower Street.* APISOGHOM AGHA, LANDLADY

APISOGHOM AGHA: Can you tell me which house is Number Two?

LANDLADY: This is it. Welcome, Apisoghom Agha.

APISOGHOM AGHA: Did they bring my bedding and trunks?

LANDLADY: Yes, they did, Apisoghom Agha, some time ago. Come in. If you wish to rest a moment, you can sit here and catch your breath. (*She leads him to a small foyer.*)

APISOGHOM AGHA: Yes, I am very tired. I would like to rest a while.

LANDLADY: Do just as you please, Apisoghom Agha. The house is yours. Rest as you would at home.

APISOGHOM AGHA: Thank you.

(*She leads him to a small room, holding a lamp that begins flickering because the oil is low.*)

LANDLADY: How have you been, Apisoghom Agha? How's everyone at home?

APISOGHOM AGHA: Everyone's well.

LANDLADY: May they always be so. And how are your children? Are they going to school?

APISOGHOM AGHA: I have no children.

LANDLADY: How's your wife?

APISOGHOM AGHA: I have no wife either.

LANDLADY: You're not married, Apisoghom Agha?

APISOGHOM AGHA: No.

LANDLADY: Well then, we must find you a pretty girl while you're here.

APISOGHOM AGHA: I do have such a purpose in mind, but first I would like something to eat. I haven't had anything since early this morning.

LANDLADY: Of course, Apisoghom Agha, of course. I'll have your dinner ready very soon. (*She leaves, opens the outside door and stands on the threshold waiting for* MANUG AGHA *who, it will be remembered, was running about looking for the midwife. Alone in the room,* APISOGHOM AGHA *picks up a book and begins leafing through it. But because it is impossible for a man to read a book when he is hungry, just as it is impossible for him to write one, he puts it down, especially since his stomach keeps reminding him that it is his body, not his mind, that needs nourishment. He begins pacing.*)

LANDLADY (*reentering the room*): I beg of you, Apisoghom Agha, make yourself as comfortable as you would in your own house.

APISOGHOM AGHA: I'm not uncomfortable, only hungry. And I'd like to eat.

LANDLADY: Dinner is being prepared; it's almost ready. (*She leaves to resume her vigil in front of the house.*)

APISOGHOM AGHA (*mumbling to himself*): What kind of woman is this? She tells me to be comfortable and keeps me hungry. Can a hungry man be comfortable?

LANDLADY (*returning*): Just look upon me as your sister or daughter. Don't hesitate one bit. Ask for whatever you want, and I'll be happy to bring it.

APISOGHOM AGHA: Thank you.

LANDLADY: I wouldn't want any guests in my house to be the least bit uncomfortable.

APISOGHOM AGHA: I quite understand. Right now there is nothing I need besides dinner.

LANDLADY: Dinner is almost ready, so don't worry about that at all. (*Further elaboration is interrupted by the doorbell. She rushes out, expecting to admit her husband, get the things he brought, and begin preparing the long delayed dinner. It is not her husband, however, but the local parish* PRIEST.)

Scene 5

The PRIEST, LANDLADY, *then* APISOGHOM AGHA

PRIEST (*as the door is opened*): Greetings, Madam.

LANDLADY: Bless me, Father.

PRIEST: How are you? Well, I pray.

LANDLADY: Well, thank God.

PRIEST: I just ran into Manug Agha and he told me you had a visitor, so I thought I'd drop in to say hello.

LANDLADY: That's good of you. Please come in. (*She leads him to the small foyer,*

where APISOGHOM AGHA *is still preoccupied with his hunger.* APISOGHOM AGHA
gets up when he sees the PRIEST.)

PRIEST: Greetings, Apisoghom Agha.

APISOGHOM AGHA: Bless me, Father.

PRIEST: When this humble sinner heard of the arrival of your benevolent eminence, he hurried over to inquire about the esteemed well-being of your most
devout person. How are you, Apisoghom Agha?

APISOGHOM AGHA: Well.

PRIEST: May you always be so. May the Lord grant heavenly rest to your departed
ones, and to the living a long and blessed life.

APISOGHOM AGHA: Thank you. And how are you, Father?

PRIEST: Don't ask about our well-being. It is these times we should be worried
about. May the Lord God keep you from all danger and evil. When the people
are well, the priests rejoice.

APISOGHOM AGHA: It's so, Father. (*He cannot take his eyes off the door, through
which he expects his dinner to be brought.*)

PRIEST: The times are very bad. The people are burdened with much suffering,
and their piety seems to be declining steadily day by day.

APISOGHOM AGHA: That's so.

PRIEST: But what is there to do? What can we do besides be patient? As the Holy
Bible says, "He that endureth to the end shall be saved."[1]

APISOGHOM AGHA: How true.

PRIEST: If we are not patient, we will seethe with anger, and as the Prophet says, "If
you become angry, yet do not sin."[2]

APISOGHOM AGHA (*not having heard anything that has been said, but annoyed by
the* PRIEST's *presence since his only concern at the moment is his dinner*): Without question.

PRIEST: "Man shall not live by bread alone, but by every word of God."[3] (*The*
PRIEST *takes his snuff box from his pocket and inhales a pinch in each nostril,
and then extends the box to* APISOGHOM AGHA.) Have some. (APISOGHOM
AGHA *takes a couple of pinches.*) That's hardly enough to have any effect,
APISOGHOM AGHA. I beg of you, take some more. Snuff is not harmful.
(APISOGHOM AGHA *takes another pinch to end the matter, hoping that the guest
will then be content and leave.*) Why don't you take a good pinch, Apisoghom
Agha? You hardly took anything at all.

APISOGHOM AGHA: Thank you, Father. I don't use it as a rule.

PRIEST: I beg of you. Don't refuse this humble sinner. Surely you can tolerate some
more.

----

1. Matthew 10:22.
2. Psalms 4:5.
3. Deuteronomy 8:3.

APISOGHOM AGHA (*aside*): Yes, but not of you. (*He takes another pinch.*)

PRIEST: The Prophet David says that, "As for man, his days are like grass."[4]

APISOGHOM AGHA: He says that about snuff?

PRIEST: No, about us. And we have to labor and help others in this brief and transient life, succor the poor, and sometimes pray for the repose of the souls of our dear ones.

APISOGHOM AGHA: By all means.

PRIEST: We must be prepared to go whenever we are called.

APISOGHOM AGHA: At any time.

PRIEST: This humble sinner is going to venture to ask something of your gracious person, and I hope you will not refuse since this humble servant is well aware of your unbounded goodness and generosity.

APISOGHOM AGHA: What can I do for you?

PRIEST: May God keep His inexhaustible treasury open and available to such magnanimous people as you.

APISOGHOM AGHA: Thank you.

PRIEST: May He return a thousandfold every one you give, and a million for every thousand, for the glory of our sacred church and the betterment of our people. What I would like to do is have a service next Sunday for the souls of the departed members of your family. Forgive my audacity, but it is my duty to remind people always not to forget their dead.

APISOGHOM AGHA: You're right, Father.

PRIEST: Let me know if you agree, and I will make the necessary arrangements. And don't think that the cost will be excessive. Two pounds will take care of it all. And, of course, there will be a special announcement in church that day that the service is for the repose of the souls of the deceased members of Apisoghom Agha's family.

APISOGHOM AGHA: I'd be grateful.

PRIEST: Not at all. It's no more than our duty.

APISOGHOM AGHA: Here are the two pounds for the service.

PRIEST (*extending his hand for the money*): There's no hurry. You don't have to give it right away.

APISOGHOM AGHA: No, no, please take it.

PRIEST: Only because you insist so much, I will take it. I have no wish to break your heart. Bless you. May God keep your house prosperous and your purse full. May He fulfill your every wish, endow all your work with success, and protect you from all misfortune. (*The* PRIEST *says good-bye and departs.*)

APISOGHOM AGHA: At last I'm free of him. All I have had is trouble since I set foot in Constantinople. I was hardly off the boat when some editor chewed at my ears for two hours. I managed to escape him, only to run into a thousand oth-

---

4. Psalms 103:15.

er difficulties before I found this house. Here I wanted only to catch my breath and eat something. And the woman of the house seems to have one mission in life and that is to starve me. She keeps running in and out, begging me not to worry about a single thing besides my own comfort. And as though that were not enough, now this man barges in, forces me to take snuff, tells me all about the prophet David, manages to get two pounds out of me, and leaves. I'm glad of that at least. And I had to go through all this on an empty stomach. Why aren't they bringing my dinner? Are they going to keep me hungry all night? It's a disgrace. (*As* APISOGHOM AGHA *goes on muttering, the lamp, whose light is already feeble because the oil is running out, flickers one last time and dies, leaving the guest in darkness.*) This is the last straw. Either I must pick up my things and go somewhere else or I have to call that woman and give her a piece of my mind. I'm not used to this sort of treatment. Back home I have two servants always on call. They set the table early and tend to all my needs. Why should someone accustomed to servants have to put up with these inconveniences?

LANDLADY (*as she opens the door*): What happened? Did the lamp go out?

APISOGHOM AGHA (*trying to restrain his increasing anger*): Yes, it went out.

LANDLADY: Don't let it bother you, Apisoghom Agha, it's our job to see to such things.

APISOGHOM AGHA: Yes, yes, but I'm hungry and I can't wait much longer.

LANDLADY: Don't let anything at all upset you. Leave everything to me. I'll attend to it. I don't want you to be disturbed. (*She runs off to the neighbor, returns with oil and relights* APISOGHOM AGHA's *lamp.*)

(*Not very long after the light comes back on,* APISOGHOM AGHA *is confronted by yet another visitor, a young man who doesn't appear to be a merchant or a banker; nor does he look like an artisan or a laborer. What he looks like, finally, is something that doesn't look like much of anything. He is barely past thirty, with blue eyes and blond hair, and a short beard, which in the capital is a sign either of mourning or of poetry. His clothes are so old as to excite the interest of antique dealers. If, however, his clothing is repulsive, there are attractive qualities in his face. He is a* POET.)

Scene 6

APISOGHOM AGHA *and the* POET

POET (*in a loud voice, as he enters*): Honorable sir, I'm Your Eminence's servant.

APISOGHOM AGHA (*recoiling, apprehensive*): What is it? What do you want?

POET: Honorable sir, as soon as I learned of your arrival, I hurried over to place before your feet the most profound expression of my respect and admiration.

APISOGHOM AGHA (*thinking that the man perhaps had brought him a gift of slippers*): At my feet? Very well, put them there.

POET (*removing his hat and leaping on the table*): Thank you, most exalted sir. (*The spectacle thoroughly confuses* APISOGHOM AGHA, *who wonders what in the world the young man is up to. The* POET *pulls out a paper from his pocket and, looking straight at* APISOGHOM AGHA, *intones with all his might.*) Ladies and gentlemen . . .

APISOGHOM AGHA (*Startled by the sudden explosion of sound, he bolts from his chair and, unable to contain himself, shouts excitedly.*): Who is this man? An idiot escaped from the asylum? Or one about to be committed?

POET (*lowering his voice a little*): The Armenian nation is undertaking a great celebration today dedicated to our bravest hero—

APISOGHOM AGHA: What are you talking about?

POET: There was a time when the darkness contended against the light, ignorance against knowledge, the past against the future, the revolutionary against the traditional, the sword against the pen, hatred against love, fire against water, meat against vegetables. Now those times have passed. They are the past, and we the future. They are darkness, and we are light. They are ignorance, and we wisdom. They are the sword, and we are the pen. They are hatred, we are love. They are fire, we water. They are meat, we vegetable. They are cucumbers, we apples. They are the thorn, we the rose. Gone, gone are those centuries when mankind rocked back and forth, back and forth, in the cradle of ignorance.

APISOGHOM AGHA: What's on your mind, my boy? I haven't done anything to you. What do you want from me? Go make your speeches to those who have disturbed you.

POET (*continuing his speech*): Yes, man was tormented, humiliated by pitiless tyrants and had no one to go to, nowhere to protest.

APISOGHOM AGHA (*beside himself, muttering*): God have mercy, God have mercy. It looks like we have a lot more to suffer yet. I can pull him off the table, but he's a madman. He may pull out a gun and shoot me.

POET (*oblivious to* APISOGHOM AGHA's *consternation*): And when knowledge blossomed and drove out ignorance, as light did the dark, as love conquered hate, the pen the sword, the future the past; then, yes, at that very instant . . . yes, I say at that very time, only then, was it understood that words like mankind, people, nation were not intended simply to take space in dictionaries but were words stamped indelibly, in letters of iron, on all minds, spirits, and hearts.

APISOGHOM AGHA: I beg of you, Friend. Get down from there, and let's see what the matter is. (*The* POET *is trembling so violently on the table that* APISOGHOM AGHA *is afraid the lamp will topple. His patience gone, he shouts.*) Get down from there.

POET: I beg of you, don't scold me.

APISOGHOM AGHA: Get down, or else.

POET:Don't break a heart that beats so warmly for our people.

APISOGHOM AGHA: Whatever you have to say, come sit here beside me like a civilized human being, and say it. What's the point in climbing on tables?

POET: I beseech you, allow me to finish. You can't imagine how emotional I get when I make a speech.

APISOGHOM AGHA: Get down. (*The* POET *gets down and sits on the chair indicated by* APISOGHOM AGHA.) Now tell me what's on your mind.

POET: I beg you, don't be angry.

APISOGHOM AGHA: But what do you want? Tell me. Now!

POET: Don't treat me with such cruelty, I'll kiss your feet. My heart's so full. You'll make me cry. (*He starts to cry.*)

APISOGHOM AGHA: What's there to cry about?

POET: Your servant wants to serve his people with his writing. But our people treat their writers with ingratitude and contempt.

APISOGHOM AGHA: Is that my fault?

POET: No, not at all; if anything, you are altogether innocent. I've written some patriotic poems . . . exquisite pieces . . . beautiful lines in which imagination, emotion, spirit, excitement, take wing and soar.

APISOGHOM AGHA: Good, but is that any reason to cry?

POET: Our people don't recognize the value and significance of my poems. They dismiss them as puerile exercises and abandon their author to starvation and neglect.

APISOGHOM AGHA: What am I supposed to do about it?

POET: I beg you, be gentle with me.

APISOGHOM AGHA: What have I done to you?

POET: I was going to plead with you.

APISOGHOM AGHA: What? What? Tell me quickly.

POET: Don't shout, if you have any mercy at all. You'll make me cry again (*He begins to cry.*)

APISOGHOM AGHA: Good Lord, give me patience.

POET: My problem is this. I would like to print the speech I read to you.

APISOGHOM AGHA: Go ahead and have it printed. Is anyone stopping you? Has anyone tied your hands?

POET: I was going to beseech your graciousness to pay for the printing costs.

APISOGHOM AGHA: Why? What reason in the world could there be for me to give money for your speech? Who has heard of such a thing? Someone is going to print a book for his own benefit and expects Apisoghom Agha to pay the costs?

POET: I beg you, my heart is already broken. Don't open any new wounds.

APISOGHOM AGHA: Open what wounds? Go about your business, my friend, you have been nothing but trouble to me.

POET: Do you know how painful it is for a writer to hear such words?

APISOGHOM AGHA: I don't know and, what's more, I don't care.

POET: A poet's heart is very delicate. It can be hurt by even the mildest rebuke. I've written a poem on just that theme. I'll read it to you.

APISOGHOM AGHA: I've no time to listen to poems.

POET: Don't be harsh with my poem, I beg you. I worked on it for two months, and you don't even want to listen to it. And when I see it demeaned in this manner, my dignity is wounded. Please don't say anything bad about my poem. Please allow me to read it to you once.

APISOGHOM AGHA: I didn't come here to listen to poems.

POET: I've written a tragedy, too. Perhaps we can go over that together.

APISOGHOM AGHA: No, no. I'm hungry. I must have my dinner now.

POET: Fine. I can deliver a lecture on food.

APISOGHOM AGHA: I've no time to listen.

POET: I beg you not to speak those words again. There are no harsher words for a writer. How painful it is to create this work and then be told that there's no time to hear or read it. Most honorable Sir, treat our authors with kindness.

APISOGHOM AGHA: Shall I arrange a seat for you on top of my head?

POET: I'll kiss your feet, don't make fun of me. Why should you place me on your head?

APISOGHOM AGHA: What else am I to do? Must I give you my purse to prove my kindness to our authors?

POET: No, only enough to print my speech.

APISOGHOM AGHA: How many pounds will that cost?

POET: Four should take care of it. It's really not much. You will be my patron. And I'll put your name in a dedication at the very front of the book.

APISOGHOM AGHA: On the cover?

POET: Yes.

APISOGHOM AGHA: Why?

POET: So everyone will know that the book was printed with your money.

APISOGHOM AGHA: All right, all right. (*He takes four pounds from his purse and gives it to the* POET *who praises him a thousand times and leaves.* APISOGHOM AGHA *calls after him.*) Isn't it possible to put the names of my servants on the cover, too, and also to add that Apisoghom Agha owns cows, sheep, donkeys, and farms in his city?

POET: The things you mention belong more properly to pastoral poetry.

APISOGHOM AGHA: I don't understand.

POET: Poems can be written on that theme. If that is your desire, I can write one.

APISOGHOM AGHA: What would I do with a poem?

POET: We'll have it printed in a newspaper.

APISOGHOM AGHA: Will they print it?

POET: Why not? If you give them half a pound, they'll print it forty times.

APISOGHOM AGHA: Good. Write it then.

POET: It'll be my privilege.

APISOGHOM AGHA: But it has to be something good.

POET: Of course.

APISOGHOM AGHA: Everybody has to like it.

POET: Certainly.

APISOGHOM AGHA: Will you bring it to me tomorrow morning?

POET: Tomorrow morning? What are you saying? It'll take at least a month.

APISOGHOM AGHA: One whole month?

POET: At least. It may be easy to read a poem; writing it is another matter. A beautiful poem will take two months at the very least.

APISOGHOM AGHA: Really?

POET: Yes, but I'll try to finish it in a month.

APISOGHOM AGHA: What a difficult thing it must be.

POET: What did you think? I have to wait two months for my muse to come and inspire me. A poem can't be written without the muse.

APISOGHOM AGHA: And if the muse doesn't come?

POET: She has to come.

APISOGHOM AGHA: Is there any way to write her a letter or something and persuade her to come earlier, so you won't have to wait two months?

POET: She comes on her own. She doesn't need any letters, most honorable Sir.

APISOGHOM AGHA: Where does she live? Is it very far?

POET: Very far, but she will come.

APISOGHOM AGHA: Over land or sea?

POET: No, my gracious Sir, no.

APISOGHOM AGHA: Who can this strange creature be? Where will she be coming from? Tell me. Maybe we can think of some way to get her here sooner. If we were to give her one or two pounds, would she come this week?

POET: Yes, yes. For two pounds it may be possible to arrange the matter; the muse will get here in a hurry, this week even.

APISOGHOM AGHA: Write to her at once, and give her my special regards. Tell her Apisoghom Agha wants to see her.

POET: On my honor. Good day, Sir. I am most grateful to you. I remain the servant of Your Graciousness and beg you to accept the assurances of my deepest respect. I am the most humble servant of Your Eminence.

APISOGHOM AGHA: Good, good.

(The POET finally departs, {having promised to summon his muse for two pounds, something others do for much less. At the present time a muse's wage is less than a carpenter's. It will be observed that APISOGHOM AGHA forgets his hunger whenever someone promises to get his name in the paper or announce it from the altar, and

that he opens his purse and rewards anyone who agrees to spread his name in public.
Vanity is a kind of hunger, too, that people satisfy with money. Vanity, regarded by
some as a vice and by others as a virtue, can be found in abundance in all classes of
our people and makes APISOGHOM AGHA *even forget momentarily about his hunger*
and worry only about the poem. Will it be the way he wants it to be? Will the muse
come in a few days? And if she doesn't come, will another one be found? He is re-
viewing these questions in his mind when} the LANDLADY *comes in. It is already four*
o'clock.)

LANDLADY: Dinner's ready. Please come in, Apisoghom Agha.

Scene 7

The dining area, adjacent to the kitchen. MANUG AGHA, APISOGHOM AGHA, *then the*
LANDLADY

(APISOGHOM AGHA *is greeted by* MANUG AGHA *who is busy placing chairs around the*
table which has at last been set.)

MANUG AGHA (*pointing to the head of the table*): Please sit here, it will be most
    comfortable for you.
APISOGHOM AGHA: Please, after you.

(*They sit.*)

MANUG AGHA: Forgive the delay in serving dinner. You can dine at any hour you
    choose hereafter. There were urgent reasons this evening that prevented us
    from getting things ready on time. I will tell you about them later. How are
    you, Apisoghom Agha?
APISOGHOM AGHA: I'm very well.
MANUG AGHA: We're very pleased. How is our friend in Trebizond?
APISOGHOM AGHA: He sends his special regards.
MANUG AGHA: May the bearer of the tidings flourish. May I offer you a glass of raki?
APISOGHOM AGHA: One glass only. (*He takes a glass from* MANUG AGHA *and swal-*
    lows it in one gulp, the raki that is, not the glass.)
MANUG AGHA: To your good fortune, Apisoghom Agha.
APISOGHOM AGHA: Thank you.
MANUG AGHA: To your health.
APISOGHOM AGHA: And long life.

(MANUG AGHA *mixes his raki with water and drinks it in four sips, toasting the guest each time.*)

MANUG AGHA: While my wife finishes her preparations and brings in our dinner, we can talk and pass the time. Would you like that, Apisoghom Agha?

APISOGHOM AGHA (*in a tone that leaves no doubt that it would be far better to eat first and talk later*): Yes, of course.

MANUG AGHA: Just listen to the things I had to go through today. I've been involved with a representative's election campaign for the past few weeks. Now you must be saying to yourself, "What's the representative's election to you?" But we really can't be indifferent, Apisoghom Agha. If I'm not concerned with the public interest, and you're not, and he's not, who'll there be to look after things? To say, "What do I care?" is very bad. That's an excuse for everyone to withdraw, and the public interest is neglected. I think that everyone should take as much part as he can in public work. Let's have another drink, Apisoghom Agha. It'll whet our appetite.

APISOGHOM AGHA: It's not my habit to drink more than one.

MANUG AGHA: But the glasses are small, and remember that the Constantinople air gives raki a special flavor.

APISOGHOM AGHA: Very well.

(*They drink another glass to each other's health, before* MANUG AGHA *resumes his discourse.*)

MANUG AGHA: This morning, on my way to the coffeehouse, I ran into my friend Melkon Agha, an honorable man, but no more so than you. This Melkon Agha was married to the daughter of Bartoghimeos Agha who, from the old days, was always pointed out as a good man, hospitable, patriotic, and kind. And he had a lot of stores in the marketplace, from which he earned considerable income. In a few years Melkon Agha's wife passed on, and he later married saddler Nigoghos's daughter who had several brothers, one of whom served as a secretary for Ampagum Agha. This Ampagum Agha had a son who lost a lot of his father's money gambling and, in the end, ran off to Russia. This boy was the child of the brother of the grandson of the sister of Bishop Markar. The other brother is a goldsmith, a tall, good-looking man. A third brother was unemployed for a long time, altogether without means, and was on the verge of starvation, but then was elected representative and in a year or two got back on his feet. To make a long story short, after Melkon Agha married Nigoghos Agha's daughter, he enjoyed a very comfortable life for a few years. But then his luck changed, misfortune followed misfortune, and he lost everything he had. I'll bring him here one day so you can see for yourself what kind of man he is. He has a brother, too, who is a master watchmaker. He used to live in Büyük Dere,[5] and later in Üsküdar,[6] and still later in Kum Kapi,[7] where he was unable to stay for very long either. And I don't know where he is now. Still, he was an excellent watchmaker. Toros Agha wouldn't entrust his watch to anyone but him to clean. Do you know Toros Agha? He's a different kind of man altogether. Let me tell you a story about him and see if you think it's possible to find a man like this anywhere on earth.

LANDLADY (*her head appearing in the door*): Shall I serve dinner now?

MANUG AGHA: Be patient a little, Woman. Let me finish what I'm saying, and then bring it in. Isn't that so, Apisoghom Agha? We must have a little time to talk. If you feel I'm boring you, please say so.

APISOGHOM AGHA: How can you think such a thing, but—

MANUG AGHA (*interrupting*): This Toros Agha is a furrier, may his ears be burning, and lives a very comfortable life with his family. Whatever he needs in his house—food, clothing, furniture—he buys with his own hands; he trusts no one but himself, may his ears be burning. He will buy a piece of meat from the butcher, and weigh it as soon as he gets home, and without fail he'll find it an ounce or two short. Then he rushes back to the butcher, gets into a heated argument, and doesn't leave until he gets an additional couple of ounces of meat. This is the sort of man he is, may his ears be burning. One day, this Toros Agha, may his ears be burning, took his watch to have it cleaned and, after lengthy bargaining with the watchmaker, agreed to pay fifteen piasters, but on one condition—that the work be done in his presence because Toros Agha, may his ears be burning, not trusting anyone, as I said, was afraid that if he left the watch there, something might be stolen from its works or that the watchmaker would deliberately damage something to create more work for himself, as many watchmakers are not above doing, especially when business is a little slow. The watchmaker took this as an insult to his honor and got very angry. If you were in his place, wouldn't you?

APISOGHOM AGHA (*not having heard a word of the story, his thoughts on nothing but dinner*): I certainly would.

MANUG AGHA: Toros Agha, may his ears be burning, was in turn enraged by the watchmaker's anger and said some very harsh things, which he really shouldn't have said. Isn't that so?

APISOGHOM AGHA (*mechanically, agreeing in the hope that this will bring the story to an end, and hasten the arrival of his dinner*): That's so. That's so.

---

5. A suburb of Constantinople.
6. The quarter of Constantinople on the Asiatic shore of the Bosphorus.
7. A quarter of Constantinople on the European shore (lit., Sand Gate), where the Armenian Patriarchate is now located.

MANUG AGHA: The watchmaker threw Toros Agha out, may his ears be burning, and Toros Agha, may his ears be burning, refused to leave, considering such behavior somewhat beneath his dignity. If you were in his place, you wouldn't leave either.

APISOGHOM AGHA (*not knowing what place he was in or out of*): I wouldn't leave either.

MANUG AGHA: Then the fight really began. The watchmaker slapped Toros Agha, may his ears be burning. Toros Agha, may his ears be burning, punched the watchmaker. In the circumstances, I think there was nothing else he could do. May I kiss your feet, Apisoghom Agha, tell me, could he have done anything else?

APISOGHOM AGHA (*suddenly*): You make it with tomatoes here, too?

MANUG AGHA: Tomatoes?

APISOGHOM AGHA: Yes, in other places they make it with tomatoes.

MANUG AGHA: The watch?

APISOGHOM AGHA: Which watch?

MANUG AGHA: Toros Agha's watch.

APISOGHOM AGHA: Who is Toros Agha?

MANUG AGHA: Then you weren't listening to my story?

APISOGHOM AGHA: I was, of course I was. I was listening very carefully.

{*But his question about tomatoes made it clear that his mind was going from soup to tomatoes, and from tomatoes to how soup was made with rice in Constantinople, and that he was paying no heed at all to* **MANUG AGHA**'s *rambling. He had a perfect right not to listen to his host's long speech, especially on an empty stomach. There are people in the world who think they have the right to grab someone by the nose and talk his head off for hours. There are others who think so highly of what they have to say that they make a special point of hunting down people to listen to them, and if they can't find volunteers, are willing to pay people to do so. Some even have listeners on monthly retainers. The author has been trapped in such situations on occasion, pretended to listen, all the while thinking about other matters, giving agreeable answers to all questions, saying, "That's so," when asked, "Is that not so?"; acknowledging, "That is true," when asked, "Is that not true?"; responding with, "You are most certainly right," when confronted with, "Am I not right?" All in the hope of bringing the talk to an early conclusion. The trouble starts when your tormentor begins to ask the sort of question to which answers cannot be arranged so easily, and a judgment is satanically forced on you. After a long and tedious story, of which you have not heard a single word, he may, for example, suddenly ask: "Now you be the judge, was Margos Agha right, or Giragos Agha?" What can you say? You have no idea about the issue in question, and you may never have even heard of Margos Agha or Giragos Agha. There is also the matter of your tormentor's feelings, which you can hurt irreparably by picking the wrong man. The author has found a way out of this, too, with answers* *like these: "The matter should be resolved amicably"; or "Yes, but who is right in-deed?"; or "What's the use? You can't do anything with an unreasonable man"; or "Yes, but I ask you, tell me if you can, which of them is right?"; or "Why do you insist on an answer, my friend. It is as clear as two and two make four." Many have been satisfied with answers like these, but there are those not so easily put off who seem prepared to turn you over to the police if you do not say right out whether it is Mar-gos who is right or Giragos. To escape from their clutches, it is best to mention some urgent business, just remembered, and rush off. The author has noticed lately that this sort of action sometimes actually encourages the talkative, and has been forced to put politeness aside and say: "Sir, for listening to you for two hours, I think I am entitled to two pounds. I will not accept even one piaster less than two pounds." One man offered half a pound, which was refused with righteous indignation, the rejec-tion itself serving to stop all further talk. The same man later found two people who agreed to listen to him for a quarter of a pound each. You have to envy some of our newspapers which, instead of paying their readers, are actually paid by them.* APISOGHOM AGHA *would not behave in this manner; and when with his talk of toma-toes he revealed that he had been less than attentive and had heard nothing the lec-turer had been prattling about, he tried immediately to cover up his discourtesy, by insisting: "I did. I listened very carefully." Should he have said this? Obviously not. He should quite simply have said:* "MANUG AGHA, *look here, my friend, when some-one begins to speak, he should not set conscience aside. I have been hungry for eight hours and feel no real need to know whose son Mardiros Agha is, or whose father Kevork Agha is, or that the watchmaker slapped Toros Agha, and that Toros Agha hit him back, may all their ears be burning. He should respond unhesitatingly in this manner not only to a social bore but also to the priests who preach for four hours for the sole purpose of speaking at great length and are offended if even one of the faith-ful dares to leave the church during the marathon, for whatever reason. The author made a point of this to a bishop on one occasion, as he was leaving church after de-livering a five-hour sermon. "Where are you going, Your Grace?" "I perspired a great deal during the sermon and must go and change my clothes. Where are you going?" "I am going home to change my clothes, too." Since that time the bishop's sermons have been mercifully brief.* APISOGHOM AGHA *could not summon such audacity, and* MANUG AGHA *felt encouraged to continue, addressing himself first to the question of the tomatoes.}*

MANUG AGHA [*with sudden gusto*]: We use tomatoes in soup, in pilaf, and in all sorts
of meat dishes, but never in watches.
APISOGHOM AGHA: Thank you. So you do use it in soup. That's what I wanted to
know.
MANUG AGHA: Do you like soup with tomatoes?
APISOGHOM AGHA: I like it with tomatoes.
MANUG AGHA: Good. Let's get back to the story now. Where were we? Oh, yes,

Toros Agha. He's a strange man, that Toros Agha, may his ears be burning; he has a lot of strange stories. They'll keep for another night. It'll be a nice way to pass the time. Not to go on too long, I ran into Melkon Agha this morning—

LANDLADY (*entering with food*): Here it is. Eat it while it's hot.

APISOGHOM AGHA: Yes, yes. Let's eat now. I'm starving.

LANDLADY: Please begin.

APISOGHOM AGHA: Thank you. (*He leaps in the air as the first spoonful barely touches his lips.*)

LANDLADY: It must be too hot. Please excuse me, Apisoghom Agha.

MANUG AGHA: Drink some water, quickly, Apisoghom Agha.

APISOGHOM AGHA: No harm done, no harm.

MANUG AGHA (*scolding his wife*): Madam, why aren't you more careful about how hot the soup is?

LANDLADY: I beg you to overlook our shortcomings tonight.

APISOGHOM AGHA: It's nothing. Please, nothing at all.

MANUG AGHA: While the soup is cooling off, I can at least fill the time by telling you about all that's happened today.

LANDLADY: Manug Agha, don't pester Apisoghom Agha so much this evening. Maybe he'd rather not hear these stories.

MANUG AGHA: I only want to help him pass the time. I don't want him to be bored.

LANDLADY: Save it for another night. Tired as he is, how can he listen to you?

MANUG AGHA: I'm sure it's a pleasure for Apisoghom Agha to hear about our nation's affairs.

APISOGHOM AGHA: Yes, a great pleasure. But as your wife says, maybe we can leave it for tomorrow night. I really am very tired.

MANUG AGHA: Of course, however you wish. But our council's doings are very amusing. If Melkon Agha were here, he could tell stories that would split your sides.

LANDLADY: The soup is cool enough now.

(*As soon as he hears these words, APISOGHOM AGHA falls upon the soup with his spoon.*)

MANUG AGHA: How about another raki, Apisoghom Agha?

APISOGHOM AGHA: No, thank you.

MANUG AGHA: Madam, pour Apisoghom Agha some wine.

LANDLADY: Manug Agha, you're saying some very peculiar things tonight. Whoever heard of drinking wine with soup?

MANUG AGHA: And why not? Let's see if he'll appreciate our vintage.

(*The woman goes out and brings in the meat dish. APISOGHOM AGHA eats with such an appetite that he begins gulping down the meat without chewing it.*)

APISOGHOM AGHA: Praise God. We're full and content again. (*He makes the sign of the cross, while murmuring the Lord's prayer, then rises, looking for water to wash with.*)

LANDLADY: You wash after dinner?

APISOGHOM AGHA: If there's water.

LANDLADY: It's not our custom, but I'll bring some for you to wash with.

(APISOGHOM AGHA *washes and dries his hands. Lights dim in the parlor. With a lamp in her hand, the* LANDLADY *leads him to a room on the second floor, above the dining room area. A true measure of its size can best be communicated by saying that the width of the room matches* APISOGHOM AGHA's *height. The bed is in front of the room's only window, which opens on the street. The furnishings include a chair, a small square table, a small mirror, a pitcher of water and a glass, and a comb and brush. As soon as he is in the room,* APISOGHOM AGHA *crosses himself in a prayerful manner. Then he quickly undresses and throws himself into bed.*)

Scene 8

APISOGHOM AGHA's *bedroom.* APISOGHOM AGHA *alone*

APISOGHOM AGHA (*muttering into the pillow*): I know what I will do from now on. I won't see anyone at all. I don't like the people here at all. They either want to get their hands on your money or talk your ears off for two hours. What have I to do with any of them? I came here to find a wife. If I see a girl I like, I'll ask for her hand. If I am accepted, I'll take her and go home. And if I am not accepted, if I'm not . . . but why shouldn't I be? Can they find anyone better? If that paper prints some nice things about me tomorrow, they'll all beg me to take their daughters. But what will I do with more than one? I'll pick a very nice one, make all the arrangements, get engaged and then married right away. (*Having so decided everything to his satisfaction, he goes to sleep.*)

ACT 2

Sitting room of the house at Number Two Flower Street (APISOGHOM AGHA *is extremely tired and sleeps soundly that night, and may very well have slumbered through the next day but for the raucous sounds of the street vendors disturbing his sleep, a way station of death, which is not only a haven for the weary, but also a comfort for painful ailments. {Blessed are they who sleep and wake up late or not at all, since they feel none, or at any rate very little, of the pain that wracks and ruins man. But in Constantinople there is no freedom even to sleep. At night the watchmen bang the ground so hard with their staffs, and in the morning the street vendors shout so loud the virtues of their wares, that sleep is altogether confounded and doesn't know which way to turn. If on the day of the Last Judgment, the Angel Gabriel does not succeed in waking the dead with his trumpet, he might prevail on the night watchmen and vendors of Constantinople.}* APISOGHOM AGHA, *whose room faces the street, is up early and goes down to the sitting-room, where he is greeted by the* LANDLADY.)

Scene 1

Sitting room. The LANDLADY, APISOGHOM AGHA, *later the* PHOTOGRAPHER

LANDLADY: Good morning, Apisoghom Agha.
APISOGHOM AGHA: Good morning.
LANDLADY: There's someone here to see you.
APISOGHOM AGHA: Have him come in.
LANDLADY: Tell me, please, do you take coffee with or without milk?
APISOGHOM AGHA: I take milk without coffee.
LANDLADY: Shall I bring milk then?
APISOGHOM AGHA: Yes, bring some milk. (*She leaves.*) (*Muttering to himself*) Who can this man be? Maybe he has a daughter he wants to marry off and heard of my arrival and came to talk about it. But I won't jump into anything until I'm absolutely sure about the girl's character. I have to know everything about her, look her over very carefully, and then ask my father's consent. Even if I like her, that's not enough. My father has to like my wife, too. And not only my father, everybody has to approve. I can't have a wife people don't like.

(*A vigorous-looking, thirty-year-old man enters the room, walks quickly to* APISOGHOM AGHA *and shakes his hand.* APISOGHOM AGHA *gets up and submits to the handshaking, which takes place to the accompaniment of a thousand and one expressions of felicitation and solicitude. The visitor is a* PHOTOGRAPHER.)

PHOTOGRAPHER: Good day, most glorious sir. Please remain seated, Apisoghom Agha, I beg you. It's not appropriate for you to be standing. (*He releases the hand he has been shaking and, bowing and scraping, steps slowly back to an armchair and sits down.* APISOGHOM AGHA *lounges on the couch.*) I should have been here yesterday to welcome you on your arrival, but I learned of it much too late. And for this I humbly beg your pardon. (*He rubs his hands together.*)
APISOGHOM AGHA: You've done nothing wrong by coming today, so there's no need to beg any pardon.
PHOTOGRAPHER: It's your kindness that makes you say that. But I'm always aware of my shortcomings and am indeed at fault. For so noted a man as yourself to vis-

it our capital and not be greeted immediately by a photographer is the fault of all faults. And there's no way that's not a fault.

APISOGHOM AGHA: Not at all. I wouldn't even count it a fault if you hadn't come at all.

PHOTOGRAPHER: You're too generous.

APISOGHOM AGHA: I'm not generous at all.

PHOTOGRAPHER: Whatever you say. There's no need to argue that now. I just want to place myself at your disposal and await your command. If you wish, we can have them taken here, or if you'd honor our office, we can do it there. It's all the same to me. However you please.

APISOGHOM AGHA: What are you going to take? My blood pressure's fine.

PHOTOGRAPHER: I wasn't alluding to your health. What I want to take is your picture.

APISOGHOM AGHA: I've never had my picture taken, and I can't see any reason to do so. Anytime I want to see myself, I can look in a mirror.

PHOTOGRAPHER: If you wanted to give your picture to someone, could you send him the mirror, Apisoghom Agha?

APISOGHOM AGHA: Why should I send a picture? I'd go myself.

PHOTOGRAPHER: You can say what you like. But I won't rest easy until I've taken your picture. It's an indignity for me not to be able to take your picture, and I hope you share that feeling.

APISOGHOM AGHA: Why?

PHOTOGRAPHER: Have you ever heard of a celebrated man like yourself visiting our great city and not having his picture taken? Do you want the whole world to laugh at you?

APISOGHOM AGHA: Why should anyone laugh?

PHOTOGRAPHER: The answer's obvious. Great men naturally have great friends. You are a man of some importance and soon will certainly be receiving visits from other important men. Many of them will present their pictures to you, and you will be obliged to do the same.

APISOGHOM AGHA: And if I don't, will they laugh at me?

PHOTOGRAPHER: Laugh? You'll be ridiculed everywhere.

APISOGHOM AGHA: Strange.

PHOTOGRAPHER: It's simply unheard of for so noble a man not to have his picture taken. Really a disgrace.

APISOGHOM AGHA: Disgrace?

PHOTOGRAPHER: A great shame. Going about without underwear is not nearly as demeaning as being without pictures.

APISOGHOM AGHA: I didn't know all this.

PHOTOGRAPHER: Sophistication, enlightenment, civilization even, make it a duty for all of us to have pictures of ourselves.

APISOGHOM AGHA: Will the newspaper report that Apisoghom Agha has had his picture taken?

PHOTOGRAPHER: That's not a matter of special interest to the newspapers.

APISOGHOM AGHA: Then there won't be any announcements about it in our churches either?

PHOTOGRAPHER: Why should there be, Apisoghom Agha? Are you trying to ridicule me?

APISOGHOM AGHA: Ridicule you? Never. I'm against that sort of thing. What right do I have to ridicule anyone?

PHOTOGRAPHER: Don't get angry.

APISOGHOM AGHA: I will get angry. It's my nature to want everything just right.

PHOTOGRAPHER: I'll make sure of that. How shall I have you pose?

APISOGHOM AGHA: I have no intention of having a picture taken. It seems absurd.

PHOTOGRAPHER: How can you say that? What could be more useful? If you want to pay a visit to a friend and have no time, you can simply send a picture, and that'll take care of the matter. If you're married, you can send it to your wife whenever you're away, to ease her longing. If you're not married, all the girls will see your picture and find out who you are, so that you'll be talked about everywhere. These days a man needs a picture of himself more than bread. You should see this and not put off another moment having your picture taken.

APISOGHOM AGHA: How will the girls see my picture? Where will they see it?

PHOTOGRAPHER: Didn't I say that you'll be giving them to friends who will, of course, place them in special albums at home and show them off to every-body?

APISOGHOM AGHA: What will that accomplish?

PHOTOGRAPHER: What do you expect? People will always remember you and talk about you.

APISOGHOM AGHA: What will I lose if I am not remembered? You think I care if I'm not remembered? They can remember me or not, it is all the same to me. I won't pay good money for such a trivial pursuit; besides, I don't believe what you say.

PHOTOGRAPHER (*affecting a French accent*): This is something of an *insulte*.

APISOGHOM AGHA: Who is this *insulte*?

PHOTOGRAPHER: Sir, are you aware you've deeply wounded an *artiste*?

APISOGHOM AGHA: I?

PHOTOGRAPHER: Yes, you.

APISOGHOM AGHA: Are you making accusations simply because I refuse to have my picture taken. I don't know of anyone I've offended.

PHOTOGRAPHER: You offended me just now.

APISOGHOM AGHA: Go tell the police about it. I've no time to listen to such non-sense.

PHOTOGRAPHER: There's no need to go to the police. I beg only that you reconcile your words with your graciousness.

APISOGHOM AGHA: I don't want to get into an argument. Go find some people who are fighting and reconcile them.

Scene 2

The same setting. MANUG AGHA, APISOGHOM AGHA, *the* PHOTOGRAPHER

(MANUG AGHA *enters with* APISOGHOM AGHA's *breakfast, puts it on a small table and invites him to have his milk.* APISOGHOM AGHA *sits in front of the tray and begins to drink his milk.*)

MANUG AGHA: Have some breakfast, Apisoghom Agha. (*To the* PHOTOGRAPHER) What have you decided? Are you going to take Apisoghom Agha's picture from the waist up or full figure?

APISOGHOM AGHA (*interjecting*): Not from the waist up or from the waist down.

MANUG AGHA: Oh, then you will be seated in a chair?

APISOGHOM AGHA: No.

MANUG AGHA: Lying down?

APISOGHOM AGHA: No.

MANUG AGHA: Profile?

APISOGHOM AGHA: No.

MANUG AGHA: How have you decided to do it then?

APISOGHOM AGHA: We've decided not to do it at all.

MANUG AGHA: But that's impossible. These days everybody, from the young to the very old, has his picture taken a few times a year. The only ones who don't are still in their mother's womb. And someday they'll find a way to have their pictures taken, too.

PHOTOGRAPHER: I was unable to persuade Apisoghom Agha, who seems to think I came here to cheat him.

MANUG AGHA: No, no, our photographer's not that kind of man.

PHOTOGRAPHER: I told him that a celebrated figure like himself simply has to have his picture taken.

MANUG AGHA: Yes, he must, and several kinds. He should have twelve small ones, for example, twelve medium-sized, twelve large, twelve standing, twelve seated casually, twelve taken from the side, twelve more seated erect, twelve with his legs crossed, twelve with one hand on the other, twelve with his head resting on one of his palms, twelve with his hand on the table, twelve lying down, twelve with a cane in his hand, twelve smiling, twelve with a serious expression, and twelve neither smiling nor serious. Even if one set of these is omitted, Apisoghom Agha, it'll reflect very badly on your honor.

APISOGHOM AGHA: You can't be serious.

MANUG AGHA: I've no reason to lie. If you don't have pictures, people simply won't look at you with favor. All important men have them.

APISOGHOM AGHA: Men of real importance have them, are you sure?

MANUG AGHA: Positively.

APISOGHOM AGHA: Ordinary people have them too, you said?

MANUG AGHA: But they don't have so many. They have two or three, or at the very most six sets.

APISOGHOM AGHA: It never occurred to me that having pictures mattered so much here.

MANUG AGHA: Yes, that's the only thing they seem to admire now. The better the pictures, the more important the man.

APISOGHOM AGHA: Since everybody seems to have pictures, how will anybody know that I'm important? They shouldn't allow everybody to have them, so there could be no question.

PHOTOGRAPHER: But there's a great difference. For important men the pictures are large and on glossy paper.

APISOGHOM AGHA: Couldn't we have my servants in the picture, too—waiting on me?

MANUG AGHA: Why not?

APISOGHOM AGHA: Really?

PHOTOGRAPHER: Of course.

APISOGHOM AGHA: I have farms with cows, sheep, horses, geese, ducks. Can't we get them into the corner of the picture somewhere?

MANUG AGHA: That would be difficult. (*He turns to* PHOTOGRAPHER.) But servants are feasible, aren't they?

PHOTOGRAPHER: Most assuredly.

APISOGHOM AGHA: Then, can you print under the pictures that this man has farms, cows, horses, donkeys?

PHOTOGRAPHER: No. It can be done, of course, but that's not the custom. Why should it be necessary? Everyone will know soon enough.

APISOGHOM AGHA: Can we take a picture of me mounted on a horse?

PHOTOGRAPHER: Yes.

APISOGHOM AGHA: With the horse galloping?

PHOTOGRAPHER: That would be very difficult.

APISOGHOM AGHA: All right, we'll see about it tomorrow.

PHOTOGRAPHER: If you wish, I can bring the camera here.

MANUG AGHA: Good idea. Bring it here. It would be inappropriate for Apisoghom Agha to come to your studio. Important men always have their picture taken in their homes.

PHOTOGRAPHER: My pleasure. (*He rises, rubbing his hands together, and stammering as though he has something further to say but doesn't know quite how to say it. It is quite obvious to the audience that anyone who has something to say but hesitates can only intend to ask for money.*)

APISOGHOM AGHA: Bring the camera here tomorrow.

PHOTOGRAPHER (*continues rubbing his hands and stammering*): Very well.

APISOGHOM AGHA (*impatient that the* PHOTOGRAPHER *is not leaving*): Tomorrow, as I said. You'll bring it tomorrow.

PHOTOGRAPHER: Yes, I understand. I will bring the camera tomorrow. But we have a custom . . . that . . . pardon . . .

APISOGHOM AGHA: Speak up, speak up.

PHOTOGRAPHER: I beg you not to be offended.

APISOGHOM AGHA: I won't be offended.

PHOTOGRAPHER : Our custom is that if we take the camera to someone's house, we ask for a retainer. Not because we don't trust the person, you understand, but only out of respect for an established custom.

APISOGHOM AGHA: What a hideous custom that is!

PHOTOGRAPHER: Still, it's a custom.

APISOGHOM AGHA: Will two pounds be enough?

PHOTOGRAPHER: Quite satisfactory.

(APISOGHOM AGHA *pays the* PHOTOGRAPHER, *who leaves without any further hesitation or stammering.*)

Scene 3

The same setting. APISOGHOM AGHA, MANUG AGHA

{*There are people who make a great show of what they do not have, and there are those who prefer not to show what they do have. There are also those who have something to show and want very much to show it.* APISOGHOM AGHA *was among these. He wanted the whole world to know he had farms and spared no expense to realize this wish. When he was told that important men had their pictures taken, then of course there was nothing left but to have his picture taken. But he was suspicious that he might have been cheated and separated from his money without purpose.*}

APISOGHOM AGHA (*to* MANUG AGHA, *after the* PHOTOGRAPHER *leaves*): If I don't have my picture taken, you think that no one will have any respect for me?

MANUG AGHA: I wouldn't say that. But since men of your station do so, it's proper for you to act accordingly. If someone asks for your picture, and you tell him you haven't had any taken—

APISOGHOM AGHA: What would happen?

MANUG AGHA: Nothing would happen . . . but—

APISOGHOM AGHA: But what? Would my farms be taken from me?

MANUG AGHA: Of course not.

APISOGHOM AGHA: Would they snatch my sheep and cows from me?

MANUG AGHA: By no means, but they'd regard you as unenlightened. They wouldn't give you the recognition important men always receive.

APISOGHOM AGHA: I see. How shall I have the picture taken then, so there'll be no mistaking me for an unimportant man, since you yourself said that ordinary people have their pictures taken, too?

MANUG AGHA: There'll be no doubt at all if it is a large picture, and if you're seated grandly in a handsome armchair.

APISOGHOM AGHA: I should be dressed in my new suit, shouldn't I?

MANUG AGHA: Yes.

APISOGHOM AGHA: With my watch showing?

MANUG AGHA: Certainly.

APISOGHOM AGHA: Maybe taking snuff like this? And with two men bowing to greet me and one behind me ready to help.

MANUG AGHA: Yes, yes.

APISOGHOM AGHA: What else should we do to make it even more impressive?

MANUG AGHA: What you've mentioned seems sufficient.

APISOGHOM AGHA: Can't the picture show me beating my two servants and driving them out of the room? Could that be done? Or maybe beating just one of them? Or scolding my foreman? I could be screaming at him: "Scoundrel, how many times have I told you to treat our workers with kindness, to be gentle with our animals. And since you continue to disobey me, I'm going to throw you off my land." And he can fall at my feet, wiping his eyes with his handkerchief, begging and pleading: "Forgive me for my children's sake. I've eaten your bread for so many years. You're my benefactor. I held you on my knees when you were a little boy, loved and cared for you." Can't we get things like this into the picture?

MANUG AGHA: Let's work that out tomorrow. Now, maybe we can go on with yesterday's story, which was interrupted right in the middle. As soon as Melkon Agha saw me . . .

APISOGHOM AGHA (*speaking at opposite purposes throughout this scene*): Or maybe I can lie down like this, and my servants can be pulling off my trousers?

MANUG AGHA: . . . and he came up to me . . .

APISOGHOM AGHA: Won't it be more impressive with me smoking a water pipe?

MANUG AGHA: . . . took hold of my hands and warned me: "If we don't get down to business, all our opponents will be elected to the council."

APISOGHOM AGHA: With a tube say about ten feet long?

MANUG AGHA: We can worry about that tomorrow, Apisoghom Agha. Let me get on with the story. Melkon Agha grabbed me by the arm and took me to the clubhouse where some young men were playing cards.

APISOGHOM AGHA: I really think that if the tube of the water pipe were a little shorter, it'd look better in the picture.

{*The author has witnessed such a scene at least a hundred times in his lifetime, in which the two actors keep snatching the words from each other's mouths at least a hundred times, twice perhaps in social gatherings, and all the rest in sessions of our national assemblies. This is the hundred and first occasion, and the devil is tempting the author to tell one of these men: "Let the other finish what he has to say, then speak." But because he has hurt people in the past by speaking up in this manner, the author decides to remain neutral and leave them to their own devices, hoping that it will not end—as is always the case in the national assemblies—in a fight.*}

MANUG AGHA: You're absolutely right. It would be better shorter. But in any event, anybody elected as representative must be honest and upright.

APISOGHOM AGHA: Do you know a good one?

MANUG AGHA: My knowing one is not enough. The choice is made by voting.

APISOGHOM AGHA: Voting?

MANUG AGHA: Yes, according to the constitution[8] the voting decides.

APISOGHOM AGHA: What are you talking about? The people have to vote to pick a good water pipe?

MANUG AGHA: We're talking about a representative.

APISOGHOM AGHA: Where did the representative come from? We were talking about a water pipe.

MANUG AGHA: Don't be upset, Apisoghom Agha.

APISOGHOM AGHA: Why should I be upset? We'll go buy one tomorrow.

MANUG AGHA: Of course.

Scene 4

The same setting. The MATCHMAKER, MANUG AGHA, APISOGHOM AGHA

(*The door opens and a woman's head appears; she is an intermediary of love, a matchmaker. She finds women for men, arranges men for women, and, on getting them married, accepts wages for her labor. And sometimes she even separates the man and the woman, for which she also expects to be paid. If you ask her, she is thirty-six years old; if you were to ask the author, he would say forty-six, since it is my custom to add ten years to any age a woman admits to. Measles left its traces on her face, a long black face, in the center of which her nose stretches out, more lavish as it descends, bearing at its source two small black eyes, which always seem to be looking in four di-*

---

8. The reference is to the Armenian constitution ratified by the sultan in 1863, which granted the millet a measure of democracy in providing for an elected assembly to counterbalance the previously absolute authority of the Armenian patriarch.

rections. Her forehead is barely two inches wide. Her eyebrows have fallen out. When the rest of her enters the room, she speaks.)

MATCHMAKER: If you're discussing confidential matters, I'll leave.

MANUG AGHA: No, not at all. We were talking about the council.

MATCHMAKER (*She nods to* APISOGHOM AGHA, *goes to the couch and sits.*): That council business is getting to be a nuisance.

MANUG AGHA: It's good to see you, Madam.

MATCHMAKER: It's good to be here. How are you, Apisoghom Agha? How do you like our city?

APISOGHOM AGHA: I like it very much.

MANUG AGHA: What brings you to this neighborhood? Is there an engagement?

MATCHMAKER: I was visiting across the street and thought I'd drop in to see you. I want to arrange something between Antaram's daughter and the boy across the street. And the matter was practically settled. But because Martha wanted him for *her* daughter, she told a lot of stories about Antaram's daughter, and he cooled off a little. I came to see him today to persuade him. But he wasn't home, so I'll have to come by again tomorrow.

MANUG AGHA: Why don't you find a nice girl for Apisoghom Agha?

(APISOGHOM AGHA *smiles.*)

MATCHMAKER: Your wife already informed me downstairs that Apisoghom Agha is not married and, to be honest, that's why I came upstairs. (*She dabs her nose with a white handkerchief.*)

APISOGHOM AGHA (*getting up and offering the* MATCHMAKER *a cigarette*): I do have such an intention.

MATCHMAKER: If you have such an intention, I can find the kind of girl you want. I've been in the business for more than twenty years. I know everybody. Give me some idea of the kind of girl you have in mind. (*Seeing that* APISOGHOM AGHA *and the* MATCHMAKER *will be talking about this particular matter for a time,* MANUG AGHA *leaves the room, reluctantly reconciled that the story of the councilman will have to be finished another time.*)

APISOGHOM AGHA (*laughing*): I want a nice girl.

MATCHMAKER: Of course you want a nice girl. One who is rich, too?

APISOGHOM AGHA: Yes.

MATCHMAKER: Of good character?

APISOGHOM AGHA: Of course.

MATCHMAKER: Sixteen to eighteen years old?

APISOGHOM AGHA: Exactly.

MATCHMAKER: Should she know how to play the piano?

APISOGHOM AGHA: She should.

MATCHMAKER: And dance?

APISOGHOM AGHA: That would be nice.

MATCHMAKER: I know just such a girl. But you have to understand that girls like this don't do any work around the house. From morning to night, they cross their legs and sit around, sing, dance, and go out. I want to warn you now, so you won't hold me responsible later. There are the good ones, too, of course, but they are very hard to find. Then there are those who fall in love with someone else and run off with him, while you wait patiently for her to come home.

APISOGHOM AGHA: Really? I don't want anyone like that.

MATCHMAKER: Then there are those who'll worship you.

APISOGHOM AGHA: That's the kind I want.

MATCHMAKER: Some will live a month with their lovers and not even mention your name.

APISOGHOM AGHA: I don't want anyone like that.

MATCHMAKER: Others won't leave your side for a minute.

APISOGHOM AGHA: I'd like that.

MATCHMAKER: Don't reproach me for saying this. There are men, too, who let their wives take all sorts of liberties and overlook everything because they can squeeze some money from their fathers-in-law.

APISOGHOM AGHA: I can't believe such charlatans exist?

MATCHMAKER: More than the hairs on my head.

APISOGHOM AGHA: But who would even look at people like that?

MATCHMAKER: Everybody. They excuse the woman by saying that she's been possessed by the devil, and they make a saint out of the man by claiming that the poor soul doesn't know what his wife's up to.

APISOGHOM AGHA: Ah, I can't take it. I won't go through with it. Forget the whole thing. I'll get married when I go back home.

MATCHMAKER: But there are girls so nice they'd give their soul for you.

APISOGHOM AGHA: Find me someone like that, and I'll get married.

MATCHMAKER: And that's just the kind of girl I'm going to find for you. I only asked all these questions to get some idea of what you fancied

{She is perfectly justified for being so meticulous, since every day we see such marriages as can only make us wonder. Once, as a matter of curiosity, the author kept the accounts of the romantic involvements of a married man he knew. When he closed the ledgers at the end of the year, he found that the man was a moral bankrupt. The author stopped having anything to do with him but was surprised to find that the man continued to be held in high esteem in the community and was respected everywhere as a person of exemplary character. The author's interest was reawakened, and he was prompted to go over the ledgers again, this time finding that the wife, whom *he had casually entered as a partner, had been listed by her husband as an asset. If a realistic and accurate bookkeeping system for romantic relationships were developed one day, a lot of accountants would be deeply distressed. There are countless men who, in their marital accounts, list their wives as a general disbursement; others under furnishings; still others under household items. Some carry them as receivables, others as payables. There are very few men who count their wives as partners in their matrimonial enterprise.}*

MATCHMAKER: Marriage is a very sweet thing. If you find the right girl, you'll be in heaven every day.

APISOGHOM AGHA: That's just why I want to get married.

MATCHMAKER: And if you don't get along, you'll be in hellfire everyday.

APISOGHOM AGHA: That's just why I'm afraid to get married.

MATCHMAKER: Let me tell you, Agha, since you're a celebrated man, you will, of course, want a wife from a very substantial family.

APISOGHOM AGHA: Yes, yes, from a substantial family.

MATCHMAKER: I'll proceed on that basis. Does your honor know French?

APISOGHOM AGHA: Do I have to know French to get a girl from a substantial family?

MATCHMAKER: Yes, because girls from substantial families speak French, and when a woman speaks a language her husband can't understand, he can easily get jealous.

APISOGHOM AGHA: Then I'll learn French.

MATCHMAKER: Besides, happiness is seldom found in marriages when the wife knows more than the husband.

APISOGHOM AGHA: That's true. I'll go along with that completely.

MATCHMAKER: Does your honor have any knowledge of European music?

APISOGHOM AGHA: Not a bit, and it bores me to hear it besides.

MATCHMAKER: What'll you do if your wife spends hours at the piano playing European music?

APISOGHOM AGHA: I won't permit it. It will be a torment for me.

MATCHMAKER: But it'll be a pleasure for her.

APISOGHOM AGHA: What right does a woman have to give her husband a headache?

MATCHMAKER: What right does a husband have to deny his wife such pleasure?

APISOGHOM AGHA: If the matter comes down to this, I will not get married.

MATCHMAKER: That won't do either. All you really have to do is to please your wife by learning how to play the piano.

APISOGHOM AGHA: Will I be able to learn?

MATCHMAKER: Why not? It'll be much easier for you to learn how to play than for your wife to forget.

APISOGHOM AGHA: If that's the case, we've found a way out of that problem, too.

MATCHMAKER: I'm telling you this because I don't want my honor stained in any way. I'm spelling everything out at the start so there'll be no cause for complaint later. I know girls of every class—high, middle, and low—and have merchandise in all three classes. Your Honor must consult with his purse and tell me: "I want a girl from this class." Obviously the upper class would be very expensive, the middle less so, and the low not expensive at all.

APISOGHOM AGHA: I don't want anything cheap.

MATCHMAKER: Good. Do you prefer a fair complexion or dark?

APISOGHOM AGHA: I like a fair complexion.

MATCHMAKER: Black or blue eyes?

APISOGHOM AGHA: Come to think of it, I like black and blue.

MATCHMAKER: It has to be one or the other. I don't know of any girls who have one black and one blue eye.

APISOGHOM AGHA: All right then, blue.

MATCHMAKER: Her height and hair?

APISOGHOM AGHA: Long, long.

MATCHMAKER: Her waist?

APISOGHOM AGHA: Slender. But I don't want anybody sickly. I want her flesh to move when she walks.

MATCHMAKER: I understand. This is enough to go on. I have just the girl for you. She is modest and virtuous and is the kind who will worship her husband.

APISOGHOM AGHA: That's exactly the kind I want.

MATCHMAKER: Perhaps she will fall in love with you the moment I mention your name to her. Let me have a picture of you to show to her.

APISOGHOM AGHA: I'm having my picture taken tomorrow.

MATCHMAKER: Tomorrow? It'll take eight days to get prints. Do we have to wait eight days then?

APISOGHOM AGHA: Why wait? We'll go tomorrow. Is she from a substantial family?

MATCHMAKER: Yes.

APISOGHOM AGHA: Is her father rich?

MATCHMAKER: Very rich, but he doesn't flaunt it.

APISOGHOM AGHA: Has he a lot of stores?

MATCHMAKER: Twenty.

APISOGHOM AGHA: Houses?

MATCHMAKER: Forty.

APISOGHOM AGHA: Good. We'll visit her the day after tomorrow.

MATCHMAKER: It'll be my pleasure. I'll come by in the morning and we'll go together. Good day, Apisoghom Agha, rest easy. I won't disappoint you. I'm not like the others who wouldn't care if they fitted you out in a hair shirt. I'll be back the day after tomorrow. (*She leaves.*)

Scene 5

The same setting. MANUG AGHA, *the* LANDLADY, *and* APISOGHOM AGHA

(*As soon as* MANUG AGHA, *who has been downstairs drinking coffee, sees the* MATCH-MAKER *leave, he puts down his cup and goes up immediately to rejoin* APISOGHOM AGHA.)

MANUG AGHA (*starting to speak as soon as he sees* APISOGHOM AGHA): Melkon Agha took my arm like this, and we entered the reading room together. It was once a tavern, run by Gomig Agha, a good man, God rest his soul. A sickness came over him. Doctor after doctor examined him, but I suppose he was beyond any cure, and the poor man died.

LANDLADY (*entering with a newspaper for* APISOGHOM AGHA): The honorable effendi[9] has special regards for you. (*She leaves.*)

APISOGHOM AGHA (*opening the paper hastily and reading*): "The following is reported from Van."[10] That's not it. This must be it. "Our friend in Mush has submitted the following for publication."[11] That's not it either. (*He keeps searching the paper.*) "The following report is from the *Courrier d'Orient*.[12] Let's see what's on the next page. "The Times reporter has telegraphed the following." My name's not here. Let me look at . . . "There was a recent addition to the elite of our city. The noted merchant and owner of many farms, the well-known patriot, linguist, and benefactor Apisoghom Effendi, arrived in the capital yesterday on the Trebizond steamer and is staying at Number Two Flower Street in Pera. The visit of someone of Apisoghom Effendi's stature will cause considerable joy in our community." (*Turning to* MANUG AGHA) See what they've written about me. (*He reads the story aloud again.*)

LANDLADY (*returning*): The honorable effendi sends his special regards. It seems he expects a subscription fee.

APISOGHOM AGHA: Right away. (*He gives her the money, and she races downstairs again. To* MANUG AGHA) He doesn't write too badly, does he?

MANUG AGHA: Not bad at all.

----

9. Effendi is a Turkish title of Greek origin applied to men of education and significant social standing.

10. Van is a city on the south shore of Lake Van, center of the eponymous vilayet in this period.

11. Mush is a city in a fertile plain, to the northwest of Lake Van. At this time it had a significant Armenian population.

12. A French newspaper of Constantinople.

APISOGHOM AGHA: It's a fine paper.

MANUG AGHA: The very best.

LANDLADY(*entering once again, this time with a letter and a large package*): The honorable effendi has special regards for you.

APISOGHOM AGHA (*opening the letter and reading*): "Having learned of your arrival in our capital, I hasten to welcome you and send ten copies of my newspaper. It's my hope that you will support us by subscribing to our paper, thus encouraging one who has dedicated his entire life as an editor in the thankless service of our people. Yours respectfully, editor of . . ." What'll I do with ten copies?

MANUG AGHA: We will read them until they come out of our ears.

(*The* LANDLADY *is there again, with still another letter and package.*)

APISOGHOM AGHA (*opening and reading the letter, as before*): "Honorable Effendi, your renowned patriotism encouraged me to send you fifteen copies of my paper. My heart is warmed by the hope that you will accept them as a patron of our journal, which, because of limited readership, is going through a very rough time. Your devoted servant, editor of . . ." (*He has not yet folded the letter when the* LANDLADY *bursts in again.*)

LANDLADY (*with another package and letter*): More greetings and respects. (*She leaves.*)

APISOGHOM AGHA (*tearing open the letter and reading*): "Honorable Effendi, I thought it appropriate and worthwhile to send you forty copies of my last book, containing the poetic expressions of my heart. I devoutly hope you will do me the honor of accepting them and in that way giving me the encouragement to continue and have my new poems published. I beg you to accept assurances of my highest esteem, and remain your Honor's humble servant . . ." (*He puts the letter away.*)

(*The* LANDLADY *comes back again.*)

I suppose the honorable effendi has special regards again.

LANDLADY: No, one of the porters is here asking for his money.

(APISOGHOM AGHA *gives her twenty piasters, and she leaves.*)

MANUG AGHA (*resuming his story*): There were a few people sitting in the corner of the reading room, preparing the slate of council candidates. They were not on our side and were working to get their own corrupt people elected.

LANDLADY (*back again with a package of books*): Some boy came and dropped off these books. It seems the honorable effendi has special regards and would like to see you today or tomorrow. (*She sets books down on the table.*)

APISOGHOM AGHA: What'll I do with these, open a bookstore? I don't want them. If they bring any more, don't accept them. Tell them Apisoghom Agha isn't here and get rid of them.

MANUG AGHA: You can't do that. You don't know our editors. If you support one, you'd better support them all. Some of them won't stop at anything. If they hear that you supported their competitors and refused them, they'll attack you with all sorts of unimaginable insinuations.

APISOGHOM AGHA: If that's the case, accept everything they send. What can I do? I'm caught in the middle. But don't accept any books.

(The woman nods and leaves.)

MANUG AGHA: Even though those men were working to elect their own people to the council, there was division among them, too. The jeweler wanted his best customer to get elected. The baker was supporting the man who bought ten loaves a day from him. The tailor thought that the young man for whom he made two suits a week would be an excellent candidate. The saddler wanted to vote for the rich man who ordered several saddles every year. The editor wanted to see all his subscribers on the council. The doctor wanted to turn over the community's leadership to the gravely ill, and the tavern keeper to those who drank the most wine and raki. And so there was among them a—

(Here he is interrupted by still another visitor, a well-dressed young man, his round, white face framed in a black beard, streaked with yellow and not very becoming. There are pictures that look much better with frames, and there are those that must have frames to look good at all. If nature had not forbade women to enclose their countenances in frames, so many of them would have had beards today. On entering the room, the young man, who is a DOCTOR, *removes his long black hat and greets the two men.* MANUG AGHA *mutters as he leaves.)*

In all my life, nothing like this has ever happened to me. They won't let me say two words. I barely open my mouth when someone else walks in and starts talking, and what I have to say stays stuck in my mouth.

Scene 6

The same setting. APISOGHOM AGHA *and* DOCTOR

DOCTOR(*after settling himself on the couch*): Have I the honor of addressing Apisoghom Agha?

APISOGHOM AGHA: Yes, I am Apisoghom Agha.

DOCTOR: Thank you for being Apisoghom Agha. I read of your arrival in the paper and was elated that our nation doesn't lack for such noble-hearted patriots as yourself, since a nation without patriots is no nation at all.

APISOGHOM AGHA: Quite so.

DOCTOR: And, conversely, a patriot without a nation isn't a patriot.

APISOGHOM AGHA: Unquestionably.

DOCTOR: These two are so inextricably connected that if they were to be separated, they would shatter beyond repair.

APISOGHOM AGHA: That's so.

DOCTOR (*portentously*): And a nation that doesn't recognize and encourage those who work for it has no right to be considered a nation.

APISOGHOM AGHA: You speak very well.

DOCTOR: When such a professional doesn't receive his due from his nation, he's naturally disheartened and is sometimes tempted to throw himself into the sea.

APISOGHOM AGHA: That would be childish.

DOCTOR: Forgive me, Apisoghom Agha, if I speak so frankly at our first meeting.

APISOGHOM AGHA: No matter.

DOCTOR: Your humble servant spent six years in Europe studying medicine.

APISOGHOM AGHA: An excellent profession.

DOCTOR: I've gone sleepless, working and studying nights, to be able to learn and come back to serve my people.

APISOGHOM AGHA: A man should serve his people.

DOCTOR: I've been back for two years and have had no more than four patients in all that time. You can see how our doctors are encouraged here.

APISOGHOM AGHA: That's awful. Don't the people here have any inclination to get sick?

DOCTOR: Oh, yes, they get sick. But it seems there's no national sensitivity in the sick. They've no idea at all about Armenia.

APISOGHOM AGHA: You can't mean that?

DOCTOR: Yes, very much so. When an Armenian gets sick, he calls a doctor of another nationality, without realizing that only an Armenian can cure the ailments of an Armenian, without comprehending that a foreigner can't possibly make him well. We have more than two thousand Armenian doctors here, and only two or three, or at most five or six, lead comfortable lives. The rest wait and wait, day after day, for someone to treat, for some way to make a living.

APISOGHOM AGHA: It must be very trying.

DOCTOR: What can our nation's doctors do when our nation's sick go to foreign doctors? Ah, (*He raises his eyes to heaven.*) when will we be rid of this xenophilia?

APISOGHOM AGHA: Xenophilia is not a good thing.

DOCTOR: Especially when, in the first place, there isn't enough sickness among our people to support our own doctors. And for a nation with so little inclination to sickness, it's too much to hope that our doctors will have the skill of Europeans; just as a nation with little inclination for literature cannot reasonably expect to have talented, creative authors. Without encouragement, talent and genius expire.

APISOGHOM AGHA: That's very true.

DOCTOR: You can't imagine, Apisoghom Agha, how discouraged I am. A thousand times I have regretted, two thousand times cursed the day I became a doctor. I would rather be a patient, instead of a doctor, and die. Among our people it's better to be a patient than a physician; ignorance is regarded more highly than knowledge, superficiality is respected more than seriousness; fanatics enjoy more honor than the moderates. As God is my witness, I've taken an oath that if I ever have the privilege of treating one of our noted compatriots, I am going to sing his praises in the newspapers.

(*This last remark arouses* APISOGHOM AGHA, *arouses his vanity, that is. He is all ears when he hears that the* DOCTOR *intends to have his patient's name printed in the paper, and he feels a sudden irresistible urge to be sick.*)

APISOGHOM AGHA: It's a good thing you dropped in, Doctor. I haven't been feeling too well these past few days.

DOCTOR: What's wrong?

APISOGHOM AGHA: I feel an uneasiness.

DOCTOR: Where?

APISOGHOM AGHA: Where?

DOCTOR: Yes.

APISOGHOM AGHA: Everywhere.

DOCTOR: How's your appetite?

APISOGHOM AGHA: Good.

DOCTOR: Do you digest your food easily?

APISOGHOM AGHA: Yes.

DOCTOR: Do you sleep well?

APISOGHOM AGHA: Very well. But I've a feeling of discomfort.

DOCTOR: Does your head ache sometimes?

APISOGHOM AGHA: Yes.

DOCTOR: A feeling of lethargy?

APISOGHOM AGHA: Exactly.

DOCTOR: Sometimes a little shivering?

APISOGHOM AGHA: Yes, yes, a little shivering. (*Under his breath*) I've never shivered a second in my life.

DOCTOR: And after that a fever?

APISOGHOM AGHA: A fever.

DOCTOR: And then perspiration.

APISOGHOM AGHA: Perspiration.

DOCTOR: A bitter taste on your tongue in the morning?

APISOGHOM AGHA: Yes, a bitter taste.

DOCTOR: I see. It's really nothing. You've caught a slight chill.

APISOGHOM AGHA: That's just what I thought; it feels like a cold.

DOCTOR: There are many, many doctors who don't understand this illness, prescribe the wrong medicine, and make the patient sick of something else.

APISOGHOM AGHA: I'm glad you were able to diagnose it. You can give me something to cure it right away.

DOCTOR(*He pulls out a pad, scribbles something on it, tears off the top sheet, and gives it to* APISOGHOM AGHA.): This is a red liquid. Take a tablespoon every hour. It's a little bitter but very effective.

APISOGHOM AGHA: I'll have it sent for right away.

DOCTOR: I forgot to ask you how your bodily disposition is?

APISOGHOM AGHA: My disposition? Well, I don't like devious men. I try to deal equably with—

DOCTOR: No, no. I mean do you go out every morning? (*He gesticulates to make his meaning clear.*)

APISOGHOM AGHA: I've been here two mornings already and haven't been able to go out yet.

DOCTOR: Really?

APISOGHOM AGHA: Why should I lie to you? There's no reason—

DOCTOR: Then I'll give you another prescription. (*He writes on the pad again.*) First take this medicine so you will be able to go out tomorrow morning; then you can drink the other.

APISOGHOM AGHA: If I take this medicine, I'll have to go out tomorrow morning?

DOCTOR: Without question.

APISOGHOM AGHA: What miraculous medicine! And what if visitors keep coming and keep me involved with their talk?

DOCTOR: How can that matter?

APISOGHOM AGHA: How can it not matter? I've been wanting to go out for two days, and they haven't given me a chance. They come and chew my ear off for hours. But tomorrow I'll have to go out anyway . . . to have my picture taken.

DOCTOR (*trying another approach*): How is your stomach?

APISOGHOM AGHA: Like everybody else's stomach.

DOCTOR: Is it hard or soft?

APISOGHOM AGHA: Who knows? The truth is, it has never interested me. Why should I care whether it's hard or soft?

DOCTOR: Very well. I'll drop in to see you again tomorrow morning.

APISOGHOM AGHA: That'll be fine.

DOCTOR: Don't worry one bit. I'll make you as good as new with a few medicines.

APISOGHOM AGHA: Thank you. (*As the* DOCTOR *is about to leave,* APISOGHOM AGHA *calls to him.*) Don't forget what you have to write.

DOCTOR (*puzzled at first, but quickly recovering*): I haven't forgotten. I'll see about the newspapers without fail. Good day.

APISOGHOM AGHA: Good day. (*After the* DOCTOR *leaves, he muses to himself.*) I was afraid he was going to tell me I wasn't sick at all. But there was nothing to worry about. He had no idea what was going on. He even gave me medicines to cure me of sicknesses I don't have. Ah, my dear doctor, you don't understand anything at all. My mother was right. She never called a doctor. There's nothing the matter with me, dear Doctor. I became ill only to get my name in the paper. (*Then, feeling some remorse*) Anyone who hears me might think I was pretending to be sick. But, in reality, I haven't been feeling all that well these past few days. I can't get over this feeling of discomfort. I have trouble eating and sleeping, and with that cough that keeps me awake at night. Is it really true that vanity often makes fools of the intelligent, and wise men of fools?

Scene 7

A street in Pera. APISOGHOM AGHA, TEACHER

(APISOGHOM AGHA *crossed to the dining area to get a bite to eat, but when he noticed some people waiting to see him, he rushed out of the house. If he had done otherwise, if he had received every visitor, he would not have had time to eat, sleep, or wake up. He remembered a restaurant in Pera, which is frequented by notables, and decided to go there. Before he has taken a few steps, a fifty-year-old man in ragged clothing, who turns out to be a* TEACHER, *steps in front of him.*)

TEACHER: You're the honorable Apisoghom Agha, are you not?

APISOGHOM AGHA: Yes, I am.

TEACHER: May I speak to you a moment?

APISOGHOM AGHA: What is it?

TEACHER: I've created a new textbook with a completely new approach to education, and I'd like you to accept one hundred copies. Forgive my boldness, but what can I do? Our people have forced this audacity on me. They don't encourage our educators and allow them no more than a miserable existence. If I am unable to place these books today, the printer will have me jailed. I haven't paid him yet, and he threatens me every day.

APISOGHOM AGHA: And what am I supposed to do with the textbooks?

TEACHER: Give them to your friends. I beseech you, don't refuse me. At six piasters each, it comes to only six hundred piasters, and that's not a large sum for you.

APISOGHOM AGHA: Which way is it to the French restaurant?

TEACHER: Down this street. I'll be happy to direct you there.

APISOGHOM AGHA: Thank you.

TEACHER: We can walk and talk at the same time. Teachers are considered servants of the nation and, as such, are scorned by the nation, when in reality they are the masters of the nation. A nation progresses through them. But what's the use? No one realizes this or cares about it. A teacher is given a position one day and is dismissed the next. Why? Because he didn't humble himself before a member of the school committee. If he serves for a few months and asks for his salary, he's dismissed for being so presumptuous as to make such a request. And people never stop saying to him: "You're supported by public funds . . . you're a burden to our people . . . go make a proper living . . . leave us free of your demands." Ah, Apisoghom Agha, you can't imagine what our teachers in Constantinople have to endure. They have achieved the zenith of poverty. I can't believe that, after hearing this, you'll be able to refuse to accept one hundred of my textbooks.

APISOGHOM AGHA: Is that restaurant very far from here?

TEACHER: No, we're almost there. It's not only the teachers who are in this position. EDITORS, authors, publishers, book dealers, all who are dedicated to books are destined for misery. We scream for progress but stumble toward darkness. We point to the right and go left. We speak of the future and scurry into the past. Ah, always big brave words but deeds that are like stable droppings . . .

APISOGHOM AGHA: How is the food in that restaurant?

TEACHER: Very good. Shall I send the hundred books to the house or—

APISOGHOM AGHA: I'll let you know about it in a few days.

TEACHER (*as they arrive in front of the restaurant*): Here it is. Please go in, APISOGHOM AGHA.

Scene 8

The French restaurant in Pera. APISOGHOM AGHA, TEACHER, *then* WRITER *and* LAWYER

APISOGHOM AGHA (*entering and seeing only mirrors on the sides*): They must sell mirrors here. This is the wrong place.

TEACHER: No, no, it's the right place. (*They're seated at a table.* APISOGHOM AGHA *takes the menu from the* WAITER, *examines it, turns it over, looks at the other side, and lays it on the table.*) What would you like to eat?

APISOGHOM AGHA: Something with meat.

TEACHER (*after he calls the* WAITER *and places their order*): That's how it is, Apisoghom Agha. Don't you feel sorry for the condition of our teachers?

APISOGHOM AGHA: Is it possible not to feel sorry?

TEACHER: And is it fitting for our nation to have its educators live like beggars?

APISOGHOM AGHA: Not at all.

TEACHER: If it's convenient, I can drop off the books tonight.

APISOGHOM AGHA: No, no, not tonight. We'll talk about it some other time. (*When the* WAITER *brings their dinner,* APISOGHOM AGHA *crosses himself and begins to eat, then turns to his companion.*) Can such a small portion satisfy anybody? Tell that creature to bring some more.

(*The* WAITER *is asked to bring some pilaf. A heavy-set young man of medium height, a package under his arm, enters the restaurant and walks right up to* APISOGHOM AGHA. *He turns out to be a* WRITER.)

WRITER: I believe I have the honor of addressing Apisoghom Agha.

(APISOGHOM AGHA *looks up at him blankly.*)

I believe I have the good fortune to be in the company of that great man who has come to the capital to be accorded due recognition as a benefactor.

(*Unfamiliar with such formalities,* APISOGHOM AGHA *picks up his spoon and begins to eat his pilaf, which the* WAITER *has just brought. The* TEACHER *begins to exhibit some concern that the newcomer will hinder his own plans and so tries determinedly to ignore him.*)

WRITER (*undaunted*): I believe I have the supreme privilege of being with the noble individual whose name appeared in the newspaper the other day.

(*Occupied with his pilaf,* APISOGHOM AGHA *still doesn't respond, and the newcomer is constrained to be more direct.*)

I think, honorable sir, that you are Apisoghom Agha.

APISOGHOM AGHA: Yes, yes.

WRITER (*He pulls up a chair and sits. To the* WAITER *who comes back to see what he will have.*) Fried eggs. (*He places his package on the chair beside him. Meanwhile* APISOGHOM AGHA *finishes the pilaf and orders broiled fish.*) Ah, Apisoghom Agha, I deem it a great honor to be in the company of so noble-hearted a man as you. Your servant is the humblest of our writers and something of a poet, too. I've written a few tragic plays and would like to present you with twenty copies of each.

(*Still another man, a* LAWYER, *suddenly, smilingly approaches the table.*)

LAWYER: Ah, Apisoghom Agha, welcome to our city. It's good to see you.

APISOGHOM AGHA: Thank you. It's good to see you, too.

LAWYER: I'm an attorney. I heard of your arrival and hastened to offer my respects, and at the same time to ask that you allow me to take care of all your legal affairs.

APISOGHOM AGHA: I have no legal affairs.

LAWYER: Then why have you come here?

APISOGHOM AGHA: For other business entirely.

LAWYER: It's impossible for a man like you not to have legal problems. Not only impossible, an utter dishonor. Someone like you should have hundreds of lawsuits and a string of lawyers to attend to them. If someone like you doesn't have any lawsuits, do you think that poor people are going to have them?

APISOGHOM AGHA: I have no legal problems with anybody.

LAWYER: Amazing. And there's nobody you want to sue?

APISOGHOM AGHA: I've no reason at all to sue anybody.

LAWYER: Do you have to have a reason to go to court? You just go ahead and sue somebody and that's that.

APISOGHOM AGHA: Oh? And how will I benefit by doing that?

LAWYER: You may not benefit, but your lawyer will, and he'll pray for you. That's what important men do these days. To support their lawyers, they bring suits of honor against anyone they see.

APISOGHOM AGHA: I don't get involved in such disgraceful things.

LAWYER: I was jesting, Apisoghom Agha. But seriously, all jesting aside . . . (*Assuming a grave attitude*) I heard that you had a dispute with someone on the steamer and that he said some things that touched on your honor.

APISOGHOM AGHA: No such thing.

LAWYER: And that you said some things, too.

APISOGHOM AGHA: Nothing.

LAWYER: And that there was a fight.

APISOGHOM AGHA: Nothing like that happened.

LAWYER: And that you struck him on the head.

APISOGHOM AGHA: It's a lie.

LAWYER: And that he slapped you.

APISOGHOM AGHA: Altogether false.

LAWYER: And that a third party entered the—

APISOGHOM AGHA: There was no second party. How could there be a third?

LAWYER: . . . who pulled your arm.

APISOGHOM AGHA: Wrong.

LAWYER: And grabbed your hand, too.

APISOGHOM AGHA: False.

LAWYER: And in this way separated the two of you.

APISOGHOM AGHA: No.

LAWYER: And that you, as the injured party, have determined to sue.

APISOGHOM AGHA: Nonsense.

LAWYER: And that you are looking for a good lawyer.

APISOGHOM AGHA: Lies.

LAWYER: And that you wanted to retain me —

APISOGHOM AGHA: Never.

LAWYER: . . . to defend you. That's why I'm here.

APISOGHOM AGHA: No such thing.

(*In the course of this conversation, two or three others gather, all of them for the purpose of presenting him with books or persuading him to subscribe to a newspaper, and all of them partake of a complete meal in the process of putting forth their proposals. Cursing a thousand times the fate that brought him to the restaurant,* APISOGHOM AGHA *calls the* WAITER *and asks for the check, which amounts to 40 francs which, converted, comes to 176 piasters.*)

APISOGHOM AGHA: 176 piasters! I couldn't have eaten that much.

LAWYER: No, you didn't, but you had guests joining you for dinner.

GUEST ONE: It is really a shame for Apisoghom Agha to assume the obligation for our dinner.

GUEST TWO: Yes, that's very true. It is our duty to have him to dinner, too.

GUEST THREE: Forgive this discourtesy. The next time you must promise to be our guest.

(*Without answering,* APISOGHOM AGHA *counts out the money and rushes out, determined never again to enter a restaurant.*)

Scene 9

APISOGHOM's *room at* Number Two Flower Street. APISOGHOM AGHA, MANUG AGHA

(APISOGHOM AGHA *returns home, still in a rage at the self-invited Guests who dined with him at the restaurant, and finds more than a score of letters addressed to him. He goes up to his room, opens the letters one by one, reads them, crumples them, and tosses them to the floor. He paces the floor briefly, then stops.*)

APISOGHOM AGHA: Do these people intend to lead me around by the nose and rob me of my last piaster? I haven't been left to myself one minute since I arrived. One barely leaves before another enters to ask for money. They are practically running into one another. Did I come here to give everybody money? What shameless people! Unheard of, anywhere, ever. And if I decide to throw them all out, how will I be able to manage it? Where will I begin? I will have to hire four or five people to do nothing else but throw these beggars out all day long. And if I refuse to see these people, they'll gossip about me everywhere in the city, saying I'm discourteous and rude, that I've no money, and God knows what

else. I don't want them to say such things about me. What an awful predicament, dear God. I wish I'd never set foot in this place. The best thing is to find a
girl quickly and get on a steamer, before these people bankrupt me. It's unbearable, enough to make one burst. Work hard, bleed and sweat to earn a little
money, and then come here to distribute it to teachers and poets and doctors
and editors and God knows what else? Where has such a thing been heard of?

MANUG AGHA (*opening the door and entering slowly*): You seem to be angry this
evening.

APISOGHOM AGHA: Anger is hardly the word. Anyone else in my place would have
exploded by now.

MANUG AGHA: My dear man, what happened?

APISOGHOM AGHA: What do you think happened? Nobody leaves me alone for a
minute. I stay at home and they pounce upon me and beg for money. I go out
into the street and they surround me and beg for money. I go to the restaurant
and they pop up all around me and beg for money. To get away from their
clutches, I dash from the house to the street, and from the street to the house.
I beseech you, show me a hole I can crawl into to escape them.

MANUG AGHA: You've every right to be annoyed. Do you think I don't understand?
Didn't I go through the same thing? Did they give me a minute's peace to finish the story I was telling you about the council?

APISOGHOM AGHA: I tore up twenty letters just this minute.

MANUG AGHA: What did the letters say?

APISOGHOM AGHA: One wanted to come back with me to teach in my home; another wanted to dedicate a book to me, but I was to give him twenty pounds, of
course; a few wanted me to subscribe to newspapers; another . . . but what's
the point? How can I keep track of them? It's impossible to endure.

MANUG AGHA: The poor wretches are impoverished. What can they do?

APISOGHOM AGHA: They can find work and support themselves. They can learn a
trade. They can do whatever they want. Is it my fault? Am I responsible that
they come and fling themselves at my feet? Shall I take everything I have and
give it to them?

MANUG AGHA: Why should you do that?

APISOGHOM AGHA: A man should have a little pride. To go up to a stranger and say:
"Good day to you, sir, give me some money." Would you be able to do that?

MANUG AGHA: May God never show me that day.

Scene 10

The same setting. APISOGHOM AGHA, MANUG AGHA, *and* ACTOR

(*The door opens and a young man, an* ACTOR, *about twenty-five and of medium
height, comes in and, with some hesitation, gives* APISOGHOM AGHA *a letter.*)

APISOGHOM AGHA (*without opening the letter*): What do you want?

ACTOR (*trembling*): It's all in the letter.

APISOGHOM AGHA: I don't care what's in or out of it. Tell me what you want.

ACTOR: I'm presenting a play tomorrow night, and I brought your honor tickets for a box.

APISOGHOM AGHA (*throwing the envelope in the young man's face*): I don't want them.

MANUG AGHA: You can't force yourself on someone in this manner.

ACTOR: I've trod the stage for ten years—

APISOGHOM AGHA (*shouting*): You should've sat down.

ACTOR (*continuing*): . . . as our people's servant.

APISOGHOM AGHA: You could've been their master for all I care. What's it to me? These are all empty words.

MANUG AGHA: He's right, you know. Empty words.

ACTOR: For the past ten years I've been teaching in the service of our people.

APISOGHOM AGHA: What's that to me?

MANUG AGHA: What's that to him?

ACTOR: And I've the right, I feel, to invite someone like you to a performance dedicated to myself.

APISOGHOM AGHA: I'm not interested.

MANUG AGHA: He's not interested.

ACTOR: If you don't accept a box, who else can I possibly expect to take one?

APISOGHOM AGHA: Take it anywhere you wish, it's none of my business.

MANUG AGHA: None of his business, young man.

ACTOR: I beg you, don't refuse these tickets. If you refuse, you'll be responsible for my being disgraced in the streets.

APISOGHOM AGHA: Go about your business. I am tired of hearing that sort of thing.

MANUG AGHA: He's tired of hearing that sort of thing.

ACTOR: If I leave here empty-handed, it'll be my end.

APISOGHOM AGHA: I've no time to listen to such rubbish.

MANUG AGHA: He has no time to listen to such rubbish.

ACTOR: It's only a matter of one pound. I beg you to take a box. I came here with such high hopes. Don't turn me away hopeless.

APISOGHOM AGHA: Get out, now, for God's sake. Must we listen to you all day?

Scene 11

The same setting. APISOGHOM AGHA, MANUG AGHA, *and* PRINTER

(*The door opens again and the* PRINTER, *an older man, past fifty, with salt and pepper hair, bursts in and confronts* APISOGHOM AGHA.)

PRINTER: Aren't you ashamed of yourself?

APISOGHOM AGHA (*confused*): Why should I be ashamed?

PRINTER: Why have you kept this young man waiting here for two hours?

APISOGHOM AGHA: Who kept him waiting? Who wants him to wait? I want him to leave but he won't go.

PRINTER: So you'll throw him out without giving him the one pound you owe?

APISOGHOM AGHA: Who owes him anything?

PRINTER: You do. And if he hadn't told me that he was going to collect his debt from you this evening and give it to me, I'd never have printed those tickets and the playbill. I've been waiting in the street for two hours for him to come down and pay me, and you've been up here tormenting the poor boy.

APISOGHOM AGHA: What's this all about? I owe him? Impossible.

MANUG AGHA: Did you hear? Impossible.

ACTOR: Sir, I didn't say that it was a debt. I merely said that I'd give him a box and get a pound for it.

PRINTER: Why did you deceive me, liar?

ACTOR: So the announcements wouldn't be delayed.

PRINTER: You think you can toy with me?

APISOGHOM AGHA: Do you think you can toy with him?

ACTOR: Why should I toy with you?

PRINTER: Wretch, deceiver, cheat, liar.

ACTOR: You're all those things.

PRINTER: You.

ACTOR: Not I, you.

(*A scuffle follows on the "not I, you" exchange between the* ACTOR *and the* PRINTER, *and* APISOGHOM AGHA *and* MANUG AGHA *succeed in separating them with great difficulty.*)

APISOGHOM AGHA (*when peace is restored*): Get out of the house, both of you. Go outside and fight.

PRINTER: What right do you have to interfere in our dispute? You can't throw me out. I want my due, and I can follow my debtor wherever he goes.

APISOGHOM AGHA (*to the* ACTOR): Get out.

ACTOR: How can I leave? You saw with your own eyes what he did.

PRINTER: I won't move from here until he leaves.

ACTOR: I can't leave until he goes away.

APISOGHOM AGHA: Then we'll leave, Manug Agha.

(*The* ACTOR *wraps himself around* APISOGHOM AGHA's *knees and begs him at least to lend him a pound.* APISOGHOM AGHA *resists as long as he can, but seeing no other way of escaping their clutches, grinds his teeth, pulls out a pound note and gives it to the* PRINTER *who thanks him and leaves. The* ACTOR *begs his forgiveness and follows.*)

What do you say to this, Manug Agha?

MANUG AGHA: There's nothing left to say, Apisoghom Agha.

APISOGHOM AGHA: Please go down and lock the door, and see to it that it's not opened.

MANUG AGHA: Very well.

APISOGHOM AGHA: I want to spend a quiet evening and think about what I must do.

MANUG AGHA: You've every right.

APISOGHOM AGHA: Hurry, hurry, or they'll keep coming.

MANUG AGHA: I'll go immediately. (MANUG AGHA *leaves.* APISOGHOM AGHA *lays his head on the pillow for some rest.*)

Scene 12

At the PHOTOGRAPHER's *Studio.* APISOGHOM AGHA *and* PHOTOGRAPHER.

(APISOGHOM AGHA *slept on the couch for a few hours. Judging from the sounds that exploded from his sleep however, it is obvious that he had not escaped the editors, teachers, and poets, who seemed to be provoking him to shout from time to time: "Get out, get lost, I've no money to give you." After three hours of such uneasy sleep, he suddenly opened his eyes and groaned: "Ah, dear God, have mercy. I can't even sleep in peace," as though an editor is squeezing his throat, threatening to choke him if he did not subscribe to his newspaper. In the morning, anxious to escape his tormentors, he decided to go to the* PHOTOGRAPHER's *studio to have his picture taken. The studio was not yet open, and* APISOGHOM AGHA *walked around the streets of Pera until four o'clock when, as per Turkish custom, it opened. He goes up a flight of stairs and into a room, decorated with photographs, where the* PHOTOGRAPHER *is sitting, reading.*)

PHOTOGRAPHER (*putting down his paper*): Good day, Apisoghom Agha, good day. Please step this way. (*He indicates to his Secretary to bring some coffee.*)

APISOGHOM AGHA: Let's take care of this matter quickly. I have some urgent business to transact with some very important people.

PHOTOGRAPHER: There'll be no delay.

APISOGHOM AGHA: I want the picture to be very impressive. I'll be seated in an armchair, with two servants ready to do my bidding, one of them a maid. Make it appear as though I'm on a farm, with crops showing off to one side and cows being milked on the other; sheep grazing here, and there some planting being done, and farther off some reaping, plowing, yogurt being made, watermelons gathered, butter churning, ducks swimming in the pond, trees being cut in the woods, wheat being transported in carts—everything that takes place on a farm should be part of the picture.

PHOTOGRAPHER: It's impossible to do all that. All I can do is perhaps have a couple of servants standing beside you.

APISOGHOM AGHA: Why is it impossible?

PHOTOGRAPHER: Because it can't be done.

APISOGHOM AGHA: How do you manage it for other important men?

PHOTOGRAPHER: They have their portrait taken sitting in an armchair or simply standing.

APISOGHOM AGHA: How can anyone tell whether they are important?

PHOTOGRAPHER: The picture will be large and glossy.

APISOGHOM AGHA: Mine will be that way, too?

PHOTOGRAPHER: By all means.

APISOGHOM AGHA: Standing or seated?

PHOTOGRAPHER: As you wish.

APISOGHOM AGHA: Which would be better?

PHOTOGRAPHER: Standing will suit you better.

APISOGHOM AGHA: All right. With my servants before me?

PHOTOGRAPHER: Yes.

APISOGHOM AGHA: I'll appear as though I'm scolding them, and they'll look properly penitent.

PHOTOGRAPHER: Wonderful.

APISOGHOM AGHA: I'll pretend I'm about to beat them, and then relent.

PHOTOGRAPHER: Excellent idea.

APISOGHOM AGHA: Are my clothes suitable?

PHOTOGRAPHER: They couldn't be better.

APISOGHOM AGHA: I've another watch, too; shall I hang it from the other side?

PHOTOGRAPHER: One watch is enough. Any more would be too much.

APISOGHOM AGHA: I paid fifty pounds for these clothes. How can anyone tell from the picture that the material is the finest and most expensive?

PHOTOGRAPHER: Don't worry. It'll be obvious.

APISOGHOM AGHA: How?

PHOTOGRAPHER: Don't worry about it.

APISOGHOM AGHA: I don't want people to think I'm wearing a cheap suit.

PHOTOGRAPHER: Don't let that bother you.

APISOGHOM AGHA: Well, if you're sure about it.

PHOTOGRAPHER: I'll get things ready in the next room. In a few minutes you can come in.

APISOGHOM AGHA: All right.

PHOTOGRAPHER: If you wish, we can call the barber next door to comb and fix your hair and beard, while you're waiting for me.

APISOGHOM AGHA: That's a good idea.

Scene 13

The same setting. APISOGHOM AGHA *and* BARBER

(*The* PHOTOGRAPHER *sends his Secretary to fetch the* BARBER *who comes in soon after, nodding and bowing his respects to* APISOGHOM AGHA.)

APISOGHOM AGHA: Come and fix this hair a little.

BARBER: It's our privilege.

APISOGHOM AGHA: Do a good job because I'm going to have my picture taken.

BARBER: On my honor.

APISOGHOM AGHA: I pay a great deal of attention to my head.

BARBER: And why shouldn't you, most honored sir? Ah, if someone like you didn't, who would? How I wish I had only that much to occupy my mind.

APISOGHOM AGHA: Come, get on with the work.

BARBER: I know how guilty I am for not having come to welcome you, but what could I do? Circumstances didn't permit me to perform that duty and so left me without the confidence to ask your most exalted being.

APISOGHOM AGHA: We can talk later. Just comb my hair, the man is waiting for me.

BARBER: Don't worry, he'll wait . . . (*continuing*) . . . to beseech your exalted being, if you would be so kind, for fifty or sixty pounds . . . after all, I'm one of our nation's servants, too.

APISOGHOM AGHA: What do you mean, fifty or sixty pounds?

BARBER: I beg you, don't be angry. Just a loan then. I have to send fifty or sixty pounds to my son in Paris so he can pay his debts, get his doctor's degree, and return here and work and, in a few years, return your money, with interest. But what's the use? I can't even venture to make such a request, because of my discourtesy in not coming and welcoming you properly. If I'd done that, I'd have dared to beg you to take care of this small matter. But since I failed so wretchedly in extending to you the basic courtesies, you've every right to reject my plea, in spite of my service as a devoted artisan of our nation.

APISOGHOM AGHA: I've no time to listen to that now. Do whatever you're supposed to do. What a strange city this is! "Hello, good day, give me money." God have mercy, it's risky just to greet someone. Everything has a limit, Effendi. I have to get out of this city as soon as possible. There's no other way.

Scene 14

The same setting. APISOGHOM AGHA *and* CLERGYMAN

(*A* CLERGYMAN *enters, somewhere between fifty and sixty, and commiserates with* APISOGHOM AGHA.)

CLERGYMAN: It appears they've angered the effendi.

APISOGHOM AGHA: It's unbearable, Father.

CLERGYMAN: Bless you. Though you don't know me, I know full well who you are. How are you? How is your honorable disposition?

APISOGHOM AGHA: Not so well, in fact.

CLERGYMAN: May God prevent it. With God's help may you soon be better. I wanted to see you privately for a moment. (*To the* BARBER) Would you please leave us alone? I'll speak on your behalf, too. I'll discuss your problems with the effendi and persuade him to help. (*To* APISOGHOM AGHA) Effendi, our barber, you know, is one of our people, too. Armenian blood flows in his veins. We can't ignore that. (*The* BARBER *leaves. He changes the subject.*) The reason for a special private meeting with you is to talk about your wanting to get married, and why shouldn't you want to get married? When I heard of it, I was extremely happy, and why shouldn't I be happy? People like you should get married and bless our nation with more fine, wealthy children. It seems you're looking for a suitable bride, and why shouldn't you look for a suitable bride? If I were in your place, I'd look for one, too. You want her to be well off, and why shouldn't you? Marrying someone who hasn't at least some money isn't a very good thing. Now I happen to know a few girls who are both very nice and very rich.

APISOGHOM AGHA: Thank you. We'll take a look at them someday. If you wish, you can wait a little. I'll have my picture taken, and we'll go. To tell the truth, I've no other business here. I came to find a wife and can only stay a few days. If I find one, I'll get married and leave with her. If I don't find one soon, I'll leave anyway because they don't leave me at peace here. I'm getting sick and tired of it.

CLERGYMAN: You're altogether justified. Times are bad, too, Effendi. An economic crisis is choking everything. The nation has many poor. I'll wait then, and we'll go together.

APISOGHOM AGHA: That worthless man came to fix my hair and—

PHOTOGRAPHER (*entering*): Please, come in now.

APISOGHOM AGHA: What about my hair?

PHOTOGRAPHER (*leading* APISOGHOM AGHA *into the sitting room*): No matter, I'll comb it.

{*Alone the* CLERGYMAN *begins turning some thoughts over in mind. But how can we divine what is turning over in his mind? From his expression, of course. Faces can often be very eloquent. The tongue, with rich and poor alike, is on the face as often as it is in the mouth. You can tell by looking at someone's face that "this man has come to ask me for money" or that "he has come to give me some money." There could be no mistaking the* CLERGYMAN's *expression: "What is the best way to get enough money for this winter's coal and wood from this man?" The* CLERGYMAN *is deep in such thoughts when the* BARBER *reenters.*}

Scene 15

The PHOTOGRAPHER's *waiting room.* BARBER *and* CLERGYMAN

BARBER: Father, you ruined my plan. If you hadn't butted in, I'd have squeezed a few pounds out of that man. He's a giver, they say, a giver. He's given some money to editors and teachers and God knows who else.

CLERGYMAN: But, my son, aren't they the ones who are making it impossible for poor people like us to get a little help from these visitors? Someone barely sets foot in the city before all the editors and teachers descend on him like the plague-damned abominations.

BARBER: What are we going to do now?

CLERGYMAN: I'll put in a good word for you. And you intercede for me. We ought to be able to put the touch on him.

BARBER: All right.

CLERGYMAN: He'll be coming out soon. I'll whisper to him to keep this barber content because he goes in and out of many rich homes, and he can, if he is so inclined, damage your prospects.

BARBER: What's he after?

CLERGYMAN: He's looking for a rich bride.

BARBER: Good. And I'll tell him to trust no one but the priest.

CLERGYMAN: Agreed.

BARBER: This is a good plan.

CLERGYMAN: I never saw anyone so naïve.

BARBER: He's gullible, all right. But they fleeced the man already, fleeced him good. We came very late.

Scene 16

The same setting. BARBER, CLERGYMAN, APISOGHOM AGHA, *then the* PHOTOGRAPHER

(APISOGHOM AGHA *returns from the sitting, jovial and happy.*)

BARBER: Pardon me, Apisoghom Agha, for bringing up that personal matter, but I thought that I could be of some service to you as well.

CLERGYMAN (*on cue*): Apisoghom Agha, you must be aware that our barber effendi is welcome in practically all the wealthy homes of the capital and knows all their eligible daughters.

APISOGHOM AGHA: You don't say?

CLERGYMAN: Yes. And he's a kindly, deserving man. Help him. He needs your support.

BARBER: If you're thinking of getting married, don't leave the side of our Reverend Father for even a minute. Those who've been married by him have always been happy. I'm delighted that you've entrusted your affair to so good and reliable a person as our priest. You can be sure that you'll be happy in your marriage.

CLERGYMAN:(*to the* BARBER): But you must help me, too.

BARBER: But what can I—

CLERGYMAN: Your cooperation is essential.

BARBER: Of course, I'm ready to do whatever I can.

CLERGYMAN: I'm grateful. After all, Apisoghom Agha isn't a stranger, he's our compatriot. He's come to be married. It's our duty to help him.

BARBER: Of course. I've no ill feeling toward Apisoghom Agha, especially since he's so kind and virtuous a man.

CLERGYMAN: It may be embarrassing to say it in his presence, but he's a remarkable man.

BARBER: A man of great honor.

CLERGYMAN: One look at him is enough to see the refinement oozing from every pore.

BARBER: Whoever says otherwise is my enemy.

CLERGYMAN: The thing is, whenever anyone asks about him, you must give him a warm recommendation.

BARBER: What else could I do?

CLERGYMAN: Apisoghom Agha isn't an ungrateful man. He'll reward you later.

BARBER: On my honor. Ah, if my son could only get his diploma.

PHOTOGRAPHER (*entering*): The pictures will be ready in a few days.

APISOGHOM AGHA: Very well. (*He goes out, accompanied by the* CLERGYMAN *and the* BARBER.)

Scene 17

Street outside the PHOTOGRAPHER'*s studio.* CLERGYMAN, APISOGHOM AGHA, *and* MATCHMAKER

(*The* MATCHMAKER *learns from the* LANDLADY *that the* CLERGYMAN *has gone to the* PHOTOGRAPHER'*s studio looking for* APISOGHOM AGHA. *She runs panting to the stu-*

dio, arriving at the very moment when the CLERGYMAN, *having cleverly gotten rid of the* BARBER, *is ingratiating himself with* APISOGHOM AGHA.)

CLERGYMAN: Forgive me for being so late in apprising you of the truth about the barber. This is a man altogether without shame. He grabs hold of everybody who comes to Constantinople and tries to wheedle money from them. A complete scoundrel. It's my duty, as a clergyman and confessor, to caution you about such people who ingratiate themselves with the wealthy, with the sole purpose of getting money from them. How I despise people like that!

APISOGHOM AGHA: I appreciate your concern and kindness.

CLERGYMAN: Don't pay any attention to such people.

APISOGHOM AGHA: I won't.

MATCHMAKER (*as soon as they are in range of her voice*): Father, what business do you have with Apisoghom Agha?

CLERGYMAN: A small matter.

MATCHMAKER: No. You'll have nothing at all to do with him. People should have some sense of shame. You tend to your own affairs, and let us take care of ours. Let's go, Apisoghom Agha.

CLERGYMAN (*pulling* APISOGHOM AGHA *by the arm*): No, control yourself a little. I've a small matter with Apisoghom Agha. Let's go, Apisoghom Agha.

MATCHMAKER (*pulling him by the other arm*): The way you're acting doesn't befit a clergyman.

CLERGYMAN (*continuing to pull on* APISOGHOM AGHA*'s arm*): Silence.

MATCHMAKER (*also pulling*): I won't be silent.

APISOGHOM AGHA: Let go of my arms.

MATCHMAKER: I won't. It's my right. I was here first.

CLERGYMAN: It's mine, we've already made arrangements.

MATCHMAKER: Do you want to make the man miserable just to get a few piasters? You don't know any girls.

CLERGYMAN: Don't shout. You think I'll leave this noble man to be robbed by you?

APISOGHOM AGHA: Why are you fighting? Aren't you ashamed of yourselves? I don't want a girl.

MATCHMAKER: That won't do at all. We're going to find a suitable girl for you. But if you let the priest take over, your name will be mud.

CLERGYMAN: On the contrary, what more honorable way is there to find a bride than through the intercession of a clergyman? It's time we were off, Apisoghom Agha.

MATCHMAKER: I won't let him go.

CLERGYMAN: We have to go, Apisoghom Agha.

MATCHMAKER: I won't let him go. I've already arranged for him to see some potential brides.

Scene 18

The same setting. MANUG AGHA *and* APISOGHOM AGHA

(*A small group of passersby gathers and watches with amusement.* MANUG AGHA *enters on an urgent mission to find* APISOGHOM AGHA, *sees him being pulled one way by the* MATCHMAKER *and the other way by the* CLERGYMAN, *frees him, severely reprimands the* MATCHMAKER *and the* CLERGYMAN, *and sends them off.*)

MANUG AGHA: Ah, it's your own fault. You encourage everybody to bilk you for what they can get.

APISOGHOM AGHA: Really?

MANUG AGHA: Why should I lie? If you want to get married, fine. I'll find some suitable prospects for you. You choose and marry the one you want.

APISOGHOM AGHA: I'd like that.

MANUG AGHA: I'll show you daughters from the finest families.

APISOGHOM AGHA: Show them to me.

MANUG AGHA: Finding a wife through a matchmaker is passé.

APISOGHOM AGHA: Is that so?

MANUG AGHA: It's even a little déclassé.

APISOGHOM AGHA: If that's the case, I won't do it.

MANUG AGHA: I'll find a girl you like.

APISOGHOM AGHA: I'd be very grateful.

MANUG AGHA: All you have to do is let me have fifty pounds now.

APISOGHOM AGHA: What! Why should I do that?

MANUG AGHA: Just a matter of fifty pounds.

APISOGHOM AGHA: What do you mean?

MANUG AGHA: For God's sake, if I ask for fifty pounds, there must be a good reason. Merciful God, I'm not going to take it and run.

APISOGHOM AGHA: You won't run off but—

MANUG AGHA: Are you afraid to give me fifty pounds? You owe me that much anyway. I've had so many expenses for you.

APISOGHOM AGHA: So many expenses? Like what?

MANUG AGHA: I'm not going to set them down item by item. My wife knows them. But let's forget about that now.

APISOGHOM AGHA: No, no, let's not forget about it. Fifty pounds? How many days have I—?

MANUG AGHA: I owe somebody money, and he embarrassed me today by demanding I pay up. If I don't, we'll be evicted from our home. The shame would be intolerable and wouldn't bring you any honor either. So give me the paltry fifty pounds now. We'll settle the account later.

APISOGHOM AGHA: I've never heard of anything so outrageous.

MANUG AGHA: When I find you a bride, I'll waive the fee. So give me the money now.

APISOGHOM AGHA: Why should I? What have I done to embarrass you financially?

MANUG AGHA: It's painful that you simply refuse to understand. Just do as I tell you. Why won't you give me fifty pounds?

APISOGHOM AGHA: I won't. And I'll leave your house at once.

(*They continue to walk a few more paces and pause again.*)

MANUG AGHA: Is fifty pounds such a big amount that you refuse to part with it? I never expected this of you.

APISOGHOM AGHA: Expect it.

MANUG AGHA: I didn't think that a man of such refinement and delicacy would make such an issue of fifty pounds.

APISOGHOM AGHA: I'll take my trunks and leave.

MANUG AGHA: You can leave, but only after paying me fifty pounds.

APISOGHOM AGHA: I won't give it to you.

MANUG AGHA: Yes, you will.

(APISOGHOM AGHA *runs offstage with* MANUG AGHA *in pursuit.*)

Scene 19

MANUG AGHA's *house on Flower Street.* APISOGHOM AGHA *and the* LANDLADY

APISOGHOM AGHA (*upon entering and seeing the* CLERGYMAN, *the* BARBER, *and the* MATCHMAKER *waiting for him, he shouts.*): Go away, go away. I don't want to see your faces. (*He knocks on the door, enters, climbs to his room, and begins packing his trunks while the* LANDLADY *looks on in amazement.*)

LANDLADY: Why are you packing, Apisoghom Agha?

APISOGHOM AGHA: I'm leaving. I can't stay here another minute. I changed my mind. I'm not going to get married.

LANDLADY: Did they upset you?

APISOGHOM AGHA: No.

LANDLADY: Why are you angry then?

APISOGHOM AGHA: I'm not angry.

LANDLADY: Dear Apisoghom Agha, Manug Agha was going to ask you for fifty pounds. Did he?

APISOGHOM AGHA: He did.

LANDLADY: I'm sorry, but a serious mistake has been made.

APISOGHOM AGHA: A mistake? Ah, I thought it was rather strange.

LANDLADY: Yes. It wasn't fifty pounds he should have asked for, but one hundred and fifty. Do this kindness for us. You're a man of great refinement. Your generosity can free us from debt.

APISOGHOM AGHA: I've had it with the lot of you.

{*Almost in a single motion,* APISOGHOM AGHA *binds his trunks, rushes into the street, brings back three* PORTERS *and has his trunks removed. The* BARBER, *the* CLERGY-MAN, *the* MATCHMAKER, *and* MANUG AGHA *follow him to the hotel and leave only after he enters, all except* MANUG AGHA, *who accompanies* APISOGHOM AGHA *in order to settle their accounts. From that moment, no one has seen* APISOGHOM AGHA. *But for several weeks, editors, authors, poets with packages stuffed under their arms were seen regularly clustered in front of the same hotel. And so the man who came to Constantinople to get married could not find time to see even one girl before he escaped in a frenzy. But he left an indelible impression on our literary men. When two or three of these writers get together, they muse on "how we let this* APISOGHOM AGHA *get away from us," and they laugh a little. And when they find themselves in financial difficulties, "God send us* APISOGHOM AGHA," *they pray, and then add, "Ask of Apisoghom Agha, and it shall be given you." The wealthy also have reason to remember* APISOGHOM AGHA, *especially when an intellectual approaches one of them for financial help, pointedly saying, "We're not* APISOGHOM AGHA." *As for this work, it was created not so much for the purpose of denigrating our authors, editors, poets, and intellectuals as much as to describe for future generations the deplorable circumstances in which the writers and intellectuals of our time existed, and the shocking indifference of our wealthy to literature and the arts.*}

ALEKSANDR SHIRVANZADE

In 1916 Maxim Gorki wrote an admiring letter to Shirvanzade, in which, with a touch of deference for a man ten years his senior, he says: "I heard your name for the first time in 1892 in Tiflis, and then in 1897 when I was in the Metekhi prison. You see! We're old acquaintances."[1]

Born on April 18, 1858, into a tailor's family from the town of Shamakh in the province of Shirvan in what is now the Republic of Azerbaijan as Aleksandr Movsesian, he adopted the literary pseudonym Shirvanzade (son of Shirvan) to indicate his affinity with his native province. He obtained his earliest education at a local Protestant Armenian school, then at the parochial school, after which he progressed to the regional Russian school. At about seventeen he left his hometown to take up employment as a clerk and bookkeeper in Baku, the city on the Caspian whose fortunes were beginning to rise as a result of the boom in oil production.

There he lived with his maternal aunt, whose son, Nerses, had contacts with progressive thinkers and thus, in part, influenced the writer's intellectual development. Family connections on his father's side assisted him in securing his first job with a rich Armenian landowner. Thereafter he was employed

---

1. Arshavir B. Kaghtzrouni, ed., *Alexandre Shirvanzade* (New York: Armenian National Council of America, 1959), p. 17.

as a court clerk and then as a bookkeeper in the offices of a petroleum company. In addition, he functioned as librarian for the recently opened reading room of the Armenian Benevolent Society, immersing himself in Armenian and Russian literature. He read with particular interest the works of Stendahl, Balzac, Flaubert, Zola, and Shakespeare, which was his greatest love, as he relates in his memoirs. He also participated in amateur dramatics and wrote the vaudeville *Tanu gogh* [Cat burglar]. Seeing firsthand the social effects of industrialized oil production, he turned his shock and anger into a literature of protest that was strikingly poignant and realistic.

Like Gorki, Shirvanzade wrote in many genres—novels, plays, short stories, newspaper articles—always with an avowedly strong social commitment. During this period Shirvanzade embarked on his career in journalism. He began by submitting articles to Tiflis papers like the nationalist *Meghu Hayastani* [Bee of Armenia], the progressive *Mshak* [Yeoman], and the reform-minded *Murch* [Hammer], then became secretary of the editorial board of the literary and cultural *Artsagank* [Echo], rising to the post of assistant editor (1889–95). His first short story, *Fire in the Oil Works* (1883), already expressed his social outrage at the inhumanity of the Baku managerial class toward their workforce. His critique of the negative impact of industrialization informed a series of novellas (e.g., *Khnamatar* [Caretaker], 1884; *Fatman and Asad*, 1888; *Tasnuhing tari ants* [Fifteen years later], 1890; and later novels (e.g., *Arsen Dimaksian*, 1893). Parallel with this, the writer also exposed the backwardness and superstition prevalent in the provincial towns of the region in his novels *Namus* [Honor] (1885) and *Tsawagare* [The epileptic] (1894), both of which he subsequently turned into plays. All these works were written in a realistic mode which he defined and defended in his apologia *Im kritikosnerin* [To my critics] (1891).

This first phase of Shirvanzade's career as an author is also marked by his increasing politicization, leading to his membership of the Hnchakian (Social Revolutionary) Party and his protests against the Hamidian massacres perpetrated on the Armenian community in the Ottoman Empire. While on a trip to Russia in 1895 to raise funds for the refugees, he was arrested and incarcerated in Tiflis's Metekhi prison, to which Gorki refers in his letter cited above. That was the matrix of his masterpiece *Kaos* [Chaos] (1896–97), the natural culmination of this initial burst of productivity. It offers the first full-blown description of the capitalist city that Baku had become, with its unrestrained exploitation of the working classes for quick profit.

Hardly was the book complete when he was again imprisoned, this time in Odessa (1898–99), as reflected in his novelette *Artiste* [The artist] (1901). He was to remain under the surveillance of the secret police until 1917. On his return to Baku, he became increasingly interested in women's issues, as evinced by his treatment of women's suffrage in his play *Evgine* (1901) and the novel *Vardan Ahrumian*, as well as his play *Uner irawunk* [Did she have the right?] (1902). The two forces, which had so far preoccupied him, capitalism and feminism, clash power-fully in his extremely polished drama *Patui hamar* [For the sake of honor] (1904). Like his narrative works, his plays were drawn from life as he saw it. Consequently he brought the realistic school of Armenian dramaturgy, promoted by Gabriel Sun-dukian, to full fruition.

Thereafter Shirvanzade moved to Paris (1905–10), where for a time, it has been argued, he became somewhat more open to liberal ideas. This period saw the ap-pearance of his political drama *Kortsanwatse* [Ruined] (1909). Returning to Tran-scaucasia, he commented on current events in the comedy *Sharlatane* [The char-latan] (1912) and the more serious play *Arhawirki Orerin* [In the days of terror] (1917). Two years later he again went abroad, this time for medical treatment, first visiting Constantinople (1919) and Smyrna, then New York (1923–24). After a fur-ther brief stay in Paris, he finally established himself on his native soil in 1926 and began work on his final play, the comedy *Morgani khnamin* [Morgan's in-law]. It focuses on capitalist ex-patriots in Europe who dream of repossessing their proper-ties, now appropriated by the state. His last years were spent preparing his complete works for publication and the finalization of his two-volume memoirs in novelistic form *Keanki bovits* [From the crucible of life].

During his life Shirvanzade was the recipient of various tributes. Already in his letter of 1916, alluded to above, Gorki had noted that "his works were known and read not only in the Caucasus but also in England, in the Scandinavian Peninsula, and Italy." On the newly established Erevan stage his dramatic legacy formed "one of the cornerstones in the growth and development of the Armenian theater," be-ginning with a performance of his *For the Sake of Honor* in 1923.[2] Recognizing the power of the cutting realism in his play *Namus*, Beknazaryan transformed the work into the first Armenian silent feature film at the Haykino studios in 1925. Several others later appeared on screen, notably *Kaos* in 1973. In 1934, one year before his death, he was invited to the First Congress of Soviet Writers in Moscow, and there-after was awarded the title of "Peoples' Writer" of Armenia and Azerbaijan. In all modes—film, novel, and drama—Shirvanzade still has the power to excite appre-ciative interest.

N.P.

---

2. In Ibid., *Two Thousand Years of the Armenian Theater* [An English digest of Professor Georg Goyan's monumental work in Russian, with an introductory address by Rev. Charles A. Vertanes and a supplementary essay by V. Vardan] (New York: Armenian Exposition Committee, 1954), p. 8.

FOR THE SAKE OF HONOR

(PATUI HAMAR, 1904)

Translated by Nishan Parlakian

CAST OF CHARACTERS

ANDREAS ELIZBARIAN: A man of fifty-five, well-built, short-cropped graying hair, sparse beard, and ruddy complexion; wealthy, a pillar of his local community.

ERANUHI: ANDREAS's wife, forty-six (but looks older), a priest's daughter, pale and thin, yet still attractive.

BAGRAT: The older son, twenty-seven, positive in his manner and of a practical and quick disposition.

SUREN: The younger son, twenty-three, a smart dresser, hearty and pleasant, but with traces of past excesses.

ROZALIA: The older daughter, twenty-four, not bad-looking but smug and conceited; follows the current fashions without much taste.

MARGARIT: The younger daughter, twenty-two, resembles her mother but is even more attractive; thoughtful, expressive eyes; dresses modestly but in good taste.

SAGHATEL: ERANUHI's brother and ANDREAS's trusted partner, about fifty; thick-skinned with a keen, crafty look about him; clean-shaven with tufted sideburns; wears baggy trousers, black satin shirt, oversized vest trimmed with gold watch chain and gold belt; wears thick-soled shoes; constantly fingers his large green "worry" beads.

ARTASHES OTARIAN: Son of ANDREAS's deceased partner and his ward, about twenty-seven, quiet and thoughtful, always dressed in black, nervously tightens jaw muscles under pressure.

ARISTAKES KARINIAN: ANDREAS's bookkeeper, forty-two, but much older looking; the typical loyal employee.

VARDAN: A young employee in ELIZBARIAN's office, speaks in the Shamakh dialect.

ZARUHI: A servant girl in the ELIZBARIAN home.

The action, which is of a time approaching the present, takes place in the ELIZBARIAN *home.*

ACT 1

A sitting room/office used by ANDREAS *and* BAGRAT ELIZBARIAN *set between the library and the bedrooms in the upper story of the house. It is a medium-sized room. At right, two windows look out onto the street. Between them is* ANDREAS's *desk. On it are papers and documents, a phone, and electric lamp. Near the desk at the wall a large arm chair; on the other side of the desk a plain chair. There are two doors in the upstage wall, one at center, the other at far left. In left wall, doors that lead to the living quarters. Near these doors,* BAGRAT's *desk with documents, pencils, engineering books, and so on. A strongbox behind. On the right, a stove. Chairs at the wall. A rug covers the floor at right. The windows are curtained.*

Scene 1

SAGHATEL *and* KARINIAN

(The curtain rises as SAGHATEL, *standing by* ANDREAS's *desk, speaks into the telephone. The middle doors are open.* KARINIAN *enters and begins to look about* ANDREAS's *desk. When these doors are open a bookkeeper's desk can be seen [with the young bookkeeper beside it]. From time to time, there appear other employees and visitors who pass to and fro in an occupied manner until the closing of the office. The sound of office machines can be heard, as well as the occasional ringing of the telephone.)*

SAGHATEL *(telephoning)*: What can I do for you? Yes, he'll be back, soon. Huh? I can't hear. Yes. Good. Send it. Good-bye. *(The bell rings and he hangs up.)* What an invention—this telephone! Good for business! Now, what was I saying, Aristakes? After you finish what you're doing, start on Bagrat's accounts. *(Derisively)* Our Mr. Engineer wants to know what his factory is costing him.

KARINIAN: But you haven't entered your expenses with the bookkeepers yet. Mr. Bagrat wants receipts for every item of expense.

SAGHATEL: That's what he's all about, your Mr. Bagrat—receipts. I've worked with Andreas Elizbarian all these years handling receipts enough. Yes, I've worked faithfully. The old man trusts me. The son should trust me, too. (*Calmly*) What are you looking for?

KARINIAN: The unpaid bill made out to the Mnatsakanians. (*He stops looking.*)

SAGHATEL: Hey, angel face. You've been working here all this time and you don't know that Andreas Elizbarian never leaves important papers on his desk.

KARINIAN: Of course. Everyone's a born thief for Elizbarian.

SAGHATEL: That's right. He thinks people will steal anything they can get their hands on. And he's right. There are no honest men on the face of the earth. We're all born thieves (*He fingers his beads, muttering, as he goes to* KARINIAN.)

KARINIAN: You know, there is such a thing as conscience in the world.

SAGHATEL: Eh? You and your conscience. If you like it, eat it. But it won't fill your belly.

KARINIAN: For some it's indigestible.

SAGHATEL: What about you? A forty-two-year-old man. Look at you: white-haired, bent over. What has saying "conscience, conscience" netted you? Tell me, if you dropped dead this minute, would your wife find some money in your pockets?

KARINIAN: Maybe not, but I'd have died in peace.

SAGHATEL (*bitterly derisive*): Sure. Peace for you. Leaving your children hungry in the streets. Conscience is a good thing. Too bad it's the slave of money and wears you out day after day. Oh yes, listen: I wanted to ask you. Has Otarian been here, today?

KARINIAN: No.

SAGHATEL: Thank God. (*He fingers his beads and turns away.*)

KARINIAN: Tell me, what's going on between the young man and Mr. Andreas?

SAGHATEL: It's a long story. And really not our business.

Scene 2

Same and SUREN

(SUREN *enters left, with hat and coat.*)

SUREN: Is Poppa home? That's just as well. (*To* SAGHATEL) Uncle, for God's sake, give me three hundred rubles, right away.

SAGHATEL (*putting his beads in his pocket*): Huh! How's that? What's the matter? You seem angry.

SUREN: No time for questions. What I need is three hundred rubles, cash.

KARINIAN: Gambling. You've lost again.

SAGHATEL: He calls them business transactions. Either gambling or some sweet young ladies.

SUREN (*angry at* KARINIAN): Listen, Mr. Ink-licker, mind your own business. I don't need your lectures. Uncle, if I don't get three hundred rubles right away, I'm finished, disgraced. It's a question of honor. If you love me, don't deny me.

SAGHATEL: It isn't a question of love, my boy. I don't have the money. What can I do? Your brother runs your father's business, now. You know that. (*He takes out his beads.*)

SUREN: My brother, my brother. Always spoiling things. But, we'll see. One day, I'll bite him where it hurts.

SAGHATEL: Hey, he's not the kind to be afraid of your teeth.

SUREN (*impatiently*): Are you lending me the money or not?

SAGHATEL: What can I do? Look. There's the box and there you are. Help yourself. Why do you bother me?

SUREN: Give me the key.

SAGHATEL (*sighing*): My boy, I don't have it. I'm not the keeper of the gates of paradise. Anyway, between you and me, there's nothing in that box except receipts and checks. That's your brother's new system. In the old days, that box always had ten to twenty thousand in it. Now, your brother keeps everything in the bank.

KARINIAN: Your brother says that you have to keep both mind and money in circulation.

SUREN: Okay, then, lend me your money.

SAGHATEL: My boy, where would I have money? I'm only a poor employee.

SUREN: Stop singing that old song. You've got money in the soles of your shoes.

SAGHATEL: God, spare me this!

SUREN: Stop muttering your old father's proverbs. You're as much like him as I am like St. Paul. Let me see your wallet—come on.

SAGHATEL: How do I get rid of him? (*He patiently puts the beads in his pocket and slowly takes out a worn, almost filthy leather wallet.*) I don't have a hundred rubles. (*He looks into the wallet with averted face.*) Not even . . . fifty.

SUREN: Give me the wallet. (*He grabs it.*)

SAGHATEL (*alarmed*): What are you doing?

SUREN: What a piece of filth! (*He begins to look through the wallet, pulling out articles one by one.*) You name it; it's here. Look at this. Old receipts. Bank notes. Labels.

SAGHATEL: You're shameless.

SUREN (*taking out a letter*): What's this? A letter on pink paper in a woman's handwriting and scented.

SAGHATEL (*ashamed before* KARINIAN) That's enough; we're not alone.

SUREN (*taking out a piece of fabric from the fold of the letter*): Here's the response to the letter. And what else have we? Bless the Lord. Drug prescriptions, eyeglass prescriptions, herbs. A whole pharmacy, by God. All we need is the doctor. Tell us what ails you so we can cure you. Aha! Here we have it. Three hundred, four hundred, a thousand!

SAGHATEL (*Uneasy, he tries to grab the wallet.*): This is out and out stealing. You see, Aristakes, in broad daylight.

KARINIAN: That's the way to rob! Not the way you do it in dribs and drabs.

SUREN: Don't worry. I won't take more than one, two, three. (*He puts the money into his pocket and returns the wallet.*) Take your wallet! It stinks like cheap oil.

SAGHATEL (*putting the wallet away*): I'm lucky I got off so lightly.

SUREN: Thanks. Now, my honor is saved. My creditors wouldn't let me gamble on credit anymore. I've got to be going. (*He starts to leave.*)

SAGHATEL: What about an IOU?

SUREN: You make it out and I'll sign it. But mind, no exorbitant interest. (*He walks into the other room.*)

(KARINIAN *shakes his head and enters the far office.*)

Scene 3

SUREN, ERANUHI, *and* SAGHATEL

(ERANUHI *enters at doors left, without a hat. She is agitated.*)

ERANUHI: Stay. Don't go.

SUREN (*He stops and waits.*): Eh, Mama, enough. How far are you going to go with your crying and complaining? I'm a sensitive man.

ERANUHI (*to* SAGHATEL): Did you give him money?

SUREN: Yes, Mama. I found your brother to be kinder than you and my brother.

ERANUHI: Take it back, Saghatel. Take it back. Money has ruined him . . . put him into the streets.

SUREN: All right, Mama. This is no time to sing your old song. They'll hear you in the accounting office. (*He shuts the doors to the office.*)

ERANUHI: Let them hear. Who doesn't know by this time that you are no son to me? You are God's punishment.

SUREN: Why? Because I want to live the way my friends live?

SAGHATEL: You mean like a prodigal son? (*Aside*) My God, what did I say?

SUREN: Uncle, don't meddle in my affairs. Your job is to keep my father's books and eat spinach.

SAGHATEL (*aside*): He put you in your place, Saghatel.

SUREN: And you. Mama, take care of your other son. He's going to end up worse than I am. Don't fool yourself. Our money's dirty. Wasting it's no sin. You'd better believe it, sweet Mother. And don't expect me for lunch. (*He goes into the other room.*)

Scene 4

ERANUHI *and* SAGHATEL

ERANUHI (weakened, sitting on a chair): They're torturing me. They're slaughtering me with a broken knife. He takes a revolver and puts it to his brother's chest. "Give me money or I'll kill you." It was too much. I could hardly see. I thought it was the end. And I don't know how I separated them. And women are supposed to envy me for being a rich man's wife.

SAGHATEL: Forget it. If one son is prodigal, the other is good. Whatever one destroys, the other builds.

ERANUHI: Eh. I don't want a destroyer or builder. For one, money is the grave. For the other, well . . . he's got his father's curse. Both are beyond God's path.

SAGHATEL: Bless the hands of the money minter. Is there anything sweeter in the world than money?

ERANUHI: Hedonist. You have no God. You worship Mammon.

SAGHATEL: Eh. Now you're echoing father's words.

ERANUHI: May light fall on his grave. He used to say money was created by the devil's hands so men could buy and sell themselves to hell.

SAGHATEL: He used to say that because he was a priest. We're in this world. What's it to us?

ERANUHI: Fear the judgment day, Saghatel. Don't worship money.

SAGHATEL: Sister, God's punishment and His goodness are of this world. There is no greater judgment.

ERANUHI (*fearful*): There is, you heretic. There is.

SAGHATEL: All right. So I'm a heretic. But ask your older son. See what he says. Luckless men have thought up such things to comfort their burned-out hearts. That's what your son says, do you hear? He says that's the voice of scientific knowledge.

ERANUHI: Curse your knowledge.

SAGHATEL: Why, because it gives us electric light instead of candlelight? Tell me, please, were the railroad, ocean steamer, telegraph, telephone, and gramophone invented through knowledge or by your priests?

ERANUHI: They know what they're talking about when they say a priest's son is unfaithful.

SAGHATEL: Ah, Eranuh, you're fifty years behind the times. Come to your senses.

See how other rich women live. They eat, drink, and enjoy themselves. Every year they travel. Whereas you . . . What judgment! (*Change of tone*) Your youngest daughter, Margarit, is just as bad. She thinks she's just invented something: preaching honesty. Yesterday she started reading me the catechism. "Uncle, people ought to be guided by truth."

ERANUHI: That's a bad thing to say, eh?

SAGHATEL: You know, my dear, when was there ever a man in this town more honest than our father? But what did he leave us? Nothing but poverty and hunger. Right after he died, we had to start looking about for handouts. Thank God, you were beautiful. Luck brought you to this house. What if Elizbarian hadn't married you? Father didn't teach me a trade. He wanted me to become a priest, too. To go hungry like him. No, Sister, I don't admire you or Margarit. You don't know how to live. Your older daughter is something else. She gives me joy. She tears out the mouth of the world. Do you see how she keeps this house in order? How chic she keeps it. You certainly don't look like a millionaire's wife. But let's drop this. Isn't that Andreas's voice?

Scene 5

Same and ANDREAS

(ANDREAS *appears in the office doors with hat and coat, one foot on the threshold talking back into the office.*)

ANDREAS: Tell them I'm not here. I know why those two fellows came here with their blessings. Get them out of here. And then close the office. Go to lunch. I won't need you till early evening. (*He enters, closing the doors behind him.*)

SAGHATEL: Who were they?

ANDREAS: The nation's vultures. You'd think I was running a public welfare office. As if I don't know whom to help and whom not to help. They're the local unemployed. They've gathered together and are going around from door to door. They want money for the workhouse. (*He gives coat, hat, and cane to* SAGHATEL. *He is dressed modishly. On his vest he carries a gold watch chain. On his right hand, he wears a big diamond ring.*) Don't I have my own workhouse? A working man has his own work and his own house for it. They collect the indolent and worthless and want them fed for free. And that's supposed to save the nation.

SAGHATEL: The words of a wise man. (SAGHATEL *takes the coat and cane into the adjoining room and returns.*)

(ANDREAS *sits at his desk and at that moment sees* ERANUHI.)

ANDREAS: Ah. You're here. Why the raised eyebrows? (*Irritated*) Don't start your doomsday preaching. Things are dark enough without you.

ERANUHI: It's a sin to deny those who come in need.

ANDREAS (*bitterly, ironically*): Hah, millionaire's daughter. Good for you. If that's the way it is, make them a donation from your dowry or from the great inheritance your father left you.

ERANUHI (*standing*): You always throw my father's poverty in my face.

ANDREAS: Didn't he always preach: "Do good." He had nothing of his own; and from others he was always calling for "goodness." What is goodness? Man is an animal. If you see him stuck in the mud, step on him. Push him in deeper. Never reach for his hand to pull him out. (*Silence. Changing his tone. To* SAGHATEL) Has that young man come?

SAGHATEL: Not yet.

ANDREAS: Why are you standing there, gaping? What do you want from me?

ERANUHI (*sighing*): Nothing.

ANDREAS: Thank God. I thought you were going to insult me.

ERANUHI: When have I ever insulted you?

ANDREAS: When? You've been insulting me without a letup for thirty years and you know it. You are my number-one enemy. (*He stands and walks to and fro.*)

ERANUHI: What do you mean? How am I your enemy?

ANDREAS: How? By your thoughts. You never think well of anything I do. (*Silence*) What has Otarian spoken to you about?

ERANUHI: Artashes? Nothing. Whatever he has said to you, he's said to me.

ANDREAS: What do you think? What kind of young man is he?

ERANUHI: He's a fine young man, a fine person. Modest, good—

ANDREAS: All right, all right, don't drag it on. Your praise is excessive . . .

(ERANUHI *sighs.*)

ANDREAS (*irritated*): Listen, I've told you a thousand times. I don't want any of your damn sighing and your "Oh my's." All your damned fearfulness. On your face, in your eyes. I'm sick of your insults. Your complaining infuriates me. You're always after me like a shadow, to see if I make a wrong move. Who do I say no to? Who do I overcharge? Who have I short-changed? Let me alone. What are you, my conscience? I don't need your eyeing me all the time. I have conscience, spirit, and God within me.

ERANUHI (*puzzled*): I can't understand anything you say.

ANDREAS: Oh, you understand everything. (*He looks at his watch uneasily.*) It's two o'clock. That young man hasn't come.

ERANUHI (*carefully*) Are you at home?

ANDREAS: Of course. What sort of question is that?

ERANUHI (*pensively*): Who knows what's on your mind?

ANDREAS: Ah, do you see? Behind that "who knows" the devil lurks. Insults, always insults. Like a snakebite. Get out! I've been hungry as a dog all morning. Prepare lunch and set a place for Artashes. I'm asking him to join us. Treat him well. It's important. If Bagrat is home, send him in here.

(ERANUHI *exists left*.)

Scene 6

ANDREAS *and* SAGHATEL

ANDREAS (*quietly*): Your sister knows everything. She must be kept from ruining everything.

SAGHATEL: If you don't stop treating her the way you do, you're the one who's going to ruin things.

ANDREAS: You're right. Sometimes I just lose control. What can I do? I've been irritated since this morning. People are starting to talk about me. Just being jealous isn't enough for them. They have to envy Andreas Petros Elizbarian's rising star. My house and lands cause mental anguish in many people. (*Silence*) Are the office workers gone?

SAGHATEL (*looking into the office*): They're gone.

ANDREAS (*muttering while pacing to and fro*): I know what he's thinking. "Half of Elizbarian's houses and properties are mine. No more, no less." (*Silence*) From time to time, I myself think it. But how can I give him half of everything with my eyes open. What would people say? "You bought the properties in partnership with my father." Yes, it's true, but when?

SAGHATEL: In patriarch Noah's times.

ANDREAS: That's right. We were partners. But didn't I put the money to work? I did it. I, Andreas Elizbarian. I, Elizbarian's grandson, made all this with intelligence and sweat, investing my ability and talent, my name and reputation. For fifteen years I served as an apprentice to Agha Musiel. I took insults, spit, and dirt. I lived a dog's life. Finally, I got hold of a small sum of money. That's when I came to know Arakel Otarian.

SAGHATEL: Heh, I see it in my mind like a dream. In the old market. You had a grocery. You used to sell vegetables, pickles. You used to buy fish to sell at Easter.

ANDREAS: What can I say? Arakel was intelligent. But if I had let myself be guided by his thinking, we'd be paupers now. He had no smell for things. I said to him over and over again, "Arakel, let's buy those cheap properties; in time, they'll turn to gold." We started to buy some marshy garbage dumps for as little as fifty kopecks. Arakel didn't want to. I insisted. I made my fortune. It's mine. Only mine. Now that bastard comes along and says, "Give me half." Am I that insane? If I'm crazy, why haven't they locked me up in an asylum? (*Irritated*) Welcome! Here's what you get for your benevolence. I raised him as an adopted son in memory of his father, I educated him to be a gentleman and supported his mother and sisters, and this is what I get for my troubles. Blind ingratitude.

SAGHATEL: Fine. Don't get excited. One way or another, we'll make a deal and send him on his way.

ANDREAS: That's right. We've got to make a deal. I can't afford to go to court with him. He'll have me in some stinking lawyer's hands . . . take it or leave it.

VARDAN (*He enters from the anteroom dressed in a yellow and black peasant costume with silver belt. He speaks carelessly, in the accent of Shamakh.*): Artashes has come. He wants to see you now.

ANDREAS: He's welcome.

(VARDAN *leaves.*)

ANDREAS: SAGHATEL, stay in the office a while and come in later.

(SAGHATEL *enters the office, closing the door behind him.* ANDREAS *sits in a chair girding his strength and trying to appear pleasant.*)

Scene 7

ANDREAS, OTARIAN, *later* BAGRAT, *still later* SAGHATEL

(OTARIAN *enters from the anteroom bowing to greet* ANDREAS.)

ANDREAS (*affectionately*): Welcome, Son. It's been quite some time. Have you forgotten us?

OTARIAN (*shaking* ANDREAS's *hand*): I was at your house yesterday.

ANDREAS: Ah, but they didn't tell me. Sit. Today you'll have lunch with us. Let's talk a little. Then we'll go in. Have you found work?

OTARIAN (*sitting near* ANDREAS's *desk, facing out*): Private lessons.

(BAGRAT *enters at doors left, wearing boots and a working jacket. He looks at* OTARIAN. *Shaking his head, he appears indifferent. He sits at desk left and immediately is occupied with work. He draws with a compass while still attending to the conversation.*)

ANDREAS: Lessons? After all that education. Teaching?

OTARIAN: What can I do, Mr. Andreas? For the time being, I have to.

ANDREAS: But that's not for you. It can't be enough. My son, we'll have to find a place for you in our business. What do you say, Bagrat? Maybe, an executive position in your factory. Something appropriate, of course.

BAGRAT (*cutting*): My factory's only half-built.

OTARIAN: Thanks, Mr. Andreas. I don't think I want to work for anybody. In any case, if I did, it wouldn't be for your son.

ANDREAS: Why is that?

BAGRAT (*bitter tone, without interrupting his work*): He wouldn't want his lily-white plumes to get blackened with bourgeois work. He's an idealist.

ANDREAS: You're friends! I don't understand why you have to bait each other this way.

BAGRAT (*ironically*): Friends, huh. No, Father, it's never been friendship.

ANDREAS (*scolding*): Bagrat!

BAGRAT (*throwing the pencil and compass down*): Father, I think it's about time you talked straight with this fellow. What does he want? What's he after with you?

ANDREAS (*firmly*): That's not your concern. Mind your own business.

BAGRAT (*standing*): Please, Father. Don't expect me to say nothing. It's an attack on our name, on our honor. And from someone who is still wearing the clothes we bought him.

OTARIAN (*He stands, emotionally, while still controlling himself.*): Mr. Andreas, control your son. I don't want to be forced to argue with him.

BAGRAT: All right, then; tell me what you want of us.

ANDREAS (*irritated*): I told you, that's not your business. Keep out of it.

BAGRAT: But, Father, I'm not going to be put down like that. I just want to ask him a few things. (*Turning to* OTARIAN) Have we been generous with you or not?

OTARIAN (*controlled*): Yes.

BAGRAT: Who has always provided for you and educated you?

OTARIAN (*controlled*): Your father.

BAGRAT: You confess it, and you still dare to show ingratitude. You heard him, Father. And you expect me to take his impudence.

ANDREAS: I told you, it's not your business. You don't understand.

OTARIAN (*to* BAGRAT) Listen, sir. I really didn't come here to talk about any of this. But if that's what you want, I 'll speak. Sure, I was raised by the Elizbarians. You looked out for me and protected me, for nine years: my mother and sisters, too. But how? Only I know that. How I felt all those years. You poisoned every penny you touched before you gave it to us.

ANDREAS: Did I so much as once flaunt my good deeds in your face?

OTARIAN: The question is, did you ever trouble yourself to discuss my condition with me? You were outwardly polite. But what you didn't say with words you said with your eyes, gestures, movements. You denied my self-esteem when I had to ask for help. You poisoned my self-respect.

BAGRAT (*ironically*): It's amazing! For years you have said nothing and now you speak.

OTARIAN: I kept silent to spare my mother and sisters. If I angered you, you would have denied them a piece of bread. Inside, I said: "I'll take these insults now and then one day I'll pay the Elizbarians back, and be free." My mother was silent, too. But what kind of silence? (*To* ANDREAS) Giving her twenty-five rubles a month, you insulted her twenty-five times. "You've spent too much. Live in cheaper places, on lower floors, in basements. Take in sewing and laundry. Send your daughters out to do housecleaning."

ANDREAS (*impatient*): I beg your pardon! (*Aside*) Good Lord.

OTARIAN: One day you went so far as to suggest that she go into a poorhouse. Your words pierced her heart like needles. My sisters can't think of it without crying. Why did you do it? Who was my mother? Wasn't she your partner's widow? As rich as you? When she wept out the whole story, my blood froze. I felt helpless, beside myself. I wanted revenge and couldn't find the way. That's when my mother showed me what I—

ANDREAS: She told you I had robbed your father. Yes, of course. Sure.

BAGRAT: She turned on her benefactor; she defamed him.

OTARIAN (*paying no attention to* BAGRAT): Yes, sir. She told me my father's words at the end. "I'm dying in poverty. My partner robbed me. Here are the papers. Give them to my son when he's older and can understand."

ANDREAS (*excited*): Papers? What papers?

OTARIAN: Signed agreements between partners which prove that half your holdings belong to me. You took advantage of my father's illness; you tricked him again and again till you turned everything in the partnership into your name.

ANDREAS (*hurt*): That's a lie! Whatever I have, I have legally, through notarized documents.

OTARIAN: Yes, but without payment of a kopeck. You've been able to twist the laws. And my father's papers will prove that everything I say is true.

BAGRAT (*furious*): Get out of here, you liar!

OTARIAN (*proudly furious*): Sir, think of your father—

ANDREAS (*Slamming the table, he rises.*): Silence. You infuriate me.

(SAGHATEL *enters.*)

BAGRAT: But he wants to dishonor you. He called you a thief.

ANDREAS (*controlling himself*): Let him talk. Who believes him? He's young. He doesn't understand anything. He's excited. (*Turning to* OTARIAN) Son, all that you've said is empty. I forgive you like a father. Let's talk like grown-ups. I know how your blood boils. You want to live a better life, but can't. You've thought and thought and now you've come up with this.

(OTARIAN *shows he is wounded.*)

ANDREAS: Don't get excited. We'll talk calmly. I've done all I could for you, for your father's sake. And I'll do more. Here, take a few thousand rubles and give me a paper saying you have no further claim on me. That way we'll save both of us further headaches.

BAGRAT (*flatly, positively*): Never. I won't allow you to give him a kopeck.

ANDREAS: For God's sake. Will you shut up!

SAGHATEL (*aside to* BAGRAT): Let him alone. You don't know what's going on.

BAGRAT (*unheeding*): It's ridiculous to give him money! It means we're afraid of him. Let him go to court. I'll defend you against him. I know what he's up to.

OTARIAN: Be careful, sir. Those words will cost you dearly.

BAGRAT: Don't threaten me. I know what you're made of. That's why I despise you. But why should we waste words? This is it, short and sweet: Do whatever you want. (*He takes up some papers from the desk.*) Uncle, I'm going in the factory. Tell the salesman to fill the pipe order immediately. Father, I won't be in for lunch. (*He hurries out looking scornfully at* OTARIAN.)

SAGHATEL: Good for you, boy. A ball of fire.

Scene 8

Same, without BAGRAT; *later,* MARGARIT

ANDREAS: Look here, my son. We of the older generation are kinder than you young ones. You can have three thousand rubles. Take it, and let's make up.

OTARIAN (*frowning*): Anything else?

ANDREAS: Then you're agreed? (*Giving* SAGHATEL *the key to the strong box*) Saghatel, get me the checkbook.

OTARIAN: Good-bye.

(SAGHATEL *stops.*)

ANDREAS: Where? Wait. Settling accounts is one thing—friendship is . . . friendship. You're dining with us.

OTARIAN: Good-bye.

MARGARIT(*entering, left, in a simple housedress*): Mother invites you to lunch.

(OTARIAN, *walking to the anteroom, stops.*)

ANDREAS: You see how everyone likes you in this house? And you want to walk away in a huff!

MARGARIT (*surprised, looking at* OTARIAN): You're leaving? Why?

ANDREAS: Who knows? He's caught in a shifting wind. But you'll bring him around.

SAGHATEL: Let's go. Margarit may shame him into coming.

ANDREAS: But, Son, don't make us wait too long. (*He goes out the doors at left with* SAGHATEL.)

Scene 9

MARGARIT *and* OTARIAN

MARGARIT: What is it? (*She holds his hand affectionately.*) Why are you so flushed?

OTARIAN: It's nothing.

MARGARIT: What happened? Why won't you stay for lunch? Why did my father say you were walking away from us?

OTARIAN: I can't tell you, now. Please don't ask.

MARGARIT (*hurt, dropping his hand*): All right! I won't ask. If you can't stay, I won't keep you.

OTARIAN: Oh, Margarit, please. Don't be childish. You're not like other women.

MARGARIT: But you treat me like a child. You're the one who said there should be no secrets between people in love. Have you forgotten?

OTARIAN (*perplexed*): There are things you can't be concerned with. You're too sensitive. (*He takes her hand again.*)

MARGARIT: But I thought there was nothing that could concern you and not me. (*Taking her hand away*) Go away. You've hurt me. (*She turns away from him.*) You're being cruel. And you say you love me.

OTARIAN: What have I done? Sometimes wounded pride makes us cruel.

MARGARIT: Pride? Whose pride is wounded? Yours? Who wounded it? My father? My brother? (*Pause*) You're silent. You turn your back. I've had enough. My patience is gone. I hate hypocrisy. Say it out, plainly and clearly. What's happened? Ah, I understand. You spoke to my father about me. You asked him for my hand. He refused . . . But no, what am I saying? My father likes you. And besides, his rejection couldn't hurt you as long as I love you. I have my own mind. (*Pause*) Wait . . . I suspect something else. You've spoken to him about me . . . But you're not the kind to bargain with him.

OTARIAN: You're pushing me, Margarit. I told you. There are some things you should not be concerned with.

MARGARIT (*with feeling*): No. You mustn't keep even the smallest secret from me. Love me that way or leave me. I won't have it any other way.

OTARIAN (*with a decisive movement*): All right. I guess, I just can't make you understand.

MARGARIT (*breathy*): Well. Well?

OTARIAN: Tell me, Margarit. Do you love your father?

MARGARIT: My father? (*positively*) Why, yes.

OTARIAN: I don't mean as a daughter. Not as your father. I mean as a person.

MARGARIT: I don't understand.

OTARIAN: What I'm saying is: Do you respect him as a man?

MARGARIT: Of course. Isn't my father a man?

OTARIAN: And a decent man. Isn't that right?

MARGARIT: That's right. My father's no villain.

OTARIAN: Are you sure of that?

MARGARIT: Very sure. I know of nothing dishonorable that he has ever done. I respect him as a man, who, after many years of hard work, managed to provide for his children's needs. He was uneducated, but he didn't stint on his children's education. (*Pause*) Why are you looking at me like that? Don't you believe I'm telling you what I think?

OTARIAN: So you find no fault in your father?

MARGARIT: What do you mean? He likes money. He examines his accounts closely. Thinks only of his work. But aren't all businessmen like that? There's nothing indecent about that. (*Pause*)

OTARIAN: What would you do if one day you found out he's dishonest?

MARGARIT (*hurt and angry*): Artashes.

OTARIAN (*heatedly*): Yes, yes, dishonest. At least in the past.

MARGARIT (*same tone*): Artashes. Do you realize what you're saying?

OTARIAN: I'm saying what I know. Your father has been . . . far from faultless.

MARGARIT: And what exactly was his fault?

OTARIAN (*stressing his words*): A callous lack of charity.

MARGARIT (*shaking*): Whom has he denied?

OTARIAN: A fatherless and needy family. His own partner's children.

MARGARIT: You?

OTARIAN: Me, my mother, my sisters.

MARGARIT: Ah. (*Shaken, she sits in a chair and covers her face with her hands.*)

(*Long pause*)

OTARIAN: That's the truth.

MARGARIT (*Gaining strength, she stands.*): You'd better be able to prove that. Do you hear? Otherwise, I'll despise you as a slanderer. No, no. You couldn't slander your benefactor. You always loved and respected him. There must be some explanation. You've got to explain. He's my father, you're my happiness. For me, you're both equal. But above everything else, we have to have the truth.

(ZARUHI, *the maid, appears at doors left.*)

ZARUHI: They're waiting for you in the dining room.

MARGARIT: I'll be right in.

OTARIAN: I don't suppose I have the right to come here anymore.

MARGARIT: No, no. You must come. I know you can't say anything that will make it right. Not now. You've got to go. But tomorrow, you'll tell me; you'll explain.

(*Turning away, he hurriedly walks out to the anteroom. Weakly, she walks to the left, stops, and leans against the door.*)

The curtain falls slowly.

ACT 2

The ELIZBARIAN *living room, richly but not distinctively furnished. At right, two doors: one leading to the anteroom, the other to* ANDREAS'*s room, a sitting area with armchairs, a round table with a silk cover and an electric lamp. At center, doors to the dining room and the passage leading to the girls' rooms. At left, the door to the rooms of* BAGRAT *and* SUREN. *Also at left, another sitting area with chairs set about a circular table with knickknacks on it. Upstage a piano. Above it, on the back wall, a glass-framed mirror. Chairs of gold and velvet, cushions, vases, statues, tropical plants, etc., etc. The floors are fully carpeted, the doors colorfully draped. A large electric chandelier with many branches overhead.* ZARUHI, *the maid, is seen through the open doors of the dining room putting the cloth on the table preparing for lunch. A few minutes after the curtain rises, the dining room clock strikes twelve noon.* VARDAN, *the servant, enters in a red costume with a large cap on his head. Loaded down with all sorts of packages, he carefully manages to hold onto a hat box.*

Scene 1

VARDAN *and* ZARUHI

VARDAN: Ooph! As God's my witness. My soul's in my mouth. My back's broke. (*He puts the packages down on the floor one by one, still holding onto the hat-box. As he wipes the sweat from his face with his shirttail, his cap falls to the floor.*)

(ZARUHI *enters wiping a coffee cup with a towel.*)

ZARUHI: So you're back? Pah, pah, pah, look how many things you've brought.

VARDAN: Oh, my poor back. This cap on my head, squattin' on the wagon like a cossack. Drive and drive. She didn't miss a single department store. Seems to me she didn't leave a damned thing for anybody else. Like it was a matter of life and death.

ZARUHI (*Interested, she puts the cup and towel down and unties her apron.*): She bought everything, clothing, shawls, blouses. What kind of a hat's this?

VARDAN (*keeping the hatbox from her*): Hey! Don't touch. She don't want nobody to see it. You might drool over it.

Scene 2

Same and ROZALIA

ROZALIA (*entering from the anteroom*): Mon Dieu! Am I tired! I've been in and out of every shop in town, and this is all I could find. Paris ruined me. Nothing pleases me here. (*To* VARDAN) Imbecile, why are you kneeling on the floor? (*To* ZARUHI) Pick up those parcels and take them to my room. Leave the hat here. (*While* ZARUHI *and* VARDAN *wait for orders,* ROZALIA *puts the hat box on the table, goes to the mirror, removes the hat she is wearing, opens the hat box, takes out a large red plumed white hat and looks at it admiringly.*) I still think it's beautiful. (*She puts it on her head and looks in the mirror.*) That Miss Iltarian kept saying it was brought here just for me. Still, it's not bad. Eh, Zaruhi?

ZARUHI: It's beautiful, Miss!

VARDAN (*gesturing*): Like a big . . . a big pomegranate!

ZARUHI: Heavens! It must have cost twenty rubles.

ROZALIA (*disdainfully*): Don't be silly. Any ordinary hat costs twenty rubles today. This one's from Paris. It's ninety rubles.

VARDAN: Ninety rubles? The hell with it. With ninety rubles you can . . . you can have a whole house built back in Shamakh.

ROZALIA (*without looking at him*): Are you still here?

VARDAN: You're the boss. What ever the hell you want, just speak out.

ROZALIA (*turning toward him*): What's that? Watch your tongue! You're not talking to your sister or one of your old Shamakh friends!

VARDAN: Ah, well. We're peasants.

ROZALIA: Now it's "we." Where do you people come off with your royal airs? "We." Go and tell Ivan I don't need the carriage anymore.

(*Puzzled,* VARDAN *goes out to the anteroom, forgetting his hat on the floor.*)

(*To* ZARUHI) Who's home? (*She puts the hat in the box.*)

ZARUHI: My mistress and Miss Rita.

ROZALIA: Tell my little sister to come in here. And take this hat to my room.

(ZARUHI *carries the hatbox off.* ROZALIA *removes her coat, puts it on a chair, and straightens her hair at the mirror.* VARDAN *enters.*)

VARDAN: My hat. I don't know where I left it. Ah. Here it is. (*He picks it up.*) One day you'll break your owner's neck. (*He hits his hat with his hand.*)

ROZALIA (*furious*): What are you doing? Get out, you . . . you animal.

VARDAN: When an ass brays at your door, you don't have to let him in. (*He goes into the anteroom.*)

(ZARUHI *enters.*)

ROZALIA: What a job, to train a beast of a man like him! And he was supposed to be our liveried coachman. I'll have to hire a foreigner.

(ZARUHI *takes the coffee cup and towel into the dining room.*)

Scene 3

ROZALIA *and* MARGARIT

(MARGARIT *enters, dressed simply, carrying a paperback book.*)

ROZALIA (*derisively*): My, how like Margarit in the opera *Faust*. A book in your hand, modest, shy. I wish I knew what you find in reading. (*She sits on the sofa.*)

MARGARIT: Where did you go? (*She puts the book down on table left and sits.*)

ROZALIA: Oh, I couldn't begin to tell you. I'm dead tired. Finally found a hat. You'll see it later. Beautiful. I spent three hundred rubles today. Father'll be angry. But what can I do? I just had to have every single thing.

MARGARIT: Rozalia, you just can't be such a spendthrift.

ROZALIA: Oh ho! You're scolding me.

MARGARIT: Call it that, if you like. You're just too extravagant.

ROZALIA (*ironically*): Is that the way it is? If you're jealous, you can be extravagant, too. Anything else bothering you?

MARGARIT: Maybe there is.

ROZALIA: Oh, you seem very wrapped in thought today. So tell me, what's happened? You seem so preoccupied.

MARGARIT: ROZALIA, you've got to understand what's happening in this house. You're spending money that's tainted. (MARGARIT *stands.*)

ROZALIA (*standing quickly*): Who's tainting it? Who? Your Artashes Otarian? A filthy, shameless slanderer.

MARGARIT (*calm, scolding, but hurt*): Rozalia!

ROZALIA: Now, you listen! Don't you dare defend him to me. I hate that man with all my soul. He's as treacherous as a snake. Father took him into the heart of this family. He should have shown him the door, long ago.

MARGARIT (*sighing*): Don't be so sure he's blameless.

ROZALIA (*pausing briefly, and serious*): Rita, you're going too far! How could you be so callous as to take a slanderer's words against your father's?

MARGARIT (*same tone*): Ah. I don't want to . . . but—

ROZALIA (*cutting*): But you're afraid of losing him. Isn't that right?

MARGARIT: What are you saying? That I love Otarian? Yes, I love him. Very much. And don't any of you forget it. (*She paces back and forth.*)

ROZALIA (*derisively, with hate and jealousy*): How brave you are. A real heroine. I knew all about it long ago. Only I never believed you loved him so much that you'd be willing to dishonor your father's name for him.

MARGARIT: It's not a clean name.

ROZALIA: What do you mean?

MARGARIT: Oh how I wish he were wrong! As God is my judge, if I were convinced he owed his partner nothing. (*Fatigued, bitter voice*) But to this day, father hasn't brought a single proof against Artashes's accusations. Our family's committed a great injustice. It's too hard to bear. I just can't face it. I can't. (*She sits and puts her head on the table.*)

ROZALIA (*sarcastically*): Do you think you're the only one in this family with a sense of honor or pride? The rest of us are nothing, I suppose. (*Pause*) Either you're insane or that man's a demon. There's no other way to explain your attitude. (*After a short silence, she approaches her sister.*) Listen, Rita. I'm my father's own daughter. I have to love and protect him—even if he's a thief. That's all I can say. Let your Otarian trump up charges against Father. I'll have him thrown out of this house. Understand? Be as angry as you like, be my enemy. I'm going to do what I have to do. (*She moves away.*)

MARGARIT: Do what you must. I've got to listen to my own conscience. There just can't be any lying or deception between people who love each other.

ZARUHI (*at the dining room doors*): Lunch is ready.

ROZALIA: Let's go. Father will be here. You've got to tell him all these idiotic things you're thinking.

MARGARIT: I'm not hungry.

(ROZALIA *glares at* MARGARIT *as she goes into the dining room.* MARGARIT *remains at left in a pensive mood.*)

Scene 4

MARGARIT (*unnoticed*); ANDREAS, BAGRAT, *and* SAGHATEL *enter from the anteroom.*

ANDREAS: Don't contradict me. It has to be my way. You don't put out a fire with oil.

BAGRAT: If it's only a fire. We'll win if he doesn't have evidence. Let him go to court. We'll beat him in a civil suit. It's got to be this way for you, me . . . for family honor.

ANDREAS: Even if you put a rope around my neck, you won't get me into a court with him.

BAGRAT: Father, I've known, ever since I was a child, that you earned everything we have by honest sweat.

ANDREAS (*irritated*): I've said that, and I say it again. But don't keep repeating it. Even though that young fellow accuses me falsely, I want to go easy with him.

BAGRAT: I don't understand. I just don't understand.

ANDREAS: Saghatel, go to my office and send someone to Otarian. I want to see him here. (SAGHATEL *goes out by the anteroom;* ANDREAS *sees* MARGARIT, *at left.*) Ah, you were listening. God, God, I don't have a moment's peace in the house. You all seem to have sworn an oath to drive me out of my mind.

MARGARIT: Forgive me. I'm going.

ANDREAS: Good. Don't excite yourself. I'm not guilty of anything. Your brother has upset me. And you, too. You're like your mother. You don't care for me.

MARGARIT (*hurt*) Father! . . .

(ERANUHI *and* ROZALIA *appear in the dining room doors.*)

Scene 5

Same, without SAGHATEL; ERANUHI *and* ROZALIA

ANDREAS: Go ahead. Leave. I'm not your father. You're a stepchild. I'm a stranger in this house. A stranger. No one thinks about me. I'm a porter in your eyes. That's all.

ROZALIA: You've no business saying that to me, and you know it. (*Going toward him*)

ANDREAS: Ah. They're all here. You're no different, too. You think about me only when you have to pay your bills at the department stores. You people just eat me up, you wreck me. (*Getting more and more irritated*) I'm nothing to anybody. Not to outsiders nor to family members. You take me for a bag of gold. Nothing more. Respectful to my face, yes. But behind my back, contempt.

When they need me, they come running. When they don't, I don't exist for them.

BAGRAT: You've got to admit he's right on that point.

ANDREAS: That's how it is, all right. I'm not a fool. I know how people are, in their souls. Always thinking of themselves. And you're one of them, yourself. That's a lie? You don't love me either. You respect me for my money. Yes, yes. I'm not a person for you. Only a money box. But you can't fool me any longer. I won't give you another kopeck.

BAGRAT: Father, take it easy.

ANDREAS: No, I won't give you a thing. Your factory can stay half-built. Did I ever receive any money from my father that you should come begging to me? Spat on, working in dirt, with a hungry belly, that's how I became a man. Go and sweat blood. Then I'll say you're worth something. All of you, go and live by your own work. Look here. See what a home they've fixed up. What's it to me to have these fancy furnishings? Who am I? A prince's son? Heh? A poor boy. A boy raised on bread and cheese. Why are you ruining me? You're to blame for Otarian's abusing me. Yes, yes, you. He sees you wasting my money recklessly, and he wants to do the same. You've made enemies for me . . .

(MARGARIT *cries quietly.*)

Tears! Cry your eyes out. I've had it up to here. You've choked me to death. Enough. Get out. I hate tears. Don't ever cry or laugh in Andreas Elizbarian's presence.

(*With labored breathing,* MARGARIT *goes to her room.*)

ERANUHI: How can you be so heartless! To wound her like that. She's a lamb of God.

ANDREAS: A lamb of God. Like your father. I hate God's lambs. Give me Satan. I get along better with him than with lambs of God. Get out of here. Why do you circle around me like vultures? They won't leave me in peace. They want to strap me, drive me to the poor house, throw me into the streets. At least give me some peace. Get out of here. Out! (*He sits in the armchair, right.* ERANUHI *and* BAGRAT *go into the dining room.* ROZALIA *stays.*)

Scene 6

ANDREAS *and* ROZALIA

(ANDREAS *sits in deep thought, suffering.* ROZALIA *wants to come near to talk but is not sure of herself.* ANDREAS *sighs as he bangs on the table.*)

ANDREAS: Akh.

ROZALIA: Father. Why are you torturing yourself like this?

ANDREAS (*raising his head, indifferent*): None of your business.

ROZALIA: Forgive me, Father. What troubles you troubles your children.

ANDREAS (*turning, aloof*): I don't have any troubles. (*Nervously quick, he stands.*) Anything else?

ROZALIA: Yes, Father. But I don't know if I dare say it.

ANDREAS: Get to it. I don't have all day.

ROZALIA: Do you know, Father, that this ingrate who wants to take you to the cleaners has an accomplice here?

ANDREAS (*interested*): What are you talking about? Speak plainly.

ROZALIA: Margarit is in love with Otarian.

ANDREAS: In love? Who says so?

ROZALIA: She said so herself only a half-hour ago.

ANDREAS: And? Does he love her?

ROZALIA: I suppose so. Though it's hard to believe a man like that.

ANDREAS (*He thinks a few moments. All of a sudden his face brightens with happiness.*): Margarit told you herself?

ROZALIA: Yes, Father. I know they see each other, every day. Father, I had to tell you. I think they ought to be stopped for the family name. Margarit is acting indecently, but she's still your daughter. Otarian isn't fit to be your son-in-law.

ANDREAS (*He keeps thinking.*): It's true. It's true. Thanks for warning me. Call Margarit. Tell her to come here.

ROZALIA: But don't be angry with her. She's a fool. She doesn't understand.

ANDREAS (*impatient*): Tell her to come here.

ROZALIA (*aside*): Now we'll see how you defend your lover. (*She leaves.*)

Scene 7

ANDREAS *and* MARGARIT

(*Until* MARGARIT *enters,* ANDREAS *paces to and fro, betraying his thoughts.* MARGARIT *enters calmly.* ROZALIA *follows immediately, stands by a moment, looks at them, and then goes into the dining room, closing the doors.*)

ANDREAS: Come here, my crying angel. How long can a father be angry with his daughter? Eh? Tell me: what would you do, you spoiled children, if you had parents like ours? When Father slapped me behind the ears, I saw stars. Well, good. If you can appreciate that, you won't hold a grudge against your parents.

MARGARIT: Father, I don't hold a grudge against you.

ANDREAS: Bless you, my daughter. I know you've got a good heart. Let's make up.

(*He approaches and kisses her forehead.*) But I'm annoyed. You know what, my daughter? You're not frank with me.

MARGARIT (*looking surprised*): Frank?

ANDREAS: Why are you surprised?

MARGARIT: Father, it's the first time I've heard you say any such thing. If you can say that, it means you don't take me seriously.

ANDREAS: But you . . . you keep your distance. You probably think, well, my father is a shrewd businessman no doubt, but ignorant. It's not worth confiding in him.

MARGARIT: No, Father, you're wrong. I believe in you. I've always been ready to confide in you, fully and sincerely, if only you'd consider me worth listening to. But you . . . you've always stopped me with your bad tempers.

ANDREAS (*pretending happiness*): Have I done that? Forgive me. Now, tell me why you're sad these days.

MARGARIT (*confused, embarrassed*): I don't know . . . I . . . I'm not sad.

ANDREAS: You see? You want to be frank, but aren't. Want me to answer for you? You're sad because lately you've been convinced that your father is not a good man.

MARGARIT: Father. . . .

ANDREAS: Yes, my dear. You can't keep secrets from me. I can tell from a person's movements what they're thinking. (MARGARIT *is altogether confused and blushes.*) All right. Don't be ashamed. I know everything. Don't be afraid. I won't be angry. I don't say Artashes is a bad fellow. If I thought he was, I would have closed my door to him. Only, my dear, he's still a child! He doesn't know what he's doing. He forgets my kindness. Eh, God help him. One day, he'll come to his senses and see how wrong he's been.

MARGARIT (*happy and suspicious at the same time*): Yes, he's wrong about you.

ANDREAS: Of course. What did you think?

MARGARIT: Father, why should I hide it? I've never questioned your business practices. Why should I? But now he's trying to persuade me that—

ANDREAS: That I robbed his father, isn't that so? But how? With words or actual proof?

MARGARIT: Father, I can't ask for proof, not from you or him.

ANDREAS: So without proof you're ready to judge your father, eh? (*He feigns being hurt.*) Shame on you, Margarit, shame. You've dealt me a blow . . .

MARGARIT (*hurt and embarrassed*): Father—

ANDREAS (*still pretending to be hurt*): Leave me alone. What kind of father am I when my own daughter calls me a thief without proof? Leave me. Go to him. He's precious to you. But who am I? What am I? Nothing but . . . dirt.

MARGARIT: You're right to hate me, Father. I was too hasty to judge you. Please forgive me.

ANDREAS: What's the good of pleading forgiveness? You've got to set things right.

MARGARIT: But how, Father? What can I do? Tell me. I'll make it up to you.

ANDREAS: Yes, and how. Listen. He says he's got his hands on written proof. You
. . . (*Looking about him*) This is no place to talk. I think they're coming. Let's
go to my room. I'll explain what you should do, there. Let's go.

(*They exit right.*)

Scene 8

SUREN *and* SAGHATEL

(*They enter by anteroom doors.*)

SUREN: Yes, Uncle, you can't imagine how funny it was. Abulov is the town's greatest playboy and biggest spender. Suddenly, there he is by the stage door with
his nose out of joint. And your sister's son has the beautiful Arlova by the arm
and gets in the carriage beside her.

SAGHATEL: If you don't mind my asking, what's there to brag about?

SUREN (*continuing spiritedly*): We were the focus of attention. Everyone looked on
jealously. Abulov's eyes shot flames. Fiery Ali Baba makes the carriage fly with
lightning speed and brings us to the Grand Hotel. Servants wait on us hand
and foot. The table is laid out. The guests are waiting—

SAGHATEL: If you don't mind my asking, what guests?

SUREN: Admirers, like me. They applauded us. The coachmen brought in the bou-
quets from the theater, half of them my gifts. Never had she received such an
ovation. And then what fun. What laughter! Champagne flowed like water.
Everyone drank to Arlova's health. Then to mine. One, two, three. All of a sudden, I'm under the table. I take Arlova's foot. She, laughing and joking, looks
under the table. I stand with the beauty's shoe in my hand. I fill it with champagne and drink her health. The spirit is inexpressible. Arlova is radiant. She
says, this is the first time I see you, a person like you, worship my art! Ah,
charming, marvelous. She's not a woman; a goddess . . . (*He slaps* SAGHATEL
on the shoulder.) Now, her heart is mine, Uncle, all mine. (*Hitting* SAGHATEL
in the stomach) You want me to introduce you? Ah? Staunch family man like
yourself.

SAGHATEL: Mind your own business. How much did all that merrymaking cost?

SUREN: Really, all things considered, a bagatelle. A mere nothing. Six hundred
rubles.

SAGHATEL (*turning, amazed*): Six hundred rubles! Pah. You'd better pray you can
keep your head above water!

SUREN: That hit you, didn't it!

SAGHATEL: Six hundred in one night. If you don't mind my asking: When are you
going to pay off your debt to me?

SUREN: At the time we agreed.

SAGHATEL: You mean I have to wait till your father dies?

SUREN: Sure. What's wrong with that?

SAGHATEL: But he's healthier than me. He'll bury ten like me before he kicks off.

SUREN: What can I do? You're the one who put me up to it. You gave me three hundred and you'll get two thousand at my father's death. (*Pause*) Ah, Uncle, my head is splitting. I'm exhausted. Drained. After a big party, life seems trivial and boring. (*He sees* ERANUHI, ROZALIA, *and* BAGRAT.) Ah ha, here comes the dream family.

Scene 9

The same and ERANUHI, ROZALIA, *and* BAGRAT

(*They enter from the dining room.*)

ERANUHI (*to* SAGHATEL): Tell Zaruhi to give you breakfast.
    (SAGHATEL *goes into the dining room.*) (*To* SUREN) No need to bother about you. I'm sure you stuffed yourself last night.

SUREN: I'd never turn down a little yogurt soup.

ERANUHI: Where were you all night?

SUREN: I was busy stargazing, Mama. The stars came down to the opera house.

BAGRAT: Don't you ever feel ashamed? How could you take the Dilbarians' rent money and squander it?

SUREN: Respectful engineer. I think I'm as much my father's son as you are.

BAGRAT You've polluted the family name.

SUREN: That's just the question. Was it me, or you, Mr. Profiteer? I spread the filth around, but you worship it. Eh. Don't start that business with me. I've got a wicked tongue, and don't you forget it.

ROZALIA: You've got a wicked tongue, all right. Mother, he called me a jackass, yesterday.

SUREN: And today, I'll call you the Marchioness of Bath Scrubbers. What are you so high and mighty about? Really, you were laughable yesterday. You had Vardan dressed in that stupid outfit sitting up front in the carriage. Wasn't it enough that you changed your name from Rosylea to Rozalia? Now you play the part of a chic princess. Heh. . . . Elizbar, the bath attendant's granddaughter. Come off it. You're all ridiculous, except poor old Mama.

(MARGARIT *enters from her father's room.*)

(*Indicating* MARGARIT) If any of you has a right to insult me, she has.

Scene 10

The same and MARGARIT

ROZALIA: Coming from him, that's a glowing recommendation.

SUREN (*Bitterly*): At any rate, it's better than having Otarian break off with you.

ROZALIA: Mother, stop him. He's trying to hurt me. (*To* SUREN) It's a lie. I broke off with him.

SUREN: Yes, on the day you realized you weren't the one he had his eye on. But before that, when he was a student? You all but lit candles in his name. Everything I've said is as true as the fact that in my pockets right now all I have is air. (*Pause*) Where's Popa?

BAGRAT: None of your business.

SUREN: Okay, keep everything from me. I know everything, anyway. The wolf's caught in the trap. He's gnawing at his own legs.

BAGRAT: That's enough.

ROZALIA: He's drunk. Don't waste your breath talking to him.

ERANUHI: He's insane.

SUREN: Eh. What are you all looking so amazed at? The whole town is talking. We've got to stop the gossipers. One way or the other. Either Otarian is right or he's wrong. If he's wrong, he should be punished. (*To* BAGRAT) Ah, you're afraid. You're shaking already. Threatening to take him to court?

BAGRAT (*with wounded pride*): What about the coward who gets his face slapped over a woman and simply takes it.

SUREN: Shut up, you dog. (*Lunging toward* BAGRAT)

ERANUHI (*going between her sons*): In heaven's name. God help us!

MARGARIT: Oh God. What a family!

ANDREAS (*appearing at the door without a jacket*): What's that racket? (*He looks at* SUREN.) Ah, is that you, you good for nothing? I'll choke you like a dog. (*He lunges at* SUREN.)

SAGHATEL (*running out of the dining room, his napkin still tucked around his neck, at* ANDREAS*'s words*): Calm down, Andreas . . . (*He grabs him by the arm and pulls him back.*)

ANDREAS: Get out of here. I told you I didn't want to see you around.

MARGARIT (*holding* SUREN*'s arm*): This is disgraceful. Come to your senses. (*She takes him to doors left and returns alone.*)

ANDREAS: What a life! I can't even put my feet up and have a rest. (*He lets* SAGHATEL *take him to his room.*) Damn the lot of you.

ROZALIA (*to* MARGARIT) You snake. You put him up to it.

MARGARIT: You ought to be ashamed of saying a thing like that, Rozalia.

ERANUHI: Now the two of you are at it. What kind of household is this? Lord God!

ROZALIA (*to* MARGARIT): Just you wait. Someday I'll get even with you. (*She starts to go to her room, but stops on seeing* OTARIAN.)

Scene 11

ERANUHI, MARGARIT, OTARIAN, *and* ROZALIA

(OTARIAN *comes through the anteroom doors, looking happy.*)

OTARIAN: Hello, Mama. (*He kisses* ERANUHI's *hand.*) Hello, Miss Rozalia. (*He extends his hand to shake hers.*)
ROZALIA (*with an offended air*) Sir, we're not acquainted.
OTARIAN (*hurt*): What do you mean, Miss?
ROZALIA (*sarcastically*): Lovers! (*She goes to her room.*)

Scene 12

ERANUHI, MARGARIT, and OTARIAN

(OTARIAN *looks puzzled. He shakes* MARGARIT's *hand mechanically.*)

OTARIAN: I don't know what I've done to provoke her.
ERANUHI (*sitting in armchair at right*): It's nothing, my son. Don't let it trouble you. We had a little family squabble. Her feelings were hurt.
OTARIAN: If I've offended her in any way, I'm ready to apologize.
ERANUHI: Don't concern yourself. She's a child. She doesn't understand. Sit down. How's your mother?
OTARIAN (*controlling himself*): Thank you, Mother. You're very kind to us.
ERANUHI: I love you like my own son. I'm happy that you've grown up to be such a fine person, a gentleman. I've heard that there's some kind of disagreement between us. That makes me very unhappy, my son, very unhappy.
OTARIAN: Mother, you're above all the disputes. No matter how things work out, I'll always love and respect you.
ERANUHI: God bless you. All I want is for family and friends to live in peace, and not to turn away from God for the sake of money.

(ZARUHI *enters.*)

ZARUHI: Madam, your daughter is asking for you. (*She goes into the dining room and returns with a carafe of water and glasses.*)
ERANUHI: So the hysteria has started up again. (*She goes out hurriedly.*)

Scene 13

MARGARIT *and* OTARIAN.

OTARIAN (*approaching* MARGARIT, *impatiently*): What's happened here? Tell me.

MARGARIT: The usual arguments. Suren picked on Rozalia, and then he and Bagrat insulted each other.

OTARIAN: But what have I done that made your sister so rude to me?

MARGARIT: Forgive her. Rozalia can't control herself. I'm sure she'll regret her behavior later.

(*At this moment,* ZARUHI *enters carrying a carafe and a glass.*)

(*To* ZARUHI) How is she?

ZARUHI: All right. She cried a little and then calmed down. (*She enters the dining room.*)

MARGARIT: Let's drop that subject. There's a more important matter. My father sent for you.

OTARIAN: Yes. Where is he?

MARGARIT: He's in his room, resting. Please sit down. It's really you and I who have to talk. Please sit.

(*They sit on the sofa.*)

You've put me between two fires. I believe you. And I want to believe my father. Help me out of this dilemma. One of you, either you or my father, is in the wrong.

OTARIAN: Listen, Margarit. I've told you that this matter is important to me from a moral standpoint. Believe me, money isn't the main issue here.

MARGARIT: Don't you think I know? But you must understand that what's going on between you and my father can destroy me. I don't know what to do. I'm frightened.

OTARIAN: Darling Margarit, it's all very confusing, but you mustn't let it distress you. I know you adore your father, but I'm not so much in opposition to him as to your brother.

MARGARIT: Bagrat isn't good-natured.

OTARIAN: He's slandered me among my friends. He insults me everywhere he goes. He's called me a freeloader many times. I've worn a beggar's badge long enough. I want to feel I deserve your love. Do you understand why I've brought up this whole business?

MARGARIT: I understand. I understand completely. But what can I do? You know I love you very much. But I also love my father. I could have died of shame at the things he said today. I don't think he could have said such things if he really felt any guilt. He asked for proof of what you say, and he wants me to check it.

OTARIAN: And you yourself want to check it. You're torn between two equal feelings. Faith in your father and faith in me.

MARGARIT: That's it. You see my dilemma exactly.

OTARIAN: All right. I'll take you out of it.

MARGARIT: Please. End it for me.

OTARIAN: I'll show you the proof.

MARGARIT: I couldn't ask you. But there's no other way.

OTARIAN: That's it then. You're the best possible judge for me. All I ask is that you tell your brother I'm not a freeloader. Grant me that and I'll give up my inheritance. I could have gone to court, but I won't because of you. So you'll be our judge.

MARGARIT: Thank you, really. And believe me, I'll be an honest judge.

OTARIAN (with a slight tremor): Ah, that's what frightens me.

MARGARIT: Why?

OTARIAN: MARGARIT, promise me that when the truth comes out you won't become bitter.

MARGARIT: Don't even say it. You said yourself that the important thing is honesty. Bring me the papers. I want to end all these lingering doubts. And I won't weaken, whoever turns out to be right. I know I stand to suffer in either case, whether the ground opens between my father and me or between you and me. Bring the papers. I'm your fiancée. That makes a difference.

(OTARIAN watches her as she speaks and is disturbed. When she stops, he is calm.)

OTARIAN: Very well, I'll bring them. (He gets up.)

MARGARIT: Today?

OTARIAN: I'll be back in a few minutes.

(MARGARIT walks with him to the door, and he goes out.)

Scene 14

MARGARIT and SUREN

SUREN (entering left): I couldn't sleep. I'm uncomfortable. A man's peace of mind is surprisingly connected with the contents of his pocket. When this damned little sack is empty, whatever anyone says, it's hard to sleep. Yes, dear Margarit, I've made a new spiritual discovery. In the meantime, can't you, perhaps, reconcile me with naughty Morpheus.

MARGARIT: I don't have money.

SUREN: I think Father gives you three hundred rubles a month allowance.

MARGARIT: It's ages since I stopped taking money from Father.

SUREN: That's it. You hate money. You're a philosopher.

MARGARIT: What use is money to me when everything I need is supplied at home?

SUREN: That's true. But I need it. I need it badly. Without money, I'm a cripple. I hate money, too, and all the time I'm trying to get rid of it. When I have a few bills locked up in my pockets, you see, they immediately gnaw away like moths. Eh, I'm forced to leave the pockets open. But meanwhile, it's sad being without money. Ah, Margarit, life's insane. (*Short pause*) It's sad, very sad. I'm really tired of life.

MARGARIT (*pacing sadly, reprimandingly*): Twenty-three years old?

SUREN: Is it so little? Time enough to have seen a lot, felt a lot, and tired quickly. Happy thought. Sometimes I'm afraid of myself. (*He takes a revolver from his pocket.*) Look, with one shot, I'm across the Rubicon.

MARGARIT: Stop it. Don't do anything idiotic. It might go off accidentally.

SUREN: It can't go off accidentally. (*He demonstrates.*) This is the way to fire a revolver. You've got to pull this back, squeeze this with your finger, and it's ready.

MARGARIT: Give it to me. I don't want you near it. It's dangerous.

SUREN: I was going to put it away. (*He gives it to her.*) Put it away. Let's keep the devil at a distance. (*Pause*) So you don't have any?

MARGARIT: None. (*She looks at the revolver and puts it on the table.*)

SUREN (*after a moment*): Not even fifty rubles?

(MARGARIT *shakes her head.*)

It hurts. It hurts a lot. It means I won't see Arlova today. That's impossible. What a disgrace. She'll say that the Armenian boy ran from the expense. And she'll turn to Abulov. (*He sits on one of the armchairs, thinking. Pause. Then he slaps his head.*) Eureka! I'm an Edison. I'm an Edison. Where's Rozalia?

MARGARIT: In her room.

SUREN: She'll have money. (*He goes to doors left.*)

MARGARIT: After the way you hurt her, do you dare to ask?

SUREN (*stopping*): I meant no harm. She knows I have a good heart. It's only my tongue that's wicked. We'll make up. It won't be hard. I'll stroke her, praise her beauty, and she'll ease up. (*He goes into the girls' room singing a Russian song.*)

Scene 15

MARGARIT *and* OTARIAN, *later* ANDREAS.

(OTARIAN *enters wearing a coat.*)

OTARIAN: Here you are, my dear. That's the lot. (*He gives her a packet.*) My honor, my self-respect, my reputation.

MARGARIT: Thank you for your faith in me.

OTARIAN: I know your hardheaded brother would think me an idiot for agreeing to do this. But it's a simple matter. I love you and believe in you. (*He kisses her.*)

MARGARIT: You'll get it all back in a day or two. My word's my pledge.

OTARIAN: That's good enough for me. Good-bye.

MARGARIT: Good-bye. (*She goes to the door with him.*)

(ANDREAS *appears at the entrance to his room.* MARGARIT *returns to center. She is about to go to her room.* ANDREAS *pretends he did not see* OTARIAN.)

ANDREAS: Who was that?

MARGARIT: Look, Popa. Everything's here. Now I'll see which of you is in the right.

ANDREAS: Bless you, my dear. Examine it well. (*He kisses her forehead.*)

(*They go to their own rooms.*)

Curtain

ACT 3

Same scene, evening. The stage is dimly lit at rise of curtain. Except for the doors of the anteroom, which are partly open, all the doors are closed. A band of light falls on the piano where MARGARIT *sits playing a sad melody. Her body is in darkness; only her head is clearly visible. She is alone. In the distance the sound of an electric bell can be heard. From the dining room,* ZARUHI *enters and passes to the girls' quarters.*

Scene 1

MARGARIT and BAGRAT

(BAGRAT *enters wearing a jacket with the insignia of the Technological Institute. He is putting on his tie.*)

BAGRAT: Always the same sad melody at the same time of day.

MARGARIT (*playing*): They say that each time of day has its own mood. In the evening I'm sad and emotional and always remember this melody.

BAGRAT: And you play in darkness like a romantic lover. But forgive me. I hate darkness. (*He goes to the doors and switches on the ceiling lights.*)

MARGARIT: That's enough. (*She stops playing and closes the piano lid. She notices* BAGRAT's *jacket.*) Where are you going?

BAGRAT (*standing by the mirror, adjusting his tie*): To the Technological Institute dance. Get dressed; I'll take you with me. Rozalia is getting ready. You'll meet the best of our local intelligentsia there.

MARGARIT: Why the best?

BAGRAT: Only engineers. None of the old-time elitists such as lawyers and doctors.

MARGARIT: It seems you have a high regard for your profession.

BAGRAT: The most earnest and intelligent representatives of the times are engineers. Do you realize that?

MARGARIT: I don't feel a bit inclined to meet your engineers.

BAGRAT: What a way to talk! Inclined. It's up to a person whether he's inclined this way or that. This damn thing won't tie right.

MARGARIT (*coming forward to help him*): It's easy for you to say. You're reconciled to taking life as you find it.

BAGRAT: Why not, if circumstances don't warrant resistance? If things were different, I'm clear-headed enough to know what to do about it.

(MARGARIT *fixes his tie.*)

Thank you. (*He looks at his hands.*) Don't you realize, sweet Sister, that in our time, reason is king? That's why I can't take your moodiness as anything but provocation.

MARGARIT: Believe me, I'd much rather be a carefree bird, like my sister. I'd have preferred not to think about anything except my own pleasures. But what do you want? I can't help what I am. (*Crying, she puts her elbows on the piano.*)

BAGRAT (*ironically*): You're in love. You're suffering for an incomparable young man, an uncommon idealist. (*Pause*) That's enough, Margarit. I have no right to scold you. But I just can't keep silent, anymore. That's enough. You mustn't be childish. You're a grown woman. You have to understand that you have no right to love a man who slanders your parents.

MARGARIT (*raising her head*): And if he's not a slanderer, then what?

BAGRAT: You're certain.

MARGARIT (*positively, with feeling*): I'm convinced, more than I ever thought I would be.

BAGRAT: Sister, you're becoming emotional about it. You've got this stupid feeling of love and it's as if you're drunk. If you continue this way, I'll end up hating you the way I hate him.

MARGARIT: It makes no difference to me now what you say. I have the proof—papers that could convince even stones that Father robbed a bereaved family, and robbed them without mercy. I asked Otarian to show me his proof. Father himself urged me to do it. Now I have the papers. Bagrat, whatever he's said is absolutely true. Just thinking about it drives me out of my mind. (*Overwhelmed by the thought, she paces back and forth. Pause.*)

BAGRAT: You've confused me completely. Where are the papers exactly?

MARGARIT: In my room. In my desk.

BAGRAT: Have you spoken to Father?

MARGARIT: Yes.

BAGRAT: What has he said about them?

MARGARIT: What can a guilty man say when he has been photographed red-handed? He was confused; he reddened and got tongue-tied. But he couldn't refute it. You go to your dance. In the morning, if you want, I'll show you the papers.

BAGRAT: What dance? I've forgotten everything. Is he really threatening us with bankruptcy?

MARGARIT: Ah, it's the bankruptcy that bothers you. What bothers me is the dishonesty. Obviously, for the present, everything hangs on Otarian.

BAGRAT: Is he going to disgrace us and force us into bankruptcy? You know, he holds a tremendous grudge against me. Show me the papers. I want to see them with my own eyes and be convinced, personally.

MARGARIT (*thoughtfully and earnestly*): Please be careful. I've guaranteed their safety with my honor.

BAGRAT (*hurt*): I'm not a thief, Margarit.

MARGARIT: All right. Come and see for yourself. You'll know whose money it is you want to use for your big deals.

(*They go out.*)

Scene 2

ANDREAS *and* SAGHATEL

(*They enter from the anteroom.*)

ANDREAS: She's not my daughter. No. She's my judge. I haven't slept all night. And I've been in agony all day. I thought those papers were lost. Eh, I used to say, she's a woman; she can't understand these matters. Is it so uncommon to have women burn their husband's important papers? But this one's not one of your fools. She held on to them so her son could one day heap all these troubles on my head. Like an avenging spirit, the dead father demands that I bend my neck before that whelp, demands that I ask forgiveness and give him half my wealth.

SAGHATEL: Did you see the papers yourself?

ANDREAS: I saw them. But no. She read them to me, at a distance, in front of her mother, and reminded me of everything. Then she put them into her desk.

SAGHATEL: And no doubt her mother added whatever details were lacking, telling everything she herself knows.

ANDREAS: Oh, your sister is God's curse on my head. Instead of defending me, she dishonored me all the more in front of my daughter. I got furious and pounced on her and was going to kill her on the spot. Fortunately Margarit intervened in time and prevented me. She threw her arms around her mother's neck. You should have seen how she was weeping. She won't cry as much over my bier. And then when she revived, what words. Dear God. What language. Father, she said, you can make a mistake, but you ought to be able to regret it. Not to regret it is indecent. Where did she learn such things?

SAGHATEL: Where? From that whelp. God knows what else he's taught her.

ANDREAS: I tried to justify myself. I said that when my partner died the stocks had no value. They brought no income. What could I have given the bereaved? I told them they rose in value later, lucky for me. Because if the dead one had been lucky, he wouldn't have died. But I, in any case, didn't forget my partner's family. I helped them. And I want to help them now. I always took them by the hand to help them. No, he says, you're obliged to give us all that's legally ours. Do you hear, Saghatel? To give all. He thinks that's possible. He thinks stolen money isn't money. But forget the money. What about my honor? What will people think when they hear such things?

SAGHATEL: What will they think? They'll say that Elizbarian was a crook and, being afraid of a court judgment, gave back what he stole. Then try to appear in public. They'll spit your eyes out. And I, I'll consider you an idiot.

ANDREAS: One thing could have solved the problem. And I tried it. I said: Daughter, you love that young man. He loves you. That's good. Let me get you two married with a good dowry and set you up in a fine home. Give me the papers.

SAGHATEL: Huh. What did she say?

ANDREAS: No, Father. I prefer honor to money for a dowry. As long as the wrong to your partner is not righted, I can't marry his son. At any time, he'd have the right to throw it in my face. "Your father robbed my father." That would be too much of an insult to take in my marriage.

SAGHATEL: What a tongue. She talks like a philosopher.

ANDREAS: Ah. Margarit is like her grandfather, like your father. Yesterday, when she spoke, it seemed like Grandfather Simon was standing by the wall behind her, the scripture verses spouting from his mouth.

SAGHATEL: My father was a spiritual man, obliged to preach the truth. But we're of this world. It's different for us. Why don't the women understand that?

ANDREAS: Now give me some advice. What am I going to do? How shall I save myself from that pup?

SAGHATEL: What are you going to do? Your fear points the way. Do what you think is right.

ANDREAS: Yes, I must do it! There's nothing else for it. I tried to get Margarit to give me those papers.

SAGHATEL: But you must get them, right away. Tonight. Tomorrow will be too late.

ANDREAS: Quiet. I hear footsteps. They're coming. Let's go to my room. We'll work out what must be done.

(They go out.)

Scene 3

MARGARIT, BAGRAT, *and* ROZALIA

(They come out together from the girls' quarters.)

BAGRAT *(emotionally)*: It's worse than I believed. The danger is inescapable.

ROZALIA *(Dressed for a dance, she puts on her gloves.)*: And yesterday I asked myself, "What are those papers my sister is looking through?" She hid them when she saw me. What's she up to? Are they love letters from someone famous? No. They're contracts, business papers—phoo . . . *(She goes to the mirror and looks at herself.)*

*(*BAGRAT *is preoccupied. His arms akimbo, he moves to stage right.)*

BAGRAT: Tell me, Margarit, can you keep those papers here for a few days?

MARGARIT: No.

BAGRAT: Why?

MARGARIT: I've promised to return them tomorrow.

BAGRAT: Before returning them, I think it's important to think this matter through.

MARGARIT: What do you want from me? Say it clearly.

BAGRAT *(wavering)*: I don't think it's wise to put such a gun back into our adversary's hand.

MARGARIT: What then? You're asking me—

BAGRAT *(coldly)*: Not to return those papers.

MARGARIT *(hurt)*: So that you . . . You should be ashamed, with that emblem on your jacket.

BAGRAT *(irritated)*: Drop those empty phrases, for God's sake. I know what's happened. Your suitor has turned your thinking upside down. But we're not living in the age of chivalry.

MARGARIT *(ironically bitter)*: You think that common decency is a matter of chivalry.

BAGRAT: Everyone has his own ideas about decency. Essentially it comes down to this: If those papers pass into Otarian's hands, I lose my factory. You know very well that I've staked my future on that, my strength, effectiveness, and fortune. I want to be known as a capitalist titan with great financial powers.

ROZALIA: A person who can open the door of employment to thousands and feed poor families. I understand you, Bagrat.

MARGARIT: And all that, with someone else's money?

BAGRAT: Children are not responsible for what their fathers have done. Our parents' past is dead for us.

MARGARIT: The one who died is reincarnated and stains our entire family.

BAGRAT: Then he must be choked and put back in his grave.

MARGARIT (*deeply angered*): Bagrat!

BAGRAT: What father hasn't cheated someone or another in this way or that? In the end, who hasn't defrauded or oppressed someone? The difference is that the old-timers stole in old ways and the new ones in new ways. Margarit, today you have to be more calculating than sentimental.

MARGARIT (*deeply indignant*): That is to say, more materialistic than reputable, to allow the parent to rob a bereaved family and leave them in the street? Take his part in his crime. Continue what he began. And why? So that we can live in this lavish palace? With gold-trimmed furniture? Get together and dress up and attend balls and dances? No, no. I'm not able to do it. I can't. (*She moves to the left.*)

ROZALIA (*with hatred, irritated*): Da, da, da, da. How brave you are. I didn't know. You're a perfect heroine.

BAGRAT (*feeling that she's lost*): Margarit, I respect your views, but don't be taken in. Think of the situation we live in. No one we know is going to praise you. On the contrary, many will think you're insane.

MARGARIT: I'm not acting for the benefit of people, but for my conscience.

ROZALIA (*ferociously*): I'm sick of those phrases. (*To* BAGRAT) It's useless to try to make her understand anything. Only force will affect her. Take those papers and it's all over.

(ERANUHI *appears in the dining room doors.*)

BAGRAT (*in the same calm tones*): At least, don't give them to him tomorrow. Wait a few days. We'll think it through. You're intelligent. You don't want to put us into the hands of our enemy.

MARGARIT: Here's Mother. We've talked enough. Let's hear what she has to say.

Scene 4

Same and ERANUHI; *later* ZARUHI

(ERANUHI *comes forward her hands on her bosom, sad.*)

ERANUHI: All these years, I kept my children from knowing what that man had done. God knows how I suffered. Night and day, I've thought and thought about it. From time to time, when I opened my mouth to speak, he'd cut me off by shouting. So I kept quiet—all this anger pent up in me.

MARGARIT: Do you hear?

BAGRAT: Mother, you're too stirred up against Father.

ERANUHI (*indignantly*): Quiet. You don't know anything. Your father has sold his soul to the devil. Last night I saw the dead man in my dream standing by our door, head bowed, with his hands on his breast, pale and worn. He was saying, " Eranuhi, you know how we were partners and worked together to get up that fortune. Why have you allowed my children to be deprived of a crust of bread?" Ah, I want to prevent so many things. But who's listening to me. Bagrat, Bagrat, for nine years that man has cursed us from his grave.

BAGRAT (*irritated*): Two yards of earth bury the curses of the dead.

ERANUHI: Ah, don't talk like my brother. It's a sin. We must all go before the frightful judgment. I am responsible for failing to prevent your father's evil schemes. I tremble with fear.

MARGARIT (*hardly able to control her emotions*): No matter, Mother. Father is good and decent. He'll set his mistake straight.

ERANUHI (*with a hopeless movement of her hand*) Eh, that one. . . .

(ZARUHI *enters.*)

ZARUHI: There's a phone call from the club.

BAGRAT: Ah, I forgot. I'm in charge of the party.

ROZALIA: Let's go. We're late.

BAGRAT (*coming close to* MARGARIT): I hope you'll change your mind by morning.

MARGARIT (*Having been affected strongly by her mother's words, she puts her arms about her neck.*): You've got a good heart, Mother.

ERANUHI (*caressing her head*): Come, Daughter. You're my only consolation. Their souls are different. They're strangers to me. (*She kisses* MARGARIT.)

BAGRAT: Don't be self-righteous. I despise it.

(ROZALIA *and* ZARUHI *follow* BAGRAT *out.*)

Scene 5

MARGARIT, ERANUHI, *and* SUREN

(SUREN *enters from left.*)

SUREN: Did he go, finally, that ardent man of commerce, that ingeniously sharp speculator, that well-larded American? Bravo, Margarit. I heard everything from inside. Mama, this time your wayward son agrees with you. Let me kiss your hand. I met Otarian today. (*To* MARGARIT) Will you let me speak freely with Mother, here?

MARGARIT: I have no secrets from my mother.

SUREN: I must confess, he's a gentleman. I never really got to know him. But I like him a lot now. He told me, "I'm poor and would willingly stay poor if Margarit would not stop caring for me." Do you hear? He's got to have a big heart to give up an inheritance for love.

(ZARUHI, *having returned, is eavesdropping.*)

Get out of here. Why are you eavesdropping?

(ZARUHI *goes into the dining room.*)

MARGARIT: And what did you say to him?

SUREN: Me? What do you think? What can a fool like me say? I told him, "Artashes, my sister is a proud girl. She won't accept such a sacrifice from you. You can't top her with your pride."

MARGARIT: Thank you.

SUREN: That's all we said. Now listen. After all, I'm a member of this family, too. If it's proven that Father cheated Otarian, we must all demand that those who have been deprived are taken care of.

MARGARIT: Mother, did you hear?

SUREN: Eh, why ask your poor mother to listen to me? She's crossed me off her list. I'm a charlatan. Finished. But I want you to know that I'd rather give up my part of the inheritance than have people say to my face, "You're a thief's son." That's final. (*He lights a cigar.*)

ERANUHI: I don't understand you at all. At one and the same time you say that and yet steal from your father.

SUREN: Ah ha, you're talking about my *ious*, Mama. I didn't invent that situation, as God's my witness, but my uncle, your respectable brother. He's Shylock's relative. He lends me money only on condition that he gets ten for one at my father's death. But greed sometimes drives a person insane. Now, my uncle's afraid that he'll go to upper Jerusalem before my father. Mama, don't get angry. Your brother's not a man. He has a wolf's appetite and a fox's cunning. But I, although I'm a prodigal, am a gentleman. Yesterday Bagrat called me a coward because I let myself be slapped in the face. Do you know why I took it?

ERANUHI: I don't want to hear such things. I don't want to.

SUREN: No. You must listen. I took the slap for a very respectable woman. If I hadn't taken it, I'd have had to fight. And had I fought, that woman would have been disgraced. Listen, here's how it happened.

ERANUHI (*closing her ears*): I don't want to hear. I don't want to.

SUREN: All right, let it be. Do you hear, Margarit, Father must prevent his name from being shamed. (*He looks at his watch.*) Oh, it's ten thirty. I must rush.

ERANUHI: Where are you going in the middle of the night, prodigal?

SUREN: To study the stars. Arlova is waiting for me. *Arrivederci.*

(*He goes out by the anteroom doors, singing.*)

MARGARIT: Say what you like, mother, your wayward son has got a sense of honor. More than his brother.

(ZARUHI *enters by the dining room doors.*)

ZARUHI: Cook is asking if you're ready for dinner.

ERANUHI: I don't want anything. Ah, I have a headache.

MARGARIT: I'm not eating either.

(ZARUHI *goes.*)

Mother, why don't you lie down. Your nerves are frayed. I didn't sleep all night either. My head throbs from lack of sleep. (*She kisses her mother and then goes to her room.*)

ERANUHI (*looking after her, sadly*): I hope you're luckier than me. Ah . . . (*She goes into the dining room.*)

Scene 6

ANDREAS *and* SAGHATEL

(*They enter, right, when* ERANUHI *goes off.*)

ANDREAS: Thank God. Finally. They've gone. Yes. Night's better than day. Darkness is a friend of sin.

SAGHATEL (*drawing his beads, one at a time*): Order-disorder, order-disorder, order-disorder. Order! No matter how I say it, order always comes up.

ANDREAS: But my heart tells me that what we're doing isn't good.

SAGHATEL: It'll be worse if you don't do it. You've explained and asked and begged. And nothing happened. What else can you do? You can't just let your enemy destroy your reputation.

ANDREAS: Ring the bell. Let's see what they're doing.

SAGHATEL: There's not a sound to be heard. (*He presses the electric bell button, right. The weak sound of the bell is heard behind the scene.*)

ANDREAS: What does it matter to you? You're safeguarding yourself with five hundred parcels you're getting from me.

SAGHATEL: Didn't I urge you to involve me in this work?

ANDREAS: Good, then.

(ZARUHI *enters.*)

Who's in the dining room?

ZARUHI: No one.

ANDREAS: Then why do you have the lights on?

(ZARUHI *is about to go.*)

What's your mistress doing?

ZARUHI: Nothing. She went to bed. She's got a headache.

ANDREAS: That's all we needed. Call Margarit here.

ZARUHI: She's sleeping.

ANDREAS: Sleeping. Already? Good. You can go. We're going to the club. Tell your mistress. You can go to bed. I'll lock the doors. You're not needed. Put out the lights. You don't know the meaning of economy. You think I mint money or steal it, you're all so extravagant.

(ZARUHI *goes to the dining room; a short while after, the lights go out there.*)

SAGHATEL: One's sick; the other's sleeping. God himself is helping you.

ANDREAS: Don't bring up God's name here. He'll get madder than ever at us. Hum, a good thing I said we were going to the club. See who's in the next room.

(SAGHATEL *looks into the anteroom.*)

Close the doors. (*With quiet steps he approaches the door of* MARGARIT's *room and listens. He looks at his pocket watch and returns to center stage.*)

(*After looking into the anteroom,* SAGHATEL *closes the doors.*)

SAGHATEL: There's nobody there. You couldn't have picked a better time. (*He puts his beads in his pocket.*) What are you thinking about?

ANDREAS: When the devil puts an evil idea in your head, he also puts fear in your heart. Close the dining room doors.

(SAGHATEL *closes them.*)

They're like eyes watching us. Come here. (*He sits in the armchair.*)

(SAGHATEL *goes downstage.*)

SAGHATEL: Eh. You've done a lot. You can handle this one, too.

ANDREAS (*whispering*): Done. I haven't done them alone. You've always been with me. Eh. Your father's image appears before my eyes. He used to say, evildoers will lose themselves in evil ways.

SAGHATEL: Eh. You've found the time to remember my father, too.

ANDREAS: I'm a fifty-six-year-old man. I've passed a thousand and one hazards. I've perjured myself to destroy others, fooled the innocent, chiseled and robbed the pitiable. Three times, I've bribed my way out of court. But I've never been in this kind of situation before. How did I get into it? Look at me: I'm in a cold sweat.

SAGHATEL: Tomorrow, this time, you can count on the fact that seven hundred thousand rubles in property is still in your hands.

ANDREAS: Greed. Avarice. There's nothing else.

SAGHATEL: Eh. You're beginning to make judgments. Hurry up. The night is passing.

ANDREAS: Don't think I'm doing this only for the money. No. That fellow has to be taught a lesson. (*He gets up.*)

SAGHATEL: Of course. There's a matter of honor here. What's money?

ANDREAS (*grinding his teeth*): Disdainful. He wants to choke me. I, who can choke a hundred with these hands. Ah, if I get my hands on those papers, I'll show you who I am. Quiet. What's that noise?

SAGHATEL: I don't hear a sound.

ANDREAS: Andreas, don't weaken. It's a shame. Do this one thing, too. Whatever will be, will be. (*He tiptoes into* MARGARIT's *room.*)

SAGHATEL: The wolf has entered the lamb's pen, my father used to say. (*He goes to the dining room doors and turns out the lights. The stage is dark.*) This is best. They can't see me.

(*Pause. The dining room clock is heard striking eleven.*)

Now I'm afraid, too.

(*A long pause.* ANDREAS *appears in the doorway extremely changed and shaking, but happy. He holds a packet of papers, tightly. Pause.*)

ANDREAS (*whispering*): Saghatel.

SAGHATEL: I'm here. (*He turns on the light.*)

ANDREAS: Ah ha, here is his soul. Ah ha, here is the thing that keeps me from sleep and rest. My wealth, my name, my honor. Seven hundred thousand saved.

SAGHATEL: Let's go. Let's get out of here.

ANDREAS: Wait. Let me see if it's them or not. (*He inspects the packet.*) We've done it! How smoothly it went. She was sleeping like a child, a book held to her bosom. The keys were under her pillow. I took them without a sound.

(*He puts the packet in his pocket quickly.*)

SAGHATEL (*uneasy*): I hear something. Let's go.

(*From the street the sound of a police siren is heard.*)

ANDREAS: The police have probably caught a thief. Some pitiable wretch forced to steal bread because of hunger. Quiet. Let's go.

(SAGHATEL *goes to doors right, pauses briefly, and goes out.* ANDREAS *follows.* MARGARIT *appears in a nightgown. She seems distressed. Looking about, she sees her father violently shaking and about to leave and cries out weakly.*)

MARGARIT: Father. (*She runs forward and cries louder.*) Father!

(*Looking back terrified, he disappears.* MARGARIT *sinks to the floor in tears.*)

The curtain descends slowly.

ACT 4

Same scene as in the first act. It is the next evening. The electric lamps on the desks are lit. The office doors are open. There is no one there. When the curtain rises, BAGRAT *is sitting at his desk, left, looking at papers related to his factory.* KARINIAN *stands nearby offering explanations.* SAGHATEL *sits near* ANDREAS's *desk, feet crossed, drawing on his beads calmly.*

Scene 1

BAGRAT, SAGHATEL, *and* KARINIAN

BAGRAT: I owe eight thousand rubles for pipes. Twenty-seven thousand, two hundred, went on machinery. The whole comes to three hundred twelve thousand . . . (*Aside*) And I'm able to handle all this. All. (*Getting up*) Finish these calculations and then show them to my father. Old merchants fear new ventures. For them, today's kopeck is more precious than tomorrow's ruble.

SAGHATEL: It's the same with me. Small but sure. (*He mashes the beads in his hand as he draws snuff.*)

BAGRAT: The mentality of a shopkeeper. (*To* KARINIAN) You're free to go.

KARINIAN: (KARINIAN *takes the account books off the desk.*) I wanted to remind you—

BAGRAT: About your pay? I know. I'll think about it.

KARINIAN: You've been saying that for six months. A hundred rubles a month for my hard work is too little.

BAGRAT: It's sufficient if one takes into account your limited education. The times require talent and education.

KARINIAN: And does long, unselfish service mean nothing?

BAGRAT: Well, you can go. I don't like to be preached to by employees. Good-bye.

(KARINIAN *goes to the office with a dissatisfied look. The lights go out there.*)

Scene 2

BAGRAT *and* SAGHATEL

BAGRAT (*impatiently*): Uncle, what's new?

SAGHATEL: Thank the Lord, everything's in order. (*He stands quietly and goes to the edge of the stage.*)

BAGRAT: Has Otarian been here?

SAGHATEL: I don't know. I'm not his keeper. (*He paces back and forth with a heavy tread.*)

BAGRAT: Is it possible to find out if he's seen Margarit?

SAGHATEL: It's possible he has or he hasn't. God knows.

BAGRAT: I haven't seen Margarit all day. She's locked herself in her room and won't let anyone in. Why?

SAGHATEL: God knows.

BAGRAT: It's plain a kind of strange sadness has taken over the house today. Don't you feel it? Father seemed changed during lunch. I never heard him speak so disconnectedly before. And he was drinking more wine than usual. You'd think, as sober as he is, he wanted to get drunk deliberately.

SAGHATEL: God knows.

BAGRAT: What is it with you? I don't understand. You keep referring to God.

SAGHATEL: I always refer to God. You'd like to turn my thoughts away from Him with your scientific explanations. But you can't.

BAGRAT (*He pauses, looking at* SAGHATEL *deeply*): You're scolding me? That's not bad, not bad. I was about to chastise you a bit.

SAGHATEL: Chastise me? For what? What have I done?

BAGRAT (*He gets closer, putting his hand on* SAGHATEL's *shoulder, half friendly, half seriously.*): By the way, reverend Uncle, why don't you confess that you wanted to be convinced that (*raising his hand to heaven*) there is nothing there?

SAGHATEL: I should hope so. What do you want to say? Speak plainly.

BAGRAT: I want to say, reverend Uncle, that for men like you there is no help there. (*Raising his hand to heaven*) You may be afraid but not in here. (*He puts his hand on* SAGHATEL's *heart.*)

SAGHATEL: And what are you? You? What or of whom are you afraid? Heathen.

BAGRAT: Me. Ah ha. (*Striking his forehead*) What should I be afraid of? My only God is reason. Now Uncle, let's turn our attention to the practical. Tell me, in twenty-five years, how much have you stolen from the Elizbarians?

SAGHATEL (*shaken, pretending to be hurt*): What have I stolen? Are you drunk, or what?

BAGRAT (*with cold seriousness*): I'm never drunk. You've created problems for my father; he's forgiven you. That's his business. But I ask most respectfully: Keep your hands clean concerning my work.

SAGHATEL: Oh Lord God, oh Lord God. This fellow is mad.

BAGRAT: A little while ago when I was examining the books of my factory, I saw that the materials ordered through you were bought at twice the prices. You haven't shown any authenticating receipts. The sums you show are false. In other words, you've pocketed the difference. I know what you've done is routine for employees. But with me, you'd better be careful.

SAGHATEL (SAGHATEL *is hurt. He makes various gestures of protestation to the wall.*) Listen to him. He's not ashamed. He calls his own uncle a thief. And the heavens don't thunder and the walls are silent. Alas, for us. Alas, for our generation.

BAGRAT: Eh. Drop those gypsylike ways. They don't fool me. I've begged you, again and again. Keep your hands clean. I'm a man who's alert and vengeful. I wouldn't even spare my mother's brother.

SAGHATEL: Shameless. He doesn't even begin to turn red from what he says.

Scene 3

The same and ANDREAS.

(ANDREAS *enters, disturbed but trying to appear calm.*)

ANDREAS: Now what shall we do, Saghatel? I think it wouldn't be a bad idea to go to the club. I haven't been there in a long while. Hum? What do you say, Mr. Engineer?

BAGRAT: I'm happy to see that you want to get out and around. When you don't go to the club, a thousand and one tongues start wagging maliciously. But I'm surprised that you're so calm.

ANDREAS: Why shouldn't I be calm? Praise God, my house hasn't burned down and I'm not in debt. (*He looks uneasily at the doors from which he came.*)

BAGRAT You weren't talking that way, yesterday.

ANDREAS: Yesterday was yesterday. Today is today. Saghatel, give me those beads.

(SAGHATEL *hands them over.*)

Eh, praise be to God. Great is Your mercy. (*He sits at his desk.*)

BAGRAT: Father, so you're not afraid of Otarian anymore.

ANDREAS (*mocking with feigned nervous laughter*): Heh, heh, did you hear that, Saghatel? Are you afraid of Otarian? (*To his son*) Who is Otarian? When have I ever been afraid of him or anyone? Andreas Elizbarian is not one of your fearful types. (*He looks again at the doors left.*) Saghatel, see who's in the other room. (*To* BAGRAT) What you've said is idiotic.

SAGHATEL: There's no one there.

ANDREAS: I thought I saw someone in the corner of my eye wearing a white dress, with long hair. Close those doors. Otarian no . . . dog, cat, mouse, lizard.

BAGRAT (*looking at his father carefully*): I'm amazed. Yesterday, Otarian's name was enough to frighten you. Today you make fun of him. But I, on the contrary, I looked on him with scorn yesterday, and today I can't.

ANDREAS: That's your affair. Do what you will. Saghatel, shall we go to the club or not?

(SAGHATEL *gestures in agreement.*)

BAGRAT: Yesterday I saw Margarit and read those papers whose contents you know. If Margarit returns them to Otarian, I don't know how you can stay so calm.

ANDREAS: You don't have to worry about such things anymore. Your factory will be completed.

BAGRAT (*cheering up*): How's that, Father? Explain. Doesn't this business concern me as much as you?

ANDREAS (*hurt*): Are you going to stop or not? You're making my head swim. I'm not in the mood to discuss these things.

BAGRAT (*Doubtfully, he looks at his father and then* SAGHATEL.) I don't understand a thing. I've got to see Margarit. I'll go and force myself into her room. There's something here you're keeping from me. (*He goes out, left.*)

Scene 4

ANDREAS *and* SAGHATEL

ANDREAS: Ah. (*Nervously impetuous, he throws the beads on the desk and stands.*) I almost let the secret out. I can't, Saghatel. I can't. No matter how I try, I'm not able to look calm.

SAGHATEL: Even a murderer owns his fault in the end. The thing is, in time, you forget and it's done.

ANDREAS: Her appearance in the middle of the night, her horrified face, her voice, I won't forget it to the grave.

SAGHATEL: You're a child. There's nothing to it. You'll talk about all this with others in such a way they won't guess a thing. What's it to Margarit? She's your daughter, she'll forgive you.

ANDREAS (*pacing back and forth*): Don't say that. You don't know how it feels. (*Shaking*) See who's in the office. I heard someone there.

SAGHATEL (*He looks in.*): No one's there. (*He closes the door, then picks up his beads.*)

ANDREAS: I hear sounds everywhere. Everywhere I see people. What does she think about her father? She's probably dying of shame. "Father," she called horrified. My legs got weak. I almost fell at the doors. Saghatel, it seems to me that she's my avenging angel. She follows me like a shadow and in the end will catch me by the collar and say, "Give me an accounting. I'm your judge." What will I say, Saghatel? You and I have done much, but this thing we can't swallow. It'll stick in our throats. You'll see.

SAGHATEL: That's how it'll be if you feel that way. You're putting yourself into jeopardy. You've got to act cool. Think of the fortune you've saved. In that way what you've done will seem trifling. (*Silence*) Yes. While it's on your mind keep your promise. Give me a paper transferring five hundred parcels of land in the city to me.

ANDREAS: For God's sake, you're only thinking of yourself. Greedy.

SAGHATEL (*ironically*): Greedy. You give me one out of twenty and you call me greedy.

ANDREAS: All right. I'll give it to you later.

SAGHATEL: No, no. Now. Later you'll deny it. I know you.

ANDREAS: Later I said.

SAGHATEL (*looking at him thoughtfully*): It's up to you.

ANDREAS (*reading his mind*): Satan, you'd turn your father's grave upside down for a piece of gold. (*He goes to the desk.*) Give me some paper.

SAGHATEL: I've already written up the document. All you've got to do is sign it. (*He takes out a document from his pocket and gives it to him.*)

ANDREAS (*reading the paper*): The devil. You've written it like a notary. Five hundred parcels in the heart of town; one of my best properties. It's too much. I can't afford to give you that much.

SAGHATEL (*coldly*): You promised.

ANDREAS: I say it's too much. I ought to give half to the city for a college. They've been asking me for it a long time.

SAGHATEL: Someone else might construe that as a good deed. Sign.

ANDREAS: I say it's too much.

SAGHATEL (*coldly, reaching to pick up the paper*): You know. I thought that a respectful businessman would keep his word.

ANDREAS (*grinding his teeth*): Ah, brute. (*He signs.*)

(SAGHATEL *picks up the paper, blots the signature, and puts it in his pocket.*)

SAGHATEL: Thank you. You can depend on me in the future. Now, don't think too much. Sin is sin only when it's exposed. What have you really done? You've taken out the wolf's teeth. It's done and gone. Let him roar later all he wants that Elizbarian robbed his father. We'll ask him for proof.

ANDREAS (*listening carefully with an intent expression so as the more to be convinced*): Yes, we'll ask for proof. Let him go to court then. Now, I'm the judge. "Sir," I'll say to him before the judges, "prove, bring evidence, and receive your inheritance." He has no proof. Ha, ha, ha. He hasn't any papers. They are lost and gone. And I'll spit in his face and have my revenge. Oh, Saghatel, I suffered so much. (*He opens the desk chest with a key.*) Ah ha, here is his tongue, pride, soul. (*He takes out the packet and looks at it.*)

SAGHATEL: Burn it. Why hold on to it?

ANDREAS: Oh, I'm going to make a pyre so you'll enjoy it. But let it stay for now until I'm satisfied looking at it. (*He puts the papers back.*) Go in there. The angel Gabriel couldn't save you from Andreas Elizbarian's hand. Eh, who shall I be afraid of? My daughter?

SAGHATEL: She'd never betray you.

ANDREAS (*Shaking, he puts the key into his pocket.*): Ah, I heard steps. See who's coming. We've got to look calm.

SAGHATEL (*He goes to the anteroom doors, opens them, and looks.*): It's him. (*Speaking toward the anteroom*) Come in. (*He moves back, bowing to* OTARIAN.)

Scene 5

Same and OTARIAN

(OTARIAN *enters with an uneasy appearance, bowing to* ANDREAS, *inattentive to* SAGHATEL. *He wears a coat.*)

OTARIAN: Forgive me for disturbing you. Tell me, for God's sake, what's happened in your home. They told me that Mother and Margarit have taken ill suddenly.

ANDREAS: We thank you, sir, for thinking about us. But there's no one ill in this house. Anything else?

OTARIAN: Mr. Andreas, I know you're aware of what goes on here. I wouldn't let them know that Margarit's health is of concern to me. This is the third time I've come today. They don't let me in, saying she's sick. That frightens me. It's impossible that Margarit would not see me because of a small indisposition. She must be very sick.

ANDREAS (*ironically*): Saghatel, do you hear? The man is suffering. Rest easy, sir, my daughter is not sick. She just doesn't want to see you. Saghatel, it's time to go to the club.

SAGHATEL: That's right. (*He signals to* ANDREAS *to act cool.*)

ANDREAS: Eh, good-bye, Mr. Sweetheart. Forgive us, we've got work to do. If you want, you can sit here and rest. Bagrat is at home. Maybe he'll see you. (*He goes to front center to exit.*)

OTARIAN (*watching him silently for a few seconds, in amazement*): It's amazing. Completely incomprehensible.

ANDREAS (*coolly looking at his watch*): What's so amazing, Mr. Philosopher?

OTARIAN: The tune you're playing. Your ironic look. Your coolness.

ANDREAS (*getting angry*): How would you like me to speak, my lad, huh? You want me to bend my neck, be frightened, beg, implore? (*Serious and formal*) Enough. You didn't know your place. I humbled myself like a Christian. You pressed me. Patience has a limit. Now you can go where you want. The doors of my house are closed to you.

SAGHATEL (*to* ANDREAS, *aside*): Don't get angry. It's not good.

OTARIAN (*Emotional and stupefied, he looks on silently.*): What's this? The tongue-tied are talking. So you've forgotten what happened here yesterday. Today you close doors to me that yesterday were open for my return. Tell me, Mr. Andreas, do you really want to hurt me or are you joking?

ANDREAS: I don't joke with fools.

SAGHATEL: Andreas, Andreas.

ANDREAS (*hurt*): Leave me alone. What favors I did for the whelp.

OTARIAN (*becoming furious*): Sir . . .

ANDREAS: Roar all you want. Your voice will rise to the seventh heaven, but it won't reach God. Continue. Why are you silent? "In helping me, you hurt me. I'm a proud man. I've suffered. You took care of me with my own monies. Half your fortune is mine. Give it to me." Disrespectful. For six months I've had no comfort, sleep, or appetite. Your gossip has made me suffer night and day. Because of you, people were beginning to call me a thief and they were just short of spitting in my face. My work of forty years, my name, my reputation, were being trampled underfoot. Now . . . Now, it's enough. You threaten to take me to court. You're welcome to do so. Your road is open. You can take it. But the doors of my house are closed to you, and they won't open for eternity.

SAGHATEL (*aside*): This man is going to ruin everything.

(*Restraining himself,* OTARIAN *listens, amazed and hurt.*)

OTARIAN: And is this glib-tongued speaker Andreas Elizbarian? The person who tried to bribe me with a few thousand rubles so I would give up my just demand? Are you still ridiculing me? Tell me what kind of transformation this is? Who or what saved you from yesterday's pitiful position? Who inspired you with such courage?

ANDREAS: I'm not frightened by your threats, not by so much as a hair's breadth.

OTARIAN: You lie, sir. You yourself this minute admitted that I kept you from sleep and comfort. That means you were convinced your security depended on me. You believed that if I simply wished it, you'd be crawling at my feet.

ANDREAS: Shameless . . . (*He springs at him.*)

SAGHATEL (*going between them*): Andreas, Andreas.

(*A pause*)

OTARIAN (*clenching his fists, wants to fight but holds back.*): No, no. No insanity. I've got to find out what's happened here. I can't say anything. I must see Margarit. She'll tell me the truth. One of us. Either I've been fooled by that girl or this man is evil personified. Margarit will tell me the secret. She is obliged to explain. I believe in her as in the last judgment. I'll see her even if she's on her deathbed. (*He walks toward the anteroom.*)

ANDREAS (*to* SAGHATEL): Tell the servants not to let him in.

OTARIAN (*stopping*): Be careful, sir. You'll lose your daughter's respect. (*He moves quickly into the anteroom.*)

ANDREAS (*loudly*): Vardan. Throw him out. Throw him out. (*He goes to the anteroom.*)

SAGHATEL (*holding him by the arm*): Patience, for God's sake. Patience. Think what you're doing.

ANDREAS (*coming to his senses*): You're right. I shouldn't get angry. It's better if he's angry. But what can I do? He vexes me in the extreme. See where he went.

SAGHATEL (*looking through the anteroom doors*): They've opened the door. Bagrat is asking him to enter.

ANDREAS: What shall we do if Margarit tells him?

SAGHATEL: Am I not the witness? I haven't seen nor heard anything.

Scene 6

ANDREAS, MARGARIT, *and* SAGHATEL; *later without* SAGHATEL

(MARGARIT *enters from left and stops at the doors. She is drowsy. Her deep suffering and drowsiness are visible on her face.* ANDREAS *trembles upon seeing her but controls himself. A few moments of tableau. He goes to center stage.* MARGARIT, *at left, does not look at her father.* SAGHATEL *crosses to right and, with beads in hand, stares at the ceiling.* MARGARIT *wants to speak but is annoyed by* SAGHATEL's *presence.*)

MARGARIT: Uncle, Mother wants to see you, I believe.

SAGHATEL (*aside*): She's calling me. (*As he is quietly going off from right to left he notices papers on the floor, picks them up, and puts them on* BAGRAT's *desk.*)

(*After getting* SAGHATEL *out,* MARGARIT *closes the doors behind him.*)

ANDREAS: You are supposed to be ill. Why are you up?

MARGARIT (*Wrapped in her own thoughts, she does not respond to her father.*): Father, he's waiting to see me. He's tried three times. I can't see him. I can't face him. Father, it's up to you whether I can ever face him again.

ANDREAS: What are you talking about? What do you want from me?

MARGARIT (*with a trembling voice, but firmly*): Decency.

ANDREAS: I am what I am. No more, no less. Who do you think you are, speaking to me like this?

MARGARIT: Don't torture me, Father. I can't endure your dissembling.

ANDREAS: If I'm dissembling, you forced me to it.

MARGARIT: I was trying to save your good name.

ANDREAS (*sarcastically*): Save? You were plunging me into total disgrace. You wanted to sacrifice me to your lover.

MARGARIT (*wounded*): Father, don't say that. Don't say it.

ANDREAS: Why shouldn't I say it? Ever since he started with you, you don't think about your parents. A kiss from him is dearer to you than my good name.

MARGARIT: You're wrong, I swear it. Yes, I love him. But the honor of our family means more to me than happiness.

ANDREAS: Silence. Have you no shame? How dare you talk to me about your love? You wanted my money—that's what you wanted—so that you and that adventurer could live together in luxury. My dowry for you was too small.

MARGARIT: Don't say that. You can't believe it. You know I never thought of your money.

ANDREAS (*mockingly*): Of course! You're not of this world. You're not born of a mother. Enough! You have no feeling for me. You hate me. You are my enemy.

MARGARIT: Very well, if that's what you believe. But one day you'll understand that no one cares for you as much as I.

ANDREAS: Why are you plaguing me? Tell me in a word what you want.

MARGARIT: Give the papers back. Give them back.

ANDREAS (*laughing bitterly*): Give them back. Andreas Elizbarian, do you hear that? Give the sword to your enemy, bow your head so he can cut it off. No, my child. God bless us. I'm not insane yet.

MARGARIT: Father, don't make fun of me. I can't endure it.

ANDREAS (*changing his tone*): What papers do you want? What papers? I haven't seen any papers. I haven't had any papers. And I don't have any papers now. Tend to your own business.

MARGARIT (*wringing her hands*): My God.

ANDREAS: You've dreamed the whole thing.

MARGARIT: If only it had been a dream! No. I heard the keys in the night and I awoke. I saw your huge figure in the dim light. I could hardly believe it. I was petrified to see you.

ANDREAS: You must have been dreaming. Yesterday, all day, I wasn't even at home. Your uncle's my witness.

MARGARIT: Father. If I don't count, at least think of yourself. Those papers will bring a curse on you.

ANDREAS: That's enough. Don't try my patience. Your attitude is insufferable.

MARGARIT: You can't frighten me. Not after what you did last night.

ANDREAS: Get out! You're shameless. Get out before I do something rash.

MARGARIT: Father, don't think I'm not going to implicate you when I have to tell about the theft of those papers.

ANDREAS: Before you could open your mouth, I'd tear out your dirty tongue and throw it to the dogs. So keep your mouth shut, and the devil take it.

MARGARIT (*hopelessly*): I don't know what to do. Don't be so heartless. Father, please give me those papers. I've got to return them today. I've given my word. He's waiting in the other room. I've avoided him like a thief. Give them up, if you have the least respect for me.

ANDREAS: Damn you, you devil. I told you, I've nothing to give you.

MARGARIT: Father, you don't know me. I can't say all I feel, but I've thought through this whole business. I'd die for your honor. But what about mine? Must I defile it just for your riches? Spare me this shame. That's your duty as my father. Give me my honor. Without it, I can't live.

ANDREAS (*in a great rage*): Get away from me. My blood's gone to my head.

MARGARIT: I won't go until I get those papers. Deny me everything. Disown me. I'd rather make my own way than be known as a thief. I couldn't bear that. He's good. He thinks I'm a good person. He respects me. I don't want him to think me a thief. Never, Father. You're kind and decent and won't let that happen.

I'm pleading with you. (*She kneels.*) Pity me. Listen. I'm speaking about my life. Don't do this Father. Don't do this. Stealing is a great sin.

ANDREAS (*struggling with himself*): Get up. Have you no shame? Someone may come in.

MARGARIT: No. I'll stand only if you return me my honor. Listen to your conscience. Don't turn away. I swear I won't judge you. Not with a word. Not with a glance. I'll be silent, and I'll respect you as before. I know that you're confused and that you regret what you've done. Father, give me the papers.

ANDREAS (*with a decisive movement, pulling away*): I've had enough. (*He crosses to the desk, quickly opens the strong box, and takes out the bundle of documents.*)

MARGARIT (*mistaking his intentions*): I knew you couldn't do this. Thank you, Father. You've cleared my name.

ANDREAS: Get your hands off. I'm going to end this once and for all. You're insane. (*He tears up the papers and throws them into the stove.*) This is where they belong.

MARGARIT: What are you doing?

(*She leaps forward, screaming, trying to save the papers. He prevents her from reaching the stove.*)

ANDREAS: Get away or I'll throw you in there, too. At last, I'm free of you. Burn! Turn to ashes. You've burned my heart enough. (*Father and daughter struggle.*)

MARGARIT: Let go. Let go. You're burning me. (*She tries to scratch her father's hands.*) I don't have the strength to fight. But I'll shout. I'll call everyone, so they can see your thievery. Let go. (*Freeing herself from her father's grip, she approaches the stove.*) Ah, it's too late. They're burned. Everything's lost. (*She calls out.*) Come here. Rozalia, Bagrat! Everyone, come here. See what's happened here. A father has burned his daughter's honor. Ah, all is lost. (*Weakened, she falls against a chair. Silence.*) So be it.

(*She goes to doors left and meets* OTARIAN *entering. She is shocked and freezes.* BAGRAT *enters by the same doors a while after* OTARIAN. ANDREAS, *arms akimbo, stands at left.*)

OTARIAN: At last I've found you. You're not sick. You've been hiding from me. Your father has dishonored me and ordered me out of his house. In his eyes I'm a thief, trying to get his wealth illegally. Show him my papers. Show him I'm in the right. I've been dishonored. Show him my proof.

(MARGARIT *stands by the wall—silent, pale, and trembling.*)

Your brother plays a different tune today. We've switched roles. Yesterday, your father wanted to bribe me; today, your brother. For God's sake, explain what's happened. (*Silence*) You're silent. You stand there as though you're guilty of something. I swear by my oppressed father's grave that either you or I is insane. Speak. Is this a conspiracy? Didn't I make you a judge in this matter? What have you done with my papers? Bring them here.

MARGARIT (*faltering a long moment*): I don't know.

OTARIAN: Why are you silent? Margarit, bring me those papers.

MARGARIT (*with the coldness of death*): I burned them. In there.

(*She points to the stove. Full of anguish, she takes a long look at her father. Then, turning from her father, and with slow steps, she leaves by doors left.* OTARIAN *and* BAGRAT *go to the stove.* BAGRAT *closes the stove's doors.*)

OTARIAN (*looking surprised from one to the other*): She burned them? Then this whole thing became a trap for her. Margarit couldn't be an ally of a thief. No, that couldn't be. I'd never suspect her. I know she's a saint. She lied and took the blame herself. The culprit here is someone else. (*To* ANDREAS) Clear her name before she's destroyed by all this.

(SAGHATEL *enters left.*)

ANDREAS: Saghatel, let's go to the club. (*He strides toward the vestibule.*)

(*Behind the scene, a gunshot is heard, startling everyone.*)

SAGHATEL: What was that? (*He runs toward doors left.*)

(BAGRAT *follows.* OTARIAN *and* ANDREAS *stand immobile.* SUREN *runs in from doors left, pale, faltering. Silence.*)

SUREN: Margarit's killed herself.

ANDREAS (*bellowing and striking his head*): I've killed her.

OTARIAN: You burned them. Monster! (*He tries to leap at* ANDREAS, *but* SUREN *comes between them.*)

SUREN: He's been punished enough. (*He looks contemptuously at his father.*)

OTARIAN: Margarit. Margarit. (OTARIAN *runs to the left and, leaning weakly on the door, exits.*)

The curtain descends slowly.

LEWON SHANT

Lewon Shant was born in 1869 into the well-to-do Seghbosian family of Constantinople, which had become an increasingly significant center of Armenian culture. He was orphaned at age six, after which his paternal aunt became his legal guardian.

His early schooling at the junior college in Üsküdar was in Western Armenian. After graduation in 1884, along with the future musicologist Komitas, he was one of eight pupils from Constantinople to be accepted into the Gevorgian Academy of Ejmiatsin, founded in 1869 by Catholicos Georg IV. During his seven-year stay there he was exposed to Eastern Armenian, affording him an unusual range and depth of literary expression. As a result, his writing is marked by a unique blend of lexical elements from both modern standard forms of the language. Languages, literature, history, and science formed the mainstay of the curriculum at the academy. The most distinguished Armenian institution of higher education in Transcaucasia, it was established to prepare clerics and teachers for church schools; however, during his study years there, it became increasingly open to free thinking.

The year 1891, marking both his graduation from the academy and his acceptance of a teaching post in Constantinople, also saw his debut as a writer. Starting with essays and poetry, he progressed through the years to short stories, novels, and plays, adopting Shant [lightning bolt] as his pen name.

His desire to obtain a rounded tertiary level of

education led him to Germany, where he attended classes in pedagogy, history of literature and the arts, psychology, and physiology at the Universities of Leipzig, Jena, and Munich (1892–99). During this period Shant published the novels *Leran Aghjike* [The daughter of the mountain], *Eraz Orer* [Dream days], *Drsetsiner* [Outsiders], and *Verzhin*; the short stories *Dardze* [The turning point] and *Derasanuhi* [Actress]; and a collection of lyric poems *Erger* [Songs].

In 1899 Shant moved to Paris and worked as the business manager of a theater, an experience that marked a transition in his career. Henceforth he transferred his artistic talents to the theater. His early plays illustrate the individualistic outlook of Nietzschean thought: *Esi marde* [The "I" Man] (1901); *Urishi hamar* [For someone else] (1903); and *Chambun vray* [On the road] (1904). These were all realistic in nature and contemporary to the author's own life and times.

When Shant returned to Transcaucasia in 1903 he married Chavo Nersesian. He served as principal of the Gayanian Girls' College of Tiflis, capital of the region (1906–1908), and taught at the local Armenian school of Erevan. He became a productive member of *Vernatun* [Upper room], an Armenian literary group, and, with its support, his first plays were published and performed.

In 1908, while bedridden with a lengthy illness in Erevan, Shant began to write his first historical play, *Hin astuatsner* [Ancient gods], a drama that revolutionized the Armenian literary world. The Armenian theater was dazzled by its debut on the Tiflis stage in 1913. Subsequently it was translated into German and Russian, then into Italian and French. The outbreak of World War I disrupted efforts to stage it in the state theaters of Germany and Russia. In 1917, however, it drew record crowds in Rostov, where it was directed by Stanislavsky.

The royalties from staging *Ancient Gods* allowed Shant to return to Europe in 1913, where he remained for the next five years, except for two visits to the Caucasus — once to perform his play there, another time to assist in the Armenian Volunteer Movement.

The ferment of World War I, together with the impact of the Armenian Genocide, led Shant to probe the Armenian past. Interlacing fact with fiction he created characters larger than life, as Shakespeare had done in his chronicle plays. His *Kaysr* [Emperor], published in Tiflis in 1916, chronicles the events of the years 963–969, reflecting the rise and fall of Emperor Nicephorus Phocas and the ascension of John Tzimiskes, who appears in *Kaysr* under the guise of Ohan Gurgen. It is the most historically accurate of his plays. In it the characters function both as real people and symbolic abstractions. He contrasts the lust for power with the glory of kingship and its burdens. It is the drama of all great men whose ambition often clouds their vision, with tragic consequences.

After the armistice of 1918 Armenia proclaimed itself an independent republic. Subsequently, in 1920, Shant headed a commission to Moscow to secure the republic's recognition by the Bolshevik government. When Armenia accepted Soviet rule later that same year, officials of the former government were imprisoned,

Shant among them. He was freed, however, when a new underground movement succeeded in liberating hundreds of prisoners in 1921, after which he fled to Teheran.

The horror of the Armenian Genocide scarred the hearts and minds of its survivors, and Shant was living with the burning memory of the suffering and loss of his people. Severely disillusioned with the fall of the Armenian Republic as a result of internal discord, Shant begins to reflect his preoccupation with Armenian history and the disunity that characterizes it in his dramaturgy of this period.

The result was the creation of *Inkats berdi ishkhanuhin* [The princess of the fallen castle], which depicts the victorious revenge of the author's most powerful heroine, Princess Anna. Written during a brief interval in Teheran, it was published in 1923. The action occurs at the beginning of the twelfth century. Shant gives a vivid portrayal of the political intrigue, tyranny, and internal strife emblematic of the era. His heroine is the pure embodiment of revenge.

Shant's other historical plays include *Shghtayuatse* [The chained] (1918), written in Lausanne, and his last drama *Oshin Payl* [Bailey Oshin], written a decade later in Beirut, where he lived and worked for the rest of his life. The former depicts social unrest in the Bagratuni capital of Ani in the aftermath of the Seljuq invasion of Anatolia in the second half of the eleventh century. The latter play treats intrigue in the Armenian kingdom of Cilicia in the eastern Mediterranean during the fourteenth century.

In 1929 Shant and Nicole Aghbabian founded the Armenian Academy of Beirut, which Shant directed over the next twenty years. He published a series of graded textbooks, which were widely employed in private Armenian schools throughout the Middle East. Although he never composed any more plays, he helped found the first permanent theatrical company in the Armenian Diaspora, the Caspar Ipekian National Theater Group. *The Princess of the Fallen Castle* was the group's first play in 1942, after which the plays of Shant became a regular part of its repertory.

In 1951 Shant died of a serious liver condition and was buried on December 2, in Beirut. Despite the rain, thousands came to eulogize the great man of letters.

A.T.V.

ANCIENT GODS

(HIN ASTUATSNER, 1908)

Translated by Anne T. Vardanian

CAST OF CHARACTERS

FATHER SUPERIOR: Abbot of the monastery of
    Sevan.

MAN IN WHITE

MONK ADAM

STONECUTTER

A SEXTON

MONK MOVSES

OLD MONK

MONK ANTON

MONK ADAM

MONK DAWIT

MONK ZAKARIA

THE PRINCE

MONK SIMON

MONK GHAZAR

YOUNG MONK

SEDA: Daughter of the prince; she appears in the
    drama as a figment of the young monk's imagi-
    nation.

BLIND MONK

DEACON

PRINCESS MARY: Sister of the prince.

NURSE

STEWARD

MASTER CRAFTSMAN

HERMIT

PAGAN PRIEST

CULT MINISTER

VETERAN

BURLY SOLDIER

VAHAGN: An Armenian pre-Christian deity; god of thunder, war, and, in the later
    period, the sun.

ASTGHIK: An Armenian pre-Christian deity; VAHAGN's consort and goddess of
    beauty and fertility.

FIRST PSALMODIST

SECOND PSALMODIST

A YOUTHFUL MONK

BUILDING LABORERS

VARIOUS MONKS

SOLDIERS

TEMPLE GIRLS AND YOUTHS

NYMPHS, BREEZES, WAVES

ACT 1

Scene 1

The summit of Sevan. A ruin amid the rocks. Twilight.

(FATHER SUPERIOR *is seated on a rock, his chin resting on his hand, as he pensively
looks down. From under a partially destroyed arch, the Man in White emerges.* FA-
THER SUPERIOR *is tall, has thick, graying hair, and is bareheaded. The Man in
White is likewise bareheaded and has long black hair and a splendid black beard,
braided in the Assyrian manner. For a moment they stare at each other in silence.*)

MAN IN WHITE (*jeeringly*): Oh, how you survey your kingdom!

FATHER SUPERIOR: Who are you?

MAN IN WHITE: Behold that sight! See those few, small flimsy cells. Didn't you
    build them? And that chapel which you've built in haste! And lastly, look at
    your new church, whose dome soars upward day by day, and on top of which,
    with your own hands, you shall soon affix the cross.

FATHER SUPERIOR: Yes, if the Lord so wills it.

MAN IN WHITE: Look and take pride! Isn't that all born of your selfish will?

FATHER SUPERIOR: Who are you?

MAN IN WHITE: You, garbed in black! Why have you gathered those black-robed
    and black-souled people about you? Why have you come to this ancient isle?

FATHER SUPERIOR: Who are you?

MAN IN WHITE: Arise, arise! Drive that miserable, morose throng back to life again.
    Get out, you who want to dry up the senses and suppress all passions. Out of

this isle, you who are enemies of all beauty, all life and movement, all strength and creation. Out! Do not defile this holy paradise of my gods!

FATHER SUPERIOR: There is no paradise here! I founded my monastery on this piece of rock. Hereafter, this isle shall be called a desert.

MAN IN WHITE: A desert? On the bay of this smiling sea, facing this brilliant sun? Go away! The spot you tread upon is an ancient altar of the gods! Away! I speak to you from the threshold of the ancient gods.

FATHER SUPERIOR: From the ruins of the ancient gods!

MAN IN WHITE: Men like you piled up these stones. They have been destroyed, but the temple of life is indestructible, as is life itself. Stones will crumble, names will change, but the gods endure forever!

FATHER SUPERIOR: Here died your gods!

MAN IN WHITE: Here and wherever man treads, they shall be immortal and eternal.

FATHER SUPERIOR: Here died your gods, and, upon their ruins, I built my God's temple. Look, see the apex of the dome, almost completed, still visible in the dusk. There reigns only the spirit; there reigns the breath of God alone.

MAN IN WHITE: There reigns the instrument of suffering and death!

FATHER SUPERIOR: It is suffering that elevates the soul and torment that cleanses it. And the most unfathomable mystery of life is death.

MAN IN WHITE: Suffering is the submission to a life of pain, and the willful waste of life is death.

FATHER SUPERIOR: Through you speaks primitive mankind.

MAN IN WHITE: It's ailing mankind that speaks through you!

FATHER SUPERIOR: Enough! Who are you that speak so profanely? Be gone! There is no place on this island for you and your gods.

MAN IN WHITE: This island is also part of the world. Oh, you bewildered fool, pay homage to the eternal gods!

FATHER SUPERIOR: Go away!

MAN IN WHITE: Accept them and pay homage!

FATHER SUPERIOR: Go away!

MAN IN WHITE: The day will come when you will accept their power. (*He disappears.*)

FATHER SUPERIOR (*looks about uncomfortably*): Who was that? He vanished! An apparition, a doubt? No, never! The world cannot enter this island. The world shall never enter this island. Never!

Scene 2

A courtyard in front of the church under construction. On one side of the stage there is an open door frame, through which several wooden ladders are seen. Here and there are planks, partially carved stones, a sieve, and tools. Upstage center there are trees through which one catches a glimpse of the sea. Throughout the scene it is windy. Occasionally there is a vigorous gust of wind. The rustle of leaves and the distant, muffled sound of the sea are heard.

Part 1

One or two STONECUTTERS *run through the trees toward the sea. The* SEXTON *passes swiftly through the upstage area, carrying a long pole on his shoulder. Out of the church emerges* MONK ADAM, *who struggles to pull a rope out of the church.*

MONK ADAM (*fervently*): God help us! May God help us!

STONECUTTER: (*He enters from the direction of the sea, drying his hands. His legs and arms are bare.*) Drop it, Father, drop it! There's no need for it. They got out. They all made it to the shore.

MONK ADAM: All? All of them, you say? Even those who fell overboard?

STONECUTTER: All of them, though we'd completely given up hope. We stood there dumbfounded and helpless. It's such a furious sea! We said, "Now it'll smash the boat against the rocks on shore and shatter it to pieces with all on board." My God, they got away lightly!

MONK ADAM: Glory to you, holy Mother of God! And who fell overboard? Were there many?

STONECUTTER: Only two, our young monk and a young lady.

MONK ADAM: Young lady? What young lady?

STONECUTTER: The prince's daughter.

MONK ADAM: Oh, was she with the prince, too? Well, is she alive? Is she conscious?

STONECUTTER: Yes, it seems so. Her father and his men took her to Father Abbot's cell. You should have seen how pale the prince was!

MONK ADAM: Poor man! Why did they embark in weather like this?

Part 2

Enter MONK ANTON, MONK MOVSES, *and the* OLD MONK.

MONK ANTON: Wait, wait, let me catch my breath! Don't keep asking me what happened next. What followed was awful! Ooh, my arms feel like they're going to fall off!

(*He sits on a high rock. During the course of the dialogue that follows, those present gather about* MONK ANTON *as he relates the events. A few Laborers and* MONKS GHAZAR, DAWIT, *and* ZAKARIA *also enter and join those listening.*)

MONK MOVSES: Get on with your story.

OLD MONK: Wait, Son, until he catches his breath.

MONK ANTON (*briefly covers his face with his hands, then suddenly looks up, taking his hands away*): We were already halfway across. Again and again we climbed to the top of the waves and were hurled down below. All on the boat clung to their places, pale and stiff. The young monk and I were pulling at the oars with all our might. When I turned my head and glanced around, I saw that we were approaching the shore! The oncoming waves, smashing against the rocks, were like mountains of foam rising before us. Why hide my fear? My heart sank. I said, "It's all over." Yet, hope against hope, I forcefully bent to my oars, repeating again and again, "Oh, Lord Jesus." I told everyone, "Sit tight, don't be frightened!" Suddenly, just as I said this, I saw one enormous wave approaching from the distance. It looked as though it was torn from the shore and was heading straight for us. (*Standing up*) And the rest . . . Oh, how can I describe it? I only know that all of a sudden the boat listed sharply at the crest of the wave overhanging the gaping abyss. Then we heard a sharp cry. It seemed as if something fell out of our boat and slipped into the sea. The prince cried, "My daughter, my daughter!" There was chaos and confusion. I hardly knew what had happened when the young monk jumped up from my side, flung off his waistband, and leaped into the water. The boat swayed violently, and I was left with one oar. It's a good thing a wave was driving us to the island shore, but I knew that the rip tide would push us out again. If you hadn't thrown us the ropes in time, we'd all have been lost. A half-minute longer . . . just a half-minute, and it would all have been over!

OLD MONK: A miracle from God!

MONK ADAM: And the young lady?

MONK ANTON (*proudly*): Our young monk rescued her!

MONK ADAM: He swam back with her?

MONK DAWIT: Yes, he did! He brought her ashore!

MONK MOVSES: You mean the young monk can swim so well?

MONK DAWIT: But when did he learn? Who would have thought it!

MONK MOVSES: It's a miracle!

OLD MONK: I tell you the hand of God is in this!

MONK ADAM: But really, why did you set out in this weather, Father Anton?

MONK ANTON: I warned them at Tsamakaberd not to. Our saintly princess herself pleaded along with us, but no one took any heed. Her brother, the prince, ordered his men to board the boat. "If you're afraid, don't come," he said. How could I refuse? I said, "It's God's will."

MONK MOVSES: Well, what about his daughter?

MONK ANTON: She's another one, just like her father!

OLD MONK: No! This was the will of the Mother of God. (*Straightening himself up on his cane, excitedly*) Who can we thank for building this shrine dedicated to the Mother of God? Our saintly princess, of course. Who keeps this monastery in good repair? Who has built our cells? Who in time of need has consistently helped the prayerful servants of the Mother of God?

VOICES: It's true, it's true!

MONK ZAKARIA: May God bestow long life on our patron, the saintly princess!

OLD MONK: She, who has left all courtly life and pleasures, her children, her palace, and has come to the feet of the Mother of God in the solitude of her castle by the shore, to dedicate her remaining days to self-denial and prayer.

MONK DAWIT: Long live our pious saint!

OLD MONK: Yes, because of the princess's dedication, the Mother of God performed this miracle for us, by rescuing the princess's brother and his daughter from the waves. Let all those wanting in faith observe and be convinced that our Mother of God does not turn away from her servants and her worshipers. May we be generous with our prayers, and may she be generous with her blessings upon us and our saintly princess. Glory to the name of the Mother of God! Glory to the name of her only begotten Son, forever and ever!

THE GROUP: Amen!

VOICES: The prince! The prince!

Part 3

Immediately the group divides itself into two parts. They line up and stand by humbly. The PRINCE *and* FATHER SUPERIOR *enter with a few followers and* MONKS.

PRINCE (*heading directly toward the building*): So this is the church so loved and cherished by my sister. It's a cozy, little church, and rather pretty. (*To his followers*) I said that I would see this church today, and, despite the adverse elements, I am here now, safe and sound.

FATHER SUPERIOR: That was a bold step you took, Your Grace!

PRINCE: Your desert is one thing, Father Superior, but outside this cloister it's quite different. Out there, the world belongs to men of daring! And, after all, who knows when I'll pass through these parts once more? I have so many things to attend to. I felt I ought to see my sister's church at least once. Shouldn't I kiss its holy altar before going back?

FATHER SUPERIOR: You might have come tomorrow, Your Grace?

PRINCE: Tomorrow? I'm taking leave of my sister tonight!

FATHER SUPERIOR: Are you crossing over again today?

OLD MONK: Do not tempt God, Your Grace!

PRINCE: God forbid! We have a few hours on the island. I hope the sea will calm down by then.

FATHER SUPERIOR: If you are not concerned about yourself, you ought to be thinking of your child, at least.

PRINCE: My daughter is up to the task! She was frightened a bit and took in some of your Sevan water. That's all. She's young, she'll get over the shock. But her experience will always stay with her. After all, I gave her an exciting storm to treasure in her youthful storehouse of memories.

OLD MONK: You shouldn't toy with life, Your Grace!

PRINCE: What do you really know about life, old man? You've lived so long, you've forgotten life is just a game.

OLD MONK: Life, my son, is a cross we must bear on our shoulders till the Lord calls us. The Mother of God spared you this time. Don't transgress in that way again!

PRINCE: And I'm thankful to her, Father. I'm on a pilgrimage to her shrine and haven't come empty-handed. I am donating an embossed oak door and a velvet curtain embroidered in gold thread to this shrine of the Holy Mother, for the main altar.

OLD MONK: Bless you! The name of your house shall never be erased from these walls!

PRINCE: Moreover, I have ordered my steward to send ten measures of wheat from my barns to your desert every year, as long as my house stands. May you enjoy it, and may you include my parents and children in your prayers!

VOICES: God bless the memory of your parents! May your fields and orchards be bountiful! God keep your children! May God increase your estate and your fortune!

PRINCE: And now (*to* FATHER SUPERIOR), where is the young monk?

FATHER SUPERIOR: Coming, your Grace. I've sent for him. Ah! Here he is now.

Part 4

The YOUNG MONK *enters, accompanied by* MONK SIMON *and a scribe. He is dejected, his face immobile, his eyes downcast and rather listless.*

PRINCE (*after briefly studying the* YOUNG MONK): What a handsome lad you are, and how young!

FATHER SUPERIOR: He is the youngest in our order, Prince.

PRINCE: Oh, if only you were not garbed in that black cassock, then I'd know what to do. I'd give you my favorite stallion. I'd give you my very own sword, which for thirty years has served me faithfully. And I'd take you into my palace as my very own son. My black stallion would have been a fitting gift for you. And your hand, I see, would have quickly gotten accustomed to my sword. Had my horse and sword not sufficed, I'd have given you my daughter—

FATHER SUPERIOR: Your Grace!

PRINCE: . . . whose life you saved today. She'd already be yours by right. In the outside world whatever you lay hands on is yours.

FATHER SUPERIOR: Your Grace!

PRINCE: I know, I know. This holy monastery is not the place for this kind of talk. But what can I do? I want to give him something. I want to do something to show my gratitude somehow to this selfless, valiant hero! What a pity! That black cassock binds my hands! (*Moving closer to the* YOUNG MONK) My son, your prince stands before you impoverished and utterly powerless to repay you. What I'd like to say would seem inappropriate here, what I'd like to give would be useless to you here.

FATHER SUPERIOR: All we need is the sun to shine on you and your daughter.

PRINCE (*to the* YOUNG MONK): Well, then, I remain indebted to you. It's not a good feeling. I'm not accustomed to being indebted. At any rate, give me your hand. Here's mine. It has never been weak before our enemies and has never committed an unjust act. It is only proper that you take it in your own, which today rescued my daughter from the waves. (*The* PRINCE *firmly clasps the* YOUNG MONK's *hand.*) Father Superior, let's go into the church.

(*The* PRINCE, FATHER SUPERIOR, *several followers and* MONKS *enter the church.*)

MONK SIMON (*gently taking the* YOUNG MONK's *arm*): Let's go. We should go now so you can rest a little. Your color is completely gone, and I sense your body is still trembling. (*Half supporting the* YOUNG MONK, *he leads him offstage.*)

Part 5

MONK GHAZAR (*approaching* MONK ADAM, *in a thoughtful manner*): Now, how long does the Young Monk have to do penance before the doors of the church are open to him again?

MONK ADAM: Do penance? Why?

MONK GHAZAR: Well, hasn't he touched a woman?

MONK ADAM: But . . . but in a situation like this—

MONK GHAZAR: It's all the same, a sin is always a sin. (*More thoughtfully*) I saw them, clinging to each other as they emerged from the waves. The Prince's men practically forced the girl out of his arms!

MONK ADAM (*angrily*): You're speaking nonsense!

Scene 3

Evening. The YOUNG MONK's *cell. A low, small room with unplastered stone walls. Upstage center there is a simple wooden bed; on it is spread a piece of rawhide and a hard rough pillow. A coarse coverlet has partially fallen to the floor. In the middle of the room stands a low, wide bookstand, upon a piece of old carpet. On the bookstand, there is a large open manuscript. On one side of the room there is a rough wooden table; on it are a black wooden cross, a clay water jug, and an oil lamp that flickers.*

Opposite the table is the entrance to the room. The YOUNG MONK*'s cassock hangs from the wall at the head of the bed.*

Part 1

The YOUNG MONK *is sitting on the edge of his bed, his hands are folded across his chest, staring at the floor. Next to him, on a low wooden stool, sits the* BLIND MONK, *erect and immobile, both hands on his cane, his head held high.*

BLIND MONK: Where are your thoughts, Young Monk?

(*Startled, the* YOUNG MONK *raises his head.*)

BLIND MONK: Wandering again?

YOUNG MONK: Yes, I know it's a sin, a great sin. No, I'm not going to think about it anymore! There's no need to! I must erase this day from my mind, everything, everything, the sea, the wind, the boat, the waves, oh, those waves! (*Suddenly he jumps up.*) But what a wonderful thing it was to fight them. They push their wet breasts against you, splashing their foam against your face, blinding you. One of them leaps on your shoulder, another rolls across your chest. One pushes, the other pulls, crushing you. And all of them, all of them, want to drag you under. And you, always on the surface, rocking with their undulations, overcome all their attempts to draw you into the deep with controlled arm strokes. Ah, for that fight!

BLIND MONK: Fighting is about life, Brother. This is a desert.

YOUNG MONK: Yes, a desert! (*Contrite*) I have sinned against you, my God; I have sinned.

BLIND MONK: Careful! Examine yourself well, Brother, pray!

YOUNG MONK (*kneeling in front of the cross*): I'm a lost sinner, save me, Lord. I'm an abject transgressor, help me, Lord. I'm drowning, take my hand, Lord. I'm adrift in the sea of sin, in the sea . . . the sea. (*He rises, covering his face with both hands.*)

BLIND MONK: Say it, say it!

(*The* YOUNG MONK *suddenly uncovers his face and looks directly at the* BLIND MONK*'s statuelike face.*)

BLIND MONK: Say it. Out with it!

YOUNG MONK: Say what?

BLIND MONK: What's out there in the deep!

YOUNG MONK: The deep, the deep.

BLIND MONK: Say it, say it!

YOUNG MONK: Who can see that far into the deep? Who can speak about the deep?

BLIND MONK: I . . . I can see. I can speak!

YOUNG MONK: You, a blind man can see? (*Sarcastically*) Then speak! Tell me what you see.

BLIND MONK (*staccato*): In the boat, when the oar in your hand was cutting through the water, who was there in your soul?

YOUNG MONK (*frightened*): Quiet!

BLIND MONK: For whom was your heart throbbing? What was the word clinging to your lips, when everyone around you was calling out to God in the midst of the storm?

YOUNG MONK (*horrified*): I wish your eyes were open so you could not see!

BLIND MONK: When all glances were turned toward heaven, when all were awaiting help from above, where were your eyes fixed? And before whom did your soul genuflect?

YOUNG MONK: Be quiet, be quiet! You have no right to see everything! You can't see into everything.

BLIND MONK (*pitilessly*): Speak! What was your desire? What were you seeking?

YOUNG MONK (*pleading*): I don't know, I don't know anything . . . that's enough!

BLIND MONK: And in the sea, when she, like a serpent, was wrapped around your neck, her body against your body, her breath against your breath, as you cut through the waves, tell me you still don't know what it was you desired!

YOUNG MONK (*dreamily*): I remember, I remember! With all my being I wished that there would be no end to that watery road, that there would be no end to that moment!

BLIND MONK: Impious!

YOUNG MONK (*shattered*): But it did come to an end!

BLIND MONK: And you reached the shore. Then, when they took your burden out of your arms and you, exhausted, fell to the sand, you were already a lifeless corpse!

YOUNG MONK: That's true! That's just how I felt.

BLIND MONK: Even now, you are a corpse. A body from which the breath of God is gone!

YOUNG MONK: Oh, my God, I've lost my soul!

BLIND MONK (*standing up*): Fall to the ground and lament. Wear the sackcloth and repent. But first, go at once to Father Superior and confess.

YOUNG MONK: Confess? To Father Superior? What? Why? Oh, anything, but that one thing. Never. Never! And you, too, Father, you won't, you—

BLIND MONK: No. I'm blind, deaf, and dumb; but go yourself, to Father Superior, and willingly confess.

YOUNG MONK (*sharply*): To Father Superior? Never!

BLIND MONK: Are you afraid?

YOUNG MONK: No, but . . . but . . .

BLIND MONK: Of course! You want to secretly venerate your little new goddess in a distant corner of your heart.

YOUNG MONK: Have pity, have pity on me . . . you merciless—

BLIND MONK: And you, do you pity yourself? You heathen, remember the commandment, "Thou shalt have no other gods before me."[1]

YOUNG MONK: Shalt not have . . . shalt not have.

BLIND MONK: "Thou shalt not make unto thee any graven image, or any likeness of anything that is in heaven above, or that is in the earth beneath, or that is in the water under the earth."

YOUNG MONK (*trembling*): "Or that is in the water under the earth."

BLIND MONK (*slowly walking toward the door*): "For I, the Lord thy God, am a jealous God, visiting the iniquity of the fathers upon the children . . ." (*He goes out.*)

Part 2

YOUNG MONK (*goes to the crucifix and kneels in front of it and, with arms outstretched, fervently prays*): Save me, Oh God, for the waters are coming into my soul. I sink in the deep mire, where there is no respite; I am come into deep . . . into deep waters, where the floods have overwhelmed me.[2]

(*He becomes weaker and weaker, and bows his head on his chest.*)

Part 3

Slowly the table and the cross become enveloped in mist; everything becomes hazy and blurred. Against the background of this mist, a girl's form gradually becomes visible. She appears to have just emerged from the water, dressed in a simple, delicate and close-fitting white tunic. Her hair is loose and damp, covered with a few strands of seaweed entwined in it. The YOUNG MONK *raises his head slightly. Suddenly he sees her and jumps to his feet in terror.*

YOUNG MONK (*backing away*): You . . . You?

SEDA: Yes, me . . . Weren't you expecting me?

YOUNG MONK: My God!

SEDA: You're alone?

YOUNG MONK: I . . . I am always alone.

---

1. In the following exchange the text is drawn from Exodus 20:3–5.
2. Psalms 69 [68 LXX]: 1–2.

SEDA: And now I've come as your companion. And I've come like this, at midnight, so we could be alone, you and I. You, my hero . . . my sun . . . my savior!

YOUNG MONK: That's enough!

SEDA: Why? Isn't it because of you I am alive now, since you saved me from the deep and gave me back life? And how sweet is that life you gave me! All these years I've lived . . . seventeen in all, I had no idea how precious life is. There we were, there in the waves. My hair is still damp . . . Take it in your hand . . . take it . . . here, stroke it.

(The YOUNG MONK backs up, bewitched by the sight of the girl.)

SEDA: You have such strong, agile arms. How aroused I still am, despite my fatigue! (She attempts to sit on the YOUNG MONK's bed.)

YOUNG MONK (attempting to prevent her): Young lady!

SEDA (sitting on the edge of the bed): I am "young lady" to my servants. I am "young lady" to our subjects. My lord must address me in some other manner.

YOUNG MONK: Seda!

SEDA: Oh, my! You know my name!

YOUNG MONK: That's the name your father used.

SEDA: Yes, Seda is my name. And what is your name?

YOUNG MONK: They call me Brother.

SEDA: But before . . . before . . . when you were in the world and of the world?

YOUNG MONK: My world has always been the monastery ever since I came of age.

SEDA: Oh, how chilly it is here. How cold I am!

YOUNG MONK: You're cold?

SEDA: Put something 'round me to warm my soul.

YOUNG MONK: I don't have anything.

SEDA (Without turning her head, she points to his cassock, hanging on the rear wall.): That would do.

YOUNG MONK: My cassock?

SEDA: I'm cold!

YOUNG MONK: My cassock?

SEDA: You hesitate! But you did not hesitate to risk your life for me. You did not hesitate when you plunged after me into the raging waves.

YOUNG MONK: No, I did not hesitate. That was different.

SEDA: Yes, that was different! There it was a battle in the stormy sea! Here, it is quiet and peaceful . . . like a grave. Oh, how chilly it is here. I'm so cold! (She stands up.)

(The YOUNG MONK runs toward the cassock. His hand reaches for it, but again he hesitates and stops.)

SEDA (*pleading*): Bring it, here . . . here . . .

(*The* YOUNG MONK *suddenly grabs the cassock and turns toward the girl, who has already disappeared. He remains immobile, holding the cassock in his outstretched hand.*)

Part 4

Offstage, the SEXTON's *voice is heard, in a monotone, as he calls worshipers to the service in a melancholy chant. The sound grows gradually closer. The cassock falls from the* YOUNG MONK's *hands.*

YOUNG MONK (*mumbling*): Jesus . . . (*He tries to kneel before the cross, but jumps back like a madman.*) No! No! What if she suddenly appears again? (*He turns his face toward the bed.*) Oh, my God has turned away from me! (*Sobbing, he falls to the foot of the bed and buries his face in the bedding. Outside, the* SEXTON's *chant continues, gradually becoming more and more distant, eventually fading away.*)

Curtain

ACT 2

Scene 1

At the spring, under the shade of a huge old tree.

Part 1

The OLD MONK *is seated on a wooden bench under the tree and seems to be napping. The* MONKS GHAZAR, MOVSES, DAWIT, *and* ZAKARIA, *and the* DEACON, *are gathered near the spring. They speak in whispers and appear uneasy. The* YOUNG MONK *is near them. With eyes downcast, he listens.*

MONK MOVSES: Is it true? Again?

DEACON: He said it jumped on the bed, grabbed him by the throat, and started throttling him.

MONK MOVSES: Jesus Christ!

DEACON: The poor man almost died of asphyxiation!

MONK DAWIT: The Evil One has obviously turned against Father Barsegh! How many times has it happened to him?

MONK ZAKARIA: What form did the demon assume?

DEACON: I don't know. He merely said that it rose like smoking sulfur and vanished through the beams of the ceiling.

MONK MOVSES: The damned thing! A curse on it!

DEACON: Ah, it's horrible. We can't escape its clutches!

MONK DAWIT: At night, I can never fall asleep until I've looked under my bed and all around it!

MONK MOVSES: Me, too! Yesterday evening I entered my cell, and what did I see? There it was, like a woman wrapped in a gray sheet, squatting in the corner. I was terrified! Immediately I made the sign of the cross, and it disappeared!

MONK GHAZAR: Yes, roots of apostasy come in female forms. They come in groups and perform any and all shameless acts you can think of.

MONK ZAKARIA: But, to me, they always appear in the form of our villagers; the tavernkeeper Usep, our neighbor Gabo, blind Akob the flute player, the drummer Minas. They come and gather about me, carrying wine and *arak*, skewered roasts, and foods of all kinds. The heavenly aroma of stew fills my cell. It's as if the demons have swarmed into the yard and are cooking sacrificial meats! How they urge me to indulge! And how they tempt me! Not until I utter the name of our holy Mother of God do they vanish, never to return.

MONK MOVSES: Why do you punish us with this, Oh Lord our Savior?

MONK ZAKARIA: Then contrarily they steal our Lady's name from my mind! I search and search for it, and . . . there, there . . . it's on the tip of my tongue, but I just can't say "Holy Virgin Mary."

DEACON: Ah, how can we escape from the clutches of these foul spirits? Where do we run, how do we flee?

MONK MOVSES: And what do they want from us, us of all people?

MONK DAWIT: He, who comes to this desert, will be tempted by Satan, as was our Lord Jesus Christ.

MONK MOVSES: May Jesus Christ be our protector!

THE CROWD: Jesus Christ!

DEACON: And they are everywhere, all over, no matter where you go. How do we know that one of them isn't sitting here right now, behind us? (*He changes his place.*) There, in the crevices of the rocks on the bank, or even above us. Yes, in the shade of the foliage. Do you see it . . . do you? There's one, deep in the shadows . . . It's moving! And another one here . . . Yes, it's here . . . in the spring! Look, look, how it bubbles! (*Horrified, stepping back from the spring*) Jesus Christ! (*He comes face to face with* FATHER SUPERIOR.)

Part 2

FATHER SUPERIOR (*sternly*): What is it? What are you afraid of, Deacon?

DEACON (*falling to* FATHER SUPERIOR's *feet*): Holy Father.

MONK MOVSES: Father Superior, the Evil One gives us no rest!

MONK GHAZAR: Powerful is the treachery of the Evil One!

FATHER SUPERIOR (*with disgust*): Are you still talking about that old demon to me? (*Angrily*) On your feet, Deacon!

(*Covering his face, the* DEACON *gets to his feet.*)

FATHER SUPERIOR (*He looks at the* DEACON *for a short while, then turns to the others, emphasizing each word.*): Let him be afraid of the Evil One, who has not conquered his body and his natural instincts. Satan's rule is over the natural instincts only!

OLD MONK: And who is he, Father Superior, who has conquered his body and his natural instincts?

FATHER SUPERIOR (*proudly*): He who has come to this desert, Old Man.

OLD MONK: We are merely men, all of us, Father Superior.

FATHER SUPERIOR: No, Father, he who has come here with me, to my desert, must be superior to ordinary man. And he, who has not severed all his ties with the world, with his past, with his memories, with his sorrows and his joys, let him be afraid of the Evil One.

OLD MONK: And who is he, Father Superior, who has been able to sever all those ties?

FATHER SUPERIOR (*proudly*): He who has come to this desert, Old Man.

OLD MONK: We are only men, all of us, Father Superior.

FATHER SUPERIOR: He, who is man, and only man, belongs to the world. Then let him return to the world. There, Father Anton's boat is ready. I didn't summon you here so you could scare yourselves silly with demons. (*Enthusiastically, he raises the simple cross hanging from his chest.*) Here is the cross of the Lord. There are no demons here!

(*All fervently make the sign of the cross.*)

There are no passions here, there are no natural instincts here. Only the Holy Spirit is here, only the mind is here, soaring upward toward truth, toward God! Know this well, and leave the satans to the world. Now go in peace, and may the Lord be with you all.

ALL: Amen! (*They scatter, each in his own path.*)

Part 3

FATHER SUPERIOR *is standing alone. He looks after them, sadly shaking his head. The* YOUNG MONK *approaches him quietly, from the side. He bends and gently raises the hem of* FATHER SUPERIOR'*s cassock and kisses it.*

FATHER SUPERIOR (*He suddenly senses the movement and turns around.*): What are you doing, my son? What is it?

YOUNG MONK: Father . . .

FATHER SUPERIOR: What's on your mind, my son?

YOUNG MONK: How sublime you are, Father, how very sublime!

FATHER SUPERIOR: We all aim high, my son.

YOUNG MONK (*ironically, sighing*): We all . . . It seems as though your voice comes from heaven . . . far away, from on high . . . (*sighing*) we all . . . . As far back as I can recall, I have been under your wing, taken your advice, and looked to your example. And there was a time when I believed that I, too, would reach those heights.

FATHER SUPERIOR: And now, my son?

YOUNG MONK: Now . . . Now . . . (*Curtly*) I'm not one of the spiritual elite you're searching for, Father.

FATHER SUPERIOR: What are you saying, my son? How you slander yourself! You, my favored one, you, who have soared above all the others.

YOUNG MONK: I soared . . . perhaps when my wings were free and light.

FATHER SUPERIOR: And now, what happened to your wings?

YOUNG MONK: Now? Now, my wings have been drenched, Father!

FATHER SUPERIOR: Drenched?

YOUNG MONK (*mysteriously, approaching* FATHER SUPERIOR): Now I, too, am afraid, Father.

FATHER SUPERIOR: Are you, too, afraid of Satan?

YOUNG MONK: Satan? No! Not of Satan.

FATHER SUPERIOR: What, then?

YOUNG MONK: I'm afraid . . . of the sea!

FATHER SUPERIOR: The sea?

YOUNG MONK: The sea. Waves, storm, excitement, struggle, all of it!

FATHER SUPERIOR: I understand, my son. That incident the other day has shaken your soul. It'll pass. What could there be between you and the sea? Your heart is tender, merciful, and compassionate. And you rescued someone your age from death! May you be blessed!

YOUNG MONK: But since that day, Father, it seems to me that the sea is the heart of nature.

FATHER SUPERIOR (*looking straight at the* YOUNG MONK, *then somewhat sternly*): Look to heaven, my son. Heaven is the mind of nature, profound and peaceful.

YOUNG MONK: Yes, profound and peaceful, when the sky is a bright sea-blue. But my thoughts are more like gray, gloomy days, when everything is hazy and blurred. (*Breaking down*) I'm not one of your spiritual elite, Father!

FATHER SUPERIOR: Is that really you speaking this way, Young Monk? You, who were my pride and joy, whose soul I have shaped, you in whom I have instilled my most precious thoughts, my very own soul, who, after I'm gone, should continue my work. I like humility, Young Monk, but from the mouth of one, who is to be my heir, I'd rather hear more spirited words!

YOUNG MONK (*suddenly covering his face and sobbing*): Ah, you don't know yet . . . you don't know yet, Father!

FATHER SUPERIOR (*Completely altered, he straightens up. Suddenly, in a stern tone*): Look at me! Look into my eyes!

(*The* YOUNG MONK *sobs.*)

FATHER SUPERIOR: Can my suspicions be true? Young Monk, look me in the eye!

(*The* YOUNG MONK *continues sobbing.*)

So weak, so pitiful! You, whose soul I thought was as strong as granite, a pure and immaculate, exceptional soul. Your head proudly held high toward heaven, in the sea of life—just as this untouched, solitary island of mine in the sea. Pathetic wretch, do you want to bow that beautiful, that proud head from these heights where our God is to this sea below?

YOUNG MONK: God has turned His face from me!

FATHER SUPERIOR: Silence! Silence! So frail, so pitiable . . . at the first temptation!

YOUNG MONK (*kneeling*): Father . . .

FATHER SUPERIOR (*pulling back*): Get up, get up. Many times I've seen you at my feet, but not like this, not like this! I can't see you this way. Get up, get up!

(*The* YOUNG MONK *stands.*)

FATHER SUPERIOR: And be gone! Go and become your old self again, just as you were before, and then come to me. As you were, as you were . . . (*He stops short and remains grimly fixed.*)

(*The* YOUNG MONK *leaves silently, with head bowed.*)

Part 4

FATHER SUPERIOR: The world wants to enter my island. There, the demons; here that girl, and the young monk, my young monk. No, it can't be. (*Turning toward the peak of the island and seeing the* MAN IN WHITE) Eh, you . . . you . . . What's your name? You there in white?

[*The* MAN IN WHITE *sneers.*]

No! What happened here was an accident. Don't gloat over a mere accident. It's over and done with.

Scene 2

A stretch of the seashore among the rocks. Stage left is a steep bank, stage right has scattered clusters of rock, center stage is flat and sandy. Upstage center is the sea, extending to the foot of the rocks. In the background is the outline of the mountains. It is a bright sunset. The rocks, the trees, the sea, everything is bathed in the orange-red rays of the sun. During the course of the scene the colors glimmer as they gradually change.

Part 1

For a short time the stage is vacant. GIRLS' *high-pitched giggling is heard. To the right, on one of the lower rocks, a nymph appears. She looks around gaily and, turning back, cups her hands over her mouth and calls.*

FIRST NYMPH: Hoh! Hoh!

(Another nymph appears on the adjoining rock. She boldly and playfully motions with her hands and calls to her companions in the distance.)

SECOND NYMPH: Over here. Here!

(The two of them, hand in hand, lightly jump to the sand. Meanwhile, from atop and behind the same rocks, singly and in groups, NYMPHS *pour onto the stage, delicately and lightly, nimble and lively. They are wearing light blue or green netlike garments adorned with foamy ornaments. All have their hair loose, with matching colored headbands. They jump, they run, they romp about. There is laughter and jostling. On the edge of the same rock the* YOUNG MONK *appears, like one who is fleeing his pursuers. Other* NYMPHS *follow him. The* YOUNG MONK *looks off from the rocks, then hastens to descend. He stumbles, falls, and ends up sprawled at the foot of the rock. There is general giggling and gaiety. The* YOUNG MONK *cautiously rises from where he stumbled, gloomy and dazed. And with a hopeless gesture, he covers his eyes with his hand. The* NYMPHS *become silent and motionless.)*

THIRD NYMPH *(slowly approaching the* YOUNG MONK *and shouting in his ear)*: Seda!

(The YOUNG MONK *is startled and immediately uncovers his eyes. There is a general wave of giggling, which is quickly repressed.)*

ALL NYMPHS *(from various sides and positions, echoing each other)*: Seda . . . Seda . . . Seda . . .

YOUNG MONK: Go! Vanish! In the name of Jesus Christ! In the name of this cross (*making the sign of the cross over them*).

A GROUP OF NYMPHS (*surrounding him, jeeringly*):

> Pity this poor handsome boy,
> Pity this poor handsome boy.
> Your cross is just a broken toy.

YOUNG MONK (*again breaking down*): My prayers are impotent. My cross is powerless.

FOURTH NYMPH: Hey, hey, don't dismay.

FIRST NYMPH: Everything here is happy and gay.

YOUNG MONK (*discouraged*): Oh, what do you want, let me be!

THIRD NYMPH: We want your soul afire and free.

SECOND NYMPH: We haven't hurt your views.

FIFTH NYMPH: We've only brought good news.

THIRD NYMPH: Tidings of love, from hills above.

SECOND NYMPH:

> To love with love,
> To love with love,
> The rule is this
> For centuries.

YOUNG MONK (*rubbing his eyes*): But no, this is a demonic dream!

FIRST NYMPH: Demonic?

ALL NYMPHS (*Arm in arm they encircle the* YOUNG MONK, *then sing and dance around him.*):

> Demons, demons, arm in arm,
> Let's sing and dance, arm in arm.
> His heart will then feel lighter,
> This loveless, wingless mortal.
> Wings, wings,
> Rapture and love,
> Give him wings
> To soar above.

YOUNG MONK (*attacking the* THIRD NYMPH):

> Tell me, tell me, what are you
> To sound as sweetly as you do?

THIRD NYMPH (*jumping back lightly*):

> I'm not a demon, nor a pixie,
> I've brought you tidings from the sea.

YOUNG MONK: Then you are living, and you are real.
THIRD NYMPH: Yes, as real as you, now standing here.
YOUNG MONK: Where is your home, where is your nest?
THIRD NYMPH: First here, then there, just anywhere.
FIRST NYMPH:

> Nymphs of the land, nymphs of the sea,
> We are as sweet as sweet can be.

YOUNG MONK: Never before have I seen you.
FIRST NYMPH: First . . . you must feel love in you.
SECOND NYMPH: Yearnings and dreams of every hue.
FIFTH NYMPH (*pushing her companions aside, coming forward*): But we're acquaint-
ed, you and I.
YOUNG MONK: We are acquainted? You and I?
FIFTH NYMPH: Yes, that morning . . . do you recall?

> The wave—you at its crest, Seda at your breast,
> And in your ear, the storm, the squall . . .

YOUNG MONK (*excitedly*): When I fought the waves!
FIFTH NYMPH:

> It was us you fought,
> And kicked with such zest
> Striking me hard right
> Between my breasts.

YOUNG MONK (*compassionately*): Was it painful?
FIFTH NYMPH (*to her companion*):

> Painful? And what is pain?
> But from the blows so widely thrown,
> I turned into a ball of foam.

YOUNG MONK: You, foam and mist?
SIXTH NYMPH (*tenderly embracing* FIFTH NYMPH):

Sweet Sis,
Foamy Miss,
Just one,
Little kiss?

FOURTH NYMPH (*with a dismissing wave of the hand*): It's so funny! What a tease.
FIFTH NYMPH (*annoyed*): Oh, that's enough, let me be!
YOUNG MONK: But when did you leave the sea?
FIFTH NYMPH:

Before the cool descended,
The warm noon not yet ended.

YOUNG MONK: You willingly ascended?
FIFTH NYMPH: Father Sun called us, on high.
YOUNG MONK: Father . . . Sun . . . called you, but why?
FIFTH NYMPH (*echoing him with laughter and amazement, to her companions*):
    Why?
FIRST NYMPH (*echoing the last phoneme*): Ay! Ay!
SIXTH NYMPH:

To fly, to fly,
To embrace the breezes with our kisses.

YOUNG MONK: The breezes?
SECOND NYMPH: Ay! Ay! They've come!
A GROUP FROM BACKSTAGE (*voices*): They're here, here.
FOURTH NYMPH: Breezes! Breezes! Run away far!
ANOTHER GROUP (*coming on with a hop and a skip*): Breezes! Breezes! Here they
    are!

Part 2

*There is general confusion. The Breezes enter, scrambling about. They are young,
slender adolescent boys with thick hair. Their clothes are gray, pleated, and flowing.
They enter upstage center and, mingling with the NYMPHS, pair off embracing one
another. Then they pull the NYMPHS away with them as they exit downstage, noisily
skipping and laughing. A couple speaks as they cross the stage.*

NYMPH: Again, you kept us waiting.
BREEZE: In the hills we were fighting.
NYMPH: With whom this time, may we know?

BREEZE: With those who dwell in the snow.
NYMPH:

> For them such hatred I hold.
> They are so crude and so cold.

(*They exit. A small group enters, tugging at one another.*)

BREEZE: Into the bush and its embrace.
ANOTHER BREEZE: Into the sea's open face.
NYMPH: Oh, to song and dance unending.
ANOTHER NYMPH: To joy and pleasure ever tending.

(*They exit. A large group enters, arm in arm, forming a chain.*)

BREEZES: You're the sweet breath of the sea.
NYMPHS: You're ethereal passion till eternity.
TOGETHER:

> In warm embrace we entwine,
> Oh, what a life, pure divine!

(*They exit. A group, which has fallen behind, enters hurriedly.*)

A NYMPH (*looking back at the* YOUNG MONK):

> Come on, boy. Come on!
> You, too, can come with us.

ANOTHER NYMPH (*embracing her Breeze*):

> Oh, no! He cannot,
> For he has neither mate,
> Nor friend.

THE GROUP (*going off*): Nor friend.

Part 3

YOUNG MONK (*He looks after them for awhile, until the sound dies away. He sadly shakes his head.*): Neither mate nor friend. (*He is silent for a moment, then he suddenly speaks from the depths of his heart.*) Oh, if I only knew that this ascetic life were not in vain! What kind of life is it? A neglected candle before the crucifix, alone and pale, that burns and melts away. (*He covers his face with his hands, hangs his head, and remains immobile.*)

Part 4

(*From the edge of a high, steep rock bank, a* HERMIT *appears, disheveled and half-naked. The* YOUNG MONK *stands near the opening of a pit.*)

HERMIT (*yelling*): Hey, who's there? What business have you there, at the opening of my pit?

(*The* YOUNG MONK *looks up, startled.*)

Hey! I'm talking to you! What are you up to, down there? (*He quickly climbs down the cliff, appearing and disappearing behind the pointed edges of the rocks.*) Why have you come here, Man, to these uninhabited parts?

YOUNG MONK: Oh, you must be that hermit who came to this island all by himself, long before us, to lead an ascetic life. But hasn't he been dead for a long, long time now?

HERMIT: And you, haven't you been dead for a long, long time now?

YOUNG MONK: Me?

HERMIT: Vanity! Now, tell me this. Why have you come to these uninhabited parts?

YOUNG MONK: I don't know. They brought me here.

HERMIT: Who brought you here?

YOUNG MONK (*pensively*): I don't know. But wasn't your hermitage farther up, on the other side of these rocks?

HERMIT: But this is where my pit is!

YOUNG MONK: Pit? What pit?

HERMIT: Look there, at your feet; the Pit of Vanity!

YOUNG MONK (*He looks down. There is a gravelike hole in the ground.*): Vanity?

HERMIT: Careful! Don't cave it in!

YOUNG MONK: Is it true, Hermit, that you were lord and king of entire countries, that you lived in palaces, that hundreds catered to your every whim? That your joys and pleasures were boundless? Is it true, Hermit, all that they say?

HERMIT: Vanity!

YOUNG MONK: They say you have left it all—palace, festivities, kingdom, and glory. You left everything, put on the habit, and went among the people to preach repentance, mercy, charity, and humility. Is it true, Hermit, all that they say?

HERMIT: Vanity!

YOUNG MONK: Is it true that you had your fill of that, too? You came to this solitary place to find tranquility and to meditate on the salvation of your soul?

HERMIT: Vanity!

YOUNG MONK (*intrigued*): Hermit, what are you talking about? Vanity? Then why this hermit's life?

HERMIT (*indifferently*): Stand back from the edge of my pit. Don't cave it in!

YOUNG MONK: Yes, this pit! It must be your grave, since you fret over it like that. But it is open and empty!

HERMIT: The grave . . . also Vanity! I have no grave.

YOUNG MONK: Yes, that's true, I know! They say you threw yourself into the sea—there, from that high cliff, on the other side. Weren't you afraid of losing your soul? Didn't you fear the afterlife?

HERMIT: That in itself is another Vanity—your soul and your afterlife!

YOUNG MONK (*horrified*): Be silent, you wretch! What you say is blasphemy.

HERMIT: Your alarm is groundless! Stand back from my pit!

YOUNG MONK: Then why the pit? And to what end? What's more, why did you dig that hole and guard it with such obsessive care? Even now that you're dead?

HERMIT (*shaking his head*): Aha, that's it, that's it! Vanity of Vanities! I dug, I dug . . . See, with my fingernails, my mind, my heart! I dug constantly, from the day I was born till I drew my last breath. I dug and sought to find something at the bottom, something of value. I dug and protected the pit, so that all my work would not be in vain. And now I protect it because I dug it—it's the only thing I own, my creation! The only thing, that pit, that empty pit, that perpetually empty pit, that becomes emptier the more you dig. Empty, empty! Do you understand that it will never, never be filled? With anything, anything. You go, too; go and dig your own pit and leave mine to me. (*He starts to leave.*)

YOUNG MONK: Wait, wait! I have a final question for you, you who are so wise.

HERMIT (*still partially visible behind the rock*): Man—wise? Vanity! (*He disappears completely.*)

Part 5

The YOUNG MONK *goes again to the head of the pit. He looks at it thoughtfully, with a sad, gloomy expression. From amid the rocks, a form emerges, completely wrapped in a mistlike veil. Slowly and deliberately, she comes forward and stands facing the* YOUNG MONK.

VEILED ONE: Here I am. What's your desire?

YOUNG MONK (*raises his head, looks somewhat surprised, yet unconcerned*): You, too—a nymph?

VEILED ONE: Why did you summon me?

YOUNG MONK: I . . . summon you?

VEILED ONE: Your soul called me, and here I am.

YOUNG MONK: My soul?

VEILED ONE: Why is your soul so burdened? What were you thinking of?

YOUNG MONK: My soul?

VEILED ONE: Tell me, and don't be so sad.

YOUNG MONK (*pointing to the pit*): There, look!

VEILED ONE: What about it?

YOUNG MONK: It's life!

VEILED ONE: Life? That dark, narrow pit?

YOUNG MONK: Yes, the Pit of Vanity.

VEILED ONE: Frightened by that empty pit? Shall I fill it?

YOUNG MONK (*eagerly*): Fill it?

VEILED ONE: Right away, there's nothing to it. (*She moves closer and stands at the edge of the pit; then she begins her chant with evocative beckoning movements. From above, a misty fog descends over the pit, beneath the red rays of the setting sun. In the descending fog, barely distinguishable, are images of faces, different parts of the body, leaves, flowers, sparks and colors.*)

VEILED ONE:

Descend,
Dreams descend.
Dreams,
Gently descend.
Caressing,
Sweet dreams,
Descend,
Tender dreams.
Flowers, foliage,
Freshly woven,
Murmur of fortune
And hopes,
Quivering, fleeting,
Full of longing.
Secret tears,
Hesitation,
Contradiction
Of mind and sense,
Ever expecting
A new life's dawn.
    Descend.
    Dreams descend
    Dreams,
    Gently descend.
    Caressing,

Sweet dreams,
Descend,
Tender dreams.
Gentle love and smiles,
Color and scent.
Sparkling eyes
And kisses,
Endless desires
Inexplicable
Torment and yearning,
Ever raging.
Lullaby and excitement
Agitating,
Hearts aflutter,
With song and love.
    Descend,
    Dreams descend.
    Dreams,
    Gently descend.
    Caressing,
    Sweet dreams,
    Descend,
    Tender dreams.
Enchanting stars,
Flames and sparks,

Deliriums burning
And flickering.
Belief in strength
And greatness.
In existence of glory and will.
Tumult and thunder,
Pride,
And wisdom,
Myriad dreams.

Descend,
Dreams descend.
Dreams,
Gently descend.
Caressing,
Sweet dreams,
Descend,
Tender dreams.

VEILED ONE: So, come, don't be sad anymore.

YOUNG MONK (*looking at the pit*): It's filled! I'd like to step on it.

VEILED ONE: Go ahead.

YOUNG MONK (*places one foot on the pit*): So now I'm standing on the Pit of Vanity!

VEILED ONE: Now you're standing on dreams!

YOUNG MONK: Yes, and the pit is filled. (*Suddenly, he jumps back joyously and calls out spontaneously.*) Hey, Hermit! Hey, Vanity! Your pit is filled, filled. But who are you, veiled charmer?

VEILED ONE: Me? I, too, am a dream.

YOUNG MONK: A dream?

VEILED ONE: I'm the one you've been waiting for, years and years without knowing . . . the one you called in the loneliness of your cell during those long, long nights, without uttering a word . . . for whom your young, eager heart thirsted, endlessly, without admitting it. I'm the one without whom the island is a desert, whose presence makes paradise bloom in the desert. And now I've come to you.

YOUNG MONK (*excited*): Blessed is your arrival, oh veiled one! Tell me, what shall I call you?

VEILED ONE: Call me whatever your heart desires. My names are countless. You loved the sea so well. Call me Mermaid, if you like.

YOUNG MONK (*dreamily*): Yes, the frolicking waves of the sea, at the foot of these rocks, have always spoken of you to me.

VEILED ONE: And the gentle wind in the leaves, the birds beneath the bushes, the gurgling of the spring . . . All, all, every day and everywhere, they spoke of me to you.

YOUNG MONK: I want to see your face. Uncover it.

VEILED ONE: Don't, you may be sorry!

YOUNG MONK: I want to see your face. Uncover it!

VEILED ONE: All right, come and uncover it yourself.

YOUNG MONK (*fearfully, trembling*): Me?

VEILED ONE: Come, uncover it.

YOUNG MONK (*Trembling, he approaches her; his hands shaking, he takes hold of the tip of the veil and draws it back. It slips on to the girl's arms, and there stands* SEDA, *just as she was in the first act. The* YOUNG MONK *pulls back in wonder and frenzy.*) Seda!

SEDA: It's me.

YOUNG MONK (*becoming gradually more and more enraptured*): Oh, you! You charm of my very being, you queen of my thoughts, you sea of my heart, you storm of my soul. You are the fire of the sun. You are the tumult of the seas. You are Nature's gift to me . . . (*He prostrates himself before her.*) Let me kiss the ground you walk on—kiss the immaculate hem of that white dress. (*He tries to wrap himself about her. The girl's image fades into the mist and disappears. The* YOUNG MONK *remains motionless where the Pit of Vanity was, in the same embracing position.*)

Part 6

MONKS ADAM *and* SIMON *emerge from behind the rocks upstage, each carrying a stuffed handkerchief.*

MONK SIMON: What a hellish road. Here, take my hand.

MONK ADAM (*helping* MONK SIMON *climb down from the rock*): Look, Father Simon, what's that over there? It looks like a man fallen on the ground.

MONK SIMON (*making the sign of the cross*): In the name of Jesus Christ! A man? So far from everything? Let's hope he hasn't met with some misfortune! (*He climbs down the rocks, and they both approach the* YOUNG MONK *cautiously.*)

YOUNG MONK (*Hearing their footfalls, he turns his head toward the noise, then looks back at where* SEDA *was, bewildered.*) She's gone! (*He looks to see where she's gone, rises partially, and then sits again.*)

MONK SIMON: Ah, is that you, Young Monk? Were you praying? But why so far from everything?

MONK ADAM: You scared us!

(*The* YOUNG MONK *stands up, looks at them in confusion, then, suddenly and in earnest, he begins to search for something on the ground.*)

MONK ADAM: What are you looking for, Young Monk?

YOUNG MONK: Where is it? It should be right here. Where's the pit? Where's that pit?

MONK ADAM: What pit, Young Monk?

YOUNG MONK: Oh, that's right, I forgot. Of course, she filled it up!

MONK ADAM: Filled it up? Filled what up? Who?

YOUNG MONK: She . . . it . . . the dream!

MONK SIMON (*smiling*): Oh, you had a dream? You fell asleep, did you?

YOUNG MONK: A dream? (*Suddenly, he flings himself on* MONK SIMON, *shaking him roughly by the shoulders.*) And you're not?

MONK SIMON (*pulling back*): Lord Jesus, protect us from evil!

YOUNG MONK: This, me? The monastery, this desert? How do I know what's a dream and what's waking? She and they there, or you and me here?

MONK ADAM: Wake up, Young Monk, wake up! What dream? That's Father Simon, and this is me, a humble sinner. We were at the peak of the island and climbed down to gather mushrooms, going from rock to rock, until we got here. There are excellent mushrooms hereabouts. I've gathered a full hand-kerchief. They'll make marvelous soup!

YOUNG MONK (*suddenly*): But what if you, yourself, are only a mushroom, a wonderful mushroom, sprouting in the shadow of a rock? And you are merely dreaming, in sleep, that you're a monk out gathering mushrooms?

MONK ADAM: Come to your senses, Young Monk! What are you talking about?

YOUNG MONK (*continuing*): Or maybe you are the shadow of that cliff, the shadow of a piece of rock fallen here, dreaming that you are a saint who has overcome his sins. What's a dream and what's waking? Tell me, if you know, what dreaming really is?

MONK SIMON (*frightened and attempting to change the subject*): Let's go, let's go, Young Monk. It's late now. These paths are hellish, look about you. A tortuous stairway to hell!

MONK ADAM: Let's go so we're back in time for supper. We have vigil tonight.

YOUNG MONK (*resigned*): Let's go. Let's eat the mushroom soup to stand through vigil. That, too, is a dream, a long, long dream. Isn't that so, Father?

MONK ADAM: I don't know what you mean, Young Monk.

Scene 3

A spacious medieval columned hall in PRINCESS MARY'*s castle on the shore opposite the island monastery. At stage right a deep alcove with long narrow windows. In front of the alcove is a wooden armchair with a cushion on it and another on the floor as a footrest. Next to it, a small, low round table, and on it a few articles for feminine grooming, and a beautiful manuscript. At stage left, a long divan. There are rugs all around. Upstage center are columns, separating the outer from the inner hall. There are dark-colored curtains hung between the columns. All is pleasantly tranquil.*

Part 1

The PRINCESS *is seated in the armchair, her forearms resting on the table. Her beauty has not yet faded, her hair is slightly graying. She has the appearance of a woman in mourning, simple and elegant. Slightly to the side and upstage of the* PRINCESS, *on a rug, sits her elderly* NURSE. *She is dressed in black, is alert and agile, though old and gray. Standing before the* PRINCESS *is the* STEWARD. *He is bareheaded and holds a parchment scroll in his hand.*

STEWARD: Yes, if it please the Princess.

PRINCESS: Good. As you know, I agree.

STEWARD: And what of Prince Sepuh?

PRINCESS: My son? I'll see to it.

STEWARD: Good. Does the Princess have any further instructions?

PRINCESS: No. Give my love to them all. Anna should take good care of herself, she's so delicate. Tell her, "Mother is very concerned."

STEWARD: The Princess should not have left us. Your absence is deeply felt at the palace.

PRINCESS: Oh, the palace gets by without me. At their age a mother's attention is almost superfluous. I've raised them and have seen to their marriages. I've fulfilled my obligations. After all, I've paid my duty to the world, and now I need rest to care for my soul.

NURSE (*to* STEWARD): Oh, let her be! You and your palace. My lady has been a martyr all her life. Now you want her to knuckle under the grinding wheel of life again? No, we've had enough! We need rest now in our latter days. I wouldn't trade this peaceful, quiet cloister for any royal court!

STEWARD: That's right, this castle by the shore is a beautiful place, beautiful and restful . . . on Lake Sevan facing the island.

PRINCESS: And, after all, I want to be close to my church and watch it being built before my eyes.

STEWARD: I'm aware of my lady's piety, her merciful heart, her generosity. Right here, with every step I take, people speak of her goodness and compassion. I know many who have been aided by her kindness. Indeed, they don't call her a saint for nothing.

PRINCESS (*smiling*): Really? Let them. A name does not change anything. Even in a solitary, forlorn corner like this, shouldn't I reach out to the needy, if I can?

NURSE: That goes without saying for a kind heart like my lady's, accustomed, as she is, to providing and caring for others.

PRINCESS: To be a woman is to be caring, Elisa, and to be a mother is to provide.

STEWARD: Do I have the Princess's permission to leave?

PRINCESS: When do you want to set out?

STEWARD: In about an hour.

PRINCESS: Good. God be with you!

STEWARD: May the Princess be well! (*Bowing, he humbly kisses her hand and exits through the curtains.*)

Part 2

PRINCESS (*She is momentarily silent, then sighs.*): Ah, how little life has to offer us.

NURSE: Don't fret. A little or a lot, whatever life has to offer, it has given you.

PRINCESS: Is that what you think, even you?

NURSE: That's the truth.

PRINCESS: If so, life is very poor and niggardly.

NURSE: Perhaps.

PRINCESS: Oh, how sad my heart is today!

NURSE: It's a cloudy day.

PRINCESS: It's cloudy outside, but raining in my heart. Bring me my Bible.

NURSE (*She stands up and after searching for it awhile says*): There it is, next to your elbow.

PRINCESS (*picking it up and opening it*): Oh, yes, I forgot.

Part 3

MAID (*A woman, dressed in black, draws back the curtain and speaks humbly.*): It's the abbot. He wishes to see the Princess.

PRINCESS: The abbot?

MAID: Yes, my lady. What is my lady's pleasure?

PRINCESS (*putting the Bible down*): Show him in.

(*The Maid exits.*)

NURSE: Ah, that's good. Now you will cheer up a little. You're always happy when they talk to you about your church.

PRINCESS: Draw the curtains aside.

Part 4

The NURSE *draws aside the curtains between the columns and respectfully stands there holding them.* FATHER SUPERIOR *enters and goes directly toward the* PRINCESS, *who stands.*

FATHER SUPERIOR: God's blessing upon you, Princess.

PRINCESS: And you too, Father Superior. What news from the monastery?

FATHER SUPERIOR: Only prayers and blessings.

PRINCESS: No, I mean the church.

FATHER SUPERIOR: Day by day it nears completion and becomes a house of prayer and deep contemplation.

PRINCESS: What about the alcove in the right wing?

FATHER SUPERIOR: Just as we decided it should be, the other day.

PRINCESS: Then it's behind the two columns with an arch of its own.

FATHER SUPERIOR: Yes. No! How could it be behind the columns? It is next to the columns.

PRINCESS: Behind the columns. Aren't the columns this way? Elisa, bring me the plans.

(*The* NURSE, *who has been standing away from them with her arms folded across her chest respectfully, brings a parchment scroll from the wall cabinet.*)

PRINCESS (*spreading out the parchment on her small table*) Be seated, holy Father. There it is, see!

FATHER SUPERIOR: Here is the right wing, and here the columns.

PRINCESS: That's right. It's just that I haven't seen that part in actual construction yet. Imagining it is not the same, even though I've pored over this plan many, many times. Often I've spent the whole night thinking about that building, you know, every corner, every detail, and its every stone. It's so close to my heart—it's part of my soul. You'd think I'd placed its every stone, that I'd built it myself.

FATHER SUPERIOR (*jokingly*): Yes, Princess, I thought it was I who built it, but now, you have built it.

NURSE: That's right! That chapel for Mary, Mother of God, is the creation of my Princess Mary.

FATHER SUPERIOR (*thoughtfully*): Yes, you did build it, Princess.

PRINCESS: No, holy Father, I didn't build that church. We built it, you and I. Together we planned, together we were inspired, together we formed it and gave it shape. And it has all been so woven together that now I hardly know what was created by me and what by you! Remember those long hours poring over the plans, holy Father?

FATHER SUPERIOR: I remember, Princess. Building itself is a privilege, all the more so, a shrine where one's God shall reside.

PRINCESS: You said it beautifully! (*Dreamily*) The sweetest moments of my life were spent at this table, creating and constructing that edifice in our imagination.

NURSE: And high upon its facade your name shall be engraved as a testimony of your devotion and love of God, for ages to come.

PRINCESS: Enough of your nurse's maternal vanity, Elisa. Now leave us in private, and don't disturb us.

(*The* NURSE *exits, grumbling.*)

Part 5

PRINCESS: Yes, they were the sweetest moments of my life. I'm not ashamed to re-peat it. I won't be ashamed. Why do you lower your eyes? You shouldn't look down. All my life I have looked everyone straight in the eye, and I want every-one, for whom I hold respect in my heart, to be able to look me straight in the eye, too.

FATHER SUPERIOR: I don't understand the Princess's drift. I've no reason to lower my eyes before anyone.

PRINCESS: But the truth is that you and I are afraid to look deeply and directly into each other's eyes!

FATHER SUPERIOR: Princess!

PRINCESS: Let me have my say. How long must I restrain my lips? My cup is spilling over. My enforced silence weighs heavily upon me. Why should I have to bear it? What sin have we committed?

FATHER SUPERIOR (*rising to his feet*): Will the Princess excuse me? I must leave.

PRINCESS: No, no, holy Father, don't run off. What's the use of running? You can't escape yourself. Sit, sit down. I have to talk. I've been here a whole year. And for a whole year now this question has lingered on my lips. I've always been afraid to utter it. And that fear is a deep offense to my dignity. You'd think we were two sinners, standing face to face, obliged to hide our souls in shame.

FATHER SUPERIOR: I don't understand what the Princess means.

PRINCESS: You don't understand?

FATHER SUPERIOR: I understood nothing of what you said!

PRINCESS: Nothing, Hovhannes?

FATHER SUPERIOR (*as though stung*): Princess! (*Slowly he rises to his feet.*)

PRINCESS (*rising in the same manner*): Do you remember that evening at twilight, on the edge of our little pool, at the summer palace, just twenty-five years ago?

FATHER SUPERIOR: And now, twenty-five years later, the Princess still recalls those few casual words we exchanged then?

PRINCESS: I have remembered them always!

FATHER SUPERIOR: I'm flattered, Princess. It's a great honor, I never dared imagine. (*After a short silence he gradually raises his head.*) Except that the Hovhannes, whose name the Princess has surprisingly not forgotten, died a long time ago. While now, there stands before you a monk, practically an old man, far from court and society, who has come to discuss building costs with you.

PRINCESS: Perhaps Hovhannes is dead for you, I don't know. But not for me! He has always been alive in my heart and shall stay so. His image, Father Superi-or, is the only bright spot in my whole life.

FATHER SUPERIOR: Are those the words of a woman who has had a husband?

PRINCESS (*interrupting him*): And a very worthy one, too, whom I always respected deeply. I also suffered deeply, since I wasn't able to give him anything more than respect.

FATHER SUPERIOR: Are those the words of a woman who has had children?

PRINCESS (*sternly*): I did my duty. But it lay heavy on my heart to know that I was unable to give my children anything beyond the bounds of duty. I've had everything and gave it all to my family. Yet I've given happiness to no one, and received none from anyone in return.

(FATHER SUPERIOR *stands silently, his eyebrows arched.*)

PRINCESS: Listen, I must get it off my chest to remove this unpleasant tension between us once and for all. Look at me, a middle-aged woman, and you your-self said, a little while ago, that you are but an old man. We have nothing to fear and nothing to be ashamed of, since our conscience is clear. This mask that distorts our feelings does not become us, neither you nor me. Listen to what my lips have never uttered, although the thought has filled my entire being. In the gray skies of my life you've been a star of light, my reason for living. Without that light, that consolation, I don't know how I could have lived.

FATHER SUPERIOR (*pressing his hands against his forehead*): Enough! Enough!

PRINCESS: Your image has been before me, in all my moments of solitude. And I don't really know whether my fervent, heartfelt prayers were more directed to the image of Christ Crucified or to your image. The truth is that I have wor-shiped your image along with that of my God.

FATHER SUPERIOR: And didn't you fear God?

PRINCESS: God? (*Lifting the Bible from the table*) God is love, Father!

FATHER SUPERIOR (*thoughtfully, shaking his head*): That's true. (*Suddenly*) And now?

PRINCESS: Now? Now, too. See this window that looks out toward your island and into your window, your little window, where the light burns until midnight. It seems you read and pray there. And from here, I try to read your thoughts and prayers. Can it be that you didn't feel this in your soul?

FATHER SUPERIOR (*cuttingly*): Never!

PRINCESS: Really? Wasn't your soul filled with me—as mine was filled with you?

(FATHER SUPERIOR *is silent.*)

PRINCESS: Answer me! Wasn't your soul filled with happiness? Here—in this soli-tude, as we sat face to face, talking and planning for hours on end. Answer me!

FATHER SUPERIOR (*uncomfortably*): I don't know. I don't know a thing!

PRINCESS: You don't know! I know. I've always been certain that I dwell in your soul, even though, over these long years, we only met occasionally until I

came here. And we exchanged little more than a word or two, merely polite
clichés. Tell me, isn't this true? Isn't it?

FATHER SUPERIOR: Leave off, Princess! Those days are gone, past and forgotten.
What's the use of reviving them?

PRINCESS: Holy Father, give me your honest answer. Today, we must settle our old
scores.

FATHER SUPERIOR: What do you want from me, Woman? For half my life you've
given me nothing but misery and bitterness. You've shattered my life, wracked
my youth; and now you want to rekindle the ashes?

PRINCESS: My poor Hovhannes!

FATHER SUPERIOR: Even now, what has life given me besides pain, both before you
and after.

PRINCESS: Oh, I felt your pain.

FATHER SUPERIOR: Let's end this. What's the sense of stirring those old, smoldering
ashes?

PRINCESS: Smoldering ashes?

FATHER SUPERIOR: Yes. I tore those haunting memories from my heart with the rest
of my worldly cares the day I donned this cassock.

PRINCESS: You tore them from your heart?

FATHER SUPERIOR: When those last worldly sparks faded.

PRINCESS: Those sparks never faded.

FATHER SUPERIOR: Princess!

PRINCESS: No, I tell you. Those sparks never died. You tried to extinguish them,
but you deceived yourself. You numbed your soul and convinced yourself that
you had put them out. But you didn't . . . you couldn't!

FATHER SUPERIOR (*sternly*): Princess!

PRINCESS (*softly*): If you had extinguished them, then what is this church, our
church?

FATHER SUPERIOR (*drawing back, fearfully*): Silence. Be silent, Princess!

PRINCESS: The truth, Father Superior! We haven't built that church for your exalted God, as you keep repeating. Don't deceive yourself. We built that church
for ourselves, for the God of our love!

FATHER SUPERIOR (*devastated*): Mary!

PRINCESS: Yes, your church is not dedicated to Mary, Mother of God, but to me,
your Princess Mary. Tell me that isn't true!

(FATHER SUPERIOR *is still silent, his head lowered.*)

Part 6

Suddenly the MAN IN WHITE *appears in the corner.*

MAN IN WHITE: Tell me, isn't that true?

(FATHER SUPERIOR *is shaken. He straightens up, stares at the* MAN IN WHITE, *and freezes.*)

PRINCESS: What's happened to you?

MAN IN WHITE: Tell me, to whom is that church dedicated? That newly built church of yours.

(FATHER SUPERIOR *is silent.*)

Tell me. Out with it. Confess!

FATHER SUPERIOR (*crushed*): Yes, it's true. That church is dedicated to . . . the ancient gods!

MAN IN WHITE: To my gods!

FATHER SUPERIOR: Your gods!

(*The* MAN IN WHITE *vanishes.*)

FATHER SUPERIOR: That's true! I'm a miserable fool, blinded by my own conceit! I closed my eyes and thought I was soaring. I spread my arms proudly in flight and thought I had reached heaven.

PRINCESS: Don't talk like that! The link that binds our hearts together, our love, has been pure, warm, and noble—like the murmur of a fervent prayer, like the fragrance of rare frankincense rising heavenward.

FATHER SUPERIOR (*fixing his gaze at the spot where the* MAN IN WHITE *appeared, as though addressing him*): No, no! That's all true, but you're not victorious yet! It's still too soon. We'll meet again. . . . (*He quickly exits without turning toward the* PRINCESS.)

PRINCESS (*confused and fearful*): Hovhannes . . . Hovhannes . . . holy Father! (*Exhausted, she collapses into her chair.*)

Curtain

ACT 3

Scene 1

FATHER SUPERIOR's *cell. Upstage is a square, low window with plain wooden shutters. On one side of the window are several rows of recessed shelves in the wall, filled with scrolls and manuscripts of various sizes and shapes. In front of the window is a wooden table piled with books and other small items. Downstage from the table is a door.*

Part 1

From the open window, a wide, bright, golden ray of sunlight falls on the floor and table. FATHER SUPERIOR *is seated at the table, bathed in this light. His elbows rest on the table, and his head is buried in his palms. There is a brief silence. The door opens slowly and the* MASTER CRAFTSMAN *enters, wearing a workman's dusty, dirty clothes. He takes a step toward the table, then stops.*

MASTER CRAFTSMAN: Did you send for me, Father Superior?

(FATHER SUPERIOR *does not move.*)

Holy Father, did you send for me?

FATHER SUPERIOR (*raising his head slowly and looking at the* MASTER CRAFTSMAN): Yes. (*Slight pause*) So tell me, what are we going to do now?

MASTER CRAFTSMAN: Do? About what, holy Father?

FATHER SUPERIOR: What are we going to do with that building now?

MASTER CRAFTSMAN: The church?

(FATHER SUPERIOR *nods affirmatively.*)

What do you mean, holy Father? You already know that by the Feast of the Dormition we'll have the dome on. The rest's only minor details.

FATHER SUPERIOR (*pensively*): By the Feast of the Dormition.

MASTER CRAFTSMAN: What's troubling you, Father Superior?

FATHER SUPERIOR: So it'll be finished by the Feast of the Dormition? Hmm . . . Are you sure of that?

MASTER CRAFTSMAN: I'm a man of my word, holy Father.

FATHER SUPERIOR (*heatedly and cuttingly*): I, too, am a man of my word.

MASTER CRAFTSMAN: Well, then . . .

FATHER SUPERIOR: How many years have you been an artisan?

MASTER CRAFTSMAN: Me? I don't know? Say twenty.

FATHER SUPERIOR: Then for twenty years you've built and built, but have you ever had to destroy something you built?

MASTER CRAFTSMAN: Destroy what I built? But why?

FATHER SUPERIOR: Why are you so surprised? Isn't it true that the real difficulty is in building? Destruction is always easy.

MASTER CRAFTSMAN: Yes, destruction is easy when it's someone else's work you're destroying. But it's very difficult to destroy what you've built yourself, holy Father.

FATHER SUPERIOR (*He gazes outward, through the window, dreamily.*): It's difficult . . . of course! Especially when it's bound to old memories, emotions, and sorrows; when it's bound to your past, your youthful years! Isn't that so, Master Craftsman? It's difficult, of course. (*He stares silently out the window, briefly. Then, suddenly turning his head, he is stern and sharp.*) Close this shutter!

MASTER CRAFTSMAN: Close the shutter?

FATHER SUPERIOR: Yes, the shutter!

MASTER CRAFTSMAN: But there's such a pleasant sun. So warm and glowing.

FATHER SUPERIOR: And that's exactly why you should close it!

FOREMAN: But—

FATHER SUPERIOR: The sun . . . Of course, we need the sun, the warm, glowing sun. We're still sun worshipers. We can't live without the heartening sun, the bright, warm sun. A window, at least, or a crack, even a sneaking ray of light creeping in . . . (*Suddenly, slamming his fist on the table*) No, close it, I tell you! Why are you frozen to the spot?

(*Astonished, the* **MASTER CRAFTSMAN** *closes the shutter. The room is almost dark.*)

FATHER SUPERIOR: That's it! That opening must be shut, by which the sun, the mainland, and the world intrude.

MASTER CRAFTSMAN: But now your dwelling is dark and gloomy, like a tomb.

FATHER SUPERIOR: You mean like a church!

(*The* **MASTER CRAFTSMAN** *shrugs his shoulders;* **FATHER SUPERIOR** *gets up and speaks thoughtfully.*)

Why are you afraid of the dark? The dark is dark only to near-sighted eyes. All great concepts have come into being in the bosom of the dark. All great profundities are only perceived in the dark. And that light you worship—isn't that the offspring of the dark? An offspring that is mortal. It's only the dark that exists; only the dark is immortal and eternal!

Part 2

FATHER SUPERIOR *is silent and pensive. The* **MASTER CRAFTSMAN** *is also silent. The* **YOUNG MONK** *enters and stands near the door, silently and humbly.*

MASTER CRAFTSMAN: Does Father Superior have new instructions for me?

FATHER SUPERIOR: Yes! In a moment. First, I have another matter to settle. You may go now. Thank you, and the Lord be with you. (*Turning to the* **YOUNG MONK**) Why have you come, Young Monk?

Part 3

YOUNG MONK (*He waits until the* **MASTER CRAFTSMAN** *has left. Then he lowers his head further.*): I have something to tell you.

FATHER SUPERIOR: Each man must forge his own path, Young Monk.

YOUNG MONK: I know that the way to your heart is closed to me now. I realize that, as far as you're concerned, I'm a base, unworthy creature. And to me, you are a . . . (*He stops.*)

FATHER SUPERIOR: Speak up, don't hold back!

YOUNG MONK: I would tell you if I knew. I myself don't know. I just feel that we've become irreconcilable enemies.

FATHER SUPERIOR: Enemies? And is that what you've come to tell me now?

YOUNG MONK: No! I've come to reveal something else.

FATHER SUPERIOR: Go on!

YOUNG MONK: You've said that once other gods dwelled here on this island.

FATHER SUPERIOR (*repressing his shock*): And so?

YOUNG MONK: You said that was many, many years ago.

FATHER SUPERIOR: So then?

YOUNG MONK: You said that now they're all defunct.

(**FATHER SUPERIOR** *is silent.*)

Long defunct.

(**FATHER SUPERIOR** *remains silent.*)

But now I've come here to tell you that you're wrong! Those gods are not defunct!

FATHER SUPERIOR (*terrified and rattled*): How do you know that?

YOUNG MONK (*softly and mysteriously*): I saw—

FATHER SUPERIOR: You saw? You saw it in me. How did you see it?

YOUNG MONK: In you? What do you mean? No, I saw it there . . . Out there . . .

FATHER SUPERIOR: Where do you mean?

YOUNG MONK: Beside the old hermits' cells.

FATHER SUPERIOR: What did you see there, around the hermitages?

YOUNG MONK: I saw those others . . . the creatures of the ancient gods.

FATHER SUPERIOR: Creatures?

YOUNG MONK: You're wrong, Father Superior. I tell you, the ancient gods are alive, and with them lives their ancient life. While we, here in our dark and narrow churches, are prostrate and penitent, there, they live freely under the warm, bright sun, on the blue sea, in the blustery wind, on the sandy shore. They live their carefree, impassioned lives, full of vigor and excitement. We pray, while they live. This sea, these mountains, this island, are all theirs. Ours are only these cells and the church.

FATHER SUPERIOR: No, not even these cells with their windows that let in the light are ours; nor is our church. These, too, are theirs, all theirs!

YOUNG MONK (*at first confused, then fearful*): Father, is that what you really believe?

FATHER SUPERIOR: Our God has nothing here, nothing!

YOUNG MONK: Father!

FATHER SUPERIOR: It's all theirs. (*Moving closer to the* **YOUNG MONK**, *softly*) And it will all be destroyed, Young Monk. By the Feast of the Dormition, not a stone will remain. Not one stone of these cells nor of the church.

YOUNG MONK: Father, are you mocking me? You're making a bad joke!

FATHER SUPERIOR: My words have been a mockery until today, and my deeds have been a bad joke until now. But from now on everything's going to be serious. All shall be changed on this island. Nothing will remain here. Neither its modern buildings nor its modern souls.

YOUNG MONK: And the ancient gods, Father?

FATHER SUPERIOR: Pull yourself together, my son. Summon up your will and cast out all those ancient gods within you. Destroy them! If necessary, shatter your soul to pieces! Your soul is noble . . . It's worth the effort. (*He exits.*)

Scene 2

The courtyard of a temple. On both sides of the stage is a double row of tall, majestic columns. Upstage center is a large, wide arch between two sets of columns, draped with a curtain. Behind the columns at a distance is a stone wall upstage. On the dark rose-colored curtains in the archway is a golden picture of a radiant sun. In front of the curtain at center is a small stone altar, with smoke rising from it, on either side of which are long stone tables and benches running diagonally so as to create a horseshoe-like pattern. In front of the columns are tall candelabra and suspended torches. Amid all this, a chain of flowers and foliage is twisted about the altar, the columns, and the torches.

Part 1

Only the two torches on either side of the altar upstage center are burning, so that the tall mass of the structure shimmers in semi-darkness.

SEDA (*She appears from behind the downstage left columns, walking backward across the stage, in the same clothes. She leans forward, earnestly beckoning with her arms.*): Come. Come.

YOUNG MONK (*appearing*): Seda! Seda!

SEDA: Come!

YOUNG MONK: Give me my peace, give me my prayers. Give me faith in my actions, my life, my strength. Everything is crumbling about me!

SEDA (*continuing to walk backward stage right*): Come. Come.

YOUNG MONK: There's no peace for me anymore! Not in the loneliness of my cell, not outside, not even under the arches of the church. In the Psalms I hear your voice. Beneath the dark arches your eyes smile at me. In the aroma of incense I smell the fragrance of your wet tresses. Why, oh why do you torment me?

SEDA: Come! Come!

YOUNG MONK: Give me back my pride, my spiritual meditations. Give me back my faith, my God. Give me back my God!

SEDA: Come. Come. (*She withdraws and disappears behind the columns downstage right.*)

Part 2

YOUNG MONK: She's gone again. Alone again. (*He is in the center of the building, stage center. He pauses, raises his head, looks all around him in astonishment.*) Where am I? Where has she led me?

(*From offstage a distant noise and clamor can be heard. An elderly cult official with a lamp in his hand enters hurriedly and quickly lights the candles and torches.*)

YOUNG MONK (*suddenly approaching him*): Old Man, what building is this? Where am I?

CULT MINISTER (*in a shrill, startled voice*): You scared me, as the sun's my witness! Who are you?

YOUNG MONK: Is this a church?

CULT MINISTER: A church? What kind of foolish talk is that? This isn't a place for the vanquished or crucified. Relax!

(*The outside noise gradually gets closer.*)

YOUNG MONK: How joyful it is here, how festive!

CULT MINISTER: Of course! We've been given life to enjoy!

YOUNG MONK: A man your age is saying this?

CULT MINISTER: Yes. Growing old is hard, but my soul is still fresh, and my heart is young. I can still enjoy life and will do so, as the sun's my witness, till my last breath! Of course, to be as young as you, ah, that's very fortunate! It's a pity that those wild, reckless days will never return. Ah, here they are! (*He goes off toward the noise.*)

(*The* YOUNG MONK *withdraws, walking backward, and hides in the shadows behind the columns.*)

Part 3

The PRINCE *enters from upstage columns at left with thirty of his comrades-in-arms, accompanied by about the same number of nubile* TEMPLE GIRLS *and young Armor-Bearers holding torches. The building is immersed in light. The men are accoutered with helmet, shield, and sword. The* GIRLS *are dressed in sheer white, and in their hair they wear star-shaped ornaments. First, a few torchbearers and a group of lively, spirited* GIRLS *enter. Then the* PRINCE *enters, surrounded by his magnates. After them, the Soldiers and* GIRLS *enter, mingling with joyous exclamations. There are torchbearers all about them.*

FIRST GROUP OF GIRLS (*as they enter from the columns*): Long live the victors! Long live the brave!

ALL WOMEN: Long live, long live the victors!

(*The* PRINCE *goes to the altar and stands before it, and they all gather 'round him. From behind upstage column at right, a* PAGAN PRIEST *appears, dressed in white. Two other* PAGAN PRIESTS *appear from the right and left columns.*)

PAGAN PRIEST (*going before the* PRINCE): Hail, Oh Prince. Hail to you, warriors.

PRINCE: We have come to lay our arms before the altar of Vahagn the Brave and to worship his holy dawn.

PAGAN PRIEST: May his holy dawn protect you! May your arms be always powerful, your swords always sharp, and your shields impenetrable. The blessing of Vahagn, the Light and Sun, be with you! You who are victors in the Battle of Life. May success and victory always be yours!

A GROUP OF SOLDIERS: Success be with us! Victory and triumph!

GIRLS: The blessing of Vahagn the Brave be with you!

PAGAN PRIEST: There is still plenty of time until our Lord of Light rises, Prince. Sit and take your rest. Sit at the table of Vahagn the Great and Astghik the Radiant. Sit and enjoy yourselves, you who are warriors in the great Battle of Life. Warriors and victors, yours the triumph, yours the pleasure!

A GROUP OF SOLDIERS: Ours the victory, ours the pleasure!

PAGAN PRIEST: Girls, set the Lord's table, the table of Vahagn and Astghik. Bring unmixed wine and merriment, bring beauty and charm. Bring them, that we may be worthy of worshipping Vahagn, born of light, and Astghik, born of foam. Spread the table of bounty, Girls, the table of pleasure! (*He exits with his two fellow priests.*)

Part 4

The PRINCE *and his comrades-in-arms doff their helmets and shields, hand them to the Armor-Bearers who take them and exit through the columns. One group of* GIRLS *runs out through columns left. They bring flowers and strew them abundantly over the stone table. They bring candelabra and large silver vessels filled with wine. They also bring gold and silver goblets, as well as cups, and mugs made of twisted ram horn.*

YOUNG SOLDIER (*coming forward*): What a heated battle it was.
OLDER SOLDIER: May the holy art of war never vanish from life!
YOUNG SOLDIER: The enemy was trounced!
ANOTHER (*jokingly*): If you felt sorry for them, you should have spared them!
PRINCE: Who's speaking of mercy? Never, my sons. In the battle of life, never pity anyone. Mercy is a weakness, pity a defeat! Strike at those who oppose you, who stand in your way. Those who restrict your freedom are your enemies!
YOUNG SOLDIER: Strike! We are the victors!
ANOTHER: It's great to be a victor!
YOUNG SOLDIER: To return from battle as victor!
PRINCE (*going to the head of the table*): There, now come and let us sit at the Lord's table. A just reward for our fierce battle.

(GIRLS *and* SOLDIERS *mingle and mix at the table. Several* GIRLS *stand in attendance and wait on those seated, as others come and go. The Armor-Bearers line up and stand, statuelike, behind their lords. Some of the crowd is already seated, some are still standing during the conversation that follows.*)

SOLDIER (*raising his cup*): Hail to battle!
GIRL (*next to him*): Long live the warrior!
SOLDIER (*nearby*): Hail to beauty!
ANOTHER: Long live love!
GIRLS: War is the way of the world!
SOLDIERS: Love is the joy of the world!
PRINCE (*laughing*): Wait, wait, don't rush. You, Battle . . .You, Love . . . Don't get carried away. Calm down. Let's honor the ancient custom. Raise your cups. I offer a libation to our great god!

(*The* GIRLS *pour wine from the vessel in the center. Profound silence.*)

PRINCE (*Taking a large, wine-filled ram's horn, he stands before the altar, facing the curtain, and raises the horn.*): To you, oh Great God, Vahagn the Valiant, you the glowing sun of the world, you the life and vital force, the battle, the power. You the light and the redeemer, the savior of glory. You who have conquered evil, darkness, gloom, and the black clouds of the overcast sky, as well as the devil and the dragon at the gates of hell. To you, born of daybreak; born of the rays. To you, I dedicate this horn of pleasure, filled with pure heady wine. You, who give us the intoxicating passion to live and fight. Lord, accept our libations. (He pours a few drops into the fire, which flares up.)

VOICES FROM ALL SIDES: Accepted, accepted!

PRINCE (*returning to his place*): The victor's libations are always accepted on the divine Victor's altar. Let us drink! Here's to life and its struggle!

ALL (*Amid the general noise and clamor, as they are seated, they strike one another's cups as they toast.*): To life and its struggle!

(*They drink and sit. Silence.*)

Part 5

YOUNG MONK (*Trembling, he shyly edges forward, looking down, with his hand outstretched.*): Give me a cup, too. I want one, too.

(*There is an overall wave of amazement followed by general silence.*)

PRINCE: What business do you have here? You, in the black robes?

YOUNG MONK: Give me a cup. I want one too.

PRINCE: He who wants to drink from this horn should come from the battlefront.

YOUNG MONK (*pleading*): Just one cup, Prince. Is it such a big request? Just once, only one sip from your horn of pleasure and battle.

PRINCE (*sarcastically*): At the Lord's table, you miserable wretch, pleading will get you nowhere. Go to the table of beggars!

A SOLDIER (*ridiculing the* YOUNG MONK): Hey, friend, what winds have blown you here?

A YOUTH: The abstainer's nose has caught the whiff of wine!

PRINCE: I've donated ten measures of wheat a year from my fields to your desert. Go, sit and have your fill there.

VETERAN (*mocking*): And pray to your gods for our sins.

BURLY SOLDIER: Sins. (*Holding his stomach, and laughing heartily*) Pray for our sins. Our countless sins.

(*General raucous laughter*)

YOUNG MONK: Prince, don't you recognize me?

PRINCE: What an impudent fellow. (*Angrily*) Are you going to leave or not'?

VETERAN: I recognize you. Aren't you that contemptible coward, who threw down his sword and ran from the battle of life?

YOUNG OFFICER: Out, and be quick about it, you vile creature!

ANOTHER: Get out, you renegade!

VETERAN: Aren't you that arrogant idiot who scorns our majestic Vahagn's supreme gift of life! And you refuse to bow your miserable head before his radiant image!

ALL: Be gone! Be gone!

ONE OF THE CROWD: Get off this holy ground!

YOUTH: Apostate!

VETERAN: Aren't you that insolent wretch refusing to worship our golden Astghik, born of foam, who won't accept her gift of love, nor womanly beauty and charm?

GIRLS: Out with that insolent fellow!

ANOTHER: Imbecile!

VETERAN: Desecrator of the body, the wonderful creation of Vahagn and Astghik?

A GIRL (*pointing to the boy next to her*): Disdain this body? This strong healthy body?

GIRLS: Sacrilege!

YOUTH (*pointing to a girl next to him*): This tender, this beautiful, magnificent body!

ALL THE YOUTHS: Desecrator!

YOUNG MONK (*The abuses have a shattering effect on the* YOUNG MONK, *who lowers his head by degrees and withdraws step by step until he is back in his original position behind the columns, out of sight.*)

Part 6

PRINCE: Never mind him! I have libations to offer. Here, take the cups.

(*They all fill their cups.*)

> (*The* PRINCE *again goes up to the altar and raises his ram's horn cup.*) To you, oh Sublime Goddess, Astghik born of the sea. You, so pure and wondrous, like the foam from which you sprang! You, the supreme beauty, with resplendent charm and tenderness, like the light you radiate! You, who are the fountain of love, of desires and passions, like the waves that caress you. To you, born of the sea, I dedicate this horn of pleasure, filled with pure heady wine! You who give us the pleasure of beauty and love, its delight and intoxication!

Oh Goddess, accept my oblation! (*He pours a few drops into the fire, which flares up.*)

ALL: Accepted! Accepted!

PRINCE (*returning to his place*): The victor's oblation is always accepted on the altar of beauty. Let's drink! Here's to beauty and love!

ALL (*There is noise, laughter, and jesting, as they strike their cups together.*): Long live beauty and love! (*They drink and sit.*)

Part 7

YOUNG MONK (*In the ensuing quiet he ventures out of his corner. He approaches the* BURLY SOLDIER, *putting his hand on his shoulder, and says cuttingly.*): Make room for me!

(*All are amazed.*)

BURLY SOLDIER: Not again, you beggar?

YOUNG MONK (*more cutting, arid, scornful*): I want to sit at this table, too!

BURLY SOLDIER: There's no room for you at this table!

YOUNG MONK (*riled and quivering with rage*): I shall sit at this table!

BURLY SOLDIER: We told you there's no room. There's no room here for anyone without a sword! Why do you stick to us, you horsefly?

(*Suddenly, the* YOUNG MONK *attacks the* SOLDIER, *pulls him up from the chair, then knocks him to the ground. At first, there is uncomfortable tension and confusion, which suddenly gives way to a vigorous round of collective laughter.*)

YOUNG MONK (*Putting his knee on the chair and pounding the table with his fist*): I shall sit at this table!

BURLY SOLDIER (*Springing up, furious, he draws his sword and hurls himself at the* YOUNG MONK.): Stand aside, you blockhead! I don't want to defile this holy temple with your filthy blood!

YOUNG MONK (*With strong, firm steps, he approaches him. For a moment, they stare at each other fiercely. Suddenly, the* YOUNG MONK *strikes the* BURLY SOLDIER'*s arm with all his might, causing his sword to fall. The* YOUNG MONK *immediately grabs it, and places his knee on the chair.*): Here I am, Prince, and here's my sword!

(*General excitement, clamor, and admiration*)

GIRLS (*to one another*): What strength!

A GIRL: What arms of steel!

BURLY SOLDIER: No, Prince, you saw the way he tricked me! You saw it all! That's my sword!

VOICES (*scoffing at him*): No, no, no!

YOUNG SOLDIER: You fell on your rear end!

PRINCE: The sword belongs to him that holds it now!

ALL: Long live our just Prince!

VOICES: Long live our new champion! Welcome to our ranks!

ONE OF THE GROUP (*approaching the overpowered* SOLDIER): Excuse me, friend, but you can see there's no longer any room for you here.

BURLY SOLDIER: I go, but we'll meet again, you there in the black robe! And when we do, you'll either give me my sword or your life!

YOUNG MONK: My life, perhaps!

Part 8

VOICES: Wine for the victor!

A YOUTH (*tossing the* BURLY SOLDIER's *cup to the* YOUNG MONK): Take his cup! It's yours now!

YOUNG MONK (*He takes the goblet and throws it after the* BURLY SOLDIER.): I don't want somebody else's castoffs!

A GIRL (*extending her arm*): Here, Champion, here's my cup!

VARIOUS GIRLS (*extending their cups*): Take my cup. Take mine!

YOUNG MONK: Prince, a moment ago I asked for the ram's horn you offered libations with.

PRINCE (*He empties his ram's horn, gives it to a girl nearby, and speaks solemnly.*): Fill this up and give it to him.

(*The girl fills it and gives it to the* YOUNG MONK *with heartfelt reverence.*)

PRINCE: You should know, Newcomer, that the first cup is always to Vahagn. That's the ancient law of the world.

YOUNG MONK: Here at your table of life, I drink my first cup according to the law of life. I drink a toast to struggle, that struggle, which is on high in the darkness and clouds, the struggle that is out there on the earth from which you come. To struggle in the depths of the sea and in the fury of the storm, where I come from!

GIRLS (*very interested, whispering one another*): From the sea? The sea?

YOUNG MONK: Blessed be the struggle of Life! (*He drinks.*)

VOICES: To your health! May victory always be yours!

YOUNG MONK: Good! Now fill the second cup!

GIRLS (*calling with gusto*): Wine! Wine!

(*The girl fills the horn again and gives it reverently to the* YOUNG MONK.)

PRINCE: You should know, Newcomer, that the second cup is always Astghik's. That is the ancient law of the world!

YOUNG MONK: The second cup is to Astghik, born of luxuriant foam, sprung from the impassioned, surging waves of love. She, who swirls around in the depths of the storm, and ravishes you. Prince, with this cup, I drink a toast to your daughter! (*He drinks.*)

GIRLS: Seda? Seda?

PRINCE: My daughter?

(*All are extremely excited and look toward the* PRINCE *with fear and expectation.*)

VETERAN: Your daughter, Prince?

PRINCE: Wait, Young Man! Your face seems familiar.

YOUNG MONK (*smiling sardonically*): Now, Prince! You must recognize me now!

GIRLS (*whispering to one another*): Who is he? Who is he?

PAGAN PRIEST (*appears in front of the curtain*): Victors, make ready, let's leave the table now. The eastern sky is flaming red, the sea is cloaked in gold, and all nature shakes slumber from its eyes to worship the great God! The morning star and the sun embrace each other now. You must prepare for worship also!

(*All immediately jump up from their places. The Armor-Bearers quickly bring the helmets and shields to their masters, who then don them and stand before the altar. They form a double line facing the curtain,* SOLDIERS *on the right and* GIRLS *on the left.*)

PRINCE (*approaching the* YOUNG MONK): Give me your hand and let us go to worship our sublime gods!

YOUNG MONK: To worship gods?

PRINCE: The ancient gods, always ancient, yet always new and forever eternal! Come!

(*The* YOUNG MONK *stands fixed and stubborn, his eyes downcast.*)

PRINCE: Come, I tell you, hurry! You, who drank a toast to struggle; you, who drank to my Seda, you must come! Give me your hand. (*He grasps the* YOUNG MONK's *arm and, slightly pushing him, takes him through the double line of people, to the front of the group. Then they stand at opposite sides of the altar.*)

Part 9

From behind the curtain, a trumpet fanfare, followed by the PAGAN PRIESTS' *joyful hymn of victory. During the singing the upstage curtain in the archway is slowly drawn aside and the lights on the rest of the stage gradually black out. Behind and above the arch is depicted the summit of Sevan and its ruins. The* PAGAN PRIESTS *are at right, all dressed in white, with golden solar discs on their chests. At left, there are priestesses, all dressed in white, their hair, adorned with star-shaped ornaments, loosely flowing. First the priests sing, then the priestesses sing, then they all sing in unison.*

The scene behind the arch depicts the meeting of sea and sky. The sky is flamered with patches of yellow. The sea has a hue of red with apricot patches. During the course of the song a huge solar disc gradually rises from the sea. When half of it has emerged from the water, the sun opens like an oyster shell so that the side facing the audience descends to the surface of the water, giving the appearance of the sun's reflection. The inside of the oyster shell shines brightly, with a dazzling, silvery, pearllike glitter. And within that intense glow stands victorious VAHAGN, *naked, tall, and straight, with a majestic physique. His right hand is outstretched, his red hair and beard are in the Assyrian style, and his eyes are fiery. On his left, leaning amorously against him,* ASTGHIK *stands upon a bed of sea moss and flowers. She is softly embracing* VAHAGN, *her head resting on his chest. She is naked, nubile, and graceful. In her hair there is a massive diamond-studded star, and on her body a few long, delicate strands of sea-weed.*

The singing continues until the oyster shell opens completely. When the song abruptly ends, the trumpet fanfare sounds again. The entire crowd immediately falls to the ground in deep adoration. The pagan priests and priestesses bow to the waist. Only the YOUNG MONK *remains standing, erect and motionless.*

PAGAN PRIEST (*observing his noncompliance, formidably, from the group*): Bow, ambivalent one!

(*The* YOUNG MONK *is motionless.*)

PRINCE (*agitated and falteringly*): Bow, you fool!

SEDA (*Appearing suddenly on the steps of the upper stage, she comes forward through the arch, quietly. She stands directly in front of the* YOUNG MONK, *gently yet authoritatively.*): Bow. Worship before the sea and its god!

(*First the* YOUNG MONK *tilts his head, then his knees buckle, and he precipitously drops to the ground. There is a tremendous clamor; everything disappears in an instantaneous blackout, in which a deep silence prevails.*)

Part 10

When the darkness upstage begins to dissipate, the scene has changed. Gradually, through the misty light, a double row of low, wide columns can be seen at center stage. It is a church. Upstage, only two lighted candles can be seen. In front of these candles are two MONKS *reading the Psalms, interchangeably. Behind them, in a semicircle, the* MONKS *stand facing the altar. It is gloomy and dark. The reading is sad and spoken in a monotone. Amid the quietly praying* MONKS, *suddenly a buzzing begins.*

A MONK (*turning his head, he whispers over his shoulders.*): Water, water, splatter some water on his face!

(*From the columns upstage left, two* MONKS *appear. They are holding the* YOUNG MONK *by the arms and supporting him as they bring him forward.* MONK MOVSES *follows, helping them.*)

MONK ADAM (*He enters hurriedly through the columns at stage right, approaches* MONK MOVSES *after the* YOUNG MONK *has been taken away. Falteringly*): What is it, what is it? What's happened?
MONK MOVSES (*always haltingly*): The young monk fainted! He was standing in front of me and praying, and all of a sudden he lowered his head. Then he leaned over a little and crashed to the floor!
MONK ADAM: Poor boy . . . He must have prayed a lot last night! Take him to the spring, take him to the spring. (*He returns to his original place.*)

(MONK MOVSES *leaves hurriedly with the rest. Everything is calm again. The monotonous, doleful, and weary sound of the psalms is heard again.*)

FIRST PSALMODIST: There is no soundness in my flesh because of Thy indignation.[3]
SECOND PSALMODIST: There is no health in my bones because of my sin.
FIRST PSALMODIST: For my iniquities have gone over my head. They weigh like a burden too heavy for me.
SECOND PSALMODIST: My wounds grow foul and fester because of my foolishness.

(*The scene fades gradually, quietly, but the psalmody continues for a brief time.*)

Scene 3

The PRINCESS's *private quarters in her castle on the mainland shore. A small, cozy room with a low ceiling, the floor entirely covered with rugs. Upstage, a couch, and next to it a low stool. In the corner, against a white background, an elegant, black*

---

3. The antiphonal reading is from Psalms 38 [37 LXX]: 4–6.

crucifix on a narrow white table. There is a vase filled with fresh roses on either side of the crucifix. A colorful Arabic lantern hangs from the ceiling. Entrances left and right.

Part 1

The PRINCESS *stands erect and motionless in front of the sofa. A short distance away, directly opposite her,* FATHER SUPERIOR *stands near the doorway. Both are looking down with an averted gaze.*

FATHER SUPERIOR (*calmly and formally*): We gave birth to the church; it bound us together and still binds us now. But there must be no tie between us. We must destroy every bond there is!

PRINCESS (*looking him in the eyes, formally*): Father Superior, no one can destroy that church. Not you, not me—no one! Its foundation is here in our hearts.

FATHER SUPERIOR (*sternly*): Its foundation, Princess, is built upon sin!

PRINCESS: What do you mean, upon sin?

FATHER SUPERIOR: Sin, I tell you!

PRINCESS (*proudly*): Sin has always been a stranger to me, and so it shall always remain.

FATHER SUPERIOR: Woman, are you still bent on deception?

PRINCESS (*stupified*): Deception?

FATHER SUPERIOR: Yes.

PRINCESS: Me?

FATHER SUPERIOR: Yes, you! Why are you so surprised? Your whole life has been nothing but show and pretense! You've lied for years and years, deceived the man who took you as his wife. You've deceived your children, who ran to your bosom for tenderness. You've deceived and bound the eyes of all who surround you. You've deceived me also without making a promise, without saying a word. And you've deceived yourself! You've seen yourself as a martyr . . . You, whose husband was no sooner dead than you rushed here to build a new shrine with me. To erect a new church to your god of deception!

(*The* PRINCESS *stands erect and proud, frowning, still and sullen.*)

Of course! Love is what you worship, isn't it? Oh, what sophistry! What is love? Is God's love carnal? Woman, your name is sin. Your soul and your world are blighted by deception! That church is built on sin.

PRINCESS: Have you had your say?

FATHER SUPERIOR: All I had to say.

PRINCESS: Well, the door's open!

FATHER SUPERIOR (*offended*): Princess!

PRINCESS: What is it? Go and destroy it!

FATHER SUPERIOR: It's my duty, as I'm well aware. But you must also know what you must do.

PRINCESS: What do you expect me to do?

FATHER SUPERIOR: You must leave here immediately.

PRINCESS: Is that an order?

FATHER SUPERIOR: That's what I said!

PRINCESS (*abruptly angering*): Who are you to tell me what to do?

FATHER SUPERIOR: I'm a monk, Princess, withdrawn to the desert.

PRINCESS: You yourself are a desert, and a stranger—a stranger to my heart, just like all of them. I've lived a whole lifetime among strangers. I've been a stranger to everyone, alienated and alone! Alone, amid the crowds of the courts. I'm all alone in my palace, in my own family, continually alone! And the only luminous star in my soul was the image of another soul, alone, forlorn, and longing like mine . . . who understood me and the heavy cross I bear. Who was close to me and who loved me! (*Pause*)

(FATHER SUPERIOR *stands motionless and tense, clenching his fists, as though ready to fight.*)

I fled from the clutches of that horrible, maddening loneliness, and took refuge here for us to be together at last. Each in union with another soul to share life together. To create a shrine with the only soul who understands me, who has been with me from a distance, all my life. And now, this is the way that very soul understands me. As a woman, sin, Eve, and a deceiver! (*Furiously*) Now leave me. Be gone!

FATHER SUPERIOR: I'll leave when you've concluded.

PRINCESS: I've nothing more to say. I've always lived alone and apart, and that's how I'll go to my grave. It's foolish to defy fate. Go. Go destroy the church, crush those stones! My shrine's already destroyed!

FATHER SUPERIOR (*frowning*): Forgive me, Princess, if I have spoken carelessly. I was speaking rather of myself than of you. I wanted to bare the truth before us. I wanted to open both our eyes.

PRINCESS: And you did. Thank you.

FATHER SUPERIOR: I'm sorry if what you've seen with your eyes open is not what you wanted. If, in this world, you want to see what your heart desires, you have to look with your eyes closed.

PRINCESS: That's true!

FATHER SUPERIOR: That truth is what I learned from you exactly twenty-five years ago! Forgive me, Princess. I believe all scores between us are settled now.

PRINCESS: Yes, now I've settled all my debts in life.

FATHER SUPERIOR: Settle your obligations with the Lord above! Good-bye,
    Princess!

(*The* PRINCESS *stands silent and motionless, while* FATHER SUPERIOR *calmly leaves,
with bowed head. The* PRINCESS *slowly and reluctantly sinks down, crushed, onto the
sofa. Her hands are weak, one resting on the sofa, the other in her lap, her lifeless
gaze is fixed.*)

Part 2

NURSE (*entering*): Are you alone?
PRINCESS (*sadly, nodding her head*): Yes, alone.
NURSE: Did he leave?
PRINCESS: Who?
NURSE: Father Superior.
PRINCESS: I don't know.
NURSE: What did he say?
PRINCESS: Who?
NURSE: Father Superior!
PRINCESS: I don't know. (*Pause*) Bring me those—
NURSE: Those what, Princess?
PRINCESS: The plans.
NURSE: For the church?

(*The* PRINCESS *nods sadly.*)

NURSE (*She exits, returns immediately, and hands the plans to the* PRINCESS.):
    Here. (*She steps back to the crucifix.*)

(*The* PRINCESS *opens the plans, looks at them, raises and kisses them, and with calm,
deliberate movements, begins to tear them up, sobbing uncontrollably. While her
chest heaves and her tears flow abundantly, she does not utter a sound.*)

NURSE (*looking back, puzzled*): What is the Princess doing?
PRINCESS (*her voice shaking*): Can't you see? I'm tearing them up.
NURSE: You're tearing them up? Why?
PRINCESS: It's . . . it's over!
NURSE (*happily*): It's over? The church is over?
PRINCESS: Yes, it's finished!
NURSE: Is it, really! Congratulations, Princess! Then why are you so sad?
PRINCESS: Sad? Who? Me? Not at all! Can't you see, Old Woman, how glad I am,
    how fortunate I am? Can't you see I'm crying?

NURSE (*deeply moved and distressed*): Yes, my princess is crying. (*Kneeling before the* PRINCESS) My lady is crying. I've never seen your tears before. After all the grief and pain you've seen, it's such a peculiar cry, that cry of joy!

Curtain

ACT 4

Scene 1

Evening in the YOUNG MONK*'s cell. In the lamplight, the* YOUNG MONK *can be seen lying in his bed. The* BLIND MONK *sits at the head of the bed, erect as a statue.* MONK SIMON *sits at the edge of the bed, constantly fingering his rosary, yawning at short intervals.*

Part 1

YOUTHFUL MONK (*Standing near the table, he toys with the lamp and speaks deliberately and thoughtfully.*): And yet there are so many, so very many fools out there. Out there in the world! Those wretches. Glory to you, Oh Lord, for illuminating our minds!

MONK SIMON (*yawning*): Glory to you, Oh Lord!

YOUTHFUL MONK: Someone should ask them: "What's the benefit of those adversities, that toil, that valley of strife and the bitterness, in what is called 'the world'?" What a senseless notion! For the sake of a few meager pleasures, a few fleeting joys, that one should sacrifice one's eternal bliss in the life hereafter!

YOUNG MONK (*speaking deliberately*): Father, have you ever seen the rising sun?

YOUTHFUL MONK: What?

YOUNG MONK: Have you ever been in the Temple of the Sun?

(*The two* MONKS *look at each other, flustered.*)

YOUTHFUL MONK (*approaching the bed and putting his hand on the weakened* YOUNG MONK*'s forehead*): No fever. Are you awake, Young Monk?

YOUNG MONK: Yes. I awoke at sunrise. What about the rest of you?

YOUTHFUL MONK: We've been talking, Young Monk.

YOUNG MONK: I heard you talking. Go see the sunrise!

MONK SIMON (*Gesturing that the sick* MONK *be left alone and they be silent; he then stands up.*): You're right, Father, it's late. Let's go so he can get some rest.

Good-night, Young Monk. Sleep well. Tomorrow everything'll be fine. (*He exits.*)

YOUTHFUL MONK: Get well, Young Monk! (*He exits.*)

YOUNG MONK (*speaking deliberately*): I'm talking to you. Have you ever seen the rising sun?

Part 2

BLIND MONK (*He listens and waits for the sound of footsteps to grow fainter. Then he leans closer to the bed, mysteriously and in a whisper.*): I . . . I have seen that rising of the sun.

YOUNG MONK (*Fully awake, he suddenly bolts and sits upright, leaning on his arm, pointing at the* BLIND MONK.): You? You? You've seen it? You, who are blind?

(*The* BLIND MONK *slowly nods his head.*)

YOUNG MONK (*in a strained whisper*): And did you bow your head?

(*The* BLIND MONK *slowly nods his head.*)

YOUNG MONK: You've seen the Temple of the Sun with those eyes!

BLIND MONK: Yes, I saw it with my own eyes. And I gouged them out, so that I could no longer see!

YOUNG MONK (*horrified*): You gouged out your eyes!

BLIND MONK (*emphatically, as though reading*): Crush that member, which causes you to stumble, and cast it away. So it is written.

YOUNG MONK: So you gouged out your eyes?

BLIND MONK: Yes!

YOUNG MONK: You gouged them out with your own hands!

BLIND MONK: No, not with my hands. I gouged them with my will.

YOUNG MONK: Your will?

BLIND MONK: Faith moves mountains. What are eyes that they should remain fixed in their sockets?

YOUNG MONK (*doubtfully*): And you say you've worshiped the sun?

BLIND MONK: Yes, I sinned, Young Monk, and that's why I understand you. I can peer right into your soul. And so I say to you, "Beware! I see the devil lurking there. The black devil within you!"

YOUNG MONK: Is that your understanding? What enchants me is beauty and light. What inspires me are the gods.

BLIND MONK: All the demons were once gods, Young Monk. They are fallen gods
. . . You must suppress them.

Part 3

FATHER SUPERIOR (*entering dejected, his body slightly bent over*): Good day.

(*The* BLIND MONK *stands.*)

FATHER SUPERIOR (*approaching the bed*): How are you? I've come from the mainland. They said you were asking for me.

YOUNG MONK: Yes, I can smell the freshness of the sea on your clothes.

FATHER SUPERIOR: I'm just off the boat.

YOUNG MONK (*with wonder*): The boat . . . the boat.

FATHER SUPERIOR (*sternly*): Why did you ask to see me?

YOUNG MONK (*hesitating a bit*): Father, I've worshiped the ancient gods!

FATHER SUPERIOR (*firmly*): That's quite natural.

YOUNG MONK: What?

FATHER SUPERIOR: Of course! I expected it! Didn't he promise you his favorite stallion, and the sword at his side, his very own daughter, and who knows, someday perhaps, his princely scepter?

YOUNG MONK (*offended*): Father!

FATHER SUPERIOR: Of course, it's perfectly natural! All that is certainly worth the
denial of your God! (*Suddenly and angrily*) But why did you call me here?

YOUNG MONK (*with reproach*): Whom else should I call, Father Superior!

FATHER SUPERIOR: You're wrong. Call Father Anton.

YOUNG MONK: Father Superior!

FATHER SUPERIOR: Only Father Anton's boat can take you to where your heart
is.

YOUNG MONK: Are you turning me out?

FATHER SUPERIOR: I'm sending you to the world you long for.

YOUNG MONK (*slowly and bitterly*): You are sending me to the world? Who gave you
the right to snatch me out of that world when you pleased, only to toss me
back to it when it suits you? Who gave you the right to shackle my soul and to
fetter my feelings? Who gave you the right to reprimand me to my face?

FATHER SUPERIOR (*contrite*): You're right! I wanted the impossible. I wanted to free
you from that long, winding road, all the bitterness and suffering, by which
man can reach this holy cloister. But since that's impossible, take off your sackcloth and go!

YOUNG MONK: Go where?

FATHER SUPERIOR: To the world.

YOUNG MONK: To the world? (*Nodding his head silently, then with a cynical laugh*)

No, Father Superior, my world's here! This is the world—this island. Here, I came to know the ancient gods, and here's where I'll continue to worship them!

FATHER SUPERIOR (*at first he stares perplexed, then firmly and decisively.*): No, I won't allow that, Young Monk!

YOUNG MONK: You will! You've willed it that way. I haven't seen another world. Here's where I've built my world.

FATHER SUPERIOR (*cuttingly*): This is a monastery, a sanctuary, where you're only a worldly guest, a passing pilgrim. And you know that pilgrims are allowed only a three-day stay! (*Walking out*)

BLIND MONK (*calling after him*): Father Superior, you're too harsh!

FATHER SUPERIOR (*looking at him sidelong*): No, Father, he's sick, so I made allowances. Didn't you hear me? I gave him three whole days. But when the three days are up, Father Anton's boat will take the lad to the mainland. (*He exits.*)

Part 4

YOUNG MONK: The boat. The boat!

BLIND MONK: Forget the boat, Young Monk! Forget that flimsy bridge that ties you to the world. Forget those planks cobbled together.

YOUNG MONK (*echoing him*): Cobbled together.

BLIND MONK: It's not too late. Stifle those memories in you, suppress that old demon, and count it a brief malaise, now gone! (*His arms outstretched over the* YOUNG MONK) Take refuge in God, Young Monk. (*He goes toward the door but stops.*) At night, if you need me, knock on the wall, and I'll come to help you.

YOUNG MONK: How can you help me, Blind One, you, who have gouged out your own eyes?

BLIND MONK (*groping for the door*): I can help somehow, Young Monk, by groping, groping. Knock on the wall if you need me. (*He exits.*)

Part 5

YOUNG MONK (*sitting in bed, clasping his knees, briefly he is silent and still; then he nods his head, emphatically.*): Groping . . . groping . . . And he says, "Forget the boat."

SEDA (*as an apparition, hardly visible in the doorway*): Forget the boat.

YOUNG MONK (*with a start, whimpering*): Seda!

SEDA : Forget Seda, too!

YOUNG MONK: Forget you?

SEDA: Forget me. I'm that black devil inside you!

YOUNG MONK: You're the white wings of my soul. I was sitting on the desert sands, dejected, thirsting and lonely. It was you who came and gave wing to my soul, awakened my senses to nature and gave my heart to the sea. The sea, from which suns are born, where I once held you in my arms!

SEDA: Forget all that! It's not too late. Be as you were, before you met me. Think . . . You've got three days!

YOUNG MONK: No, Seda. There's no turning back. I can't. I won't! I worshiped your gods, I offered libations, I drank from the horn of pleasure. Now I long only for you. Now I yearn only for your embrace!

SEDA (coming forward, invitingly): Come, I'm your woman!

YOUNG MONK (leaning forward as well): Seda. But how can that be? You're only a dream.

SEDA: Come. You, too, can become a dream!

YOUNG MONK: A dream!

SEDA: Come back.

YOUNG MONK (frightened, yet enraptured): To the sea.

SEDA: Where you once embraced me.

YOUNG MONK: Where you trembled in my arms with every fiber of your being.

SEDA: Where the storm howled and the waves swirled!

YOUNG MONK: And under my strokes, the foam seethed!

SEDA: Come there, if you want to hold me once more . . . only there! Come as the waters rage again and the sea foams.

YOUNG MONK (kneeling on the bed): Yes, when the waters rage, when the sea foams!

SEDA: Come, let's embrace, and in my arms I'll take you from one abyss to another, from one sphere to another. I'll reveal unknown mysteries of new worlds, mysteries you and your world know nothing of! Come!

YOUNG MONK: I'll come! Oh, how many, many mysteries were revealed when I held you that first time. I'll come and hold you again to learn all life's mysteries!

SEDA: Come, I will take you far, far away, beyond the narrow bounds of your life. I'll take you to a new existence, new forms and a new essence!

YOUNG MONK (ecstatically): A new life, a new existence!

SEDA: Come and merge with the sea, merge with the light and the warmth, merge with me and Astghik, with Vahagn and the gods!

YOUNG MONK: Ah, soon, soon!

SEDA (drawing backward): When the waters rage! When the sea storms!

YOUNG MONK (choking): When the waters rage! When the sea storms!

Scene 2

In front of the church under construction. The same as Act 1, Scene 2. Daytime.

Part 1

The MONKS *have crowded about, speaking excitedly. The* YOUNG MONK *is silent and in thought, as he leans against a tree.*

YOUTHFUL MONK (*amazed*): What did you say?

MONK ADAM: Whoever heard such a thing?

MONK GHAZAR (*with mocking laughter*): Father Superior is riled at the church!

MONK SIMON: Stop that insolent laughter!

ANOTHER MONK: But it's true. He doesn't come to church anymore.

MONK ADAM: Where is he now?

A MONK: He's withdrawn to his cell. He may be reading, praying, who knows?

OLD MONK: All that reading! This whole thing has a foul smell about it.

MONK SIMON: Old Man, do you know what you're saying?

OLD MONK (*drawing back*): I didn't say a thing!

MONK SIMON: He's our superior, our leader.

OLD MONK: I didn't say a thing! (*He exits.*)

MONK SIMON (*following him out*): Wait, Father, wait!

MONK DAWIT (*thoughtfully*): That's right! Arrogance is a mortal sin!

MONK ADAM: Man should be meek and humble!

A MONK: Humble, humble.

(*All three exit together.*)

MONK GHAZAR (*aside*): Father Superior is riled at the church! (*Stifling his laughter with his palm, he exits after them.*)

Part 2

The YOUNG MONK *stands under the tree.*

MONK DAWIT (*Lingering behind at center stage, he shakes his head in bewilderment and approaches the* YOUNG MONK.): Did you hear that, Young Monk?

YOUNG MONK: I hear it. I hear it. Leave me alone! Quiet, so I can hear it!

MONK DAWIT (*shocked*): Hear what?

YOUNG MONK (*pointing up stage*): Ah, listen!

MONK DAWIT : What?

YOUNG MONK (*mysteriously*): The waters are swirling. The waters are starting to churn!

MONK DAWIT: What of it? Probably a storm's brewing.

YOUNG MONK (*excited*): A storm, a storm!

MONK DAWIT (*unconcerned*): Maybe. The seasons are changing.

YOUNG MONK (*suddenly seizing* **MONK DAWIT** *by the arm*): Then, tonight . . . Do you think it'll break tonight?

MONK DAWIT: How you tremble! Poor Young Monk! Since that storm, you must be living in terror. Calm down, calm down. Come, let's go to the church. Pray, and it will ease your heart.

YOUNG MONK (*suddenly*): Come, let's go to the shore!

MONK DAWIT: The shore?

YOUNG MONK: I want to see the storm approach. But I can't go alone. You know, it's drawing me closer . . . closer. (*He clings tightly to the tree.*)

MONK DAWIT: Young Monk, you'd better go lie down. You shouldn't have gotten out of bed. Your eyes are still feverish! Let me take you to your cell.

YOUNG MONK (*Sliding against the tree, he slowly sinks and sits.*): Let me be! Let me be! I want to see the storm approach!

(**MONK DAWIT** *stands over the* **YOUNG MONK**, *puzzled.*)

Part 3

A MONK (*He enters running.*): It's Father Superior!

(*Muted voices and stirring . . .* **MONKS** *enter singly and in pairs, somber and concerned. They enter and silently form a line. A monk leads the* **BLIND MONK** *forward.*)

BLIND MONK: What is it? What happened?

MONK ASSISTING THE BLIND ONE: I don't know! Father Superior gave the order!

A MONK: Hush . . . He's here!

MONK DAWIT (*as though arousing him*): On your feet, Young Monk! It's Father Superior!

(*The* **YOUNG MONK** *looks around him and stands up.*)

Part 4

(**FATHER SUPERIOR** *enters from upstage center, burdened and sad. All the* **MONKS** *bow their heads to him.*)

FATHER SUPERIOR (*taking a long, silent look at the group*): Is everyone here?

A VOICE: Yes, Father Superior.

FATHER SUPERIOR (*He sits on a high rock. There is an expectant silence.*): I have something to tell you. (*Pause*) Do you see this church, nearly completed, where for some time now the sweet savor of our prayers has risen to our God? This church is not dedicated to our God!

(*General wave of dismay*)

MONK SIMON: What did you say, Father Superior?

FATHER SUPERIOR: This church is not dedicated to our God. When I was building it, I hadn't yet severed my ties with the world.

(*Murmurs from the crowd*)

I used to think I had. We, all of us, who have left the world and come to the desert, have brought with us a portion of that world deep in our souls. A secret longing for hidden pleasures, an exquisite desire for veiled delights, a delicate, clinging network of our past lives, struggles, emotions, and involuntary recollections. These were all with us while we were building this church. Those hidden, veiled passions have built this church. That portion of the world we have insinuated into the desert has built this church. The church is the world's; it is not our God's! We can no longer pray under its arches! They must be destroyed!

VOICES (*dumbfounded, horrified*): Destroyed? Destroyed . . .

MONK ADAM: Our church destroyed?

A YOUTHFUL MONK: Our new church destroyed?

FATHER SUPERIOR: Yes, we must destroy it and build a new one!

VOICES (*shock and disbelief*): A new one? A new one?

MONK ADAM: Build a new one?

FATHER SUPERIOR: Yes! And we are going to build that new church ourselves. Money that comes from the world is the gift of worldly sentiments. Worldly craftsmen have worldly notions and worldly arts. A temple dedicated to one's God can only be built by one's self, with one's hands, with one's back, with one's mind. As for the form our new church should have, I myself am not yet certain. Let's sit and deliberate together. We shall deliberate, and then we shall build.

OLD MONK (*sarcastically*): Fine craftsmen we'd make, Father Superior. What can we build, even if we wanted to?

FATHER SUPERIOR: Willpower, Old Man. Will it and you shall build—if you have faith in your will, though it be the size of a mustard seed!

OLD MONK: Oh, those times are gone.

FATHER SUPERIOR: No, they're not gone. They've still to come. We'll reach them through my new church.

OLD MONK: Listen, Father Superior, I'm an old man, listen to me! You've read so much you've addled your brain. Your chosen path is crooked! Don't torture yourself. That's the path of heretics!

FATHER SUPERIOR (*proudly*): That's the path of the Apostles. Christ himself trod that path.

MONK GHAZAR: Ooh! Listen to him.

(*Uneasy murmurs from the crowd*)

OLD MONK: Don't speak so mindlessly, Father Superior!

MONK ADAM: Nor so arrogantly!

MONK ANTON: Leave us alone with our church. We don't need newfangled forms. This is the form we have inherited from our forefathers.

A MONK: We're not stonecutters. We're not masons!

MONK ADAM: We haven't come here to tear down walls and build new ones.

ANOTHER MONK: We've just come here for peace.

MONK ZAKARIA: Yes, for peace and prayer.

A YOUTHFUL MONK: Destroy our beautiful new shrine?

MONK ZAKARIA: On which so much money and labor were expended?

MONK GHAZAR: And what of the Prince and Princess, who have underwritten the task?

VOICES (*mixed*): Of course, of course, the Prince, the Princess!

MONK ZAKARIA: Then who's going to give us our tithes of wheat and all these gifts?

VOICES (*mixed*): Yes, yes, our tithes, the wheat!

MONK ADAM: Leave us our livelihood!

MONK ZAKARIA: Will that church of yours give us our daily bread?

MONK DAWIT: No matter how frugal our fare, we still need bread to live!

OLD MONK: So the cares of life won't drown us!

MONK MOVSES: So our prayers won't be disrupted!

OLD MONK: Come to your senses, Father Superior, while there's still time, and leave our desert in peace and quiet!

FATHER SUPERIOR (*Having lowered his head, oppressed by the torrent of words, he then looks up at those around him, somewhat confused.*): You stand before your Father Superior as members of my order. (*Smiling*) A brotherhood . . . What sort of brothers are you and me? (*Rubbing his eyes*) It is as though the scales have fallen from my eyes! How could I have missed something as obvious as this? Together, we've made it here to this desert. I was able to bring you here, but from now on you're on your own. You're right. That church must stand. It's your church. Go occupy it. It will sustain endless prayers and offer consolation. It'll open to you the doors of the Kingdom! It'll free you of all demons; it'll also give you bread and comfort. Go dwell in it, and peace be with you! But that is not what I aspire to! I seek toil, the inward search, boundless and unceasing, the endless inner quest, from peak to peak, from rampart to rampart, over the chasms of doubt, sometimes surefooted, sometimes stumbling, a perpetual journey toward truth. Go into your church, and I'll go and build my own church! But this time, I alone shall raise an edifice worthy of my God, under whose arches not a word of my prayers shall sound false nor the resonance of a word ring hollow!

MONK DAWIT (*derisively*): And where are you going to build it, Father Superior, that new edifice of yours?

MONK GHAZAR (*scornfully*): And of what, granite or marble?

FATHER SUPERIOR: Granite and marble, basalt, and every other kind of stone, I leave them all to the gods of this world. This shrine shall have my reason as foundation, my will for columns, my faith its dome!

OLD MONK: That new shrine of your has a very shaky foundation, Father Superior.

FATHER SUPERIOR (*offhandedly*): If it's shaky, it'll collapse.

MONK DAWIT: And then?

FATHER SUPERIOR: I'll build a new one!

OLD MONK: But there is no end to that!

FATHER SUPERIOR: Did you expect it to have an end? As long as we live we must build. We must build our God, His shrine. We will build, and it will collapse; we will build, and we will destroy; we will build, and we will build ceaselessly . . . but we shall never finish. Should it be completed, it would no longer be the house of God, but (*pointing to the church*) a house of idols!

MONK GHAZAR (*furious*): He's blaspheming. He reviles our God!

FATHER SUPERIOR: Only the lowliest of souls can revile the God they once worshiped! I see that we no longer understand one another. Farewell; your God be with you!

(*The* YOUNG MONK *comes forward and blocks his way.*)

YOUNG MONK: Wait!

FATHER SUPERIOR: What is it? Could it be you want to follow me, Young Monk? Come, your soul has wings, I know!

YOUNG MONK: Wait! Tell me, will the rising sun be seen from that new edifice of yours?

FATHER SUPERIOR: Forget the rising sun, so that the dawn of dawns may rise for you, the sun of suns light your way!

YOUNG MONK: Wait! Tell me, will this sound be heard from that new edifice of yours? Listen! (*Pointing upstage*) Do you hear it?

FATHER SUPERIOR: What? That's the tempestuous sea you hear.

YOUNG MONK: Yes, the sea. That's what I mean!

FATHER SUPERIOR: What you seek is the primitive church men first built.

YOUNG MONK: You don't fool me any more with your lofty words! Tell me straight up, will the call of the sea reach your church?

FATHER SUPERIOR: No external turbulence or tumult will reach my church! If you want to follow me, give up your obsession with the sun and the sea!

YOUNG MONK (*letting him pass*): Go then!

FATHER SUPERIOR (*leaving*): What a pity, Young Monk, once your mind had wings!

YOUNG MONK (*calling after him*): What a pity, Father Superior, once your heart had wings!

BLIND MONK (*with both arms outstretched*): I'd like to follow you.

VOICES (*murmuring*): The blind one, the blind one.

Scene 3

A seashore. There are cliffs left and right. A steep cliff gradually rises to upstage center, creating a steep promontory where it joins the sea. It is night. The sea swells.

Part 1

The WAVES *fiercely dash against the promontory. They appear in the shape of women from the waist up. As they try to cling to the rocks, hanging for a second, they wail as they fall almost instantly.*

VARIOUS WAVES(*calling to each other, overlapping lines*):

You'll perish soon,
Yield now, at last
To my embrace,
For you're to face
A rocky doom!
Lo, we're here, a wavy rush,
The waters gush, the currents crush,
Shore to shore, we dash,
With the tides, we splash!
Splashing, splashing,
Crashing, clashing,
Whirling as we soar,
Hurling as we soar,
Now we fly, without a splash,

Now we foam, without a
   clash.
Wait, wait and call,
That's not him at all!
He is the one!
No, that's not him
'Tis all the same,
Just call his name.
We're not drifters; no time to
   spare.
No, but still, we'll call out
   there!
Cry out! Cry out!

A GROUP OF WAVES (*in unison*):

> Hey, hey, lend an ear!
> Passions, desires, await you here!
> Howling, roaring,
> The sea is calling!
> Hey, hey, lend an ear!

ANOTHER GROUP(*sarcastically, as they disappear*):

> Oh, no, no, not ever. Sit on the sand, suffer forever!

VOICES FROM THE FIRST GROUP(*from a distance*):

> Hey, hey, lend an ear! Passions, desires, await you here!

(*After a brief interval, silence prevails on the promontory, and the dull tones of the storm reverberate more clearly.*)

Part 2

The YOUNG MONK *hurls himself from the rocks, on the side. His hair is unkempt, his clothes badly disheveled, his eyes glaring wild-eyed.*

YOUNG MONK: Here I come. (*He stops suddenly, wipes his forehead, looks behind him and speaks angrily.*) Hey, farewell island, farewell desert! Farewell, you too, you murky arches of the church. Farewell, my prayers, the incense of my soul. And farewell to you, oh, implacable and vengeful God, focus of all my yearnings and prayers. Farewell to you, my little cell, my silent, solitary cell, farewell! I'll return to you no more! Ah, the dim light of my lamp still burns there, in your bosom. By morning, it'll die alone, never to burn again! Let it die! (*A fierce gust of wind. He shudders and turns to the sea, his arms outstretched with longing.*) There, welcome me to your embrace, Seda. Take me into your arms. It's time now! The raging waters are here, the rush of the storm is upon us! Open your arms and let me cling to your fragrant body once more, with your breath in mine! Let me cross into that great unknown, to that new life, that new existence you promised me. Take me into your arms, Seda!

Part 3

MONK SIMON (*From the rock above, he jumps down directly in front of the* YOUNG MONK, *panting, and cuts him off.*): Stop! (*Clutching his chest and gasping for breath*)

YOUNG MONK (*startled, then fiercely*): Out of my way!

MONK SIMON: Stop, you poor wretch, stop! Fear almighty God!

YOUNG MONK (*preparing to fight*): Don't block my way!

MONK SIMON: Before you lies the darkness of the deep!

YOUNG MONK: Stand back!

MONK SIMON: Beware of the abyss.

YOUNG MONK (*furious*): Enough! Away with your darkness! Away with your endless fears! Fear of the light and joy, fear of the dark, the torment, fear of the gods, and of hell! Get out of my way. There no darkness exists, no abyss. Only the sea and the storm await me there!

MONK SIMON: Death awaits you there, you poor soul.

YOUNG MONK: Death is what you fear. Death, the creation of your fear!

MONK SIMON: My God, he's gone mad!

YOUNG MONK: Death is this, right here! Here, in your desert, this life of fear, this wasteland. But, there—out there—is freedom, exuberance, vitality! (*Suddenly he shoves* MONK SIMON *forcefully, knocking him down.*) Out of my way! I want to live, to live! Seda! (*He jumps into the sea.*)

MONK SIMON (*rising, horrified, with a choking voice*): He's lost. His soul is lost!

Part 4

The other monks gradually appear from among the rocks, their clothes and hair blowing in the wind.

MONK ADAM: Where is he?

MONK DAWIT: Did you find him? Is it true? Did you see him?

MONK ZAKARIA: Which way did he go?

MONK GHAZAR(*dashing*): Where is he? Where is he?

MONK SIMON (*pointing to the sea*): There . . . out there!

THE GROUP (*fearfully, in hushed voices*): The sea?

MONK SIMON: His soul is lost!

A MONK: This rock is cursed! A hermit also threw himself into the sea from here!

(*Hanging on to the arm of another monk, breathless and very excited, his arms outstretched, groping wildly, the* BLIND MONK *enters.*)

A MONK: His blind companion's here!

BLIND MONK(*He stands still, straightens himself up, and speaks in the ensuing silence.*) Is it true? Is it true?

(*With bowed heads, the* MONKS *remain silent.*)

BLIND MONK (*raising his hands*): So . . . Oh, my God!

MONK GHAZAR: Yes, God! This was God's vengeance. Wanting to destroy a church can't go unavenged! The punishment of the elder fell upon the youngest!

MONK MOVSES: Oh, our poor, our good, our pure Young Monk!

MONK ADAM: So meek and modest, so kind and saintly!

THE GROUP: A saint, a saint!

MONK ZAKARIA: Let's go down to the shore, Brothers. Perhaps we can recover his body.

A YOUTHFUL MONK: Let's go and get the boat!

MONK ANTON: It'll be difficult in this swell, but we must bring it round!

BLIND MONK: The boat!

MONK ANTON: It's amazing how he saved a life from the sea, and then gave it back his own!

A YOUTHFUL MONK: Let's go look for him!

MONK MOVSES (*his eyes raised, in a prophetic tone*): Listen, Brothers, if God shows mercy and we find his body, we must bury him at the threshold of the new church. Like a sacrificial goat, slain at the threshold of a shrine.

MONK DAWIT: The Lord speaks through you. Let us bury him at the threshold of the church.

THE GROUP (*as they leave*): Let's bury him at the threshold of the church!

(*They all exit, forgetting the* BLIND MONK, *who stands alone.*)

Part 5

BLIND MONK (*devastated*): Go, bury him at the threshold of your church, at the threshold of the ancient gods. Ah, they're great and powerful, those ancient gods. They're still potent!

A VOICE: You gouged out your vibrant eyes in vain!

BLIND MONK (*deeply moved and horrified*): Who dares—

A VOICE: In vain, you gouged out your eyes in vain!

BLIND MONK (*drawing back in fear*): Whose voice is that? I want to look into the depths of your eyes!

VOICE: You gouged out your eyes in vain!

BLIND MONK: In vain?

Curtain

DERENIK DEMIRCHYAN

Derenik Demirchyan, poet, novelist, translator, and playwright, was born on February 6, 1877, in Akhalkalaki, eponymous center of a region populated by Armenians since the Treaty of Adrianople (1829), in what is now southern Georgia. In 1892 he graduated from the Ardahan School and was accepted at the Gevorgian Academy in Ejmiatsin, where he extended his knowledge of literature beyond the Armenian, by reading classics of world literature such as Lermontov, Pushkin, Tolstoy, Goethe, Heine, Byron, and, of course, Shakespeare. The following year marked his literary debut with the appearance of his poem *Apagan* [The future] in the periodical *Taraz* [Vogue]. In 1894–95 a student rebellion erupted at the academy, inspired by leftist ideas, which had been in clandestine circulation there for some time. As a result, Demirchyan decided to continue his education at the Nersisian School in Tiflis, graduating in 1897.

He gained his first work experience at the meteorological office in Ardahan and then as a technical secretary for the Armenian Benevolent Society in Tiflis. During this period he was a member of the cultural circle of the Vernatun [Upper room] which used to meet in the fifth story residence of the distinguished Armenian poet and short-story writer Hovhannes Tumanian (1869–1923). In 1899 he published his first book of poetry. This was followed by another collection in 1913 and, in 1920, a book of quatrains entitled *Garun* [Spring].

In 1903 he departed for Baku and worked as cafeteria administrator at the factory of the rich Armenian entrepreneur Aleksandr Mantashev, one of the richest men in the Russian Empire at that time. He then studied music in Moscow but returned to Tiflis owing to a nervous breakdown. From 1905 to 1909 he studied in the physics, pedagogy, and literature departments of the University of Geneva. In 1910 he taught Armenian language and literature at the Hovnanian Girls Secondary School in Tiflis. By 1923 he was teaching Armenian and world literature at the dramatic studio that opened adjoining the Armenian Art House in Tiflis. In 1925 he moved to Armenia and established residence in Erevan. From 1925 to 1928 he served as secretary of the artistic division of the Institute for Armenian Culture, and from 1927 to 1929 he occupied the position of president of the Armenian Proletarian Writers' Union.

During this period several of Demirchyan's plays were performed. His play *Vasak* was staged by the Tiflis Artistic Theater in 1914. It was based on the renegade fifth-century governor of Armenia who took a decisive stand with the Persians against Armenian national interests. Five years later his *Azgayin khaytarakutiwn* [National disgrace] was presented by the Armenian Dramatic Society of Tiflis. Subsequently the newly founded Erevan State Theater put on his *Datastan* [Judgment] on November 12, 1922, as the third work in their repertoire, under the direction of L. Kalantar.

In 1923 Armenian actors approached the poet Tumanian to dramatize his new version of the tale of *Kaj Nazar* [Nazar the brave] which he had created in 1908 (published in 1912) by collating some sixty-six sources. Sensing, however, that his end was near, Tumanian suggested that they broach the matter with Demirchyan, who was receptive to the idea and brought it to fruition. The play was performed in 1924, first by a school group in Dilijan, and then by professional troupes in Erevan, Tbilisi (formerly Tiflis), and Baku.

From the mid-twenties on, in addition to writing plays, Demirchyan began to explore other prose genres, first turning his narrative skills to short stories and then novels.

Thus the performance of his next drama, *Haghtakan siro erge* [The song of victorious love], in the Armenian Hall at Tbilisi in 1927 coincided with the publication of his collection of short stories, *Tsanotner* [Acquaintances]. Thereafter he continued to work in both genres until his death in 1956. Of his later dramas one might mention *Fosforayin shogh* [Phosphoric ray], which appeared at the Erevan State Theater in 1932; *Kaputan* [Captain] was staged in 1938 by the Sundukian Theater in Erevan; his patriotic extravaganza, *Erkir hayreni* [Fatherland], opened at Moscow's Mali Theater in 1941. Subsequently Armenian theaters in Transcaucasia also staged his dramas *Hovhannes metsatun* [Wealthy Hovhannes], *Napoleon Korkotyan* , and *Enkerner* [Comrades].

His later novels included *Rashid* and *Nigyar* in 1936, the former translated into Azerbaijani and Kurdish the same year. In addition to *Nazar the Brave*,

Demirchyan is probably best remembered for his novel *Vardanank*, devoted to the struggle the Armenians waged in the fifth century under the command of Vardan Mamikonian against Persian aggression. Despite the work's religious overtones, the Soviet authorities allowed its publication in order to lift the spirits of the thousands of Armenians fighting in World War II in defense of the fatherland. It appeared in two parts: the first in 1943, the second three years later. The novel was translated into French and published in Paris in 1963. His final novel, *Mesrop Mashtots*, a treatment of the inventor of the Armenian alphabet, remained unfinished at his death.

Armenian children learn of Demirchyan in their earliest years for his children's story *Puypuy mukike* [Puypuy the mousie] in 1934. Later, he made several other contributions to the genre such as *Arjuk-lrjuk* [The serious little bear] in 1944, *Tstapar: pisiki vishte* [Sparrow dance: The kitten's sorrow] in 1949, and *Mankakan ashkharh* [Children's world] also in 1949.

For his prolific literary output, which also embraced translations from Russian, of which his rendition of Nikolai Gogol's *Dead Souls* is considered the best, and his excellence as a writer, Demirchyan was awarded the Medal of Lenin in 1939 and the Medal of the Red Flag of Labor in 1945 and 1956. The golden jubilee of his literary activity and the seventieth anniversary of his birth were celebrated in 1945. He died in Erevan on December 6, 1956. An annual government-sponsored prize in his name was established in 1980.

A.G.S.

NAZAR THE BRAVE
A FOLK TALE-COMEDY
IN FIVE ACTS
FOR CHILDLIKE ADULTS AND
ADULTLIKE CHILDREN

(KAJ NAZAR, 1923)

Translated by Aris G. Sevag

CAST OF CHARACTERS

HOUSE MANAGER

NAZAR THE BRAVE

USTIAN: Nazar's wife

SUB-DEACON

SAKO

MASTER OF CEREMONIES

SCHOOLMASTER

GULZAR: Neighbor woman of USTIAN in the village

GIANTS OF ZORBASTAN

   GHOROBUGHA

   DANGIZ

   KHOZENI

   ARDJATOTOSH

   GHARAGHURA

   GHORONTI

   GHUZGHUN

   PERISHAN: Their sister

CHAMBERLAIN

MINISTER

VIZIER

GENERAL

CHANCELLOR OF THE EXCHEQUER

COURTIERS

TROOPS

COMMON PEOPLE

TIGER

PROLOGUE

The House Manager, coming down center before the closed curtain, is a fat, kindly, and smiling man wearing oriental garb. He addresses the audience.

HOUSE MANAGER: Members of the audience, young and old, I bid you welcome a thousandfold at this joyous time.

I have the honor of informing you that Nazar the Brave has come and is presently in the theater. He's just arrived with his entourage from the city of Nazarashen (which, as the name suggests, he built himself) situated in our hero's very own country of Nazarstan. He's changing his shirt in an outpouring of heroic sweat and, if the wood flooring of the stage doesn't cave in from the furious momentum of his bravery, the brave and robust Nazar will receive you all royally on stage.

I affirm the special love and care he has toward you. And until His Excellency himself personally comes out on stage for your delectation, he's ordered me to offer you his greetings.

I bear you many greetings from Nazar himself, his wife, Ustian *hanum*, and his decrepit sub-deacon. Also full of greetings are the heroes of Zorbastan, land of tyrants, despots, and oppressors, namely, the frightful Sako, the lively *tamada* (their master of ceremonies) the pale schoolmaster, the sweet-talking priest, and the rest.

Greetings, too, from the seven giants of Zorbastan: the wise Ghorobugha, the very intelligent Dangiz, Khozeni, Ardjatotosh, Gharaghura, Ghoronti, Ghuzghun, and their sister Perishan the destitute.

And also from the eloquent chamberlain, the vizier, the minister, the courtiers, troops, people, and tiger.

And the last to extend his warm greetings is the author of this tale of heroism, who isn't in the theater at this moment. In fact, on the advice of his critics, he's gone to take singing lessons from a rooster. As soon as the lesson is over, he'll join us as well. After all, these days he's become pretty unpretentious. So, if he doesn't get beaten up this evening, but by some quirk of fate actually hears the sound of your applause, just like his hero, he'll modestly come on stage during the final act to express his thanks.

(The House Manager bows to the audience and then departs, opening the curtain with his long staff as he moves into the wings.)

ACT 1

NAZAR THE BRAVE, *at home.*

The scene is set in the yard of his home. At left is a hut with a barn, with window and door. Facing it is the yard fence which, extending to the right, bends forward, and the yard gate is precisely at that corner. The wall then comes forward and ends where a small square forms to the right of it. A door opens from the left corner of the hut toward the rear. Behind the fence and extending to the right of it is a forest. Motley items of clothing are hung out between the hut and the yard wall. A threshing tool is at left, in the corner created by the door to the house and barn. It is very late afternoon. Sunlight is reflected in the yard, where a plantain tree gives shade. Dogs can be heard in the distance. NAZAR, a large, tall man, with lazy movements, disheveled hair, long mustache, and clean-shaven chin, has put down his goatskin in the doorway and, sitting on it at an angle, is dreaming half-asleep.

NAZAR (*waking up, without looking inside*): Ustian!

USTIAN (*An ugly, coarse, and heavy-set woman is preparing food in an in-ground oven*): What is it, Agha?

NAZAR: Listen, Ustian, it's almost dusk.

USTIAN: Are you blind or what? Don't you see I'm preparing the meal?

NAZAR: That's not what I'm getting at.

USTIAN: Well then, what are you getting at?

NAZAR: I was just thinking I should go to the village and bring home the loot.

USTIAN (*curious*): Loot? Well, if you know it's there, why don't you just go and get it.

NAZAR (*scratching the back of his neck*): Yeah, I was thinking it's time for me to get up and go. (*He gets up, drags along his goatskin cape, and drops it down next to the oven. Losing his train of thought, he sits down on it again.*) Let me go, I say, and get what's coming to me in the village.

USTIAN: Well, why did you sit down again?

NAZAR (*musing*): Yeah, that's what I was just thinking, too.

USTIAN: You were planning on going to the village to bring home the loot, weren't you?

NAZAR: That's right. I'll see if my men are in the village. If they are, I'll send them to the mountain pass. A caravan or traveler is bound to come through.

USTIAN: I don't understand. Didn't you say the loot was already stashed?

NAZAR (*yawning*): What loot are you talking about?

USTIAN: You idiot, you just said you were going for the loot, right?

NAZAR: Never mind that. I heard that Köroghlu's gang has come to the village.[1] Let me go and see if they've actually had the guts.

USTIAN: You'll be the laughing stock of the whole village. You've got no business there.

NAZAR: Yes, I do. Nazar the Brave has got to go and show them who's boss.

USTIAN: You, brave? You'd give your life's savings for a mouse hole in a storm!

NAZAR: Speak to me with respect.

USTIAN (*in a loud and threatening voice*): Respect? So you're a prince or something? I'll speak to you with respect when you're dead—maybe. Respect my foot.

NAZAR: I don't understand how you can belittle me like that. I'm known as the village prince. Don't talk like that, otherwise I'll get up and—

USTIAN: You pip-squeak, who the hell do you think you are? Are you above criticism? No way, José! Are you going to bring home the swag, or are we going to live on charity?

NAZAR: What are you blabbering about? I don't support you. You support me.

USTIAN: Me support you? Why don't you find work?

NAZAR (*threatening*): What did you say? You sure have got some nerve—

USTIAN (*surprised*): Nerve?

NAZAR: How could you even imagine Nazar working? You'd be in a pretty state if that got around.

USTIAN (*sarcastically*): Oh, really? . . . So, Your Majesty doesn't have to work. Is that it?

NAZAR: That's it. You're going to work. Not me.

USTIAN: I'll see you die first. Who in hell's name do you think you are, anyway?

NAZAR: I'm a member of the aristocracy.

USTIAN: A nobleman? In your dreams!

NAZAR: It's in the church records. My grandfather's grandfather was a king. Our family belongs to the nobility.

USTIAN: How'd your grandfather get to be a dirt farmer then? And you're not even that. First you don't work, second you pass yourself off as nobility, and now you're trying to put me down, when I'm the one of noble birth.

NAZAR: Ha! You of noble birth? A noblewoman?

USTIAN: A noble noblewoman. Those not as ignorant as you know!

NAZAR: How does an idiot like you become nobility?

USTIAN: If I weren't nobility, would my father have been so respected?

NAZAR: Get off your high horse! "Nobility!" Don't you dare say that in my pres-

---

1. Köroghlu is the hero of a Eurasian bardic epic cycle. His character seems to be based on two separate historical figures of the early seventeenth century, a minor Ottoman official and a peripatetic bard. With a band of fugitives, he leads local resistance against the central authorities.

ence. You get a kick out of abusing me. My name reverberates throughout the world. Köroghlu doesn't dare come near us because he knows of my reputation. What do you know about bravery? Nothing! Now, look what you've done, you've made me go on and on and kept me from my duties. Who knows what action I'm missing in town? Let me go now. When those Daghestani bandits catch sight of me, they'll quake in their boots and beat it.[2] (*He picks up his goatskin cape again, drags it to the door, and sits on it.*)

USTIAN: Dream on! Meanwhile, make yourself useful and chase the chickens out of the yard or I'll smash your head in with that old club.

NAZAR (*looking inside*): Just you wait and see the royal banquet I'll throw when this fight's over.

NEIGHBOR WOMAN (*entering from the rear of the house*): Ustian?

USTIAN: Is that you, Gulzar? Come on in.

NEIGHBOR WOMAN: Hey woman, what are you cooking? (*Looking about*) Isn't your husband at home?

USTIAN: He's home all right, sprawled out behind the door.

NEIGHBOR WOMAN (*whispering*): Isn't he working yet?

USTIAN: You're joking, of course. Work is out of the question for him. Every other woman's husband goes and brings home the bacon. But mine is nothing but a leech. He's not capable of robbing or working.

NEIGHBOR WOMAN: There's always someone looking for a herder. He can handle that, can't he?

USTIAN: Nazar a herder? Don't make me laugh! Say "king," "prince," or "baron" to Nazar and he's all for it. Now, do you actually think he would consider herding as suitable work?

NEIGHBOR WOMAN: Well, what's he going to live on?

USTIAN: How should I know? He lies about like a tattered rag from morning to night and talks of being an exalted leader.

NEIGHBOR WOMAN: Who knows, woman, maybe he'll become a leader. That's not so far-fetched. Maybe if he talks enough of becoming a king, he'll actually become a king some day.

USTIAN: What, that runny-nosed squirt? He can't even wipe his nose, and you say he's material for a king?

NEIGHBOR WOMAN: Stranger things have happened.

USTIAN (*thinking*): He will? Who knows, maybe.

NEIGHBOR WOMAN: Wouldn't you want him to become a king?

USTIAN: Sure. I'd make as good a queen as anyone. But I can't imagine that spineless imbecile as my consort. He deceived my father into giving me to him. Be-

---

2. Daghestan is a region located in the northeast Caucasus, bordering on the Caspian Sea.

fore, I was a princess in my father's house; now look at me. We don't even have a crust to eat.

NEIGHBOR WOMAN: If you know your husband can't cut it, why not find work yourself?

USTIAN: You can't expect me to work, my dear. My father happens to be a prince. Now tell me, is it dignified for me to work?

NEIGHBOR WOMAN: Well, what's going to become of you?

USTIAN: What's going to become of me? I'll crack his skull if he doesn't get work and put food on the table. I'll show him which one of us is nobility. Do you think I'll let him treat a princess like a washerwoman while he pretends he's a prince? I'm the one of noble stock, not him!

NEIGHBOR WOMAN: Ustian, my child keeps crying. Would you be a dear and come over to see how she's doing?

USTIAN: Let's go. I was planning to go into the village anyway.

(*They leave by the rear entrance of the house. Pause.* NAZAR *is sleeping with his head against the door. Mischievous children slowly approach him and wake him up by touching his nose with a stick.*)

NAZAR (*jumping up*): Hey, who's there? (*He runs into the house.*)

CHILDREN (*As they run off, they shout.*) Snot-nose Nazar!

NAZAR: Shut up, you little bastards! I'm not one of your ass-kissing fathers. I'll skin you alive.

CHILDREN: Nazar is a scaredy-cat. Nyah, nyah nyah!

NAZAR: You sons of bitches. I'll tan your hide.

(*The children run off.*)

NAZAR (*He lies down. Within moments, flies begin to annoy him. He shoos them away and then yawns lazily.*): These flies won't let a man sleep in peace. Hey, good-for-nothing woman of mine, come and drive them away. On top of everything, do I have to do that, too? (*He looks inside.*) Has she gone out? (*Calling*) USTIAN! (*He tries to pick up the goatskin cape to go inside, but he is too lazy to do so and stretches out again.*) Oh! Am I tired. (*Pause*) It'll soon be dark. Who knows what thieves and robbers are lurking about? (*To the flies*) Hey, get off me! . . . As if I didn't have enough to worry about. (*He drags the goatskin with his body and wriggles his way inside the hut.*) I've had enough! The devil tells me to get up and annihilate these buggers once and for all. (*Getting angry at the flies*) Just who do you think you're fooling with? (*Slapping at a fly on his face*) There, I've got you, and you, and you. I'm Nazar the Brave. Everybody kids around. I don't kid around. (*Looking at the flies fallen on the ground*) How many are there? One, two, three, four, five. (*He is too lazy to count any fur-*

ther.) Ooph. Call it an even thousand. (*Shouting*) I'm Nazar the Brave, I'll have you know. I slay a thousand with a single blow.

(*A thin, decrepit* SUB-DEACON, *with disheveled hair and carrying a parchment book, enters, leaning on a staff.*)

NAZAR: Who's there? (*Jumping up*) Oh, it's you, Sub-Deacon.
SUB-DEACON (*jumping up and down*): I throw, I catch; I catch, I throw. (*Noticing* NAZAR) Greetings, Brother Nazar, hail and well met. What's that about slaying a thousand and bagging them in a net?
NAZAR: Ah, what's this world come to! If I had the energy, I'd get up and slay everybody.
SUB-DEACON: It's a sign of the times.
NAZAR: No matter what, I've made up my mind, I'm going to annihilate mankind, and I've started with the flies.
SUB-DEACON: It's a sign of the times.
NAZAR: Just look, I struck one blow and destroyed a thousand.
SUB-DEACON: It's a sign of the times. (*Looking at the flies*) Oh, Nazar, these aren't flies, no, these are heroes. (*Excited, his speech becomes increasingly more rapid and mechanical.*) I saw a frightening hero in my dream. He had a sword in his right hand and a banner in his left. He appeared in the form of celestial fire and annihilated a thousand lesser heroes. By the grace of God, you are that hero. Wow, my dream has come true! You shall conquer the world, Nazarias, and kings shall tremble with fear before you. (*He opens his ledger and, walking around the yard, begins to look at it and mutter an incantation.*) See, I came, I found, I saw and I verified with help from the Lord. It's a great day, and my dream was auspicious. Now I shall verify, make a prediction, and depart. Behold (*He counts the flies.*) one, two, three, four, five—all in all, a thousand. (*Looking at the ledger*) It's an accurate sign. (*Approaching a white cloth spread out on the wall*) Now I shall write it on this cloth for the whole world to see. (*Sticking his finger into an ink well, he writes on the cloth and reads out loud.*)

Nazar the Invincible, Nazar the Brave,
With one blow sends a thousand to their grave.

(*Holding up the cloth*) A divine sign, a mysterious phenomenon, a banner given by heaven, a frightful statement whereby it is God's hope that you become master of the world. (*He ties the cloth to* NAZAR's *lance and extends it to him.*) Take it, (*looking directly into* NAZAR's *eyes*) take it, (*getting closer to him*) take it . . .
NAZAR: What am I going to do with it? (*Pulling back*)
SUB-DEACON: Take this God-given banner. Strike the enemy by the thousands.

NAZAR: Really? But now I feel kind of lazy. Put it over there in the corner, and to-morrow I'll get up and smash the world to smithereens.

SUB-DEACON (*putting the banner in the corner*): Now I place it at the corner of the altar, may the prophet's words come true, that (*singing*) "The wise servant shall dominate the foolish leaders." (*Removing a magic charm from his breast pocket*) Here's a magic charm. (*Picking up a few specks of dust from the ground*) Behold, the dust of giants. (*He wraps the dust in the charm and hands it to* NAZAR.) Take it.

NAZAR: What is it, what do I do with it?

SUB-DEACON: Put this charm in your breast pocket and go vanquish your enemies. (NAZAR *takes it.*)

(*The* SUB-DEACON *pauses, jumps up and down on the spot, and snickers; again in-canting*) "I catch, I throw, I throw, I catch." (*He leaves.*)

NAZAR: Sub-Deacon, stay by my side to stop me from inflicting harm on mankind. (*He tries to follow the* SUB-DEACON *but yields to lethargy.*) Oh no! (*He cocks his ear. Afraid, he tries to screw up his courage.*) It's getting dark now, it's getting dark, show the stuff you're made of, Nazar the Brave. (*Suddenly seized by fear, he runs to the hut.*) What happened to that damned wife of mine? Ustian! (*Louder*) Ustian! . . . (*Again he runs inside and, closing the door, locks it. Sud-denly there's a knock at the door.*) Who is it? (*He cocks an ear.*) Haji-Murad? (*Pause*) Gomesh-Patran, is that you?

USTIAN: What the hell's the matter with you? Did the devil eat your tongue?

NAZAR (*coming out of the hut*): Don't be foolish! You have no sense of time. What kept you? Where were you?

USTIAN: Do I ask about your comings and goings?

NAZAR: That isn't a proper response at all for the wife of a brave husband like me.

USTIAN: The way you rushed inside so terrified, one would think a robber was chas-ing you.

NAZAR: Why shouldn't a robber chase a man like me? Running away requires skill, too. I'm such a brave man, I run away and I cause others to run away. I hit and I get hit. That's the lot of the brave. Well, no matter, get the food on the table so I can eat.

USTIAN (*thrusting her fist in the air*): Eat this! Who do you think you are, a king, the way you're ordering me about?

NAZAR: I know my business. (*He sits down at the edge of the oven.* USTIAN *lights a lamp, brings a serving table over, places it under the sycamore tree, and places the food on it.*) What, is it dark already? H'mm. I can hardly see . . . I'm telling you, the bandits will attack the village at night, and our home will be endangered, too. Wife of mine, keep my sword handy.

A STRANGER'S VOICE (*from behind the fence*): Hey!

NAZAR (*entering the hut and sticking his head out the door*): Go see who's there. Lock the outer gate.

(USTIAN *eats leisurely, unmoved.*)

A STRANGER'S VOICE (*nearer*): Here I come! Here I come! Here I come!

NAZAR (*to himself*): I won't open the door. I'll look through the crack! (*The stranger's voice fades away.*) He's gone! (*The voice becomes more distant.*) If he comes again, I'll show him! Seems he didn't know whose door he was shouting at. (*He cocks his ear.*) Well, he's gone now. They must have told him in the village that this is where Nazar lives. (*Coming out of the hut*) He spoke with a Daghestani accent. Who knows, maybe it was the Lezgi Haji-Murad.[3] I thought the voice sounded familiar. Well, what do you know! Oh, the days we spent together! You, the wife of a hero, didn't have the presence of mind to invite him in for a visit. Never mind, I'll go up the mountain tomorrow myself and bring him back with me. (*He sits down and begins to eat.*)

USTIAN: How lucky I am! My husband's a hero, and I'm the queen of a golden palace!

NAZAR: Uphold your man's honor, and everything will work out.

USTIAN: I'd be fine without a man like you.

NAZAR: You'd be fine without a man like me! What man have you found that you're not satisfied with me? You've got a roving eye, right? Well, I'll blind those eyes of yours. I'm not called Nazar the Brave for nothing. Don't exhaust my patience, otherwise I'll whack you with my club. You hear?

USTIAN (*getting up*): You're threatening me with a club? (*She gets up, goes and picks up the club from its place in the corner, and attacks* NAZAR.) Well, take this!

NAZAR: Oh! Oh! Oh! . . . (*He jumps up and goes around the sycamore tree in an attempt to avoid getting hit by the club.*) Don't be afraid, I won't hurt you. Hand over the club.

USTIAN: Stay right where you are!

NAZAR: Whoever heard of a woman beating a man? Is that a humane thing to do? (*He runs under the hut, then sticks his head out.*) Stop! Where are you running off to? I'm coming! Here I am, you merciless witch. Hand over the club.

USTIAN: Come out of there so I can crack open your skull and be done with it!

NAZAR: I'm not coming out! You can count on that.

USTIAN: Ha! You're not coming out?

NAZAR: I'm a man of my word. I'm not coming out.

---

3. The Lezgis are a Caucasian mountain people.

USTIAN: Yeah? For a man like you, you're in the hole where you belong. If you dare show your face, I'll bury your boastful head! (*She pulls back.*)

NAZAR (*sticking his head out*): Put the club away, or I'll come after you.

USTIAN: Come on!

(USTIAN *throws herself on* NAZAR. *He pulls his head back, and* USTIAN *sits down.*)

NAZAR: Woman, put the club back. I've got a mean temper. The blood's going to my head. I'll get up and smash you to pieces. That's why I'm staying under the hut. Do you want everyone to know that I struck my wife? (*Pause*) So you're not going to put down the club? Okay. Any man who lets his wife dishonor him isn't worth a kopeck. Stand there and drop dead! I'm not coming out! (*He pulls his head back. Pause.* USTIAN *puts the club down.* NAZAR *sticks his head out.*) Put the club back where it belongs because I'm hopping mad.

USTIAN: The club is where it belongs.

NAZAR: Give it here!

USTIAN: Come and get it!

NAZAR (*Seeing the club on the ground, he approaches gingerly.*): I'm going to blow my top and wreck the joint, you nagging bitch. (*He runs out of the hut but, tempted by the food, sidles over to the dinner table.*) Well, I was in no mood to fight anyway. (*He sits down.*) Our clan is made up of real men; we don't raise a hand against women. (*He picks up his spoon and begins eating.*) If you were a somebody, I wouldn't mind, but considering you're a nobody, you don't think I'm going to let you hit me with the club? If you were really tough, you'd go with me into the mountains and see how the bandits take to their heels when they see me! All you know is how to act bossy within these four walls. A really brave person never lifts a club in his own house.

USTIAN: Your day wouldn't be complete if you didn't run off at the mouth.

NAZAR (*scratching his head and yawning*): I told you, I'm in no mood to fight. Clear the table and lay out my bed. I need my sleep so I can get up early. To-morrow there's going to be a clash with the Köroghlu gang in the Chakhmakh mountains, and I'll be there.

USTIAN: Oh, what a bullshit artist you are! It's easy to conquer the world with all that crap.

NAZAR: My conquests keep growing! A mere bagatelle. The whole kit and kaboo-dle's not worth one of my toenails! The world is my captive; like that (*He snaps his fingers.*) I fear no one, so I dare to release my prisoners and let them live as they wish instead of trampling the whole lot underfoot.

USTIAN: You trample the world underfoot?

NAZAR: You bet! I'm not one of your clod-hopping knuckleheads.

USTIAN: You know how to piss off a person. Nobody compares to you, right?

NAZAR: Right. There are going to be award ceremonies honoring me.

USTIAN: And you're going to become famous and wow the world!

NAZAR: Wait and see. I'm conquering everybody. Me, hero of heroes, on top of the heap.

USTIAN: You snot-nosed squirt! There's no limit to your bullshit!

NAZAR: If I weren't so lazy, I'd get up and beat the hell out of you.

USTIAN (*aside to the audience*): Well, at least he admits he's lazy.

NAZAR (*motioning to her*): Who do you think you're talking to? (*Slumping lazily*) All right, let it go till tomorrow. (*He pulls his wool coat over him and prepares to sleep.*) A man like me deserves respect. All you do is sit there and abuse me, instead of marveling at my mind. My thoughts circumscribe the world. I'm debating the future of the globe. With all my aspirations for international diplomacy you should be proud of me. (*He lies down. Pause. Musing.*) Sweetie pie, what are you going to say when you get word of my glorious victory? I'll martial my forces, get on my horse, draw my sword, ride straight through the enemy ranks to cheers of "Long live Nazar!"

(USTIAN *takes the plates into the hut.*)

NAZAR (*jumping up*): Hey. Where are you going?

USTIAN: What are you following me for? Can't you see I'm putting away the plates? Just go chase the enemy.

NAZAR: You shouldn't go alone. Wait, I'll guard you as you walk. (*He goes into the hut with her.*)

USTIAN: Just stay put! (*She goes out.*)

NAZAR (*following her*): What do you mean? With all the thieves and bandits about, I'm not going to let you leave the house alone. What would the villagers say if they found out?

(USTIAN *enters the hut.*)

NAZAR (*following her*): That a girl. Never fear, Nazar is here.

(*Again about to leave,* USTIAN *approaches the door.* NAZAR *follows her. But* USTIAN *changes her mind and turns back, preoccupied. She is about to close the door.*)

NAZAR: Ustian, leave the door open so I can see my way to the stable and check if the donkey's got barley to eat.

(USTIAN *complies grudgingly.* NAZAR *goes outside.*)

NAZAR (*calling from the barn*): Don't close the door, stay there. Why isn't there any barley here for the donkey? (*Pause*) Stay cool, I'm still here. (*Pause. The moon appears.*) The moon's out. (*Pause*) Sweetie, look what a bright clear night this is! Bring me my weapons. I'm going to ambush the khan's caravan from Daghestan.

USTIAN (*with contempt*): Just wipe your nose and crawl into your hole. You're incapable of ambushing anything.

NAZAR: My dear, don't exhaust my patience! I repeat, bring my weapons so I can ambush the caravan.

USTIAN (*aside*) I can't take it anymore. Who the hell does he think he is? (*Firmly*) So you want to ambush the caravan?

NAZAR: Right on! Don't be a pain in the butt. What's wrong with a little ambush?

USTIAN: Go to hell! (*Going inside, she slams the door shut.*) Shove your ambush!

NAZAR: What did you do that for?

USTIAN (*calling through the door*): Get lost, and don't bother coming back.

NAZAR: Open the door or I'll break it down.

(USTIAN *is silent.*)

NAZAR: Open the door. I won't beat you.

USTIAN: You beat me? Watch I don't crack your head open!

NAZAR (*urgently*): Ustian, open the door. The bandits are coming.

USTIAN: Forget it! I'm not opening it.

NAZAR: Open the door. They're here. I've got to strap on my weapons.

USTIAN (*Taking* NAZAR's *rusty sword from the wall, she picks up the banner and wool coat and pushes them through the partially open door.*): Take your junk, and get out of my life!

NAZAR: It's dark. Where can I go?

USTIAN: Try Daghestan, you jerk. I'm no longer your wife! (*She lies down.*)

NAZAR (*Picking up the wool coat, he puts it on, straps on his sword, and takes hold of the banner.*): Ustian, they're at the gate! (*He looks toward the forest and crouches near the door.*) They're here! Hey, hey, hey! (*Louder*) Hey, hey, hey! (*Louder still*) Hey, hey, hey! [*As though talking to someone*] Who do you think you're attacking? . . . I'll gouge your eyes out! Yeah! Hey, hey, hey! (*He runs behind the house from the left side.*)

SAKO (*He comes forward out of forest right, wearing a white sheepskin cap.*): Oh, my gosh, for the love of God, where are we? Is this a house or a whole village? Who's there? Help! We've lost our way!

VOSKAN (*He comes forward behind him, also wearing a white sheepskin cap.*): Hey, Sako, hitch your horse to a tree, and we'll take a look around.

SAKO: Voskan, we're done for. This place's worse than hell!

VOSKAN: God is merciful. Don't be afraid, Sako.

NAZAR (*approaching from the left but still out of sight*): I'm Nazar the Brave, the hero who destroys a thousand with one blow.

SAKO: Hey, Voskan, who's this Nazar fellah?

VOSKAN: Don't know. Sit down and keep cool.

(*They crouch in the bushes.*)

NAZAR (*as though talking to someone*): Hambo? Are you at the top of the tower? Take a good look, there's a caravan approaching. If it's Köroghlu's, ready the men for ambush. We'll grab us a high ticket item to take to Sardar's tomorrow. I'm saddling my horse, so, boys, get with it. (*Imitating the voice of Ashi, one of the village gang*) Nazar the Brave, who are you talking to? (*Answering as himself*) Ashi, I got tired playing games with Köroghlu's forces by myself, I'm taking our boys with me to annihilate them. (*Again as Ashi*) Why don't you let Köroghlu go? Give him a break. (*Answering as himself*) No way. I'll make mincemeat out of him. (*Cocking his ear*) Hey, who goes there? Hambo, somebody's standing there and listening. Go see who it is, grab him and drag him over here. Have you got hold of him? Break his neck. That's it. Good. Throw him in the bushes.

SAKO: Oh, no! We've had it!

VOSKAN: Shut up.

NAZAR (*threatening and fearful*): He-e-e-e-ep!

SAKO (*rapidly*): Jesus Christ! Jesus Christ! Jesus Christ!

NAZAR: I'll send your feathers flying! (*Silence, dashing from here to there*) Is there anybody left? Dali-Aslan, grab that hand. Gija-Ghushi, grab this hand. I'm mounting my horse.

SAKO: Voskan, let's get out of here!

VOSKAN: We can't, they've blocked the road.

NAZAR (*still acting*): I'm on my horse. Here I am. Karvan-Ghran, come quick! Jamush-Patran, strike! Grab hold of them! Hey! I'll smash them to smithereens!

(NAZAR *runs forward to the front of the stage.* VOSKAN *goes into the bushes.* SAKO *runs out of the bushes and pulls up confused.* NAZAR *comes, bumps into* SAKO *who, falling down, begins to shudder.*)

NAZAR: Huh-u, mmuh, mu!

SAKO: Huh-u, mmuh, mu, mu! . . . Nazar the Brave!

NAZAR: Köroghlu!

SAKO (*grabbing* NAZAR *by the waist and shouting*): Hey!

NAZAR (*likewise grabbing* SAKO *by the waist and shouting*): Hey!

SAKO (*shouting*): Let me go!

NAZAR (*shouting*): Let me go!

(*Both of them suddenly let each other go and each flees:* NAZAR *to the left, toward the rear of the hut;* SAKO *to the right, into the bushes.*)

VOSKAN (*coming out of the bushes*): Sako, run for your life! (*He runs toward the right.*)

SAKO: Oh! Holy Mother of God! (*He runs after him. Pause*)

NAZAR (NAZAR *falls flat on his face.* VOSKAN *and* SAKO *run over him to the right and disappear.* NAZAR *gradually gets up and begins to look over* SAKO's *horse. Tentatively*): Well, you helpless creature, did your leader escape or is he coming back? (*Pause*) No, he's gone . . . He probably high-tailed it out of here. Did he swipe anything? Nah, he just took off. (*With assurance*) Who says I'm not brave? (*Shouting*) With one blow I destroy a thousand! (*Approaching the door*) Ustian, open the door! (*Pause*) Well, from now on, to hell with any man who speaks well of women! I'm off! Make way, watch out! Nazar the Brave is on his way! (*He cocks his ear. Inside the hut,* USTIAN *is silent.*) Okay. If that's how you want it. I'll give you a beating in the morning and be on my way. (*Pause*) Okay, Bitch, I'm off! (*He gets on his horse.*) Tally-ho!

USTIAN (*Jumping up, she grabs the club, opens the door, and dashes out.*): I've had it with you! (*Striking* NAZAR *and his horse with the club*) Take this, you old fart!

NAZAR: You'll frighten the horse! (*The horse bolts.*) I told you so! Help! (*His voice becomes more distant as he continues calling out.*)

USTIAN (*going inside*): Good riddance to bad rubbish! Have yourself a heart attack and go blind, too! (*She goes inside.*)

Curtain

ACT 2

NAZAR THE BRAVE *in Zorbastan.*

The scene is set in a forest clearing; there are paths right and left. A party is in progress. The guests are gathered around a table.

GUESTS (*singing*): Hey jan, hey jan, hey jan!

A SPRIGHTLY OLD MAN (*Swaying gently and displaying his charm, he dances solo and beats out the time to himself. He is drunk*): Um, tara-ni ee-ee-ee! nee-nam! . . . um, tara-ni ee-ee-ee! nee-nam! (*He addresses one of the guests.*) Cousin Tatos[4] . . . um, tara-ni ee-ee-ee! nee-nam. Cousin Tatos, are you game? Come on dance. Show us what you're made of or I'll pluck your eyes out! . . . Um, tara-ni ee-ee-ee! nee-nam.

---

4. The Armenian term *khnami* is translated here as "cousin," suggesting a loose sort of kinship. In a narrower sense it signifies a relationship through marriage.

GUESTS (*to the dancer*): Jan, Cousin Ghunkianos, jan!

A GUEST: Jan, Cousin Ghunkianos, sit down! Hey, pour some wine for Cousin Ghunkianos.

(*They seat the sprightly old man.*)

MASTER OF CEREMONIES: Village elders, I bid you, fill your mugs.

A GUEST: Master, just say the word, you're the boss.

MASTER OF CEREMONIES: What I have to say is, God help us keep hold over our villages. May God protect our new son-in-law and village chief Tatos Matosents.

GUESTS: Hey, jan! Hey, jan! Hey, jan! Here's to you, Cousin Tatos! (*They drink. Sounds of a commotion are heard nearby.*)

MASTER OF CEREMONIES: Go see who that horseman is.

VOICES: He's a traveler.

MASTER OF CEREMONIES: A traveler is a guest sent by God. After he dismounts from his horse, bring him to the table.

(GUESTS *go out and bring in* NAZAR *who, banner in hand and sword dangling from his waist, stands with a frown on his face, looking apprehensively at the group. The guests, in turn, look suspiciously at him.*)

MASTER OF CEREMONIES (*looking quizzically at* NAZAR's *banner and appearance*): Welcome. (*To those sitting near him*) Hey fellows, make room for the guest.

(*They make way. Uncertain,* NAZAR *looks morosely all around, coughs, comes with his banner and sits next to the* MASTER OF CEREMONIES, *the* SCHOOLMASTER, *and the old men. Pause. He coughs again. The* MASTER OF CEREMONIES *likewise coughs.* NAZAR *gets up halfway, as if to flee. The guests, thinking he will attack them, move about fearfully as if to flee.* NAZAR *frowns at the guests. The guests, in turn, look at him warily.*)

MASTER OF CEREMONIES (*noticing* NAZAR's *erratic movements*): Help yourself to food and drink. Enjoy!

(*The guests lighten up and start eating.*)

FIRST GUEST (*to those sitting next to him*): Who is he? What sort of fellow is he?

SECOND GUEST: Just look, there's his banner, and there's his sword—

THIRD GUEST: He's the strong silent type.

AN OLD MAN: The way he sat down like that, banner, sword, and all, he's someone to be reckoned with.

(*Pause*)

NAZAR (*coughing*): Hem!

(*Everybody looks at him.*)

FIRST GUEST: What did he say?
SECOND GUEST: He said, "Hem!"
THIRD GUEST: What did he say?
FOURTH GUEST: He said, "Hem!" (*The same question-and-answer exchange continues, reaching an Old Man.*)
OLD MAN: Since he said, "Hem!" that means he's Köroghlu.
SECOND OLD MAN (*putting his hand to his forehead and looking at* NAZAR): No, he's Köroghlu's grandson.

(*Pause*)

NAZAR (*to the* MASTER OF CEREMONIES, *proudly*): You, good-for-nothing! I want to know just one thing about you people. Are you from Daghestan?
MASTER OF CEREMONIES: No, we're from Zorbashen.
NAZAR: What's the name of the country?
MASTER OF CEREMONIES: Zorbastan.
NAZAR (*slowly shaking his head*): Zorbastan? Okay. That's what I wanted to know.

(*Pause*)

MASTER OF CEREMONIES: And you, sir, what country are you from?
NAZAR: From Nazarstan. The city of Nazarashen.
OLD MAN: Nazarashen? I know it well. That was my grandfather's hometown.
FIRST GUEST: You and your grandfather! Find out who he is.
SECOND GUEST (*to the one next to him*): Find out who he really is.

(*Constantly egging one another on and sometimes skipping over a few guests, they ask who the stranger is, until the question reaches the* PRIEST, *who is seated next to* NAZAR.)

THE LAST GUEST (*to the priest*): Father, find out what kind of a man he is.
PRIEST (*Looking at* NAZAR's *banner and reading it, he becomes terrified. Then, turning to the last questioner, he says in a low voice*):

> Nazar the invincible, Nazar the brave
> With one blow sends a thousand to the grave.

THE LAST QUESTIONER (*To the one sitting next to him; the latter, in turn, passes it down to the* FIRST GUEST.):

> Nazar the invincible, Nazar the brave
> With one blow sends a thousand to the grave.

MASTER OF CEREMONIES: Hah!
EVERYBODY: Ahah!

(NAZAR *coughs.* SAKO *enters, sober and proud.*)

GUESTS: Welcome, Sako! Have a seat!
SAKO (*serious*): Glad to be here.
MASTER OF CEREMONIES AND THE OTHERS: Welcome. Sit down. What's brought you here?
SAKO: Hold on. I'm very tired.
GUESTS: Where's your horse?
SAKO (*sitting down and taking a deep breath*): This is what happened. I trampled over so many troops that my poor horse fell to its knees. I walked here all the way.
GUESTS: You don't say! Was there a fight?
SAKO: Boy, was there ever! We slogged it out so long that my arm nearly dropped off. After all, there are only so many you can massacre, right?
MASTER OF CEREMONIES: It's time to relax and enjoy yourself. That's quite a story you tell.
SAKO (*He fills his pipe, just itching to tell his story. Everybody is eagerly waiting to hear it. He lights his pipe, puffs on it, and begins to brag as he speaks.*): This is what happened, fellows. I was riding on my horse to Dumanlu, Chamlebel. It was dead in the middle of the night and, before I knew it, I'd reached the Gharanlukh woods. My horse was still fresh, and I whipped him to a frenzy. It was such a dark night, you couldn't see the whites of the enemy's eyes. Then I heard a sound; it was either a beast or a brigand. When I listened some more, I knew it was neither beast nor brigand. It was coming at me like a torrent. I said to myself, "What the hell could this be?" In the next instant I saw men charging at me, one after the other, like hail in a storm. (*The listeners have a terrified look about them.*) I called out, asking whose men they were. They didn't respond. So I pulled out my sword, got my horse going, rushed into them, and began slashing away. (*He puffs on his pipe as he presses the tobacco down.*)
VOSKAN (*Entering from left and seeing that everybody is occupied, he cautiously approaches* SAKO, *so as not to cause a disturbance, and stands behind him. Then, recognizing* NAZAR, *he is surprised. He nudges a guest sitting near* NAZAR.): Who's that?

A GUEST: That's Nazar the Brave.

(*Terrified,* VOSKAN *gapes at* NAZAR.)

SAKO: As I was charging, a horseman suddenly appeared and cried out, "Sakhkal-Tutan, Jamush-Patran, strike!"

(NAZAR *rises halfway and prepares to run. The attention of the others is focused on* SAKO.)

That's all I needed to hear. I urged my horse to a gallop, caught up with him, and (*demonstrating with his arm*) knocked horse and rider to the ground.

NAZAR (*losing his composure*): Bah, bah, bah, bah!

(VOSKAN *casts an anxious glance at* NAZAR.)

SAKO: This fellow wraps himself around my feet and feebly shouts: "I beg of you, Köroghlu, spare me!" I trampled him underfoot and you should have seen me wallop him in the stomach, head, and back . . . back, stomach, and nose . . . I made mincemeat out of him . . . By this time, the moon had come out. I looked down and saw that it was the so-called Nazar the Brave.

EVERYBODY(*confused*): Hey, boy, hey boy! . . . Look over here, here! (*They cough.*)

VOSKAN (*drawing* SAKO's *attention to* NAZAR): Oh, you're telling them about our adventure.

SAKO: I made mincemeat out of him . . . (*Suddenly noticing* VOSKAN) Sure!

VOSKAN (*softly*): Sako, it's Nazar the Brave! Sako, it's Nazar the Brave! (*He winks, poking his head in* NAZAR's *direction.*)

SAKO (*totally disconcerted*): Hah! Hah! Hah! Eh! . . . (*Suddenly noticing* NAZAR's *loss of composure*) Bah, bah, bah, bah!

NAZAR (*likewise disconcerted*): Bah, bah, bah, bah!

SAKO: Hah, eh! Was he carrying a banner or a sword, that nobody attacked him? Hey, Nazar the Brave. You should have seen the guy giving it to them in the stomach, back, head . . . head, back, stomach.

VOSKAN: We did pretty well ourselves.

SAKO: Yeah, a whole lot of things happened . . . bah, bah, bah . . . (*He asks the guests sitting next to him, softly.*) Who is this guy?

FIRST GUEST, SECOND GUEST, THIRD GUEST: It's Nazar the Brave.

SAKO (*looking warily at* NAZAR *and sitting down*): Really? . . . bah, bah, bah, bah!

(NAZAR *likewise sits down and looks warily at* SAKO.)

GUESTS: How did it end up? Who won?

SAKO: Who do you think? Nazar the Brave. We gave a good account of ourselves too . . . (*To those sitting next to him*) Where does this Nazar the Brave you're talking about come from?

THE ONE NEXT TO HIM: Nazarashen.

SAKO: Yeah, that's right. Nazar the Brave's from Nazarashen. Boy, how he's changed! I didn't recognize him at first.

FIRST GUEST: You know him, huh?

SAKO: Sure I do. We lived like brothers for five years during the fighting in Daghestan.

NAZAR (*menacingly*): Uhr! (*He looks at* SAKO. SAKO *turns away, cowering.*)

MASTER OF CEREMONIES: You know him, right? Well, then say so, for crying out loud!

GUESTS: You know him, right?

SAKO (*to* NAZAR): You're Nazar the Brave, aren't you? [*To the others*] You see, I know him!

(NAZAR *growls again and swipes with his hand.*)

MASTER OF CEREMONIES (*to* NAZAR): Brother Nazar. Welcome. We heard of you quite a while ago but never saw you. Now we have the good fortune to meet you.

GUESTS (*taking turns getting up and shaking hands with* NAZAR): Welcome, Brother Nazar.

FIRST GUEST (*to* SAKO): My good man, it's quite remarkable you are one of the select few who actually know Nazar the Brave.

SAKO: Did you see how quickly I identified him? Well, sure. I know two heroes between Daghestan and Hindustan; one is Nazar the Brave, the other is . . . Nazar the Brave will tell you who it is.

SECOND GUEST: I understand why he has come to these parts. This is the end of the road.

VOICES: For what?

SECOND GUEST: I'll tell you later.

SPRIGHTLY OLD MAN: I know. I know what for. (*He winks at* NAZAR.) You and I know, don't we?

AN OLD MAN (*to the* SECOND OLD MAN): I'm not going to say anything yet. Let me see if you can figure out who Nazar the Brave is.

SECOND OLD MAN: Who doesn't know Nazar the Brave? The whole world knows him. Nazar has been in these mountains of ours for forty years.

GUESTS (*chanting*): Hey jan, hey jan, hey jan!

MASTER OF CEREMONIES (*to* NAZAR): Brother Nazar, you kept still all the while we were speaking. Who knows where your mind was straying all this time? Tell us what you've brought back from your wanderings. Where were you before coming here?

NAZAR (*coughing, with pride*): My brother, let me tell you, I've come through Kafrstan. I had set out to cut off the head of Baghr Khan. I cut it off and came on here. Along the way I cut off Kyarim Khan's head, too.

GUESTS: Wow!

MASTER OF CEREMONIES: May your arm be strong forever! Do you also kill ordinary folk as well as bigwigs?

NAZAR: Like flies. A thousand with one blow.

MASTER OF CEREMONIES: You mean you strike down anyone great or small that gets in your way?

NAZAR: That's my style. That's my business. Massacring.

MASTER OF CEREMONIES: God willing, are you going to massacre the whole world?

NAZAR: That's my plan.

MASTER OF CEREMONIES: May your arm never lose its strength. Now, if that's the case, I've a request to make.

NAZAR: Let's hear it. I'm all ears.

MASTER OF CEREMONIES: Well, we are as you see us. All of us are village elders. But, unfortunately, we are also prisoners of our neighbors.

ALL: We're prisoners, we're prisoners!

NAZAR: How is it that you're prisoners?

MASTER OF CEREMONIES: We're prisoners, Brother Nazar. Prisoners. Our neighbors won't let us live on their land. Couldn't you free us from them? They've devoured us.

NAZAR: Won't let you live on their land? How so? Me being Nazar, I shouldn't be hearing such a thing! (*Addressing the imaginary oppressors, he strikes his foot on the ground.*) Is this how you abuse my people? (*They're all amazed at his bravado.*) Is that why my forefathers became kings, for you to oppress my people?

(*Everybody gets to their feet, doffing their caps.*)

NAZAR: Tell me, who are these neighbors of yours?

MASTER OF CEREMONIES: They are seven giants.

NAZAR (*jumping up from his seat, seized with fright*): Seven giants? . . . oh! oh! oh! oh! . . . (*Anxiously*) Where are they?

VOICES: They're far off.

NAZAR (*relieved*): Oh, they're far off. (*Encouraged*) Well, how have they dared to be so far away? (*To* SAKO) Comrade of mine, go see where they are and bring them here so I can eat them alive. How come they won't let you live on their land? How many heads do these ogres have, that they're giving you such trouble? What is it, don't they know that I'm a giant slayer? The other day, I pulverized a thousand of them, made flour and cast it to the winds. These two specks of dust were left so I just put them in my charm. (*He shows the charm.*)

ALL (*amazed and fearful*): Wow!

PRIEST: Present one of them as a souvenir to our village, blessed one.

NAZAR (*Opening the charm, he gives one speck to the* PRIEST.): Take it! (*To the others*) Wait, I'll make dust out of these giants, too, and give each one of you a speck as a souvenir. Now, an order from me to you elders of my people. May the land of all your neighbors be yours.

ALL: Hurrah for Nazar the Brave.

TEACHER (*as white as parchment*): The golden age has come! Our nation's hero has appeared!

MASTER OF CEREMONIES: Absolutely, Oh wise one. Right on.

PRIEST: Deep mystery, incomprehensible, without beginning.[5]

MASTER OF CEREMONIES: Blessed be your priesthood. Don't say another word, Father!

NAZAR: The devil be cursed! To think of those giants giving you trouble like that! (*To* SAKO) Tell them to give my horse some barley. Then I'll go and put an end to them.

SAKO (*to one side*): Tell them to feed our horses.

ALL (*chanting*): Hey jan, hey jan, hey jan!

TEACHER (*jumping up*): Oh Friends! Oh people! Oh nation! Now is the hour! The indomitable Nazar is going against the giants of India in a sacred cause. To regain the land of our ancestors. Nazar the Great shall reign as king. He has risen up against the whole world.

PRIEST: We are the nation of Nazar the Brave and, as such, we express our thanks to God. We are above all nations.

SPRY OLD MAN: Yahoo! We won't let another nation look askance at us. We'll send their fine feathers flying skyward. Yeah!—

TEACHER (*interrupting, getting to his feet*): Stand up! Death to the King of India! Long live Nazar the Brave!

ALL (*rising to their feet*): Long live Nazar the Brave! Blessed be Nazar! (*They sit.*)

MASTER OF CEREMONIES: Nazar the Brave, how are we going to handle the giants of India?

NAZAR: I'll wipe them out good and proper. Get ready, we're going.

MASTER OF CEREMONIES: We're off.

SPRY OLD MAN: I'm coming, too.

AN OLD MAN: Well, I'm coming, too.

ALL: We're coming, too.

---

5. The allusion is to the opening of the hymn of vesting, sung at the opening of the Armenian liturgy.

COUSIN TATOS (*questioning*): Where?

ALL (*to him*): Cousin Tatos, we're going to wipe out the giants.

COUSIN TATOS: I'm coming, too.

MASTER OF CEREMONIES (*to the duduk players*): Play the "Nazar the Brave" anthem.

(*The duduk players play.*)

TEACHER (*recites to the music*):

> Long live Nazar, congratulations, Nazar,
> Who kills a thousand, a thousand,
> Live long for our nation,
> Lopping off enemy heads like radishes.

MASTER OF CEREMONIES: Well said, Wise One. May your words inspire us in our fight.

GUESTS: Hey jan, hey jan, hey jan . . .

MASTER OF CEREMONIES (*with the music*): Nazar, we're off. (*He drinks.*)

NAZAR (*to the old man*): We're off, Chief. (*He drinks.*)

PRIEST (*Clearing his throat, and in a hoarse voice, he begins to sing spontaneously, with the duduk players and guests joining in.*):

> From the capital Nazarashen,
> From the fortress Pghndzashen,
> Came our sun, lion Nazar.
> Come, our shining sun, come.
> Come, our champion, come.

GUESTS: Jan, priest, jan. May your priesthood be blessed.

SPRY OLD MAN: Nazar the Brave, are we going to wipe them out? (*He drinks.*)

NAZAR: We're going to wipe them out, Chief. (*He drinks.*)

MASTER OF CEREMONIES: Cousin Tatos, are we going?

TATOS: We're going.

GUESTS: Hey jan, hey jan, hey jan.

(*The duduk stops playing.*)

TEACHER: Fill your glasses. I'm going to drink a holy toast. Let's drink to our brave, strong Nazar.

ALL: Nazar the Brave. To your health, Nazar. (*They drink. The duduk players give a musical toast, followed by deep silence.*)

NAZAR (*getting up ponderously and proudly*): Thank you, my people. (*He drinks and sits.*)

MASTER OF CEREMONIES (*drinking*): Down the hatch.

ALL (*drinking*): Down the hatch.

(NAZAR *toasts and drinks again.*)

PRIEST: May you have a lot of sons. I'm going to baptize them all, Nazar the Brave.

NAZAR (*roaring drunk*): Let's move it. I'll eat them alive.

A GUEST (*suddenly looking to his left*): Who's that? What kind of man is that?

ALL (*in drunken voices*): What are you blathering about?

VILLAGER (*from the depth of the forest, at right*): Help. Do something.

ALL (*uneasy*): What's your problem?

VILLAGER (*now rushing into the crowd*): Help. There's a tiger loose in the forest!

MASTER OF CEREMONIES (*chuckling*): A tiger?

ALL (*also chuckling*): A tiger?

VILLAGER (*bewildered*): Why are you laughing? I'm telling you, there's a tiger in the forest.

MASTER OF CEREMONIES (*with a relaxed smile*): So there's a tiger, so what? . . . Don't worry. Nazar the tiger killer's on hand.

VILLAGER: What Nazar, what tiger killer? It's torn the dogs to pieces.

(SAKO *coughs and, getting up, sidles toward the left entrance and suddenly bolts.*)

NAZAR (*calling to a person offstage*): Friend, give my horse some water. I'll be on my way soon. (*To the villager*) Where do you hail from, friend?

VILLAGER: From the village of Kyallagyoz.

NAZAR (*slowly shaking his head*): Yeah? What tiger are you talking about? Where is it, and how did it have the nerve to enter our forest?

VILLAGER: I don't know, but it's headed this way.

NAZAR (*jumping up and coughing*): Friend!

MASTER OF CEREMONIES: Ah, Nazar, you love a good fight, right? See how lucky you are.

NAZAR: I love . . . (*He walks around apprehensively.*) Buh, buh, buh, buh! . . . (*To the villager*) What side is it coming from, Friend?

VILLAGER (*pointing to the right*): From this side.

NAZAR (*Coughing loudly, he gets up and prepares to run off.*): I'll make it see stars! (*He runs off left.*)

ALL: Where's he going? Where's he going?

MASTER OF CEREMONIES (*at left*): He wants to circle round the tiger. I don't know why you people couldn't deal with the beast. Instead, you let him go after it.

Get yourselves over here. (*The villagers run to the left and prevent* NAZAR *from making his getaway.*) Nazar the Brave, you go after the tiger. We'll block its path.

VOICES (*offstage left*): It's coming, it's coming!

(*Confusion. Some run to the left; others to the right; still others to the back.*)

NAZAR: Buh, buh, buh . . . (*He runs downstage.*)

THOSE RUNNING TO THE BACK (*retreating to center*): It's coming this way.

NAZAR (*running back from down center to the right*): Buh, buh, buh! . . .

THOSE RUNNING FROM THE RIGHT (*retreating to center*): It's coming this way.

NAZAR (*running backward from up left*): Buh, buh, buh! . . . (*He runs out. Everybody goes after him.* NAZAR *reenters from the right side then backtracks and goes off right again, then enters from stage left.*)

VOICES: It's here, it's here!

MASTER OF CEREMONIES: Let Nazar lead! Let him go in front! (*Everyone hides behind* NAZAR.)

(*The tiger appears from the right. They push* NAZAR *toward the tiger and run off left.* NAZAR *remains rooted, frozen from fear and bewilderment. Then, all of a sudden, he climbs up a tree. The tiger comes under the same tree and stands in the bushes there.*)

VOICES OFFSTAGE: Run, run! (*Pause*)

NAZAR (*with tremulous voice, terrified*): Mercy!

(*The tiger bellows.* NAZAR *looks at the tiger with horror and shudders. Suddenly he falls from the tree right onto the tiger's back and rides it fear-struck, holding on tight. The tiger, too, is seized with fright and, springing forward, runs off left with* NAZAR *on its back.*)

MASTER OF CEREMONIES (*speaking from offstage right, near the entrance, to villagers completely offstage*): Hey fellows, come quickly. He's caught the tiger. He's caught the tiger!

VOICES: We're coming, we're coming!

MASTER OF CEREMONIES (*to the left*): Hold on tight, Nazar. Hold on tight! (*To the villagers entering right*) Hurry up, kill it!

(*The tiger enters from the left, with* NAZAR *riding it. The villagers follow the tiger with shovels, sticks, and stones. They surround the tiger and strike at it from all sides, killing it.* NAZAR, *totally overcome with fear, is still sitting on the tiger. Pause.*)

A VOICE : He's unconscious.

ANOTHER VOICE: Be quiet! . . . He's become ferocious.

A THIRD VOICE: He's ripping the tiger's skin apart.

A FOURTH VOICE: Stop him. Don't let him rip the skin.

MASTER OF CEREMONIES: Don't rip it. It'll be a souvenir.

ALL (*to* NAZAR): Get up, Nazar the Brave. That's enough.

(*They take him off the tiger's back.*)

MASTER OF CEREMONIES: Remove the tiger's skin. You're all a bunch of clods! Does Nazar have to do that, too?

(*A few drag the tiger toward the background to skin it.*)

NAZAR (*regaining consciousness*): Where's the tiger?

ALL: We killed it.

NAZAR (*Looking at the tiger, he coughs to himself.*): Yeah, hum . . . That's how you tame a tiger. (*To the tiger*) You got what was coming to you. (*Coughing out loud, he addresses the villagers.*) Come to think of it, you really shouldn't have done that.

ALL (*confused*): Do what?

NAZAR: Kill it. Who told *you* to kill it?

ALL: What else should we have done?

NAZAR: *I* was about to administer the coup de grace. Although, I have to say he gave me a better ride than my horse. Come to think of it, why even harm a tiger? After all, it's such a timid beast!

ALL: We didn't know. We won't do it again.

SAKO (*rushing in from left*): Where is it? Where's the tiger? They said a tiger was on the loose.

ALL: You're too late. Nazar the Brave has taken care of him.

SAKO (*boastfully*): We'll cut it to pieces, yeah! . . . (*Seeing the dead tiger*) Well, what do you know?

TIGER SLAYERS (*bringing the skin forward*): Here it is!

MASTER OF CEREMONIES: Bring it forward and spread it out at Nazar's feet. (*They spread it out.*) Congratulations, Nazar the Brave, our lord, our savior. May the whole world unfold like this beneath your feet. (*To the villagers*) Now get up, let's go with Nazar and massacre the giants.

ALL: Let's go!

TEACHER: Get up!

PRIEST: Get up, everyone!

TEACHER: Oh, people, let's follow Nazar the Brave. Let's save the homeland and bask in its glory.

PRIEST: And may God's will be done!

ALL: Lead on, Nazar the Brave. Bring out Nazar's horse.

(*The horse is brought out. The tiger skin is thrown upon the horse.* NAZAR *sits on it, banner in hand. Surrounding him, the people prepare to move.*)

MASTER OF CEREMONIES (*to the duduk players*): Play!

(*The duduk players take out their instruments and play.*)

NAZAR (*holding onto the horse uncomfortably*): Let's go, fellah. Buh, buh, buh!
MASTER OF CEREMONIES (*to the others*): Forward march!
SAKO (*to the others*): Forward!
MASTER OF CEREMONIES (*moving forward*): Move out! (*And immediately he returns somewhat fearfully.*)
TEACHER: Forward! (*He moves forward and also warily returns.*)
PRIEST (*coming back cautiously*): Forward arms!
ALL (*standing in their places*): Oho!

(*Suddenly* NAZAR's *horse is startled and carries him forward.*)

ALL: Let's go. Follow our leader! Onward. (*They run after him.*)

Curtain

ACT 3

NAZAR THE BRAVE *in the Land of the* GIANTS.

The scene is set in a forest clearing. The trunks of thick trees, sticking up like posts, darken the background. In front, the giants' cyclopean fortress rises. Irregular stone steps lead up to the fortress gate. Paths lead off right and left from the clearing in the center. A haughty giant with huge eyes appears. His head is shaved, but for a few wisps of hair bunched on his crown. The ends of his long mustache are tied behind his ears. He breathes like a bellows and snorts like a pig. Sticking his head through the crenelations of the fortress, he looks about.

KHOZENI: Hummm!
DANGIZ (*a lazy, slow-moving giant, with sleepy bloodshot eyes. From deep inside the fortress, he calls out in a drawl characteristic of all the giants*): Kho-ze-ni!
KHOZENI (*speaking in the same manner*): What-is-it?
DANGIZ (*drawling again*): Kho-ze-ni, can you hear me?

KHOZENI: Yeah, yeah, yeah! (*Drawling*) What is it?

DANGIZ: Look and see if there's a caravan coming.

KHOZENI: Okay. (*He looks all around, yawns, and snorts.*) Hummm!

DANGIZ (*from below*): Ghuzghun, Ghorobugha. (*Sticking his head out of a window in the fortress*) Gharaghura?

KHOZENI: They're not here. They're not here.

DANGIZ: Where are they?

KHOZENI: They're out hunting. They're out hunting, hunting!

(DANGIZ *nods comprehendingly, then draws back inside, his head scrunched between his shoulders.*)

KHOZENI (*turning toward the inner part of the fortress*): Yo, girl, Perishan.

PERISHAN (*a huge girl, naïve, with big eyes and a smiling face. From way deep in the fortress calls out in a drawl*): What is it?

KHOZENI: Big brother'll be back from hunting any minute. Put the pots on the fire.

PERISHAN (*as she exits to the rear of the fortress*): Okay.

(KHOZENI *snorts and looks this way and that while twisting his mustache.*)

DANGIZ (*from below*): Khozeni!

KHOZENI: What is it?

DANGIZ: I'm starving.

KHOZENI: Eat one of the buffaloes.

DANGIZ (*jumping out of the fortress and wrapping himself around one of the buttresses*): Can I find one? Bring one down!

KHOZENI (*As he comes down he laughs long and boisterously, as befits a giant.*): Hah! Hah! Hah! Pah! Pah! Pah! Pah! Pah! Ho! Ho! Ho! Hoo! Hoo! Hoo! Hoo! Hoo!

DANGIZ (*grabbing him*): Finish your laugh, I've got something to tell you. Finish your laugh, I've got something to tell you.

(KHOZENI *continues to laugh uncontrollably.*)

DANGIZ: Let's see, is he finished laughing?

KHOZENI (*Suddenly he stops laughing.*): Yeah, I'm finished. What's on your mind?

DANGIZ: Isn't Ghorobugha here?

KHOZENI: He's gone hunting, hunting!

DANGIZ (*He pauses, thinking.*): You said hunting? (*He pauses again.*)

KHOZENI: Well, did you get it?

DANGIZ (*pausing and thinking*): Yeah, I got it. (*He goes in and comes out right away.*) I'm going to eat what's in the big pot.

KHOZENI (*screaming*): What do you mean? (*He strikes* DANGIZ *in the head.*) How do you like that? Eh!

PERISHAN (*suddenly rushing out and sniffing the air*): I catch the scent of a man.

KHOZENI: A man? Huh!

PERISHAN (*kneeling down*): Ghoronti . . . The scent of a man is drawing near.

GHORONTI (*cockeyed, with blond hair, sticking his head out of the fortress*): The scent of a man. (*Sniffing the air, he goes out.*)

KHOZENI (*pointing to the left*): Brother Ghorobugha, Gharaghura.

PERISHAN: Our big brothers are here! (*She claps.*)

(GHOROBUGHA *and* GHARAGHURA *enter from left. The first is a colossal giant with thick eyebrows. The second is smaller. Both of their heads are shaven, but for strands bunched up on the crown. They are carrying a bear and other prey on their backs.*)

GHOROBUGHA (*Snorting, he puts his load down.*): Huhammm!

GHARAGHURA: Huham! (*Likewise he puts his load down.*)

PERISHAN: Big brother, we've something to tell you.

GHOROBUGHA: Huham! . . . What?

PERISHAN: A man's approaching. His scent's getting stronger.

GHARAGHURA (*pointing to the left*): Huhamm. Yeah, there's Ghuzghun bringing him. We bumped into them on the way home. Huham!

(GHUZGHUN *enters from the left, carrying the* PRIEST *on his back.*)

PERISHAN (*to* GHUZGHUN): Brother, what's that you've got?

GHARAGHURA (*to* GHUZGHUN): Who knows where this creature's been? He could bring sickness with him. Get rid of him!

PERISHAN: Brother, let me have him as a plaything.

(KHOZENI *approaches the* PRIEST, *smiles and looks at him with curiosity, then picks him up and deposits him in* GHORONTI's *lap.* GHORONTI *in turn sticks him in* GHUZGHUN's *lap,* GHUZGHUN *then sticks him in* GHARAGHURA's *lap, and finally* GHARAGHURA *sticks him in* DANGIZ's *lap.*)

PERISHAN (*crying*): Vay!

DANGIZ: Phew! He stinks like a corpse. Get rid of him.

GHARAGHURA: Dump him in the river. The current will carry him downstream.

GHOROBUGHA: No! . . . Wait, I've got a question.

PRIEST: Mercy, blessed ones. Let me go. My heart's going to burst!

GHOROBUGHA: Stop! Why are you acting like an enemy instead of a friendly neighbor? Why have you stopped the deliveries from your salt mines? Huhammm?

PRIEST (*jumping up*): We've used all the salt for traditional sacrifices. There's none left.

GHOROBUGHA: Sacrificial meals? What sacrificial meals? Huham!

PRIEST: A warrior has come to these parts so we've offered sacrifices to God to save us from his sword.

GHOROBUGHA: Who are you talking about? Huham!

PRIEST: Nazar the Brave.

GHOROBUGHA: Nazar the Brave? . . . Gharaghura. Nazar the Brave? . . . Ghoronti, Nazar the Brave? (*He laughs boisterously; the others laugh until they groan.*)

PRIEST: You're laughing, blessed ones, but Nazar the Brave has captured this territory. All he does is annihilate.

KHOZENI: Hah, hah, hah, ha!

GHOROBUGHA: Ho, ho, ho, ho!

GHARAGHURA: Hi, hi, hi, hi! How does he annihilate? Huham!

PRIEST: It's all right for you to laugh. But for us it's no laughing matter, blessed ones.

GHOROBUGHA: Warrior to warrior, we understand. Hahummm!

PRIEST: As a priest, it's even more difficult to understand, because we take on the sins of the world.

KHOZENI (*With a curious smile he approaches the* PRIEST, *grabs the end of his beard and feels it.*): What's this?

PRIEST: It's my beard, blessed one.

KHOZENI: Why is it so scrawny?

PRIEST: Because I fast so much.

KHOZENI (*elongating*): Really? You eat so little? Poor thing! (*Grabbing him by the beard, he drags the priest this way and that.*)

PRIEST (*in a meek and weepy voice*): Yes, blessed one, we are God's representatives. We eat little so we'll have no obstacle in ascending to our heavenly Lord. We are also the world's servants. When there's a disaster, we pray. In turn, we receive a little wheat and oil and live modestly. And, when there's massacre in the world, we lament like this. (*Wailing*) Meyaaa!

GHOROBUGHA: Are you good people?

PRIEST: Yes, blessed one, we are good people.

GHOROBUGHA: Then why would Nazar the Brave massacre you? Huham!

PRIEST: We're small fry for him. He's after bigger game.

GHOROBUGHA: You don't say.

PRIEST: With one blow he kills a thousand.

GHOROBUGHA: You've got to be kidding.

PRIEST: He holds a banner, written by the hand of saints, which reads "invincible

Nazar, Nazar the Brave, with one blow, he destroys a thousand." (*Weeping*) Oh, blessed ones, he sends them to the infernal fire.

GHORONTI: Are you trying to scare us?

GHARAGHURA: Pshaw! He couldn't scare a mouse.

PRIEST: No, blessed ones. No, it's true, as the living God's my witness. Nazar the Brave possesses greater strength than you.

GHOROBUGHA: A likely story!

PRIEST: Yes, blessed ones, flee before he arrives.

GHOROBUGHA: You're pulling my leg!

PRIEST: Mercy, blessed ones. I'm telling the truth. Flee, save yourselves. The only powerful creatures you know are giants like yourselves. You haven't seen the likes of Nazar the Brave. Nazar will wipe out your race of giants. (*In a mellow tone*) Listen, I'll tell you everything, which I have seen with my own eyes and heard with my own ears. Amazing scenes these were! Right before my eyes he destroyed five hundred giants, pulverized them and threw their dust to the winds. (*He removes a pyx from his pocket and takes out a pinch of dust.*) See, there's just this speck of dust left, which I took as a souvenir. (*He wails.*)

GHOROBUGHA (*alarmed*): Ghoronti, just a speck of dust is left! . . . Gharaghura . . . Ghuzghun?

GHARAGHURA (*holding his head*): Did he steal it? Huhamm! . . . (*To the* PRIEST) Did you steal it? . . . Huham?

PRIEST: No, God forbid.

GHARAGHURA (*approaching the* PRIEST): Didn't I tell you not to scare us? I'm going to mash you to pulp.

PRIEST (*running behind* GHOROBUGHA): I'll put a curse on you.

GHOROBUGHA: Are you joking or something?

PRIEST: I'll put a curse on you, too, so Nazar will destroy you and put you in the pyx. (*He tries to escape the ring of giants.*) Please be good enough to let me pass. This is all too hot for me to handle. (*He pants from fear.*)

GHOROBUGHA: No, we won't let you through. You put a curse on us. (*To* GHARAGHURA) He put a curse on you. Grab him and don't let him go until the curse wears off.

GHARAGHURA: Huhaam! (*About to carry off the* PRIEST)

KHOZENI (*looking to the left*): Big brother, big brother, who are they? (*Pointing to the left side*)

GHOROBUGHA: Huhaam!

PRIEST: Mercy, it's Nazar the Brave!

GIANTS (*terrified*): Huhammm!

(*Clutching the* PRIEST, GHARAGHURA *now takes him away. All the giants hide in the fortress. Thereafter* NAZAR, *the* MASTER OF CEREMONIES, *the* SPRY OLD MAN, SAKO, *the* TEACHER, *and the other villagers enter from left.*)

A VILLAGER: Brother, this priest of ours went to find the giants. He must have gotten lost.

TEACHER: He went as a scout and fell as a martyr. For the fatherland! Let's move out.

MASTER OF CEREMONIES: So the priest got lost. But what happened to the giants?

NAZAR: The giants? If they're not around, I'll smash in your heads. You bring Nazar the Brave here and lose track of the giants? (*To* SAKO) Friend, go find those giants. (*To the others*) Go get them. When you see them, attack. Don't wait for me. I know what I've got to do. Get it? Then, go!

TEACHER: Sako, go!

SAKO: Right away. (*He turns on his heels and stands where he is. To the others*) Get going, men!

THE OTHERS (*offstage, sounding the cry*): Get going, men!

(*All stand where they are and no one budges.*)

MASTER OF CEREMONIES: Well, why not sit down, Nazar, my son. Let's enjoy a meal.

TEACHER: Sit down, Hero, sit down. Let the fury of your ardor abate a while.

MASTER OF CEREMONIES: Bring the goatskin of wine.

(*They bring it and place it in front of* NAZAR, *the* MASTER OF CEREMONIES, *the* TEACHER, *and two others. Everyone sits and begins to eat and drink.*)

MASTER OF CEREMONIES (*carousing*): Hey, giants, which hole have you crept into? Come out now!

NAZAR: Not so loud! Don't shout, we don't want them to run off!

ONE OF THEM: Brother Nazar, why not forgive those giants just this once. Have pity on them.

NAZAR: No, don't ask that, I can't agree. It's God and me in this one fight. I shall annihilate these giants.

ONE OF THEM: Nazar the Brave, how come you're not afraid?

NAZAR: Afraid? Me afraid? (*He drinks.*)

ONE OF THEM: What a noble thing is courage that inspires the heart to talk so bravely?

NAZAR: Courage? . . . Courage is nonsense. This is how I'll grab hold of the giants. (*Demonstrating*) I'll strike them like this and make their heads fly. Now, is that courage? Courage is knowing what fear is. (*He drinks.*)

ONE OF THEM: There's a brave soul! Of course, that's the reason he fights fearlessly!

NAZAR: Fight? Who's fighting? You think it's me? The fight goes on of its own accord. In the middle of a fight, it doesn't even cross my mind that I'm fighting.

ONE OF THEM: Excuse me for interrupting, Nazar, have you destroyed many giants?

NAZAR: What giants? (*He fills up his wine goblet and drinks.*) As many as there are flies!

(GHARAGHURA *looks out through the crenelations;* GHOROBUGHA *and the others follow his lead. The* MASTER OF CEREMONIES *and* TEACHER *shift about apprehensively.*)

NAZAR (*jumping up*): What's wrong? Are you afraid of the giants?
MASTER OF CEREMONIES: Just go on with your story.
NAZAR: Give me wine. My heart is very sad in the absence of those giants. But just once—
TEACHER: Listen, people, listen!
NAZAR: Once there was a fight in the land of Gog-Magog. Giants attacked me. A hundred came and I massacred them. A thousand came and I massacred them. Then, more of them kept coming . . . They came, I massacred; they came, I massacred. Finally, I left it up to my hand to carry on, if it wished. Massacring left and right, I reached Abyssinia. When I woke up, I saw that I had pulverized them all and thrown them to the winds. (*He pulls out a speck of dust wrapped in a piece of cloth.*) Just this speck of dust is left as a memento of those giants. The priest has got the other speck.

(*The giants stick their heads out gawking at the speck of dust.*)

NAZAR: Now, all I've got to do is smash the heads of these giants and be done with them.

(*The giants hide their heads.*)

MASTER OF CEREMONIES (*shouting*): Hey, giants, no matter whatever hole you've crept into, come out, now!
NAZAR: Speak softer, they'll bolt.
MASTER OF CEREMONIES: I'm afraid they've hightailed it.
TEACHER: Victory! The enemy's fled! Heroic victory!
MASTER OF CEREMONIES (*to the* zurna *players*)[6]: Strike up a tune!

(*The* zurna *players play a merry tune.*)

NAZAR (*He jumps up and begins to intone.*):

---

6. The *zurna* is a high-pitched, double-reed instrument with a shrill sound, often used with the *dhol* drum to accompany dancing.

Let me get my hands on them,
I'll eat them alive;
Let me get my hands on them,
I'll turn them into dust, like the wind;
Send them up in the sky, leaving no trace.
Hey, where are you, come out into the open, giants,
I'll twist your heads off and throw them down.

ALL: Hey jan, hey jan, hey jan!

NAZAR: I'm Nazar the Brave, from the town of Nazarashen,
My lineage is noble, my forebears kings.
I pounced and struck, like lightning from the sky,
Causing fire the world over, mountain and valley.
Hey, where are you giants, come forth,
I'll twist your heads off and throw them down.

ALL: Hey jan, hey jan, hey jan!

NAZAR: Hey, Friend, bring on those giants, I'll make salad out of them, let me just get my hands on their bones, I'll crack them like this, smash and pulverize them, and then toss them to the winds.

MASTER OF CEREMONIES: Just when we want them to appear, they're nowhere to be found.

NAZAR: You shouted so much, you frightened them off. (*To* SAKO) What news?

SAKO (*entering*): We looked all over and couldn't find them.

THE OTHERS (*entering*): Nazar the Brave, the giants aren't around.

NAZAR: They're not around? You mean to tell me you couldn't find them? What kind of talk is that? You bring Nazar the Brave all this way, make him cool his heels, and then tell him that they're not around? Better say your prayers. (*He lifts the whip and attacks* SAKO *and the rest with it.*)

SAKO: Nazar the Brave, forgive me!

MASTER OF CEREMONIES: Forgive us this one mistake.

NAZAR: Keep out of this. I'll deal with them myself. (*He strikes* SAKO *and* THE OTHERS.)

ALL: Nazar the Brave, forgive us!

(GHOROBUGHA *sticks his head out of the fortress.*)

SAKO (*seeing him*): Let's get out of here! (*He runs off.*)

MASTER OF CEREMONIES: Oh, oh. (*He runs.*)

THE OTHERS: Have mercy! (*They run too.*)

NAZAR (*whipping the trees*): You can't count on anyone to find you a giant.

GHOROBUGHA (*jumping up*): Bo, bo! . . . (*Frightened, he runs out supplicating* NAZAR) Mercy.

(The other GIANTS *follow him and fall to their knees in a circle around* NAZAR. NAZAR *tries to get past* GHOROBUGHA *to escape from the circle.)*

Ha-m-m-m! . . . *(He crawls toward him, beseeching, with arms extended.)* Forgive me!

NAZAR: M-a-a! *(He runs toward* GHORONTI.*)*

GHORONTI: Ha-m-m-m! *(He crawls toward him, with arms extended.)* Forgive me!

NAZAR: M-a-a! *(He flees toward* GHUZGHUN.*)*

GHUZGHUN: Ha-m-m-m! *(He crawls toward him, with arms extended.)* Forgive me!

NAZAR: M-a-a! *(He runs this way and that and suddenly, in an intense moment of fear, shouts.)* E-hey! *(He grabs a tree by the trunk.)*

GHOROBUGHA *(Letting go of the* PRIEST, *he crawls on his knees toward him.)*: We're at your mercy, Nazar the Brave!

NAZAR: Buh, buh, buh! . . .

THE OTHER GIANTS: We're at your mercy, Nazar the Brave. Forgive us!

PRIEST: Forgive them, Nazar the Brave.

NAZAR *(seeing the* PRIEST*)*: What?

PRIEST: They're defeated. Spare them. Show them mercy . . .

GIANTS: Forgive us, Nazar the Brave!

NAZAR *(Looking suspiciously at the* PRIEST *and the* GIANTS, *he grasps the situation and comes to his senses.)*: So these guys were nothing but a bunch of phonies all along. Good for you, Nazar the Brave. *(He looks at* GHOROBUGHA *cannily.)*

GHOROBUGHA *(striking his forehead on the ground)*: Nazar the Brave, we had heard your name but never thought you'd be so tough an adversary. We beg you, come and be our leader and we'll become your vassals. Just give the command and we'll conquer the world and bring it to your feet. Only forgive us.

GIANTS: Forgive us!

NAZAR: Friend, what's this land called?

PRIEST: Giantland.

NAZAR: Giantland. Fine. *(To the* GIANTS*)* I forgive you.

PRIEST *(making the sign of the cross)*: Peace be with you. *(To himself)* We escaped by the skin of our teeth. Blessed are you, oh brave warrior.

(Pause)

GHOROBUGHA: Ha-a-m! Is it your wish that we rise, master?

NAZAR: Rise? *(He thinks.)* Rise and . . . stand a bit farther away.

GHOROBUGHA: Unsheath your sword, we implore you, and let us pass under it.

*(*NAZAR *takes out his sword and the* GIANTS *pass under it. Pause.)*

What is your next command, Master?

NAZAR: Stand at ease. (*He looks this way and that for a way out. He paces around.*)

GHOROBUGHA (*following him*): What does your heart desire now? Shall we lay out a spread here, or inside? Ha-a-m!

NAZAR (*uncertain*): A spread? Lay it out here. It'll be dark inside.

GHOROBUGHA: Whatever pleases you. (*Walking behind NAZAR*) Nazar the Brave? Would you care to sit?

NAZAR: Huh? (*He sits down and looks warily at the GIANTS.*)

GHOROBUGHA (*sitting next to him and turning toward the other GIANTS*): See to the feast. Ham-m-m!

GIANTS: Right away! (*They depart.*)

GHOROBUGHA (*calling after them*): Barbecue some bear meat. (*Louder*) Ha-mmm! Boil some buffalo. (*Louder*) Ha-mmm! Fry some camel. Ha-mmm!

(NAZAR *jumps up from his seat, increasingly unnerved with each new exclamation.*)

GIANTS: We're barbecuing, brother, we're frying! (*They go into the forest and, with ungainly movements and wide steps, quickly begin to pull up trees by their roots. They enter the fortress and bring out huge plates and knives. They pick up huge stones and place them next to each other, creating a hearth for the fire.*)

NAZAR (*with trepidation*): Giant brother?

GHOROBUGHA (*fearful himself*): Ha-a-m!

(NAZAR, *equally fearful, sits quietly.* PERISHAN *suddenly stumbles and falls on a tree, smashing it and causing branches to drop in front of* NAZAR. NAZAR *jumps up, while* KHOZENI *laughs, as do the others. Suddenly,* GHOROBUGHA *bursts with laughter, too. A storm of unrestrained laughter spreads.* NAZAR *rises and starts pacing restlessly to and fro again.*)

GHOROBUGHA (*again venturing to converse*): They're brave fellows, Master. They know how to fight.

NAZAR: Let them be quiet.

GHOROBUGHA: Be quiet!

GIANTS (*They fall silent. Only* KHOZENI *is unable to restrain his laughter. The other giants fall upon him and beat him.*): Are you quite finished? (*They get back to their work.*)

(KHOZENI *tries to snap off the large tree branch hanging above* NAZAR's *head.*)

PERISHAN (*preventing him*): Don't break it off. Don't break it off. It's rotten.

(*The giants fling* KHOZENI *into the bushes. They then finish uprooting trees and start putting the pots on the fire.*)

GHOROBUGHA (*seeing the worried look on* NAZAR*'s face*): Something's bothering you. Ha-am! Shall I bring you a bear to tear apart?

NAZAR (*alarmed*): No, that's not necessary.

GHOROBUGHA: There are some nice big ones. (*To the other giants*) Ha-mmm! Bring on the meal!

GIANTS: We're bringing it! Ha-a-m!

(*They bring the pot and lay it in front of* NAZAR. *With her sleeves rolled up,* PERISHAN *sticks her hand in the pot and stirs the food with a ladle. The giants noisily seat themselves around* NAZAR.)

GHOROBUGHA (*To* NAZAR): Ha-mmm! . . . Enjoy it, what else does your heart desire? Ox? Hammm! . . . (*Louder*) Camel? Hamm! . . . Elephant? . . . Hamm! . . . (*With his sleeves rolled up, he takes out large pieces of meat and puts them in front of* NAZAR.) Enjoy. (*To the others*) Eat. (*He pulls out a large piece of meat from the pot. The others, their sleeves likewise rolled up, begin to devour its contents.*) Haam! Town crier, go inform the king. We're going to have to fight it out. Tell him we won't let Perishan marry him. Tell him he's no longer our king.

TOWN CRIER: Right away. (*He plays the bagpipe with the fingers of his left hand, while playing the* zurna *with his right.*) Hey, king, this is to inform you that we won't give Perishan over to you. You're no longer our king. Come on, let's fight.

GHOROBUGHA (*jumping up*): Hammm!

NAZAR (*trembling*): You should have fought him earlier.

GHOROBUGHA (*pacing to and fro, impatient, disposed toward fighting*): I know, I know. (*To the* GIANTS) Arm yourselves well, we're going to fight . . . Hammm! . . .

(*Making a twanging sound, he puts on his armor, as do the other* GIANTS. *Then he climbs to the top of the fortress, observes the surroundings, runs down, and again paces to and fro.*)

NAZAR (*walking behind him*): Uh, uh, my friend, what do you say? . . . Let's think this over. Isn't peace better, eh?

GHOROBUGHA: Huh? Hah! (*He repeats mechanically.*) Peace is better. (*He runs again to the top of the fortress and then down.*) Hammm! . . . Have they come yet?

TOWN CRIER: An envoy has come from the king.

NAZAR (*coughing*): Uhuh!

ENVOY (*entering from left*):

What's this about choosing a new master
And dishonoring your legitimate king?
Quickly, depose him,
Chain his hands and feet,
And have him grovel before the king.

NAZAR (*flittering about, his teeth chattering*): Buh, buh, buh, buh! . . . Now here's
a new fix for you . . . Let's see how you get out of this.

GHOROBUGHA:

Get lost, you fool.
You haven't seen Nazar the Brave.
You only know your king and
Mosquito-like troops.
Go, tell that has-been
We don't recognize him anymore;
We pay homage to Nazar the Brave.
God in heaven and him on earth.

ENVOY: I'll go and tell the king to come, and when he does you'll rue your day. (*He
goes.*)

NAZAR (*looking for a way to escape*): For crying out loud, where have they taken my
horse? (*He paces around restlessly.*)

GHOROBUGHA (*to the* GIANTS):

Hammm! Arm yourselves, get ready,
Follow Nazar the Brave.
Come together—line up one by one,
The fight is going to start now.(Horns sound.)

TOWN CRIER: Are the enemies in sight?

GHOROBUGHA: Ham! . . . Quickly bring Nazar's horse.

NAZAR: Friend, what's the rush? (*He coughs.*) I haven't finished my dinner yet.

GIANTS:

Bring out Nazar's horse,
The enemy's in sight.

VILLAGERS:

Long live our great Nazar the Brave,
See how he massacres a hundred thousand.

(Armed, all move right; the villagers stand at the ready, while the giants, except GHOROBUGHA, *go up to the top of the fortress. Horns sound from afar, followed gradually by the shouts of attacking troops.)*

TOWN CRIER: Troops are coming, bah, bah, bah, bah!

GIANTS: Troops are coming, vah, vah, vah, vah!

GHOROBUGHA: Nazar the Brave is here, hah!

GIANTS: Let's run for it, brother. There's too many of them. Vay, vay!

GHOROBUGHA: Where are you scurrying off to, you scoundrels? I'll flay you, hah! Nazar the Brave won't tolerate cowards? Hahmm! . . . Take hold of your maces.

GIANTS *(above)*: Big brother, come up and see how many they are.

GHOROBUGHA *(He climbs up to the top of the fortress)*: Bo-o-o-o! . . . what's this? *(He comes down and falls at* NAZAR's *feet.)* Hammm! . . . Help us, Nazar the Brave!

NAZAR: Help!

GIANTS *(likewise falling at* NAZAR's *feet)*: Help us, Nazar the Brave!

NAZAR: Help! *(He flees unarmed.)*

GHOROBUGHA: Where's he going unarmed? Grab him.

(The giants grab NAZAR, *bring him back, strap arms onto him, and sit him down.)*

GHOROBUGHA: Bring me a horse. *(They bring it.)* Sit him on it!

NAZAR *(Astride the horse, he is extremely restless. He looks all around for a way to escape. Fear robs him of his judgment and inhibitions, and he lunges into the melee with ardor.)*: Into the fray. Show me your mettle, hai-haaai!

GHOROBUGHA: Easy does it!

(Seeming to charge forward, NAZAR *is actually trying to find a way to escape. Suddenly he sees a rotten tree branch, which is hanging above his head. He moves his horse under the limb and tries to pull himself up onto it. From afar the commotion is heard which grows increasingly louder.)*

VOICE OF THE KING *(offstage right)*: Where is that foolish rebel? Bring him here.

GHOROBUGHA *(looking out, to the King)*: Hold your horses, he'll come out now! *(To* NAZAR*)* Now show us your mettle, Nazar the Brave.

GIANTS: Attack, Nazar the Brave!

NAZAR *(screaming from fright)*: Ehe-e-e-y! . . . *(He turns around, sits facing the horse's rump, and stretches his hands toward the tree branch. The giants are shouting. Suddenly the horse is startled and jumps forward. The branch breaks, remaining in* NAZAR's *hand. Astride the horse, he surges toward the enemy.* NAZAR *shouts.)* Mercy!

ENEMY TROOPS (*offstage*): He's uprooted the tree. Let's get out of here!
GHOROBUGHA: The enemy's retreating . . . Let's get them!

(*The giants attack the enemy troops.*)

TROOPS: Mercy. Nazar the Brave's upon us!
GHOROBUGHA: Annihilate them!

(*The fighting, shouting, and commotion gradually subsides.*)

VOICES OFFSTAGE: Good for you, Nazar. Look at him go. Did you see how he uprooted the tree? Just look at him slaughter! They've taken to their heels.
(*Pause*) They're leading Nazar back.

(*The voices of the victors swell and soon the giants and villagers enter, leading* NAZAR
in on his horse. He has fainted from fright.)

GHOROBUGHA: Take the tree from his hand. Lift him off the horse. Long live Nazar
the Brave!

(*They get* NAZAR *down from the horse and take the branch out of his hand.*)

GHOROBUGHA: Bring carpets, arrange pillows. Let Nazar the Prince relax. Go bring
the spoils of war from the field.
PRIEST (*coming out of hiding*): Set up the pots to cook the sacrificial animals.
TEACHER: Set the table for everybody.
TOWN CRIER (*from the tower*): An envoy has come from the enemy in flight.
GHOROBUGHA:

> Ha-a-mm!
> He's in a tight spot.
> Let's see him squirm.
> We'll rip his head off.

(*They bring the envoy in.*)

ENVOY:

> I've come on behalf of
> Our defeated, yet valiant troops,
> People and country,
> To make a request of Nazar the Brave.

GHOROBUGHA: Hammm! . . . Speak up!

ENVOY: Our king was killed in the fight. Our people and country are left kingless. Now our decimated troops and our entire kingdom requests that Nazar the Brave unite our country with yours and become our joint monarch.

GHOROBUGHA (*to* NAZAR): Nazar the Brave, do you wish to become joint king?

NAZAR (*regaining consciousness, his voice muffled*): I do.

GHOROBUGHA (*to the envoy*):

> Go, tell your brave troops,
> People and kingdom,
> That our leader Nazar
> Has become our mutual king.

ENVOY: Now I'll report this to our brave troops, people, and country. (*He departs.*)

TEACHER: Long live the king, our savior Nazar. He slew a thousand, he massacred ten thousand!

PEOPLE: Long live King Nazar!

(*The* zurna *players play.*)

Curtain

ACT 4

King NAZAR THE BRAVE.

The setting is a palace hall in oriental decor; on the right is the royal divan, with a tiger skin hanging on the wall behind it; the entrance, upstage center, is covered by a curtain. At left is a balcony that opens onto a square. The CHAMBERLAIN *enters and stands to the right of the curtain. He is an unemotional, quick-footed, short-paced individual with mousey eyes, and mechanical, ceremonial movements.*

MINISTER (*humbly greeting the* CHAMBERLAIN *as he enters*): My lord.

CHAMBERLAIN (*greeting him with a Persian gesture*): My lord.

VIZIER (*greeting the* CHAMBERLAIN *and* MINISTER *separately upon entering*): My lord.

MINISTER *and* CHAMBERLAIN: My lord.

(*The other officials now enter:* GENERAL, CHANCELLOR OF THE EXCHEQUER, COURTIERS, *and various members of the court. After greeting one another, they stand in two rows at attention and wait respectfully.*)

MINISTER (*to the* CHAMBERLAIN): Is the Supreme One awake?

CHAMBERLAIN: He slept soundly until dawn, rose with the sun, and will soon beam before us with brilliance.

MINISTER: These are unforgettable days! What was our ship of state during the reign of our former defeated king, if not a storm-tossed bark?

VIZIER: Yes, ever since the Supreme One defeated our former greedy, puny king, I've been so happy I haven't slept.

MINISTER: I, too, have lost sleep. Indeed, lucky for us King Nazar brought our state contentment, so now it is fitting that he rest a while.

COURTIER: Happiness forced the sleep from my eyes, too. I'm enjoying a perpetual insomnia, which is like heavenly sleep.

MINISTER: Happiness! This king of ours was manna from heaven! And worthy of the throne! Since he became king, I annexed six provinces to the lands under my authority.

VIZIER: I, in turn, annexed four provinces.

GENERAL: I got my hands on some prime real estate owed me by the former king.

COURTIER: He enriched the clergy, too.

MINISTER: We have all flourished.

VIZIER: And there's more to come, my lord.

COURTIER: God is great. May He grant us a nice profitable war.

MINISTER: The God that gave us a new king won't deprive us of a war.

GENERAL: Our valorous king will lead us to new victories.

MINISTER: Well, gentlemen, let's stand by the king in all he does.

(*All present accede with shouts of approval.*)

MINISTER: May God protect the king.

CHAMBERLAIN (*He runs out and then pokes his head back in through the curtain.*): The Supreme One!

(*All bow and remain with their faces turned to the floor.*)

CHAMBERLAIN (*He darts in and, with trembling hands, draws the curtain aside.*): Stand in fear!

(*King* NAZAR *enters and, passing by the bowed heads, crosses to the divan where he stands facing the* COURTIERS. SAKO, *wearing new clothes and carrying the banner, follows in the same manner and stands behind* NAZAR.)

CHAMBERLAIN: Joyous greetings to King Nazar on the thirtieth day of his reign. Move forward in obeisance. May the Lord protect our king.

ALL (*They stand in a semicircle in front of* NAZAR *and then humbly prostrate themselves.*): Amen! (*They remain prostrate.*)

CHAMBERLAIN (*Coming forward and, taking out a parchment scroll, he bows to* NAZAR *and begins to read.*): Brave King, Sun of Justice, Sea of Intelligence, Arm of Ability, Mouth of Truth, I take the liberty of reading to all the order you gave last night, as follows: "I, Nazar the Thousandth, by the incomprehensible will of God, king, and chief priest of Nazarstan, Titanstan, Gog and Magog, Achuch and Pachuch, etc. Ruler of the world, victor over everybody and everything, I hereby command, dispose, proclaim, and order that today the sun rise from the east and set in the west, that people be born and die, that all human endeavors which are pursued continue to be pursued. May the word of God and the law of man be carried out. For it is true that as 'kings command, so the world turns.' Signed: 'Nazar the Thousandth.' I, secretary of secretaries, Baghakhorik am witness to the document."

(NAZAR *motions approval with his hand.*)

I dare to raise my eyes skyward, to your face, Oh Center of the Universe, to await your further bidding.

NAZAR (*taking a key out of his pocket and extending it to the* CHAMBERLAIN): Go get some raisins from the royal cupboard.

CHAMBERLAIN: Palate of Fine Taste, would you perhaps like grape preserves from India or from Abyssinia?

NAZAR: What's he spouting off about? Bring whatever kind of raisins you have.

CHAMBERLAIN: Your sure command is a mouthful of truth. So let me go and bring whatever raisins there are.

NAZAR: Yeah, yeah, any raisins, you jackass, just hurry up.

(*The* CHAMBERLAIN *exits.*)

NAZAR (*Settling on the divan, he puts his right foot up on it and lets his left foot dangle.*): Now, look here. Are the affairs of state in order? Is everyone pulling his weight? What say you, Minister . . . Vizier?

MINISTER and VIZIER: Everything is in order, Oh Righteous King.

NAZAR: General, are the troops ready?

GENERAL: Ready for battle, Oh Brave King!

NAZAR: Chancellor, how's the exchequer?

CHANCELLOR: There's money to burn, Your Eminence.

NAZAR: Now, my ministers, go and inspect every corner of the kingdom down to a T—troops, trade, treaties, tribunals. I'll smash your heads to pieces, if you scoundrels disobey my command. There shall be no stealing in the kingdom, especially the spoils of war. So guard them well. Do you understand?

ALL: We understand, Lord King.

CHAMBERLAIN (*entering*): Oh, Storm of Anger. The new princes are awaiting an audience with you.

NAZAR: Huh?

MINISTER: The master of ceremonies from Zorbashen and Consul Ghorobugha with his contingent.

NAZAR: His what?

CHAMBERLAIN: He means the chamberlain from Brnashen, along with Varazeni and his adjutant.

NAZAR (*impatiently*): Whoever they are, tell them to enter.

(*The* CHAMBERLAIN *invites the* MASTER OF CEREMONIES, GHOROBUGHA, *and the other giants, all wearing new princely garments, to enter.*)

NAZAR (*Seeing them, he addresses the* CHAMBERLAIN.): Oh, it's the master of ceremonies from Zorbashen, Ghorobugha, and the other Giants. Well, why didn't you say so? (*To them*) So, you've come?

MASTER OF CEREMONIES: We've come. Long live the king.

NAZAR: How do you fare?

MASTER OF CEREMONIES: Thank God, we're fine. Long live the king.

NAZAR: I appointed each of you as ruler of a separate territory. Did you receive land and people?

ALL: Yes, we have. Long live the king. Thanks for your beneficence! Long live the king.

NAZAR: Now, hear my command. All you lords of Zorbashen and you giants shall live in my palace. You shall become masters and put your lands in the hands of managers. The common folk will toil, and you'll eat off their work. It's my command that you not work. Now you're all nobles. Do you understand?

MASTER OF CEREMONIES: We understand. Long live the king.

NAZAR: Ghorobugha, do you understand?

GHOROBUGHA: I understand. Harumph! Oh, King!

NAZAR: Speak softly! Intone politely. This is a palace, not a stable, you beast! (*To all*) Well, I wish you well. (*To* SAKO) Prince Sako, plant the banner.

(SAKO *plants the banner at the edge of the divan. The* COURTIERS *bow and depart.* SAKO *follows them; the* CHAMBERLAIN *follows him.* NAZAR *settles comfortably on the divan.*)

This is the life!

(*The* CHAMBERLAIN *enters with a* COURTIER *who is holding a tray of raisins. The* CHAMBERLAIN *signals to the* COURTIER *to offer them to the king. The* COURTIER *momentarily genuflects, approaches* NAZAR, *and serves him the raisins.*)

NAZAR (*slapping the* COURTIER): Why are you twisting and turning like a monkey? Just serve the raisins.

(*The* COURTIER *puts the raisins on* NAZAR's *divan.*)

Now, get out of my sight!

(*The* COURTIER *departs, making effusive gestures of respect.*)

(*To the* CHAMBERLAIN) Why are you standing around like a horse's ass?
CHAMBERLAIN: For you, Picture of Beauty. Today your face has yet to be royally washed and anointed.
NAZAR: What?
CHAMBERLAIN: Oh, Reflection of the Sun, wouldn't you perhaps like to freshen up with rose water or some other fragrant lotions applied to your face?
NAZAR: I don't understand.
CHAMBERLAIN: Oh, Pureness of Driven Snow, you have not yet performed your matinual ablutions.
NAZAR: What's the big deal about washing every day?
CHAMBERLAIN: It's the rule for kings, oh Keeper of the Law.
NAZAR: What an asinine rule. Wash every day!
CHAMBERLAIN: Won't you please go to the bath, oh Voice of Good News?
NAZAR: The bath?
CHAMBERLAIN: Yes, my lord, the bath.
NAZAR: Wet the face cloth and bring it here. Let's get it over and done with. I don't feel like getting up.
CHAMBERLAIN (*bowing deeply*): I'm the executor of all your wishes. Is there anything else you ordain, Oh Divine Inspiration?
NAZAR: No, that's enough, get a move on it. (*He gives him a kick, and the* CHAMBERLAIN *bows humbly and departs.*) Bath? My grandfather died in the bath, you horse's ass.

(*The* CHAMBERLAIN *enters with two servants, one carrying aromatic lotions, the other with wash cloths and towels draped on his arm. Following the* CHAMBERLAIN's *instructions, they first wash* NAZAR's *face and then anoint him, as dictated by the* CHAMBERLAIN.)

CHAMBERLAIN (*instructing*): First anoint the nose of the Solar Beauty. (*Motioning*) Like that. Now apply the towel. (*The servants wipe* NAZAR's *nose. The* CHAMBERLAIN, *again motioning*) Right. Now drip seven drops of Indian rose water on the chin of His Majesty, the Fountain of Blessings. (*Motioning*) Exactly. Towel. (*They wipe the chin.*) Three drops of Arabic incense on the nape of the

Marvelous One's neck. (*Motioning*) Good. Apply drops of Shiraz rose water on the eyebrows and the edges of the nostrils three times. (*Motioning*) Just so. Towel.

NAZAR (*twisting his face and blinking his eyes*): Stop, stop, you idiots, my eyes are burning.

CHAMBERLAIN: Hold it a moment.

NAZAR (*sniffing the air*): Hum! . . . The accursed thing's got a nice smell. Pour a little of that rose water into that cup and bring it here. (*A courtier hands* NAZAR *the cup and he drinks from it.*) It's good. Hey . . . why are you wasting it on my face? Don't lose another drop of it on unnecessary bathing. I'll have a glass or two of it every day. Now move it!

(*The courtiers gather up the bottles and towels and depart. The* CHAMBERLAIN *follows them.*)

NAZAR (*He leans back, eating raisins, and begins to sing, with* SAKO *joining in.*): Aman hey, ay jan, jan, jan, eh aman, aman!

CHAMBERLAIN (*entering*): Ear of Mercy, a peasant woman is here and requests an audience with Your Excellency.

NAZAR: So what? You horse's ass!

CHAMBERLAIN: A peasant woman is here. Do you deign to consider her worthy of your sunlike countenance?

NAZAR: I don't understand what you're saying. Go say (*intoning*) "Yes!"

SAKO (*imitating* NAZAR): "Go say yes!"

(*The* CHAMBERLAIN *goes.* USTIAN *enters and stands at the threshold.* NAZAR *doesn't notice her and continues to sing.* USTIAN *moves a step forward.*)

NAZAR (*looking toward her*): Huh, who's there?

USTIAN (*coming forward*): So, you don't recognize me. It's me, Ustian!

NAZAR: Hey . . . Ustian, Old Girl, is that you? Come here, come here!

USTIAN: For goodness sake! Is this for real? What's going on here? Is this a dream or what? (*Coming forward and looking at* NAZAR *with surprise*) What's become of you, Nazar?

NAZAR: Well, you can see for yourself. I've got the world by the tail.

USTIAN (*doubtfully*): That's what I heard, but I didn't believe it. Now, tell me, is this for real?

NAZAR: It's for real, Ustian *hanum*, it's for real.[7] (*He goes right up to* USTIAN's *face.*) Remember how you used to say I wouldn't amount to anything? Well, now

---

7. *Hanum* is a Turkish term of respect for a married woman.

you see what I've become? You used to say I was cowardly. You see me now, right? Now, who is braver than me, wiser than me, richer than me? Well, tell me. Do you know that whole kingdoms quake at the mention of my name? Do you know to what distant borders my realm extends? I dare you to lock the door on me again! Well, there you go, now I'm king. How do you like that? (*He goes to his divan.*)

USTIAN (*looking at him out of the corner of her eye*): I just don't understand how this happened . . .

NAZAR: What's there not to understand? Take a real good look around. Do you believe what you see? I'm a king!

USTIAN: What can I say? It's true, you're a king.

NAZAR: Why, of course I'm a king and the world trembles before me. Now, do you still think you're so smart?

USTIAN: What can I say?

NAZAR: No, tell me, did you make any sense back then?

USTIAN: What can I say? The way I thought before, this wasn't how it was supposed to be. Now it appears that my reckoning was wrong.

NAZAR: Oh yeah? That's for sure. Well, now, come over and kiss my hand and become my queen.

USTIAN: Yum, yum! . . . I'll die for you, if all this is for real! (*She kisses* NAZAR's *hand.*) I can't believe it! Me a queen?

NAZAR: Well, you came in with your old clothes and your old way of thinking. Now go change your clothes and your thinking, too. (*Calling offstage*) Hey, you, Chamberlain!

SAKO: Hey, Chamberlain.

(*The* CHAMBERLAIN *enters.*)

NAZAR: Have a nice set of clothes from the last queen's wardrobe brought down for Ustian *hanum.* Do you understand?

CHAMBERLAIN: I humbly understand, Oh Herald of Orders. The only thing, Pinnacle of Thought, shall the garment be for the queen's coronation or . . . for a mistress?

NAZAR (*testily*): Come close.

(*The* CHAMBERLAIN *approaches, scratching the back of his neck.*)

There you go running at the mouth, that tongue of yours is still wagging, huh? (*Giving him a kick*) Get going now!

CHAMBERLAIN (*He goes and comes back.*): I relayed your order to the party concerned. Oh Source of Life, the garment shall be expedited with the greatest of speed.

NAZAR: Good. Bring my sable coat, put it on me and go. Bring some snacks for Ustian *hanum* while her garments are being prepared. Bring them on that gold tray so she can admire it.

(*The* CHAMBERLAIN *goes out and then comes back with waiters who bring* NAZAR'*s mantle, along with the gold tray bearing various sweets and dried fruits. Following the* CHAMBERLAIN'*s bidding, the waiters put the mantle on* NAZAR *and then place the tray before* USTIAN *who, overcoming her peasantlike shyness, partakes of the sweets.*)

Now go and bring my gold crown.

(*The* CHAMBERLAIN *goes.*)

(NAZAR, *stretching out on the divan, lets out a deep sigh of joy and speaks to himself.*) Hey, being a king is a good thing. Too bad I was such a fool and hung around in the village so long. I didn't do a thing to improve my situation. All I did was eat, drink, sleep, get up and wander around the garden, lean back on the pillow and smoke my water pipe. (*He sings.*) Aman, aman, hey, jan!
(SAKO *joins in. The* CHAMBERLAIN *brings the crown and, again with trepidation, puts it on the head of* NAZAR *who is still singing.*) Don't press so hard, you animal! (*To* USTIAN) From morning till noon I sit on the divan and give orders. Then they bring my lunch—more than I can eat—fine butter, honey, sweet rolls, and pilaf, with choice morsels of spring lamb.
USTIAN: You make it sound like I only served macaroni at home.
NAZAR: My palace is a sea of riches. Upstairs alone there are drapes with a hundred and five thousand folds, quilt-covered mattresses with fine bed frames. (*To the* CHAMBERLAIN) Bring the globe, let me gaze on it.

(*The* CHAMBERLAIN *goes.*)

USTIAN: Gosh, how nice it is! So now we'll finally get to enjoy life.
NAZAR: Yes we will . . . We'll live a comfortable and secure life. (*He sings briefly.*) Aman, aman, hey jan!
USTIAN: Not only will we live as such but we won't say insulting things to each other either. We're man and wife, so what is there to divide us? Today you're the king and I'm the queen. Now, as far as I can see, it doesn't become us to behave like commoners and fight.

(*The* CHAMBERLAIN *escorts a servant carrying a globe, which they present to* NAZAR *and then leave.*)

NAZAR: I fell into a good life. Ustian, it should have been like this before. You say it's a dream now. (*Calling offstage*) Hey, Chamberlain.

(*The* CHAMBERLAIN *comes in.*)

Come close! (*Giving him a light slap*) Huh!

CHAMBERLAIN: What is your command, my lord?

NAZAR (*grabbing him by the nose and shaking him*): Huh! (*He waits.*) Does it hurt?

CHAMBERLAIN: It hurts, my lord!

NAZAR (*grabbing the* CHAMBERLAIN *by the ear, to* USTIAN): Aha, now look. (*He exerts pressure. The* CHAMBERLAIN *endeavors to restrain his tense facial constrictions.*) Is this a dream? (*To the* CHAMBERLAIN) Get lost!

(*The* CHAMBERLAIN *leaves.*)

No, my dear, just enjoy yourself. This is not a dream, everything's real. (*He sings.*) Aman, aman, hey jaaan! (*Straightening up*) Phew! . . . (*Feeling bored*) Well, what shall we do now? (*Calling offstage*) Minister, Vizier.

(*The* MINISTER *bumps into the* VIZIER *and falls over him as they come through the doorway.*)

VIZIER: At your command. Long live the king!

NAZAR (*calling offstage*): General! Chancellor!

GENERAL AND CHANCELLOR (*stumbling in*): At your command. Long live the king! (*Silence*)

MINISTER: What is your command, Master?

NAZAR: What is my command? (*Enunciating clearly*) I command nothing. Go.

(*They all leave.*)

USTIAN: Why did you summon them?

NAZAR: No reason, just for the hell of it! (*Straightening his mantle and his body, too*) Phew! Do you see, Ustian, how they're like spinning tops all around me? (*Observing* USTIAN *eating*) Enjoy yourself, Ustian, there's plenty more where that came from. Put some in your pocket, too, so you can have a snack in the garden. Try the Baghdad dates. They're great.

USTIAN: So, it appears we're not going back . . . home.

NAZAR: Home? What the hell would we go back to? That home is history! You said this is a dream. No, no. That back there was the dream.

CHAMBERLAIN (*entering, along with maids bearing clothes for* USTIAN): If the queen would consent to be dressed, the maids are ready.

NAZAR (*watching him closely, impatience lining his face*): Bring, bring, bring, bring, bring!

CHAMBERLAIN: So what's your command regarding the arrangement, Oh Legislator of Blessings?

NAZAR (*sticking his tongue out, grimacing*): Bring, bring, bring, bring . . . speak . . . what do you want?

CHAMBERLAIN: The queen's dresses are ready, Master.

NAZAR: Well, say so, you horse's ass. (*To* USTIAN) You put on your dress while I go to the colonnade and survey my kingdom to see if everything is in order. When you're done, let me know, and we'll go out to the garden. Prince Sako! Take the banner.

(SAKO *holds the banner.*)

Consul! Chancellor!

CONSUL AND CHANCELLOR (*stumbling in*): At your command. Long live the king!

NAZAR: Come, let's go and see how the people are faring.

(*The* CONSUL *and the* CHANCELLOR, *bent over, lead the way.* NAZAR *follows them onto the balcony, which is visible from inside, and begins to survey the surrounding area.* SAKO *stands by* NAZAR *with the banner. The* CONSUL *and the* CHANCELLOR *are partly masked by* SAKO *and* NAZAR.)

USTIAN (*She gets up to go, but suddenly stops and turns to the* CHAMBERLAIN.): I've got something to say, you malingerer. Are you paying attention?

CHAMBERLAIN: Yes, Your Highness. I'm all ears.

USTIAN: Do you know how he became king? After all, my Nazar was somewhat timid back home.

CHAMBERLAIN (*attempting to be gracious, but terror-stricken*): I don't believe I hear you right, Oh Virtuous Queen.

USTIAN (*louder*): I was saying, this man was timid before, so how did he become king? Now do you hear me?

CHAMBERLAIN: I'm not hearing straight, Angelic One, spare me, I'm not here . . . I'm gone . . .

USTIAN (*moving toward the door*): I'll be damned if I understand anything. (*To the* CHAMBERLAIN) Are we going out by this door?

CHAMBERLAIN: Most Truthful One, yes, by that door, oh Beatitude of Universes.

USTIAN: I'm telling you, it's a dream. (*She exits up center, the* CHAMBERLAIN *following.*)

NAZAR (*calling out from the colonnade*): Hey, hey, hey, hey, hey, who's that scoundrel? Without paying the tax, he's taking a horseload home, huh? Give him a shot in the head. Give the scoundrel a whipping. Here I come now!

(The CHAMBERLAIN *returns, cowering like a bat by the curtain, and waits. The* MINISTER *and* VIZIER *enter, then the* GENERAL *and other* COURTIERS.)

MINISTER *(nodding to the* CHAMBERLAIN): My lord!
CHAMBERLAIN *(nodding)*: My lord!

(The VIZIER *and the others, nodding to the* CHAMBERLAIN, *exchange the same words.)*

MINISTER *(to the* CHAMBERLAIN): Where is His Excellency?
CHAMBERLAIN : He deigned to step out on the balcony to look over the kingdom personally.
MINISTER *(cautiously)*: Aren't there still rumors of war?
CHAMBERLAIN: Not anymore.
MINISTER: Has His Excellency said how he'll spend the day with our budding queen?
CHAMBERLAIN: Nothing in particular.
MINISTER: So, gentlemen, let's not stand idle. Let's go help our king in his just cause. Let's go up to the balcony and review the kingdom.
ALL: Let's go. *(They turn to the* CHAMBERLAIN *and bow.)* My lord!
CHAMBERLAIN *(nodding to them)*: My lords.

(They depart and disappear on the balcony. The CHAMBERLAIN *goes out and, returning right away, pulls back the curtain in the doorway.* USTIAN *enters dressed as a queen, comes forward solemnly, and sits on the divan. The* CHAMBERLAIN *cowers by the curtain. An indistinct noise comes from offstage. The* CHAMBERLAIN *rushes toward the balcony.)*

TOWN CRIER'S VOICE *(coming from offstage)*: Sound the trumpets! Up and at' em! Ring the bells!

(The sound of trumpets is heard.)

NAZAR *(He runs inside, with* SAKO *following, and addresses the* CHAMBERLAIN.): Hey, rascal, what's up? [*To* USTIAN] Ah, Woman, what's happening?
USTIAN: I don't know.
NAZAR *(to* SAKO): Go see what's happening.

*(*SAKO *fearfully approaches the curtained entrance and, going out partially, suddenly cowers.)*

SAKO *(running inside after him)*: It's a fierce storm.

NAZAR: What storm?

CHAMBERLAIN: He means confusion.

NAZAR: Go and find out exactly what's going on.

(SAKO *and the* CHAMBERLAIN *exit on the run; the* MINISTER *and* VIZIER, GENERAL, *and other* COURTIERS *enter running.*)

What's going on? What's all the commotion about?

MINISTER: Brave king, a messenger has come and said that enemy troops, led by ten kings, have violated our nonaggression pact. They're invading our territory from the north, south, east, and west.

NAZAR: What could they possibly want?

MINISTER: They want to seize our kingdom and your crown.

NAZAR: Seize my crown? How so? . . . (*Removing the crown and giving it to the* CHAMBERLAIN) Rascal, take it and put it away. I'd rather the dogs had it!

(*The* CHAMBERLAIN *takes the crown away.*)

GENERAL: Brave king, shall we assemble troops or will you again crush the impudent enemy with your bare hands? What is your command?

NAZAR: My command? Go and fight!

GENERAL: What? We're going to do the fighting, brave king?

NAZAR: Why, of course! Did you expect me to fight?

GENERAL: Brave king, lead and the troops will follow.

NAZAR (*whistling*): I'm done with it all! Nazar shall go into battle no more. You do as you please.

GENERAL: Bravely did you command, brave king. But if you don't come, the troops must stand alone against the enemy.

NAZAR: Let them stand alone. Do I have to lead every time?

MINISTER: Long live the king! The situation, however, is extremely grave.

NAZAR: Grave?

MINISTER: Our troops will be totally massacred.

NAZAR: If they're going to get massacred, so be it. That's not my concern.

MINISTER (*rejoicing*): Then we have your permission to get slaughtered!

ALL (*greatly rejoicing*): How fortunate for us!

MINISTER: So, at least forty thousand men will be killed.

NAZAR: Forty thousand? How does that compare with our total male population?

MINISTER (*opening the portfolio and consulting it*): Exactly one million, one thousand, nine hundred and five men.

NAZAR: Well, that's a mere nothing. Let them be massacred. Go and tell them to fight.

ALL (*extremely glad*): May God protect the king!

(*They bow and depart. Outside can be heard the sound of horns, martial clamor, commotion, hurrahs, the crier's voice calling "War," etc., all of which gradually recede.*)

NAZAR: Well, I've fulfilled my regal obligation. Now let them fight, and we'll go enjoy ourselves. (*Calling offstage*) Hey, you rascal!

(*The* CHAMBERLAIN *enters.*)

Go bring my crown. Bring some snacks, too.

(*The* CHAMBERLAIN *goes.*)

(NAZAR *leans back on the pillows.*) Phew! . . . (*He sings.*) Aman, aman! . . . hey, jan! . . . USTIAN, now that you've become queen, you're downright irresistible. (*Looking at her admiringly*) What do you think? Aren't you enjoying yourself? Look how far you've come!

USTIAN (*quite seriously*): I'm at peace with God. This happened according to the wishes of my father, the village elder. My family was of nobility, of course—

NAZAR: You're harping on your family's nobility again?

USTIAN: Listen, what's the secret? How did you become king?

NAZAR: By God's will. It's written that way in the royal manifesto: "By the incomprehensible will of God."

USTIAN (*making the sign of the cross over her face*): Of course . . . His power be praised.

(*The* CHAMBERLAIN *has the servants bring various fruits and offer them to* NAZAR *and* USTIAN, *then departs with the courtiers.*)

NAZAR (*a little annoyed*): Tell me, why do you insist on knowing how this all happened?

USTIAN: Because I'm dying to know.

NAZAR: I made it, that's all that counts.

USTIAN: Did you fight a battle?

NAZAR (*whistling*): Boy, did I ever!

USTIAN: Did you often find yourself in narrow straits?

NAZAR: Narrow straits? . . . We passed through the eye of needles and crossed bridges of hair . . . Are you kidding? There were fights when the earth quaked underfoot.

USTIAN: But it takes bravery, brains, and bravado to become a king.

NAZAR: Why, of course! Uncommon bravery, brains, and bravado. (*He thinks.*) Ee! ee! ee! Ayshi! What bravery? What brains? What bravado? It's a matter of luck, sheer luck! If you're lucky, the world is yours. Enjoy it. The wind swirls wealth and dumps it on your head. (*He sings.*) Look here, isn't what we have here a matter of luck? Now there's fighting. They're dropping like flies. Now I ask, for whom are they being massacred? For Nazar, of course. While they're being massacred, we're having a ball, eating and drinking. Soon the fighting will end. What's it to me if they are massacred? And if they don't get slaughtered, who gets the credit? Nazar, of course. What good is intelligence? Who needs bravery? It's all a matter of luck!

USTIAN: Luck. Is that it?

NAZAR: The truth is there was a time when I got scared in a jam. Then I saw things took care of themselves. Now, the way I see it, to hell with everything, just enjoy life. People are so idiotic, they hand you a victory without realizing it. The world is crazy, people are crazy. The world was crazy before, and it'll go on being crazy. (*He sings.*) Aman, aman, ay jaaan!

TOWN CRIER (*offstage*): Ring the bells!

(*The offstage commotion grows louder.*)

NAZAR (*jumping up*): Hey rascal? Chamberlain?

(*The CHAMBERLAIN runs in.*)

Rascal, what's going on?

CHAMBERLAIN: The situation is becoming most grave, my lord.

NAZAR: Stop babbling and call my top honchos.

(*The CHAMBERLAIN runs out and comes right back in with the MASTER OF CEREMONIES, SAKO, GHOROBUGHA, and the other giants.*)

NAZAR: Let's hear the latest military report.

MINISTER (*rushing in*): The fighting has spread, King of Kings. It's a crisis. (*He rushes out.*)

NAZAR (*to the others*): Take up your post outside the door.

(*The MASTER OF CEREMONIES, SAKO, and GHOROBUGHA go out.*)

USTIAN: What a misfortune! Why did those dogs have to wait for me to become queen before attacking?

NAZAR (*tense, calling the CHAMBERLAIN*): Rascal! What's going on? (*Alarmed at the increasing commotion, he runs on to the balcony, shouting.*): They've entered the city. (*Pacing back and forth, holding his stomach*) Vouy, vouy, vouy, vouy!

USTIAN: Hey, Nazar, what's happening?

NAZAR: A terrible tragedy—the kingdom has fallen, vouy, vouy, vouy, vouy!

USTIAN: What?. . . the kingdom?. . . Lord, preserve us! (*She darts about, sticking various precious items into her pockets. Suddenly she stops and cocks her ear.*) Huh? (*The commotion increases.*) Just listen to that crowd. (*She stuffs various objects into her breast pockets.*)

NAZAR: Vouy, vouy, vouy, vouy! (*He runs helter-skelter.*)

CHAMBERLAIN (*running inside*): Oh, oh, oh!. . . Sublime One, come to our aid! (*He runs outside.*)

SAKO (*running inside*): Buh, buh, buh, buh!

NAZAR (*Distracted, he sees* SAKO *without recognizing him.*): Who the hell are you? (*He darts back and forth.*)

SAKO (*He grabs the banner and runs after* NAZAR.): Buh, buh, buh, buh!

NAZAR (*running offstage*): Buh, buh, buh, buh!

(SAKO *follows him off.*)

NAZAR (*crying out fearfully*): Ooh ah! (*Shouting, he goes on to the colonnaded balcony.*)

VOICES (*from outside*): Nazar the Brave! Nazar the Brave!

GENERAL: Attack!

OTHER VOICES: Run for it!

STILL OTHER VOICES: Attack!

USTIAN: Holy Mary, Mother of God, I'd die for you. (*She makes the sign of the cross.*)

(*As the commotion intensifies,* NAZAR, *having just reached the colonnade, quickly runs back, then sneaks under the royal divan. Meanwhile,* SAKO *races mindlessly around the room.*)

(*General acclamations of victory offstage.*)

NAZAR (*poking his head out*): Huh? Who won? (*Calling offstage*) Rascal, who won? (*To* SAKO) Buh, buh, buh, buh. Bolt the door. (*He draws his head back under the divan.*)

(*Trembling,* SAKO *goes to bolt the door, with* USTIAN *looking on through the curtain curiously, but he is interrupted by a loud knocking at the door.*)

CHAMBERLAIN (*running in*): Victory, brave king!

USTIAN: Hey, we've won!

MINISTER AND THE OTHERS (*entering*): Brave king, victory!

NAZAR (*looking out from under the divan*): Who won? Our side? Really?

CHAMBERLAIN: My lord, victory is ours!

NAZAR (*He relaxes and, wiping his sweat, comes out from under the divan.*): Yes! Lucky our side won; otherwise I was about to destroy the world. (*He coughs.*)

PEOPLE (*offstage*): Victory! Long live the king!

NAZAR: Luck's smiled on you again, Nazar the Brave. You've pulled it off again. Ustian, wait till you see the kind of loot this brings in.

USTIAN (*jumping for joy*): Boy, nothing like these royal perks!

NAZAR: Now, this is what I call a good time. (*To* SAKO) Open the door, idiot!

(SAKO *opens the door, comes back in and, taking hold of the banner, positions himself next to* NAZAR.)

CHAMBERLAIN (*coming in with his hat of office, affectedly*): King of Kings, the Minister, Vizier, and Courtiers request an audience.

NAZAR: Bid them enter.

(*The* CHAMBERLAIN *goes out. The* MINISTER, VIZIER *and* COURTIERS *enter.*)

What's up? What are you so excited about?

MINISTER: Long live the king. We bring you tidings of great joy. The ignoble enemy is crushed.

NAZAR: So we've got it made?

MINISTER: When they saw your formidable and imposing figure, they disappeared. Furthermore, ten kings have been killed on the battlefield. Our gallant troops demolished the enemy with an unequaled assault, thanks to the wisdom and courage of your regal intelligence.

NAZAR: So we've got it made!

MINISTER: Long live our brave king!

ALL: Long live our brave king!

MINISTER: Brave king! The populace is impatiently waiting to see your heavenly countenance. They request that, on this great day of your victory, you requite them by coming out to receive their greeting.

NAZAR: Fine. (*He gets up and goes onto the balcony;* SAKO *follows him, carrying the banner.*)

SAKO (*to the people*): The king!

PEOPLE (*offstage*): Long live our brave king!

NAZAR (*gesturing that the people be silent*): My deep thanks to you, my people.

MINISTER AND THE OTHERS (*with tears in their eyes*): What bliss!

PEOPLE: Long live, long live, l-o-n-g l-i-v-e! Long live, long live, l-o-n-g l-i-v-e!

NAZAR: Feed the troops and the people.

MINISTER AND THE OTHERS: What generosity!

MINISTER (*going onto the balcony and proclaiming*): Oh, people! Our compassionate king not only defeated the enemy through his courage but also sparkles
with his generosity. Go, eat and bless the king. So, long live, long live our noble king.

PEOPLE: Long live, long live, l-o-n-g l-i-v-e! Long live, long live, l-o-n-g l-i-v-e!

(*The* MINISTER *comes inside.*)

VIZIER (*coming forward*): Long live the king! Now where shall we put the spoils?

NAZAR: In the granaries.

VIZIER: You command very wisely. (*Calling offstage*) The king commands that the
spoils be piled up in the granaries.

NAZAR (*to the* CHAMBERLAIN) Hold on, rascal! Bring some of those spoils and show
them to Ustian *hanum.*

(*The* CHAMBERLAIN *runs out and returns with servants who carry various brocades,
shawls, silks, dresses, plate of gold, etc.*)

Well, Ustian *hanum,* take whatever your heart desires. There's a lot more
where that came from.

USTIAN (*examining the spoils, awestruck*): I'm afraid it's a dream.

NAZAR: Bite your finger.

(USTIAN *bites her finger and ogles the spoils.*)

PEOPLE (*singing*): Invincible Nazar, brave Nazar, kills a thousand with one blow.

NAZAR (*to the* MINISTER): Rascal, tell them to get lost.

(*The* MINISTER *is about to go, when* SAKO *beats him to the balcony.*)

SAKO (*addressing the* PEOPLE): Gather round, Citizens.

(*The* PEOPLE *assemble in the square.*)

Listen to me, you rascals. When I tell you to get lost, you'll do as I say.

PEOPLE [*staggered*]: Okay.

SAKO: Now, get going, you knaves.

(*Sounds of the populace dispersing*)

NAZAR (*apprehensive*): Beh, beh! . . . is he angling for my job?
MINISTER: Prince Sako!

(SAKO *comes in from the balcony.*)

NAZAR AND SAKO (*looking at each other suspiciously*): Beh, beh, beh!
NAZAR: What's up?
SAKO: Bah! . . . bah . . . nothing . . .
NAZAR: Then get lost!

(SAKO *goes.*)

MINISTER: Do we dare depart, Oh Source of Life?
NAZAR: Not yet, you rascals. Come tomorrow morning. I shall make a royal speech
    to my entire kingdom. Now it's my pleasure that you get lost.
ALL: May God protect the king! (*They go.*)

(*As soon as they go,* USTIAN *stands up and begins to search for something in various
corners. Finding a wide piece of fine cloth, she brings it out into the open and wraps
it around herself like a sash.*)

NAZAR: Hey, Wife, what are you up to?
USTIAN: Let me hold on to this and keep it tucked away somewhere. You say it's not
    a dream. Who knows? The world turns, and suddenly we find that this is a
    dream. Then, at least we'll have this to show for it.
NAZAR: Enjoy yourself, my dear. Luck is with us. Aman, aman, hey jaaaan!
USTIAN (*pulling on the sash of the garment she's wearing*): Hey, my man, this is no
    time to play. (*Giving the end of the sash to him*) Pull on it, let's make it tighter.
    Pull on it!

(*The two of them tighten it.*)

Curtain

ACT 5

NAZAR THE BRAVE's *end.*

The same palatial hall as in the previous act. NAZAR *sits on the divan. Behind him,*
SAKO *holds the banner.* MINISTER, VIZIER, GENERAL, COURTIERS, PRIEST, MASTER

OF CEREMONIES, GHOROBUGHA, *and the other* GIANTS *stand opposite* NAZAR *and wait timidly for him to speak. Silence. Led by the* CHAMBERLAIN, *servants enter with censers in hand and proceed to diffuse incense all around* NAZAR. *Then, together with the* CHAMBERLAIN, *they discreetly and reverently depart.*

NAZAR (*Pensively fingering his worry beads and mulling things over, as though faced with very serious and important decisions, he coughs and begins speaking.*): Look at me, you rogues. I shall give you a command and speak my regal thoughts. I fought many a battle and was always the victor. You saw, thank God, that we emerged victorious again in this last major encounter. What do you call this? What is the meaning of this? What gift is this? This gift is such, this rule is such, that I see the finger of God in all this. And in His law it is especially written of me that I shall triumph every time.

PRIEST: God is our witness.

(*All bow down as a sign of profound piety.*)

NAZAR: And now, you rogues, I'm telling you that my clan is holy; know, too, that the populace is born, lives, and dies for me. The people shall work, and I shall eat. For that very reason I wish to be classified with the saints.

PRIEST: May it be so!

(*All piously bow down.*)

NAZAR: Now look at me, you rogues. Until now, God was helping me. Now I shall do my own work. Now I shall triumph over all. For that very reason, I now wish to conquer the whole world. What's the need for those many kingdoms and kings? I alone suffice.

PRIEST: So be it!

ALL: Amen!

MINISTER: Shadow of God, a felicitous thought seems to have risen in your regal head. Command, and we shall execute it.

NAZAR: Now I shall give a royal command. Go and assemble new battalions. Relay my command to our troops to go throughout the world, ravage and plunder, and bring back the spoils to me. Levy new and higher taxes on our countrymen. Understand?

ALL: We understand, Holy King!

NAZAR: Ghorobugha, do you understand?

GHOROBUGHA: Hammm, I understaaand, Your Majesty!

NAZAR: Hey, stop your nonsense! Speak in pleasant tones, for heaven's sake! Unfortunately, I didn't have the chance to teach you good manners. Beast! (*To the* PRIEST) Spiritual Father, you go, too. Assemble the clergy and lead me to church with cross and banner. I shall say a prayer for the salvation of the world. (*To all*) When that's done, I shall have a regal consultation with my wife.

ALL: May God protect the king! (*They leave, except the* MINISTER *and* VIZIER.)

CRIER (*offstage*): W-a-a-a-r!

(*A commotion is heard, followed by the sounds of drum and fife.*)

MINISTER (*going out to the balcony*): Listen, Soldiers and Countrymen. After liberating our country from numerous enemies, our savior and holy king is rising up, by the power of the divine Holy Spirit, to liberate the entire world from unworthy kings. It is his express command that the people pay taxes and that the soldiers go out and conquer the whole world. Success to our king and victory to us!

SOLDIERS AND PEOPLE (*offstage*): Long live our brave king!

(*The sounds of bugles,* zurnas, *gunshots, and song are heard, then gradually fade.*)

CHAMBERLAIN (*entering*): Smile of Hospitality, the queen desires to be received.

NAZAR: Huh?

CHAMBERLAIN: The queen approaches.

NAZAR: So let her come. Why are you running ahead, like an ass before a herd of cattle?

(*The* CHAMBERLAIN *goes.*)

(*To himself*) Behold the queen. She looks like a fragile egg that'll crack any minute now.

(USTIAN *enters in her royal robes.*)

USTIAN (*Advancing deliberately and daintily toward* NAZAR, *looking for a pillow by him and not finding it, she summons the* CHAMBERLAIN.): Chamberlain!

(*The* CHAMBERLAIN *enters.*)

You old goat, where's my pillow!

CHAMBERLAIN: Oh my, they haven't brought the pillow! (*He trembles.*)

NAZAR (*striking the* CHAMBERLAIN *with his staff*): You dog! You're all dogs! Queen Ustian comes to sit by me, and you don't bring her a pillow?

CHAMBERLAIN (*falling to his knees*): The keeper of the wardrobe is at fault, spare him, spare him, oh Hail of Anger!

NAZAR: Cut off his head!

(*The* CHAMBERLAIN *exits.*)

USTIAN: My goodness! The queen comes to sit, and they don't put a pillow under her. What am I supposed to sit on, the bare floor?

CHAMBERLAIN (*entering*): Long live the king! They cut off the wardrobe keeper's head.

USTIAN: It's a good thing they did so! I'll bury his head! Look at this terrible gown!

(*The* CHAMBERLAIN *goes out and has a pillow brought in by a court page and placed under* USTIAN.)

NAZAR: You oaf, you should have brought a softer pillow. Ustian *hanum*'s skin is delicate.

USTIAN: You've become so testy.

NAZAR (*assuming a more serious demeanor*): I have not.

USTIAN: I don't know, you've been out of sorts since yesterday.

NAZAR (*somewhat upset*): This is no time for quibbling and chitchat, Ustian. I've got a kingdom to run. That requires the utmost concentration. Today, the eyes of the world are focused on me. Now, my movements, my words, my mind, my honor are an example to all. From one day to the next, my mental capacity grows. Now, I'm a new man!

USTIAN: Anybody would give their right arm to be in your shoes.

NAZAR (*drowsily stretching*): Today, the affairs of state hung heavy on my shoulders! I'm pooped. Let's relax a bit! (*To the* CHAMBERLAIN) Hey, rascal!

(*The* CHAMBERLAIN *enters.*)

Bring food!

(*The* CHAMBERLAIN *goes.*)

Let's have a grand dinner. What do you say, Ustian *hanum*?

USTIAN (*very seriously*): Well, if that's your pleasure, we'll eat.

(*The* CHAMBERLAIN *enters, followed by servants with trays of delicacies, adorned with flowers. They lay the trays on a round wooden table in front of* NAZAR *and* USTIAN. *Two court pages go behind the couple. With various towels draped over their arms and shoulders, they wait on them during their meal. They unfold the towels and, when* NAZAR *and* USTIAN *wish to have their mouths and fingers wiped, they turn halfway around so the servants can do so.*)

Oh, what transport of delight!

(*Suddenly, as one of the pages wipes* NAZAR's *mouth, a grain of rice slips into* NAZAR's *nostril.*)

NAZAR (*sneezing and contorting his face*): Eh, eh, eh!
USTIAN: Mercy, what is it?
CHAMBERLAIN: Oh horrors! Alarm! Ring the bells! . . . A grain of rice has gone up His Excellency's nose!

(*All the* COURTIERS *rush in; the commotion can be heard from offstage.*)

Horrors!

(*They ring the bells.*)

ALL: Oh! Horror, horror! (*They bow low.*)
NAZAR (*He sneezes, whereby the grain of rice is discharged from his nose.*): Thank God, I'm finally rid of that annoying grain of rice!
MINISTER: The cook is at fault.
ALL: What a crime!
VIZIER (*calling offstage*): Cut off the cook's head!

(*The* COURTIERS *go to carry out the order.*)

NAZAR: Give me some rice pilaf!
PRIEST: Miraculous salvation for our king!
ALL: Praise the Lord! (*They weep.*)
CHAMBERLAIN (*calling to those offstage*): Rejoice, people! . . . (*sounds of joy, bells ringing, etc., outside*) The grain of rice has fallen from His Excellency's nostril.
COURTIER (*entering*): Great king, the cook's head's off.
USTIAN: He got his just desserts! And I'll sew his mouth shut, to boot! Is this any way to cook royal pilaf?
NAZAR: Okay, be off, and quick about it!

(*They all exit.*)

What was I saying? They're such asses. They won't let me concentrate on anything. Oh, I know! Bring over some of that pilaf.

(*They bring the dish to him, and he eats.*)

Phew! Pour some wine.

(*The* MINISTER, VIZIER, GENERAL, *and* COURTIERS *run in.*)

MINISTER: Brave king! A thousand seven hundred more men have been massacred.

NAZAR: How so? Were they going after pilaf? (*Pause*) Well, why were they slaughtered?

MINISTER: They can't fight, my lord.

NAZAR: Go and tell them they can. For heaven's sake, what's so difficult about fighting that they can't do it? [*To* SAKO] Prince Sako?

SAKO (*fearfully*): Long live the king! What is it?

NAZAR: Go and destroy the enemy . . .

SAKO: Buh, buh, buh, buh! . . . Me go?

NAZAR: Go! Smash them!

(SAKO *exits and hides behind the door.*)

MINISTER: What else do you command, my lord?

NAZAR: Here's my order. Put the civilian forces on the front line to fight the enemy, and then bring our malingering regular troops to me so I can ascertain the cause of their inaction.

MINISTER: I'll dispatch the civilian forces immediately. (*Going onto the balcony and calling down to the* CRIER) Crier, I have a new command. Muster the people.

CRIER: Assemble! . . . new orders!

(*There is a commotion and the people summon each other loudly.*)

MINISTER: Oh, people! New happiness. Our brave king rules the world in order to save you. I give you the strictest of commands, to go to the assistance of your gallant troops. So, onward, you who have always been ready to die for the king, now go and die.

NAZAR (*to the* COURTIERS *in attendance*): Get lost. My patience is wearing thin. The affairs of state await my attention. The food has gotten cold. I've got work to do. I'm ready to eat. Do you understand, you fools? From now on, keep fighting till the enemy surrenders. And if you come back and start blabbing about the battle, I'll split your heads in two. Do you hear?

ALL: We hear, Oh Shadow of God.

NAZAR: Buzz off!

(*They go.*)

And now to our personal affairs. (*To the* CHAMBERLAIN) Get over here and clear the table. [*To his wife*] Ustian, let's go and sit on the roof and have a smoke. (*To the* CHAMBERLAIN) Have them bring the water pipe to the roof. Prince Sako? Get the banner.

(SAKO *picks up the banner and follows* NAZAR *and* USTIAN. *After they leave, the* CHAMBERLAIN *calls the servants and motions for them to clear the table. They do so and leave. Then, going out for a moment, he suddenly rushes back and, cowering, clings to the curtain.*)

GENERAL (*running inside*): Where is our brave king? All the troops have fled the battlefield and are in retreat.

CHAMBERLAIN: His Excellency is puffing his water pipe for the good of the fatherland.

GENERAL: He must be told immediately. And since the brave king forbids us, under pain of death, to speak to him about the troops and war, I earnestly beseech that, for love of the fatherland, you yourself do so at the risk of death. Convey the news to the king.

CHAMBERLAIN: Absolutely. I have kept my person intact just to sacrifice it for the sake of the fatherland. It's just that I can't convey the news right away, since His Excellency has not yet finished his first smoke. Once he has had a couple more smokes, I'll inform him.

GENERAL: I'm counting on your self-sacrifice, my lord.

CHAMBERLAIN: You may do so completely, my lord.

(*The* GENERAL *exits. The* MINISTER *and* VIZIER *enter.*)

MINISTER AND VIZIER (*bowing to the* CHAMBERLAIN): My lord.

CHAMBERLAIN (*bowing*): My lords.

MINISTER: We hope you've relayed the latest news to the king.

CHAMBERLAIN: I'm not aware of anything new. Do you know anything, gentlemen?

MINISTER: Absolutely nothing.

CHAMBERLAIN: So, what is the latest news, gentlemen?

MINISTER: Forgive me, my lord. It seems you said "latest news."

CHAMBERLAIN: No, that was simply a slip of the tongue.

MINISTER: And what do you know, my lord?

CHAMBERLAIN: I'm hard of hearing and I'm so preoccupied . . . (*Pause*) As for—

MINISTER AND VIZIER: Yes!

CHAMBERLAIN: Did you say something, gentlemen?

MINISTER AND VIZIER: Nothing.

VIZIER: All is well with you?

CHAMBERLAIN: Utterly blissful. May God protect the king! (*Pause*) Is all well with yourselves, gentlemen?

MINISTER AND VIZIER: Completely, my lord.

CHAMBERLAIN: In that case, let me withdraw a moment and predispose the king that there's no news.

MINISTER: Quite right, my lord.

(*The* CHAMBERLAIN *seems to exit but stays behind the curtain to eavesdrop. His outline is visible from behind the curtain.*)

MINISTER (*to the* VIZIER, *in a low voice*): He hasn't gone, he's eavesdropping.

VIZIER (*softly*): All the better. And it appears that he's aware of the bad news.

(*The* CHAMBERLAIN *looks through the slit in the curtain.*)

VIZIER: Oh, how can we inform the king that we don't believe that there is no news?

MINISTER: Listen, my lord. I have an idea. I'll say that the people have revolted against the king.

VIZIER: Then I'll say that they're swarming around the palace.

(*The* CHAMBERLAIN *looks out through the slit in the curtain. The* MINISTER *and the* VIZIER *likewise look at the* CHAMBERLAIN. *The three of them, in turn, are caught motionless, staring one another in the face.*)

MINISTER: My eyes are so sore that I can't see clearly.

VIZIER: It's as if I've gone blind from misery.

MINISTER: How is the King of Kings?

CHAMBERLAIN: Calm as the bottom of the ocean.

VIZIER: Thank God!

MINISTER: After all, there are kingdoms, whose populations are in revolt against their kings.

CHAMBERLAIN: Yes, there's constant change and continual tribulation.

MINISTER: If the king's life is threatened, his merest thought would suffice for us to fly to his aid as swift as an arrow.

VIZIER: And we'll triumph over his foes.

CHAMBERLAIN: Gentlemen! My heart and spirit follow you like a shadow. In case of need, my faith is in you.

MINISTER and VIZIER: And ours in you. (*They bow.*) My lord!

CHAMBERLAIN: My lords!

(*The* MINISTER *and* VIZIER *bow and depart. Voices behind the curtain are chanting*

"The child was stewed, blessed be he. Bring another." The CHAMBERLAIN *hides in the folds of the curtain.)*

NAZAR (*singing*): Aman, aman, ay jaaaan! (*Returning from the roof with* USTIAN)

(*The* CHAMBERLAIN *enters and takes up his position, smiling.*)

NAZAR (*to the* CHAMBERLAIN): Well, what's all this skittering like a mouse? What's going on? Get out of my sight!

(*The* CHAMBERLAIN *stands motionless.*)

NAZAR: Are you deaf and dumb, you old goat?
CHAMBERLAIN: Source of Life! The queens of the three kings defeated in the last war have come and request the pleasure of basking in the brilliance of your presence.
NAZAR: Three queens? . . . What do they want?
CHAMBERLAIN: The minister knows, oh King of Life.
NAZAR: Summon the minister.

(*The* CHAMBERLAIN *goes.*)

USTIAN: If you had any sense, you'd send them off and be rid of them.
NAZAR (*sitting on the divan*): Ahhh! . . . Phew! . . . Hey, Ustian! We've become king and queen of the world. How does that strike you?
MINISTER (*entering and somewhat slowly approaching* NAZAR): Divine King, the queens of our enemy kings, seeing that their husbands were killed in the war and hearing of the reputation of your intelligence and bravery, have fallen in love with you and have come to fall at your feet and solicit your love.
NAZAR: Are they attractive specimens?
MINISTER: As radiant as the full moon.
NAZAR: Go and tell the *hanums* on my behalf that I love them and have them come in.

(*The* MINISTER *goes.*)

USTIAN: You're not listening. Keep them out and you've got no problem.
NAZAR: How can I do that? It's a king's duty, and they're noble queens.
USTIAN: What do you mean by "noble queen"? A queen is a queen, and that's it!
NAZAR (*relaxed*): No! There are low-class queens, and then there are queens who belong to the nobility. The queen of nobility is the queen of the world.
USTIAN: Use your head. Listen to me. Get rid of them. Send them packing.

NAZAR: I can't do that. It's my duty to see them. Even if it causes me heartache, I've got to fulfill my obligation.

USTIAN: Is that obligation good or bad? That's what I'd like to know.

NAZAR: Don't annoy me. Don't interfere in matters beyond you.

USTIAN: Beyond me? Nothing's beyond me.

NAZAR (*feigning sincerity, crudely*): Listen, Ustian. I have a little bit of royal business to attend to, so why don't you go to the other room.

USTIAN: Pardon me! Taking in pretty women's not royal business, it's monkey business.

NAZAR: That's right, Ustian *hanum*, that's the way it is.

USTIAN: Listen, I'm the queen here and I'll have the final say!

NAZAR (*annoyed*): The queens are coming. I've got a royal appointment to keep. Go to the other room.

(NAZAR *waits for* USTIAN *to go. The* CHAMBERLAIN *peers out through the slit in the curtain.* NAZAR *sees him doing so and coughs.*)

USTIAN: Listen, Nazar, why can't I be the noble queen of the world?

NAZAR: You can't.

USTIAN: Can too.

NAZAR: No way!

USTIAN: Come on now, what's there to stop me?

NAZAR (*singing softly*): Aman, aman, ay jaaan! (*To* USTIAN) Royal business is a weighty matter, very onerous . . . (*To the* CHAMBERLAIN) Hey, scoundrel!

(*The* CHAMBERLAIN *comes in.*)

Go bring some lotion and sprinkle it on me.

(*The* CHAMBERLAIN *runs out.*)

Eh! . . . (*Feigning displeasure*) The weight of the world is crushing me. I've got to give advice, display courage, do this, do that. Ignoramuses, once and for all, leave me alone. Let me collect my wits.

(*The* CHAMBERLAIN *comes running in with servants who sprinkle the sweet-smelling lotion on* NAZAR *and quickly exit.*)

USTIAN: Well, since you're entertaining other queens, does that mean I'm no longer up to the mark?

(NAZAR *makes a clicking sound with his tongue.*)

Why not?

NAZAR: Because.

USTIAN: No, come on, tell me why.

NAZAR: I'm going to take a wife of noble lineage so my dynasty may become truly noble.

USTIAN: Is that a proper thing for you to do?

NAZAR: I'm a doer, Ustian *hanum.*

USTIAN: No, I won't let you do it.

NAZAR: I'm getting hot under the collar. Don't annoy me. I'm going to consort a little with nobility. I don't have time to waste. Go about your business!

USTIAN: My dear, what's all this talk about nobility and lineage? Come out and say it, your heart desires another woman. Do you realize what it is you're doing?

NAZAR: Peace! Cut it short!

USTIAN: You're going to marry them, is that it? That's the long and short of it? (*Pause*) Well, now what am I supposed to do?

NAZAR: How should I know? I'll give you money and possessions. Go back home.

USTIAN: Oh, no! I'm not leaving.

NAZAR: You'll go, Ustian *hanum,* you'll go!

USTIAN: I won't go! I'll shame you!

NAZAR: How?

USTIAN: I'll say you're a coward.

NAZAR: Me a coward?

USTIAN: Yes, you!

NAZAR: Sure, I'm such a coward that I strike fear throughout the world!

USTIAN: Those are mere games, my dear. It's nothing but a lie. I wonder what tricks you pulled. Now, let's see what happens to you when I reveal your true self.

NAZAR (*attacking* USTIAN): I'll show you, you spoiler!

(*Before he can finish, the* MINISTER *enters, with* VIZIER, CHAMBERLAIN, COURTIERS, MASTER OF CEREMONIES, GHOROBUGHA, *and the three queens they are escorting. They move forward, smiling coquettishly, and approach* NAZAR.)

(*Addressing* USTIAN *sternly*) Ustian, now we're having a meeting. I'm all confused. Step into the other room for a while.

USTIAN (*with feigned politeness*): Oh, is that so? It's a meeting, is it? Fine! (*She gets up to exit.*) But, I don't wish you well. (*She looks askance at* NAZAR.)

(NAZAR *looks at* USTIAN *with suspicion and moves to strike her, but the appearance of the queens dazzles him and he forgets about her.*)

(*Departing,* USTIAN *looks at the queens and mutters.*) Look at those bitches. They're in love! . . . I'd like to bury you all! (*She exits.*)

NAZAR (*smiling to his entourage*): Are these the queens? So buxom! Be seated, please.

(*The queens sit.*)

A table has been set in the garden. Shall we go and sit among the flowers? (*To the* CHAMBERLAIN) Order a nice spread of appetizers. Have the musicians accompany us into the garden.

(*The* CHAMBERLAIN *goes and quickly returns.*)

(*Turning to the* COURTIERS) You, in turn, will escort us to the garden and then go about your business. Keep a close eye on the affairs of state, make sure they're in order; otherwise, I'll have you skinned alive. Hah! You understand?

ALL: We understand, Center of the Universe.

GHOROBUGHA: Hamm! We understand!

NAZAR: Who told you to yell in the presence of the *hanums*? You horse's ass! (*Addressing the queens*) Well, my *hanums*, how are you? Are you in good spirits?

(*The queens giggle coquettishly. The musicians enter and give obeisance to* NAZAR.)

Well, my friends, play something catchy. *Hanums*, let's go. (*He puts the crown on his head.*)

(*The queens giggle. The musicians play and sing.*)

USTIAN (*Entering, she listens to the music, then comes downstage.*): Huh!

(*The musicians play more softly as* USTIAN *comes forth.*)

Look at snot-nosed Nazar. He couldn't even divide a pail of barley between two asses. Now, look at where he's got! When you think about the ways of the world, you can go berserk, trying to figure out how it happened. I don't know, it's a matter of luck. That's all I can say.

(*The musicians play even more softly.*)

Do you see how he has made the world an object of scorn and laughed at it, making it out to be ridiculous? Did you notice how those idiots turned into rabbits before that mouse? It's a matter of luck, I tell you.

(*The musicians continue playing. The queens are giggling.*)

So, you're on top of the world, huh? You'll be lucky if I don't bury your shameless heads. His, too, for he's got no sense of shame either. Hum! (*Thinking and shaking her head*) All said and done, he's always been lucky. It's a matter of luck, I tell you.

(*The musicians play a dance tune. The queens take turns dancing.*)

NAZAR: Ay jan! (*He too dances.*)
USTIAN: Just you wait, I'll fix your wagon. (*She picks up a stick lying in the corner.*)
NAZAR: Mercy, mercy, ay jan!
USTIAN (*She runs forward, stick in hand.*): So, that's your royal meeting, huh? (*Hitting* NAZAR *on the head with the stick*) Take that, you old fart!

(*The queens and musicians run off hastily.*)

NAZAR (*running to one side*): Beh, beh, beh, beh!

(USTIAN *runs after him but, noticing the* CHAMBERLAIN *enter, she restrains herself and pulls back.*)

(NAZAR *goes and sits cross-legged on the divan.*) Chamberlain, you rascal, call the Minister and Vizier . . . I have a complaint against the state.

(*The* CHAMBERLAIN *exits.*)

USTIAN: You're dead meat!

(*The* CHAMBERLAIN *returns, accompanied by the* MINISTER *and* VIZIER, *the* GENERAL *and* COURTIERS.)

MINISTER: We're at your command, Center of the Universe.
NAZAR: I command that—

(USTIAN *looks at him crossly.*)

(*Controlling himself and remaining silent*) Hem! . . . (*Then losing patience*) Beh! . . . (*Jumping up out of his seat*) Beh! . . . (*Jumping up again*) What are you trying to say? I'm not king? Am I supposed to keep my mouth shut?

(*A commotion is heard offstage. There's a knock on the door.*)

Rascal, is that the people out there? Haven't they gone to fight?

MINISTER: No, my lord!

NAZAR: You don't say! . . . What are they saying, you rascal? Whoever heard of a
king declaring war and the people not going off to fight? (*Turning to* SAKO)
Sako, go!

SAKO (*extremely frightened*): Sh—, sh—, shall I go?

NAZAR: Get going, you good-for-nothing. If you want to become king, you have to
fight for it.

ALL: Prince Sako, onward!

SAKO (*going to the balcony and addressing the people*): Fellow countrymen, the
king commands . . . (*Terrified, he runs back.*) Mercy!

NAZAR (*to the* COURTIERS): Yeah, yeah! . . . just go and punish the people. Hang
the traitors. Chamberlain, go; General, go, Minister and Vizier, Ghorobugha,
go, go, go!

USTIAN (*Having returned in the meantime and having heard the last words, she proceeds to strike* NAZAR *on the head with her fist.*): I'll stick your royal head in the
mud. Never mind sending them. You go!

(NAZAR *looks at* USTIAN *in fear. The* COURTIERS, *in turn, are terrified of* NAZAR *and
wait to see what he will do.*)

USTIAN: You think everyone's so afraid of you? Well, I'm not one of them. (*She lifts
the stick and strikes* NAZAR.) Take that, you old fart!

(NAZAR *runs out. The* COURTIERS *are bewildered.*)

COURTIER: Gentlemen, what's happening here? Can the king be afraid?

SECOND COURTIER: How could he be? There's something here that doesn't meet
the eye. A miracle's about to happen.

NAZAR (*running in followed by* USTIAN): Beh, beh, beh, beh!

SECOND COURTIER: Now a miracle will take place.

USTIAN (*hitting him on the head with the stick*): I'll crack your skull open!

(NAZAR *runs from her.*)

CHAMBERLAIN (*running toward* USTIAN): Virtuous queen—

NAZAR: I'll hit you so hard you'll see stars! (*Continuing to avoid* USTIAN)

CHAMBERLAIN (*running toward* NAZAR): Brave king!

USTIAN (*running after* NAZAR *and hitting him with the stick*): I'll smash your head
in!

CHAMBERLAIN (*running after her*): Virtuous queen!

NAZAR: I'll rip her to pieces! (*He runs and crawls under the divan.*)
CHAMBERLAIN (*running toward him*): Brave king!

(*The* COURTIERS *and* SAKO *move toward* USTIAN *in a supplicating manner.* USTIAN *delivers a blow to* SAKO's *head and shakes the stick in the direction of the other* COURTIERS.)

SAKO: Mercy! (*He runs out.*)

(*The* COURTIERS *retreat.*)

NAZAR: Come on now, enough is enough, have you no shame?
USTIAN: Should I be ashamed, or should you? I'll have your head!

(*She pokes the stick at* NAZAR *under the divan.*)

NAZAR: Bo, bo, bo! . . . Go on, seize her . . . Ustian!
USTIAN (*rolling the divan to one side*): Now, stand up. I'll beat the daylights out of
     you in front of the others, so they can see what you're really made of . . .
A COURTIER: Here comes the miracle.
NAZAR (*running out*): Mercy!

(USTIAN *pursues him.*)

COURTIERS: Did you see the miracle?

(*Suddenly a ripple of laughter breaks out, which begins to increase unrestrained in intensity, filling the hall. The* GIANTS *pour in and look on with amazement. Above all,* GHOROBUGHA *is the most astonished. Suddenly realizing what is going on,* GHOROBUGHA *bursts into raucous laughter, as do the other* GIANTS.)

(*The* COURTIERS *begin plundering the palace, filling their pockets with valuable objects and then, fearing some threat, move toward the door to escape.* USTIAN *rushes in and fills a bag with various objects. The curtain falls.*)

(*Shouting from either side downstage,* NAZAR *and* SAKO *rush upon each other and fall to the floor terrified. Natives of Parzashen enter and surround* NAZAR *and* SAKO *with derisive laughter. Black out. Then lights fade in. The forestage is empty.* USTIAN *enters, stick in hand and a sack slung on her back. She looks all around. She is confused.*)

USTIAN: Now, didn't I say it was a dream . . . a matter of chance? (*She exits.*)

HOUSE MANAGER (*coming in from the rear with a candle and advancing to stage front*):

> Ustian , it's not by chance, you silly sage,
> That people are hoodwinked in every age,
> Entrusting scarecrows with scepter and rule
> So that fool plays king or king plays fool.
> That bad old dream has gone, I vow.
> There's no more king, no Nazar now
> To concern us further or cause remark,
> Like this stage here (*blowing the candle out*), one puff and
>   it's dark.

Black out.

PERCH ZEYTUNTSYAN

Perch Zeytuntsyan was born in Alexandria, Egypt, in 1938. Ten years later, he moved with his parents to Soviet Armenia at a time of severe economic hardship as the country struggled to come to terms with the aftermath of World War II. While still at the Aghayan School in Erevan, Zeytuntsyan published his first short story *Nvere* [The gift] in 1953. Three years later, while studying at the Pyatigorsk Pedagogical Institute for Foreign Languages, his first collection *Nra arajin enkere* [His first companion] appeared to critical acclaim, winning second prize at the Soviet Youth Festival. He also produced a series of translations from English, including works of Erskin Caldwell, Graham Greene, and Ernest Hemingway.

Subsequently Zeytuntsyan published a series of novels and novellas, for example, *Mer taghi dzaynere* [Sounds of our neighborhood] (1959), *Mezanits heto* [After us] (1963), *Parizi hamar* [For Paris] (1965), *Klod Robert Izlerli kam xx dari legend* [Claude Robert Izerli or a twentieth-century legend] (1968), *Katakergutyun arants masnakitsneri* [Comedy without participants] (1975), *Arshak Erkrord* [Arshak the second] (1977), *Verjin arevagale* [The last dawn] (1989), and *Goghatsvats dzyune* [The stolen snow] (1995). Many of these works have been translated into Russian, Czech, Bulgarian, Hungarian, and the languages of the Baltic Republics.

Zeytuntsyan wrote his first work for the theater

in 1974, *Amenatkhur marde* [The saddest man], a tragicomedy that was staged in Erevan. Thereafter ten of his plays have been produced there and later published in the Armenian Republic, some also appearing in Russia. Of these one might mention *Avervats kaghaki araspele* [The legend of the ruined city] (1975), *Astvatsneri kanche* [The call of the gods], *Anavart menakhosutyun* [Unfinished monologue] (1981), *Mec lrutyune* [The great silence] (1984), *Otki, datarann e galis* [All rise, the court is in session] (1988), and *Tsnvel e u mahatsel* [Born and died] (1995).

The leitmotif of Zeytuntsyan's prose works is the relation between the individual, society, and the exercise of authority. He has analyzed different aspects of this complex triangle in his various works, employing artistic means to illuminate its diverse facets. Thus, in *Arshak II* he treats the tragic situation of one of the last Armenian Arsacid kings, who committed suicide rather than submit to the suzerainty of his Persian Sasanid counterpart in the latter part of the fourth century. Similarly, his latest hybrid novel/play, *The Stolen Snow*, focuses on the struggle for freedom of religion waged by the general and governor Vahan Mamikonian in the second half of the fifth century against the Persian attempt to forcibly reintroduce Zoroastrianism into Armenia. In a manner anticipating the twin maxims of glasnost and perestroika, characteristic of the later Gorbachev era, Zeytuntsyan presents the main character's dogged perseverance against the strictures of a rigid centralized bureaucracy in *Unfinished Monologue*, compelling him to lead a double life, which brings him to the edge of self-destruction. Most recently, the destabilizing social effects of the post-Soviet transition to democracy and a market economy are reflected in Zeytuntsyan's *Born and Died*. It problematizes established theatrical conventions from an absurdist perspective, highlighting the issue of self-censorship and the actor's yearning to escape the control of the director and playwright.

Most of his plays draw their subject matter from Armenian history, particularly episodes with special relevance to contemporary problems. Among these, one of the main themes of Zeytuntsyan's more recent prose and theatrical works has been the genocide of the Armenians in the Ottoman Empire, reflecting the growth of nationalist sentiment in the republic during the last years of Soviet rule. To this topic are dedicated his novel *The Last Dawn* and his dramas *The Great Silence* and *All Rise, the Court Is in Session*. The first play deals with the murder of Taniel Varuzhan on April 24, 1915, along with several other Armenian intellectuals and community leaders in Constantinople. Cut down in his prime, this poet had been in the forefront of a movement for national cultural revival, evoking its deepest and oldest symbols and rekindling them in his poetry. The second dramatizes the tense trial of Solomon Tehlerian, who was acquitted by a Berlin court in 1921 of assassinating Talat Pasha, the Ottoman Minister of the Interior responsible for the massacre and deportation of large sections of the Armenian population of the eastern vilayets. These plays have been frequently performed in Armenia, as well as in different parts of the Armenian Diaspora.

Zeytuntsyan held the post of executive secretary of the Writers' Union of Armenia (1975–81). Later, he became Minister of Culture in the first post-Soviet administration of the Republic of Armenia. He received the State Prize of Armenia, the republic's highest award, as well other honors for his prolific output. He was also elected a corresponding member of the Tiberina Academy of the Social Sciences and Arts of Rome.

After graduating from an advanced course in screenwriting in Moscow (1962–64), Zeytuntsyan worked at the Hayfilm center in Erevan, later becoming the senior editor of the art film section of the Erevan studio for television films (1968–75). The striking film *Erevanyan oreri khronika* [Chronicle of Erevan days], shot by the renowned director Frunze Dovlatyan (1973), was based on his screenplay. He also wrote a number of speeches and newspaper articles focusing on significant sociopolitical issues affecting the Armenian Republic. One collection of these pieces appeared in 1990 under the title *Tsulere der ayntegh en* [The bulls are still there] and won the Golden Pen Award of the Republic's Union of Journalists.

S.P.C.

UNFINISHED MONOLOGUE
A DRAMA IN TWO ACTS

(ANAVART MENAKHOSUTYUN, 1981)

Translated by S. Peter Cowe

CAST OF CHARACTERS

RAFAYEL AVETYAN: Head of a construction crew in the Ministry of Public Works; currently engaged in building a rail link. At various points he is referred to endearingly as RAFIK or RAFO.

ANAHIT: His wife

HASMIK: His daughter; a divorcee looking for a husband

VIGEN: His son; a teenager applying for admission to a university

ARSEN: His father

RAFAYEL'S MATERNAL AUNT

BENO: His cousin

ELEONORA: His sister; recently separated from her husband

ELYA AND NORA: ELEONORA's children

LOVER-BOY SHAHEN: RAFAYEL's school friend

HAYK MARKOSYAN: RAFAYEL's superior at the ministry

MARKOSYAN'S SECRETARY

HAMO: RAFAYEL's right-hand man; humorous and practical

ZHANNA: RAFAYEL's secretary; habitually late for work

RAFAYEL'S CONSTRUCTION CREW:
    KARAPETYAN
    HAMBARDZUMYAN: His deputy
    AZATYAN

RUBEN

VANIK

ARSHALUYS

SARGSYAN

CHILINGIRYAN

SONYA: An employee at the ministry

NORA: An employee at the ministry, whose major attribute is her lovely legs

A PHOTOGRAPHER

LUCY EDVARDOVNA: Wife of COMRADE Arshakyan, with whom RAFAYEL has a relationship of some intimacy and standing

COMRADE ARUSHANYAN: An upper official at the Ministry for Public Works, who becomes deputy minister in the course of the play.

FIRST OFFICIAL

SECOND OFFICIAL

THIRD OFFICIAL

A NEIGHBOR

ACT 1

RAFAYEL AVETYAN's *house*

ANAHIT: You know, Rafik, I'm glad you get sick once in a while. You stay home and we get to see your face. You seem to need me more when you're ill. I like that a lot.

RAFAYEL: Okay, what's it this time? If it's not the plumbing, it has to be the furniture. Right?

ANAHIT: I don't have to say a thing. It's obvious the house is in ruins. Some people change their furniture every two years. Looking at myself in the mirror I realize the furniture's as old as I look. We both need a makeover.

RAFAYEL: You old? Never! You'll always be the young thing I married. You know we can't afford new furniture just now. It's a waste of breath speaking about it. If you can hang on a few more years with the same furniture, you'll both get a facelift. A shoemaker's wife has no shoes. You know the old saying. That's life.

(RAFAYEL's *aunt enters in a smock.*)

AUNT: Rafik, dear . . .

RAFAYEL: Auntie? I thought you were leaving this morning.

AUNT: I'm in no hurry. Are you tired of me already? How many aunts do you have anyway? Here I am in the big city, and what do you do? You should take me out places, show me around, and get me a few souvenirs of the trip, like having our photograph taken together.

ANAHIT: I'll take you wherever you want, Auntie.

AUNT: That'd be nice. Oh, and while I'm complaining . . . Do you think I could sleep on this soft divan instead of that hard cot in the back room?

RAFAYEL: By all means, Auntie dear. Sleep wherever you want.

AUNT: How good of you. You wouldn't want me to go without sleep, now would you? If you really loved your aunt, you'd use your pull to get my son, Beno, a job. All he wants is to be a busboy at the station buffet. I'm sure if you called Serob on our district council, he'd see to it that that lazy so-and-so Vagharshak gave Beno the job. That's not asking much. Besides, the poor boy has six kids, ooh . . .

RAFAYEL: Six?

AUNT: It'll be seven tomorrow.

(*The doorbell rings.*)

That doorbell of yours never stops. Can't we have a little peace to deal with Beno's problem? I tell you what. You don't get him the job, and your aunt's going to be here for a long stay. (*She goes into the next room.*)

(ANAHIT *goes to open the door. She returns with* HAMO. HAMO *takes off his shoes.*)

HAMO (*laying a package on the table*): Boss, you sure as hell found the right time to have a heart attack.

RAFAYEL: A touch of angina, that's all. Forget it. (*Pointing to the package*) What've you there?

HAMO: Brandy, boss. The best.

ANAHIT: You shouldn't have, Comrade Hamo. You're too kind.

RAFAYEL: Hold on, Anahit. (*To* HAMO) Take this brandy back with you. You know I don't like expensive gifts.

HAMO: But, boss, this is my first visit. I couldn't very well come empty-handed.

RAFAYEL: Did you hear what I said? Do I have to spell it out for you? Bring flowers instead. They're cheap, and pretty.

ANAHIT: Actually, dear, flowers aren't that cheap any more. (*She realizes her presence is superfluous and exits.*)

RAFAYEL (*furious*): How many times have I told you not to set foot in this house? I don't give a damn what's going on in the office. Never come here.

HAMO: A man from the ministry was snooping around in our books, boss. Can you imagine, he didn't take any money. Some young kid, just out of training.

RAFAYEL: What's his name?

HAMO: Karapetyan.

RAFAYEL: Did he find anything?

HAMO: We filed paperwork for a paycheck to be issued to a workman while he was on leave at a state spa. The money wasn't appropriated, because the job was allocated to a subcontractor. Okay, we messed up. But it's a misdemeanor, not a crime.

RAFAYEL: That's it?

HAMO: For now. But he's digging around, and he's bound to find something. If the jerk discovers we're way over budget, laying thirteen kilometers of rail link for the industrial complex instead of the specified four—

RAFAYEL: Okay, okay. Keep your voice down. Let's wait and see. You say he's an honest guy.

HAMO: That's just the trouble. His honesty could get in the way of our plans. Let him keep it to himself, I say, and let us get on with our lives. Don't you agree, boss?

RAFAYEL: Shower him with money. Drown him in the stuff. And see if he comes to his senses.

HAMO: Where's the dough coming from, Comrade Avetyan.

RAFAYEL: Me. Here's the key to my safe. Give him as much as you can carry. If some finds its way into your pocket, no matter, take it. I don't keep tabs on how much there is.

HAMO: I don't know, boss. Maybe you should handle it. I'm not the smooth talker you are.

RAFAYEL: No, I don't like dealing with rookies. I can't help sympathizing with them.

HAMO: Oh, to be in his shoes. He's probably never seen so much money.

RAFAYEL (surly): He won't take it.

HAMO: Who are you kidding, Comrade Avetyan? He'll take it all right.

RAFAYEL: He won't.

HAMO: Of course he will, and how!

RAFAYEL: No way. I know the type.

(RAFAYEL's *father*, ARSEN, *comes in*.)

ARSEN: RAFIK, Sahak next door went to senior citizens' bureau to see about a pension increase. The clerk on duty demanded a pay-off. You've got to help him. Tell his superiors to rap the creep over the knuckles and raise Sahak's pension. Do me this favor, Son, okay?

RAFAYEL: I'll look into it, Pop.

ARSEN: Remember, I gave Sahak my word. Your word and mine are the same, right?

RAFAYEL: Right, Dad. Don't worry.

(*Pause.* ARSEN *looks quizzically at* RAFAYEL, *then at* HAMO. *He realizes he has interrupted their business.*)

ARSEN: See you later. (*Unable quite to tear himself away*) I'm going to visit a teacher friend of mine. I'll bring him here one of these days so you can meet him. What a refined vocabulary he has. No ordinary cookies for him, only dainty sweetmeats. Well, okay, bye now. (*He goes out.*)

HAMO: So what's our plan, boss?

RAFAYEL: Relax. Forget what I said before. Of course he'll take the money. Grease the kid's palm. Enough to bury him. Then, if he takes it, bring him to see me.

HAMO: Didn't you say not to come here?

RAFAYEL: I'll see the guy, if he goes for the dough.

HAMO: Okay, I'm off, boss. God help me.

RAFAYEL: On your way back, buy some carnations for my wife. And, by the way, don't take off your shoes in the house. Wipe your feet on the mat before coming in. Got that? Okay. Here's money for the carnations.

HAMO: What's that for, boss? If you're so keen on carnations, I'll bring you a hundred fresh every day. (*He is about to go.*)

RAFAYEL (*suddenly serious*): Hamo, don't even try to cross me. I keep close tabs on my money.

HAMO: That's for sure. Oh, I almost forgot . . . [*Handing* RAFAYEL *a lottery ticket*] Here you are, boss. Enjoy it. You've won the lottery.

RAFAYEL: What's the prize?

HAMO: You know. The Zhiguli you wanted. With air conditioning.

RAFAYEL: How much did you give the lotto official on top of the price of the ticket?

HAMO: The going rate. Enjoy.

RAFAYEL: Good. Take the brandy with you.

HAMO: Don't get me wrong, boss. I brought it to make my coming here look like a social visit.

RAFAYEL: Hamo, don't do me any favors I don't need.

HAMO: Sure, boss. Enough said. (*He goes out.*)

RAFAYEL (*as if talking to the auditor*): Comrade Karapetyan, do you hear me? I've never met you, but I want to give you some advice. Auditing's not for wimps. Be a man, okay? Resist it . . . one moment. Just resist it for a moment. The rest's easy. I've cursed that Hamo's hide. Count to ten and you'll win . . . count . . . count . . . what is it? Have you forgotten how to count? It's not like a prayer that you can forget so easily. Don't give in. Please don't forget—one moment, one moment at least . . . (*He is about to go.*)

ANAHIT (*entering, concerned*): Where do you think you're off to? . . . In your condition, you're not supposed to—

RAFAYEL: I'll only be gone ten minutes. I'm taking a turn round the block to get some fresh air.

The scene is set at the Comptroller's office of RAFAYEL's *construction plant.* RAFAYEL *is at a staff meeting with the members of his crew.*

RAFAYEL (*addressing his staff*): I suppose you thought I'd had it? You'd never see me again?

(RAFAYEL's *secretary,* ZHANNA, *enters.*)

ZHANNA, is that you late again? What happened this time?

ZHANNA: Excuse me, Rafayel Arsenich, I almost fell under a tram.

RAFAYEL: What tram?

ZHANNA: Number eight.

RAFAYEL: Who are you trying to kid? I don't want to hear any more of your stories.

ZHANNA: Shall I put on coffee?

RAFAYEL: No.

ZHANNA: Are you in, if anyone calls?

RAFAYEL: No. (*To* ARSHALUYS) Arshaluys?

ARSHALUYS: Yes, Comrade Avetyan. (*Standing up in* AVETYAN's *presence*)

RAFAYEL: Sit down when you speak, lad. Before I fell ill, you said you wanted a transfer. Where's your application? It's not on my desk. Bring it so I can sign it, and you can go. Sahakyan will take your place.

ARSHALUYS: Excuse me, Comrade Avetyan. That was only talk. I was running a temperature the day I thought about the transfer.

RAFAYEL: Chilled out now? Back to normal?

ARSHALUYS: I'm fine. Thanks.

RAFAYEL: As for you, Chilingiryan, you're out. I've no time for your speeches now. I'll talk to you on the fifteenth. [*Adding pregnantly*] On the other side of the bridge.

CHILINGIRYAN: We won't complete that section of track by then, Comrade Avetyan.

RAFAYEL: If you're still on this side of the bridge, you're out, as I said, despite your application to stay on here. Look alive. [*To* AZATYAN] Listen, Azatyan, I'll be at the site tomorrow at noon to check whether the fitters have received their bonus for all the overtime they're putting in.

AZATYAN: No can do, Comrade Avetyan. I'm forty percent over budget.

RAFAYEL: I'll cover your deficit.

AZATYAN: How?

RAFAYEL (*humorously*): With a pep talk.

AZATYAN: Then what?

RAFAYEL: If I have to, I'll fire you.

AZATYAN: What? That's not fair. How would that help?

RAFAYEL: It'd help us lay those thirteen kilometers of rail track. You'll go, but those thirteen kilometers will stay. Ultimately we'll all go, but the rail link will be around forever. See what I mean?

AZATYAN: You're looking at a law suit, Comrade Avetyan.

RAFAYEL: Arshaluys, what percentage of the overall budget is required to cover Azatyan's deficit?

ARSHALUYS: Whatever you need it to be.

RAFAYEL: Did you hear? There you go, Sargsyan. Fix it. Don't waste your breath trying to talk me out of it.

SARGSYAN: We can't move ahead without the wire shipment. It would have been better if you'd talked with the suppliers yourself.

RAFAYEL: Wire, wire. Hamo, take a note. I've got to line up a hundred tons of wire.

HAMO: That blows my mind.

RAFAYEL: Write it down, I'm telling you. Anything else?

HAMBARJUMYAN: The trench is ready to lay the pipes, but we're completely out of them. Ceramic, and cast iron.

RAFAYEL: How many meters?

HAMBARJUMYAN: A thousand.

HAMO (HAMO *dials a telephone number and hands the receiver to* RAFAYEL): Galust.

RAFAYEL: My regards. How are you, Galust? Did you ever have those hothouses inspected? Too bad. How can I help you? Glass? How many meters do you need?

HAMBARJUMYAN: We don't have any here.

RAFAYEL: Three hundred? I'll give you four hundred meters. After all, what are friends for? It just so happens I need a thousand meters of pipe . . . cast iron . . . ten to twelve dumes . . . You put the order together and I'll have it picked up. The girls in the planning office won't create any problems. Hamo will take care of them. Good for you. (*He replaces the receiver.*) Hamo, take a note: trench, planning office, girls, pipe.

HAMBARJUMYAN: Where are we going to get glass from?

RAFAYEL: Think pipes, pipes, pipes.

HAMO (*He picks up the phone and dials.*): Perfume department? Aharon . . . Hold on. (*He hands the phone to* RAFAYEL.)

RAFAYEL: Aharon? Hello. Rafik. Okay, I'm fine. No problem, it was a minor thing, nothing serious. Listen, Hamo's coming over. Give him some French perfume. Do you have any of that popular *Fiji* brand? Excellent. Take care. (*Replacing the receiver*) Hamo, take those bottles of *Fiji* perfume and give them to the girls in the planning office and bring me Galust's paperwork for the pipes.

HAMO: A bottle of *Fiji* costs thirty to forty rubles.

RAFAYEL: Put in a requisition order for the perfume, and I'll think of something.

HAMO: How should I fudge it?

RAFAYEL: Put down anything, just get it on paper. Write it off as funeral expenses for your granny.

HAMO: My granny's died twice this year already. Remember? Once when we had to call in the firemen, the other time to cover my car repairs.

RAFAYEL: Okay. Vanik. *You* handle the paperwork.

VANIK: My granny kicked the bucket this year as well, I think.

RAFAYEL: Ruben, How's yours doing?

RUBEN: Both my granny and grandpa are gone.

RAFAYEL: Is there no one in the office with a granny who's still alive and kicking?

HAMO: Not this year, boss.

RAFAYEL: Sargsyan, what news of the joists?

SARGSYAN: The joists are Poghosyan's baileywick.

RAFAYEL: Poghosyan, what happened to the joists?

POGHOSYAN: Joists? That's Chilingiryan's baby.

RAFAYEL: Chilingiryan, what's up with the joists?

CHILINGIRYAN: The joists have been here for ages.

RAFAYEL: Where are they?

CHILINGIRYAN: They're here.

RAFAYEL (*shouting*): Where are they?

CHILINGIRYAN (*turning pale*): Actually, the joists are Manik's responsibility.

RAFAYEL: Manik—

SARGSYAN: Manik's out sick.

HAMO: Boss, what are those joists for?

RAFAYEL: Didn't you hear? I promised to get Galust some glass. Since we don't have any, how am I going to get my hands on some? We'll exchange the joists for glass, give the glass to Galust, the perfume to the girls in the planning office, and transfer Galust's budget to our account. Meeting's over. Back to work. I'm off, Zhanna.

The scene changes to HAYK MARKOSYAN's *office. Bent over the table,* COMRADE MARKOSYAN *is busy writing.*

SECRETARY (*entering*): He's waiting.

MARKOSYAN: Let him wait.

SECRETARY: It's time for your lunch break, Comrade Markosyan.

MARKOSYAN: Already? (*Looking at his watch*) All the better. Let him wait.

(*The secretary pours tea from a small samovar, hands it to* MARKOSYAN, *and exits.* MARKOSYAN *lays the papers to one side, pulls out a modest packet from a drawer, and begins to eat. The door opens noisily, and* RAFAYEL AVETYAN *bursts in furiously. He is taken by surprise seeing* MARKOSYAN *at his break. He hesitates a moment in confusion, then, without saying hello, goes up to the smallish table in the corner, takes bread and cheese from* MARKOSYAN's *packet, and begins to eat and drink tea. Both eat in silence.*)

MARKOSYAN: Waiting gets on your nerves, doesn't it?

RAFAYEL: Is that what you called to tell me?

MARKOSYAN: I've been waiting a year and four months for you to move the project ahead.

RAFAYEL: Here's an application form. I've brought it so as not to keep you in suspense any longer.

MARKOSYAN: Another application. Time for a transfer, is it? Throwing in the towel again?

RAFAYEL: Just don't try to change my mind. It's a waste of time.

MARKOSYAN: Try to appreciate what I'm saying. How can I cover for you when you flit from one position to another? What do you mean? You're the only decent guy around here. Everyone else, me included, is petty and corrupt. Forget it, RAFIK, the rest of us can't all be bad. Anyway, no one will buy it.

RAFAYEL: Okay, pal. I'm the bad lemon. Are we done?

MARKOSYAN: What do you think? That's what they're going to say. I can't give you unconditional support against all of them. I don't have the right. Even if I think you're justified.

RAFAYEL: You're right. When have you ever been wrong? On this side of the door, everything's right. You're right, every one of you.

MARKOSYAN: At school your son said hello to me, and I didn't even recognize him. He said, "It's me, Uncle Vigen." I said to myself, "Damn your father, for not letting me get to know you." Eat up, eat up, don't leave your sandwich half-finished. From now on you have to change your tactics and start portraying me, not yourself, in a bright light. Even if you and I put our friendship aside when it comes to business, the people around us don't miss a thing, Rafik, not a thing. I can't afford to have them start badmouthing me.

RAFAYEL: Am I to blame that people like you keep up with friends from your student days? Don't make inquiries, so you don't have to get in touch with me.

MARKOSYAN As for that rail link, put it out of your mind. It's impossible, Rafik. Forget it right this instant.

RAFAYEL (*agitated*): Don't broadcast the rail link to everybody, I beg you, Hayk. I really beg you. I'll pass on, but those thirteen kilometers will stay. Then you'll go, but the railway will still be there. (*He wants to have a smoke, but he can't get the lighter to work.*) People often present you with lighters. Can I have one?

(MARKOSYAN *opens a drawer and hands* RAFAYEL *a lighter.*)

MARKOSYAN: As soon as you run into difficulties, you file an application for transfer and run up the white flag. Did you think I didn't know you were secretly building that rail link? All thirteen kilometers of it instead of the original four. Did you think I didn't realize that without those thirteen kilometers the industrial complex wouldn't be constructed on time, and, after construction, would only function at half capacity? What difference does it make whether I grasp that or not? It's all over and done with. You didn't submit your review of the plans in time.

RAFAYEL: That's good. You're answering your own question.

MARKOSYAN: I'm asking the question, Rafik. You're the one who has to answer it ultimately. Don't forget that. By the way, this is a no-smoking area.

RAFAYEL (*extinguishing his cigarette*): You put me in a cage and then tell me to get out. It can't be done. You can't force me. It's not my fault you've become incapable of assuming responsibility for things. If you don't want to, so be it, but please don't get in the way of others.

MARKOSYAN: Who the hell do you think you are? Who are you to make decisions on your own? You're supposed to carry them out. That's your job description. What? Are they going to set up a statue in your honor? Are they going to say, "This guy thinks he runs the country, he took the responsibility on his own shoulders, let's give him a round of applause." (*Pause*) You know what? If you want it that badly, damn you. I'll go along with you. Go and do it.

RAFAYEL: Okay, but thirteen kilometers, not four. And, of course, you know nothing about it.

MARKOSYAN: Nothing at all.

RAFAYEL: All hell will break loose the day you do hear about it.

MARKOSYAN: Yes, Rafik, be warned. It'll be hell.

(RAFAYEL *gets up and moves toward the door.*)

RAFAYEL: One more request, Hayk, a personal one.

MARKOSYAN: It better not have more than three points.

RAFAYEL: You have to find me four extra apartments. I've invited experts to work on the railway. They've nowhere to stay. I promised.

MARKOSYAN: Anything else? What about something for yourself?

RAFAYEL: I'm the only master builder in the whole project. You have to assign three more to my staff.

MARKOSYAN: Anything else?

RAFAYEL: I owe you big just for that.

MARKOSYAN: You let me off easy this time. Good luck then.

RAFAYEL: You're making light of this in vain. Let's see if you're still smiling once it's over.

MARKOSYAN (*smiling*): Only one person makes threats in this office, Comrade Avetyan. Only one.

The scene changes to RAFAYEL AVETYAN's *house.*

VIGEN (*agitated*): Who's this Mnakyan? Mom said he's an acquaintance of yours. Is that right? He said he could help me get through the entrance exams.

RAFAYEL: Mnakyan's not an acquaintance, Son. He's a close friend. Not only can he help, he can guarantee you'll be accepted.

VIGEN: You're so laid back about the whole thing. Every applicant needs pull to get in, right?

RAFAYEL: Pull, and more—

VIGEN: Money?

RAFAYEL: Loads of money. You know, money?

VIGEN: I wasn't born yesterday.

RAFAYEL: So you know. (*Caught off guard*) And without my bringing up the subject? Absolutely right. (*He shouts.*) Anahit!

VIGEN: What's up, Dad? Did I say something wrong?

RAFAYEL: No. Not at all. But why should you be right? (*He shouts angrily.*) Anahit! [*To* VIGEN] What else do you know? (*He somehow manages to control himself. Putting the best face on it*) Vigen, it doesn't always work that way. If Mnakyan helps you, he'll get you in through his connections.

VIGEN: Why are you making such a big deal out of it?

RAFAYEL: I don't want you to go with the flow and follow the crowd. You need to make your own road in life.

VIGEN: But if you don't dress like them, think like them, and live like them, you're out.

RAFAYEL: I don't believe my ears. You grew up before my eyes, and I never realized . . . I can't forgive myself for being so blind. I only saw you getting taller and the stubble forming on your chin. And when your last birthday came round I suddenly said to myself, my boy's growing up. I should have realized your mind was maturing as well.

VIGEN: So I'm not a kid anymore. Big deal, Dad. Now tell me, is Mnakyan going to come through or not?

ANAHIT'S VOICE: Phone, Rafik.

RAFAYEL: Off you go, Vigen.

VIGEN: I'm going nowhere without Mnakyan.

RAFAYEL (*picking up the receiver*): I knew it was you. What about the pipes? Have you sent them? Who went with them? What do you mean, nobody? Are the pipes going to sprout tongues to talk their way through the red tape? Get in your car right now and catch up with the train. Yeah, yeah, if push comes to shove, you'll be on the road for three months. Your family's not going to pine away. What are they going to miss, your pea-sized brain? You can sleep with the pipes. Don't let me see you without the rails. We can't make any progress without them. If you can't take the heat, go ahead, send in an application for transfer. (*He lays down the receiver.*) Idiot.

ARSEN (*coming in*): Rafik, let me have your car to go for a checkup. My blood sugar's way up.

RAFAYEL: Okay, Dad. Gegham'll take you, as soon as he gets back. (*To* VIGEN) If your head's screwed on right, you'll pass the test with flying colors, no matter who grades it. After all, the professor's human too. Out of twenty-four hours, surely he can be human for fifteen minutes, can't he? I want you to be one of the exceptions to get in under your own steam, Son. By the sweat of your brow. That way you'll have done it yourself, without depending on others.

VIGEN: What if I don't pass?

RAFAYEL: That means you're mediocre. You couldn't pass muster. So you'll just try again next year. No matter what it takes till you're admitted on your own merits. You may get a couple of bloody noses, but you'll have the satisfaction of making it on your own.

(ANAHIT *comes in.*)

ANAHIT (*overhearing their conversation, frightened*): He'll have to do military service.

ARSEN: So what? We served, too, and we're the better for it.

RAFAYEL: He's right. The army'll make a man of him.

VIGEN: Okay, say I make it on my own, does being a rugged individualist mean going without a proper suit or shoes?

RAFAYEL: Your mother'll give you something out of the household allowance. I don't need any hints from you that I'm not doing right by you. I'm doing the best I can. I don't have to tell you how hard I work, day and night. And I make a pretty decent living. What can I do if we're struggling to make ends meet?

VIGEN: Maybe Mom could get a job.

RAFAYEL: You really are street-smart. That's none of your business. I'm surprised at you, Vigen.

VIGEN: I was just asking, that's all.

ANAHIT: I'm very disappointed in you. So you think taking care of a home isn't a full-time job?

RAFAYEL (*ironically*): You see, Anahit, how much more sense sons have than their fathers. Did we ever have time to enjoy life when we were your age, Son? Maybe we were born at the wrong time. Maybe that was our fate. Just don't pretend you have it so different from us. No, Son, we knew what life was about. We saw and heard a thing or two, things that never enter your head. That's what life's really all about, Son. You young people haven't a clue.

VIGEN: I know you saw war and starvation. You ate rinds and peels. You spent all night standing in line. You wore galoshes. Is that what made a man out of you? Am I to blame there's no war and starvation now? Is it my fault I don't wear galoshes?

RAFAYEL: It's not your fault, Son. But I wasn't to blame either for wearing my friend's old worn suit when I married your mother. Even now I only buy a new suit once every five years. So, should your mother work at her age so I can buy one every four years and you can have a new one every year? (*He seizes* VIGEN *by the collar.*) Listen, Son, if you don't learn how to live within your means, you'll never be happy in life, even if you're a millionaire.

VIGEN: Stop lecturing me. I'm tired of hearing the same thing every day. (*He takes hold of his father's hand, which is tightly gripping his neck and pushes it away.*)

(RAFAYEL *looks at him in astonishment.*)

Sorry, Dad. You were hurting me. Sorry.

(RAFAYEL *smiles, helpless and dismayed.*)

Sorry, Dad. I didn't mean to.

RAFAYEL (*taking out his wallet in confusion and handing* VIGEN *money*): Here, go and get yourself whatever you want. Your mother'll give it to me out of her allowance later.

VIGEN: I'll need more than that. You can't get what I want off the rack. I'll have to get it on the black market.

RAFAYEL (*still dazed*): Sure, sure. Here. Take this, too. If you need more, you can have it. I don't know the going rate.

VIGEN: That's enough. See you later. Sorry, Dad, about . . . you know. You were really hurting me. (*He goes out, followed by* ARSEN.)

RAFAYEL: Anahit! Vigen's a good boy, a very good boy. He's decent, bright. Does he have a girlfriend?

(ANAHIT *shakes her head.*)

No? He's a good boy. That's what I thought. We did a fine job raising him. He's okay. (*Suddenly he shouts.*) He knows how to bargain. Even with his father . . . sort of subtly. And did you see the kind of strength he had? I don't know how he got so strong. He saw I was vulnerable and started bargaining to get over the awkwardness of the situation. To save his father's face, he acknowledged my authority. And I, your husband, Anahit, flattered him by giving him lots of money to keep our father-son relationship intact. [*Returning to his normal tone of voice*] He asked for money, and I gave him some. That's all it was. Nothing more to it. No use imagining anything more. [*Musing*] You know, his suit did look out of date. The guys he hangs out with all wear the latest. So, Anahit, everything's okay.

ANAHIT: Seriously, Rafik, why shouldn't I get a job? I made an excellent housewife. I'm sure I could do just as well in the job market. [*Raising her hand to keep* RAFAYEL *from interrupting.*] Don't try to shut me up as you do others.

RAFAYEL: Okay, Anahit. Go ahead. I'm in a mild panic. But go ahead.

ANAHIT: You remember, when we got married, I left dentistry and devoted my whole life to you.

RAFAYEL: So?

ANAHIT: I learned how to match your shirts and ties.

RAFAYEL: Out with it, Woman. What are you getting at?

ANAHIT: I want the old you, Rafik, the man I married thirty years ago. No sooner were we married than I couldn't say hello to any other man. You wouldn't allow me to take the trolley-bus. What would have happened if someone had touched your wife? You forced me to quit work so I'd have no contact with people.

RAFAYEL: Would you have wanted me to be jealous all these years, you, a woman above reproach?

ANAHIT: I want you to pay more attention—to show more interest than before.

RAFAYEL: Haven't I always been there for you?

ANAHIT: How do you know what *I've* been up to?

RAFAYEL: Mind your tongue!

ANAHIT: You can say things about me, but I can't say things about you? If you ask me, you've got a lot to answer for.

RAFAYEL: Have you had your say? (*He embraces her.*) You're still beautiful, Anahit, believe me. The whole time I've wanted you all for myself, not out charming dental patients. If anyone gives you the come-on, do you know what I'd do? If you hadn't given up work, I wouldn't have been the man I am, and the father of our children.

ANAHIT: You must be kidding, Rafik.

RAFAYEL: Would I kid you?

(ARSEN *comes in.*)

ARSEN: Rafik, what are those bulldozers doing in our street. They're not building a skyscraper, are they? Go to the city council and complain they've overlooked the historical status of our neighborhood. There's virtually none of the old parts of town left. Better take me with you.

RAFAYEL: No need, Dad. I'll go myself.

ARSEN: See you talk to an older clerk. The young ones don't have any sense of nostalgia. Who gives a crap today about Kond, Kozer, Ghantar, Afrikov, and the other famous old quarters of town. They really knew how to build houses in those days. Ah . . .

(*The telephone rings.*)

RAFAYEL: I'll tell them, Dad.

ARSEN: I know you will, my boy. If you set your mind to do something, you do it.

(*He goes out.*)

RAFAYEL (*picking up the receiver*): Did that fool go yet? I feel sorry for him, but what can I do if he's an idiot. I told him, didn't I, to send someone with the pipes. We have to receive shipment of the rails on time, Vanik. Tie a knot in your handkerchief. Even if you get knotted yourself. Though you have to steal them before their very eyes. He'll come through. He's a fool, but he's a sharp bastard. If he weren't so cunning, why would I keep him on? Don't you go hanging your head. I put a high price on you, too. You're no less crafty. Hang in there. (*He hangs up, sits down on the sofa, and starts to read the paper.*) Anahit, see if you can find the lottery tickets we put in one of these books. Check the numbers against the draw in the newspaper. People ask why I do the lottery. Well, you can't win if you don't play. Have you found it? Great. Check it then.

(ANAHIT *checks the lottery tickets.*)

(RAFAYEL *feigns indifference and continues reading his paper.*)

ANAHIT: We're in with a chance. The first number matches.

RAFAYEL: Close the ventilator, there's a draft. Pass me my glasses. You get all excited and then become frustrated afterward. Watch I don't miss the time for my next pills.

ANAHIT: We've got that one, too. Yes, yes. (*She cries.*) We've won, Rafik. We've won!

RAFAYEL: What've we won? Sure, maybe a sewing machine, if we're lucky.

ANAHIT: Rafik, we've won a Zhiguli with air conditioning.

RAFAYEL: Okay. Don't go jumping over the moon.

ANAHIT: Darling Rafik, we've won!

RAFAYEL: You see. Sometimes we can get lucky, too. It's not for nothing people say, when God closes a door, he opens a window.

ANAHIT (*excited*): If all goes well, we'll sell this Zhiguli and get some ready cash. It'll be a tidy sum, I'm sure.

RAFAYEL: I'll say. It'll be the cost price of the car and double that on the black market.

ANAHIT: Do we need all that money, Rafik? Let's not get in over our heads.

RAFAYEL: But, Anahit, who buys a car these days at the manufacturer's list price? I'm not against what you say. Honesty's a good thing, don't get me wrong. But idiocy's nothing to brag about either. Are we saints, or what?

ANAHIT: You know best, Rafik. You're the man of the house.

RAFAYEL: Get on the phone. Call your family, call your friends. Make everybody happy.

ANAHIT: Of course. Right away. There's nothing worse than keeping your joy to yourself.

RAFAYEL: Maybe I should look through the rest of the tickets? Now that we've begun, I might as well finish the job.

(ANAHIT *goes out.*)

(RAFAYEL *continues looking through the tickets in a perfunctory way. Suddenly he cries out.*) Anahit, Anahit, we've won! As sure's I'm sitting here, we've won. (*To himself*) Wow, how did this come about? What a real stroke of luck! Anahit!

(ANAHIT *rushes in, in amazement.*)

(RAFAYEL *beams with joy.*) Check the ticket against the paper.

ANAHIT: What've we won?

RAFAYEL: A fridge, a Saratov. A neat little fridge.

ANAHIT: What's got into you? You hardly made a squeak over the Zhiguli, and now you're making a big deal out of a small fridge. What am I going to do with a Saratov?

HASMIK (*entering in a joyful mood, almost running, carrying a paper*): It's in the press. It'll appear tomorrow. Here are the proofs. (*Seeing her father, she falls into an embarrassed silence.*)

RAFAYEL: A daughter of mine, a published author. What is it, a poem, a short story, a review?

ANAHIT: Hasmik and I placed a personal ad in the *Rainbow* magazine. She's looking for a husband.

RAFAYEL (*He snatches the paper out of his daughter's hand and reads.*): "Twenty-seven years old, divorced, no children, lives with parents, college degree. Height: one meter 70; weight: 65 kilos." (*Furious*) What kind of a caption is *Keen to Marry*? You'll make a laughingstock out of me. I'll never be able to live this down. (*He quotes.*) "Seeking to marry a handsome young man, 28–30, attractive, college graduate, professional, likes poetry and music, tall, with sky-blue eyes, and black hair, has an apartment with ambience. Contact Hasmik Avetyan, Box 212, c/o Central Post Office." How did you come up with such a vulgar scheme?

HASMIK: Daddy—

RAFAYEL: Don't Daddy me. You're sending a brazen solicitation to men. And it's some hell of an invitation. Why didn't you come right out and say, "I implore you. Please come and marry my one meter 70 height and 65 kilograms weight."

HASMIK: The ad department at the magazine wrote it up. I had nothing to do with it.

ANAHIT: Don't forget, Rafik. You precipitated your daughter's divorce. "I won't allow my daughter to live in poverty." Does that ring a bell? You're trying to train your son to live modestly. Why should your daughter have a life of luxury?

RAFAYEL: I didn't say "a life of luxury." I said a normal life. Not on two hundred and ten rubles, with both of them working.

ANAHIT: What could the poor boy do? Steal?

RAFAYEL: I don't know. Maybe people like that can run the country, but they can't keep house.

ANAHIT: So your whole family should live honestly, except him? It doesn't make sense. It didn't then, and it doesn't now.

(*The phone rings.*)

(ANAHIT *picks up the receiver and answers with annoyance.*) What's that? What do you want? There's no *katanka.*[1] What can I do about it? Let the industrial complex grind to a halt. It's already at a standstill . . . Even if it's my father's house they were building, they wouldn't move any faster. You'd think *katanka* was the only thing they're out of and they're swimming in everything else.

RAFAYEL (*removing the receiver from her hands*): What on earth do you want from me? I haven't been sick in years. Now I'm off sick and I'm on sick leave. Don't I have the right? To hell with your factory. (*He puts down the receiver, pensively.*) So there's still no *katanka*? I don't know what the hell to do.

HASMIK: Let's end the talk about my marriage. I married him, but I didn't love him. I'm to blame for everything. No one else.

RAFAYEL (*embracing his daughter*): Thank you, my girl. Thank you. People often like to blame their misfortunes on others. It's the easy way out. Still, if it'll help, I'll take the blame.

HASMIK (*pulling back from his embrace, and walking away*): Don't do me any favors, Dad. I'm not blaming anyone.

---

1. *Katanka* refers to a type of rolled sheet metal employed for various industrial purposes.

RAFAYEL: Hasmik, did you know we won a fridge?

HASMIK: What sort of fridge?

RAFAYEL: A Saratov. In the lottery.

ANAHIT: Never mind about the fridge. Tell her about the Zhiguli, Rafik.

HASMIK: What Zhiguli?

ANAHIT: We've won a Zhiguli, Hasmik. A Zhiguli. With air conditioning. For thirty kopecks. Can you imagine?

HASMIK: I don't believe it. A Zhiguli?

ANAHIT: I didn't believe it either.

RAFAYEL: Why don't you get out there and find a husband yourself, Hasmik? Any man would fall for you on your good looks alone.

HASMIK: I don't know, Dad. It doesn't always work out like that.

RAFAYEL: What do you mean, "it doesn't work out?" You must have met a guy you liked. So go for it. Grab hold of happiness. Take a chance. What can you lose?

HASMIK: I don't know what you're driving at, Dad?

ANAHIT: What's got into you, Rafik?

RAFAYEL: I'm talking about happiness, real happiness. What's there not to under-stand? The happiness life owes us. Everyone of us should be happy. Look at Hasmik. "It doesn't work out." So she throws in the towel. This ad's an admission of failure before the world. I'll show you what to do. (*Suddenly he embraces his daughter again.*) Pick a guy, any guy, and I guarantee he'll marry you. Do you hear me? Guarantee. He'll declare his love for you on bended knee. He'll grovel before you. Just say the word and I'll do it. Forget about this piece of trash. Okay?

(HASMIK *breaks away from her father's embrace and runs out;* RAFAYEL *and* ANAHIT *are silent.*)

How do you think I handled it? I mean, really? I can't read your mind. I want to know. Am I right or wrong?

ANAHIT: Wrong. Call Mnakyan, Rafik.

RAFAYEL: Wrong for parents to solve their children's problems day and night. When they were students, we did their homework for them. We got them admitted to the university, and now we're running their family life, too. Small wonder they're so late maturing these days. It's only after they're fifty they can take on any serious work. We do everything for them and then wonder why they can't do a thing.

ANAHIT: That doesn't mean we should throw Vigen into the lions' den to survive by his wits.

RAFAYEL: That's the only way to learn.

ANAHIT: He'll be eaten alive before he learns anything.

RAFAYEL: That's the risk you take in life.

(RAFAYEL's *sister,* ELEONORA, *and her two children come in, carrying two suitcases.*)

ELEONORA (*scolding him*): Remember me? It's me. Your sister, Eleonora. And these are your nieces. This one's Elya and that's Nora. [*To the children*] This is your Uncle Rafik.

RAFAYEL: What's up? Why are you giving me such a hard time?

NORA: Mom and Dad have broken up again.

ELYA: Because Daddy's cheating on Mom.

RAFAYEL: Good for you, Sis. You've done a good job educating them.

ELEONORA: Don't you like us? You don't even know where we live. If only you'd come over once in a while. You'd have been a positive influence on the kids. And you could have stood up for your sister and taught that moron a thing or two. (*In tears*) The whole city envies me for having a brother like you. So get me a decent job. I have to work to support these kids. They're both high flyers at school and help out a lot at home. Guess who they take after? Give me a hundred rubles. I'll pay you back. When I get the job. We can't go back to that house.

RAFAYEL: So, stay here.

ANAHIT: Stay, stay. Your brother's house is your house.

ELEONORA: Oh hi, Anahit dear. You look great. Maybe a little heavier? (*To* RAFAYEL) How's your father? Does he still get around?

RAFAYEL: He's fine, Eleonora Arsenovna.

ANAHIT: Okay, okay. Don't start again. Let's go, Elya. Come on, kids.

ELEONORA: This is my luck, Rafik. (*Taking the suitcases*) They saw me off, and now they've seen me back again.

(*They all leave.*)

RAFAYEL (*to himself*): You're welcome. Welcome.

(*The doorbell rings.*)

Anahit, it's Vigen, home with the good news. Go congratulate your son. He's through. I was right about him, and I'll prove myself right about you, too, Hasmik. I'm always right.

(HAMO *comes in, accompanied by* KARAPETYAN, *a personable young man.* HAMO *carries a large bunch of carnations.* RAFAYEL, *taken by surprise, looks quizzically at* HAMO.)

HAMO: This is Karapetyan, boss. The one I said was a man of gold.

RAFAYEL: Hello, Comrade Karapetyan. Hamo's told me a lot about you. Sit down. (*Taking* HAMO *aside*) Hamo, I've got a job for you.

HAMO: Fine, boss. You know me.

RAFAYEL: It's a tough one.

HAMO: Right up my alley.

RAFAYEL: Ever heard of the *Rainbow* magazine?

HAMO: Isn't it the supplement to the *Evening Erevan*?

RAFAYEL: Tomorrow morning's edition mustn't get into circulation.

HAMO: I'll buy the whole run.

RAFAYEL: What? All of it?

HAMO: I can't do anything about subscribers, boss. That's beyond my powers, and yours too, boss.

RAFAYEL: Buy whatever you can. Price is no object. Take them to your summer-house. I want the pleasure of setting fire to them myself.

HAMO: Why did you say just now I'd told you a lot about Karapetyan? I only saw the guy's face for the first time today.

RAFAYEL: I just felt like saying it. So he took the money.

HAMO: No.

RAFAYEL: He didn't take it. (*Exultant*) See! You think you can buy and sell everybody. He's fresh out of college. See, he had your number. I guess you're not the fast-talking fixer you thought you were.

HAMO [*laughing*]: The joke's on you, boss. He took it.

(RAFAYEL *is dumbfounded and undergoes a dark mood swing.*)

RAFAYEL (*sneering*): Swindlers, twisters. And you call yourselves men. Low-life bastards.

HAMO: Who are you talking about, boss?

RAFAYEL: Thieves, bloodsuckers, filthy swines.

HAMO: What's the problem, boss?

RAFAYEL: Did you give him a lot?

HAMO: So much he started to cry. (*He looks at* KARAPETYAN) You cried, didn't you?

(KARAPETYAN *has pressed the briefcase tightly between his knees.*)

RAFAYEL (*pointing to the briefcase*): Holds a lot, I can see. Czech, isn't it?

KARAPETYAN (*confused*): It's mine.

RAFAYEL: It's yours? It looks very Czech. (*Pause*) Do you have any children?

KARAPETYAN: Two.

RAFAYEL (*playing cat and mouse with* KARAPETYAN): I expect you sit them on your lap a lot. You must be very fond of them. You take care they don't fall. Though why should they fall—

HAMO: Any parent would do that.

RAFAYEL: Ah, tell me. Were there many violations at the construction works?

KARAPETYAN: The usual routine stuff.

RAFAYEL: There's bound to be some shortcoming, surely. (*He pours cognac only for himself.*) To your health! You're on the job, or I'd offer you one. (*He drinks.*)

KARAPETYAN (*mumbling*): Enjoy.

RAFAYEL: So what have you got to say? Just what do you have to tell me?

KARAPETYAN: What's there to tell, Comrade Avetyan.

RAFAYEL: Then I'll tell you something. I've just won a fridge in the lottery.

KARAPETYAN: Congratulations.

RAFAYEL: Small, compact. A Saratov.

KARAPETYAN: Good. Well, I'd better be on my way, Comrade Avetyan.

RAFAYEL: What's your hurry? We're sitting here enjoying ourselves, shooting the breeze. So no violations, huh? An inspector goes to a construction works and finds nothing wrong? You seem like a decent guy. Where are you from?

KARAPETYAN: From the Kalinino district.[2]

RAFAYEL: Where exactly?

KARAPETYAN: The village of Sarchapet.

RAFAYEL: So you're a country lad, eh? That's good. When they talk about "the people," they mean people like you.

HAMO: Villager Hambo's household got into a fight.[3]

RAFAYEL: I'm not a villager. I was born in Erevan. On Amiryan Street, right in the center of things. [*Getting down to business*] By the way, what's the lowdown on that alleged violation in the pay code regarding one of my workers?

KARAPETYAN: Paperwork was filed to issue a paycheck to a worker on leave at a state spa.

RAFAYEL: What? They paid a worker his salary when he was on leave at a state spa? At a state spa? (*Threateningly*) Hamo!

HAMO : A subcontractor was—

(*He doesn't get a chance to finish what he has to say.* RAFAYEL *lunges at him.*)

RAFAYEL: Well I never. Paying a worker at a state spa. Is that a fact?

KARAPETYAN: Don't concern yourself, Comrade Avetyan. The money wasn't appropriated—

RAFAYEL: To a worker. A worker on leave at a state spa.

KARAPETYAN: Contain yourself, Comrade Avetyan. They didn't appropriate the money.

RAFAYEL (*He lets* HAMO *go and moves toward* KARAPETYAN.): Really? I almost had a heart attack. Good you clarified it. So, Hamo, the money wasn't appropriated.

---

2. A region of the Armenian Republic near Lake Sevan.

3. An allusion from the short story "Gikor" by the Armenian poet Hovhannes Tumanian (1869–1923).

Too bad you didn't come across anything major. By bringing it to our attention you'd have done us a good turn. We're only human, right? We need all the help we can get.

KARAPETYAN: Next time, Comrade Avetyan.

RAFAYEL: You'd like to inspect our plant again? (*Pause. He looks long at* KARA-PETYAN *from head to toe, scrutinizing him carefully.*) Let me see that report. (RAFAYEL *takes the report from* KARAPETYAN, *folds it up carefully, and puts it in his breast pocket.*) So then, let me tell you the major infractions we're committing. The kind all inspectors dream of exposing.

KARAPETYAN: No, no. There's no need. I believe —

RAFAYEL: Just listen to this. Four kilometers of rail track were scheduled to have been laid to link the industrial line to the trunk line. Those four kilometers were a joke. A toy railway. According to our calculations, it should be thirteen. And it's needed right now. First to complete the complex as fast as possible. Then after it's built, to deliver raw materials from the main line on time and pick up blue-collar workers from the surrounding villages. Otherwise, what's the point, if we're pinning our hopes on that one village alone. So we're now laying thirteen kilometers of track. Not four. Do you grasp the consequences? Have you ever seen an infraction on that scale in your life?

KARAPETYAN: It could be subject to legal proceedings.

RAFAYEL: If you're afraid of wolves, keep out of the forest.

KARAPETYAN: But you're jeopardizing your career, Comrade Avetyan.

RAFAYEL: Don't worry about me. You've more need to worry about yourself.

KARAPETYAN: But why?

RAFAYEL: What do you mean, why?

KARAPETYAN: Why are you sticking your neck out like this?

RAFAYEL: What neck? What danger? I'm doing something necessary and worthwhile. I'm doing what some namby-pamby guy sitting behind a desk doesn't dare leastwise understand. But I understand. My head works. What shall I do? Cut it off? Do you think I'm doing it for my own good?

KARAPETYAN: Well, who for?

RAFAYEL: What do you mean, who for? For your two children. I don't want to build a huge factory that serves no real purpose. My conscience won't allow it. Yeah, that's right. My conscience. Does that seem bizarre to you? Isn't this my country? (*The phone rings.* RAFAYEL *picks up the receiver.*) Who's this? Who? Who? Oh, it's you, Mnakyan. Quickly—what did he score? . . . Passed with flying colors? Well done. Did you pass him the envelope with the sweetener? . . . Thanks, Mnakyan. Thanks a million. Wait a minute, why am I thanking you? Wouldn't I do the same for you? Good you remember what I did for you in the past. (*He puts down the receiver. To* KARAPETYAN.) I know what you're thinking. And you've a right to. I don't have a high opinion of myself either.

But the fate of the country rests on shoulders like mine, not yours. Hand over the money.

KARAPETYAN (*Bluffing, as though misunderstanding*): What money?

RAFAYEL: Come on, hand it over. Don't play dumb. (*Grabbing him by the collar*) When you woke up this morning you were an honest, decent man. Why do you want to wake up tomorrow a crook? Isn't it a shame you didn't resist the temptation for a minute. Even one rotten minute, Karapetyan. No! You had to come here and be humiliated? You were a man above reproach. Now you're a piece of shit! If you were a man, you'd throw all that money down and spit in my face. That moment of triumph would have been worth all this wealth. Sure, with all the wheeling and dealing I've had to do, I've forgotten what that triumphant pleasure feels like. But you? It's not too late. Go on, spit at me. You can't offend me. After all, it's easy to take money from Hamo. Who the hell's Hamo to incriminate anybody?

HAMO (*sneering*): Who the hell's Hamo—

RAFAYEL: All right, Karapetyan, hand over the money. I could tear it out of your hands. But that wouldn't be nice. You have to hand it over to me yourself. (KARAPETYAN *takes the briefcase in both hands and extends it to* RAFAYEL, *who does not take it.* RAFAYEL *is silent and looks at him for a long moment.*) Are you giving it back out of fear? (KARAPETYAN *shakes his head.*) Tell me the truth. If you're doing it out of fear, it's all pointless.

(KARAPETYAN *shakes his head.*)

Keep it. Keep it. You have a wife and kids. Go and have a decent life. Who the hell knows? Maybe it's the right thing to do. Keep it. Seriously, from my heart. Get out of here.

(KARAPETYAN *again extends the briefcase to him.* RAFAYEL *smiles gently and takes it.*)

KARAPETYAN: Thank you, Comrade Avetyan. I . . . I . . .

RAFAYEL: That's enough. Thank *you*, Comrade Karapetyan.

(KARAPETYAN *runs out, as if relieved of a heavy burden.*)

HAMO (*puzzled*) The jerk gave it back.

RAFAYEL: Hamo, tell them to continue working nights on the track. We'll distribute this money to the workers. Everyone should get a bonus equal to his regular wages. Don't give it off the books. Make them sign for it. Then tear up the sheet and throw it away. Distribute every last kopeck of the dough in this briefcase. I keep close tabs on my money.

HAMO: Sure, sure, boss. Oh I gave the carnations to Auntie Anahit.

RAFAYEL: Don't call her "Auntie." She hates it.

HAMO: Mrs. Anahit. If you like, I'll bring you a hundred fresh carnations a day.

RAFAYEL: Get going, Hamo. And never set foot in this house again.

HAMO: Whatever you say, boss. (*He leaves.*)

VIGEN (*coming in*): I got shot down in flames, Dad . . . Didn't you hear me? And I made such a fuss about connections. Well, there you are. The examiner took the money and flunked me.

RAFAYEL: Look me in the eye. You're putting me on, right? You knew your stuff. You couldn't have failed.

VIGEN (*bursting out laughing*): You're right, Dad. Sure, I was well prepared and Mnakyan must have worked his magic. I passed with flying colors.

RAFAYEL: Really, Vigen? Tell me the truth. You're not trying to kid me? (*Moved, patting his son on the back*) Well done, Son. Congratulations. Congratulations on your first success on your own steam. As for that Mnakyan. Do you hear me? Forget about him.

VIGEN: But the guy gave me a leg up. If it hadn't been for him, even with eyes in the back of my head I'd never have gotten through the exam.

RAFAYEL: Never mind about Mnakyan. You made it on your own. Everybody's got a Mnakyan. That's how things are done. But I know in my heart that you have what it takes. You always showed promise from elementary school on. So don't give undue credit to anyone else. You did it, and I'm proud of you, Son. We've got even more to celebrate. We've won a fridge, Vigen, a Saratov. Yeah, and a Zhiguli.

VIGEN: A Zhiguli?

RAFAYEL: A Zhiguli with air conditioning.

VIGEN: This is too much, Dad. A pass in physics and a Zhiguli, too.

RAFAYEL: Pretty soon we'll be coming into a bit of money, and we'll be able to get some decent duds. I know you think your pop's old fashioned and has no sense of style. But just you wait, Son. I'll show you.

VIGEN: You're okay, Dad.

RAFAYEL (*taken by surprise*): Oh yeah?

VIGEN: You bet.

(RAFAYEL *discretely wipes away some tears.* ARSEN *comes in.*)

ARSEN (*He comes in and kisses his grandson's brow*): Good for you, Son. You'll grow up to be a big shot like your father.

(VIGEN *goes out.*)

Good for you, Rafik. You gave me a great sense of accomplishment.

RAFAYEL: How so, Dad?

ARSEN: You know. You said you'd look into Sahak's case. With no further ado, they raised his pension. They didn't get a measly kopeck. And the deadbeat clerk got fired.

RAFAYEL: But I haven't spoken to anybody yet.

ARSEN: Really?

RAFAYEL: Really.

ARSEN: How's that, then? When the old geezers on the block heard about the raise, they wanted to come see you. I told them, "Hey boys, he's not a member of parliament." But they insisted you're no less of a man. There's no way out of it, Rafik. I think you've got to do something to help them.

RAFAYEL (*with a sad smile*): Sit down, Dad. I'd like to talk to you.

ARSEN: Fire away, Rafik.

RAFAYEL: Tell me what happened in 1928 when they sent supplies by train from Russia . . . you know, and you had to keep an eye on them.

ARSEN: Sure, why not? You're very fond of that story. I don't know why. Well, as you were saying, I was keeping an eye on things. Me, pegleg Arsho—oh yes, and my buddy foxy Garsevan. And just our luck, the winter that year was atrociously cold. We were stuck between starvation on the one hand, and bitter cold on the other—

RAFAYEL (*suddenly*): Just a minute, Dad. Get up, let's go. Upsy daisy, Dad.

(*He takes his father carefully by the hand and guides him along.*)

RAFAYEL's *construction works: comptroller's Office*

RAFAYEL *has brought his father with him and sits opposite him.*

RAFAYEL: Tell your story, Dad. Let them hear it.

ARSEN: It was back in 1928. Supplies had been sent from Russia by train. We were keeping an eye on it. Me, pegleg Arsho, and foxy Garsevan. And just our luck, the winter that year was atrocious. With starvation on the one hand, and bitter cold on the other. And we had no heavy clothes. Whatever we had, we bundled up in. We were young and hardy in those days. Besides, we knew that was the way of the world. It was going to be bitter cold with a lot of starvation. On empty bellies we guarded the loaded train night and day. Nobody thought of breaking into it. Sure, we'd joke about it. One day, someone did think of it. The devil tempted foxy Garsevan. Suddenly we noticed a biscuit fall out of his pocket. He looked at us, scared. You won't believe it, but we were even more scared. We emptied his pockets and found four more.

VANIK (*in* RUBEN's *ear*): Four biscuits? What's he wasting our time for?

RAFAYEL: Shut up. Listen carefully. Go on, Dad.

ARSEN: We took the five biscuits and turned them in, and called the whole village to Foxy's trial. From that day on, Garso never showed his face. He packed up everything and left the village. Every now and then we'd remember him, but we couldn't get our tongues round the word "fox." We used to call him that out of love. Then we really felt sorry for him, I guess.

RAFAYEL (*to the chauffeur*): Gegham, take Dad home.

(*With the utmost care, they lead the old man out.* ARSEN *does not quite know where he has come and why he told that story. He entrusts himself to these strangers' caring hands and goes out confused.*)

Well, you heard my father. But what did you learn? . . . Okay, here goes. Avetyan's not going to be your servant or wait on you hand and foot. Shape up or ship out. You have to go and get what you need. If you can't get it, I'll get rid of you. I'll get rid of you all, one by one. From tomorrow on, we're working by the book. I'll give the orders, you carry them out. *Katanka, katanka!* I'm round the bend with *katanka*. Go and build the thing without *katanka*. Make the concrete without cement. Bring the water without a pipe. Lay the track without rails. Learn to work by the rules. If they give us the materials, we'll build. If not, we can't.

CREW MEMBER: Give us the word, and we'll quit work.

RAFAYEL: Who said that? Who was it? You'll work all right. And how. Don't blame the regulations for your lack of ability, as if you could perform miracles if they weren't there to restrict you. We all need discipline today, like air and water. Every day we need a new dose of it. They ought to spoonfeed it to people, like codliver oil. The only thing we need today is discipline—at home, in the street, in the office. Discipline, only discipline.

(*Some voices are raised in dissatisfaction and gradually blend into a hum. Just at that moment, as if he had planned his entry to the minute, the old treasurer comes in.*)

TREASURER: All of you, get yourselves to my office on the double to receive your bonus for this quarter. I'm not allowed to keep money in my desk overnight and I'm leaving at seven.

AVETYAN's *house*

(ANAHIT, ARSEN, *the* AUNT, BENO, ELEONORA, *her two children, and one or two neighbors and friends are sitting around the kitchen table.*)

AUNT (*passing her plate*): I'd love some, Anahit. Put some on Beno's plate, too. Eat up, Beno. Eat up, don't be bashful. This is our house, too.

BENO: Unemployment's killed my appetite.

AUNT: Rafik'll see you'll get a job in the buffet.

NEIGHBOR: Rafik, let's drink to good neighborliness. I hope I'll always be welcome in this house.

ELEONORA: Just a minute, don't drink. Elya, first you. Just listen, Rafik.

ELYA (*She stands up and immediately begins to recite.*):

> Look, the in-laws are in the hall,
> Ano, Eghso, and Nushi, too.
> They've come to see the dowry on cue
> Before they agree to marry the doll.

GUEST: Rafik, you're an educated man. Are the bears at the North Pole gradually dying out?

RAFAYEL: Yeah, that's right. (*To* ANAHIT) Who's that?

(ANAHIT *shrugs her shoulders.*)

ARSEN: I propose a toast to Vigen. He passed with flying colors.

ELEONORA: One minute, please. Don't drink yet. Nora, now it's your turn. Just listen to this, Rafik.

NORA (*She stands and immediately begins to recite.*):

> I want to be an engineer,
> In policeman's blue or fireman's red.
> A school director has no peer,
> But I'll be an architect instead.

(*She cannot remember the rest and sits down in tears.*)

AUNT: Don't worry, Beno. Rafik'll find you a job in the buffet.

(*The telephone rings, as a relief.*)

RAFAYEL (*getting up and quickly leaving the kitchen*): Hello, Hayk. Congratulations? What for? . . . Me, deputy minister? You're out of your mind. Hayk, thanks a lot. I'm very touched, but that makes no sense. I don't know how you set it up, but take it down the same way. I don't want it, no. That's all. I just don't want it. You didn't arrange it? Well, then, who did? Who else knows my predicament? Besides, I've had a heart attack. And the position's not like going to a state spa. Anushyan'd make a perfect candidate. He's wanted a shot at the job for years. Why offend the guy? Can't I say something good about an enemy? If I'm giving it to my enemy, I must really not want it. Of course, I know him well. We were in the same graduating class. He even proposed to Anahit. You can say she's lucky to have turned him down. It's not for me to say. Let's see which one of us is right.

(*He hangs up and sees* ANAHIT.)

ANAHIT: They want you for deputy minister and you refuse?

RAFAYEL: It's none of your business.

ANAHIT: Whose business is it then? Only yours?

RAFAYEL: Anahit, don't get me riled up. Don't meddle in my affairs.

ANAHIT: What are you running from? The position, the office, the high life? You don't know any of them. Where are you running to?

RAFAYEL: Leave me alone, please. I have to quash this business.

ANAHIT (*With heavy irony*): You've had your fill of living high on the hog. Of course, you're tired of the good things in life. Maybe you're even sick to your stomach of them. That's so like you.

RAFAYEL: Did you want me to say I'm fed up and tired of you?

ANAHIT: I'm going to see Hayk. He's the only one who can straighten you out.

RAFAYEL: Don't you dare, Anahit. If you do, don't bother coming home.

ANAHIT: I'm going, Rafik. With a warped mind like yours, you still need me.

RAFAYEL: Anahit, don't you understand what's happening? They're washing their hands of me. They want to put an end to the headaches I've given them. They couldn't care less about the thirteen kilometers of rail link, even though they know I'm right about it. And that's exactly why they want to make life even more difficult for me. Don't you understand, Anahit? They're kicking me upstairs to get rid of me.

(ANAHIT *is perplexed, keeps silent, and goes off with her head bent.* RAFAYEL *goes out.* VIGEN *and* HASMIK *come in.*)

VIGEN: I think the ad you put in the paper was a disgrace.

HASMIK: Try to understand me, Vigen.

VIGEN: You don't get married unless I like the guy.

HASMIK: I'm glad you're concerned. This is the first time we've sat and talked sister to brother.

VIGEN: Don't give up. Everyone gets their portion of happiness. All you have to do is reach out for it. At any cost. No one's going to give you a freebee. I'll show you how.

HASMIK: You sound like Rafayel Avetyan.

VIGEN: I sound like me. Tomorrow I'll round up my pals and go from kiosk to kiosk to buy up all the copies of the paper.

(RAFAYEL *and* HAMO *come in.*)

RAFAYEL: I want a word with Hamo in private.

(VIGEN *and* HASMIK *go out.*)

(RAFAYEL *closes the door tightly.*) Take a letter.

(HAMO *sits at a desk and writes.*)

Dear Comrade Mazmanyan: We are a group of veteran builders and learned with surprise that Rafayel Avetyan has been nominated deputy minister of public works. Have you got all that? We regard it as our duty to inform you that R. Avetyan's experience and temperament make him unsuitable for such an elevated position of responsibility.

HAMO (*continuing the letter on his own*): It is not accidental that although he has always occupied supervisory positions, he has not enjoyed the love and respect of his subordinates. Moreover, he has continually failed to complete projects within their assigned time schedule and budget, in consequence of which he has periodically been moved from one assignment to another.

RAFAYEL: You write well, Hamo.

HAMO: Comrade Avetyan, for you I can do anything.

(RAFAYEL *rushes to answer the phone.*)

RAFAYEL: Azatyan? Listen to me. What's the allocation for this quarter? Speak up, I can't hear you. We're already eight percent over budget? Document it as ninety percent. No more questions. Ninety and be done with it. We won't get a bonus? Yes we will . . . out of your pocket. We'll all pitch in. (*He puts down the receiver.*) Hamo, I suspect someone's leaking information. I'm afraid the bigwigs at the ministry will move to abort the rail link, and it'll be too late. We have to get some leverage. Something really effective. Let's go.

ARUSHANYAN'*s Office*

(ARUSHANYAN *and a few officials from the ministry have come together with doleful expressions.*)

ARUSHANYAN: It's a stroke of bad luck. What's there to say?

FIRST OFFICIAL: Even with you in place, they're going to bring in someone from outside?

SECOND OFFICIAL: After all this, how are we supposed to work with him?

ARUSHANYAN: How's *he* going to work with us? What sort of approach will he adopt?

THIRD OFFICIAL: I've thought of something . . .

(*The door turns on its hinges and* RAFAYEL *enters, followed by* HAMO *and a few other people. Without looking around,* RAFAYEL *walks straight up to* ARUSHANYAN. ARUSHANYAN *automatically stands up, rather confused.* RAFAYEL *swiftly goes up to him and slaps him without saying anything. Then he turns quickly and goes out with his companions.* ARUSHANYAN *and his colleagues, perplexed, look toward the door, which has been left open, without comprehending what has happened.* RAFAYEL AVETYAN *and his supporters triumphantly walk along the corridor of the ministry.*)

RAFAYEL: Now let's see who they appoint. At least it was good to get some revenge in the process. I had some old scores to settle with him.

Curtain

ACT 2

RAFAYEL's *construction works; comptroller's office*

(*All the construction crew is present.*)

RAFAYEL (*on the phone*): I can barely hear you, Sedrak Vardanich. Are you calling from your car? Sevan? That you should be so lucky. I don't have time to wash, far less go for a swim. I'm in a really tight spot, Sedrak. Help me out, eh? I need a wagonload of ties. No, I don't have a budget. You have to do something. I could include it in the proposed budget for our next assignment. Then you'll forget, or I will. (*He laughs.*) Yeah, we'll say we've got Alzheimer's. Is he a good guy? Okay, send him over. How's the site director? He can come, too. I'll give him the authorization. Listen, could you scare me up a thousand meters of glass? No, I've got cash flow problems there as well. But the money should come through. Friendship's for tough times, isn't it? I hear music. But it's crackling a lot. No, not the tape. Your player's no good. I can get you a new one. Not on your budget. And a dozen tapes along with it. That's what I have to offer. You also promised a roller. What happened? I know you can't give it to the industrial consortium. Yeah. You give it to our ministry. Count it as mine. I'll siphon it off. Say "You saved my bacon" then. Have a good trip, Sedrak.

(ZHANNA *enters.*)

Late again, Zhanna?

ZHANNA: Rafayel Arsenich, I almost fell under a tram.

RAFAYEL: What tram? You've already used that excuse.

ZHANNA: By the way, what do you think I saw in the store? Apple juice. My kid really loves the stuff. I just had to get her some. UNESCO has declared this year the Year of the Child, you know.

RAFAYEL: You've come up with that one, too.

ZHANNA: The utilities department suddenly turned on the hot water. Mom had a bath, then we washed Granny. Are you saying I shouldn't have jumped in, too?

RAFAYEL: I've heard that one as well. What am I going to do with you, Zhanna?

ZHANNA: Do what you like.

RAFAYEL: Enough of your crap. Sit down.

ZHANNA: Shall I put on the coffee?

RAFAYEL: No.

ZHANNA: If anyone calls, you're not in today, right?

RAFAYEL: Right. How many kilometers are left till the rail link's finished?

ARSHALUYS: Three. But we've come up against rocks.

RAFAYEL: Do you get it? Has it penetrated your thick skull that we're already at the tenth kilometer? Come on, guys. Keep it up. We're almost there.

HAMO: Guys, you can do it. Give it all you've got.

RAFAYEL: Just wait till you hear what I'm going to do for you. Not that I'm sitting around idle now. When are we going to start blasting?

VANIK: If they don't blast us out of the water first, we'll get to it tomorrow.

RAFAYEL: Enough of your riddles. Talk straight.

VANIK: I meant that Juto won't allow us. If he doesn't give permission, what are you going to do?

RAFAYEL: What's this about Juto?

VANIK: Juto's not happy about us blasting next door to his barbecue joint.

RAFAYEL: Who's this Juto fellah?

VANIK: He says he won't allow a train to pass right under his nose. Customers would run a mile from the noise.

RUBEN: It's no ordinary business, Rafayel Arsenich, it's Juto's turf. Would Juto permit us to dynamite right next to it?

RAFAYEL: I see. So Juto's not just a name, he's a force to be reckoned with. He's not afraid of me, but I'm afraid of him.

ARSHALUYS: Force, you say? He's a little punk, and his place [*gesturing*] is no bigger than this.

RAFAYEL: All the same, I'm afraid. That's the truth. Surely the draftsman was aware that Juto's barbecue joint was right next to our site?

VANIK: Juto's only recently put it up, Comrade Avetyan.

RAFAYEL: In broad daylight, before our very eyes. How could that be? How come the town planning office didn't stop him?

AZATYAN: Stop Juto? You're kidding, Comrade Avetyan. The place's not a kindergarten or school that you can withhold planning permission.

RAFAYEL: So when are we going to start blasting? Any suggestions as to how to deal with this Juto guy?

ARSHALUYS: Let's send Zhanna.

ZHANNA: In the interests of the project I'll go, if I have to.

RAFAYEL: Okay. Any other bright ideas?

VANIK: Suppose when we weren't looking, his barbecue grill happened to set fire to the joint?

RAFAYEL: Getting warmer. Any more?

ARSHALUYS: After all, the guy makes a really mean barbecue. We can't pass that up.

RAFAYEL: Trust you to think of your stomach. Eating's what you do best. Anything else?

AZATYAN: Brainstorming's your department, boss. Leave the implementation to us.

RAFAYEL: Hambardzumyan, you're the meanest of the bunch.

HAMBARDZUMYAN: Comrade Avetyan—

RAFAYEL: In the best sense, of course. Get the boys together and have a bite at Juto's. I know you're not a drinking man, but have a good drink that day to loosen your inhibitions. If he brings you something hot, say it's cold, if he brings you something juicy, say it's dry. If the food's tasty, say it's bland. Then start an argument over the bill. Hamo, you take charge of that part.

HAMO: Beat my dog, would you? You ain't seen nothing yet.

RAFAYEL: That's the spirit. The rest of you take your cue from Hamo. Then you'll tell me, Hamo, who was active and who was passive. The point is to prepare the ground for a formal complaint. Are you with me? Hambardzumyan, you're the only literate one among them. Write a proper complaint, polite but indignant, and have everyone sign. Let me go over the text beforehand. Underneath you'll spell out the address in big letters so that he'll come right here.

CHILINGIRYAN: You think he'll come? I have my doubts.

RAFAYEL: He'll have no other alternative, pal. I'll deal with him personally. Just let him fall into my hands. I know what I'll do with him then. Let's move on to the next issue.

AZATYAN: Rafayel Arsenich, you haven't forgotten that the commission's going to visit us tomorrow.

RAFAYEL: I remember. We'll put them up at the Hotel Ani or the Armenia. Don't pay for the rooms. Let them do that. It's their responsibility, if you follow my drift. Take them on a tour of Erevan the whole day. Hamo, write down the statue of David of Sasun, Saryan's house-museum, the Genocide Memorial. No, I'll take them to the Genocide Memorial. Hambardzumyan, as the only literate man in the crew, you'll go with them. The Youth Palace, Erebuni. Next day you'll take them to Garni and the cave monastery of Geghard, then on to Lake Sevan.[4] Make sure to stop at the Charents' arch. Zhanna, you go with them.

ZHANNA: "I love the sun-ripe word of my sweet Armenia."[5]

RAFAYEL: That's my girl. The next day you'll bring them here. (*He gets up, goes over to the plan of the industrial complex, and indicates with a pointer*) You'll come in by the main entrance. Park the car right here. Avoid going anywhere near the rail link. Put up a nice placard to block it off from view, Vanik, with your skull on it. Underneath write in big letters—

VANIK: Danger. Keep out.

RAFAYEL: By the way, did you see the write-up they gave us in the paper? Have you ever heard the likes of it? Congratulations to one and all. What did I tell you? Good workmanship never goes unnoticed. Sooner or later it's appreciated for what it is. Azatyan, read it to us. I know you've read it, but we should all hear it one time and savor it together.

AZATYAN (*reading*): "The sun's early rays had just parted the infinity of the sky, but the construction crew were already hard at it. The whirr of machinery—

RAFAYEL: That's no way to read. Read it properly with clear enunciation and feeling. Make sure to trill the "r"s. Whirr-r-r . . .

AZATYAN: "The dance of the cranes soaring in the sky united with the men's animated activity to create a mighty symphony, the builder's harmonious unity of word and deed. The results achieved over the last three months stand as objective proof of what the construction crew is capable of. Take, for example, the rail link they are building to connect to the industrial complex—

RAFAYEL: Hold it. The rail link they are building to connect to the industrial complex? . . . One of you's been hob-nobbing with the press. (*Calmly*) Who is it? Nice interview. I liked it.

---

4. The reference is to various Armenian historical sites: Erebuni, Urartian fort near Erevan; Garni, site of a tomb from the classical era; Geghard, significant partly rock-carved monastery from the thirteenth century; David, central hero of the oral epic *Daredevils of Sasun*; and Martiros Saryan, one of the most important modern Armenian artists of the first half of the twentieth century.

5. The citation is from the Armenian poet Eghishe Charents (1897–1936).

AZATYAN (*falling into the trap*): Me.

RAFAYEL (*furious*): Did the flattery go to your head? Or are you so stupid that you didn't realize what you were doing? With a smile on your face, in broad daylight, you blew our cover, you Judas. I've told you a thousand times. No journalists, no articles, no publicity. We don't exist. There's no complex under construction. Not even a fly should come here without my say-so. It's nothing to be amused about. Okay, meeting's adjourned. Hamo, you stay behind.

(*Everyone except* HAMO *leaves.*)

Hamo, what about the newspaper?

HAMO: I have the whole print run at the summerhouse, boss.

RAFAYEL: Okay, wait at reception till I call you.

(HAMO *goes out.*)

(*dialing*) Lucy Edvardovna? Hello. It's Rafik. How are you? It's ages since I heard your voice. (*Screwing up his face*) A voice constantly beckoning me. I can't talk to you without waxing poetic . . . even someone as prosaic as me. How is Comrade Arshakyan? (*Feigning surprise*) Really? On a business trip? Moscow again? How can he leave a woman like you on her own? It's no laughing matter. It's a serious business. If someone wanted to take advantage of his error, now would that be a crime? Who might that be? I might be up to something like that myself. Merely to teach him a lesson, of course. You don't think I have any ulterior motives? He does deserve a lesson though, right? Okay. Till this evening.

(*He lays down the receiver and presses a switch on the switchboard.*)

Zhanna, tell Hamo to come in. Don't forget, I'm not here.

(HAMO *enters.*)

(RAFAYEL *opens the wall safe and removes a wad of notes.*) Here's two thousand rubles. Go buy a really nice ring.

HAMO: No problem, boss. But what if you don't like it? Your taste's very different from mine.

RAFAYEL: Never mind. Two thousand rubles will get you something decent, however bad your taste. By the way, Arushanyan's sending someone over. I hope he hasn't read Azatyan's interview and smelled a rat.

HAMO: You mean, about the rail link.

RAFAYEL: He's just taken over as our supervisor and wants to meet us. Except he's keeping his distance and sending his assistant—what's his name—instead.

HAMO: I think it's Aghabek Vardanyan.

RAFAYEL: Really?

HAMO: He's no greenhorn. (*He dials, then hands* RAFAYEL *the phone.*) Sokrat.

RAFAYEL: Hi, Sokrat. How are things? Me? What do you think? I've no time to be ill. Listen, Sokrat. I'd like you to do me a favor for a VIP. Can you arrange a sea cruise? Any place'll do, provided it's wet. He's a real big shot. Aghabek Vardanyan. We're in business. The poor guy hasn't been back to Italy for years. Okay, Sokrat, thanks a lot. Regards to your family. Bye. (*He lays down the receiver.*) [*To* HAMO] You know what you have to do, right?

HAMO: Take the money to the accounting office, fourth window, and get the ball rolling. What piece of dirty business have you got lined up for me, so I can go to the seaside?

RAFAYEL: Your turn'll come. Okay. Get out of my sight.

HAMO: You bet, boss. (*He goes.*)

(SHAHEN *walks in.* RAFAYEL *looks at him quizzically.*)

SHAHEN: Hello, Rafik. Don't you recognize me?

RAFAYEL: Hello. Do I know you?

SHAHEN: Shahen, Rafik. Lover-boy Shahen. Remember, from sixth grade? The kid whose parents were always being called to school. And I always brought Arshak, the bouncer, to smooth things out with the principal.

RAFAYEL: Shahen? Doesn't ring a bell.

SHAHEN: It'll all come back to you—I'm the one who always hit you. We were all amazed. We'd beat the daylights out of you, but you'd never cry.

RAFAYEL: Okay, Shahen. To what do I owe the honor of this visit?

SHAHEN: It's my son-in-law, Rafik. He's not a bad kid. He's young, he made a mistake. Don't ruin his career. He was only twenty-eight rubles short. And he lost his job over it? That's a misdemeanor, not a crime. The rest of the crew are saints, I suppose. If you let him off this one time, I'll see he doesn't do it again.

RAFAYEL: Vazgen Badalyan's your son-in-law?

SHAHEN: What good did it do to fire him? They're struggling to get by. Besides, what I make's not enough to tide them over. They don't have much to live on, but they really love each other and get on well together. That's no small thing, Rafik. Of course, you were within your rights, don't get me wrong, but you're going against your conscience. I said to myself, let me go and have a word with him.

RAFAYEL: What's your own line of work, Shahen?

SHAHEN: I'm a driver. I drive a heavy-duty truck.

RAFAYEL: You look up an old friend when you're stuck, is that it? It's not a good idea, Shahen. At least you should have come to the house. I guess you don't even know where I live.

SHAHEN: My mistake, Rafik. I'm sorry.

RAFAYEL: I did your son-in-law a favor, Shahen. What difference does it make whether you're one ruble short or a thousand? You and I call it a "misdemeanor," but the real name for it is stealing. How come we're so quick to forget that? No, Shahen, your son-in-law'll have to take the rap. Too bad he's just a kid. If you're honest, you should support me in this. We should both come down on him.

SHAHEN: Are you telling me my son-in-law's the only one to do something like that? Can't you see beyond the twenty-eight rubles?

RAFAYEL: Listen, Shahen. I've broken my back building houses over the years. Who ever said, "Well done, Rafik"? Who ever said even a tight-lipped thank you. Who's ever had anything good to say about me? Instead, they got off their behinds and cursed me and wagged a finger in my face. What do you expect? But now, what a turn-around over sacking Vazgen. You'd think it's the best thing I'd ever done. Now they're all patting me on the back and holding me up as a model of principle and a crusader against injustice. They ignore all the houses and bridges I've built and can only think about the twenty-eight rubles. Now do you see how important your son-in-law is to me? I'd no idea this sort of thing was going to come along, but now that it has, I can't let it go. Now I can work in peace, thanks to your son-in-law, and go ahead with my plans. No, Shahen. He's got to leave the unit. You see why. But since you were my bully at school, I'll make sure he finds a good job.

SHAHEN: Thank you, Rafik. I'll keep in touch from now on. We'll be real friends again.

RAFAYEL: There's no need. Take care.

SHAHEN: You remember me now, don't you?

RAFAYEL: No, I don't.

ARSHAKYAN's *apartment*

LUCY EDVARDOVNA, *a woman in her forties whose beauty has begun to fade, lies wrapped up in a shawl on the bed.* RAFAYEL *sits on the bed and buttons his shirt, straightens his tie, and puts on his jacket.*

LUCY: How did you happen to remember me?

RAFAYEL (*in the character of a romantic hero*): "You said, 'It's time for us to part. I'm tired of your crazy lifestyle. It's time for me to receive guests.' It was just my fate to slide down further . . ." Lucy Edvardovna, do you recall how a young man and woman saw each other for the first time. Such a sense of fulfillment radiated throughout the woman's being that it found automatic expression now in her sparkling gaze, now in her smile. The woman deliberately expunged the light in her eyes, but it found an outlet despite herself in her scarcely observable smile. Can you guess, Lucy Edvardovna, that I was that young man, and you the young woman?

LUCY: That was the first meeting of Vronsky and Anna Karenina, Rafik. It's your luck I've just finished rereading it.

RAFAYEL: Really? So Tolstoy thinks on the same wave length as I do. What a coincidence.

(*The telephone rings.*)

LUCY: Wrong number. What? Avetyan? [*To* RAFAYEL] Rafik, it's for you. Urgent. Are you a doctor or something that you leave a contact number wherever you go?

RAFAYEL (*taking the receiver*): They won't give us any? You saw they have it with your own eyes? You keep the guard talking, while the rest smash the windows and enter. What are you afraid of? When was I ever stuck for an answer? (*He replaces the receiver.*)

LUCY: Rafik, why do you lie to me about being in love? You can't lead a woman my age up the garden path. What if I were to believe you?

RAFAYEL (*ingenuously*): How did you work that out, Lucy Edvardovna? Really, I never thought about it. What if you believed me?

(RAFAYEL *takes the ring from his pocket and puts it on her finger.*)

LUCY: It's lovely, Rafik. Thank you.

RAFAYEL: Naturally, your finger deserves a much more exquisite ring.

LUCY: What's it this time?

RAFAYEL (*almost in tears*): Katanka.

LUCY: *Katanka?* What sort of thing's that?

RAFAYEL: Your husband'll know.

LUCY: Let me write it down before I forget.

RAFAYEL: One hundred tons. That's all.

LUCY: I'll tell him tomorrow when he gets back. You're dressed very lightly. See you don't catch cold. Let me give you one of Arshakyan's jumpers. Don't worry, you don't have to return it.

RAFAYEL: In that case Arshakyan won't have any left soon.

LUCY: So what. Shall I make some more coffee?

RAFAYEL (*unsettled*): No, no, Lucy Edvardovna. I'm in a hurry. Next time I won't be in a rush. We'll take our time. Sip tea. Read each other poetry, Esenin,

Blok, Teryan, Tsvetaeva.[6] Just now "I'd like to hear the *zurna* play and stay in-toxicated till morning."[7] One hundred tons. Don't forget.

HAMO's *house*

It's night. RAFAYEL *and* HAMO *are burning bundles of newspaper in the orchard. Noise, music, and drunken shouts are heard from inside.*

RAFAYEL: Is it me you serve, Hamo, or my title?

HAMO: What's the difference, boss?

RAFAYEL: Is it Rafayel Avetyan you work for, or the program director?

HAMO: Do you want the truth or—?

RAFAYEL: No. Tell me a white lie, and I'll get at the truth.

HAMO: Since it's a lie you want, I work for you, boss.

RAFAYEL: Thanks for your candor, Hamo.

HAMO: I could have tried to lie, but you'd have seen through it. I knew this is the answer you wanted at this moment.

RAFAYEL: If I'm replaced and you get a new boss tomorrow, would you—

HAMO: Stab you in the back? Never. Do you know why? The new boss wouldn't like it. New bosses like to appear decent. They don't like you to badmouth their predecessor. That's how things are now.

RAFAYEL: And you'd work for him just the same?

HAMO: How do you mean "just the same"? Depends what he expects from me. If he wants an honest day's work from me, that's one thing, if not . . . It all comes down to what type of guy he is.

RAFAYEL: What did I ask of you?

HAMO: My hands are clean, boss. You've no idea what I did for previous bosses. In comparison, you're a lamb, an angel. Don't get annoyed, if I speak like this. You're a worker. You know how to roll up your sleeves. You really care about that industrial complex. That's no small thing. Before you, no one cared about anything other than lining their pockets.

RAFAYEL: Let's go, Hamo. The fire's done its job.

---

6. The reference is to the following Russian poets: Sergei Aleksandrovich Esenin (1895–1925); Aleksandr Aleksandrovich Blok (1880–1921); Marina Ivanovna Tsvetaeva (1892–1941); and the Armenian poet Vahan Teryan (1885–1920).

7. The citation is from the work *Sayat Nova* by the Armenian poet Eghishe Charents. The *zurna* is a high-pitched, double-reed woodwind instrument.

Inside HAMO's *house*

(*There are fifteen people, including* HAMBARDZUMYAN, AZATYAN, HAMO, RUBEN, VANIK, ZHANNA, SONYA, *and* NORA.)

RAFAYEL (*a bit drunk*): It's boring partying with you guys. All these years we've had fun together and you've never yet come out with any interesting thought or idea. You don't read papers, let alone books. That doesn't apply to you, Hambardzumyan. You're the only sensible person in the bunch.

NORA: I've read *The Three Musketeers*, Rafik. Really, I have. You remember, the girl died of TB.

RAFAYEL: You mean *The Woman with Camellias*.[8] You're excused reading, Nora. At least you have lovely legs. What do the rest have going for them?

SONYA: What about me, Rafo?

RAFAYEL: You have to read a little, at least. You've no other saving grace.

SONYA: Oh! You should be ashamed of yourself.

RAFAYEL: From now on we'll begin every week with book reports from the lot of you.

RUBEN (*laughing*): Do that and I'll put in an application—

RAFAYEL: Be honest about it. Honesty's never done anyone any harm. Have you seen any? Try it some time. Just give it a try.

SONYA: Rafik's in a trance today.

VANIK: We're too good, guys. This world doesn't deserve us.

RAFAYEL: If you really love me, Nora, give me a few years of your youth.

NORA: Gladly, Rafo. Not only a few years. I'll give it all.

RAFAYEL: Do you know what I'd do with it?

NORA: You wouldn't do a thing.

RAFAYEL: I'd turn the world around. No. You don't love me.

NORA (*from boredom, she reads a piece torn out of a newspaper*): More people have been arrested for bribery in Kirovakan. The title's in really huge letters: "The Ground under Their Feet Should Burst into Flames."

RAFAYEL: If your mind's set on catching crooks, look around you. Check out the discrepancy between how much they earn and how well they live. Anything new on the rails, Azatyan?

AZATYAN: Rafayel Arsenich, we're at a party, can't we have a bit of fun?

RAFAYEL (*banging the table with his fist*): Anything new on the rails?

AZATYAN: Gugush's bringing them. He left a while ago.

---

8. The novel *The Three Musketeers* (1844) was written by Alexandre Dumas senior, whereas *The Woman with Camellias* (1847) is the work of his son.

RAFAYEL: What sort of a name's that? Tell him to change it. When will he get here?

AZATYAN: Three days at the latest.

RAFAYEL: Get a move on. Aghabek Vardanyan'll be back from his cruise in ten days. We have to finish the rail link before that reptile shows his face.

NORA: Take it easy, Rafik. All this shop talk. We're having a good time here. Give us a song. Go on.

RAFAYEL: Sing? I'll do anything for you, get you an apartment, a car, whatever you like, only keep up the good work. (*He starts to sing. The rest join in.*) I'm not a bad singer, eh? Just keep at it, keep at it, and I'll see you get time at the state spa, a summerhouse, furniture, anything you want. (*He continues to sing. Suddenly he falls silent.*) Are you making fun of me?

THE OTHERS (*startled*): What on earth are you saying, Rafayel Arsenich?

RAFAYEL: No, seriously. You're not making fun of me?

THE OTHERS: No way, Rafayel Arsenich. The very idea!

VANIK: Guys, let's drink to the Armenian people. With this little glass, but a big heart, let's drink to our nation's health. On your feet. (*He begins singing at the top of his voice.*) "We're Armenians, Brothers, we're Armenian."

RAFAYEL (*interrupting him*): Just a minute. Listen, Vanik. Who are you to speak for the people?

VANIK: What did I say, boss?

RAFAYEL: Who are you to speak for me, or for the country, for that matter?

HAMO: He's right.

RUBEN: But Rafayel Arsenich, does that mean I don't love my country?

RAFAYEL: Hamo, you tell me, does he love his country or not?

HAMO: He's one thing, the country's another. The two don't mix.

RAFAYEL: People are turning patriotism into a profession. Just as they become doctors, teachers, factory workers, engineers, even waiters, so they become professional patriots. It's a new specialization. They'd better give me a wide berth.

RUBEN: What did I say wrong, boss?

RAFAYEL: Don't take it personally. I was talking about myself. Actually, it was a general comment. Isn't that so, Hambardzumyan? How many self-appointed patriots have you seen running around with the nation's problems on their shoulders? Suppose someone were to ask, where are you rushing off to? Careful you don't slip. What a shame if those issues should fall into the mud. Isn't that just self-promotion, Hambardzumyan? You're a sensible guy. Don't they realize that by lugging those issues around they're just adding a new problem for the nation to shoulder.

SONYA: Right on.

NORA: Rafik, I couldn't agree more. Only I can't put it as well as you.

RAFAYEL: You keep out of this. At least you have lovely legs. What have the rest got to show for themselves? Who's going to get down to business? There are thousands of people with their heads down, hard at work, creating something. Great or small, they're making a difference. How else is the country going to move forward? I suppose they're not patriots. How come patriotism became divorced from work and family and started putting in an appearance when people relax around the table? Can you explain that, Hambardzumyan?

AZATYAN: Let's drink Comrade Avetyan's health.

HAMO: Comrade Hambardzumyan, how come you're not drinking?

THE OTHERS: Lighten up. Leave the guy alone.

HAMO: You don't get it. Is the guy going to have his say or not? Drink up, Comrade Hambardzumyan.

(HAMBARDZUMYAN *lifts his glass to drink.*)

Hold on. Why don't you make a toast?

HAMBARDZUMYAN (*He gets up.*): Your health, Rafik. I'm not going to speak good or ill of you today. Only the truth, as I see it.

RUBEN: What are you talking about, Comrade Hambardzumyan? You should walk in the boss's shoes before talking about "truth."

RAFAYEL: Don't interrupt, Rubik. Let him speak.

HAMBARDZUMYAN: You're a man, Rafik, who's always lived dangerously. You still tread a fine line, constantly having to make decisions that could just as easily pull you down as get you across to the other side. Here's to good judgment, Rafik. You'll need it, because willy-nilly you can't stay up on the high wire for too long. You've got to get off on one side or the other. There's no other option.

SONYA: I don't get it.

VANIK: I didn't understand a thing either.

RAFAYEL: All the better. You're not supposed to understand. Go on, Hambardzumyan.

HAMBARDZUMYAN: You've an amazing talent for combining several different personalities in one. Effortlessly, without being disturbed by doubts or internal conflict. You've heard that the end justifies the means. But that's not so. As you proceed, despite yourself, you lose your sense of direction. Somehow, the end and the means have to be in sync, Rafik. To your health.

RAFAYEL: Sing something, boys. Why are you sitting around silent? Are we partying or what? (*He drinks a large glass of vodka.*) Can I help it if I don't get drunk. So what if I enjoy living at the edge of the precipice? Why can't I take it in the future like I have up to now? People should always live at the edge of an abyss, like a tightrope walker, Hambardzumyan. What I like about it is that it stops you from getting soft. With all the mistakes I've made, for good or ill, I've created something. You, with all your correct opinions, are only a spectator. Which do you prefer, Hambardzumyan? I wouldn't swap even one of the walls I've built for all your words of wisdom. Maybe I'll fall into the ravine. But the wall I built will endure. You'll ascend to heaven, Hambardzumyan, but won't leave any trace behind on earth. Which of these is better?

VANIK (*inspired by the rhetoric*): Don't ever think of transferring, Comrade Avetyan.

RUBEN (*toasting*): Forever together, Rafayel Arsenich.

AZATYAN: Here's to your great heart, boss.

RAFAYEL: What can I do about it, if I don't get drunk?

NORA (*disappointed*): What kind of party is this? No one's fighting, no one's insulted Sonya and me. Nothing's smashed.

HAMO: Everything'll work out okay, boss. Don't worry.

SONYA: So what do you think, should I do my striptease routine now? Would somebody please say something.

(ARSHALUYS *enters, gasping, and collapses on a chair. He tries to speak but cannot, either from fear or from his exertion in running. The others pepper him with anxious questions, "What happened?" "Is it your heart?" "Bring some water." "Should we call the paramedics?"*)

RAFAYEL: No need. Let him rest. He's come to see me. Out with it. I can take it. My hide's gotten pretty tough, Arshaluys. What's happened? Let's have it.

ARSHALUYS: Arushanyan. The deputy minister. He came and caught us. He's standing at the tenth kilometer of the rail link.

RAFAYEL: I knew it. I was puzzled why he didn't show up at the ninth, the eighth, or even the fifth for that matter. What else?

ARSHALUYS: He stood there talking to the guards, asking questions.

RAFAYEL: Go on.

ARSHALUYS: He said, "Arshaluys Vardanich, your boss won't swallow this one. This is the end of his fun and games."

RAFAYEL: So that's the rail link up the spout? At the tenth kilometer? We sent his deputy on a cruise and now Arushanyan's caught us, Hamo.

HAMO: Don't worry about a thing, boss. We'll send Arushanyan on a longer trip.

RAFAYEL: Go on, Arshaluys.

ARSHALUYS: Find that boss of yours Avetyan, even if he's ten feet under, and tell him to come to the ministry immediately. He's sitting waiting for you, Rafayel Arsenich.

RAFAYEL: Didn't you say anything, Arshaluys? You didn't explain the rail link is essential for the industrial complex. Without that, it's . . . it's . . . What am I babbling on about? What happened then?

ARSHALUYS: He got in his Volga, furiously slammed the door shut, and drove off.

RAFAYEL: Tell me again, Arshaluys.

ARSHALUYS: He said, "Your boss won't swallow this one."

RAFAYEL: Then.

ARSHALUYS: He said, "He should come to the ministry immediately." He's sitting waiting, Rafayel Arsenich.

RAFAYEL: Again. In more detail.

ARSHALUYS: He said, "Find Avetyan, wherever he is."

RAFAYEL: Give it to me straight. "Even if he's ten feet under, find that boss of yours Avetyan." I want his exact words.

ARSHALUYS: He said, "This is the end of his fun and games. Your boss won't swallow this one."

RAFAYEL: That's enough. So the rail link's up the spout. At the tenth kilometer. I won't allow it. It simply can't be. The rail link has to be finished. What's the point of a rail link that goes nowhere?

HAMBARDZUMYAN: Maybe you'd like to be left alone?

RAFAYEL: Alone? Already? So soon?

HAMO (*dialing, then hands the phone to* RAFAYEL): Hayk Markosyan.

RAFAYEL: It's me. Sorry to call you at home. The clouds are gathering. I need your help. Just for a day or two. Can you? You have to. There's only three kilometers left. We'll work night and day. I'll be with them. It's essential. (*Despairingly*) He hung up. (*He paces around and suddenly catches sight of* VIGEN *and* HASMIK.) Vigen, what are you doing here? Is everything okay at home?

[*Somewhat embarrassed,* RAFAYEL *draws* VIGEN *and* HASMIK *aside. The construction crew pull back to a corner and tone down their raucousness.*]

VIGEN: What's going on here?

RAFAYEL: We're having a little party, can't you see?

HASMIK: Let's go, Vigen. Please.

VIGEN: Let me say what I have to say.

RAFAYEL: What's this all about, Son?

VIGEN: I've heard all about your double life.

HAMO: That's no way to talk to your father.

RAFAYEL: Don't believe it, Son.

VIGEN: Your salary's not enough. My suit money has to come from Mom's allowance. You preach self-sufficiency to me. [*With deep irony*] Poor Daddy.

RAFAYEL (*deeply shaken*): What's all this leading to?

VIGEN: Is that all you have to say? Aren't you mad at me? I'd have thought by this time you'd have beaten me to a pulp. After all, I'm only your son. What right does a son have to talk to his father this way?

(RAFAYEL'*s hand reaches for a chair.*)

It's too late, Dad. You let the moment slip.

RAFAYEL: And you believed all the garbage you heard?

VIGEN: Why don't you ask who told me? It came straight from the horse's mouth. Someone right in this room.

RAFAYEL: There's no one like that here. [*To* HASMIK] What do you say, my girl? I know you don't believe any of this. I see it with my eyes. Good for you, girl. I knew you wouldn't let me down.

VIGEN: The guy told me everything. Point by point. Your whole life.

RAFAYEL: And you believed him. You let him slander your old father?

VIGEN: Fiftyish is old?

RAFAYEL: I'm not really old? You should love your father all the more, the older he grows.

VIGEN (*shouting*): No. Don't lay a guilt trip on me with this old age routine. All I want to know is why we can't live like everyone else. Why do you deprive us of everything? Who are they that you should spend your money on them? What are we, then?

RAFAYEL: What? You mean, all this is about money? I don't spend money on you? I don't give you anything? Is that it, you ungrateful son of a bitch? (RAFAYEL *furiously removes his belt and lunges toward* VIGEN.) Finally, it's come to this. (*He begins to whip* VIGEN *with his belt.* VIGEN *dodges this way and that to escape the blows.*) I thought you were blaming me for my wheeling and dealing. But it turns out you had something else in mind. Take this . . . Your stupid dad almost had a heart attack. Are you worth having a heart attack over? You made me feel ashamed. I wanted to run away from you. I couldn't look you in the eye. [*Hitting him again*] Take this . . . So you want your share, eh? You never thought of blaming your dad for his business dealings. I'd have given you my life if you'd told me to clean up my act. So that's the kind of man you've become? (*Suddenly, throwing the belt at him*) Take it and beat me for everything you think I've done wrong. Go on, hit me. All those who want to whip me have run into their holes for cover. You're justified. At least you hit me. (*Exhausted, he slumps into a chair.* VIGEN *retreats into a corner, fearfully.*) Vigen, Vigen. I was so ashamed I wanted the ground to swallow me. What have you done? When did everything fall apart? You were my shining light . . . (*Unexpectedly* ANAHIT *enters. Everyone pulls back into a corner in surprise. There is a long pause*) What have you done? When did everything fall apart? . . . Anahit?

ANAHIT (*to* HASMIK *and* VIGEN): What are you doing here? Who gave you permission to come? I told you not to. (*Flustered, to the members of the crew*) Hello. . . . (*To* HASMIK *and* VIGEN) Can't your father have a party once in a while?

RAFAYEL: Anahit.

ANAHIT (*to* HASMIK *and* VIGEN, *and secondarily to the others*): After all, what life has he seen? From the time he opened his eyes it was work, work, work. His health's not all that good either. He never complained. You should see how devious and cunning he had to be to handle superiors who were far from his equal. Do you think he did it for himself. He never did anything for himself. (*Approaching her husband*) I've no complaints, Rafik. Only how were you able to keep your life a secret from us so well?

RAFAYEL: I lived like a dog. I was scared at home and outside.

ANAHIT: No problem, Rafik. No problem. I've just come to take the kids home.

RAFAYEL: Even if you forgive me, if you can do that, I'm going to live with you like a lodger. There's no other way. I can't drag you all down with me. It would completely destroy you.

ANAHIT: Come on, up you get. Let's go home.

RAFAYEL: Now that it's all come out, wouldn't you prefer I kept everything secret, that you had no idea where I worked?

ANAHIT: Maybe, Rafik.

RAFAYEL: But you found out. Now we're all going to suffer the consequences.

ANAHIT: Home, kids. Get going. [*To the others*] Excuse us for disturbing you. (*To* RAFAYEL) Rafik, don't be too late. You've got your work tomorrow.

RAFAYEL: Anahit. Do you know what *katanka* is?

ZHANNA (*sneeringly*) How would she know?

RAFAYEL: When you find out, you'll start to understand me. You'll understand the whole story.

(ANAHIT, VIGEN, *and* HASMIK *leave.* RAFIK *gesticulates to indicate that the others should go, too. Quietly, they all go their own way.*)

NORA: Rafik, do you want me to stay?

(RAFAYEL *shakes his head no.*)

(*To* SONYA) What are *you* hanging around for?

(*They both leave. Only* HAMBARDZUMYAN *is left.*)

HAMBARDZUMYAN: I've got wheels. Do you want a ride?

RAFAYEL: You remember you once told me you gave your dog poison to put him down. Recently our dog's been barking so much we can't get any sleep at night. Do you think you could get me some of the stuff?

HAMBARDZUMYAN: Sure. When do you need it?

RAFAYEL: When you get a chance. Today, if you can make it, or tomorrow. Today would be better, though.

HAMBARDZUMYAN: Okay. I'll bring it over in half an hour.

RAFAYEL: My conscience is giving me a hard time, but there's no other way. It seems the poor thing's got rabies. Will he suffer a lot?

HAMBARDZUMYAN: There's no easy way to say it. Sure he'll suffer.

RAFAYEL: Too bad. He's served us faithfully for twenty years. He grew up with the kids.

HAMBARDZUMYAN: You've got so much on your plate, and you're worrying about that?

RAFAYEL: We're talking about a live animal, Hambardzumyan, one with a soul.

(HAMBARDZUMYAN *goes out.*)

Hamo, I know you're there behind the door.

(HAMO *comes in.*)

Your neighbor's a photographer, isn't he? Go and call him. I want my photo taken. I've never had time for photographs. I'd like him to come and take my picture. Ask him to come. Why are you looking at me with such a puzzled expression. Go and call him.

HAMO: Right away, boss. (*He leaves, looking surprised.*)

RAFAYEL: A guy should have a lot of photos. They should tell his life story. You only realize that once you start growing old. (*He goes up to the tape recorder, turns it on, sits beside it, and listens to music.*) You only realize that once you start growing old . . . (*He gets up and dials.*) It's me, Khosrov. Did I surprise you? How many years is it we've been out of touch. I'm glad you recognized my voice at least. I guess I should say why I've called. I want to ask your forgiveness and put our differences to rest. What's done is done, but that's all in the past. You could hang up on me, but please hear me out. We don't have to become bosom buddies. A friendship patched up with sticky tape doesn't have much of a chance. But I do want us to make up. I don't want you to think ill of me. Forgive me, if you can. Tell the folks I said hello. Okay. Good-bye. (*He turns off the tape recorder.*) You only realize that once you start growing old.

(HAMO *comes in with his* PHOTOGRAPHER *neighbor in his pajamas.*)

PHOTOGRAPHER: What's got into you that you want your picture taken in the middle of the night?

RAFAYEL: I'll pay you well.

PHOTOGRAPHER: That goes without saying. You're not really drunk either.

RAFAYEL: Very well.

PHOTOGRAPHER: You bet.

RAFAYEL: I'd like to be seated.

PHOTOGRAPHER: Sure. Seems you know a thing or two about the game. (*He sets up the tripod and prepares to take the picture, asking* RAFAYEL *a few questions as he works.*) Where are you from? What year were you born? What did your parents do for a living? Have you read *The House of Cilicia*?

(RAFAYEL *looks sternly at the camera. Seeing that his questions remain unanswered, the* PHOTOGRAPHER *proceeds to take the picture.*)

RAFAYEL: One more. I want this one to be happy.
PHOTOGRAPHER: Whatever you say.

(RAFAYEL *becomes even sterner. The* PHOTOGRAPHER *takes the picture.*)

HAMO: Why not take one together, boss?
RAFAYEL: I want to be alone. One more, please.
PHOTOGRAPHER: Since you won't answer my questions, at least change your posture. Otherwise everything'll turn out the same.
RAFAYEL: Just take care of the picture. It won't be the same.

(*The* PHOTOGRAPHER *comes forward and tries to fix his pose.*)

Take me as I am. This one with an even bigger smile.

(*The* PHOTOGRAPHER *goes back rather quizzically and takes the photograph.*)

Make lots of prints. I'll pay you whatever you ask.
PHOTOGRAPHER: You sure will, and more besides for . . . You get the picture?
RAFAYEL: I'd like the two of you to go now.

(A *car horn is heard.*)

It's Hambardzumyan. He's brought something for me. Go get it, Hamo.

(HAMO *goes.*)

PHOTOGRAPHER: Good-night. Why don't I take your photo during the day sometime. But you have to respond to my questions for the picture to be successful. I talk to the client to get to know his character, what makes him tick.
RAFAYEL: See you. Good-night.

(*The* PHOTOGRAPHER *goes. Then* HAMO *comes in with a bottle of medicine and gives it to* RAFAYEL.)

HAMO: Since you're keen on photos, there are albums in that dresser. Take them out and have a look before going to sleep. That way you'll get a better idea about my family.

RAFAYEL: Good-night, Hamo.

HAMO: Sleep well. Everything'll be all right in the morning. (*He leaves.*)

(RAFAYEL *clears the table, straightens out the room, combs his hair in front of the mirror, brushes his suit for some reason, then opens the medicine bottle, takes a good swig, and throws the instruction form into the waste basket. Then he switches on the tape recorder, places the microphone in front of him, counts up to five, rewinds the tape and plays it back to check that everything is in working order. Then he rewinds the tape again. Suddenly remembering something, he gets up and turns on all the lights, one by one, closes the curtains, then takes his position again and begins to record himself.*)

RAFAYEL: I'm glad to have this chance to relax and unwind. You said you were tired of seeing me strong, Anahit. I'm tired of being strong. I grew up without a mother from the age of ten and scarcely saw my father's face. I looked around me constantly for fear someone would trip me up. I had to be strong. I wasn't born strong. I had to force myself. I took charge of my potential and betrayed the real me. And so a ten-year-old boy came across as strong and invincible. That's what you thought, too, Vigen and Hasmik. That was the expression of my weakness, my darlings. If you want to know the truth, I used strength to conceal my weakness. Now you see me without the mask, now that I've decided to take my leave of you—as well as everything I have ever loved and hated. But love always won out over hate. I guess I can say that honestly. What was my work all about? My whole life I never knew what it was to relax. Wasn't that love? When I die—in a few hours I won't be with you anymore—bury me alongside the rail link. At the thirteenth kilometer. Just as I built it inconspicuously, I don't want any fuss over my funeral. But be sure to say that here lies a man who lived constantly on the wire, who could hold his head high or fall to the ground. His faults were his own, but his strengths belonged to his time. I don't know whether that applies to me exactly, but you should say it in any case. Not for me, but for yourselves who are still alive.

My darlings, Anahit, Hasmik, Vigen, forgive me, if you can. I humbly ask your forgiveness. Maybe you know, maybe you don't, Vigen—how would you know?—what a heavy burden a father's forgiveness can be. So much so that you'd prefer my last word to be a curse. My forgiveness is a demand, Son. Become a real man: honest, straightforward, loving your work and your country. Did you think my forgiveness would sit lightly on you?

Do you all remember how I was? The kids won't, but you will, Anahit.

You ought to remember. I was always in first place. Work, study, partying, fighting, in meetings. Everywhere. I was never afraid to look truth in the face. Did you ever see me give in and compromise? Did you ever see me shrug with indifference? I didn't know the meaning of surrender. When did I learn? How did I learn? When did I let myself float with the current? Now I'm the last to speak my mind. I look at all the eyes, read all the glances, and figure out what they want from me and wait till the rest have had their say. Anahit, think back when I slipped up and be at Vigen's side in case, God forbid, the same thing happens to him.

The family should be close-knit, Anahit. And keep the old traditional customs. At mealtimes everyone should sit round the table together. Mother, with her apron on, should serve the food. She should serve her husband first, then the children, then herself. I get a real kick, Anahit, when I recall the synchronized clatter of knives, forks, and spoons in my father's house. What a heavenly sound it made. The son shouldn't smoke in his father's presence. The daughter shouldn't come home late at night. The kids should remember their parents' birthdays and get them a little something. There should never be enough money for everything, Anahit. Do you understand?

Do you remember what a great day it was when we won a fridge—a Saratov, no less. I'm not going to mention the Zhiguli, because that was won with someone else's ticket. I paid off someone to get it. Foolishly I thought at least once in my life I'd give you a break. What was the upshot? Now that I've confessed to it, you've got even more worries. You can't spend the money or get rid of it. Forgive me, Anahit. Forgive me, if you can. Don't tell my father about the ticket. I couldn't live it down.

Now on the table right in front of me there's a bunch of flowers. You know I've been indifferent to flowers all my life. I never appreciated their smell or saw how beautiful they could be. But you know that all too well. That may be why it never crossed my mind to give you flowers. Right now, though, I'd like to get up. Take one of them from the vase and become really tender for a moment. You can't imagine how. But believe me, I don't know how to go about it. I've never gone about smelling anything like this before. Maybe I should put it in my pocket and you'll laugh in the distance at my gaucheness and lack of savvy. How firm the rock is, my darlings, how brittle the soil, how blue the sky, how cold the water, how fiery the flame, how high are Mt. Masis and Mt. Aragats, how close is the house opposite that I see through the window, and how distant is yours. Yours and perhaps mine. Will you allow me to call the house mine, the house where we once knew what happiness was? Now I'm taking leave of specific, concrete things, firmness and brittleness, high and low, near and far, because my separation from you, from my work, my friends, my Erevan, to which I devoted my whole life, is just as specific and concrete.

I'm taking leave of all those questions, whose answers no longer matter to me, but which will pursue you with every step you take. How to live, how to tell good from evil, white from black. After all, there are so many shades in between that you can easily be misled. I was misled, I, your father and husband, who appeared to you like a god. A father should be a god! But I went off the straight and narrow. It seemed that the path I took was inevitable, there was no other way. It seemed I had stumbled onto that path without thinking, that life had taken me and placed me there. No, darlings, I made that choice. I searched it out and found it. For a number of years things go smoothly, but ultimately the road doesn't lead anywhere. You hit a dead end. You have to face the consequences. Hambardzumyan, even Hambardzumyan, who struggles to make ends meet, is going to come out the victor, Vigen. Rejoice in your father's defeat. Your father's defeated on both fronts, at home and outside. But you rejoice . . .

I'm taking my leave. But, as you can see, there's no end to my going. After I'm gone, you'll still be there, you and the wide world, complex and incomprehensible, disconnected. Isn't it strange, Anahit, that we know what's happening in the furthest corners of the globe, who's oppressing whom and where, but we've no idea what suffering oppresses our next-door neighbor, and we're not inclined to find out. We take the distant, unknown captive to our heart, because it's easy to love him. He makes no demands on us. We give him nothing of ourselves. We don't put our health on the line for him. We only shake our heads, drink our tea, and watch television. Loving someone close, on the other hand, is really hard, tremendously hard. It's almost impossible to love me, you or the guy over there, to love a concrete person. Who understood my situation? Who lent a helping hand? How can we live like this? What ring broke the big chain, that the repercussions reached our house, found me, and you, Anahit? And instead of holding his head high, your husband fell into the ravine. What sort of ring was that? You've no idea how I want to justify myself to you. Do you think I can't? That I can only do it to other people? I can't do it. Accept me as I am and forgive me, if you can.

Why did they allow me? How did they let me? Why didn't someone take me by the hand? Where did they all run and hide? Maybe it was during a break. But the break's lasting an awfully long time. Haven't we taken enough time off? What if it suddenly dawns on us that we've forgotten how to reach out to someone who's had a fall? What will we do then?

My God, how the list of endangered species has expanded! The air's already in there, along with the water, the earth, the honor of an honest day's work, a circle dance, the intoxicating smell of newly cut grass, family photographs, the good old custom of writing letters, belief in the three apples of folk tales: one for the teller, one for the listener, and the third for the world of creation. The chain's broken, Anahit. Watch out that it doesn't strike our house again. Keep the doors tightly closed. Tight! So it's farewell to this wonderful, maddening world, whose fate today is dangling by the thinnest of threads. And you, and a million other people like you, brittle, defenseless souls, are hanging from it for dear life. When my thread was cut, it was me that cut it. Others will cut yours.

Farewell to these somber thoughts, which is all I have and which I bequeath to you. Farewell to my friends and enemies, my mistakes and frailties, the places I visited and didn't have a chance to go, all my loves, every individual person, known and unknown, and all their struggles and concerns. And perhaps also in part to me, in an indistinct undertone . . .

If you're ever asked who your father and husband was, tell them, without hesitation, Rafayel Avetyan, Rafo. He came to the world as a laborer and that's how he lived and died. Tell them, don't be ashamed. That's the greatest accolade a man can receive. If you can, and if you care to, take pride in my accolade. Be proud and you won't regret it.

(HAMBARDZUMYAN *comes in. He looks around the room, then approaches* RAFAYEL *who is asleep in the armchair, and covers him with a blanket. He sits in an armchair opposite him, takes some papers out of his pocket and looks through them.* RAFAYEL *begins to move around and gradually wakes up.*)

HAMBARDZUMYAN: Good-day, Rafik. Excuse the interruption. I've brought a few papers for you to sign.

RAFAYEL: That's good of you. Let me see them.

HAMBARDZUMYAN: The *katanka* will be here this morning. One hundred tons.

RAFAYEL: Good. That's one less thing to worry about.

HAMBARDZUMYAN: Everything's still in play. Don't give up hope.

RAFAYEL (*suddenly*): You're the one who gave me away, Hambardzumyan. You're the one who had a talk with my son. You told him about the rail link business. And you know only full well, you bugger, that you've brought me to my knees. Now I'm just a plaything in your hands.

(HAMBARDZUMYAN *smiles and shakes his head in the negative;* RAFAYEL *grins ironically.*)

So you brought a sedative?

HAMBARDZUMYAN: You can overdose on sedatives, too, but I brought just enough for you to experience the pleasure of seeing us again.

RAFAYEL: I've got a splitting headache.

HAMBARDZUMYAN: You'll soon get over it.

RAFAYEL: Some laborer I am. I lived like a clown and that's what I'll continue to be. Poor clown . . .

HAMBARDZUMYAN: Forget it. The rail link'll be completed in ten days. Meanwhile, first they'll have to prepare the charges against you, then examine the case, then reach a verdict, and then see about sentencing.

RAFAYEL: And you know, Hambardzumyan, that after this you're going to be my closest companion. Because you're the only one who knows my darkest secret, the most shameful page in my life. I'm going to love you out of effrontery, if nothing else. You and I are bound by a chain. The chain's tight, you bastard, it's biting into my hand.

HAMBARDZUMYAN: Let's go, Rafik. Let's stop for a bite on the way and be off. If you like, we can stop at my place. It'll be quicker that way.

RAFAYEL: From now on, whatever you say goes, Hambardzumyan. That's what you were angling for, isn't it?

HAMBARDZUMYAN: The commission's gone. We saw them off this morning. I think they were satisfied. They particularly enjoyed Sevan.

RAFAYEL: Okay, let's go to your place. I haven't seen your folks in a long time. I always liked chatting with your mother. Say, Hambardzumyan, you're going to be fifty, aren't you? Let's put you up for an award. After all those years of service. Don't you worry. It's as good as done.

HAMBARDZUMYAN: However you see fit, Rafik. Let me help you on with your coat. (*He holds the coat for* RAFAYEL *to put on.*)

RAFAYEL: Off we go, Hambardzumyan. My head's bursting. (*At the door*) How did you put it, Hambardzumyan? The ends and the means have to cohere. Know why I remember? Because you said it. Let's go.

RAFAYEL's *house*

HASMIK: I've never seen you with a suitcase before.

RAFAYEL: You've always seen me with a briefcase.

HASMIK: Even when you were going to be away for a long time.

RAFAYEL: It's good that I thought of buying one . . . for a rainy day.

HASMIK: I'm amazed you fitted everything into that small case.

RAFAYEL: It's not that small, Hasmik. It holds quite a lot. Three shirts, five ties, a pair of shoes.

HASMIK: It's really small, Dad. Don't pretend. Is this your whole life? This little case? Where are you going?

RAFAYEL: The world's a big place. I'm bound to find a corner somewhere.

HASMIK: No, Daddy. You're the kind of person who has nowhere to go. Don't you see that?

RAFAYEL: I'll be all right. Don't worry.

HASMIK: Don't get me wrong. I know you've got a lot of friends, and maybe a few girlfriends, too. But that's not the same as having somewhere to go.

RAFAYEL: Maybe you're right. But I'm going all the same.

HASMIK: I want you to know, I love you. Vigen, too, and Mummy. It's not that I want to keep you back. I just want you to go in peace, to know you're missed.

RAFAYEL: Thank you, my girl. But you know you've got a sting in your tail. You know you're not making it easy for me by what you said. That's not what you wanted. You wanted to make your father feel guilty with your love.

HASMIK: We'd be very happy for you to come back. And we'd live just like before.

RAFAYEL: Like before? What do you mean?

HASMIK: Just like we used to live.

RAFAYEL: Watch out, young lady. Maybe I won't forgive you for those words. I'm the only one who has a right to live like before. Not the rest of you.

HASMIK: What should I say to Mum and Vigen?

RAFAYEL: Tell them I love you all, too.

HASMIK: I won't.

RAFAYEL: Yes, you will. Word for word. You see how much love there is? We're drowning in this sea of love.

HASMIK: Nobody knows but us, just the four of us. Nothing's changed, Dad, nothing.

RAFAYEL: Don't try to justify me. Four people's no small thing. Four people's an entirety. Don't be afraid, you won't starve. I'll take care of you at a distance. You'll still dress well. You won't want for anything. You'll go to the Black Sea coast in the summer. You'll have many more suitcases than me. Don't try to whitewash your father.

(HASMIK *goes, scarcely holding back her tears.* ARSEN *comes in.*)

ARSEN: Where are you going, my boy?

RAFAYEL: On a business trip.

ARSEN: The guys have come. They're waiting to see you.

RAFAYEL: Why are they waiting? What's up?

ARSEN: You recall you helped Sahak. Now the rest of my cronies are giving me a hard time wanting to meet you. Basically they've come to tell you, "Rafik, you've got to help us. You're our only hope."

RAFAYEL: Me? What exactly do they want done?

ARSEN: I can't say. Each one has a different problem.

(RAFAYEL *puts down his suitcase and hugs his father.*)

RAFAYEL: How are you, Dad?

ARSEN: Okay, Son.

RAFAYEL: Tell me that story again. It's ages since I heard it. You know, the one about the supply train from Russia in twenty-eight. You remember.

ARSEN: How could I forget? The time I was on guard duty. Let's see now, there was me, peg-leg Arsho and foxy Garsevan. Who knows where they are now and what they're up to. If they're alive, may God grant them long life. If they're dead, may God have mercy on their souls. What a harsh winter it was. Starvation on one side and bitter cold on the other. But we were young and hardy. On empty bellies we guarded the loaded train night and day. Nobody thought of breaking into it . . . till finally one of us cracked. The Devil entered him, Rafik. A biscuit fell out of foxy Garsevan's pocket. "What were you putting your hand in your pocket for?" we asked him. He looked at us, scared. But we were even more scared. We emptied his pockets and found four more. We took the five biscuits, turned them in and held a trial. We put the biscuits on the table, as material evidence. No one looked at Garsevan, everyone's gaze was fixed on the biscuits. All the witnesses were focused on the biscuits as they spoke. From that day on, Garso never showed his face. We couldn't find neither hide nor hair of him in the village. No one called him foxy after that. We used to call him that out of love. Let me call the boys now.

(RAFAYEL *doesn't answer, smiles vaguely, then picks up his suitcase and leaves. Going out the door, he is caught by surprise by the sight outside. A group of seven or eight elderly men, still as statues, are staring at him. Their gaze is full of entreaty and expectation. They stare at him without saying a word.* RAFAYEL *cannot endure the weight of their glance, lowers his head, and heads off. After going a little way, he suddenly turns and, overwhelmed and bitter, directs his words to* ARSEN, *who stands at the threshold.*)

RAFAYEL: Dad, how did that story go again?

EPILOGUE

RAFAYEL's *Construction Site*

(RAFAYEL's *entire team are seated around the table.* HAYK MARKOSYAN *sits in* RAFAYEL's *chair.* RAFAYEL *stands by the door.*)

MARKOSYAN: Any comments? (*Pause*) None of you has anything to say?
ARSHALUYS: What's there to say, till you explain what the man's done wrong?
CHILINGIRYAN: What difference does it make what we say. You simply can't remove Avetyan.
HAMO: Rafayel Arsenich, I know I'm not exactly your bosom buddy. But wherever you go, I'm going too.
VANIK: Avetyan's built half of Erevan. Did we ever get together like this and show him how much we appreciate him?
ZHANNA: Rafayel Arsenich, you know I was always late for a good cause. I've made

a resolution from tomorrow on never to be late again. But what's the use . . .

RUBEN: Just a minute. Just a minute. Wait, let's get this straight. Are you removing Avetyan for what he didn't do—or what he did do, and did extremely well?

RAFAYEL: Avetyan was guided by honorable motives. He also constructed the rail link out of these same honorable motives. But there has to be order in the world. There's such a thing as laws, right? Just imagine what would happen if everybody decided on their own to set everything to rights.

SARGSYAN: I still can't fathom how we were able to keep the rail link project under wraps. It's not as if we're on some desert island.

MARKOSYAN: Comrade Hambardzumyan, how come you haven't said a word yet? After all, you're Avetyan's deputy.

HAMBARDZUMYAN: Do you know what sort of thing *katanka* is?

ZHANNA: 'Course he does.

(MARKOSYAN's *glance meets* ZHANNA's. *Startled, she hides her head behind the back of the chair next to her.*)

HAMBARDZUMYAN: When you know, only then will you begin to understand Avetyan, and everything'll become clear.

MARKOSYAN (*getting up*): That's it then, Comrades. Now with regard to the rail link—

HAMO (*through his teeth*): One word about the rail link and I'll kill you.

(*Realizing what he has done, he diffidently conceals his face with a folder. Some of the others burst out laughing.* MARKOSYAN, *who does not understand what is going on, looks at them quizzically.*)

MARKOSYAN: Since the rail link's a fait accompli, apart from the final one and a half kilometers, I think we should finish the task. We'll draw up the resolution as follows. Rafayel Avetyan should be removed from the project for infringing work regulations, making illegal decisions, and exploiting his office, and the case should be handed over to the appropriate judicial bodies. Any objections?

[*No one raises a hand.*]

The meeting's adjourned, Comrades.

(*They all get up.*)

You stay behind, Avetyan.

(*Gradually the room empties. Only* MARKOSYAN *and* RAFAYEL *are left. They look at each other for a long time in silence from opposite ends of the rather long table.*)

MARKOSYAN (*He gets up and goes toward* RAFAYEL. *Extending his hand, he then suddenly embraces him tightly and whispers.*): Well done, Rafik. Well done.

Curtain

ANAHIT AGHASARYAN

Anahit Aghasaryan was born in Erevan on August 28, 1959. Thereafter, till the age of eight, she lived with her grandparents in a small village in the autonomous region of Nagorno Karabagh. Growing up in such an idyllic natural environment left a lasting impression on her. Back in Erevan with her parents, she began her formal schooling. However, she struggled under the regimentation of both environments until finally she demonstrated her feisty independence by running away from home.

Nevertheless, she graduated from school with a gold medal in 1977 and took the entry examination for the faculty of physics and mathematics at Erevan State University. Although she achieved high scores in her major fields, her unconventional approach to the subjects of Armenian language and literature did not meet with the examiners' expectations, and her application was rejected. She immediately decided to enter the theater where she could voice her views through her artistic roles.

Thus she entered the Sundukian State Academic Theater's acting studio, grounding herself solidly in the dramatic arts through stage and television performance. After graduation, she continued acting at the same theater until 1985, appearing in such varied productions as Saroyan's *My Heart's in the Highlands* and *The Time of Your Life*, Euripides' *Iphigenia in Aulis*, and Shakespeare's *All's Well That Ends Well*.

In 1986 she entered the Erevan Institute of Fine

Arts as a dramaturgy student. There she wrote her first dramatic works. Her play *Prkek mer hoginere* [Save our souls] was performed by the State Academic Theater in 1989 to enthusiastic reviews. This iconoclastic drama centers on a twenty-two-year-old homicidal drug addict, recently released from prison, who has difficulty coming to terms with life at large.

Subsequently, in 1992, two of her works were performed, the drama *Khelagar-nere bolor erkrneri miatsek* [Madmen of the world unite!], translated here, and the controversial melodrama *Uilli Titi Jig ev erekn el mi aghjik* [Willy, Titi, Jig: All three one girl], which played at the Metro Theater. The troubled protagonist adopts a new name at different stages of her life but, despite her adversities, finds the courage and hope to go on with her life.

Three years later, Aghasaryan's light comedy *Khelahegh or* [A crazy day] entered the basic repertoire of the State Musical Theater and has since appeared in the republic's provincial theaters, as well as in Tbilisi, Syria, and Lebanon. It tells the story of a sly but amiable crook, who contracts marriage with a rich, ugly woman several years his senior for personal gain.

Her most recent drama, *Anarak hor veradartse* [The return of the prodigal father] premiered in 1999 at the Erevan National Theater. It treats the urgent contemporary issue of emigration from the Armenian Republic, which has led to the exodus over the last few years of about one-third of the population. The play focuses on a man's return to Armenia after thirty years with the sole intention of taking his daughter, whom he has never seen, back with him to Los Angeles.

In addition to playwriting, Aghasaryan is involved in drama criticism, journalism, and writing for comedy shows on television and radio.

S.P.C.

MADMEN OF THE WORLD, UNITE!

(KHELAGARNERE BOLOR ERKRNERI MIATSEK, 1992)

Translated by S. Peter Cowe and Nishan Parlakian

CAST OF CHARACTERS

ARAMYAN: A fixer who acts as an agent for several political parties

HASRATYAN: A senior official of one of the political parties

AMATUNI: A member of parliament and president of the Committee on Women's Rights

SHAKE: An alias employed by **AMATUNI** in act 3 when she disguises herself as a waitress in a bar

SHAMAMYAN: A member of the current presidential cabinet; he disguises himself as a doctor in act 3

BRTUJYAN: A representative of the Armenian Revolutionary Federation Party

STATUE: A representative of the Communist Party who disguises himself as one of a set of three life-size model statues of **MHER** that are being prepared to adorn his grave

MHER ASTVATSATRYAN: An actor who has had himself committed to a psychiatric facility

PROFESSOR: An astronomer who has been committed to the same facility

GENERAL: An inmate of the facility who became unstable after losing his savings; he has a large collection of medals that he always wears on his chest

GHOST: An inmate who sees apparitions of ghosts

GIRL: An inmate who is constantly seen with a doll in her arms; she wants to have a child

MRS. ARMENIA: A variant on Mother Armenia, the personification of the Armenian homeland, watching over its people

FIRST DOCTOR

SECOND DOCTOR (DAVTYAN): A physician at the facility; in league with ARAMYAN and HASRATYAN

MEN IN BLACK: Rather nondescript security guards associated with the various parties

PHOTOGRAPHER

GLOUCESTER: A brief role in imitation of the character in *King Lear*, taken by one of the inmates

MASTER OF CEREMONIES: Oversees the presidential election press conference and inauguration ceremony

ACT 1

Presidential Election Press Conference

The scene is set in a medium-sized conference room. Men in black suits check the wings, under the podium, bring in a new carafe of water, remove the old water, and test the new. A PHOTOGRAPHER *stands at the ready with his camera. The room is full of journalists and government officials. The atmosphere is solemn and strained. Everyone waits in silence.* ARAMYAN *rushes in late and takes his place next to presidential contender* HASRATYAN. *Stony silence.* ARAMYAN *wipes the sweat off his brow with a handkerchief, and then observes the proceedings attentively.*

MASTER OF CEREMONIES: Moving right along now, I'd like to call on our next speaker, Mrs. Amatuni, member of parliament and president of the Committee for Women's Rights, to outline her party's platform.

(AMATUNI *goes to the podium. The photographers immediately set to work. On her way,* AMATUNI *strikes a few poses for them like a mannequin. Applause.*)

ARAMYAN (*aside to* HASRATYAN): I've come up with someone for our scheme. (*He joins in the general applause for* AMATUNI.)
HASRATYAN (*also applauding*): Who is it?
ARAMYAN: Someone expendable. He's made three suicide attempts already. (*Tapping his briefcase*) I have his dossier right here.
HASRATYAN: What guarantee is there that he'll go through with a fourth attempt?
ARAMYAN (*applauding again*): He's crazy.
HASRATYAN: That's no guarantee.
ARAMYAN: I should add, he's an actor.

HASRATYAN: That's a different story.

(*Pause*)

AMATUNI (*speaking from the podium with great animation*): Fellow Armenians, the presidential elections will soon be upon us. The women of Armenia have proposed my candidacy. Their longing, hopeful eyes say it all. When I see them, I simply cannot refuse to run. (*She sips some water.*)

(*Applause*)

HASRATYAN: That's a new one. Before, it was men she couldn't refuse!

AMATUNI (*continuing her speech*): Fellow Armenians, our party opposes the election of any man to the presidency. We mustn't make the same mistake again. A man should not be elected president for three simple reasons:

First, compare a woman's body with that of a man. Which of them is specifically attuned to intellectual activity? One glance at the male physique is enough to show it's only intended for physical labor.

Second, a man is naturally subservient to a woman. As a child, he is under his mother's control. When he marries, his wife assumes the direction of his life. When the husband finds a mistress, she immediately takes over. Finally, when he loses her, too, in old age, for obvious reasons, he simply drops dead.

Third, a woman's body is delicate and vulnerable. That's why she must resort to wiles, pretense, and deceit. Her self-defense instinct makes her a born diplomat, and diplomacy is essential to statesmanship. Women are never straightforward: For them, directness is a sign of inexperience, almost as unsophisticated as a man. And so only a woman should be elected president. (*Applause*) It's time to admit once and for all that the equality of men and women before the law is a myth, a legal fiction. The lesson to be drawn from nature is loud and clear. Men have always been children, and will stay children. Is it right to trust a child with running the country?

(*Applause*)

HASRATYAN: Nice work. I want to see that actor of yours tomorrow.

ARAMYAN: That's not possible.

(HASRATYAN *looks at him with a puzzled expression.*)

ARAMYAN (*defensively*): He's in a psychiatric facility.

HASRATYAN (*sharply*): Aramyan—

ARAMYAN (*justifying himself*): He's healthy, perfectly healthy.

MASTER OF CEREMONIES: I now call on our final presidential candidate, Mr. Hasratyan, member of parliament, whose candidacy is supported by a three-party socialist coalition.

(*Applause*)

HASRATYAN (*from the podium*): Friends, Ladies, and Gentlemen, anyone can advance his candidacy for president and participate in the upcoming elections at this time of great historic importance. But the winner can only be someone whose very being and temperament are in step with the times. He will automatically have truth and justice on his side, since his victory will have been dictated by the demands of the time. We, that is I, am, of course, not exempt from certain alleged flaws that have been continually ridiculed in the opposition press. (*He smiles.*) We, that is, I, have been called, by turns, harsh, heartless, wily, deceptive, and so on. I urge you not to take that as self-incrimination. (*He smiles.*) That's pure self-slander. But we're advancing our candidacy because our cause is the most in tune with our times.

(*Applause*)

Caesar was a crook, to quote the English writer Chapman.[1] But Caesar won. Cato was the embodiment of probity, but the people did not elect him, so he lost. Caesar won because Rome needed a dictator. Cato lost because he wanted to defend the republic. Was Cato wrong to be just? No. Was Caesar wrong to be a crook? No way. Individuals in history are not responsible for their characters and actions. Society gives birth to them in order to understand itself. That's why, right or wrong, I'm calling on you to give me your vote, so you can know and understand yourselves better.

(*Applause*)

[HASRATYAN *descends from the podium, shaking hands with supporters as he goes, amid shouts of congratulation.*]

BRTUJYAN (*to* ARAMYAN): Just look at that double chin Shamamyan has developed.

ARAMYAN: You'll get one just as big if your man becomes president.

---

1. The reference is to the play *Caesar and Pompey* by George Chapman (c. 1559–1634). For details, see *The Plays of George Chapman: The Tragedies with Sir Gyles Goosecappe*, ed. A. Holaday et al. (Cambridge: D. S. Brewster, 1987), pp. 529–99.

(AMATUNI *approaches* BRTUJYAN.)

BRTUJYAN (*sarcastically*): Hearty congratulations, Mrs. Amatuni. Your speech struck a real blow. To the foundations of legal equality, the foundations of the state, and your election hopes as well.

AMATUNI: How many minors have you registered to vote, you monster?

(BRTUJYAN *explodes.*)

MASTER OF CEREMONIES: Ladies and Gentlemen, your attention please. The presidential debate will begin in five minutes.

HASRATYAN (*to* SHAMAMYAN): Congratulations on your appointment to the cabinet, Shamamyan. Keep the seat warm till I take over.

SHAMAMYAN: You don't think you can win the elections, do you? (*With a loud guffaw, then ironically*) We're up a creak without a paddle, I suppose?

(*Some waitresses come in with drinks to serve on trays. Light music is playing in the background.*)

You haven't a chance. We hold all the trump cards: the people, the military, the church, and, after all, the supreme patriarch's our man. (*He picks up a glass.*) Incumbents in office are always the favorites, Hasratyan.

HASRATYAN (*smiling*): But then there are democratic, socialist, and communist forces working against you. (*He takes his glass.*)

SHAMAMYAN: Aren't you embarrassed to wrap yourself in those smelly old cliches? Don't you see they're piled high with dust. (*Loud guffaw.*)

HASRATYAN (*ironically*): Here's to your success! Since you hold all the cards.

(*They clink glasses.*)

SHAMAMYAN: And yours, Hasratyan. (*He drinks.*)

(*One of the waitresses whispers something in* SHAMAMYAN's *ear.*)

Excuse me. (*He leaves.*)

(AMATUNI *approaches* HASRATYAN.)

AMATUNI: What was that greasy swine talking about?

HASRATYAN: What's a card shark going to talk about if not poker? Congratulations, Mrs. Amatuni, on your excellent speech.

AMATUNI: Can you imagine? That pig's proposing I withdraw from the race to help the president's chances of reelection. The presumptuous ass, asking me to pull out. [*Confidentially*] Was he really talking about poker? I find it hard to believe.

HASRATYAN (*sipping his drink*): Yes. Political poker, that is. But that fool doesn't know I've got an ace up my sleeve.

AMATUNI: I'm dying to see you play your hand. I'd love his head on a silver platter.

HASRATYAN: Silver? Where's your class? Gold! On a golden platter, with fireworks and all the trimmings.

(*Both laugh aloud, clink glasses, and drink.*)

MASTER OF CEREMONIES: Ladies and Gentlemen, the presidential debate is about to begin. Will all those present please move into the auditorium and take their seats.

(HASRATYAN *gestures to* ARAMYAN, *who is wiping the sweat off his brow in heated conversation with someone. All the people onstage exit gradually.* ARAMYAN *approaches* HASRATYAN.)

ARAMYAN: Okay, what's up?

HASRATYAN: Give me the nut's folder. (*He takes it from* ARAMYAN *and flips through the pages.*)

ARAMYAN: Does the guy really have to commit suicide?

HASRATYAN: Don't you get it, you idiot? He's going to be our tool to get the president to resign. When he commits suicide in the name of the nation, the people will rally behind us and shame the president into resigning. The trick is to keep it under wraps that we knew the nut would kill himself. I can't get to be president if it comes out we were implicated.

ARAMYAN: I'm surprised it took us so long to track down this actor when he was under our plant's nose the whole time. After all, we were paying Dr. Davtyan good money to keep his eyes open for a suicidal maniac. Strange he never showed up in any of Davtyan's reports from the facility.

HASRATYAN (*examining the papers*): Is this clown an alcoholic?

ARAMYAN (*offended*): Twice he attempted to choke his wife in a blind rage. That's why he checked himself into the loony bin. Davtyan says he's perfectly sane. Now he regrets going in and wants out, but they won't let him leave.

HASRATYAN: Why not, if he's healthy?

ARAMYAN: He keeps the patients occupied, so they're less trouble for the doctors. The inmates feel so good, they don't bother to take their medication.

HASRATYAN: What does he do to amuse them?

ARAMYAN: He's turned the madhouse into a theater. He puts on plays with the inmates as actors.

(HASRATYAN *gives* ARAMYAN *a long quizzical look.*)

HASRATYAN: If this scheme falls through . . . I'll string you up by the short hairs.

(ARAMYAN *laughs nervously.*)

HASRATYAN (*continuing to read*): This actor fellow has a child. Good. A mental
    clinic's a terrific cover. Surely our plan's foolproof.
ARAMYAN: If it falls through, we'll say he's wacky.
HASRATYAN: There's no such thing as failure, Aramyan. Understood? (*He thinks.*)
    Are you glued to the spot?
ARAMYAN (*sheepishy*): Well, what am I supposed to do?
HASRATYAN: Look sharp. There's no time to lose. The elections are just around the
    corner. Go and get acquainted with him. See what makes him tick, engage
    him in small talk . . . put on a hospital gown to gain his trust. Tell Davtyan to
    give you one. Prepare the groundwork so I can take over. When everything's
    set up, give me a call. Take care how you handle him. Play it cool. Bullshit
    with him first to break down his defenses, then go for the kill.
ARAMYAN: Okay.
HASRATYAN: I'll be at my place. (*Going out*) Wait a minute. Take a bottle of vodka
    with you. Not for yourself, you understand. You're on the job, mind. Not a
    drop, Aramyan, not one drop, got it?
ARAMYAN: I hear you. (*He exits.*)

Curtain

The scene changes to a large ward in a psychiatric facility.

(*As the curtain opens, we see people dressed in hospital gowns. One is kneeling beside the wall. A hangman's noose dangles from a beam in the ceiling. One of the patients brings in a chair, and puts it under the noose. He wipes the chair with his cuff
and quickly takes his place. Everyone is waiting. From backstage* MHER *enters,
shrouded in a sheet, with bare feet and a crown of thorns on his head. One of the patients says "oof" and claps his hands. Another holds a cello.*)

MHER (*placing his hand on a patient's shoulder*): Pray, innocent one, and beware of
    the evil demon. The Lord calls me and says Nero's hunting frogs in the Sty-
    gian lake of hell. Is that right?

(*The patient nods.*)

Tell me, Uncle, is a madman an aristocrat or a plebeian?

PATIENT: He's a king.

MHER: No, he's a plebeian with an aristocratic son. Any plebeian's mad to give his son a hand up before ensuring his own advancement. (*To another patient*) Is that evil demon biting your stomach?

SECOND PATIENT: Yeah.

MHER: You're mad, my son.

SECOND PATIENT: Yeah.

MHER: A madman is somebody who believes in a wolf's naïvety, a horse's hooves, an adolescent's love, or a slut's oaths. Come, sit here, prudent judge. You, wise man, sit there. Now it's your turn, foxy ladies. (*He assigns them all different places.*) How are you, my lord, don't stand in such amazed confusion. Lie down here . . . (*To another*) Don't chirp, black angel, I don't have any food for you. (*To another*) You, sir, draped in robes of justice, be seated. (*To another*) You, his colleague on the bench, take your seat beside him. (*To others*) And you members of the jury, you sit down, too. (*To another*)

> Merry shepherd, do you sleep or wake?
> Your flock has been at pasture since daybreak.
> If you but whistle with your soft lip's charm,
> You'll keep your flock from every harm.

PATIENT: Pr-rr, the black cat's gray.

MHER: So it's singed. Let the trial commence. [*To the judge*] First call her, she's Goneril. [*To* MRS. ARMENIA] Come forward, lady.

[*She steps forward.*]

> Is your name Goneril?

MRS. ARMENIA: Yeah.

MHER: Pardon me, I thought you were a chair. Here's the second accused. (*He brings forward the* GIRL *carrying a doll.*) And now the third, whose evil eyes reveal the fabric of her heart. Stand there.

(*The girl runs away.*)

> (*He is shocked.*) Bribery holds sway even here! You false judge. Why did you permit her to get away? (*In someone else's voice*) Oh, this is most regrettable. Lord king, where's your much vaunted patience? (*In someone else's voice*) The puppies and the whole pack, Blacky, Blanche, and Beauty, are barking at me. (*In someone else's voice*) Get lost, you flea-ridden curs, don't bother the old man . . . (*He pats the judge on the shoulder.*) Sir, I accept you into my inner circle. Only I don't like your style of clothes. I suppose you'll tell me it's an Iranian costume, but couldn't you wear something else?

PATIENT: The dogs are barking at me.

MHER:

> Oh, those hounds again. Listen up, guys,
> Should your muzzle be white or black,
> Should your teeth form poisoned plaque,
> Pit bull, greyhound, and mongrel with fleas,
> Retriever and spaniel, whelp eager to please,
> Whether you're docked or still have a tail,
> Short or long, you'll all weep and wail.
> If I should only show my face,
> They'll bolt the fence without a trace.
> Du-Di, Du-di, Off . . .

THE PACK: Du-di, Du-di, Off . . . Du-di, Du-di, Off . . .

MHER: Don't make a noise, don't make a noise. Pull back the curtains like this, like this, like this . . .
(*He climbs on the chair. Silence. Everyone waits. He sings an aria from the opera* I Pagliacci. *He suddenly stops and pauses; then, serious and sad*): But if King Lear should happen to come by, tell him he's late . . . the jester's hanged himself with pain in his heart. (*He puts the rope around his neck.*)

(*The cellist begins to play. All look at him expectantly. He kicks the chair away. The others watch spellbound as he hangs. The hospital alarm goes off. Doctors rush in. They take down* MHER.)

MHER: What are you doing? The show's not over yet—

DOCTOR: Enough. You've had enough fun for one day. (*To the* SECOND DOCTOR) Remove the noose from his neck. Pull down the rope. (*To the patients*) Back to your rooms.

MHER: Let go. Keep your hands off the rope. Why have you got mixed up in this, what's up?

SECOND DOCTOR: What would be up? Do you want us to get a citation and lose our foreign humanitarian aid because of you?

MHER: Tuh! Oh what a crock! I'm wearing a vest, not a straightjacket. You guys should be wearing the straightjacket, not me. Look, distinguished doctors, I won't do it again. Put that out of your head. Mher Astvatsatryan will never again undertake a suicide attempt as long as this puky world rotates on its axis. Leave the rope, doctor. It's a stage prop. We need it for the play.

DOCTOR: I'll go off the deep end one of these days, from all the crap I have to take.

MHER: This is a vest, I tell you, not a straightjacket. I've learned some sense by now.

(*Emphasizing the words*) I'm not going to hang myself again. It's over. I'm already dead. I don't exist. Can the dead hang themselves, Uncle?

DOCTOR: It's impossible to tell when he's joking and when he's serious.

MHER: You're mad, my son.

DOCTOR: You're mad if you believe in a wolf's naïvety, a horse's hooves, an adolescent's love, and a slut's oath. (*To the* SECOND DOCTOR) Let's go.

MHER: Well done, doctor. I'll give you a part in my next production. You'll play Polonius.

DOCTOR: Yeah, that's all I need. We've played all your games. Now the fat lady's about to sing. Two days ago my wife said, "Why are you home so late? You're not on the graveyard shift. You think I don't know what hanky panky's going on." I said, "We were putting on a play by Shakespeare." She looked at me in disbelief, picked up the pillow, and marched to the other bedroom. Yesterday she called the psychic hot line to find out what her husband's up to. (*To the* GIRL *with the doll crouched beside the wall*) What are you doing here . . . are you still laying eggs?

GIRL: Doctor, let me push a little harder. It's about to come out.

SECOND DOCTOR: Come here, come on. The beer I put in the fridge has frozen solid. Off with you.

DOCTOR: Get up now. You've finished laying. Upsy daisy!

GIRL: You can't fool me, Doctor. An inner voice tells me I haven't laid.

MHER: Tuh! I didn't get a chance to recite my last monologue. These doctors have spoiled everything.

DOCTOR: Get up a moment. (*He picks up the imaginary egg.*) Isn't this an egg?

(*The* GIRL'*s eyes sparkle.*)

Take hold of it gently. (*He gives the imaginary egg to the* GIRL.) Off you go. Easy does it. Careful you don't break it.

(*The* SECOND DOCTOR *watches his colleague in amazement.*)

DOCTOR (*to the* SECOND DOCTOR): What are you gaping at? Let's go.

(*The Doctors exit.*)

MHER (*left alone*): Devil take them. (*He calls.*) Mrs. Armenia! Goneril! These quacks have messed up everything. Goneril!

MRS. ARMENIA (*coming in*): Why the devil are you shouting at the top of your lungs?

MHER: Another rat's fallen into the trap. Take it away, I bristle at the very sight of them. (*He gradually takes off his theatrical costume.*)

MRS. ARMENIA: Where is it?

MHER: Under the bed. Use this piece of paper to pick it up. Here you are. (*He hands her the paper.*)

MRS. ARMENIA (*bending under the bed*): How big these rats are. [*To the rats*] That's the end of you.

MHER: Take them away. Leave the trap here. (*He puts on his hospital gown.*)

MRS. ARMENIA (*going out*): Oh, don't squirm again. Take it easy.

MHER: Make me a cup of coffee. Those doctors have put me in a foul mood.

MRS. ARMENIA: No way. You haven't paid your rent for four months. How long am I going to keep you in my house for free? I'm not making you any coffee. (*She goes out.*)

(ARAMYAN *comes in, carrying a large bag. With swift, precise movements he takes various things out of the bag: a cup, a plate, a fork, some packets, and arranges them on the small table.* MHER *scrutinizes his every move.*)

ARAMYAN: What's the state of the nation?

MHER: I don't understand. Are you one of us or one of them?

ARAMYAN: What's the difference? It's one world, one universe. I've come from outer space. Just now. God says hello.

MHER: Mystery solved. When were you admitted?

ARAMYAN: I wasn't admitted exactly. I was sent. They said, "There's a tough assignment, Aramyan. Get yourself over there on the double." That German fox of a boss . . . "Psyche him up first," he said. "How should I go about it?" I said. "Work in from the side," he said. "Where's the side? Do you know how to find the side?" I said. " Aramyan, take this, Aramyan, bring that." Is Aramyan supposed to grow blind looking on all day while they fry trout. It's twelve thousand Armenian dram a fillet, you know? No Lake Sevan ersatz, a real trout. Who cares what Aramyan thinks?

MHER: Who's this Aramyan guy?

ARAMYAN: Oof! be quiet. I can't take that German fox of a boss. [*Mimicking* HASRATYAN] "I'll be at my place," he said. Liar. He's never at his place. [*Addressing the absent* HASRATYAN] Aramyan knows well enough whose place you're at. [*Turning to* MHER] I'll tell you where! He's with that Cleopatra with the dyed hair. Jet black. And her feet start way down here. Oho! They're using her like a football. [*Feigning a soccer pass*] First Shamamyan had her, then passed her to that German fox. But what do you care? All we want's a piece of bread. But even that's too much to ask. "Dangling sky high," to quote our poet Tumanian.[2]

---

2. The reference is to the Armenian poet Hovhannes Tumanian (1869–1923).

MHER (*clapping with joy*): Good that you've come, Uncle. I didn't have a Polonius for my new production. Have you played Shakespeare's Hamlet?

ARAMYAN: You mean that nut who runs around bumping people off? Jumping on everyone, accusing them all, abusing his mother, driving his girlfriend crazy and throwing her into a stream. He kills five, six people in one day.

MHER: But have you considered why he kills them?

ARAMYAN: Because there was no psychiatric facility. They were forced to keep loonies at home. If there'd been an asylum, they'd have committed him there and those innocent people wouldn't have died. He took it into his head that his uncle had poured poison in his father's ear. [*Engaging Hamlet in debate*] Hamlet, baby, kiddo, how did you come to the conclusion you were told this by "My father's spirit."[3] What father's spirit? Come on, snap out of it. [*Acting Hamlet*] "Yes, my father's ghost came and told me." Hey, Son, could it be you were dreaming? What's this about a ghost? What are you getting at? [*Hamlet*] "No, no, I saw it." Where, Son? You're sick. You're running a fever. Where did you see the ghost? [*Hamlet*] "In my soul's eye."

MHER (*He gradually approaches* ARAMYAN *and grabs him by the collar.*): Okay. Just tell me who you are and why you've come. You're no lunatic.

ARAMYAN: What? I really am sick. As schizoid as they come.

MHER: Only a normal guy would talk like that. Tell me who you are.

ARAMYAN: I'm your uncle. Didn't you call me uncle?

MHER (*pinning* ARAMYAN *against the wall*): Are you making fun of me, Buster? Has my wife sent you? Speak up! You think I'm crazy, right? . . . Has she sent you to check up on me, eh? Son of a bitch!

ARAMYAN: Let go, you psychopath. Help!

MHER: I'll fix you up now so no word'll ever come out of your foul mouth again. Sure, I'm psychopathic. Go and tell her she can sweat in someone else's bed. She's spent her whole life dreaming about it. Tell her she's free.

ARAMYAN: Let go, you fool, you're choking me. Help!

MHER: Don't waste your breath. Prepare to meet your Maker. Say your prayers, Uncle.

ARAMYAN: Help! Get him off me! (*He deftly takes a container of mace from his pocket and directs it at* MHER, *who tumbles to the floor.*)

(*The* DOCTOR *comes in.*)

ARAMYAN (*straightening his clothes and tie*): You said he was harmless. He just attacked me. If it weren't for this mace, he'd have choked me.

---

3. See *Hamlet*, act 1, scene 2, l. 254.

DOCTOR: Don't be afraid. He was kidding around. It's hard to tell when he's joking and when he's serious. We've gotten used to it. He's really a wonderful guy.

ARAMYAN: Some joke. He was about to kill me.

DOCTOR: I can't imagine what things would be like for us here if he were to go.

ARAMYAN: Didn't you assure us he's not dangerous?

DOCTOR: Calm down, he wouldn't hurt a fly. [*Pointing*] In case of emergency, press this button. (*He presses the button on the wall, which emits the sound Pee-Paah! Pee-Paah! He presses it again. Pee-Paah! Pee-Paah! He cannot tear himself away from the button. Mesmerized, he presses it again. Pee-Paah! Pee-Paah!*) . . . Neat, isn't it?

(ARAMYAN *looks at him timidly. The patients and doctors pile in noisily.*)

DOCTOR: What's going on? Why are you all milling around in here? What's the big deal?

SECOND DOCTOR: The alarm went off. What's happened to Mher?

DOCTOR: He fell asleep. He'll wake up any minute. Go, go, go. Nothing's the matter. Go on . . . break it up.

(*They all start to leave.*)

GENERAL (*to* ARAMYAN): Got any connections at the Swiss Bank? (*He heads off.*)

DOCTOR: Do you play chess?

ARAMYAN: No. (*Leaning over* MHER) Seems to be coming 'round.

DOCTOR: Too bad. (*He goes out.*)

ARAMYAN: Mher? Mher?

MHER: Go to hell.

ARAMYAN: Give me your hand.

MHER: Go to hell. (*He gets up.*) What was that all about?

ARAMYAN: Self-defense. What was I supposed to do? Let you choke me?

MHER: Ooh! My head's spinning. Today's not my lucky day. Did my wife send you? Does she want a divorce? Get a note from Davtyan and take it back to her. The court'll immediately grant a divorce. Go on. Get lost.

ARAMYAN: Don't you want something to eat? Just look what I've brought. (*He opens up the packets he had laid on the table earlier.*)

MHER: Take your chow and beat it. I've had a tough day. And I've been in a pretty lousy mood this last decade.

ARAMYAN: I've no contact with your wife. I don't even know her. I've come to see you on some other business. I know you're at loggerheads with yourself and the world. You were a heavy drinker and ended up on the street completely destitute. One day you showed up here among the crazies and felt at home. You've found your niche. You help people, you've got a roof over your head, they feed you, they like you. At last you've found a place where you feel useful, after being useless for so many years. But the most important thing is that here you can perform roles you never could as an actor. (*Pause.* ARAMYAN *digs into some of the food with a hearty appetite.*) I haven't had a bite to eat since morning. I've been rushing around all over the place. What a life!

MHER: Who are you?

ARAMYAN: Difficult question. To explain who I am, I have to say why I've come. To say why I've come, I have to tell you what I want from you. But if I tell you what I want from you now, you'll kill me. Or my boss Hasratyan, that German fox, will do the job for you, if I mess up. I have to psyche you up for what you're gonna hear.

MHER: Shoot. You're whetting my interest. Is it a detective story?

ARAMYAN: It's a dreadful story. And they've stuck Aramyan in the middle of it again.

MHER: Who's this Aramyan guy anyway?

ARAMYAN: Okay. It goes like this. (*Pause*) Where shall I start?

MHER: At the end.

ARAMYAN: Sure, why not? (*Having memorized this by heart*) You have no money, no work, no family, no home, you're stuck in a madhouse, nobody visits you. They've all forgotten you, no one needs you. You're superfluous, you're through. I mean, you basically don't exist. Nothing in life's worked out for you. Not even suicide. But one decision can change all that. You've dreamed of fame but never achieved anything. Now's your chance for greatness. Everyone will know your name. You'll redeem yourself in your wife's eyes, though she's always regarded you as a jobless, lazy freeloader. Your child will be proud of you. Your mother will sing her son's praises, and your name will be on her lips till her dying day.

MHER: That was a superb ending. Now double back to the start so I get an idea of what you're talking about. (*Suddenly he is jolted.*) Wait a minute. Are you a director? Are you offering me a part? (*He slaps his head.*) I should have cottoned up to you right away. Out with it, out with it. Hurry up. What's my part? I'll be damned. I always felt that one day I'd make it in a film or in theater.

ARAMYAN: You must be mad to think—

MHER (*eagerly*): I'm only mad when the wind blows from the northwest. But when it's from the south, I can tell a hawk from a jay. Let me introduce myself. I'm Mher Astvatsatryan. I've played . . . actually I haven't played that many roles. Let me see. I've played Nazar the Brave. I used to dream of playing the part of the actor in Gorky's *The Lower Depths*.[4] You remember? He hangs himself at the end. Tell me what part you're offering me?

---

4. Maxim Gorki's play *The Lower Depths*, published in 1902.

ARAMYAN: Something similar.

MHER: Does he hang himself at the end?

(A *man with tousled hair comes in screaming. In the hospital he goes by the name of* GHOST. *The others follow him in.*)

GHOST: Mher! Mher! He's come back. Over there. Go talk to him. Tell him to leave me alone. I'm afraid, Mher!

MHER: Tuh! Oh, just my luck.

GHOST: He's at the palace next door. The door's bolted on the inside. He's putting his hand through the wall and wants to catch me. Chase him away, Mher. Drive him from the palace.

MHER: Okay, okay. I'll go this instant. Don't budge from here. (*He rushes out.*)

(*Everyone moves about the room uneasily.*)

ARAMYAN: Who bolted the door on the inside?

GHOST: Hey, Dude, I'm just sitting there minding my own business. I look down at my writing pad and suddenly this ghost appears.

PROFESSOR (*interjecting*): It's not a ghost. It's a space alien.

GHOST (*furious*): That's it. I'm not saying another word.

ARAMYAN: There, there. Don't be upset. So what did the ghost do?

GHOST: Why did that egghead interrupt me? I refuse to go on.

PROFESSOR: Forgive me, dear friend. Forgive me.

GHOST: Okay. So I was sitting there minding my own business. I looked at my pad for quite a while.

ARAMYAN: How come?

GHOST: What do you mean, "how come"?

ARAMYAN: How come you were looking at your pad for such a long time?

GHOST: It's red.

ARAMYAN (as if comprehending): Aha . . .

GHOST: Suddenly he starts moving toward me slowly, slowly, ever so slowly, snatches my pad in a flash and throws it at me. Now tell me, what was that all about? What have you got to say to that?

PROFESSOR: It's that menace from the Ophiuchus constellation. [*Aside to* GHOST] That's snake charmer to you. That's who attacked you.

GHOST (*annoyed at the interruption*): Who does he think he is? I'm not saying another word.

PROFESSOR: My fault again. Forgive me.

GHOST: A while back I was counting money at work. Suddenly this hand appears out of the wall, coming closer and closer. It suddenly tosses the bills into the air and disappears. That evening my wife pulls the notes out of the rice she's straining for dinner. So tell me, what's going on? [*Snubbing the* PRO-FESSOR *and posing the question to* ARAMYAN *instead*] No, you tell me what's going on?

(MHER *returns.*)

MHER: I spoke to your ghost. He unlocked the door and left. He's gone. So you can go, too.

GHOST: Did you tell him to stop bugging me?

MHER: Sure, sure. Off with you. Off you go. (*He shoos the patients out.*)

PROFESSOR (*to* ARAMYAN): Look here. (*He has laid out a stellar chart.*) Look care-fully. This is the constellation of Scorpio.

MHER: Later, Professor. Not now, later. This fellow's come to see me on business.

PROFESSOR: One second, just one second, Mher.

MHER: Tush! . . . Professor.

PROFESSOR: Look here. (*Pointing to the map*) This is Scorpio. This is the constel-lation Libra, above is the constellation Hercules. Before, the Ophiuchus con-stellation was here . . . Look. But now it's not here. It's moved. You under-stand? It's moved. It's entered the zodiac.

MHER: Professor.

PROFESSOR: One moment. He should know the Ophiuchus has entered the zodi-ac. The question arises, why?

ARAMYAN: Why?

PROFESSOR (*cryptically*): Because he has a plan. He has something in mind.

ARAMYAN: What?

PROFESSOR: To destroy the world. Look—

MHER: That's enough, Professor.

ARAMYAN (*to* MHER): If you find this boring, don't listen. (*To the* PROFESSOR) Go on, Professor.

PROFESSOR: Look. Here in the Ophiuchus constellation a star of exceptional bril-liance was observed in the year 1604. Previously there'd been no trace of such a thing. However, in March of 1605 that star burned out. The question arises, why? After all, its light was a billion times brighter than the sun.

ARAMYAN: Why?

MHER: What the hell . . . Professor.

PROFESSOR (*with emphasis*) Because Satan set foot on it. That's why the star burned out. Satan's the lord of darkness. Now he's ruling us from there and has gone into the zodiac. Do you understand? He's using it to realize his age-old scheme.

ARAMYAN: What scheme?

PROFESSOR: Spiritual annihilation.

ARAMYAN: So how does he go about it?

PROFESSOR: Magic.

MHER: PROFESSOR. (*To* ARAMYAN) He can go on forever.

ARAMYAN: Don't interrupt. (*To the* PROFESSOR) So then . . .

PROFESSOR: The star I referred to was a neutron star, you understand. They're fascinating objects. Their diameter's smaller than the earth's radius, but their density's enormous. One cubic centimeter of these stars weighs millions, billions of tons.

ARAMYAN: Sheer madness . . . (*to* MHER) Can you imagine? (*Gesticulating*) A cube this size. . . a million tons.

PROFESSOR (*enthusiastically*): Those stars, you see, rotate at an extremely high velocity. They possess vertical radiation and an awesome magnetic field. Now perhaps you understand the sort of radiation we're up against. What powerful rays Satan's sending our way from the constellation I mentioned. Consider its name more closely. Ophiuchus, the snake charmer. It's him, him. The lord of the snake in the Bible. Satan. It's him, I tell you.

ARAMYAN: Wow, what are our scientists thinking, sitting back with their arms folded? We have to blow up that constellation. Blow it up and destroy it forever. Can you think of something?

MHER (*exploiting the opportunity*): Good idea, Professor, good idea. Think it through. Only you can find a solution. Off you go.

PROFESSOR: Me? What can I do? I'm just a poor scholar.

MHER: Think it over carefully.

PROFESSOR: I'm powerless against Satan's tricks. With a snap of his fingers he can conjure up all sorts of things.

ARAMYAN: Like what?

PROFESSOR: Like what? Like the parliament of Armenia, the first Christian nation, seriously debating polygamy. The people are all opposed, but, diabolically, their representatives seem to be in favor. One after another, poets are lining up to join the police force.[5] Can you imagine a more astounding trick? I want to scream. My heart's bursting. I want to jump right out of my skin. I'm going mad. My brain's turning to pulp. I'm powerless against Satan, powerless. Do you understand, Mher? Don't abandon me. You swore you'd help me.

MHER: I won't leave you, Professor, no way. Go and take a sedative and lie down.

ARAMYAN [*to the* PROFESSOR]: I'm with you on this. Together we'll beat Satan.

PROFESSOR: Really? Promise? Swear! I can't do anything on my own, you understand. Atheism's my undoing.

---

5. An oblique reference to the poet Vano Siradeghyan, who became Minister of the Interior for a time in the Ter Petrosuan administration.

ARAMYAN: What's atheism got to do with it?

MHER: Phoo! He's off again.

PROFESSOR: Investigating the stars and their movements gives rise to a thousand unanswered questions. You know what I mean? These strain human reason to the breaking point and the mind goes into overdrive. It begins to warp with the effort. The only reason there are scientists out there who haven't been committed to a place like this is that they're shielded against these unanswered questions. They've taken up arms.

ARAMYAN: What arms?

PROFESSOR (*in a whisper*): God. But I'm an atheist, you understand. There's no salvation for me! None at all! Wars, plagues, gaps in the ozone layer, the neutron bomb . . . (*He grasps his temples firmly with his hands and gradually falls into a trance.*) . . . blood, flood, earthquakes. Our ship's foundering in space. Save us, we're sinking. Oh God. (*He prays, his head twisting and his body writhing.*)

(ARAMYAN *watches him in terror.*)

MHER: Professor, Professor . . . (*He presses the alarm button.*)

(*The blare of the siren fills the hall, drowning out the* PROFESSOR's *shriek. The doctors and patients pile in.*)

DOCTOR: Back . . . back . . . keep away.

(*They take the* PROFESSOR *away.*)

SECOND DOCTOR: Who got him talking? (*To* MHER) Why did you let him talk?

ARAMYAN: (*guilty*) I had no idea—

SECOND DOCTOR (*to the patients*): Out with you. It's dinner time. Get a move on.

GENERAL: What's on the menu? Surely not milky gruel again?

SECOND DOCTOR: No. Beluga caviar and roast lamb. Out with you. (*He takes the patients out.*)

GENERAL (*As he leaves, he whispers in* ARAMYAN's *ear*): Haven't you any connections with the Swiss Bank to help me get my money out?

ARAMYAN: What?

SECOND DOCTOR: Out you go. Out, out. (*He pushes the* GENERAL *out.*)

ARAMYAN (*to* MHER): Who is this guy?

MHER: He was a prominent local government official. When Armenia left the ruble zone and everything had to be converted to Armenian dram, he lost all his savings in the exchange. He thinks I'm his grandson. We've had a rough day today. Everything's going wrong. Nothing's worked out.

(*They are silent and sad.*)

ARAMYAN: Are the medals his? Is he a real general?

MHER: Yeah, they're real. He collects insignia. After losing his money he's afraid he'll lose them as well. He doesn't take off his jacket when he goes to sleep. But that's neither here nor there. You came on business, didn't you, Sir? What is it you're proposing?

ARAMYAN: Why are you suddenly so polite to me?

MHER: Oh, I don't know. Can you tell me what part I'm auditioning for. Is it in a play?

ARAMYAN :(*sadly*) No.

MHER: In the movies?

ARAMYAN: No.

MHER: You've got me there.

ARAMYAN: In life.

MHER: You've really got me.

(*Pause*)

ARAMYAN: Okay. Let's have a drink . . . if I don't have one, I won't be able to say what I have to. (*He removes the bottle of vodka from the bag and opens it.*) To think that a cube this size weighs a million tons. (*He pours.*)

MHER (*becoming irritated*): Just what do you think you're doing?

ARAMYAN: I'm pouring you a drink. Don't you want one? It's dinner time.

MHER: Is it vodka?

ARAMYAN: No, rabbit piss.

MHER: Put it away. You keep the bottle to yourself.

ARAMYAN: Why?

MHER: I won't be drinking.

ARAMYAN: Do you think this is my idea? I was forced into it. "Take the bottle along, but mind, not a drop for you, Aramyan, do you hear?" The boss was very insistent on the point. "Get him to have a drink, but don't you touch a drop." Is Aramyan supposed to open the bottle and not have a drink? Is he to swallow down his saliva as he watches other people having a good time, eh? Can you imagine? We're on a mission of great political sensitivity. So here's to you, German fox. (*He drinks.*) How can someone who's seen so much not drink? What's to stop me? What? (*He bites into a gherkin.*) What a punch this has. My mouth's still stinging . . . What are you staring at? Go on, pick up your glass.

MHER: I'd like to know who's crazy, you or me?

ARAMYAN: We're all crazy. Me, you, all of us. Haven't you seen people walking along the street talking to themselves?

MHER: I don't understand a thing. (*Undoing the zipper on his pants, he goes back-stage. Soon after, the sound of urine dribbling is heard.*)

ARAMYAN: Oof, the country's swarming with nuts and moochers. And who's to blame? The government, of course. The nation's hanging itself in shifts: one batch today, the next tomorrow. Then there are others like me who want to hang myself, but . . . never quite get around to it.

MHER (*from offstage*): I don't know. I don't understand politics. Even during the turmoil of the late eighties under glasnost I didn't attend the demonstrations and shout. I had more serious things to do.

ARAMYAN: Like what?

MHER (*He comes in, straightening his pants.*): I was into drinking, hanging myself, and vomiting in the streets.

ARAMYAN: Exactly what I was getting at. So much for the intelligentsia. History's being made on the square and they're vomiting in the streets. But who has the nation's interests at heart? Me? . . . Aramyan again?

[MHER *starts to leave.*]

Hold on, where are you off to?

MHER: To see Davtyan. I want to clear up who you are and why you've come. "I like not that," says Iago.[6] Vodka, then mace. It's suspicious. Decidedly odd, I'd say. (*Suddenly he attacks* ARAMYAN.) Enough of your hemming and hawing. Are you going to tell me or not? Stop stalling, you bloody Sadist!

ARAMYAN: You're off your rocker, Mher. Let me go.

MHER: I don't care about the spray you've got. I'll just plaster you to the wall. They'll have to scrape you off. Speak up, and none of your crap.

ARAMYAN: Where were we when the Ghost came in? How far had I got to? (*He tries to recall.*)

MHER: My mother's lips.

ARAMYAN: I need another drink to keep up my spirits. (*He pours.*) Care to join me?

MHER: No.

ARAMYAN: Just as well. I'm going to tell you something now that'll make your eyes flip up to your forehead. (*He drinks.*) Ooh! . . . (*He bites into a cucumber.*)

MHER: Hm!

ARAMYAN: Are you psyched up for it?

MHER: Sure. Out with it.

ARAMYAN: Basically we're asking you to . . . How can you say this to someone?

MHER (*He seizes* ARAMYAN *by the collar and yells.*): Are you making fun of me, you

---

6. The reference is to Iago's comment in *Othello*, act 3, scene 3, l. 35.

son of a bitch? Either tell me or get lost. (*He grabs hold of* ARAMYAN's *tie and yanks him toward himself.*) You good-for-nothing bastard. Get lost before I smash your face in.

ARAMYAN: Hold on now, my boy.

MHER: You stink, you lap dog.

ARAMYAN: I want to help you, stupid. I've come to do you a favor. I want to help you become rich and famous.

MHER (*He lets him go.*): What's that? Me, rich and famous? How are you going to do that? Tell me!

ARAMYAN: For that I need to get to know you better. First, I have to sort out whether you're the man we're looking for. Got it, stupid? I have to gain your confidence, then offer you the part. But you keep throttling me. Sit down . . . sit down across from me. Come on. First let's get to know each other better.

MHER: Okay.

ARAMYAN: Pick up your glass. Let's drink to your sweet memory.

MHER: Oh yeah? You're hard to figure out. Davtyan will have a lot of explaining to do if it turns out you're mad. (*He picks up the glass rather slowly and warily.*)

ARAMYAN: Davtyan's one of our boys. He's in on everything. Down the hatch! Here's to you, German fox. (*They drink.*) Do you know who this German fox is? He used to translate German authors: he was down and out. Just look at him now, a party leader. You don't know him. He's a spider and he's caught me in his web. I'm buzzing like a fly. Mher, what's up? You're not upset, are you? Stick a piece of this in your mouth.

(MHER *tears off a piece of bread with his hand.*)

Don't pass out now. The committee's got to decide when you're going to die. Mher . . .
(*He fills a glass and hands it to* MHER.) Have a drink and snap out of it. (*He pushes the glass to* MHER's *lips.*) Take this, too. Eat up. (*He forces* MHER *to eat.*) Feeling better? Vodka's good after gas. Right?

MHER: Right.

ARAMYAN: Take it from Aramyan. Aramyan knows what he's talking about.

MHER: So you're Aramyan.

ARAMYAN: Yes. Azat Aramyan. As my name indicates, I'm free and independent. And you're Mher Astvatsatryan, shackled like your mythological namesake. Let's drink to friendship. Cheers.

(*They drink.*)

MHER: How good of you to come.

ARAMYAN: Let's get down to business. When you look around you, what do you see?

MHER: A hospital ward, a madhouse, a watchman's hut, a woodcutter's cottage, a drunkard's hideout, an actor's last resort . . . What exactly are you getting at?

ARAMYAN (*ejaculating*): You can't even talk to this guy. Are you stoned? (*Irritated*) What is it you see? (*He draws a circle with his hands.*) Death warmed over. That's all there is. Gloomy people, gloomy streets, plagues, catastrophes . . . Is life worth living?

MHER: No, it's not.

ARAMYAN: A spinning ball. They call it a planet. And us on it. Round and round. Just tell me why you're turning. Who are you trying to impress? Our heads are giddy already. Isn't yours spinning?

MHER: It sure is.

ARAMYAN: I've got palpitations. I can't take it any more. I'm going to throw up. (*He retches violently and* MHER *apes him.*) That's why I've taken such a shine to him. (*They drink.*)

MHER: How good of you to come, Comrade.

ARAMYAN: Say that word again and the deal's off. Do you think Aramyan's come here to mess around? Watch your mouth when you talk to me.

MHER: I'm all ears. (*Half-drunk*) I'm in your hands, Azat you optimist? If I had a thousand and one lives I'd gladly sign a thousand over to you.

ARAMYAN: That's why I like you so much. Fill it up. (*He holds up his glass.*)

MHER (*gesturing toward the bottle*): It's empty . . .

ARAMYAN (*taking out a second bottle*): They sent me off with only one bottle. What good's that to Aramyan? (*He hands it to* MHER.) Twist it open and fill up. (*They drink.* ARAMYAN *suddenly bursts into tears.*)

MHER: What's the matter, brother optimist?

ARAMYAN: To think a nice guy like yourself will have to give up—

MHER: Give up?

ARAMYAN (*in tears*): That's right.

MHER (*drunk*): I'm ready to give up my life for you, old buddy.

ARAMYAN: I don't want it. They do. I'm just small fry. What is it we want? A piece of bread, and even that's beyond our reach, as Tumanian put it.[7] He was no drinker, you know. But his words really touched Aramyan.

GENERAL (*entering, carrying a tray*): Here are my rations, Mher. I ate half and brought you the rest. (*To* ARAMYAN) There are your rations. Eat up. So you'll grow big and strong. (*He puts the food in front of him.*)

MHER: Pops, you shouldn't have. I'm full already.

———

7. See note 1.

ARAMYAN: Pull up a chair and listen. (*To* MHER) They want you to do a bit of dirty business for them. (*Disgusted*) That's why they assigned me to the case. (*He takes out the hospital gown and starts putting it on.*) I'll explain.

GENERAL: Have you any connections in Swiss banks to help me get my money out? I'll give you ten percent.

ARAMYAN: What?

GENERAL: Not so loud. Fifteen percent.

ARAMYAN: I'm supposed to run off to Switzerland for you. Hello—good-bye. While you sit here comfy? So Aramyan's going to get hitched again. (*Adjusting his gown*) What's this then?

GENERAL: An Iranian costume.

ARAMYAN: No. I was given this to blend in as a patient. Why? So I could win your confidence. It's all conspiracy. Do I look like a madman, or what?

MHER: Hell, no. I'd sooner believe in a judge's justice.

ARAMYAN: Well, it's on now, as instructed. But then whom do I look like?

GENERAL (*to* MHER): Isn't he your chemistry teacher?

ARAMYAN (*answering for* MHER): No, I'm the spitting image of Aramyan in a gown.

GENERAL (*to* MHER): Who is this Aramyan fellow?

ARAMYAN: I was. Once.

GENERAL: We got that. (*He stuffs money into* ARAMYAN's *pocket.*) Take it, take it. Leave my grandson here alone, Comrade Chemistry Teacher. My grandson shouldn't go blind poring over books. Do you catch my drift? Patvakan Smbatovich won't let you turn his grandson into a nerd.

ARAMYAN: Who's Patvakan Smbatovich?

GENERAL: I was. Once. As you were once Aramyan.

ARAMYAN: I'm really warming to you. Come, Friend, let's down a glass or two.

GENERAL: No. Davtyan'll beat me. I'm very afraid of being beaten. I shake when they beat me on the head. They used to beat us all, but since my grandson Mher came along, they've stopped. No. I'm off. I don't want—

ARAMYAN: They used to beat the inmates? (*He is moved.*) What kind of life is that? I don't want to live. I'm weary. I can't go on.

MHER: Forget it, Stranger. Come, Friend, let's have another. To hell with it all. (*He hands* ARAMYAN *a glass.*)

ARAMYAN (*pushing it away*): No. I don't want any. I've had it up to here. What kind of life is this? (*He is about to fall.* MHER *catches hold of him.*) Let me go. I'm off.

MHER: Where?

ARAMYAN: I'm going to hang myself. (*He goes up to the rope.*)

MHER: Excuse me, but that's my rope. I'm going to hang myself with it.

ARAMYAN: What, you got your name on it?

MHER (*pushing* ARAMYAN): Keep your hands off. It's my rope. I convinced them to leave it up. Go find your own rope to hang yourself with.

ARAMYAN: What an egoist you are. Let's both hang ourselves.

MHER (*without interrogation*): Together, then.

ARAMYAN: Ah! You're so cute. (*He sings.*) Oh, to have a good, handsome, faithful friend . . . (*They both stagger, getting up on a chair, scarcely finding room to stand. Side by side they take hold of the rope and start singing. In walks* HASRATYAN.)

HASRATYAN: What the hell's going on, Aramyan?

MHER: You jerk, you've ruined our song.

HASRATYAN: What did I send you for? We've lost four hours already.

MHER: Your face looks familiar to me, Uncle. Where have I seen you?

ARAMYAN: This is Hasratyan.

MHER: Oh, Mr. Big. If you pass me some dough, I'll make you two crowns.

ARAMYAN (*assuring him, drunk*): He'll do it.

HASRATYAN: Get down immediately, Aramyan. What's going on here?

ARAMYAN (*slurring*): Nothing, Mr. Hasratyan. All the action's in the snake charmer's constellation.

HASRATYAN: What's gotten into you, Aramyan. You're drunk. I hope you're not going bonkers.

ARAMYAN: You bet I am. How could I not be. This much cubed and a million tons.

HASRATYAN: Get your ass over here on the double. You can go.

(ARAMYAN *leaves immediately.* HASRATYAN *scrutinizes* MHER *long and hard.*)

MHER (*dangling from the rope with one hand*): Please press the alarm button. I need somebody to come take me down. I'm not feeling well. Do it. I'm not well.

(HASRATYAN *goes out without saying anything. Darkness. A crash. The chair falls over.*)

MHER'S VOICE: I'm not well.

ACT 2

Still in the psychological clinic. HASRATYAN, *two men in black suits, and* MHER.

HASRATYAN: Young man, I'd have you know I'm here on important business and don't intend to hang around wasting time.

MHER: Please keep those flies off my nose, Uncle.

HASRATYAN: I've been informed you've made several suicide attempts. You don't want to live and, as I've been given to understand, you haven't changed your mind.

MHER: The flies are swarming all over me. They're getting ready to feast on my corpse. Get them off me, Uncle.

HASRATYAN: You can clown around to your heart's content once I'm out of here. For the moment, listen carefully. I've a serious proposition for you.

MHER (*writhing around to gain respite from the flies*): Help me, Uncle. One's on my nose. Look how big it is. Catch it before it gets up my nose. (*He sneezes.*)

HASRATYAN: I get it. You're trying to make me lose my cool. But you've got a better chance to fly to the moon. (*Moving closer to* MHER *until they are almost face to face.*) Do you want to help your mother and your child? After all you're going to rot in this madhouse, deserted and forgotten by everyone. Or you'll flip out and jump from a window one fine day. And that'll be the end of you. Isn't it better to do something nice for your kid before you kick the bucket? What have you got to lose. I'm giving you a chance.

(MHER *does not say a word. Long pause.*)

What's going through your mind?

MHER: I'm scratching around like a chicken.

HASRATYAN: I'm offering you an assignment. Top secret. One with serious political implications. If you help me out, I'll make it worth your while.

MHER: What? Me help you? (*He laughs.*) This year's bad for madmen. The sane have all lost their heads. They're aping the insane.

HASRATYAN: Listen, clown. Are you capable of being serious for one second?

MHER: God forbid, Uncle. This is my natural state.

HASRATYAN: Look, wise guy, I'm warning you. This is the toughest day of my life. I'm ready to pop off anybody that gets in my way.

MHER (*amused, as the fool in King Lear*): Are you threatening me, my Lord? If you were my fool, I'd have you whipped for growing old without any sense.[8]

HASRATYAN (*pulling himself up*): So that's it. Amused, are you? We can play it that way, too. Okay, I'm listening. Humor me. (*He settles into a comfortable chair.*) On with the show. It's ages since I was at the circus.

MHER:

> The rugged Pyrrhus, he, whose sable arms[9]
> Black as his purpose, did the night resemble
> When he lay couched in the ominous horse,

---

8. Variation on the Fool's dialogue with Lear in *King Lear*, act 1, scene 5, ll. 39–41.

9. Citation from Hamlet's speech in *Hamlet*, act 2, scene 2, ll. 455–68. For the original Armenian version of the passage, which Aghasaryan cites here, see *Shekspir Hamlet*, trans. H. Masehian (Vienna: Mkhitarist Press, 1921), p. 52.

Hath now this dread and black complexion smear'd
With heraldry more dismal. Head to foot
Now he is total gules, horridly trick'd
With blood of fathers, mothers, daughters, sons,

HASRATYAN (*continuing*):

Bak'd and impasted with the parching streets,
That lend a tyrannous and a damned light
To their lords' murther. Roasted in wrath and fire,
And thus o'er-sized with coagulate gore,
With eyes like carbuncles, the hellish Pyrrhus
Old grandsire Priam seeks.
So proceed you.

(*Pause. They look at each other.*)

HASRATYAN (*to the men in black suits*): Leave us.

(*The men go out.*)

MHER (*slowly*): So what's your pleasure?

HASRATYAN: Exactly what you did twice already without success.

MHER: I don't get it.

HASRATYAN: This time we'll help you get it right.

MHER: Hang myself, you mean?

HASRATYAN (*smiling*): Not necessarily. We'll discuss the means later.

MHER (*He starts to laugh, but breaks off.*) What am I going to hang for?

HASRATYAN: Same as before when you tried three times to commit suicide. You tell me what for.

MHER: I just don't get it. What's in it for you?

HASRATYAN (*smiling*): We'll discuss that later. Besides, it's not essential for you to know. You do your job and get paid for it. For the moment (*opening an attache case*) all we need is your agreement. Here's the first installment. (*He shows MHER money. MHER, dumbstruck, stares at the briefcase.*) Forty thousand. If you agree in principle, you'll receive another forty in a couple of days. You wanted to commit suicide for nothing, but I'm proposing you do the same thing tomorrow and get something for it.

MHER: Tomorrow?

HASRATYAN (*with charming sarcasm*): If not . . . you'll have time to amuse yourself. The day will be decided at a closed session of the bureau. The key thing is to prepare for the event.

MHER: Event?

HASRATYAN (*pretending not to hear him*): So we're agreed then. You'll receive most of your fee posthumously.

MHER: Posthumously?

HASRATYAN: Yes. We'll transfer it to your child's bank account.

MHER (*unable to take his eyes off the money*): How much?

HASRATYAN: A six-figure sum.

MHER (*quipping, dismissively*): What? All those zeros. That's nothing. You can't making anything out of nothing, Uncle.

HASRATYAN: Damned right, my son. Nothing comes from nothing.[10]

(MHER *starts laughing convulsively. He looks at the briefcase.*)

HASRATYAN: What were you saying back there, clown? Give me some dough and I'll make you two crowns. Excellent! I'll give you two hundred thousand pounds of dough and you can help me obtain a crown.

(*They both laugh.*)

(*Haratyan extends his hand.*) Thank you and good-bye.

(MHER *shakes his hand mechanically.* HASRATYAN *is about to go out.*)

MHER: Wait . . . (*confused*) What should I do now?

HASRATYAN (*with a parting shot*): Live.

MHER (*approaching the bundles of banknotes*): I don't know what he's up to.

(*The inmates file in, carrying scripts.*)

MHER (*flustered*): What's going on? Why are you here?

GIRL: Rehearsal.

MHER (*recalling*): Ah! Okay. Have a seat. Turn to act 4, scene 5. (*He quickly hides the money.*) Ophelia, you're on. Action.

GIRL (*intoning*):

> Tomorrow's the feast of St. Valentine.[11]
> At early dawn,

---

10. Variation on Lear's line "Nothing will come of nothing: speak again" (*King Lear*, act 1, scene 1, l. 84).

11. English rendering of the Armenian version of Ophelia's distracted speech in *Hamlet*, act 4, scene 1, ll. 49–66. For the original Armenian version of *Hamlet*, which Aghasaryan is quoting here, see *Shekspir Hamlet*, p. 102 n. 9.

Standing beneath your window
I'll be your Valentine.
The youth came, and got dressed
And gently opened the house door
And took the girl to his place
And the maid was no longer a maid.

GROUP: Lovely Ophelia.
GIRL:

Jesus Christ, and the Holy Cross as my witness,
What a shameful thing it is.
Every lad, if he gets the chance,
Would do exactly the same.
The maid said, "You gave your word
That you'd make me your wife.
The youth said, "If you hadn't slept with me,
Of course I'd have taken you."

GHOST: How long have things been like that? (*To* MHER) Should I say it louder? MHER, you're not listening.
MHER: No. I wasn't listening. (*Abruptly*) Today's rehearsal is off. I'm not up to it. I'm tired. I didn't sleep a wink last night.
GENERAL: I'll lie down and we'll read to you.
MHER: No. I can't today. Tomorrow. I'll call you all tomorrow. Now off you go.

(*The* GIRL *goes out, tightly clutching her doll.*)

MRS. ARMENIA: It's okay for some people. You haven't paid your rent yet.
MHER: I paid it already. You've forgotten. I gave it to you yesterday. Oh, my head's spinning. Bring me an ice bag, Mrs. Armenia. I've had a brain concussion. (*Escorting the* GHOST *out*) Work on your monologue. You can't even read it properly. Something on your mind?
GHOST: I'm sick.
MHER: An actor has no right to be sick. The people sitting over there couldn't care less whether you're ill, have a fever, or your spleen's about to rupture. They've paid big money for their ticket and demand that you bare your soul to them. What do they care if your gallstones are giving you excruciating pain (*Pointing upward*) They've paid a hundred dram. Their wallet's the most sacred possession they have in this world.
GHOST: I understand.
GENERAL: How should I play my part, Mher? Should I follow the exhibitionist or survivalist school of acting?

MHER: Consider what kind of animal it's like and play that.

GHOST: That Claudius is a dirty bastard, turning all Denmark into a prison.

MRS. ARMENIA: What have you got against the poor guy? Hamlet's father let the country go to rack and ruin. He's hardly been dead a month. The poor man couldn't have turned the whole of Denmark into a prison in that amount of time.

GHOST: That's true. He couldn't have finished it in a month.

MHER: Well done, Mrs. Armenia. You need to get your gray cells working on your part. So off to work. Off you go.

(*They all go out.*)

PROFESSOR (*stopping short*): Mher, why did those people come? I've got bad vibes. What are they scheming? What do they want from you?

MHER: I don't know, Professor. We'll talk later.

PROFESSOR: Don't you trust me? Even after the oath we took, Mher? They're all schemes orchestrated by Him. I'm concerned about you. What's going on, Mher?

MHER: I don't know, Professor. Believe me. It's a play. I don't know how it's going to end. You know I can't resist staging plays. I love playing all sorts of roles.

PROFESSOR: What kind of a play is it?

MHER: I don't know.

PROFESSOR (*sad*): And I thought we had no secrets from each other.

(*The* GIRL *with the doll comes in.*)

MHER (*exploding*): What do you want? Look, can't you give me a minute's peace?

(*The* GIRL *turns around and goes out.* MHER *stops her.*)

MHER: Enough of your moods. It's impossible to talk to you. Tell me what's the matter.

GIRL: They've come after you. There are four cars in the yard. (*With head lowered, she squeezes her doll tight and goes out.*)

MHER (*to the* PROFESSOR): What are you looking at?

PROFESSOR: What are they here for?

MHER: They're bringing dough. I'll keep you informed.

(*The* PROFESSOR *leaves. Soon after,* AMATUNI *enters with* ARAMYAN.)

MHER: Greetings, greetings. While you were asleep in your nests, the madmen have taken over the palaces.

AMATUNI: Really? (*She looks at the ceiling.*) It's high. And spacious. The whole country's now in a total mess. Why do the inmates need so much space? The rooms should be halved to accommodate twice as many patients. Simple arithmetic. (*To* ARAMYAN) Take a note of it.

MHER: Apart from multiplication tables, have you nothing else to say, Madam? Did you bring the dough?

AMATUNI: What dough?

ARAMYAN: Dough. Just that. (*He shows her.*) A million tons of dough.

MHER: To stuff in the crown. (*He mimes being hanged and receiving the money.*)

AMATUNI: He's pretending to be mad. I have it on good authority that a second-rate party proposed you some dirty business. Do you know you could stand trial for that?

MHER: I've sunk so low, I'm singing. Would you like a concert? Free? (*He sings.*)

AMATUNI: Don't waste your energy on monkey business. It won't cut any ice. Aramyan's our agent. He joined Hasratyan to gather information for us. How much did that man-eating monster offer you?

MHER (*holding his nose and pretending to be overcome by a pungent odor*): Which one of your hands is smeared?

AMATUNI: What's he talking about? Translate, Aramyan.

MHER (*holding his nose*): When you were wiping your butts, whose finger got smeared? One of you stinks.

AMATUNI: This guy's really deranged.

ARAMYAN: No. He thinks you're here to arrest him or put him in jail. Mher, pull yourself together. These people will double Hasratyan's offer.

(MRS. ARMENIA *comes in with a broom. She moves forward, sweeping as she goes.*)

AMATUNI: Who's this?

ARAMYAN: Lear's daughter.

AMATUNI: What?

ARAMYAN: Goneril. She's dangerous.

MRS. ARMENIA: Feet.

AMATUNI: What?

MRS. ARMENIA: Move your feet, damn it. First it was the rats, now this bunch. (*To* MHER) Don't you have anyone to talk to, dearie? Just holler if things get rough. We're standing at the ready. (*She leaves, sweeping as she goes.*)

AMATUNI: It's dangerous to stay here too long. Listen, you clown, you misunderstood me. I'm not threatening you. On the contrary, I'm proposing you make a deal with our party. I'll pay you more than that monster Hasratyan. You'll do the same thing, only for us. I'm sure we can come to a better mutual understanding.

MHER: Oh, Lady. I'm ready to do anything for you.

AMATUNI: You've wasted no time in changing your colors. How can I trust you?

MHER: Madam, I can make an omelet for you right now. With my own hands.

AMATUNI (*laughing*): What an odd ball.

MHER: That's the best I can offer you as a token of good faith.

AMATUNI: What about your life? Offer us that. National interests demand it.

MHER: But I've signed an agreement with them. How can I break my promise and enter into another with you.

AMATUNI: What difference does it make, them or us?

MHER (*pondering*): Actually . . . none at all. I'm not bound to anybody.

AMATUNI: In that case, negotiate a new deal with us.

MHER (*shouting*): I proclaim the negotiations under way. Gentlemen, I'm putting my life on the line. Yesterday it wasn't worth a cent, but today I learned the nation puts a high value on it. (*To* AMATUNI) You agree, don't you? [*To the crowd*] Opposed? Abstentions? . . . Passed unanimously. (*To* ARAMYAN) Make a note of the vote. (*He shouts.*) Oy, Lear! Goneril! Look lively. Commanders, soldiers, and you servants, too. Gloucester, Kent, Regan . . . Get in here on the double.

(*The patients pile in.*)

AMATUNI (*to* ARAMYAN): What's he up to?

MHER (*pointing to the* PROFESSOR): This is my trusty friend. [*Pointing to the others in turn*] These are his ungrateful daughters, plotting to seize power. He's the Duke of Burgundy. This is the King of France.

AMATUNI: Have you gone mad? . . . This is a top secret assignment. And what do you do? You turn it into a farce. Don't you grasp the gravity of the situation? (*To* ARAMYAN) Who's this jerk you've taken up with.

MHER: You've no reason to be apprehensive or concerned, let alone paranoid. These are the loonies. They don't have a voice or ears. They don't even have a vote or say in the matter. They're voiceless, though they have a voice. They're deadbeats, though they're very much alive. None of us can leak your secret to the world, because the world's not tuned on our frequency. What fool out there would listen to a madman or pay attention to his inane ravings?

AMATUNI: We'll come back tomorrow. Try not to have contact with people. Aramyan, are the cars ready?

MHER: Your asses have gone to get the horses. (*He blocks* AMATUNI's *path.*)

AMATUNI: This is a real madhouse.

MHER: You see, Lady? This is the only place where the real's really real.

AMATUNI: Let's go, Aramyan.

MHER (*He gets down on his knees in front of* AMATUNI *in a theatrical gesture and kisses her hand.*): Madam, I agree. I'm willing to give my life. How much are you going to give? (*He extends his hand, and speaks in an imperative tone*) The first installment? (*Taking a piece of paper she hands him*) What's this, Madam?

AMATUNI: A document destined for our party's secret archives. We're not an old-fashioned mom-and-pop operation like the parties you're familiar with. All they do reeks of garlic. With us everything's documented, precise, official.

MHER: Now what am I supposed to do?

AMATUNI: Sign. Name, surname. Preferably legible.

MHER: Just a minute . . . I need to consult with my party, too. After all, I'm their spokesman. (*He calls the patients together for a consultation. They withdraw to a corner and quietly discuss the situation.*)

ARAMYAN (*to* AMATUNI): You didn't expect complications like this. A piece of cake, you said. Luckily, Aramyan has this guy figured out.

MHER (*handing over the receipt to* ARAMYAN) There you are.

ARAMYAN: What's this he's written?

AMATUNI (*She snatches it out of his hand and reads it.*): Savior Astvatsatryan. (*To* MHER) Everything has its limits. This is an official document . . . (*to* ARAMYAN) Burn it immediately. (ARAMYAN *sets fire to it with a lighter and throws it in the ashtray.*)

MHER (*cryptically*): The father ruined his daughter's life.

AMATUNI: Fool.

MRS. ARMENIA (*raising her broom in a threatening manner*): Shut up, you nympho-maniac. Who are you giving the kiss of death to?

MHER (*yelling to the patients*): Brave hearts, seize them. This is Shylock, who jeopardized his daughter's well-being for the sake of money. Oh, the intrigue of it. What would the bard have said, if he could see it now? [*Pointing to* ARAMYAN] Bring the bastard forward who sold his soul to the highest bidder.

(*The patients pounce on* ARAMYAN *and force him into a straightjacket.*)

PROFESSOR: Good God, what are you doing? (*He goes out.*)

MHER: Oh treason! Blood![12] Bind him in shackles and string him up. (*Pointing to the noose*) Pull down the rope, Gloucester, fasten the noose round his neck. Oh, hellish light!

ARAMYAN: Let go of me. Mher, these people don't understand how politics works. They're really going to hang me! Amatuni!

AMATUNI: What have I got myself into? What are you playing at, Mher?

MRS. ARMENIA: We're hanging him, can't you see? Do we have to spell it out in block letters?

---

12. Cf. *Othello,* act 1, scene 1, l. 169.

ARAMYAN: Mher! Please! Amatuni!

MHER: You must hang, my son, to expiate your sins. You see, anyone can buy you.

AMATUNI: Do you realize what you're doing? Snap out of this madness. You're murdering a man in broad daylight.

ARAMYAN: I'll submit an appeal to the Supreme Court.

MHER: We're outside their jurisdiction, pitiful gent. They often transfer people from prison to the madhouse, but never the other way round.

> Who knows exactly what you're about?
> You show up here and jeer and shout.
> And throw your agent to these rabid canines,
> Raw meat for madmen, nuts, and imbecilic swines.

ARAMYAN: Amatuni, now he's talking in verse. He means business. Do something. He'll hang me.

AMATUNI (*bolting for the door*): Help! Murder! Help!

(*The patients block her path.*)

MRS. ARMENIA: Shut up, you don't have a speaking part in this show.

MHER: Slip the noose around his neck.

ARAMYAN: Mher, I beg you. Guys, don't do it. I've a home and family.

MHER: National interests demand it. You have to die. You should be willing to die for the nation. Don't you love your country, traitor? I'll give you money. Lots of it. As much as you've given me. You can set your mother up for life and save your daughter's self-respect.

ARAMYAN: Wait, Mher. I . . . I'll do anything for you. If you want . . . if you'd like, I'll have you discharged from this madhouse. I'll settle your accounts. Send you to America. My cousin works at the American embassy.

AMATUNI: Mher, let him go. Let's get out of here and never—

MHER: Never what? Maybe you'd like to hang in his place?

ARAMYAN: Amatuni, if anything happens to me, our scheme'll be exposed. You'll enjoy your presidency from jail!

MHER: Madam, why don't you want to sacrifice yourself for the motherland? Your skin's too precious, eh? More precious than your country?

AMATUNI: Mher, we'll pay you . . . as much as you want, I promise. Just let him go.

MHER (*with pathos*): Friends, brave hearts. The captive wants to live. Tell me, what should his ransom be? How much do you want, Mrs. Armenia?

MRS. ARMENIA: My daughter's finishing tenth grade this year. She wants to go to a university. I need to cover admission costs. I don't want anything else out of life.

MHER: Your daughter's admitted, Mrs. Armenia.

AMATUNI: What? Have you any idea how much we're talking about?

MHER (*to the* GIRL *with the doll*): How about you . . . flowering basellacae. What do you want?

GIRL: An egg. So I can have a child.

MHER: I want the cost of her admission to a maternity ward.

AMATUNI: But that's highway robbery.

MHER (*To the* GHOST) And what do you need, Omnipotent Father?

GHOST: My son's in prison. They used to beat him every day so he'd confess. He wasn't guilty, but he took the blame. They tortured him. I had no money to get him released. It was that ghost again. It's his fault my son's doing time. We were strolling together down Teryan Street. Suddenly they came up and arrested him. There was hashish in his pocket. Now you tell me how come? He was wearing a sleeveless top and shorts. He didn't have a pocket. You tell me what all that was about.

MHER: See you give me enough to square things with those shysters. The boy's innocent and they know it.

AMATUNI: Are you completely out of your mind? Where are we going to get that kind of money?

ARAMYAN: I'll take care of the judge. I'll sell my house, my two cars, whatever I can scrape together. Only let me go. Tell me this is just a practical joke. Please!

AMATUNI: What are you babbling about? No matter what you sell, you'll never satisfy them.

MHER: So the hanging's on. Prepare to die, poor wretch. Here goes.

GLOUCESTER: Have you said your prayers tonight, eh? Desdemona.

(MHER *kicks the chair away.* ARAMYAN *screams. The* PROFESSOR *runs in, pushes* MHER *back, and frees* ARAMYAN.)

PROFESSOR: He's all over the place, all over. Satan's infiltrated all your brains. Poor devils, don't you understand what's happening? Who's controlling you? You're being bombarded by radiation. Get out! Get out! He's present in all of you. Get out, quick. Escape the rays. Out, out, away! (AMATUNI *and* ARAMYAN *quickly make a dash for it.*)

ARAMYAN (*to* MHER): Ungrateful son of a bitch. You're not human. (*He exits.*)

PROFESSOR: Mher, what's going on?

MHER: Just a simple conjuring trick. But now I'm in charge.

PROFESSOR: You? Good God. (*Pleading*) Mher, please, don't give in to him. I had a premonition. I felt it in my bones. Good God, you have to resist him, Mher, do you hear? Remember our oath. I beg you, don't give in.

MHER: I haven't given in. I'm in control, not Beelzebub or any other mythical force.

MRS. ARMENIA: Yeah, Mher. I'm towering at your side like a mountain. Don't be afraid.

GIRL: Are you in danger, Mher?

MHER: No, no. The Professor loves to exaggerate. Everything's fine. Off you go. The bats have left their roost. (*To the* GIRL) Look, your dolly's yawning. Go to bed. It's late now.

(*The patients file out.*)

MHER: You too, Professor. (*Feeling around on the shelf for his pills*) My sleeping pill's wearing off.

PROFESSOR: You know why he's selected you? Because all my hope's pinned on you. You're my only hope. Don't delude yourself. If you desert to Satan, I'm lost. He's tempting you to destroy me. He's laughing at me. (*He closes his eyes.*) He's laughing. Do you hear? He's laughing. I can't think straight. (*He covers his ears with his hands. He's in agony.*)

MHER: Easy, easy, Professor. Put your hands down. Relax. See, it's me who's laughing at him. (*He laughs.*) We're strong, Professor. Strong, because we're together. We are together, right?

PROFESSOR: Of course. We took an oath, didn't we? (*Suddenly relieved*) Thank you.

(*He goes out.*)

(MHER *breathes a sigh of relief. He checks to see if his money's still in his pocket. He drinks a sedative and takes off his gown. He puts out the light and lies down. Pause.* BRTUJYAN'*s silhouette is outlined in the dim light, cautiously advancing in the darkness. Suddenly he lets out a yell. Lights.* MHER *sits up and stares wide-eyed at* BRTUJYAN *standing opposite him, as he struggles hard to extricate his foot from the trap.*)

BRTUJYAN: Shh! Please! Don't make a sound. (*He removes the snare.*) It's too big for a mouse, too small for a man.

MHER: Can't I get five minutes peace? What are you doing here?

BRTUJYAN (*He takes a leaflet out of his breast pocket and thrusts it in* MHER'*s face.*): Take a look.

MHER: What's this?

BRTUJYAN: Our party manifesto.

MHER (*making a yelping sound*): Do you know what time it is?

BRTUJYAN: Ten past one. Eleven minutes past, to be precise.

MHER: What business have you in my palace at one o'clock—eleven minutes past, to be precise? Speak up. What are you here for, Comrade?

BRTUJYAN (*in confusion*): Please, please don't use that word.

MHER: Which word?

BRTUJYAN: Comrade. God forbid. There's no love lost between our party and those bastard Comrade Communists and their socialist satellites.

MHER: Listen, is all this a dream? I guess I'm asleep.

BRTUJYAN: How dare you sign a contract with the opposition and sleep peacefully afterward. And as if sleeping's not enough, you were actually going to snore. We've just got out of the Communists' clutches and now you want to hand the country over to them again? Even without that, the nation's at the edge of a precipice. Do you want to push it over the edge? (*He pushes* MHER.) Why are you pushing the nation over the edge, eh? Why?

MHER: Why?

BRTUJYAN: I'm asking *you.*

MHER: And I'm asking *you.* What do you want from me?

BRTUJYAN: Let's get down to business. We received intelligence that some third-rate party hired you for a secret mission. I'd be curious to know for how much.

(MHER *slaps his head with his hand to indicate he has fathomed the purpose of* BRTUJYAN's *visit.*)

Rather intriguing, wouldn't you say?

MHER: I guess so. But do you know what? Everyone who comes in here goes mad. So make it snappy!

BRTUJYAN: Our party's the only one today that can pull the nation out of its present crisis. The Armenian Revolutionary Federation is party no. 1. It knows exactly what has to be done. We're simply—

MHER (*He lies down, turning his back to* BRTUJYAN): A million dollars.

BRTUJYAN: I beg your pardon.

MHER: Give me a million, and I'll hang for you. Take it or leave it. Good night.

(BRTUJYAN *is rendered all but speechless.*)

BRTUJYAN: But that's outrageous.

MHER: Look here, owl face. If I weren't ready to kill myself, you wouldn't have flown by at this time of night and woken me with your squawking. (*He turns around.*) A million's the going rate. If you're up to it, buy. If not, I'll see which of the other party comes through first.

BRTUJYAN: No problem. Only . . . eh . . . there's one slight nuance. I'm authorized by the party to enter into negotiations, but you're way over my budget. I'll have to get back to the head office. (*He ponders.*) Okay, I'll get on the line to my boss, Svachyan. (*The screeching of car brakes is heard outside.*) Oh dear! It's them. What am I going to do? Where can I hide? (*He looks for a place to hide.*) Please! (*He gets under the bed.*)

(*Meanwhile* HASRATYAN *enters, along with* ARAMYAN, *a* PHOTOGRAPHER, *and men in black suits.*)

ARAMYAN: Get up, Mher. Up you get.

HASRATYAN: Hurry up. We don't have much time.

ARAMYAN: Get up, put on your clothes. Be quick about it. No, not the gown. Haven't you got a shirt?

PHOTOGRAPHER: Quick, quick.

ARAMYAN: On with it, hurry up, Mher.

MHER: What's going on?

PHOTOGRAPHER: That shirt won't do. It's creased.

HASRATYAN: Haven't you got another?

ARAMYAN: Should I give him mine?

HASRATYAN: Just be quick about it.

PHOTOGRAPHER: Your tie as well.

HASRATYAN: Straighten it. Stand here.

(*The men in suits drag* MHER *to this side and that like a mannequin.*)

PHOTOGRAPHER: The background's no good. Move him over here.

MHER: My pants—

PHOTOGRAPHER: No need. We're only going to photograph you from the waist up. Hair . . .

(ARAMYAN *runs to* MHER *and combs his hair, blows on the comb and puts it back in his breast pocket. He steps back and admires the half-naked* MHER, *whose spindly, hairy legs poke out from under* ARAMYAN'*s shirt.*)

ARAMYAN: It's for tomorrow's edition.

PHOTOGRAPHER: It's creased. His face is creased.

HASRATYAN: Give him a wash.

MHER: Listen, I'm half asleep. Tomorrow I'll do whatever you want, but today . . . I've taken a sedative. I—

(*The men in black escort* MHER *out.*)

PHOTOGRAPHER: Will we make it? Tomorrow's edition is already in press.

HASRATYAN: We'll stop the presses.

PHOTOGRAPHER: Couldn't you find anyone more stylish? This guy's a bit run-of-the-mill.

HASRATYAN: A hero should be one of the people. They love a figure they can identify with. They're not too keen on someone who stands out. And besides, run-of-the-mills cost nothing. (*He smiles.*)

ARAMYAN: It'd be good for him to make a speech on the radio, too.

HASRATYAN: Once the paper comes out, radio and TV exposure will follow. We have to schedule his appearance as part of our PR blitz closer to the election. Otherwise, the attention he gets from too much media coverage will give our actor the idea that he's the man of the moment who'll save the nation.

(*The men in black bring* MHER *back in.*)

PHOTOGRAPHER: Stand here. Look this way.

(MHER *squints.*)

HASRATYAN: Come on. Be serious. There's no time for kidding around.

(MHER *puts on a sad expression.*)

PHOTOGRAPHER: No, no, this won't do. Please cooperate. Imagine that your wife's standing here right now. Look at her.

(MHER *adopts an angry glare.*)

PHOTOGRAPHER: No, no. Why are you so angry? Relax a little. Imagine you're looking at your mother.

HASRATYAN: Aramyan, stand up.

PHOTOGRAPHER: Yeah. Look at Aramyan. Imagine he's your mother. No, no. Who looks at their mother with such disgust? Cut out all this subjectivity. Just look at the camera. (*He shoots.*)

HASRATYAN (*to* MHER): Here's the text. Take it and memorize it. When you've learned it by heart, destroy it. No slipups.

MHER: What is it? (*He examines the paper.*)

HASRATYAN: Good night . . . (*He makes his way to the exit. On seeing* BRTUJYAN's *leaflet, he suddenly halts.*) How did this get here? Who came to see you?

MHER: All of them, except the Communists.

ARAMYAN: They'll be here soon enough.

(HASRATYAN *looks at him sharply.*)

Just kidding, just kidding.

HASRATYAN (*slamming his fist on the table*): How many times have I told you?

There's a leak in our ranks. Those rotten bourgeois Armenian Revolutionary Federation blockheads have sniffed out something again. (*To* ARAMYAN) Where did it come from?

ARAMYAN: I don't deal with blockheads.

(*A strained silence ensues.*)

HASRATYAN: This is getting to be a serious matter . . .
MHER: One million smackeroos.

(ARAMYAN *whistles.*)

HASRATYAN: Let's set up a guard 'round the clock. Coordinate with Davtyan. (*He goes out, followed swiftly by the others.*)
MHER (*reading the text* HASRATYAN *gave him*): My fellow Armenians, let me introduce myself. My name is Mher Astvatsatryan. As a man of the people, I know your pains and hardship firsthand. I feel them under my skin. We struggled for freedom and independence. And we won. But the struggle goes on today. This time against those who have fraudulently abused the people's trust. And so I appeal to you all. Before going to the polls, consider carefully who you're voting for, who you're handing your future to. If the president does not resign before October 5th, I invite you all to Liberty Square at noon on that day when I will immolate myself in silent protest to stir his sleeping conscience! (*Pause.* MHER *is shaken.*)
PROFESSOR (*entering, violently shivering*): I'm on to you now, Mher. You're in league with him, aren't you? With Satan! And I had such faith in you.
MHER: Don't push it, Professor. Leave me alone.
PROFESSOR: But you swore to stay by me. How could you?
MHER: I don't want to discuss it. Just leave me alone.
PROFESSOR: Don't do it, Mher. Snap out of it. Get back on your feet, before it's too late. Don't put yourself down. Don't fall for that trick. I know it's hard. He's greater than us. But there's two of us. We'll put up a fight.
MHER: What are you talking about? What fight? What Satan? I've had enough. How long must I listen to you rambling on? I said I don't want to talk. Go away.
PROFESSOR: Don't you see, Mher? That's one of his tricks. Those people are Lucifer's henchmen. They want to enlist you, too, Mher. He's getting at me through you. Don't do it, Mher. Please! Look, I'm on my knees . . . (*Falling to his knees*) I beg you.
MHER: Stop that. Get up. Get up.
PROFESSOR: Don't abandon me, Mher. Better to die for nothing than become a stooge to the forces of evil. Don't let them jerk you around. You're a man.

MHER: Listen, you decrepit old egghead. Those snake charmers and tricks are a figment of your sick mind. They don't exist. Do you understand? They don't exist. You're a pathetic loony. You've flipped out. I'm healthy, and I'd like to do something with my life. I've never seen so much money. Not even in my dreams. Some day I'll have to die. But before I do I want to expand my horizons, not rot here listening to you rave on like this.

PROFESSOR: But you swore an oath.

MHER: Beat it, okay? I don't care. I'm half asleep.

PROFESSOR: So everything's a delusion? The snake charmer's a delusion? In that case, what have I struggled for? What?

MHER: Whatever.

PROFESSOR: So my whole life's been for nothing?

MHER: Don't know. I wasn't around then. (*Lying down*) Good night.

(*The* PROFESSOR *stands frozen like a statue.* MHER *rolls over on the bed. Feeling nothing in his pocket, he becomes suspicious, jumps up and pulls out the pocket lining. It's empty.*)

MHER (*searching furiously*): It's not here . . . my money . . . My money's not here. (*He thinks.*) I distinctly remember putting it here. (*He thinks.*) Gloucester, why are you looking at me with that goatish grin? . . . It's not here! (*He shouts.*) Gloucester, Gloucester! (*He lurches offstage. Soon after, he reappears, pulling the* GENERAL *along with him.*) Where is it?

GENERAL (*afraid*): What?

MHER (*shouting*): My money. Where is it?

GENERAL: In a Swiss bank account.

MHER (*He slaps him, then begins punching him.*): Tell me. Hurry up. I'll kill you. Tell me what you've done with it.

GENERAL: I haven't done anything. Stop hitting me. My head, my head! Mher, stop hitting me.

MHER (*continuing to lay into him*): Tell me, you son of a bitch.

GENERAL: Don't hit me. Please. Don't hit me. (*He starts crying like a child.*)

MHER (*feverishly*): Quick, or I'll kill you. Where is it?

GENERAL: I took it to buy you a bicycle. Your father won't give me any money. He says I'm spoiling his son. Ooh, my head aches . . .

MHER: Where have you stashed it? Out with it.

GENERAL (*in tears*): In my room . . . Stop it! Stop pouring water on my head.

MHER (*out of breath*): Get up. (*Dragging him along*) Come on.

(*The* PROFESSOR *stands in terror.*)

GHOST: Mher, has it showed its face again . . . that ghost? (*To the* PROFESSOR) Pro-

fessor, where's Mher? . . . The ghost's here and punching the general. Shh!
. . . It's coming this way. Turn out the light. Turn it out. (*He turns out the
light.*)

(*Pitch black. Darkness. Noises, voices, screeches.*)

VOICES: What's all the commotion about? What's happened? Why are you all out
in the corridor?
GIRL: Mom, I'm afraid.
GHOST: I saw him, Doctor. He was punching the general. [*Pointing*] They went
that way.
DOCTOR: I can't get any peace around here. Even at night. What are you shouting
about? Break it up. Break it up. Come on, off to bed with the lot of you. Easy.
Take it easy.

(*Silence. The light comes on.* MHER *stands with bundles of notes in his hands. The*
PROFESSOR's *body swings from a rope.*)

Curtain

ACT 3

*The stage is transformed out of all recognition. An idyllic scene is set for a stylized po-
etic drama the patients are rehearsing.* MHER *sits cross-legged on an Arabian throne
like the Shah of Iran, while two nubile girls, one on either side, fan him with palm
leaves.* GHOST *is dressed as a ladybug, with two antennae on his head, culminating
in small bulbous protrusions.* MRS. ARMENIA *stands like a statue with a large sword
held horizontally in front of her. The* GENERAL *is wrapped in a white sheet, with a
crown of thorns on his head and medals on his chest. The* GIRL *with the doll has angel wings and hums softly as she dances with the doll. A banner is spread out on the
ground on which the* GENERAL *is writing.*

MHER: Glorifying supernal God, the eternal Word, and Holy Spirit, to whom glory
is due from age to age, we have built this land of promise, our planet of mirth
and happiness. Oh man, enjoy the beauty of the flowers, the waving corn in
the fields, the lustrous meadows of violets, the pure fragrance of the elm and
heavenward soaring poplar.
GHOST: This is the land where the arbors and verdant vines entwine their limbs in
their passion to reach the light, and the air is redolent with the seductive fragrance of musk and frankincense. Fowls festooned in emeralds sit preening on
branches of rosebuds, fanning their plumage in dazzling array.

GIRL: The limpid brook gurgles sweetly, spraying the air with its sparkling dew, and reflects this charming scene. Flaxen steeds and gilded parrots sport freely on the azure plain of the sky. (*Nudging the* GENERAL) On the azure plain of the sky.

GENERAL (*stirring*): This is a garden—illusory, yet real—where swans glide serenely on the lake.

GHOST (*prompting*): The reed burgeons . . .

GENERAL: The reed burgeons, the cliffs resound, the mountains rejoice.

GIRL: Everywhere the great creator's holy right hand is manifest.

MRS. ARMENIA: We have left our homeland where Lucifer, Lord of Darkness, the enemy of the human race, compelled our people to root out the sublime from their minds and indulge in bestial acts.

MHER (*to the* GIRL): White dove, flowering basellacae, be happy. Here assuage your irremediable pains, violated by the lustful passion of a lascivious slave. (*To one of the girls fanning him*) Lovely dawn, red-lipped and rosy-cheeked . . . (*To the other*) and you, my songbird, peerless nightingale. Find comfort in this majestic land which our brother, the Professor, called Betelgeyze.[13] (*To the* GHOST) As for you, my honorable father of meager build, forget here fears and terror, anxiety and noisome care. And find respite in these convivial haunts, where your companion is the savage lion and the hand-tamed bear.

GHOST: We have wandered the wide universe and found this planet where there is no sin, no evil—no ghost—nor ever more shall be.

MHER (*to the* GENERAL): What of you, intimate of the dove, worthy of honor, passionate lover of honey and butter. Be diligent, tend this pleasant garden in your custody, so men can live here happy and free.

ARAMYAN (*enters wearing a blacksmith's overalls and angel wings, and carrying a watering can*):

> I've become an industrious ant,
> To till this Eden I puff and pant.
> I plant trees, and sing with all my might,
> To give the weeds a fearful fright.

MHER: What is the basic, incontrovertible law of this land, oh great, wise, experienced gardener?

ARAMYAN:

> To love one's neighbor, to relieve hunger,
> To save the victim from his oppressor;
> To forgive the one who causes unintended strife,
> And to live to the full God's gift of life.

---

13. In Hebrew, the meaning of the term is "This valley is the house of God."

MHER: But if that cursed, malicious Satan should try to enter us again, and set foot on our soil with his destructive hooves and goatish main, and infect us body and soul?

GHOST:

> Then our protectress, Mother Armenia, will rise to her feet and
>   fume.
> She'll brandish her sword and, with one blow, seal the doom of
> that wily monarch of Stygian gloom.

> (*Tired*) Oof! . . .

MRS. ARMENIA: I'll wield the lightning sword and cut Satan to pieces.

MHER:

> Betelgeyze, long live your sacred soil.
> Your citizens are honest madmen, true and loyal.

GENERAL: Ready.

(*The patients assist the* GHOST *to raise the banner. On it in huge letters is written* "Madmen of the world, Unite!")

ALL: Long live Betelgeyze!

MHER (*to the* GHOST):

> Speak up, Right-minded Noble Father.
> What long-cherished dream lies in your breast?
> What have you yearned to say, but dared not utter
> Except in this great land of liberty so blessed?

GHOST: I want to shout, loud and strong.

MHER:

> Shout. A man is free in his desire.
> May your voice outdistance any choir.

(*The* GHOST *emits a high-pitched shriek.*)

MHER (*to* ARAMYAN):

> Come, it's your turn now to say
> What your pleasure is today.

To whistle a ditty or hum a song?
Something catchy so we can sing along.

ARAMYAN: I want to whistle, Crazy Comrade.
MHER:

Whistle away, my trusty friend.
Your sweet-toned warbling may start a trend.

(ARAMYAN *gives a high-pitched whistle. The Doctor comes in.*)

DOCTOR: Aramyan, your wife's on the phone.
ARAMYAN: Hey dude, aren't I entitled to a year at the sanatorium? Since this country's become independent I haven't had a vacation.
MHER: Doctor, why are you interrupting the rehearsal?
ARAMYAN: Do we interrupt you when you're busy? Tell her Aramyan's not here, he's gone out. Oh boy!
MHER [*To the* GENERAL]:

What takes your fancy, brother Communist?
Anything but a party session.
If you'll pardon this confession,
I'd like to see you dance the twist.

GENERAL (*standing on a chair*): Eh-ge Hali-Gali . . . (*He dances.*) Eh-ge-ge, Betelgeyze!

(*They all dance to music. Soon the music stops, as does the dancing.*)

MHER: Well done. Thank you all. Tomorrow's the premiere. Go and have a rest. Rehearsal's over!

(*The patients file out.*)

ARAMYAN (*taking off his blacksmith's overalls*): It feels like I'm dreaming. I've almost reached the point of giving up and committing suicide. Tonight I had a really bad dream, Mher.
MHER (*drinking beer straight out of the bottle*): What's on the recreational schedule today?
ARAMYAN: A group of gypsy violinists, a chess club meeting with a Grand Master, a fashion show with chic models from the designer house of Koko.
MHER (*complaining about his lifestyle change since he received the million dollars*):

Damn it, how hard it can be when you're fed and watered. Who would want to be rich on a full stomach? How was the play?

ARAMYAN: My part's too small. Can't you add a poem in praise of Betelgeyze for me? Oh, by the way, yesterday a dance ensemble came by to ask for funds for stage costumes. I said you were asleep.

MHER (*responsibly, as befits his new status as national benefactor*): See they have as much as they want. What an effort it is to drag a belly around that's permanently stuffed with gourmet food. (*He sits down on a chair that wobbles slightly.*) What else is on the entertainment program?

ARAMYAN (*He reads.*): In the eastern repertoire there's the bard Gusan Perch,[14] a female vocalist singing national songs—

MHER (*interrupting*): What about the western repertoire?

ARAMYAN: A jazz-pop-rock-rap singer, Shamam Tevosyan, and a children's group playing light orchestral music. That's the one whose international tour you backed last Tuesday. Before they leave for Argentina, they want to give a concert in honor of their sponsor.

MHER: I shouldn't have eaten the third spare rib. It's giving me heartburn.

ARAMYAN: You know, schoolchildren are writing essays about you, Mr. Astvatsatryan, entitled "Little Mher."

MHER (*hurt*): Why "little"?

ARAMYAN: The "big" one's dead. Don't you remember what happens to him in the epic? Besides, it's good the children associate you with Little Mher in one way because, after your suicide, we'll tap right into tradition and comfort them with the thought that you're ensconced in a cave, as in the legend, and won't come out till wheat grows the size of grape clusters. Let them wait.

MHER: So, you're going to bury me in a cave?

ARAMYAN: You think Aramyan's kidding? Your tombstone's all ready. We've even got models of your statue. Would you care to look them over now?

MHER: Sure, why not. (*He takes out a wad of notes, puts it under the leg of the wobbly chair, and checks that it is now evenly balanced.*) Tell the gypsies to go home and not to wait around for a handout.

(ARAMYAN *goes out.* MRS. AMATUNI *comes in with pen and paper, disguised as the bellydancer* SHAKE *from a sultan's harem.*)

SHAKE: Hello, my name's Shake. I'm your new waitress.

MHER: Where's the old one?

---

14. A *gusan* is a traditional bard, singing and reciting to the accompaniment of a stringed instrument like the *saz* or *kamancha*.

SHAKE: She was elected a member of parliament. Wouldn't you like me to go over the dinner menu with you?

MHER: Don't talk to me about food. I'm sick of eating.

SHAKE: Then perhaps a little coffee, tea, a drink?

MHER: I want to go to bed.

SHAKE: Bed? I'm only paid for waitressing. I'm a girl with scruples, I'll have you know.

(ARAMYAN *returns. The* PHOTOGRAPHER *wheels in a large trolley with three full size statues of* MHER.)

PHOTOGRAPHER (*pointing to the statues*): Here they are, Mr. Astvatsatryan. Heroic, compassionate, and true to life. Take your pick.

MHER (*examining the statues*): The rugged Pyrrhus, he, whose sable arms . . . (*To the* PHOTOGRAPHER) Did you notice they were black? (*Pointing to the statues*) Leave them here. I'll think about it.

SHAKE: Excuse me, sir, I'd like to ask you something. Is it true that you're of noble birth? That your family tree can be traced back to the illustrious King Trdat III?[15]

MHER (*with a loud guffaw*): Who told you that?

SHAKE: It's the talk of the town.

PHOTOGRAPHER: You've become a national hero. Wherever you go, people talk about you. Suicide, national hero, legend . . .

SHAKE: You rescued two children from certain death when you were twenty, didn't you? One of them was about to drown in a lake. I'm not sure about the other.

MHER: He was tumbling from the summit of Mt. Elbruz, the highest peak in the whole Caucasus range. Somehow I caught him.

SHAKE: You don't say?

PHOTOGRAPHER: Let me go report to Hasratyan. Things are not good. The president's ahead in the polls, while Hasratyan's trailing in second place. Mher, all our hope's on you to ensure our party's success.

MHER (*like a potential independent presidential candidate*): How's Mher Astvatsatryan doing in the polls?

PHOTOGRAPHER (*in jest*): Way ahead of the pack. (*He goes out.*)

MHER: Leave me for a while. I'm still digesting that last course.

ARAMYAN: The government's on to you. The president's mounted a desperate search for you. They want to bump you off to stop you from catapulting us into power. [*Chuckling*] But who'd think of looking in a madhouse? Even if they

---

15. According to tradition, this king was responsible for accepting Christianity as the official religion of the Armenian court in the early years of the fourth century.

come, they'll go see Davtyan, right? Everything's under control. Digest away. (*He goes out.*)

MHER (*To* SHAKE) Listen, girl with scruples, bring me a yogurt, cold and no salt. (*He lies down.*)

(SHAKE *goes out.* MHER *sneezes.*)

STATUE: Bless you!
MHER (*sitting bolt upright*): Who's there?
STATUE: You.
MHER: Me? . . . Who's me? Oof! Who's out there?
STATUE: Us. (*The chestnut model gets down from the trolley.*)
MHER: Where the hell did you come from?
STATUE:

I've come from distant times.
On victory's path I'm bound.
My course is set for other climes,
To a future clear and sound.

(*He extends his hand.*) Let me introduce myself. I'm a present, past, and future Communist.
MHER: How much are *you* going to pay me?
STATUE: A million.
MHER (*disappointed*): That's all? Back to your place.
STATUE: Hang on, I haven't told you the most important bit.
MHER: Buzz off. Can't you see I'm digesting? Don't disturb me.
STATUE: Just a minute. Listen. We're paying you a million, but not to die.
MHER: Transfer the funds to a Chilean bank in my name.
STATUE: Comrade Mher, we want you to live. We're offering you a million to live.
MHER (*indifferent*): Interesting idea.
STATUE: In short, we're giving you a million to secure the presidency for the Communist Party. Why set fire to yourself? Today you're the only man the people would follow with any enthusiasm. Our party's already approved your candidacy. So you'll have the money and save your skin. Think about it.
MHER: Tell me, Scarecrow, who thought up that brilliant idea?
STATUE: Central Party Headquarters in Moscow. Is it a deal?
MHER (*mock heroically*): Oh fate, Oh fortune, you strumpet. Oh how easily you abandon your goal, jump into bed with everyone and reverse your role, and make some clown a king.
STATUE: What's that, Comrade. I don't follow you. Is that yes or no?

MHER (*pondering*): To die or not to die? What is nobler in the mind? To suffer the slings and arrows of outrageous fortune, or to take arms?[16] Eh, William?

STATUE: How do you know my name?

(ARAMYAN *comes in. The* STATUE *bolts back to its place.*)

ARAMYAN: Your wife called, Mher. She's bought a house in Chicago. Your kid's going to a Jewish kindergarten.

MHER: Yesterday a jester, today a suicide, and tomorrow a king.[17] Why Jewish?

ARAMYAN: The Jewish one's free of charge. Your wife's making out that her grandmother's grandmother was a Jew.

MHER: Clever gal. She's always been like that, clever, mean, gorgeous, seductive. What do you say to that, Uncle? Yesterday a jester, today a suicide, tomorrow a king.

ARAMYAN: What are you talking about?

MHER: Nothing, I'm just twirling my tongue. Good exercise.

ARAMYAN (*handing* MHER *some papers*): More bank transfer slips for your signature. This one provides aid for a hospital, this one's for an old folks home, and this one's for an orphanage.

MHER: What about the Mher Astvatsatryan Fellowship Program for scholars?

ARAMYAN: All taken care of. But if it goes on like this, I'll have to take care of your burial expenses myself. What's with all these handouts? And why privatize the madhouse? What's it all for? You've only got two days to live.

MHER: Listen, you wheeler-dealer for all the parties. Look me in the face. Do I look like a fool?

ARAMYAN: What do you mean?

MHER: I'm going to let you in on a secret. Brilliant ideas are floating around all the time. All you have to do is catch them. Grab hold of one, back stabber. See, they're whizzing about like mosquitoes swarming 'round food that's gone bad. Use your brain.

ARAMYAN: I don't know what you're babbling about. Make sense.

MHER: I had a higher opinion of your little gray cells. Yesterday a jester, today a suicide, tomorrow a king. Who would the people elect president unanimously?

(SHAKE *comes in with the yogurt shake.*)

---

16. Pastiche of Hamlet's speech in *Hamlet*, act 3, scene 1, ll. 56–59.

17. The line is broadly reminiscent of the witches' prediction of Macbeth's rise to power in *Macbeth*, act 1, scene 3, ll. 48–50.

MHER: Who proved he's ready to sacrifice his life for the people's welfare? Who are they trying to hunt down today without success? Mher Astvatsatryan. I'm the Invincible Cock. Cockadoodle Doo! (*He drinks.*) Would you like me to tell you a story, Uncle? About the Invincible Cock. Once upon a time there was a little cock that finds a piece of gold. (*Loudly, in* ARAMYAN's *ear*) Cockadoodle Doo! Little Mher, Aramyan, is not going into any cave. Quite the opposite. Little Mher has already emerged from the cave. He's going to raise dust as he walks, and the earth's going to thunder under his steps. A miracle is about to happen, Aramyan. Isn't that what the people want today? A marvel? A miracle? See, I'm completely at your disposal, all one meter and sixty-five centimeters of me. See the miracle . . . Mher Astvatsatryan, your humble . . . king.

ARAMYAN: My head's beginning to ache.

MHER (*to* SHAKE): Little Lake, why at such a loss? Why do your waves not skip and toss?[18]

(SHAKE *looks at him in amazement. The* STATUE *sways.*)

MHER: Let me tell you a story, little kiddie-winkie. As a cock picks around for food it finds a gold piece. "Cockadoodle Doo! I've found some gold," it cries. The king gets word of it and orders that the gold be brought to him. "Cockadoodle Doo!" shouts the cock, "The king lives on my money." To avoid an affront, the king orders the gold to be returned to the cock, if only to keep it quiet. "Cockadoodle Doo!" shouts the cock. "The king's afraid of me." The king immediately orders the cock to be brought to the palace. "Cockadoodle Doo! I'm going to be the king's guest," shouts the cock all over the place. The king orders the boaster's tongue to be silenced by throwing the bird into boiling water and stewing it alive. "Cockadoodle Doo! I'm taking a bath in the king's palace," the cock exclaims. Despairing and demented, the king orders the cock to be brought to the dinner table and then proceeds to eat the cock. "Cockadoodle Doo! I'm already in the king's belly, I'm the king," shouts the cock. The poor king orders his belly cut open with a sword. The king dies, but the cock jumps out and runs away. I'm the Invincible Cock who represents our people's character. And that's what our national poet wrote, Aramyan. They flay us, they rape us, but we strain our throats shouting, "Cockadoodle Doo! We're alive and kicking. We're powerful and mighty."[19]

---

18. Citation from the opening lines of the very well-known work *Ljag* [Little lake] by the Armenian Romantic poet Bedros Turian (1851–1872).

19. For the somewhat different original version of the folktale, see *Hovhannes Tumanyan: entir erker* [Hovhannes Tumanyan: selected works], vol. 2 (Sovetakan grogh: Erevan, 1985), pp. 135–36.

ARAMYAN: What an uproar. Now all the bigwigs will be in a tizzy—Hasratyan, the president, Amatuni . . .

MHER: That's nothing unusual. The atmosphere in the upper strata of government, Aramyan, is subject to frequent sharp fluctuations in temperature.

ARAMYAN (*to* SHAKE): Why are your ears flapping? Off you go. (SHAKE *goes out.*) Once you're king of the hill, Mher, what's in it for me?

MHER: You'll be my spin doctor. My grand vizier. Every king should have a wheeler-dealer like you as his sidekick. You'll keep me on my toes.

ARAMYAN: You're a monster, Mher.

MHER: You created me. When logic sleeps, the mind creates monsters. When I felt no pain at the Professor's death, I realized I was ready. I'm up to the task. I'm him.

ARAMYAN: I've got a splitting headache.

MHER: From the day the Professor hanged himself, I became a new man. You know, I didn't feel any pain at his death. I was really puzzled and annoyed at myself. I couldn't understand why I felt no pain. Then it dawned on me. Eureka! I'd ascended to a higher plane. From up there everything looks tiny. Insignificant specks of dust. When you're up there a man's life is nothing. Humanity collectively has value, but the individual is expendable. Politicians and presidents must take responsibility for exploiting us. They're precisely the ones who are supposed to defend the rights of the common man.

(*Long pause.* SHAKE *comes in.*)

SHAKE (*She takes off the wig, Arab costume, and veil to reveal her true identity—* MRS. AMATUNI.): Aramyan, go to the office, quickly.

ARAMYAN (*extremely surprised*): Amatuni? . . . Mrs. Amatuni?

AMATUNI: Shut up, you fool. So you're serving two masters, you son of a bitch. Your boss Hasratyan couldn't even run a madhouse, let alone govern the country.

MHER: We don't need invidious comparisons.

AMATUNI (*to* ARAMYAN): Rush back to headquarters and state on my authority that our party's proposing the candidacy of the Invincible Cock. Quick. I'll take you off the hook. Get going, there's no time to lose. The president's resigned!

MHER: What?

ARAMYAN: What?

AMATUNI: The president's resigned. It was announced on TV. Get going. I won't allow that monster Hasratyan to cash in on it.

(ARAMYAN *whistles.*)

MHER: What did I tell you? Cockadoodle Doo! The king's afraid of me. (*He becomes serious.*) The stew's coming to a boil. (*To* ARAMYAN) Get going,

Chameleon. If you want to change color, now's the time. There's a storm brewing.

ARAMYAN (*Elated*): My dream's coming true. (*He goes out.*)

(SHAKE *takes a long look at* MHER. *The* STATUE *sways uneasily.*)

AMATUNI (*going over to* MHER): Come here, you screwball. (*She smiles seductively.*) I haven't been able to get you out of my mind since our first meeting. (*She hugs* MHER.)

MHER (*Prying her arms loose from his neck*): Madam, what are you doing? I—

AMATUNI: You'll be the country's president and I'll be your vice . . . (*She leads him over to the bed.*)

MHER: Madam, are you trying to seduce me?

AMATUNI (*passionately*): I want an omelet. You remember, screwball. You promised. So give me a hug. Hold me tighter. Give me what I want.

MHER: What exactly do you want, Madam?

AMATUNI (*sighing*): An omelet . . . with all you've got in it.

MHER (*to the bed*): Real cool, Baby. Let's get it on.

AMATUNI: I'm yours, completely yours. Your lover, your wife, your harlot. I'm yours.

MHER: You mean "slut."

AMATUNI (*breathless*): What's the difference?

MHER (*breathless*): A big difference. Harlot's a pro. Slut's a character thing.

STATUE (*getting off its pedestal*): What's going on here, Comrade?

(AMATUNI *lets out a scream.*)

MHER: Madam, I'll explain everything. Madam . . .

(AMATUNI *continues to scream and loses consciousness.*)

MHER (*to the* STATUE): Blockhead. Look what you've done.

STATUE: You'd think I was made of plaster, too. How much of that was I supposed to take?

MHER (*lightly taps* AMATUNI *to waken her*): Madam . . . oh, damn it. I wasn't bargaining on this.

STATUE: But what was I to do? You were going to plough into an omelet, while I looked on drooling? She's coming 'round.

MHER: Get back on your pedestal. Your time's over. You belong in the historical museum now with the other past trappings of Soviet power. (*He presses the alarm button.*)

STATUE: Don't do it, please. If they discover me, I'm done for. They'll arrest me. Don't do it.

MHER (*throwing a hospital gown over the* STATUE): Put that on.

(*The* STATUE *dons the gown.* SHAMAMYAN *enters with a group of presidential hit men dressed in blue surgical attire, with masks over their faces, wheeling in a gurney and a portable screen.*)

SHAMAMYAN (*removing the doctor's mask*): Lie down, national hero. It's time for
    your injection. Your hour has come.
MHER: What injection? She's the one who's sick. She's lost consciousness.
SHAMAMYAN: You don't really get it, do you? You're going to get yours. Nobody
    does in the president without paying the piper. Were you really going to go
    through with it? Dousing yourself with gas and going up in flames? And all for
    the benefit of the people, eh? You thought so much of the people that you'd
    die for nothing? How can you save the people, you crooked, unscrupulous
    play actor? Why, you're nothing but a phony.
MHER (*stirring imaginary soup*): That's a soup I'll have to stir. Whether it comes out
    sweet or sour, I don't know myself. One thing's clear though, I'm the ladle.
SHAMAMYAN: Sitting here in the madhouse, you're turning the whole country
    topsy-turvy. You'll have to face the music. The government's on to your little
    game.
MHER: Do you want to taste it, Uncle?
SHAMAMYAN: He's crazy, or passes himself off as crazy. [*To* MHER] We're going to fix
    you once and for all. If you're sick, boy have we got a cure for you. (*Pointing to*
    AMATUNI) Take her out.

(*The presidential hit men immediately take her out. Then they return and lift* MHER *onto the gurney, holding down his arms. One of them sets up the screen in front to block the operation from view.*)

SHAMAMYAN (*behind the screen*): This is called shock therapy. Please try to relax
    . . . Stick him!

(MHER *puts up resistance and cries out. From behind the screen one of the men calls for a scalpel.*)

(*The* STATUE *winces visibly.*)

SHAMAMYAN (*coming out from behind the screen, to the* STATUE): What business
    have you here?

(*Noises of tearing are heard behind the screen as the operation gets under way.*)

STATUE (*afraid*): Who me? I . . . I'm a black . . . from Africa. I've come to see the biblical Mt. Ararat.

SHAMAMYAN: You're one of the patients. Go to your room. (*To the hit men*) Take him away.

STATUE (*opposing them*): Leave me alone. I'm not crazy. I have to get out of here. Tomorrow's our Ninth Communist Party Conference. I'll complain to our socialist comrades at the International.

(*Some of the men remove the statue. The others pull back the screen and come forward, wiping the perspiration from their heads, their gloves somewhat bloodied.*)

SECOND DOCTOR (*rushing in*): The president's resigned.

SHAMAMYAN: What? It can't be. The president? When? Who said so?

SECOND DOCTOR: They announced it on TV. Just a while ago. The president's resigned.

SHAMAMYAN: Get the cabinet members together.

(*They go out. The lights dim and an eerie cast falls over the scene. A red spotlight focuses on* MHER'*s body lying on the gurney. The* SECOND DOCTOR *bends over* MHER *and examines him. The* FIRST DOCTOR *and patients come in. They cautiously approach* MHER.)

GIRL: Is he dead?

SECOND DOCTOR: Yeah, They took out his heart . . . Too bad.

DOCTOR: Too bad . . . He was a good guy. What a heart! Too bad. The chess tournament's only halfway through. (*He puts his ear to* MHER'*s heart.*) Yeah . . . He's gone.

MRS. ARMENIA (*lamenting*): And he didn't pay the rent.

GIRL (*beginning to cry*): He's dead. He's dead. He doesn't have a heart.

GHOST: It was the ghosts, you see. They came and killed Mher. Ooh! I'll fix your . . . (*He furiously shakes his fist in the air.*)

GENERAL: If you could only see how many ghosts there are in this world.

GHOST: Apart from ourselves, I haven't seen a living soul.

(*The lights gradually brighten throughout the rest of the scene.*)

MHER (*sitting up abruptly*): It's me. I'm alive.

(*They all panic and retreat.*)

SECOND DOCTOR: That's impossible. They removed your heart.

MHER: Have you been dreaming, doctor?

DOCTOR: They operated on you.

MHER: Do you believe in fairy tales, doctor? You're no child. Remember what you said about us patients in this madhouse? "One day they'll drive me mad." Today's the day. What heart? I'm alive. We're alive. (*He shouts.*) Madmen!

PATIENTS: Yes!

MHER: Madmen of the world, unite!

PATIENTS: Unite!

GROUP (*making a fist in the air, they all spell out softly, almost in a whisper*): U-ni-ty . . . U-ni-ty . . . U-ni-ty . . . U-ni-ty . . .

(*The patients parade 'round the stage in triumphal jubilation. Two of them hoist* MHER *on their shoulders and bear him aloft offstage.*)

Curtain

MHER *has subsequently been elected President of Armenia. The stage is now set for his inauguration ceremony. Downstage, before the closed curtain, two men in black suits set up a podium. Journalists and the* PHOTOGRAPHER *throng in. One of the men places a carafe of water and a glass on the podium. Everyone is silent. The atmosphere is solemn. Then the curtain opens. Behind iron bars appear* AMATUNI, BRTU-JYAN, HASRATYAN, SHAMAMYAN, *and their aides, dressed in hospital gowns. Holding onto the bars, they watch with interest. The patients come in wearing suits, starched shirts, and ties. The* GENERAL *wears his inseparable medals at his chest.* MRS. ARMENIA *appears in* AMATUNI'S *dress.* ARAMYAN *is with them. To applause, the* MASTER OF CEREMONIES *steps up to the podium. Silence.*

MASTER OF CEREMONIES: I proclaim the solemn presidential swearing-in ceremony open. (*He applauds.*)

(*Everyone else applauds. Then they wait. A long time. From backstage* MHER *enters, changed beyond all recognition. He goes up to the* GHOST *who is accoutered in a monk's black vestments, surmounted by a pectoral cross. He gets down on his knees in front of the* GHOST *and kisses the* GHOST'S *hand. Then he gets up and slowly makes his way to the podium. Everything proceeds in stony silence.* MHER *looks dubiously at the water jug, then casts an intimidating glance at those present, surveying them all. The men in black suits immediately bring in a second carafe and glass.*)

MHER [*He begins, sober and dead-pan, but gradually accelerates oratorically, finally reaching a maniacal flamboyance as he identifies fully with the Invincible Cock.*]: My fellow Armenians, you all know me, of course. Mher Astvatsatryan. I spoke to you during the election campaign, and my words have lost none of their urgency. So let me take you back to that day. This is what I said then. "As a man of the people, I know your pains and hardship firsthand. I feel them under my skin. We struggled for freedom and independence. And won. But the struggle goes on today. This time against those who have fraudulently abused the people's trust. And so I appeal to you all. Before going to the polls, consider carefully who you're voting for, who you're handing your future to."

Now, on this solemn occasion, I call on you again for your support in taking our common cause to the next level. Graft and corruption are not a local problem only: they are the stock-in-trade of politicians the world over. These politicians neglect their people and bring their office into disrepute. This cancer must not continue. It is destroying the planet's meager resources and threatening the welfare of future generations. Therefore, in your name, I am issuing this ultimatum. If the presidents of the world do not resign before October 5th, I invite you all to the . . . Statue of Liberty. At noon on that day I will immolate myself in silent protest to stir mankind's sleeping conscience! (*He takes a drink of water.*)

(*Thunderous applause*)

SECOND DOCTOR (*entering and taking* ARAMYAN *to one side*): I've found another loser willing to commit suicide: 13 Teryan Street.

(ARAMYAN *nods to* MHER *and applauds.* MHER *nods back. He is mobbed by reporters. From different sides they thrust microphones in front of him. They fire questions in various languages.*)

Curtain

NOTES ON CONTRIBUTORS

JACK ANTREASSIAN has been editor of the weekly *Armenian Mirror-Spectator* and the quarterly magazine *Ararat*. He has edited a volume of selections from the latter, entitled *Ararat: A Decade of Armenian-American Writing*. His translations include a collection of stories, *Tales from the Armenian*; Odian's *Comrade Panchoonie*; Antranig Antreassian's short-story series *The Cup of Bitterness* and novel *Death and Resurrection*; Baronian's satirical pieces *The Honorable Beggars* and *The Perils of Politeness*; Krikor Zohrab's *Voices of Conscience*; and, with Marzbed Margossian, *Across Two Worlds: The Selected Prose of Eghishe Charents*. His own works include *Unworthy Offspring*, *The Confessions of Kitchoonie*, *Definitions & Deflations*, *Armenia: Reflections in Verse*, *Kohar:Letters to a Grandchild*, *Letters from Nowhere*, and *Memoirs of an Irresponsible*. He also served as executive director of the Armenian General Benevolent Union of America and the Eastern Diocese of the Armenian Church of America.

S. PETER COWE has held positions in Armenian Studies at the Hebrew University of Jerusalem, the University of Chicago, and Columbia University, New York. Currently he is Narekatsi Professor of Armenian language and literature at the University of California, Los Angeles. His research interests include the development of Armenian nationalism, Armenia's lyric tradition, and the Armenian theater.

The author of four books, he is now coediting the earliest extant Armenian play of 1668, as well as a contemporary short-story anthology of women writers of the Balkans. A regular contributor to Armenological journals, he recently received an International Research & Exchange grant to pursue fieldwork in the Armenian Republic.

ERVANT D. MEGERDITCHIAN was born in the Ottoman vilayet of Van in 1888. After completing his elementary education there, he continued his studies at the Gevorgian Chemaran in Ejmiatsin and thereafter at the Nersisian School in Tiflis. After graduation, he taught in Van, concurrently working as a typesetter for a local newspaper. During World War I he returned to Tiflis and then emigrated to the United States. He settled in Watertown, Massachussetts, where he applied his trade as a typesetter and operated his own press for about a decade. In 1930 he translated Baronian's *Gentlemen Beggars*, turning then to Sundukian's *Pepo* (1931) and Baronian's *Uncle Balthazar* (1933). Subsequently he married the nurse, who had miraculously revived him in the hospital when he had been taken for dead. Later he wrote a few books of his own, including a one-act play of 1934, *Kantser Vasburagani* [The treasures of Vaspurakan] (1966), describing the religious architecture of his home region, and his autobiography, *The Life of an Armenian Emigrant* (1970). He died in 1972.

BEDROS NOREHAD was editor of the *Armenian Mirror* in the 1930s, and in 1939 effected its merger with *The Armenian Spectator*, continuing as editor until he entered military service toward the end of 1942. He then extended his service to the Armenian community by serving as first editor of *The Armenian Church*, the official organ of the Eastern Diocese of the Armenian Church of America, and subsequently editor of the *Hoosharar*, the monthly publication of the Armenian General Benevolent Union. His most important literary contribution was an English translation from the classical Armenian of the fifth-century *Life of Mashtots* by Koriwn, which appeared in 1964. He died in 1988.

NISHAN PARLAKIAN teaches drama, speech, and English literature at John Jay College of the City University of New York. As artistic director of the Diocesan Players of the Armenian Church of America for a dozen years, he has staged the major plays of Shirvanzade, Sundukian, Baronian, and Asadur. He has published English translations of Shirvanzade's dramatic masterpieces *For the Sake of Honor* and *Evil Spirit* (St. Vartan's Press, New York). Both plays were subsequently produced by the Classic Theater in New York City. *For the Sake of Honor* received further visibility through the Council on National Literatures, which gave it worldwide distribution. An accomplished play doctor and playwright, he had several of his plays produced in New York, including *Plagiarized, Greta Garbo*, and most notably his ethnic *Grandma, Pray for Me*, all of which were published. Professor Parlakian is the author of many articles on Armenian studies, theater, and literature. In 1982 he also published his paper "Shakespeare and the Armenian Theater," delivered at one of several unique dramatic programs of bilingual readings featured in a five-month Shakespeare Summerfest at the American Museum of Natural History (New York, 1981). Professor Parlakian also prepared for Greenwood Press (New York) the chapter on "Armenian American Theater" in *Ethnic Theater in the United States*. He serves on the editorial board of *Ararat*, where he has published articles on the Armenian-Russian director Evgeni Vakhtangov of the Moscow Art Theater and William Saroyan. For the last twenty-seven years, Dr. Parlakian, currently president of the Pirandello Society of America, has staged, directed, and acted in dramatic programs of scenes from the plays of Luigi Pirandello for special Society programs and for the annual conventions of the Modern Language Association of America. Most recently he received the Armenian Students Association of America's Arthur A. Dadian Award for fostering the Armenian cultural heritage.

ARIS G. SEVAG is an editor, journalist, and translator. A graduate of the University of Pennsylvania, he was previously active in the fields of education and business. In the early 1980s he coedited the bilingual literary journal *Menk*, published by the Hamazkayin Educational and Cultural Society. Since 1992 he has been managing editor of *The Armenian Reporter International*. In addition, he works as a freelance translator of historical and literary works. He has translated several dozen published and unpublished works, including material by Krikor Zohrab, Kostan Zarian, and Hakob Karapents. His translations and articles have appeared in the *Ararat* and *Potomac Review* quarterlies, *The Armenian Digest* and *AIM* monthlies, and in several weeklies. He is currently translating Hagop Oshagan's novel *Mnatsortats* [Remnants].

ANNE T. VARDANIAN was born in Marseilles, where her parents were reunited after the Armenian Genocide. When she was one year old, the family moved to the United States. Growing up in New York, she was an active member of the Kimatian Armenian Youth Drama Group and starred in numerous productions. She subsequently moved to California where she continued her education, receiving her bachelor of arts degree in English and drama and her master's in theater arts from California State University, Fullerton, and her doctorate in communication arts and sciences from the University of Southern California. A theater educator for more than twenty-five years, she has directed at all levels, from preschool to university graduate classes. Her directorial credits include children's theater, classical and contemporary works, and musicals. In her retirement, she is the drama chairperson of the Armenian Allied Arts Association and a board member of the National Association for Armenian Studies and Research. In addition to being awarded several high honors over the years, she received the Distinguished Professional Achievement Award of Delta Kappa Gamma International, Honorary Teacher's Society, in 1992.

The system adopted for the Romanization of the Armenian alphabet is a slightly modified version of that employed by the *Journal of the Society for Armenian Studies*, as follows:

Ա	ա	A	a			Յ	յ	Y	y		
Բ	բ	B	b	[P p]¹				H	h²		
Գ	գ	G	g	[K k]		Ն	ն	N	n		
Դ	դ	D	d	[T t]		Շ	շ	Sh	sh		
Ե	ե	E	e			Ո	ո	O	o		
Զ	զ	Z	z			Չ	չ	Ch	ch		
Է	է	E	e			Պ	պ	P	p	[B b]
Ը	ը	E	e			Ջ	ջ	J	j	[Ch ch]
Թ	թ	T	t			Ռ	ռ	R	r		
Ժ	ժ	Zh	zh			Ս	ս	S	s		
Ի	ի	I	i			Վ	վ	V	v		
Լ	լ	L	l			Տ	տ	T	t	[D d]
Խ	խ	Kh	kh			Ր	ր	R	r		
Ծ	ծ	Ts	ts	[Dz dz]		Ց	ց	Ts	ts		
Կ	կ	K	k	[G g]		Ւ	ւ	W	w		
Հ	հ	H	h			Ու	ու	U	u		
Ձ	ձ	Dz	dz	[Ts ts]		Փ	փ	P	p		
Ղ	ղ	Gh	gh			Ք	ք	K	k		
Ճ	ճ	Ch	ch	[J j]		Օ	օ	O	o		
Մ	մ	M	m			Ֆ	ֆ	F	f		

1. The variants shown in square brackets indicate the phonetic value of the letters in West Armenian.

2. This value is employed when the letter occurs in the initial position of a word.